THE ROUTLEDGE COMPANION TO URBAN MEDIA AND COMMUNICATION

The Routledge Companion to Urban Media and Communication traces central debates within the burgeoning interdisciplinary research on mediated cities and urban communication. The volume brings together diverse perspectives and global case studies to map key areas of research within media, cultural and urban studies, where a joint focus on communications and cities has made important innovations in how we understand urban space, technology, identity and community.

Exploring the rise and growing complexity of urban media and communication as the next key theme for both urban and media studies, the book gathers and reviews fast-developing knowledge on specific emergent phenomena such as:

- reading the city as symbol and text;
- understanding urban infrastructures as media (and vice-versa);
- the rise of global cities;
- urban and suburban media cultures: newspapers, cinema, radio, television and the mobile phone;
- changing spaces and practices of urban consumption;
- the mediation of the neighbourhood, community and diaspora;
- the centrality of culture to urban regeneration;
- communicative responses to urban crises such as racism, poverty and pollution;
- the role of street art in the negotiation of 'the right to the city';
- city competition and urban branding;
- outdoor advertising;
- moving image architecture;
- 'smart'/cyber urbanism;
- the emergence of Media City production spaces and clusters.

Charting key debates and neglected connections between cities and media, this book challenges what we know about contemporary urban living and introduces innovative frameworks for understanding cities, media and their futures. As such, it will be an essential resource for students and scholars of media and communication studies, urban communication, urban sociology, urban planning and design, architecture, visual cultures, urban geography, art history, politics, cultural studies, anthropology and cultural policy studies, as well as those working with governmental agencies, cultural foundations and institutes, and policy think tanks.

Zlatan Krajina is Assistant Professor of Media Studies at the University of Zagreb, Croatia, where he teaches graduate courses on media cities, media audiences and qualitative methodologies.

Deborah Stevenson is Professor of Sociology and Urban Cultural Research in the Institute of Culture and Society at the Western Sydney University, Australia.

THE ROUTLEDGE COMPANION TO URBAN MEDIA AND COMMUNICATION

*Edited by Zlatan Krajina and
Deborah Stevenson*

NEW YORK AND LONDON

First published 2020
by Routledge
52 Vanderbilt Avenue, New York, NY 10017

and by Routledge
2 Park Square, Milton Park, Abingdon, Oxon, OX14 4RN

Routledge is an imprint of the Taylor & Francis Group, an informa business

© 2020 Taylor & Francis

The right of Zlatan Krajina and Deborah Stevenson to be identified as the authors of the editorial material, and of the authors for their individual chapters, has been asserted in accordance with sections 77 and 78 of the Copyright, Designs and Patents Act 1988.

All rights reserved. No part of this book may be reprinted or reproduced or utilised in any form or by any electronic, mechanical, or other means, now known or hereafter invented, including photocopying and recording, or in any information storage or retrieval system, without permission in writing from the publishers.

Trademark notice: Product or corporate names may be trademarks or registered trademarks, and are used only for identification and explanation without intent to infringe.

Library of Congress Cataloging-in-Publication Data
Names: Krajina, Zlatan, editor. | Stevenson, Deborah, 1958- editor.
Title: The Routledge companion to urban media and communication / edited by Zlatan Krajina and Deborah Stevenson.
Description: New York : Routledge, 2020. | Includes index. |
Identifiers: LCCN 2019026188 (print) | LCCN 2019026189 (ebook) | ISBN 9780415792554 (hardback) | ISBN 9781315211633 (ebook)
Subjects: LCSH: Cities and towns—Effect of technological innovations on. | Mass media—Social aspects. | Communication—Social aspects. | Urban ecology (Sociology) | Internet of things.
Classification: LCC HT119 .R685 2020 (print) | LCC HT119 (ebook) | DDC 307.76—dc23
LC record available at https://lccn.loc.gov/2019026188
LC ebook record available at https://lccn.loc.gov/2019026189

ISBN: 978-0-415-79255-4 (hbk)
ISBN: 978-1-315-21163-3 (ebk)

Typeset in Bembo
by Swales & Willis Ltd, Exeter, Devon, UK

Printed in the United Kingdom
by Henry Ling Limited

CONTENTS

List of Figures • x
Notes on Contributors • xii
Acknowledgements • xviii

General Introduction • 1
Zlatan Krajina and Deborah Stevenson

PART I
Trajectories of Mediated Urbanity • 7

Introduction to Part I: Trajectories of Mediated Urbanity • 9
Zlatan Krajina and Deborah Stevenson

1 An Archaeology of the Media City: Toward a Critical Cultural History of Mediated Urbanism • 13
Scott McQuire

2 The Semiotics of Urban Space • 23
Alexandros Ph. Lagopoulos

3 Understanding Urban Screen Media and Cultures • 36
Zach Melzer

4 Urban Cinema and Photography: On Cities and "Cityness" • 46
James Donald

5 Television and the City • 57
Charlotte Brunsdon

6 Journalism: An Urban Affair *Scott Rodgers*	66
7 Outdoor Advertising and the Remediation of Public Space(s): Commercialization and Beyond *Cesare Silla*	76
8 Consumption-Centered Urban Restructuring and the Mediation of Urban Life: From Spaces of Production to the Worlds of Seduction *Erika Nagy*	84
9 On the Move: On Mobile Agoras, Networked Selves, and the Contemporary City *Ole B. Jensen*	96
10 Cities of Feet and Hands: Urban Habitations *Shaun Moores*	107
11 Subjectivity in the Media City: The Media Life and Representation of the Cosmopolitan Stranger *Myria Georgiou and Jun Yu*	116

PART II
Media as Urban Infrastructure; City Spaces as Media — **127**

Introduction to Part II: Media as Urban Infrastructure; City Spaces as Media *Deborah Stevenson and Zlatan Krajina*	129
12 The City Is Not a Computer: On Museums, Libraries, and Archives *Shannon Mattern*	133
13 Urban Monuments and the Spatialization of National Ideologies *Vjeran Pavlaković and Gruia Bădescu*	143
14 Artificial Light and the Modernist Redefinition of Urban Space: Reading the "Electropolis" *Robert Shaw*	156
15 Urban Transport and Telecommunications: Dual Forms of the Communicative Skeleton of the City *Aaron Shapiro*	165
16 Global Cities as Mediated Spaces: The Role of Media in Forming Contradictory Places *Paul James*	174

17 Our Own Devices: Living in the Smart Home　　　　　　　　　　　　185
    Chris Chesher and Justine Humphry

18 Surveillance as an Urban Way of Life　　　　　　　　　　　　　　194
    Roy Coleman

19 Urban Media as Infrastructure for Social Change　　　　　　　　　204
    Naomi Schiller

20 In the Air Tonight: The Struggles of Communicating About
    Urban Environmental Quality　　　　　　　　　　　　　　　　　215
    Matteo Tarantino

21 The Promises and Pitfalls of Cyber Urbanism: Governance and
    Participation　　　　　　　　　　　　　　　　　　　　　　　　225
    Kristin Erickson

22 Tools of the Trade: Urban Planning, Urban Media and the
    Refashioning of Urban Space　　　　　　　　　　　　　　　　　236
    Sarah Barns

PART III
Media Cities as Sites of Creative Industries and Post-Industrial Urbanism　　249

Introduction to Part III: Media Cities as Sites of Creative Industries
and Post-Industrial Urbanism　　　　　　　　　　　　　　　　　251
Deborah Stevenson and Zlatan Krajina

23 From "Creative Cities" to "Media Cities": The Cases of Manchester
    and Shanghai　　　　　　　　　　　　　　　　　　　　　　　　255
    Xin Gu

24 Branding, Promotion, and the Tourist City　　　　　　　　　　　265
    Deborah Stevenson

25 "European Capital of Culture" and the Primacy of Cultural
    Infrastructure in Post-Industrial Urbanism　　　　　　　　　　　274
    Peter Campbell and Dave O'Brien

26 The Mediat(izat)ion of Urban Leisure: Screening the Event　　　　283
    David Rowe and Brett Hutchins

27 Media Architecture: Post Screens, Ante [Insert Here]　　　　　　　292
    Hank Haeusler

28 Fashion: An Urban Industry of Style   304
    Jennifer Craik

29 Digital Public Art: Installations and Interventions   314
    Martin Zebracki

30 Urban Nightlife Cultures   326
    Irina van Aalst

31 Urban Gaming: Mobile Media, Spatial Practices, and
    Everyday Play   335
    Ingrid Richardson

32 From Subculture to Scene: Urban Media Practices from Below   344
    Geoff Stahl

33 Documenting Urban Neighborhoods and Claiming the Right
    to the City   353
    Anita Bakshi

PART IV
Spaces and Practices of Daily Life in Mediated Cities   365

Introduction to Part IV: Spaces and Practices of Daily Life in
Mediated Cities   367
Zlatan Krajina and Deborah Stevenson

34 The Senses and the City: Attention, Distraction and Media
    Technology in Urban Environments   371
    Meri Kytö

35 Navigating Hybrid Urban Spaces: Smartphones and Locative
    Media Practices   379
    Jordan Frith

36 Media Audiences in the Urban Context   387
    Zlatan Krajina

37 Temporary Inscriptions: Exploring Graffiti and Street Art in the
    Age of Internetization of Everyday Urban Life   397
    Ilija Tomanić Trivundža and Mitja Velikonja

38 Creating a Situation in the City: Embodied Spaces and the Act of
   Crossing Boundaries   405
   Tina Richardson

39 Mediated Urban Protest: Practicing Dissent in Hybrid City Spaces   416
   Tetyana Lokot

40 Community, Media, and the City   425
   Andrea Medrado

41 "The Street Is the Message": Racial Violence and the White
   Control of Mobility   437
   Armond R. Towns

42 Living in the Disadvantaged End of "Dual Cities": Understanding
   the Urban Poor and the Precariat   446
   Steve Macek

43 The Politics of Sexuality in Mediated Cities   456
   Hollis Griffin

44 Methodological Approaches in Urban Media and
   Communication Research   466
   Simone Tosoni and Giorgia Aiello

Index   476

FIGURES

2.1	The Production of Space from the Major Systemic Components of Society	25
4.1	*The Skywalk Is Gone* (Tsai Ming-Liang, 2002) (Screen Grab)	47
8.1	From Informality to Controlled Spaces of Consumption: Plzen, Czech Republic, 2006 (the market was cleared off two years later)	91
13.1	Vukovar Water Tower	149
13.2	Bilice Vukovar Graffiti	151
16.1	Forms of Communication in Relation to Ways of Being and Forms of Urban Settlement	179
20.1	A Table Representation of United States EPA AQI, Using Numbers, Levels, and Colors to Express Risk	219
22.1	Ebenezer Howard (1902) *Diagram of Garden City*. Plate 2 from *Garden Cities of Tomorrow*	238
22.2	Charles Marville, *Rue de Glatigny*, 1865	241
27.1	*Orkhēstra* Installation in Frankfurt, 2014	296
27.2	*ParticipationPlus* Installation in Sydney, 2016	298
29.1	Digital Colonial Public Art? 3D-Printed Replica of Palmyra's Roman Arch, Destroyed by IS, on Display in City Hall Park, New York, 2016. User name and link blinded for confidentiality	316
29.2	Re-Wor(l)ding Urban Space with the Mobile Application *Lapse*, Miami. Shown is the author's screenshot of a GPS-based walk-through prose of the app component *The Writing*, Museum Park	320
29.3	"Although It's Not About Monuments . . . Options Are Possible" (public post, Instagram, August 17, 2017). This artist proposed playful alternatives to dismantling Confederate statues from urban public spaces. User name and link blinded for confidentiality	322
33.1	Discussion Over the Map	357
33.2	*Topographies of Memory* Exhibition	358
38.1	Phoenix Drawing on a Gravestone in the Cemetery on the University of Leeds Campus in 2013	410

38.2	An Amalgamation of Dots That Reflected the GPS Location of Individuals Walking, Driving, or Cycling Around the Area Near the University of Leeds Campus at This Time	413
40.1	Lamppost Radio "Pop Som," Pau da Lima, Salvador, Brazil	429
40.2	Screen Capture, Facebook Fan Page Maré Vive, August 10, 2017	433

CONTRIBUTORS

Giorgia Aiello is Associate Professor of Media and Communication at the University of Leeds, UK. She is lead editor of *Communicating the City: Meanings, Practices, Interactions* (2017) and the *International Journal of Communication*'s special section 'Going About the City: Methods and Methodologies for Urban Communication Research'.

Gruia Bădescu is a Research Associate at the School of Geography, University of Oxford, and a visiting lecturer at the National School of Political Science and Public Administration, Bucharest. His research examines urban reconstruction and memorialization after war and political violence, focusing on the Balkans and the Middle East.

Anita Bakshi teaches in the Department of Landscape Architecture at Rutgers University and is Associate Graduate Faculty for the Cultural Heritage and Preservation Studies (CHAPS) Program. She is the author of *Topographies of Memories: A New Poetics of Commemoration* (2017).

Sarah Barns' research explores the historical intersections between urban transformation and media innovation and uses practice-based methods to animate sites of urban change using sound, digital projection and mobile media. Sarah is Director of Public Space Media at Esem Projects and author of *Platform Urbanism: Negotiating Platform Ecosystems in Connected Cities* to be published in late 2019.

Charlotte Brunsdon's books include *Television Cities* (2018) and *London in Cinema* (2007). She is Professor of Film and Television Studies at the University of Warwick, UK where she has been Principal Investigator on *The Projection Project*.

Peter Campbell is Senior Lecturer in the University of Liverpool's Department of Sociology, Social Policy and Criminology. His work concentrates on social research methods, culture and the arts.

Chris Chesher is Senior Lecturer in Digital Cultures in the Department of Media and Communications at the University of Sydney. His research concentrates on social aspects of digital media, including robotics, computer games, mobile media, toys and the Internet.

Contributors

Roy Coleman is Lecturer at the University of Liverpool, UK. His writing and research continue to be focused on surveillance, state power, spatial injustice and governing through emotion. His first book, *Reclaiming the Streets* (Routledge), won the Hart Social and Legal Book Prize in 2005.

Jennifer Craik is Professor of Fashion at Queensland University of Technology, Brisbane, Australia. She publishes on fashion theory and culture, including *The Face of Fashion, Fashion: Key Concepts* and *Modern Fashion Traditions* (co-ed. Angela Jansen).

James Donald is Emeritus Professor of Film Studies at the University of New South Wales in Sydney, Australia, although now based in the UK. He is author of *Sentimental Education* (1992), *Imagining the Modern City* (1999) and *Some of These Days: Black Stars, Jazz Aesthetics and Modernist Culture* (2015), and editor of over a dozen volumes on film, culture and education. He edited *Screen Education* and was founding editor of *New Formations*. He is a Fellow of the Australian Academy of the Humanities.

Kristin Erickson is Senior Lecturer at Simmons University in Boston, MA and the author of *The Digital City and Mediated Urban Ecologies* (2016), which examines the phenomenon of the 'digital city' and how governmental use of digital technologies, social media and data visualization is increasingly built into the logic and organization of urban spaces, often to the detriment of already marginalized communities and residents.

Jordan Frith is Associate Professor and the author of three books and over 20 peer-reviewed journal articles. His most recent book (*A Billion Little Pieces: RFID and Infrastructures of Identification*, 2019) looks at how infrastructures of RFID work to sort and animate the physical environment.

Myria Georgiou teaches at the Department of Media and Communications, LSE. Her research focuses on media and the city, urban technologies and politics of connection, and the ways in which migration and diaspora are politically, culturally and morally constituted in the context of mediation. Her latest book is *Media and the City: Cosmopolitanism and Difference* (2013).

Hollis Griffin is Associate Professor of Media Studies in the Department of Communication at Denison University. He is the author of *Feeling Normal: Sexuality and Media Criticism in the Digital Age* (2017).

Xin Gu is Lecturer in the School of Media Film and Journalism, Monash University, Australia. Her research interests cover creative cities, culture-led urban regeneration, cultural economy and media cities. She is working on the book *Culture and Economy in the New Shanghai* (Routledge, forthcoming).

Hank Haeusler is Discipline Director of Computational Design/Built Environment at UNSW Sydney; Professor at Central Academy of Fine Arts, Beijing; and board member of the Media Architecture Institute, and is known as a researcher, educator, entrepreneur and designer in media architecture and computational design through over 60 publications.

Justine Humphry is Lecturer in Digital Cultures in the Department of Media and Communications at the University of Sydney. She researches mobile and digital media in everyday life, social media and networked publics, and digital inequalities and urban infrastructures.

Brett Hutchins is Professor of Media and Communications Studies in the School of Media, Film and Journalism at Monash University. His current research focuses on the interrelationships between sport, mobile communications and mediatization.

Paul James is Professor of Globalization and Cultural Diversity at the Western Sydney University where he is Director of the Institute for Culture and Society. He is Scientific Advisor to the Senate Department for the Environment, Transport and Climate Protection, Berlin, and a Metropolis Ambassador of Urban Innovation. He is the author or editor of 34 books including *Nation Formation* and *Globalism, Nationalism, Tribalism*.

Ole B. Jensen is Professor of Urban Theory and Urban Design at the Department of Architecture, Design and Media Technology, Aalborg University (Denmark). He holds a BA in Political Science, an MA in Sociology, a PhD in Planning and a Dr Techn in Mobilities. His main research interests are within urban mobilities, mobilities design and networked technologies.

Zlatan Krajina is Assistant Professor of Media Studies at the Department of Media and Communication, Faculty of Political Sciences, University of Zagreb, Croatia. He was awarded an MA and PhD in Media and Communications at Goldsmiths, University of London. Krajina is the author of *Negotiating the Mediated City* (2014), which was shortlisted for the Jane Jacobs Urban Communication Book Award, and co-editor of *EU, Europe Unfinished: Mediating Europe and the Balkans in a Time of Crisis* (2016).

Meri Kytö is a Postdoctoral Researcher in music studies at the University of Eastern Finland. Her previous publications have tackled sonic domestication, articulations of acoustic privacy, soundscapes of political protest, busking, football fans and public libraries. She is currently writing on sensory agency and technology.

Alexandros Ph. Lagopoulos is Professor Emeritus of Urban Planning at Aristotle University of Thessaloniki, Greece, and Corresponding Member of the Academy of Athens. He has a degree in Architectural Engineering from the National Technical University of Athens, as well as a doctorate in Engineering and a postdoctoral academic title (Habilitation) in Urban and Regional Planning from the same university, a doctorate in Social Anthropology from the Sorbonne, and an honorary doctorate in Semiotics from the New Bulgarian University, Sofia.

Tetyana Lokot is Assistant Professor in the School of Communications at Dublin City University. She studies the interplay of digital media, urban space and citizens during protests. Her research focuses on Eastern European and post-Soviet states, including Ukraine and Russia.

Steve Macek is Professor of Communication at North Central College in Naperville, IL, where he teaches courses on media history, critical media studies and urban studies. He is the author of *Urban Nightmares: The Media, the Right and the Panic Over the City* (2006) and co-editor of the collection *Marxism and Communication Studies: The Point Is to Change It* (2006).

Shannon Mattern is Associate Professor of Media Studies at The New School. She is author of *The New Downtown Library, Deep Mapping the Media City* and *Code and Clay, Data and Dirt: 5000 Years of Urban Media*.

Contributors

Scott McQuire is Professor of Media and Communication in the School of Culture and Communication at the University of Melbourne, Australia. He is one of the founders of the Research Unit for Public Cultures, which fosters interdisciplinary research at the nexus of digital media, contemporary art, urbanism and social theory.

Andrea Medrado is Senior Lecturer at the Department of Communication of Federal Fluminense University (UFF), in Rio de Janeiro. She is currently the Co-Chair of the Community Communication and Alternative Media Section of the International Association for Media and Communication Research (IAMCR) and the Co-Investigator for the eVoices Redressing Marginality Network (AHRC, UK).

Zach Melzer is a Doctoral Candidate in Film and Moving Image Studies at Concordia University (Montréal). He is a recipient of the Joseph-Armand Bombardier Doctoral Scholarship and a Québec Doctoral Research Scholarship. His research investigates the regulations and infrastructures of moving image technologies and cultures in London, New York, Toronto and Montréal.

Shaun Moores is Professor of Media and Communications, Centre for Research in Media and Cultural Studies, University of Sunderland, UK. He is the author or co-author of books including *Media/Theory: Thinking about Media and Communications* (2005), *Media, Place and Mobility* (2012), *Communications/Media/Geographies* (with Paul Adams et al., 2017) and, most recently, a volume of his selected essays, *Digital Orientations: Non-Media-Centric Media Studies and Non-Representational Theories of Practice* (2018).

Erika Nagy is Senior Research Fellow at the Centre for Economic and Regional Studies, Hungarian Academy of Sciences. She holds a PhD in social geography and her research covers economic, urban and political geography with a special focus on Central and Eastern Europe (urban restructuring, rural marginalities, state restructuring), Europe (peripheralization, border studies) and global flows (retail and food global production networks (GPNs)).

Dave O'Brien is Chancellor's Fellow in Cultural and Creative Industries at the University of Edinburgh. He has published extensively, as well as led and participated in a range of research projects, on cultural and creative industries.

Vjeran Pavlaković is Associate Professor at the Department of Cultural Studies at the University of Rijeka, Croatia. He received his PhD in History in 2005 from the University of Washington and has published articles on cultural memory, transitional justice in the former Yugoslavia and the Spanish Civil War.

Ingrid Richardson is Associate Professor in Creative Arts at Murdoch University, Western Australia. She has a broad interest in the human–technology relation, and has published widely on topics such as scientific technovision, virtual and augmented reality, games, mobile media and small-screen practices, urban screens, remix culture, and web-based content creation and distribution.

Tina Richardson is a cultural theorist and psychogeographer at the University of Leeds. She has authored a number of articles and her first edited volume, *Walking Inside Out: Contemporary British Psychogeography*, was published in 2015.

Contributors

Scott Rodgers is Senior Lecturer in Media Theory at Birkbeck, University of London. His research specializes in the relationships of media and cities and the geographies of communication. He also has interests in media production, journalism, urban politics, media philosophy and ethnographic methodologies.

David Rowe is Emeritus Professor of Cultural Research, Institute for Culture and Society, Western Sydney University and Honorary Professor, Faculty of Humanities and Social Sciences, University of Bath. His books include *Global Media Sport* (2011) and *Sport Beyond Television* (with Brett Hutchins, 2012).

Naomi Schiller teaches cultural anthropology at Brooklyn College, CUNY. She is the author of *Channeling the State: Community Media and Popular Politics in Venezuela* (2018). Her research focuses on community activism, urban social movements, environmental justice and the state in Latin America and the United States.

Robert Shaw is Lecturer in Geography at Newcastle University, and the author of *The Nocturnal City* (2018). His research exploring the geographies of the night has covered artificial illumination, night-time protest, rural electrification, night-time delivery work and the night-time economy.

Aaron Shapiro received his PhD from the Annenberg School for Communication at the University of Pennsylvania. His research focuses on the cultural politics of urban data infrastructures. His work has been published in *Nature, Space & Culture, Media, Culture & Society, New Media & Society* and *Tecnoscienza: The Italian Journal of Science & Technology Studies*.

Cesare Silla is Researcher in the Department of Economy, Society and Politics (DESP) at the University of Urbino 'Carlo Bo'. He also teaches Sociology at the Catholic University of Milan. He researches in areas of historical sociology, sociological theory and urban media studies.

Geoff Stahl is Senior Lecturer in Media Studies at Victoria University of Wellington, New Zealand. His research areas include scenes and urban culture, popular music, semiotics and, more recently, food studies. His publications include: *Made in Australia and Aotearoa/New Zealand: Studies in Popular Music* (2018), *Poor, But Sexy: Reflections on Berlin Scenes* (2014) and *Understanding Media Studies* (2009).

Deborah Stevenson is Professor in the Institute for Culture and Society, Western Sydney University, Australia. Her research interests are in arts and cultural policy, cities and urban life, and the role of gender in shaping creative practice and cultural consumption. She has published widely on these topics including nine authored/edited books. Her latest book, *Cultural Policy Beyond the Economy: Work, Value and the Social*, is due to be published in 2020.

Matteo Tarantino is Assistant Professor at the Catholic University of Milan and Lecturer at the University of Geneva. His research focuses on the intersection of sustainability, technology and urban space.

Ilija Tomanić Trivundža is Associate Professor in the Department of Media Studies in the Faculty of Social Sciences, University of Ljubljana, Slovenia. His research interests span the field of visual communication, with a special focus on the social and political role of photography in contemporary mediated communication. He is the author of *Press Photography and Visual Framing of News* (2015).

Simone Tosoni's latest book is *Entanglements: Conversations on the Human Traces of Science, Technology, and Sound* (2016). He is Associate Professor in Media and Communication at Università Cattolica di Milano and former Chair of the ECREA Working Group Media and the City.

Armond R. Towns is Assistant Professor in the Department of Rhetoric and Communication Studies at the University of Richmond. His research can be found in *Social Identities*, *Souls—A Critical Journal of Black Politics, Culture and Society*, *Communication and Critical/Cultural Studies* and *Women's Studies in Communication*.

Irina van Aalst is Senior Lecturer in Urban Geography and Head of the Human Geography Master's programme at Utrecht University, the Netherlands. Her research is positioned at the intersection of urban, cultural and economic geography. She has published on urban nightlife and surveillance, public spaces, creative industries, and cultural quarters.

Mitja Velikonja is Professor of Cultural Studies at the Faculty of Social Sciences, University of Ljubljana. Main areas of his research include Central European and Balkan political ideologies, subcultures and graffiti culture, collective memory, and post-socialist nostalgia. His latest books are *Eurosis* (2005), *Titostalgia* (2008), *Rock'n'Retro* (2013) and the forthcoming *Images of Dissent: Political Graffiti and Street Art of Post-Socialist Transition*.

Jun Yu is a PhD Candidate in Media and Communications at the London School of Economics and Political Science. His research interests include social theories, solidarity, public space and urban development, privacy and dataveillance, datafied education, and algorithmic culture.

Martin Zebracki, School of Geography, University of Leeds, conducts research at the crossroads of public art practice, social engagement, (sexual) citizenship and digital culture. Recently, he has published the Routledge volumes *Public Art Encounters* (2017) and *The Everyday Practice of Public Art* (2016).

ACKNOWLEDGEMENTS

There are many people who, in different ways, have contributed to the successful production of this collection. From Routledge, we are grateful to Felisa Salvago-Keyes for her enthusiasm for the project and careful guidance during its initial stages. More recently, we acknowledge Suzanne Richardson and Richa Kohli for seeing the book through to publication. We also thank the anonymous reviewers for the thoughtful feedback that helped improve the final volume.

Toni Kliškić's research assistance in the final stages of the process was invaluable, while Peter Hershey was generous in allowing us to use his photograph as the book's cover image. We also acknowledge the Institute for Culture and Society at Western Sydney University for providing support to engage the services of a professional copy editor.

Zlatan is grateful to Simone Tosoni for academic friendship, and his brother Dino for overall support; and Deborah thanks David Rowe for ensuring she always remembered to laugh.

Zlatan Krajina
Zagreb
Deborah Stevenson
Sydney

GENERAL INTRODUCTION

Zlatan Krajina and Deborah Stevenson

With the largest spatial concentration of media companies in China, Shanghai draws global economic success from the geographic concentration of international experts in purpose-built complexes at the same time as being less successful in engaging a local creative workforce. On the other side of the globe, in Salvador, Brazil, the uninterrupted sonic presence and open-door policy of community radio relayed through public speakers hung from lampposts articulates a sense of immediacy in collective daily living in an underprivileged neighborhood. The use of street-spoken Swahili on billboards promoting responsible sexual behavior in Nigerian cities helped reach vulnerable groups in efforts to prevent the spread of HIV. The media coverage of protests against the privatization of central green areas in Istanbul, Turkey took urban change to address the state of democracy nationwide. These cases, among countless others explored in this volume, demonstrate the communicative as a *central* dimension of modern and postmodern urbanity. At the same time, they testify to the formative relevance of material, spatial and historical articulation of media in cities.

For scholars in urban, media and cultural studies, sociology, history, anthropology and geography, who have, from their different vantage points, traced the joint trajectory of urban and media/communication developments from at least the emergence of the modern industrial city, the claim that cities and media/communication go together may be stating the obvious. Traditional definition of cities, stemming from early 20th-century observations of Chicago, USA as "a relatively large, dense, and permanent settlement of socially heterogeneous individuals" (Wirth 1938: 8), center on human association, which provides the idea of communication with its etymology (*communitas* or community). Cities are from the start imagined as much as they are materially constructed, and they only ever make sense to us through communicative practices (maps, signs, images, sights, senses, etc.). Like communication, the city is multiple and changing, and thus evades any attempt at total vision or explanation. Similarly, media elude analysis as discrete entities, since they only ever refer to other entities involved in interaction (people, objects, goods, information). Thus, it is in, and through, the city that communication becomes empirically evident in its various theorized forms: symbolic, contextualized, material, embodied, trivial and powerful. And the inverse holds equally true: it is through communication that the city is conceivable as meaningful space, poly-sectoral composite, contested terrain and practiced routine.

Thus, the two domains, cities and media/communications, become more accessible for analysis when observed alongside, against and in terms of each other: like the conjoining of raster patterns, when combined, they each elucidate something about the other, as well as producing new forms of knowledge. Despite the increasing scholarly awareness of the urgency for rehearsing shared focus on cities and media/communications, the advantages of such endeavors remain underexplored. This book brings together key themes, perspectives and global cases in an attempt to mobilize familiar, and detect neglected, connections between cities and media. We seek to demonstrate the benefits of studying urban and media/communication matters together to gain a fuller understanding of the changing nature of urban space, technology, identity and community.

Large-scale urbanization, which has spanned the globe segmentally and unevenly since the 18th century, prompted the development of mass society, which was predicated by the transfer of vital group elements (division of labor, common values) from relations defined by kinship to the depersonalized market and the state, and their incredibly sophisticated underpinning infrastructure, including class and gender inequality, the public sphere, specialization of roles, institutionalization of basic needs, the invention of selfhood, and spatial and social mobility. Not only was this tectonic shift in the organization of human association, action and experience modeled by particular communicative belief systems, such as the nation and patriarchy, but it also propelled the development of mass media, as the infrastructure of instituting connection (identification and differentiation) among strangers who found themselves living side by side in cities. In fact, the development and incorporation of communication technology (comprising vehicles, optics and telematics) into urban living was highly relevant for the rise of the modern (industrial, zoned) city and for its gradual transformation into the postmodern (service-based, polycentric, multicultural) urban territory.

Issues pertaining to the ways (face to face, technologically mediated, institutional) in which people have sought to interact and coexist in such globally diverse and complex technological environments as cities have been explored by established disciplines across the humanities and social sciences, above all sociology, which itself emerged as a response to the then new phenomenon, the modern city. In recent decades, urban media and communication ("media and the city", "mediated city", "media city", "communicative city" and other variants of emphasis) has become a separate research heading, addressed by scholarly groupings such as "urban communication" (Drucker and Gumpert 2016) and "urban media studies" (Tosoni and Ridell 2016). Most of these scholars come from a media studies background and their search for specific empirical transductions, historical connections and formal homologies between cities and media/communication is itself in keeping with interdisciplinary and experimenting origins of media studies itself (see Krajina et al. 2014).

Scholars involved in urban media and communication research argue that disciplinary research agendas become especially potent when they are shared. This interdisciplinary scholarship invites urban studies to consider more actively a media/communication angle. In matters of *planning and design* we are reminded that city spaces are imagined, in some specific way, before being constructed, and they are re-made through practical use after being built, as well as incorporating communication technologies as necessary equipment. In the area of *urban economy*, consumption that is integral to the industrial and creative industries is the prime source of post-industrial growth. In debates about *urban experience and community*, screen media such as artificial lighting, pirate radio and cinema, or practices such as social media-supported protests are recognized as essential to helping make the growing city negotiable, distinctive and globally recognizable. All standard concerns in media studies too have a relevant counterpart in urban studies: *democracy and participation* in the idea of liberal provision of public space, the idealized agora and debates about "right to the city"; *media technology* in spatial organization and navigation; *cultural identity* in questions of belonging and neighborhood/community life; issues of *representation/signification* in the realms of urban imagination, marketing and design.

Though the study of urban media and communication, burgeoning at the margins of media and communication studies, has led to considerable volumes of publications (e.g., Matsaganis et al. 2013; Papastergiadis 2016; Aiello et al. 2017; Graham 2004; Eckardt et al. 2006; Aurigi and De Cindio 2008; Haddour and Bell 2000), mainstream disciplinary research, at both ends of the media/city spectrum, still treats media and the city separately. In media research, the focus on technology usually leaves unacknowledged the generative relevance of the urban for communicative practices, whereas urban studies tends to take for granted communication issues, such as differential meanings of space. Thus, unlike many other companions which deal with established fields or themes, this book deals with familiar phenomena in new contexts and developing concerns reflecting new trends.

The consideration of urban media and communication in the *Companion* has also been driven by certain intellectual developments, such as the *spatial turn*, which spotlighted matters of multiplicity (Harvey 1982/2006; Massey 2005; Soja 1989/2011; Lefebvre 1991), the *mobility turn*, which conceptualized society beyond location (Urry and Sheller 2006), and *post-human and non-representational approaches*, which have argued for radically decentered (Rose 2016) and non-cognitional sources of meaning (Moores 2017), including *non-media-centric media studies* (Morley 2017), which has prioritized material and historical context in any discussion of communication. These developments have together contributed to the growth of a dialogical and co-constitutive relationship between cities and media. More precisely, "the city" is currently better understood as a linguistic substitute for the empirically more adequate term "the urban", which privileges process to things (Brenner and Schmid 2015; see Rodgers 2016), and is unable to deal with the complex and multi-centered and decentered nature of contemporary (often mega) cities (Stevenson 2013), and communication, rather than linear, merely symbolic and simplistically functional (assuming that messages with unchanged meanings and predictable consequences travel from A to B), is more usefully recognized as circular, contextually dependent, power-driven and inclusive in form; that is, involving "the mobility of people, goods and information" (Morley 2017).

Well aware of these lineages, our contributors aspired for a level of comprehensiveness and originality, which was commanded not only by the *Companion* form, but also by their very diverse disciplinary origins and career stage. For these scholars have previously engaged with issues outside their conventional disciplinary agenda, even if without explicit declaration. Thus, it is only partly true to say, as some earlier urban media and communication publications have done, that the kind of interdisciplinarity presented in this volume is only recent and entirely new. For instance, the urban figured as crucial in media scholar Srinivas' (2016) understanding of film viewing in India, whether in terms of recognizing convivial group attendance or the pervasive presence of filmic images in city streets as a space where the theatrical element of social life is played out. Sensitivity to media formats was essential in geographers Hoyler and Watson's (2013) analysis of distribution of media production complexes, which found that overall reliance on global profitability results in geographic fragmentation (key firms "remain firmly anchored in the three major home markets of North America, Europe and Japan", 2013: 90). Similarly, as editors—a media and cultural studies scholar from Europe (Krajina 2014) and an urban sociology and cultural policy scholar from Australia (Stevenson 2017)—we challenged our global contributors to engage with discipline(s) other to their own. They were invited to consider how culture becomes integral, space definitional, representation inescapable and technology functional in the specific form of urban media and communication they studied. Contributors were asked to rehearse parallel attention to materiality and symbolism as twin aspects of urban media and communication, to generously historicize their topics, so as to be in a better position to clarify what has changed, and to refer to specific global cases to portray depth. We sought to offer our intended readers—scholars, students and policy-makers—a wide-ranging inventory of relevant ideas and an invitation for wider recognition of urban media and communication research. Read together, the chapters in this book depict *the city and the urban* as an active and open-ended process—a meeting of different actors that results in multiple narratives and un/intended consequences—rather than a complete and indifferent supporting (technical) system operating in the background. The chapters portray *media and communication* in most diverse forms, as objects, signals, infrastructures, creative circuits and manual practices, as much as the more conventional institutions, technologies, ideologies and texts.

The book is divided into four Parts, each comprising 11 chapters. The introductory set of chapters examines formative trajectories and tropes in urban media and communication: the uneasy shift from industrial to data-driven urbanity; the formation of mediated urban subjectivity and experience; the rise of screen media intimately tied to the history of modern urbanism, such as cinema and television, practices like journalism and perspectives such as semiotics of urban space; and the centrality of urban mobility and consumption. The second Part examines how certain communication technologies and practices—transport protocols (e.g., dispatch systems and utility poles), surveillance, archives, "smart" houses, air pollution apps and citizen media—work as urban infrastructure and, conversely, how certain spaces, such as monuments, visual urban planning technologies, and global and "smart city" platforms, read as urban communication. The third Part focuses on post-industrial urbanism, which made communication its principal engine of growth. Specifically, chapters explore "media city" production centers, urban branding and tourism, European Capital of Culture projects, live urban mega events, media façade showcase, fashion, public art installations, nightlife cultures, gaming, scenes of taste and civic documentation of changing neighborhoods. Having adopted a somewhat typical structure, starting with surveys of top-down developments, in the final Part the collection focuses on the world of the everyday. Here the chapters examine such issues as multisensory experience, uses of smartphones, media audiences, graffiti, DIY architecture, protests, urban media communities, issues of poverty, and race and sexuality. The book ends with a global methodological outlook for the study of urban media and communication.

Tensions between the specific and the general, as well as conceptual and empirical, pervade all chapters, much as they have haunted urban and media studies. Ways in which general issues were refracted through specific contexts sought to aid the development of future considerations. For instance, Brunsdon's review of the field (Chapter 5) finds "the televisual city as more like the literary city than the cinematic city". James (Chapter 16) shows that the notion of "globality" in debates about "global cities" might usefully be revised by tracking from contemporary Tokyo to ancient Rome, from which vantage point we can recognize that orality, though predating, continues to coexist with the digital. Xin (Chapter 23) demonstrates that a variety of traditional media issues like convergence, vocation and ethics remain pertinent in new "media city" complexes that are usually presented as both advantageous to media production standards and hosting neighborhoods, but often end up serving neither well. In other cases, urban media and communication pairing has led contributors to invite further work on emerging phenomena: Zebracki (Chapter 29) on online participation in public art; Haeusler (Chapter 27) on the shift from planar to spline-based façades and the related issue of "density" in public space; Erickson (Chapter 21) on "cyber-transurbanism"; Coleman (Chapter 18) on the move from panoptic to "synoptic" cities; and Chesher and Humphry (Chapter 17) on the rise of the "hypermediated" home, among others.

The organization of the overall material, within and across chapters, was challenging, not least because it essentially dealt with the city, which is always multidimensional: material, symbolic, affective. The city dissects and connects very diverse domains of structure, meaning and action at once. As a result, the selection of topics—indicated by keywords in chapter titles—was informed partly by the established interdisciplinary agenda (spatial design, infrastructures, creative industries and daily life) and partly by emerging concerns (e.g., app-monitored pollution, "locative media", "urban gaming"), while some essential topics, like architecture, regeneration/gentrification, the public sphere, suburbia and gender, rather than being discussed separately, run through several relevant chapters. In-text cross-references to other chapters should help readers discover some of the ways in which shared interests were mutually defined across the book. The thematic nexus of streets, junctions and alleyways thus instituted should hopefully assist readers in weaving their journey through the book, ending up with more stimulating questions and open-ended curiosity than complete answers or "solutions".

As the book aspires to suggest, it is not enough to ascertain that social life in the 21st century is urban and mediated in general. The particular ways this mediation occurs tell us a lot about deeper orientations of issues specific to urban media and communication, such as extensive (translocal, connective) spatiality of action, group (in)visibility, mediated presence/absence and plurality of meaning (cf. Krajina 2014) that can remain unknown when emphasizing the city or media/communication alone. In its insistence on the meshing of matter, body and signal, urban media and communication research presented in this book invites us, by analogy to Venturi et al.'s (1972) landmark study on postmodern architecture *Learning from Las Vegas* and to Amin and Thrift's (2016: 2) challenge to try *Seeing Like a City*—specific in the "coming together of overlapping sociotechnical systems that gives cities their world-making power"—to also try *thinking through the mediated city*. Building from such previous initiatives, this perspective emerges as a thriving, expansive and collaborative scholarly platform for producing—advancing familiar and improvising new—interdisciplinary knowledge about cities as the dominant form and central context of human settlement and interaction in the 21st century. We hope that this diverse academic tapestry will also inspire our future negotiations of the cities in which we live.

References

Aiello, G. et al. (eds.) (2017) *Communicating the City: Meanings, Practices, Interactions*, London: Peter Lang.
Amin, A. and Thrift, N. (2016) *Seeing Like a City*, Cambridge: Polity.
Aurigi, A. and De Cindio, F. (eds.) (2008) *Augmented Urban Spaces: Articulating the Physical and Electronic City*, Aldershot: Ashgate.
Brenner, N. and Schmid, C. (2015) "Towards a New Epistemology of the Urban?" *City*, 19(2–3), pp. 151–182.
Drucker, S. and Gumpert, G. (2016) "The Communicative City Redux," *International Journal of Communication*, 10(2016), pp. 1366–1387.
Eckardt et al. (eds.) (2006) *Mediacity: Situations, Practices and Encounters*, Leipzig: Frank & Timme.
Graham, S. (2004) *The Cybercities Reader*, London: Routledge.
Haddour, A. and Bell, D. (eds.) (2000) *City Visions*, Harlow: Prentice Hall.
Harvey, D. (1982/2006) *The Limits to Capital*, London: Verso.
Hoyler, M. and Watson, A. (2013) "Global Media Cities in Transnational Media Networks," *Tijdschrift voor economische en sociale geografie*, 104(1), pp. 90–108.
Krajina, Z. (2014) *Negotiating the Mediated City: Everyday Encounters with Public Screens*, London and New York: Routledge.
Krajina, Z. et al. (2014) "Non-Media-Centric Media Studies: A Cross-Generational Conversation," *European Journal of Cultural Studies*, 17(6), pp. 682–700.
Lefebvre, H. (1991) *The Production of Space*, Oxford: Blackwell.
Massey, D. (2005) *For Space*, London: Sage.

Matsaganis, M. D. et al. (eds.) (2013) *Communicative Cities in the 21st Century: The Urban Communication Reader III*, London: Peter Lang.

Moores, S. (2017) *Digital Orientations: Non-Media-Centric Media Studies and Non-Representational Theories of Practice*, London: Peter Lang.

Morley, D. (2017) *Communications and Mobility: The Migrant, the Mobile Phone, and the Container Box*, London: Wiley-Blackwell.

Papastergiadis, N. (ed.) (2016) *Ambient Screens and Transnational Public Spaces*, Hong Kong: Hong Kong University Press.

Rodgers, S. (2016) "Theorizing Media After the Urban Revolution," *Mediapolis* No. 5, Roundtables, vol. 1. Retrieved from www.mediapolisjournal.com/2016/11/theorizing-media-urban-revolution.

Rose, G. (2016) "Posthuman Agency in the Digitally Mediated City: Exteriorization, Individuation, Reinvention," *Annals of the American Association of Geographers*, 107(4), pp. 779–793.

Soja, E. (1989/2011) *Postmodern Geographies: The Reassertion of Space in Critical Social Theory*, London: Verso.

Srinivas, L. (2016) *House Full: Indian Cinema and the Active Audience*, Chicago, IL: University of Chicago Press.

Stevenson, D. (2013) *The City*, Cambridge, UK and Malden MA: Polity.

Stevenson, D. (2017) *Cities of Culture: A Global Perspective*, London and New York: Routledge.

Tosoni, S. and Ridell, S. (2016) "Decentering Media Studies, Verbing the Audience: Methodological Considerations Concerning People's Uses of Media in Urban Space," *International Journal of Communication*, 10(2016), pp. 1277–1293.

Urry, J. and Sheller, M. (eds.) (2006) *Mobile Technologies of the City*, London: Routledge.

Venturi, R., Scott Brown, D. and Izenour, S. (1972) *Learning From Las Vegas: The Forgotten Symbolism of Architectural Form*. Cambridge, MA and London: MIT Press.

Wirth, L. (1938) "Urbanism as a Way of Life American Journal of Sociology," *American Journal of Sociology*, 44(1), pp. 1–24.

PART I

Trajectories of Mediated Urbanity

INTRODUCTION TO PART I
Trajectories of Mediated Urbanity

Zlatan Krajina and Deborah Stevenson

Cities have never been only about buildings and media have never been only about symbolic transaction. Indeed, as we emphasized in the General Introduction, outlining the central argument of this volume, the parallel study of cities and media/communication offers unique ways for deeper understanding of each other. This Part identifies key sites and origins of the media–city connection as well as highlighting phenomena particular to urban media and communication. Specifically, contributors explore conceptual issues such as historical lineages of mediated urbanity, including semiotics of space and screen cultures; institutions such as cinema, television and journalism; infrastructures such as mobility and consumption; and modes of experience pertaining to habitation and conviviality. Concepts, spaces and practices, which we identified above as key areas of this interdisciplinary scholarship, will continue to enfold in the ensuing sections and chapters that explore more specific cases.

As Scott McQuire proposes in Chapter 1, if urban processes are identified with communication, a historical perspective on this duality, an "archaeology", might help us better understand its present formation and potential future headings. As opposed to linear historicization, McQuire opts for identifying "thresholds", which, though crystalizing in different periods of time, overlap: the "big city life" of the 19th century, the "electropolis" of the early 20th century, the "suburban media city" of the postwar period and the 21st-century rise of the "digital media city". Observing those thresholds together, McQuire suggests that "creative experimentation" in combining new tech with old spaces will be needed to support conviviality in the mediated city.

Whatever the technology, it is through communicative practices, inherent to humans as social beings, that cities come to exist as meaningful environments. Immense diversification of agents and contexts engaged in sign production and exchange drives the essential slippage between the signifier and the signified. The multiplication of meanings given to social environments is, for Barthes (1986), best read from urban landscapes (of varying physical and digital variety) and semiotics remains foundational for exploring how ideas translate in space and how space is practiced as a communicative battlefield. Postmodern spatial design famously abounds in signage but particular meanings can be recognized in styles self-declared to serve "general" human needs and opposed to decoration; Le Corbusier's horizontal window can be read as the owner's camera pointing at the street and the glass kitchen door an internal surveillance system of gendered housework (Colomina 1996). Alexandros Ph. Lagopoulos in Chapter 2 provides accessible yet generous theoretical synthesis for reading "space-as-text" and "space-in-text". Along with examples like the 20th-century reconstruction of Thessaloniki and the place of Indian mandala in pre-capitalist urban planning, the chapter spans a range of perspectives, such as social and political economic.

Glass was arguably the building material that offered most opportunities for thinking about urban space as communicative interface. It embodied the modernist obsession with visibility and control through a separation between the inside and the outside thus instituted. Famous examples include 1851 London's Crystal Palace, 1976 LA's Bonaventure Hotel and 2003 Diller+Scofidio project Facsimile at the SF's Moscone Convention Center, the latter involving a moving public screen showing fictional footage of the inside and thus criticizing the unquestioned legitimacy and deceptive capacities of glass-supported surveillance. It is thus no coincidence that the essential form of urban mediation, as Zach Melzer demonstrates in Chapter 3, remains the screen, encompassing such coexisting mutations as frame, window and display. Urban screen cultures have provided cities their communicative vocabulary from as far back as the linear perspective scripted in the renaissance all the way to "Windows", the computer interface and the popular metaphor for media (Friedberg 2006).

The screen has come to figure as a key site for understanding the contradictory forces of modern, technological urbanity. Diverse as the store front and the mobile phone, the screen intervenes in transactions only to connect those involved; it diverts us from surroundings so as to expand them. Historical change in urban screen cultures that occurred during the 20th century, according to Robins (1996), was the shift from the authority of "electronic presentation" of the city, provided by cinematic narration as a space of reflection, to "electronic presence", created by pockets of networked data flows (public traffic information, advertising) offered without beginnings or endings and designed for chance encounters rather than viewing: a multi-screen impression rather than screened analysis of urban living.

The screen has embodied the tension between the desire to capture the endless city as totality and its semi-visible alleyways that are only trackable at the level of daily use and escape bird's-eye mapping. It is through the screen that we come to know the city as a gathering of segments, drawn from diverse vantage points. The primary urban media institution, cinema, gave this specific sensibility from its beginning in the early 20th century, a tangible form, through montage and perspective, as well as centering light as the equivalent of truth. First, the theater and now also more niche-oriented places, such as galleries and the multiplex (Harbord 2002), provided temporary excursions from the physical city. As Robins put it, "people went into movie houses as they went into dreams . . . aware that they were screened from actual dangers" by achieving a sense of (aestheticized) order of the city (1996: 132). Engaging with such fundamental areas of connection (representation, production and perception, Mennel 2008), James Donald, in Chapter 4, locates cinema at the origins of the modern city, which rests on the link among "the city", "the person" and "the machine". Donald explores this relationship across filmic cities such as Taipei, Berlin and New York, with a reflection on the development of this, arguably widest, area of urban media and communication scholarship.

Movement of capital between renaissance city-states circumvented other, competing forms of power such as the more static, territorial ownership by the church (Pirenne 1925). City walls, which had defined the horizon of city life, were gradually removed and cities opened up to transport connections which became vital infrastructure of communication. Now cities are gated through "data banks" (Virilio 2002). Relationships among people were given over to depersonalized social facilities of production and reproduction (factories, roads, welfare, shops) and systems of meaning (ideologies, lifestyles, aspirations); even the self was to be sought in the labyrinths of urban space and technology. Film set photography into motion to produce a meaningful presentation of movement (of people, goods, information) as the perceived essence of then-new modern city spaces (Nead 2007). In Chapter 8, Erika Nagy explores how intellectual turns (spatial, cultural) and sites (the mall, the bazaar and the street) in consumption studies harnessed issues like urban planning, policy and informality. The chapter in particular observes how urban consumption in post-socialist cities narrates an "alternative", non-binary, "modernity" to the conventional framework of "Western capitalism". Similarly, the most pronounced form of consumption-related communication in urban space—outdoor advertising—raises issues beyond matters of commercialization. In Chapter 7, Cesare Silla traces outdoor advertising in the 19th century as part of the development of "American consumer capitalism", which matched manufacturing with transport, distribution and marketing. Post-industrial developments (like "ambient marketing"), as well as concerns about "visual pollution" and social intervention (such as billboards), can challenge assumed gender roles, as exemplified in Philippine, Nigerian, Iranian and Kyrgyz cities.

Mobility is always more than transfer "from A to B", as Ole B. Jensen explains in Chapter 9. It involves different modalities, speeds and contexts (particularly access) concerning the capacity to move, hence propelling new forms of participation in the urban society. For instance, urban mobilities can combine physical stasis with virtual motion and vice-versa, as Jensen explores in the cases of Los Angeles and Beijing, leading to "mobile agoras" and "networked selves". In fact, as Shaun Moores demonstrates in Chapter 10, urban mobility, such as automatic acts of walking, driving and typing, rests on modes of being and knowing which are felt, rather than thought, and lived before being cognized and projected. These "sensuous . . . dealings" with surroundings remain precious, yet under-appreciated, sources of what we know about the urban media worlds we inhabit.

It is safe to argue that we are always in more than one location in the city, whether while standing before a back-lit storefront in a dark, cold street or engaging with like-minded others on social media in the midst of physically present and socially contrasting strangers on public transport. Separated by industrial organization, time and space were to be rejoined through technological systems such as the networked screen. As Morse famously noted, "the freeway, the mall and television" together formed the ecology of the urban postwar everyday, which involved citizens inhabiting spaces characterized by persistent "inclusion of . . . *elsewheres* and *elsewhens* in the here and now" (1990: 193–195). In Chapter 5, Charlotte Brunsdon excavates the usually ignored entanglements of television and the city: first its role as a symbolic counterpart to the physical (automobile-driven) postwar extension of the city, articulating the ideology of retreat and gendered construction of the suburban household; second, the ways in which post-industrial changes in production, distribution (broadcast to streaming) and reception (increasingly out-of-home) informed new television–city links, such as global city branding (e.g., Birmingham, drawn from BBC's images of "heritage aesthetic, dynamic violence and rock soundtrack"; Istanbul through the popularity of Turkish soaps). This circular relationship between media and cities is further elaborated in Chapter 6 by Scott Rodgers who ponders the ways in which journalism historically has infused city spaces with evocations of the public sphere by relaying "public address". Journalism continues to participate in urban place-making too, if now less from the centrally located print newsroom (which saw the analogy between "rectilinear" skyscrapers and print lines) and more in dispersed and digitally networked stations, servicing "hyperlocal" and "citizen" reporting.

If central figures of modern urbanity remain the stroller and the stranger, their navigation of city spaces can involve personal photographic tools (Kodak in the early 20th century, Instagram in the early 21st century). They enact what Gordon called "possessive spectatorship", whereby "the spectator could collect artifacts of experience with his camera, and he could just as likely be collected as someone else's artefact" (2010: 61). But what kind of visibility is good for whom? Myria Georgiou and Jun Yu raise this issue in the closing Chapter 11, on urban media subjectivity. They remind us that "tenuous commitment and proper distance" among strangers have always conditioned "freedom and cosmopolitanism in the city" and question the moral dimensions of media use in the negotiation of strangeness. Media can increase any group's visibility but also "challenge proper distance", depending on how and by whom the stranger is thus established. Contrary to celebratory visions of technology, which suggest that more communication equals more understanding, the media-savvy city is a space where difference remains constitutive of identity, and where, as Georgiou and Yu accentuate, "struggles for voice and recognition remain unresolved".

References

Barthes, R. (1986) "Semiology and the urban", in M. Gottdiener and A. Lagopoulos (eds.) *The City and the Sign: An Introduction to Urban Semiotics*, New York: Columbia University Press, pp. 87–98.
Colomina, B. (1996) *Privacy and Publicity: Modern Architecture as Mass Media*, Cambridge, MA: MIT Press.
Friedberg, A. (2006) *The Virtual Window: From Alberti to Microsoft*, Cambridge, MA: MIT Press.
Gordon, E. (2010) *The Urban Spectator: American Concept-Cities from Kodak to Google*, Lebanon, CT: University Press of New England for Dartmouth College Press.
Harbord, J. (2002) *Film Cultures*, London: Sage.
Mennel, B. (2008) *Cities and Cinema*, London: Routledge.
Morse, M. (1990) "An ontology of everyday distraction: The freeway, the mall, and television", in P. Mellencamp (ed.) *Logics of Television: Essays in Cultural Criticism*, Bloomington and Indianapolis, IN: Indiana University Press, pp. 193–221.
Nead, L. (2007) *The Haunted Gallery: Painting, Photography, Film*, New Haven, CT: Yale University Press.
Pirenne, H. (1925) *Medieval Cities: Their Origins and the Revival of Trade*, Garden City, NY: Doubleday Anchor Books.
Robins, K. (1996) *Into the Image: Culture and Politics in the Field of Vision*, London: Routledge.
Virilio, P. (2002) "The overexposed city", in G. Bridge and S. Watson (eds.) *The Blackwell City Reader*, Oxford: Blackwell Publishing, pp. 440–448.

1
AN ARCHAEOLOGY OF THE MEDIA CITY

Toward a Critical Cultural History of Mediated Urbanism

Scott McQuire

Inventing the Media City

The "media city" seems to be a recent problematic and in some respects, it is. The last decade has seen a concerted shift in which the need to think of cities and media as intimately related rather than separate fields has become more broadly recognized. The proliferation of differently spatialized digital media platforms, such as mobile devices and embedded video screens, foregrounds a distinctive mode of urban experience in which the co-evolution of built environment, media technology and social practice has become more pronounced. However, it is a mistake to assume that the media city is a function of digital media. Looked at from a different perspective, the problematic of mediated urbanism assumes a longer and more sinuous history. Take, for instance, Lewis Mumford's (1938: 479–485) assertion that the function of the city has always been as much about sociality as commerce and security. In establishing communication as a central *urban* problematic, Mumford's work signals the need to attend to the multiple historical thresholds across which different media have reworked urban sociability and communication. How far back we might push this horizon is a matter for further debate.

In Bernard Stiegler's (1998) techno-philosophical account, the elaboration of "human being" is integrally related to the co-evolution of both technics and language. Insofar as both capacities can be understood as forms of "mediation", we could argue that *media* is implicated in the unfolding of our very sense of what it is to be human. This standpoint brings into question the longstanding philosophical privilege of *presence*, which has authorized, among other things, a conceptual chain in which all forms of "mediation" are defined as secondary with respect to the assumed primacy granted to the "immediacy" of the face-to-face. It is this epoch in which mediation is inevitably parasitic and belated that may only now be coming to a close.

Even putting aside the ontological dimension of mediation, which seems to become ever more insistent as what we recognize as "media" assumes a greater role in more and more domains of social life, grasping the relation between media and urban life over a longer historical *durée* raises significant difficulties. If the broad aim is to understand how different media platforms contribute to the reconfiguration of urban sociality, it should go without saying—but frequently needs to be said!—that this cannot be figured as a neat, cause-and-effect relation. Rather, we are dealing with a complex dynamic involving multiple variables. This diversity has several consequences. While a series of eminent writers through the 20th century addressed transformations of communication, space and sociality as significant factors in the experience of modern urbanism—Simmel, Benjamin, Lefebvre, Goffman, Jacobs and Sennett, to name some of the more prominent—none, apart from Benjamin, explicitly addressed the function of media technologies as part of this problematic. Or where they did so, their responses were cast almost entirely in negative terms—for instance, Sennett's (1978: 288) pithy observation that television is "one of the means by which the very idea of public life has been put to an end". This pronounced absence of media analysis from urban studies has obscured the extent to which contemporary developments associated with networked digital media belong to a longer-standing problematic. The consequences of this foreclosure have been reinforced by the fact that the recent recognition of mediated urbanism has been approached from a number of disciplinary perspectives under a range of headings, adopting different conceptual frameworks and methodologies. The limits of both historical amnesia and disciplinary siloing set clear tasks for future critical scholarship, including the need for greater interdisciplinarity and careful attention to cultural and historical specificity.

Part of the complexity of any attempt to address mediated urbanism lies in the fact that the transformation of media platforms and communication practices is tightly implicated in the remaking of urban social experience, while the "urbanization" of media platforms—which is to say, their material instantiation in, and as part of, particular social contexts—is integral to the unfolding of their affordances. Recognizing this complexity should not be an excuse for either ignoring these issues or for lack of rigor in addressing them. Rather, it calls for the multiplication of critical empirical investigations, as well as for the probing of dominant conceptual frameworks, recognizing the need to continually interrogate assumptions and biases as they emerge.

In what follows, I focus primarily on patterns of urban development associated with the modernization of European cities and the urbanization of colonized territories such as North America and Australia. While these patterns have certainly exercised wider effects, they were never the whole story. Most significantly, the urbanizations of the late 20th century, located principally in Asia and Africa, and dominated by the rapid urbanization of China, cannot be assumed to follow the same patterns.

With this caveat in mind, I propose to trace four thresholds that might form a provisional archaeology of the media city: the "big city life" that emerges in the 19th-century industrial city, the "electropolis" of the 1920s, the dispersion of the urban into suburbs that emerges in the aftermath of the Second World War and the more recent transformations associated with the digital media city. My aim in delineating these four thresholds is not to consecrate them into a linear progression where each successive "era" is cut off from its antecedents, but to establish a frame for thinking of the problematic of mediated urbanism as an ongoing process resulting in the production of new relations between urban structures, media infrastructures, and individual and collective social life, including subjectivities and cultural forms. While certain elements persist or recur, others assume new stature or are themselves radical departures. My hope is that this approach will provide a better vantage point for assessing the current extension of networked digital media throughout urban space and, in particular, will help to broaden the narrow technocratic framing that has dominated the recent rhetoric of "smart city" debates (see Greenfield 2013). Such rhetoric, which tends to assume that it is desirable for technologies to work autonomously, represents a largely vendor-driven agenda that seems unlikely to support a rich and diverse social life in a future of intensively, if unevenly, mediated urbanism.

"Big City Life"

As Derrida has pointed out, justifying a starting point is never simple; one could always begin elsewhere. My rationale for beginning this archaeology of mediated urbanism in the 19th century is, first, that media platforms and urban life each undergo major transformations at this time. Second, and perhaps more importantly, the two domains enter a new relation at this time. This forms a critical element of "modernity" and is still recognizable in the present. Media start to become instrumental in producing what Sassen (2006) calls new "organizing logics" for grasping novel patterns of social life.

What, then, are some of the major changes in each domain? The key trajectory was undoubtedly the mass demographic movement from country to city that underpinned the inexorable rise of the urban as the dominant setting for social life. This process accelerated greatly in the 19th century, particularly in Europe, as cities expanded in scale and density in order to accommodate new production settings (factories) and a growing workforce. As major cities became increasingly crowded, dirty and susceptible to disease, pressure for wholesale change grew. If the most ambitious urban redevelopment was undoubtedly the reconstruction of Paris under Haussmann (initiated in 1853), the trajectory of "modernization" reached far wider. Myriad cities were carved apart to incorporate new transport infrastructure such as canals and railways, while their outer walls and narrow winding streets were demolished in favor of new streets and boulevards. The result was a decisive disruption of the familiar urban spaces and rhythms of the medieval city.

The remaking of the city as a space for increased circulation of both goods and people fitted the imperative of the industrializing capitalist economy, as it moved toward larger-scale integrated national (and international) markets (Harvey 2003). Reconstructed Paris, with its cafes, parks, arcades and broad gas-lit boulevards, was also the incubator for distinctively modern cultural experiences of public display—what T.J. Clark (1999) would later describe as the prototype for the modern spectacle (see also Chapter 5, this volume). The rapid growth of cities also conditioned the new social problematic formulated most influentially at the beginning of the 20th century by Simmel (1971): "big city life" was a life lived among strangers. As such, it demanded new protocols for public behavior (what Goffman [1959] would later call "civil inattention") and the new psychological disposition that Simmel (1997) famously characterized as the "blasé attitude" adopted by city dwellers as a defensive response to the multiplication and intensification of urban stimuli (see also Chapter 11, this volume).

The growing complexity and scale of urban life generated intense uncertainty as to one's proper *place* in the world: as Walter Benjamin (1999: 839) observed, the dominant literary image of the 19th-century city is of a *labyrinth*. While one prominent expression of this existential dislocation was an era of unprecedented revolutionary fervor, another was the emergence of new techniques for individual and collective adaptation to the exigencies of the changing urban environment. Notable among these were new cultural forms such as the daily newspaper and the detective story. By the mid-19th century, newspapers were evolving from vanity operations toward broad circulation mass communication platforms, extending over wider territories through rail distribution and shaping new social rhythms through practices such as multiple daily editions and the incorporation of telegraphy into reporting (Thomson 1995). At a formal level, the layout of the newspaper was distinctive in juxtaposing a multitude of apparently unrelated events in a single information space. For McLuhan, the 19th-century newspaper offered a precocious intimation of the avant-garde logic of collage. On the first page of his 1951 book *The Mechanical Bride*, McLuhan (1967a) was moved to proclaim the newspaper "a symbolist landscape", although its corporate and commercial orientation shaped his later conclusion that the newspaper's capacity to reveal the new patterns of modern urban life remained largely latent (McLuhan 1970: 192). In this respect, it exemplifies his thesis concerning media as *environment*—one that is largely invisible to those living within it (McLuhan 1967b).

Sociologists such as Benedict Anderson and Anthony Giddens subsequently offered a more historically grounded response to the same development. In Giddens's (1991: 25) account, newspapers "played a major role in completing the separation of space from place" as "geographic bundling" of news gave way to the primacy of the local "event". The collage form of the newspaper corresponds to the decline of the oral tradition of storytelling that Benjamin (2002) observed so evocatively. Instead of the physical contiguity that anchored the community of listeners who heard a story and passed it on, a new sort of continuity based on a collectively shared present-time was established by regular news reporting. Anderson's well-known formulation (1983) of the "imagined community" foregrounds the historical role of newspapers in the national extension of this fundamentally urban condition.

If, as McLuhan suggests, the potential for the news format to poetically apprehend and reveal the new patterns of urban life remained largely unconscious, it occasionally came into sharper focus. Sennett (1978: 168) argued that the exigencies of urban existence in the industrializing city, with its spatial expansion and new forms of mobility, public encounter and commodity display, generated a crisis in older forms of public life. The erosion of older forms and spaces of public sociability led to a general inability to "read" urban life and demanded the general extension of the skills of the detective: "Detectives are what every man and every woman must be when they want to make sense of the street". Exemplary of the close link between the new cultural logic of the newspaper and the detective paradigm is the figure of Sherlock Holmes, Conan Doyle's famous detective who came to public notice through newspaper and magazine serials, and was himself depicted as an avid consumer of news. Holmes the detective is a prototype who will be endlessly adapted in the new century. Capable of moving in all social strata, he is adept at scientific observation, including the pseudo-science of physiognomy, through which he reads the signs of a rigidly class-based society and pigeonholes strangers at a glance. Deploying these skills, he can penetrate the hidden order of the urban maelstrom. In the short story "The Adventure of a Norwood Builder" (published in the *Strand Magazine* in 1903), in the course of perversely lamenting the death of his arch-adversary Professor Moriarty, Holmes extols the daily paper as another touchstone for understanding the invisible patterns of modern urban life:

> With that man in the field one's morning paper presented infinite possibilities. Often it was only the smallest trace, Watson, the faintest indication, and yet it was enough to tell me that the great malignant brain was there, as the gentlest tremors of the edge of the web remind one of the foul spider which lurks in the center. Petty thefts, wanton assaults, purposeless outrage—to the man who held the clue all could be worked into one connected whole.
>
> *(Conan Doyle 1976: 16)*

Like the fetishization of visible class differences by physiognomy, the detective trope is symptomatic of growing anxiety over the forces that capitalism has unleashed.

One could equally point to the role played by new disciplines such as sociology, or new media such as photography, in generating forms of knowledge directed toward mastering the new conditions of urban life. If the former abstracts from lived events in order to build statistical portraits of urban dwellers, the latter begins to generate "visual facts" at a scale and speed previously unimagined and is yet to be constrained. The broader point I am trying to make here is that concerted deployment of different media and cultural forms including news, detective fiction and photography in this period was not only a means of responding to changes in urban form and social practices, but also actively initiated a new type of relation between media and urbanism. No longer content with embellishing the city with stable and enduring symbolic forms such as statues and reliefs, the modern media of daily press and snapshot register the industrial city's emergent spatio-temporal order, in which structure and persistence increasingly cede ground to process and ephemerality.

The Electric Media City

In 1924, Hungarian-born artist László Moholy-Nagy completed the script-collage for a film titled *Dynamic of a Metropolis*. The scenario employed a complex array of abstract and documentary elements, showcasing Moholy-Nagy's prodigious talent for working across media, including drawing, painting and photography. While never made, the project underlined the extent to which Moholy-Nagy already saw film as the primary tool for articulating a new concept of space-time. "Space creation" (*Raumgestaltung*) through the controlled use of light and movement would not only remain central to Moholy-Nagy's creative work over the next four decades, but also stands as emblematic of the desire of the early 20th-century avant-garde to address the *dynamic* qualities of the modern metropolis.

This modern city already seemed far removed from the emergent industrial city of the 19th century. As John Berger (1969) observed in his classic essay "The Moment of Cubism", the early 20th-century city became host to an astonishing array of new technologies in barely a generation. Electrical power and electric lighting, steel construction and glass-curtained skyscrapers, automobiles and airplanes, radios and telephones, synthetic materials and x-rays, air conditioning and chemical industries, subways and escalators, assembly lines and cinema were just some of the innovations transforming the urban-industrial life-world beyond recognition.

If this threshold can be seen as a problem for representation—how to show the life experience of this new urban world?—it went beyond the 19th-century need to interpret the conflictual and chaotic signs emitted by milling crowds of urban strangers. Rather, the entire urban environment seemed to have been transfigured by new experiences of speed and light. Mechanical vehicles and urban lighting rapidly became the emblematic expressions of every self-consciously modern city, not least where such elements were patently lacking. Famed "electropolises" such as New York and Berlin became social laboratories for a perceptual experience that was at once intensely pleasurable, excessive and overwhelming.

The perceived homology between this experience of the city and the then-new media of cinema—a medium distinctively produced by the combination of light moving over time—was widely remarked at the time. Many artists and writers of the period saw film as the best means for capturing the new experience of city life. The most sophisticated formulation of this relation was elaborated by Walter Benjamin (2003: 265–266), who positioned film as urban "dynamite" capable of unlocking the experiential "prison-world" of the industrial city. For Benjamin, film assumed *epochal* significance insofar as its characteristic organizing logic—based on fragmentation and reassemblage of appearances through montage—might enable citizen-viewers to grasp patterns of urban life that otherwise resisted embodied experience. Benjamin's argument had several parts. The first, influenced by Baudelaire and Simmel, was his assertion that the quintessential experience of "big city life" was *shock*. Second, drawing on his reading of Freud, he argued that consciousness routinely functions as a "protective shield" against shock by locating the effect of external stimulus in a linear temporal chain. While this enabled the individual to cope with the new urban setting, it came at the cost of reducing urban experience to a largely incommunicable private idiom.

Film offered a potential antidote to this existential isolation. Through montage and the collective viewing experience, Benjamin argued that film engendered a distinctive mode of "distracted perception" capable of eluding the habitual filters imposed by consciousness. Properly used, film could transform avant-garde aesthetics into a genuine political force, providing the key to unlocking the latent energy of the modern city. As Benjamin (2003: 264) put it: 'The extremely backward attitude to a Picasso painting changes into a highly progressive reaction to a Chaplin film". With their eyes and minds opened by the "dynamite of the 1/10th of a second", the mass of urban inhabitants could perceive their surroundings anew and begin to remake them according to their needs.

However, as Benjamin (2003: 270) recognized in the conclusion to his canonical "Artwork" essay, such an emancipatory outcome from the "technological reproducibility" enabled by media was by no means given. If distracted perception was to become a "profane illumination"—a charged and transformative insight that could be acted on collectively—a new form of political consciousness was also needed. In the absence of political awakening, the radical potential of montage risked becoming neutralized by being normalized as a purely formal technique of mass entertainment. Subsequent history confirms this fear, as cinema and the media apparatus were pressed into supporting a new global political settlement, dominated on the one hand by the hardening of the incipient spectacle into organized consumption (based on professional publicity and lifestyle advertising pioneered in the USA from the 1920s) and, on the other, by the rise of mass media propaganda and intense forms of mediated identification with the "Great Leader" that comes to dominate both fascism and communism in the 1930s.

The Suburban Media City

Benjamin himself proved unable to avoid the jaws of this political closure. By the time of his suicide in 1940, the urban environment that he hoped that film would help to unlock had already begun to further mutate. In retrospect, the 1920s can be seen as a certain zenith of the industrial city. However, its decline becomes far more evident following World War II, particularly in the USA where subsidized federal home loans for returned soldiers fueled "white flight" from aging inner-city areas to new suburban tracts such as Levittown. The scale of this shift was unprecedented: between 1940 and 1947, some 60 million Americans—nearly half the population—moved to new homes (Dimendberg 1997: 70).

As has been widely observed, the rise of the suburbs substantially altered the balance between public and private space in city life: the paucity of traditional public spaces was interpreted by Kasinitz (1994: 275) as "a turning away from the street and towards controllable domesticity". A key dimension of "controllable domesticity" was the emergence of the private home as a media center through its incorporation of radio and television. Broadcast television in particular proved pivotal in the retooling of wartime capitalism. Despite early misgivings within the industry, the rapid uptake of television in the USA from 1948 established the communication logistics necessary for the full development of large-scale Fordist production of consumer goods. As the primary conduit carrying advertising directly into the home, television went far beyond simply providing information about the new range of products and models; it also showcased model behaviors for the new era of lifestyle consumption centered in the private home.

Alongside the growth of automobility, broadcast television is closely allied with the consolidation of a particular spatial and temporal disposition of the city. The suburban dispersion that defines the postwar era inevitably placed heightened importance on linking the private sphere of the home to the public realm of work, politics and the city. Television grew to fill this *structural* need—defining itself in the process—as it became the primary mechanism carrying not only the political public sphere (news and current affairs), but also representations of cultural life and market relations *into* the home. As the habitus of broadcasting matured, the cellular architecture of network television came to typify a distinctive recasting of the relation between citizens and *polis* as one between a mass of essentially private individuals. This amounted to an historical inversion of the public–private relation of classical society: in modern suburbia, authenticity was no longer a function of public life but belonged to private experience.

Broadcasting was also critical in consolidating elements of older social routines even as it helped to propagate new everyday rhythms (Scannell 1996). With the advent of satellite broadcasting in the 1960s, television leveraged its novel capacity for the production of spatially extended experiences of social simultaneity to establish what Dayan and Katz (1992) have called *media events*, exemplified by the live broadcasting of Kennedy's funeral (1961) and the Apollo moon landing (1969). In retrospect, what is most significant about the "media event" is not the extent to which it was seemingly antithetical to the older forms of public life based on collective assembly in urban public space. Rather, it is the way it introduces a new and uncertain era in which the immediacy of "face-to-face" encounters finds itself counterpointed by a new regime of "liveness": the immediacy of relayed events that arrive in the home from distant elsewheres and can be watched in concert with a multitude of others arrayed across a multiplicity of different sites. Liveness marks a decisive shift in the operation of mediated urbanism, as the rhythms of *re*-presentation begin to be fundamentally reconfigured. Instead of media constituting a recording or record that relates to an event that has already occurred, broadcasting opens the ambiguous age in which events and their representations begin to coincide. If there is a sense in which all media function to establish feedback loops between "event" and "representation", broadcasting accelerates the feedback process to the point of undermining its formative logic by making "representation" and "event" simultaneous. However, it is arguably only with the decline of the broadcast paradigm—a process closely related to digital convergence and the rise of distributed digital networks—that the full implications of this shift become apparent.

The Digital Media City

Like most clichés, the depiction of the transition from the broadcast media environment to the networked digital media environment in terms of a shift from a "one-to-many" to a "many-to-many" paradigm carries a kernel of truth. If this is not solely about power moving into the hands of consumers, as media barons such as Rupert Murdoch like to proclaim, the digitization of production tools, the development of computers into multimedia devices, the exponential decrease in the cost of capturing, storing, retrieving and processing information, and the growth of cheap, robust global connectivity have all combined to change many of the traditional operating assumptions of media industries. These changes in the cost, ease, reach and speed of communication, notably through the profusion of Internet-enabled mobile devices, have had an immediate and significant impact on urban space.

Elsewhere, I have proposed the term "geomedia" (McQuire 2016) to situate the new affordances of digital media platforms and the way these contribute to the reconfiguration of urban social relations more generally. Geomedia emerges at the nexus of three related trajectories: ubiquity, positionality and real-time feedback. In comparison to a past defined by more restricted conditions of media access, mobile digital devices and embedded media platforms recreate the contemporary city as a space in which media content and connectivity are seemingly available "anywhere, anytime". While in practical terms access is still frequently constrained by a range of technical, commercial and politico-social pressures, connectivity has become the new default expectation. This capacity works in concert with the greatly enhanced role of location in framing media functionality over the past decade. The proliferation of location-aware devices and software, in conjunction with the growth of geocoded data, has meant that position has now become central to a wide range of social practices, commercial strategies and governmental logics enacted in contemporary urban space.

Equally as important is the recent extension of real-time communication as a general affordance. "Real-time" needs to be distinguished from the kind of social simultaneity that became a feature of modern life with the advent of live broadcasting. What is different in the present is the way the distributed architecture of digital networks opens up a potential for communication and coordination between diverse actors even as events unfold. This development can be seen in the emergence of new sorts of "media events", from the so-called "Arab Spring" uprisings to the different iterations of the Occupy movement, in which the embodied occupation of urban public space proceeded in tandem with networked forms of organization, self-reporting and publicity. Where the communication logistics for rapid mobilization of large numbers of people was once the prerogative of highly centralized institutions such as the military or the police, this capacity has now become increasingly available to other social actors including citizens and NGOs. While this development should not be hastily equated with a simple line of "democratization", it has clearly altered some of the major historical constraints on public assembly. It is also symptomatic of the extent to which the whole logic of contemporary social encounter and urban situation is increasingly articulated with the spatio-temporal affordances of digital media platforms. As a result, media, which was once predominantly considered fundamentally opposed to the logic of place, now finds itself ambiguously entangled with practices of *emplacement* and placemaking (see Chapter 10, this volume).

However, if distributed access is the harbinger of new forms of micro-sociality and collective collaborative action, the ambivalence of the emergent digital media city is found in the fact that every transaction leaves a potentially recordable, archivable and searchable trace. The kinds of tracking protocols first established on the Internet have become normalized and are now being extended throughout urban space. Corporate mass surveillance enabled through dominant media platforms including search, mapping and social media is now being counterpointed by government-sponsored "smart city" schemes for the pervasive instrumentation of the city. Under this rubric, networked sensors are being widely deployed to provide data streams relating to all kinds of urban systems, including the utilization of personal mobile devices as a means of harvesting more granular data. Urban governance of mobility and identity is fast shifting from a system based on the regulation of flows at specific border control points to become a more general *predictive* logic deployed throughout urban space.

The Future Media City?

This brief and condensed account of four historical thresholds of mediated urbanism has sought to demonstrate several things. First, there has been a significant shift in the role and function of media platforms as organizing logics of the urban. This shift relates to the distinct affordances of different media in conditioning the social relations of space and time, as well as to their distinctive spatialization *within* the city. If media function according to a general logic of enabling organized "feedback", the dominant temporal rhythms of this function have moved from *re*-presentation to broadcast simultaneity in the 20th century and are now being reworked further by distributed real-time communication practices. This is by no means a neat succession of technical thresholds, as older platforms and practices continue to exist, even as new ones emerge.

Second, the key stakes of urban communication have been significantly altered. While it is no longer so difficult for marginalized individuals and groups to gain a "voice", in the sense of producing and distributing media content, commanding attention in an increasingly crowded global agora remains a challenge. Moreover, the promise of "free expression" assumes a different hue in a social media milieu when data acquisition and analytics underpins the business strategies of the media platforms that are now the dominant corporate players of digital capitalism.

Third, the "smart city" agenda that is being leveraged on the back of urban digital networks, including personal mobile devices, has been couched largely in terms of automation and efficiency, and all too often pays only lip service to vexed issues of public participation and citizen empowerment. To contest this closure, there is an urgent need to insist on the importance of rich and complex forms of communication to an urban social life characterized by diversity and new mobilities.

In conclusion, while the mediation of urban life is not a recent invention, it has assumed new importance and urgency. Today, the mediation of urban life needs to be recognized as *constitutive*, in the sense that it reaches into and reworks all realms of social interaction, including our experience of the "face-to-face" and the "immediate" as meaningful social situations. Designing future media cities capable of providing opportunities for rich social interaction will not only require new thinking about data and privacy but will also demand creative experimentation to find new positive models for articulating—*grafting* or *jointing together*—the affordances of digital media infrastructure (network access, interfaces, ephemeral content) with the affordances of traditional urban spaces (assembly and gathering, material history, event-spaces) in productive and mutually reinforcing ways.

References

Anderson, B. (1983) *Imagined Communities: Reflections of the Origins and Spread of Nationalism*, London: Verso.
Benjamin, W. (1999) *The Arcades Project* (trans. H. Eiland and K. McLaughlin), Cambridge, MA: Belknap Press.
— (2002) "The storyteller: Observations on the works of Nikolai Leskov", in H. Eiland and M.W. Jennings (eds.), trans. E. Jephcott and others, *Walter Benjamin: Selected Writings*, Vol. 3, 1935–1938, Cambridge, MA and London: Belknap Press.
— (2003) "The work of art in the age of technological reproducibility", in H. Eiland and M.W. Jennings (eds.), trans. E. Jephcott and others, *Selected Writings*, Vol. 4, 1938–1940, Cambridge, MA and London: Belknap Press.
Berger, J. (1969) *The Moment of Cubism and Other Essays*, London: Weidenfeld and Nicholson.
Clark, T.J. (1999) *The Painting of Modern Life*, Princeton, NJ: Princeton University Press (first published 1984).
Conan Doyle, A. (1976) *The Complete Adventures and Memoirs of Sherlock Holmes*, New York: Avenel Books.
Dayan, D. and Katz, E. (1992) *Media Events: The Live Broadcasting of History*, Cambridge MA: Harvard University Press.
Dimendberg, E. (1997) "From Berlin to Bunker Hill: Urban space, late modernity and film noir in F. Lang's and J. Losey's M", *Wide Angle*, 19(4), pp. 62–93.
Giddens, A. (1991) *Modernity and Self-Identity: Self and Society in the Late Modern Age*. Stanford, CA: Stanford University Press.
Goffman, E. (1959) *The Presentation of the Self in Everyday Life*, Garden City, NY: Doubleday.
Greenfield, A. (2013) *Against the Smart City*, New York: Do Projects.
Harvey, D. (2003) *Paris, Capital of Modernity*, New York and London: Routledge.
Kasinitz, P. (ed.) (1994) *Metropolis: Center and Symbol of Our Times*, London: Macmillan.
McLuhan, M. (1967a) *The Mechanical Bride: Folklore of Industrial Man*, Boston, MA: Beacon Press.
— (1967b) "The invisible environment: The future of an erosion", *Perspecta*, 11, pp. 161–167.
— (1970) *Culture Is Our Business*, Eugene, OR: Wipf and Stock.
McQuire, S. (2016) *Geomedia: Networked Cities and the Future of Public Space*, Cambridge: Polity.
Mumford, L. (1938) "The social concept of the city", in *The Culture of Cities*, New York: Harcourt Brace and Co, pp. 479–485.

Sassen, S. (2006) *Territory, Authority, Rights: From Medieval to Global Assemblages*, Princeton, NJ: Princeton University Press.
Scannell, P. (1996) *Radio, Television, and Modern Life: A Phenomenological Approach*, Oxford: Blackwell.
Sennett, R. (1978) *The Fall of Public Man: On the Social Psychology of Capitalism*, New York: Vintage Books.
Simmel, G. (1971) "The stranger", in D. Levine (ed.), *Georg Simmel: On Individuality and Social Forms*, Chicago, IL: University of Chicago Press.
—— (1997) "The metropolis and mental life", in D. Frisby and M. Featherstone (eds.), *Simmel on Culture*, London: Sage.
Stiegler, B. (1998) *Technics and Time 1: The Fault of Epimetheus*, trans. R. Beardsworth and G. Collins, Stanford, CA: Stanford University Press.
Thomson, J. (1995) *The Media and Modernity: A Social Theory of the Media*, Cambridge: Polity Press.

Further Reading

Mattern, S. (2017) *Code + Clay . . . Data + Dirt: Five Thousand Years of Urban Media*, Minneapolis, MN: University of Minnesota Press.
McQuire, S. (2008) *The Media City: Media, Architecture and Urban Space*, London: SAGE/Theory, Culture & Society.
Mediapolis: A Journal of Cities and Culture (2016), 1(5).

2
THE SEMIOTICS OF URBAN SPACE

Alexandros Ph. Lagopoulos

Epistemological Considerations

Any scientific object is defined by the adoption of a specific epistemological approach oriented toward a specific object. A term such as "urban semiotics" is an umbrella term that covers the subject of the present chapter, but also, for example, the study of urban practices or shop signs. I shall focus on one of the central objects of this term, urban space. The term "semiotics" indicates that my approach will be concerned with meaning. Thus, the specific orientation of this chapter is the *semiotics of urban space*. Since its object is the city or part of it, it does not coincide with, for example, the semiotics of architecture, concerned with individual buildings or building complexes, and its viewpoint is differentiated from the material analysis of space—economic, sociological, demographic or other.

The semiotics of space can be studied in two manners. The first is the direct study of actually existing built space; that is, the study of space-as-text. The second is the indirect study of space through the mediation of some other semiotic system, such as religious, mythological and philosophical texts, literature, the press, painting or cinema. Such studies concern space-in-text and may be articulated with the first approach.

European semiotics is a theory of culture originating in the Francophone world and urban semiotics has developed in this tradition. There are also other theoretical perspectives on the meaning of urban space, originating in Anglo-Saxon human geography. Behavioral geography has studied cognitive or mental "maps" (e.g., Golledge and Stimson 1987); the phenomenologically based humanistic geography turned toward the existential dimension of urban space (e.g., Tuan 1977; Pickles 1985) and the "new" cultural geography studies urban space through the lens of postmodernism (e.g., Jacobs 1993).

The semiotics of space could not be constituted without the above epistemological considerations, since they delimit the field. However, this delimitation, necessary though it is, should not be interpreted as isolation from other approaches. Given the understandable tendency to extrapolate from the particular to the general, the result of isolation is partiality in the best case and, in the not infrequent worst case, misleading conclusions. Thus, I consider it necessary, before focusing on our subject matter, to touch upon the broader context within which we should understand the semiotics of space.

Political Economy and the Semiotics of Urban Space

It was Henri Lefebvre who emphasized that urban space is a social product. Simultaneously, Louis Althusser and Étienne Balibar with their "structural Marxism" defined society as a complex structured whole, composed of a set of internally structured levels or "instances." The major ones of these are the economic level, the political and legal level, and the level of ideologies and theoretical formations (philosophy and sciences); the latter two levels are determined by the economic level, but only in the "final instance," because of mediating processes, and thus are "relatively autonomous" (Althusser and Balibar 1968: 120–124). The same grid was adopted by Manuel Castells for his initial analysis of the production of urban space. Castells shows the semiotic character of ideologies when related to urban space when he posits that the spatial manifestation of the ideological system is a sign system, with the spatial forms as signifiers and the ideology they communicate as signifieds (Castells 1972: 165–280).

On his part, Lefebvre defines three aspects of social space: the spaces related to its production and reproduction (the socio-economic production of space), the "representations of space" held by urban planners, technocrats and others tending to "scientificity" (partially related to the ideological and, through it, the political production of space), and a subordinate third space, which concerns not the production but the consumption of space, including its users (Lefebvre 1974: 40–43, 48–49, 283–284).

Lefebvre's first and third aspects are also elaborated by Raymond Williams's "cultural materialism." Williams supports the dialectics between an economic field, determining in the sense of setting limits to human action and the pressure of the social subjects on society and consciousness. Stuart Hall supports a similar view. For him, the sense of economic determination is that material circumstances have limiting effects on the grid, not the content, of ideology (Hall 1996), though when he argues that they are simply "mutually determining," it is difficult to defend this as a materialist position. Williams distinguishes between a formal "official consciousness" and a "practical consciousness," which is a "structure of feeling" or "structure of experience" and is constituted by meanings and values as they are experienced actively in everyday life (Williams 1977: 83–89, 130–134). It is these meanings and values that are invested in urban space during its consumption. The same synthesis of system and practices, structure and agency, is proposed by Pierre Bourdieu, who sees the semiotic as produced from the social structure through his concept of "*habitus*" (Bourdieu 1971, 1980: 88–96, 101–102).

There is a historical precedent to these views in the "Marxist sociological poetics" of Mikhail M. Bakhtin and Pavel Nikolaevich Medvedev. According to these authors, ideology is incorporated into a "semiotic material," from language and literature to the organization of objects and people, and both are produced by economy, not as a reflection but as a refraction of it, through mediations (Medvedev and Bakhtin 1978: 7–15, 18).

The following diagram (Figure 2.1) condenses the above views, concentrating on the production of urban space. It shows the operation of the major systemic components of modern society in respect to space and is valid for any society, including those without monetary economy: the spontaneous production of space from the socio-economic system, the production of space due to state intervention (planning) and that due to the semiotic, with their dialectical interrelationships and in their articulation with space. These components are complex, being constituted by different or conflicting groups. They are analytical concepts and, in practice, cannot be isolated, because they function together dynamically as a system through continuous mediations and interactions, though these are not all of the same intensity, as the arrows indicate. The diagram shows, for example, that ideology may function *within* the socio-economic system or that it is subject to class determination, about which Hall observes that there is a tendency for ideas to arise

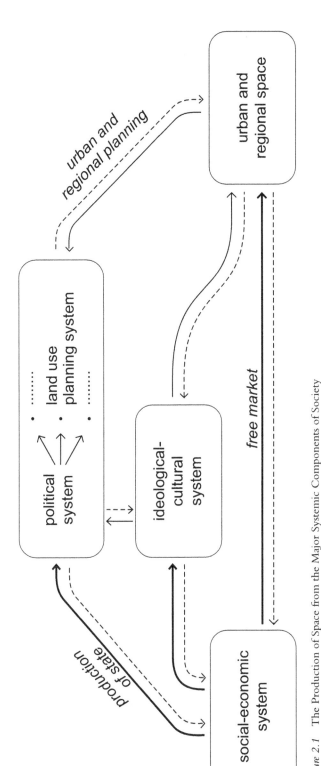

Figure 2.1 The Production of Space from the Major Systemic Components of Society

from the material conditions of social groups and classes and possibly to reflect them without any rigid link between class and ideas. The figure does not cover the consumption of space, or the circle back from it to the reproduction of the social formation.

In capitalist production, there are three stages of the circulation of capital and commodities: a circulation process before production, a process of production and a new circulation process, through which the products reach the market in order to be materially consumed; these three processes are generalizable also to societies in which goods have a non-commodity form. We observe a striking resemblance between this socio-economic circuit and the communication circuit in which an addresser produces a message that is then put into circulation and reaches a set of addressees that interpret it or pragmatically use it—that is, semiotically consume it; urban space is semiotically such a message. There is, then, a general isomorphism between the socio-economic circuit and the communication circuit (see also Lagopoulos 1993: 274).

The Semiotic Analysis of Urban Space as Place

Humanistic geography has the merit of indicating the radical difference between two kinds of spaces: (material geographical) "space" and (semiotic) "place." The concept of space refers to an external, material object and involves an intellectual, abstract, neutral and indirect manner of understanding geographical entities, while place is an internal semiotic object, a direct experience of space in consciousness, invested with meaning, values and feelings. Space is mainly produced by the dominant socio-economic system; place is by the semiotic component (Tuan 1977: 5, 17). Later, we shall concentrate on place.

Starting from Roland Barthes's position that "as soon as there is a society, every usage is converted into a sign of itself" (Barthes 1964: 106), Umberto Eco elaborated a first basis for the semiotics of space with reference to architecture. He argues that the objects of architecture are not created to communicate (the semiotic perspective) but to function (the material perspective); however, they simultaneously communicate their function. He considers architecture as a system of signs, composed of *spatial signifiers*—the perception of the form of the use objects—and conventional *denotative signifieds* of a functional nature, which are the "first functions" of architecture. Beyond these, there are *connotative signifieds* of architecture, its "second functions," which constitute a system of anthropological values, a global ideology of functions, and define the symbolic level of architecture. The first order constitutes the system of architecture *strict sensu*, but it is just syntactical; actual architecture as a whole presupposes its conjunction with systems existing outside it (the functional and symbolic signifieds), and these are the ones found in architecture (Eco 1972: 261–317).

We can improve Eco's theory in two directions. First, there are also other non-morphological denotative signifieds referring to space besides the functional ones. In a field study in northern Greece on the conception of regional space, more than two dozen unitary semantic fields (codes) of such denotations were identified (Lagopoulos and Boklund-Lagopoulou 1992: 209–217). Thus, for example, in a statement such as "[t]he western suburbs have their own way of life," we encounter a sociological denotative code. However, to do justice to Eco, the appearance of this and the other denotative codes beyond the functional one presupposes their conjunction with the functional code ("the *western suburbs*," "the *housing area* is polluted"). These codes may also function as connotative codes. There are also two codes that are always connotative: the aesthetic code ("this is a beautiful part of the city") and the experiential code ("I am fond of the neighborhood where I grew up"), covering issues of spatial and personal identity.

The second improvement to Eco's theory is outlined in the above views of Castells, focused on spatial forms. In fact, the denotations of space are not only non-morphological, but also morphological. A street pattern may be a grid, the city center may have tall buildings and, of course, various kinds of connotations may be attached to them ("monotonous arrangement," "oppressive environment"). The same code may function as either denotative or connotative.

As we saw, urban space from the semiotic viewpoint is integrated within a communication circuit. Here, we pass *from semiotics to sociosemiotics*. Elaborating on urban sociosemiotics, Algirdas Julien Greimas conceives of the producer of a city plan as a collective "actant" that may be composed of different "actors" (see below the case of the city of Thessaloniki), only one of which is the urban planner. In the process of planning, an amalgamation takes place of the values of the different actors, though sometimes contradictory, leading to an implicit ideological model of the future city (Greimas 1976: 151–153).

Approaches to the Semiotic Production of Urban Space

One of the planners who has addressed the semiotics of the urban environment is Kevin Lynch. After a detailed analysis of urban images (see the next section), Lynch formulated normative propositions for urban design. His principal goal is the "imageability" of the city (also see next section), which he considers the foundation for aesthetic pleasure. He proposes a semiotic reshaping of the city, through forms organized on different levels of generality, both in space and in their temporal development, and observes that they should take into account the basic elements of the city, traffic, land uses and the main urban focal points (Lynch 1960: 2, 91, 95).

Lynch's principles of urban design are the following (Lynch 1960: 108–109):

(a) morphological specificity and simplicity of urban elements
(b) continuity of urban space, through form, uses or rhythmical repetition
(c) use of dominant elements
(d) clarity of connections
(e) differentiation of directions, through asymmetry or gradation
(f) use of visual penetration and panoramic views
(g) creation of a feeling of movement
(h) creation of temporal sequences
(i) strengthening of imageability with non-spatial elements, such as names and social and historical references.

Lynch's proposal may work to a point for local plans, but it is over-ambitious for the scale of a whole city and one-sided because of its elitist concentration on aesthetics. Mainly, by limiting itself to morphological signifiers and their spatial or functional denotation (see the next section), it ignores the actual ideological universe projected onto the city by urban plans, which I shall try to identify with the following example.

In 1917, five years after the liberation of the city of Thessaloniki from the Ottoman Empire, a devastating fire leveled a great part of the central city. The government of Eleftherios Venizelos appointed a committee of Greek and French specialists and a first plan was prepared by the British architect Thomas Mawson, followed by a final plan by the renowned French architect Ernest Hébrard. The plan, which was partially realized, represents the first major urban intervention in Europe after World War I and still shapes the central city.

My semiotic analysis of the plan is mainly based on historical data from the historian of urban planning Pierre Lavedan (1921, 1933). Not all of its codes are semiotic (focused on urban meaning) because we also find codes of a practical planning nature; however, even these codes may be invested with semiotic connotative meaning. About a dozen major codes and certain sub-codes may be identified.

Two practical codes are a code of health and a very important economic code centered on the historic port of the city. A third practical code is the functional one covering the newly emerging principle of zoning and applied by Hébrard according to his four-zone prototype: administrative center (the central city with administration, commerce and upper-middle-class housing, which belongs to another zone of his prototype), industrial area (the west of the city, where it still is, with working-class housing areas) and leisure area (a garden to the east of the central city, in which a university is foreseen and where it is today), beyond which extend upper-middle-class suburbs. This practical functional code is invested with the connotations "modern city" (as is also the case with the economic code) and "European city," giving a specific symbolic identity to the city. These are also the connotations of his elaborate traffic code, which foresees large avenues, allowing for fast and safe traffic, and a street system securing the decongestion of the city center.

The cultural code presents special interest. It has two poles. The first is that of modernism, with the above connotations. The second is composed of three historical sub-poles. Hébrard used as a basis for his plan the Hellenistic street grid system to connote its connection to ancient Greece. He also displayed the Byzantine churches by connecting them to specially designed radial axes and making them nodal points of his plan, thus connoting the relation of the city to the next phase of Greek history, Byzantium. The Beaux-Art conception of streets converging to a monument is loaded with aesthetics and the cultural and aesthetic codes are closely linked in Hébrard's plan. For example, Hébrard created the central square of the city on the seashore, at the end of a new monumental axis oriented toward the "supernatural" view of Mount Olympus.

The third sub-pole is suggested by the writings of Lavedan, Hébrard's contemporary. Lavedan adopts an orientalist viewpoint on Thessaloniki, which combines a condescending attitude with an atmosphere of fairy-tale, exoticism and charm. The connotation "Orientalness" seems to have marked the new plan for the French.

We also encounter in the plan a kind of super-code, which is political. Hébrard was one of the cornerstones of modern French planning and his ideology was imbued with colonialism and faith in the French civilizing mission and superiority. This nationalistic code is brought out by Lavedan, who refers to the triumph in Thessaloniki of "his [Hébrard's] person, the cause of urban planning and that of France" (Lavedan 1933: 148).

Let us now pass to a sociosemiotic approach. The plan committee was a collective actant, closely related to Prime Minister Venizelos and his Minister of Transport, Alexandros Papanastasiou. The two men referred to the historical past of the city and its future as a modern city and used also in their statements the economic, the aesthetic and the health code, as well as a pronounced political code, exemplified by Venizelos's declaration: "if I am proud of the conduct of my foreign policy, I am no less proud of this work"; a work that, as Mawson writes, followed Venizelos's ideals (Yerolympos-Karadimou 1995: 81–82, 94).

The codes of Hébrard that we detected in the plan were generally also endorsed by the Greek actors. However, there are two major code conflicts in the semantic investment of the plan. First, the Greeks wanted to get rid of whatever was reminiscent of the Ottoman past and thus any connection to the Orient. Second, they opposed French nationalism.

As a last step, I shall pass to an extension of sociosemiotics, namely its articulation with the material social structure in *social semiotics*. Venizelos was the head of the Liberal party. Supported by the middle class, he was elected in 1910 with 85% of the vote, but because of his decision to cooperate with the Allies, he lost the support of that part of the bourgeoisie that believed in the "neutrality" of the ruling Bavarian king. Venizelos fought the feudal system of land ownership and attracted sections of the lower-middle class. With the Balkan wars (1912–1913), there had been a great extension of the population and territory of Greece, and irredentist aspirations continued to be a cornerstone of his politics. Venizelos's policies aimed at Europeanization and modernization; he was the founder of a modern Greek state based on the rule of law, something considered by his most powerful supporters, the bourgeoisie, as the guarantor of the unobstructed function of the economy (Mavrogordatos 1988: 11, 17–18; Svoronos 1964: 85–86, 98). Thus, the policies of Venizelos condense the aspirations of this class and may be summarized in the ideological complex "history/national identity-modernization-nationalism." This complex corresponds exactly to the dominant codes through which Hébrard's plan was interpreted by its Greek producers.

Approaches to the Semiotic Consumption of Urban Space

Lynch's urban design proposal was an extension of his field work on the image of the city held by its inhabitants. From this derives his central concept of imageability, which he defines as the quality of a physical object in the cityscape to evoke, with a high degree of probability, a powerful mental image in any observer. He states that this physical quality is due to two components: the identity of an object as a separate entity and structure; that is, the existence of relationships between objects and between them and the observer. Lynch concentrates on this "physical clarity" of the image, what in semiotics we would call the level of the signifiers, with their attached denotative signifieds, and badly underestimates his third component, the "emotional" meaning of the image, on the grounds that it is unstable and can be influenced through spatial design.

Lynch discovered—and this is to his credit and was corroborated by the great bulk of the behavioral geography studies on mental mapping that he, together with environmental psychology, inspired—that the mental image is composed of only five unitary elements: paths, edges, districts, nodes (such as squares) and landmarks. In semiotic terminology, these are the five paradigmatic categories of the visual signifiers. Lynch recognizes four different patterns of the structure of mental images, which are for him stages reflecting different degrees of precision; that is, of correspondence to physical space as referent (Lynch 1960: 1–13, 46–48, 88–89). However, as in the case of the production of space, with the two social-semiotic examples that follow, we shall see that a focus on the morphological signifiers, with their narrow denotation and aesthetics, cannot account for the richness of the actual consumption of space.

The reconstruction of Thessaloniki foresaw the expropriation of the lots of the burnt area and their redistribution, causing a great deal of social tension. As to the plan itself, there were various reactions that all concerned partial aspects of it, but there were no general counter-proposals, even if in many respects it represented a radical break with the past. On the contrary, the plan was unanimously accepted and no professional questioned its principles (Lavedan 1921: 240; 1933: 159–160; Yerolympos-Karadimou 1995: 98–107, 113–116, 125–127, 180–191).

Yet the principal addressee, the Greek public, was deeply divided between two ideologies. The first was the "Hellenist" ideology, a result of the assimilation of the imported idealizing and antiquarian neoclassicist ideas of Western Hellenism about ancient Greece and modern Greece as a direct continuity of it. The second, the "Romeic" ideology, was a reflexive adaptation of Western Hellenism to actual Greek experience, founded on a feeling of continuity with the more familiar Orthodox tradition and Byzantine culture considered as the popular culture. From the beginning of the 20th century, the clash between these two models resulted in a large number of ramifications, including the defense of two different forms of the language.

However, both parties had in common "Neohellenism": the principle of historical and cultural continuity (linked to the creation of an imaginary community), the construction of a national identity and the irredentist acquisition of a *homeland* for the nation, a place much larger than the present state, which they felt the nation deserved and which was a prerequisite for its existence and fulfillment (Herzfeld 1982: vii, ix, 4, 10, 19–23, 119, 123, 138–139; Leontis 1998: 34–37, 72, 126–148, 293, 301–305, 309).

With its integration into the Greek state, Thessaloniki inevitably was seen as a nodal point in the once desired and now, to a certain degree, acquired "place" of the nation. In this context the Hellenist and Romeic models converge and we better understand the government ideology we encountered above.

Thus, a complex intertext was produced by Hébrard, which ended up combining, as far as possible, the two ideological waves of Greek Neohellenism and the latter with Western Hellenism, but also leaving space for the conflicting Greek irredentism and French imperialism. His plan appealed simultaneously to the supporters of both parties; that is, all Greeks. The consumer, the "reader" of the city, had ideological expectations from the plan identical to (most of) the values incorporated in its production.

Our second example comes from contemporary Greece. In a questionnaire on the conception of regional space (Lagopoulos and Boklund-Lagopoulou 1992: 258–260), analysis of one of the central questions revealed marked differences between the conceptions of the region by the different social classes. The working class has no unified regional model but is split between two opposite attitudes in respect to the same set of codes, which the speakers either adopt or ignore: the codes of economic development, ecology, lifestyle and wealth. When these codes are used, a certain geographical determinism emerges, because development is associated with ecological features; this is the context for statements about lifestyle, which is associated with wealth. Similar codes appear among the lower-middle class, but they are systematically adopted and their pairings are different: ecology is here associated with a neutral descriptive code of economic activities and the code of wealth appears together with the code referring to the mentality and character of people. The codes used by the middle class are strikingly different from those of both the above classes. The middle class focuses on the relation between economic and social issues, and some of their social codes are related to aesthetic judgments; it also associates functional issues with the built environment.

If we examine gender in relation to the settlement hierarchy (metropolis, provincial city, countryside), rural women avoid references to history and markedly avoid issues of leisure, while among city (metropolitan and provincial) women, there is a balance between reference to and avoidance of these issues. City women are focused on their personal experiences. Metropolitan women, in general, avoid issues of economic development but among provincial women, there is a clear preference for these issues.

The male regional models are significantly different. Men are not attracted by issues of leisure and do not refer to their personal experiences. Provincial men show a strong tendency toward both general economic and ecological matters, while rural men show a tendency only toward the former. In general, neither men nor women make many references to politics, but rural men are divided between use and non-use of the political code (Lagopoulos and Boklund-Lagopoulou 1992: 86–91, 249–252, 257–264).

Thus, the different social groups composing contemporary society have no unified semiotic universe. Although there may be some similarities, on the whole, each group sees regional space in its own way.

The Major Semiotic Models of Urban Space

The Precapitalist Models

Modernity caused a radical break in the way urban space has been historically semiotized. I shall start with the example of traditional India, as a typical case of precapitalist societies.

There are two main images of the universe in India. The first is the Great Lotus: the womb of the divine from the center of which, located on the vertical cosmic axis passing through the summit of the universe, creation started with the emanation of the four cardinal directions of space. The universe is a lotus, but also a man. The lotus finds its equivalent in the *maṇḍala*, a cosmic drawing figuring a sacred area protected from the external profane powers. It has two forms, one combining concentric circles with a square and another that is a square oriented to the cardinal points and subdivided into a grid of smaller squares. A central square, connoting the center of the universe, is considered as occupied by a lotus.

The most important Indian treatise on architecture and town planning is *Mānasāra Śilpaśāstra*, a compilation made between 500 and 700 AD but of much more ancient origin. This book gives the description of the basic plans of all buildings and settlements. Construction starts by tracing on the ground a square oriented to the cardinal points, which is then subdivided into smaller squares, the number of which varies; the central square is dedicated to Brahma. In other words, the architectural and urban plans are constructed *maṇḍala* (Auboyer 1949: 101–102; Tucci 1961: 39, 49, 87; Zimmer 1951: 56, 90–91, 136–140, 192).

The site of each plan has its protective deity, a cosmic man from whom the universe emanated; he covers with his body the whole of the plan and his navel coincides with the central part of the grid. Thus, the universe, the body and the plans of buildings and settlements are fused into an integral whole (Acharya 1995: 36–42; Müller 1961: 119–122; Rykwert 1976: 163–165).

This case helps us to better understand the general semiotic features of the models of the precapitalist settlements, which are the following (Lagopoulos 1995):

(a) There exists a sacred semiotic model of settlement space culturally sanctified, which governs both semiotic spatial production and consumption. This model presides over the functional organization and morphology of space.
(b) It also presides over architecture, even regional space, and further, over all aspects of cultural and institutional life.
(c) It combines simple Euclidean geometric signifiers (e.g., depending on the specific culture, a circle, concentric circles, a square, quadripartition) with a structured complex of connotative codes, central to cultural ideology. This set varies between cultures, but always includes as dominant the cosmic and the anthropomorphic codes as conceived in each case. Thus, the model and the space produced on its basis are cosmograms and "anthropograms."
(d) The model may be clearly realized on the ground, or altered for topographical, social or historical reasons. However, it is always conceived in its original form and its alterations are symbolically absorbed; if they exceed a certain threshold, action is taken to restore, as far as possible, its original form.

The Modernist Models

In her work on the discourses of urban theorists, Françoise Choay classifies their 19th- and 20th-century texts up to 1964 into three discursive models. The first model, dominant in urban practice, is the "progressivist" model, which is founded on a faith in rationalism, science, technology and progress. It segregates urban functions, does not give the city precise limits, prescribes a multitude of green spaces, privileges standardized housing and, in the 20th century, promoted a geometrical and rational aesthetic. The second, "culturalist" model is systematically opposed to the previous model: it is anti-industrialist, nostalgic and proposes an "organic" city like the ancient and particularly the medieval city. It emphasizes the uniqueness of individual and interpersonal relations, seeks an atmosphere of urbanity, sets precise limits for the city, displays community and cultural buildings, encourages houses with individual character, and rejects rigid geometry, calling for irregularity and asymmetry. Finally, the third, the "naturalist," a peripheral model that derives from a strong anti-urban tradition in 19th-century USA, is founded on nostalgia for nature and incorporates elements of both the previous models (Choay 1965: 15–53).

Another work, by Raymond Ledrut (1973), combining Greimas's structural semantics with sociological analysis, studies on the basis of field work the conception of the modern French city held by its inhabitants as a structured discourse. Ledrut identifies two general urban models: an "abstract" model, correlated with the working class, which is founded on instrumentalism and functionalism, and a "concrete" one (of a "hedonistic" nature), correlated with the middle class, which has a personal and emotional character. Thus, Ledrut extends his study to social semiotics. Ledrut indicates that his first model corresponds to Choay's progressivist model, while his second presents an affinity with her culturalist model.

A third study (Lagopoulos and Boklund-Lagopoulou 1992: 217–232) converges with the conclusions above. The authors identify, on the basis of the composition of the inhabitants' codes, two opposed modern Greek regional models, the "objectivist" and the "subjectivist," closely related to Choay's and Ledrut's respective models.

Thus, the spatial models of two centuries of European urban theorists and those of the contemporary users of urban and regional space in two different European countries are closely related. The closeness of the two models found allows us to generalize them as *the* ideological urban models of European modernity. The progressivist model represents the project of the Enlightenment, while the culturalist is a byproduct of Romanticism.

The Postmodern Model

Figure 2.1 shows the intimate relation between the semiotic and the material and the foundation of the former on the latter. This is also the conclusion of Fredric Jameson and David Harvey in respect to postmodern culture. Jameson argues that it corresponds to a new stage of capitalism in which culture has lost its previous relative autonomy and become an organic part of every aspect of society, hence his conclusion that postmodern culture is the cultural logic of late capitalism (Jameson 1984: 55–58, 87).

For Harvey, the repeated crises of capitalism, due to the over-accumulation of capital, totally transform culture as a "complex of signs and significations (including language) that mesh into codes of transmission of social values and meanings" (Harvey 1989: 299). The oil crisis of 1973 opened the period of postmodernity, characterized by a new regime of capitalist accumulation, and the resulting postmodern culture is the expression of the integration of a commodified culture within market forces. Today, money, commodities and aesthetic production are integrated within the process of the circulation of capital. We witness the construction of new types of imagery promoting commodities (as is the case with advertising) and in a sense being themselves a commodity. Images are used in a variety of areas, including economic competition through brand-name recognition and image building (e.g., by sponsoring the arts). In other words, beyond the use value of commodities and together with their exchange value, their symbolic value becomes of special importance in late capitalism.

In respect to urban space, Harvey observes that in postmodernity, capital became more sensitive to the qualities of places because they create relative locational advantages that are integrated as internal elements of its logic. The great cities of the advanced capitalist world compete to attract a highly mobile capital and an equally mobile work force. One way to achieve this is to offer spectacular urban places with an ambience of tradition and a distinctive image. According to Harvey, space is seen by postmodernists as autonomous, grounded in aesthetics and detached from any social objective. They adopt the view of a fragmented city and a collage of uses; postmodern urban design wants to express vernacular traditions, but also responds to particular fancies (Harvey 1989: 54, 59, 62, 66, 77, 88–93, 124, 239–240, 287–288, 293–299, 302–307, 327–328, 344).

Among his three features of "overmodernity," Marc Augé includes spatial "overabundance," which he defines as related to a change of scale due to the acceleration of transportation, and to the creation, through television, of a relatively homogeneous fictional universe. The first phenomenon is also recognizable, according to Augé, in "non-places": infrastructure and installations such as highways and airports, the means of transportation themselves, shopping centers, big hotel chains, and recreation spaces (even refugee camps). These are just "spaces," determined by economic interests, as opposed to "places" bound to a culture localized in space and time. Spaces use history and locality as an element of spectacle and the images they embody, which show a world of consumption accessible to everybody, are the postmodern form of alienation. They create a feeling of solitude, although their experience has a certain power of attraction (Augé 1992: 41–50, 100–105, 117, 130, 133, 136–139, 144–148).

A very similar analysis comes from Mark Gottdiener, who considers Augé's non-places as pseudo-public "themed environments." Gottdiener adds to Augé's list restaurant chains, museums and historical monuments, and housing developments, extending to the thematization of nature, as in the case of Niagara Falls. According to Gottdiener, the overarching theme may be limited simply to a strongly connoted linguistic device, but it may also visually traverse a spatial complex as a whole. He identifies themes related to commercialized popular culture, such as cinema, high fashion and sports; to status; to nostalgia and fantasies; and to modernism. Gottdiener, like Augé, argues that these ephemeral spatial theme-symbols are just imitations of substantive symbols and cannot cause deeply felt meanings, but they nevertheless entertain people, create a euphoric experience and promise the realization of desires. Finally, they aim at stimulating consumption, presented as self-fulfillment, and increasing profit, serving the capitalist economy; they proliferate with increasing market segmentation (Gottdiener 1997: 2–7, 73–76, 82, 121, 142–151, 155–156).

The critical views above give an image of postmodern space as revolving around (pseudo-) history, (artificial) locality, (constructed) nostalgia and the creation of euphoric spectacle. The views from within, those of postmodern planning such as New Urbanism, Smart Growth and the Urban Village Movement, reveal an ideological nucleus focused on the neighborhood at the scale of the pedestrian, the sense of place and nostalgic architecture, social interaction in and the display of public spaces, and the use of different types of housing; it is closely related to the elusive idea of "urbanity." We see that these views are the uncritical version of the critical views above. From this whole, the postmodern model of space emerges. If we now compare it with the modernist models, a rather unexpected fact emerges: it is a neoculturalist model, a commercialized neo-Romanticism.

References

Acharya, P. K. (1995 [1934]) *Indian architecture according to Mānasāra-Śilpaśāstra*, Delhi: Low Price Publications.
Althusser, L. and Balibar, É. (1968) *Lire le capital*, vol. I, Paris: Maspero.
Auboyer, J. (1949) *Le trône et son symbolisme dans l'Inde ancienne*, Paris: P.U.F.
Augé, M. (1992) *Non-lieux: introduction à une anthropologie de la surmodernité*, Paris: Seuil.
Barthes, R. (1964) "Éléments de sémiologie," *Communications*, 4, pp. 91–135.
Bourdieu, P. (1971) "Le marché des biens symboliques," *L'Année Sociologique*, 3rd series 22, pp. 49–126.
— (1980) *Le sens pratique*, Paris: Minuit.
Castells, M. (1972) *La question urbaine*, Paris: Maspero.
Choay, F. (1965) *L'urbanisme, utopies et réalités: une anthologie*, Paris: Seuil.
Eco, U. (1972 [1968]) *La structure absente: introduction à la recherche sémiotique*, France: Mercure de France.
Golledge, R. G. and Stimson, R. J. (1987) *Analytical behavioural geography*, London, New York and Sidney: Croom Helm.
Gottdiener, M. (1997) *The theming of America: dreams, visions, and commercial spaces*. Boulder, CO, and Oxford: Westview Press.
Greimas, A. J. (1976) *Sémiotique et sciences sociales*, Paris: Seuil.
Hall, S. (1996) "The problem of ideology: Marxism without guarantees," in D. Morley and K.-H. Chen (eds.), *Stuart Hall: critical dialogues in cultural studies*. London and New York: Routledge, pp. 25–46.
Harvey, D. (1989) *The condition of postmodernity: an enquiry into the origins of cultural change*, Oxford: Blackwell.
Herzfeld, M. (1982) *Ours once more: folklore, ideology and the making of modern Greece*, Austin, TX: University of Texas Press.
Jacobs, J. M. (1993) "The city unbound: qualitative approaches to the city," *Urban Studies*, 30 (4/5), pp. 827–848.
Jameson, F. (1984) "Postmodernism, or the cultural logic of late capitalism," *New Left Review*, 146, pp. 53–92.
Lagopoulos, A. Ph. (1993) "Postmodernism, geography, and the social semiotics of space," *Environment and Planning D: Society and Space*, 11 (3), pp. 255–278.
— (1995) *Urbanisme et sémiotique dans les sociétés pré-industrielles*, Paris: Anthropos.
Lagopoulos, A. Ph. and Boklund-Lagopoulou, K. (1992) *Meaning and geography: the social conception of the region in Northern Greece*, Berlin and New York: Mouton de Gruyter.
Lavedan, P. (1921) "Un problème d'urbanisme: La reconstruction de Salonique," *Gazette des Beaux-Arts*, series V, 64 (6), pp. 231–248.
— (1933) "L'œuvre d'Ernest Hébrard en Grèce," *Urbanisme*, May 1933, pp. 148–161.
Ledrut, R. (1973) *Les images de la ville*, Paris: Anthropos.
Lefebvre, H. (1974) *La production de l'espace*, Paris: Anthropos.
Leontis, A. (1998 [1995]) *Topographies of Hellenism: mapping the homeland* (Greek translation), Athens: Scripta.
Lynch, K. (1960) *The image of the city*, Cambridge, MA: MIT Press.
Mavrogordatos, G. Th. (1988) "Venizelism and bourgeois modernization," in G. Th. Mavrogordatos and Ch. Chadziiosif (eds.), *Venizelism and bourgeois modernisation* (in Greek). Irakleio: Crete University Press, pp. 9–19.
Medvedev, P. N. and Bakhtin, M. M. (1978 [1928]) *The formal method in literary scholarship: a critical introduction to sociological poetics*, Baltimore, MD and London: The Johns Hopkins University Press.
Müller, W. (1961) *Die heilige Stadt: Roma quadrata, himmlisches Jerusalem und die Mythe von Weltnabel*, Stuttgart: W. Kohlhammer.
Pickles, J. (1985) *Phenomenology, science, and geography: spatiality and the human sciences*, Cambridge: Cambridge University Press.
Rykwert, J. (1976) *The idea of a town: the anthropology of urban form in Rome, Italy and the ancient world*, Princeton, NJ: Princeton University Press.
Svoronos, N. (1964 [1953]) *Histoire de la Grèce moderne*, Paris: P.U.F.
Tuan, Y.-F. (1977) *Space and place: the perspective of experience*, Minneapolis, MN: University of Minnesota.
Tucci, G. (1961 [1949]) *The theory and practice of the mandala*, A. H. Brodrick, trans., London: Rider and Company.
Williams, R. (1977) *Marxism and literature*, Oxford: Oxford University Press.

Yerolympos-Karadimou, A. (1995 [1985]) *The reconstruction of Thessaloniki after the fire of 1917: a landmark in the history of the city and the development of Greek urban planning* (in Greek), Thessaloniki: University Studio Press.

Zimmer, H. 1951 [1946] *Mythes et symboles dans l'art et la civilisation de l'Inde*, M.-S. Renou, trans., Paris: Payot.

Further Reading

Choay, F. (1997 [1980]) *The rule and the model: on the theory of architecture and urbanism*, D. Bratton, ed., Cambridge, MA and London: MIT Press.

Gottdiener, M. and Lagopoulos, Ph. (eds.) (1986) *The city and the sign: an introduction to urban semiotics*, New York: Columbia University Press.

Lilley, K. D. (2009) *City as cosmos: the medieval world in urban form*, London: Reaktion Books.

3
UNDERSTANDING URBAN SCREEN MEDIA AND CULTURES

Zach Melzer

Introduction

Nearly every time I come across a trashed cathode-ray tube (CRT) in my suburban Montréal neighborhood, its screen is oriented away from the domestic spaces where it once belonged. It is as though these CRTs say something about the ways the owners of these refused appliances express their own selves to others—as extraverts, performers, boasters, exhibitionists. Or perhaps the positioning of these CRTs is meant to be seen as art installations where the glass screens are re-appropriated as mirrors, embedding the passersby onto their surfaces, signaling their complicit roles in the normalization of technological waste in late capitalism. Whatever the reasons, the placements of trashed CRTs in such arrangements give us some clues about the ways screen technologies and spectatorship have been habituated as objects and practices that can be fitted in, furnished, and felt as ordinary in outdoor spaces.

I begin with the example of trashed CRTs because it reveals some of the complexities in researching urban screen media and cultures. Television sets put out on the curb point to some of the ways screen technologies and cultures are thought about, imagined, and normalized in urban spaces as urban objects and practices. It is in such temporary and transitionary instances where some of the meanings of screens and urbanism become visible and concretized. Even though the term "urban screens" is typically used to describe moving image media that are projected on or displayed in the built environment in ways that address a broad audience of passersby, there is no specificity inherent in this term. "Urban screens" is broad enough to include any and all uses of screen technologies in numerous spaces. Though lacking content, trashed CRTs nevertheless point to questions of medium specificity as well as to definitions of public space and urbanism that continue to inform the study of urban screen media and cultures.

This chapter provides a brief introduction to urban screen studies. It argues that the term "urban screens" is both insufficiently broad and problematically too narrow, but nevertheless emerges out of particular cultural anxieties with the wide range and uses of screen technologies in public places. It can be understood both as a catch-all term that describes all instances of screen or illumination media in urban, suburban, exurban, or rural spaces, as well as a category of sensemaking about screen technologies and their usages in relation to a number of many others. Screens are evermore widespread and increasingly integral to the characterizations of modern urban life, both public and private, urban and rural. The analytical problem that characterizes this area of research grows out of the inability to arrive at a commonly defined vocabulary that comprehensively articulates this area's multiple objects of study. However, the absence of a terminology that fully encompasses the diverse understandings of urban screen cultures is not to be read as a criticism of the state of the field. Instead of arriving at terms of essence, this ubiquity demands that closer attention be paid to the variety of iterations of and values attributed to screen media. In tracing the uses of the phrase "urban screens", this chapter points to the historical, cultural, industrial, and social values that are being attributed to screens and urbanism in public spaces. Rather than defining urban screen media through medium specific qualities, urban screens are best described as being found in the intersections between cinema, television, video, computation, architecture, spatial design, advertising, and a continuation of efforts to make use of screen media for purposes of public street art.

Abundance of Screens, Abundance of Genealogies

In their introduction to the *Urban Screens Reader*, Scott McQuire, Meredith Martin, and Sabine Niederer define urban screens as "screens of various scale—from the small handheld screens of mobile phones to the large screens dominating the streetscapes of global cities—exemplifying a new urban paradigm produced by the layering of physical space and media space" (McQuire et al. 2009: 9). If the term "urban screens" can be used to describe large or small projections or displays of still or moving images located on the façades of buildings or on digital billboards or electronic displays located in publicly or semi-publicly accessible urban places, then such a definition is arguably large enough to include all instances of moving image media located almost anywhere urban. Today's urban environments are furnished with movie theatre screens, television screens, computer screens, mobile screens, screens on home appliances, flat screens, curved screens, small screens, building-sized screens, wearable screens, screens alongside highways, screens in airports, stadiums, restaurants, and landfills, screens on water vessels, automobiles, and aircrafts, interactive screens, ambient screens, advertising screens, broken screens, screens at points of purchase, screens as menu boards, screens for work, screens for pleasure, screens for art, screens for commerce. According to the definition above, all screens, in any place and in any situation, can be categorized as examples of "urban screens". Clearly, then, such a definition is too broad.

In addition to the many others not mentioned, each of the screen examples listed above points to the heterogeneity of technological, technical, and cultural materializations of screen media in contemporary visual urban culture. Each are put into use by a variety of industries, networks, and cultures for a variation of reasons and aspired outcomes. As a result, instead of simply being called urban screens, the discrete characteristics of each example are highlighted as contrasting differences that inform a set of more distinct terms. For example, in the world of advertising, screen media are described as "outdoor screens", "digital billboards", "digital signage", "ambient media", "pervasive displays", and "digital out-of-home" (Kelsen 2010; Davies et al. 2014). In architecture and design circles, some of the terms that have been proposed include "electrotecture" (Taylor 1993), "hypersurface" (Perrella 1998), "mediatecture" (Kronhagel 2010), "media architecture" (Wiethoff and Hussmann 2017; Hespanhol et al. 2017), and "media façades" (Ag4 2006; Haeusler 2009; Gehring and Wiethoff 2014; Tomitsch et al. 2015). In cinema studies they are sometimes described in their relations to "expanded cinema", or "nontheatrical cinema" (Colangelo 2015a; Dell'Aria 2014). In television studies, they are put into the categories of "nondomestic" (McCarthy 2001) and "unhomely" (Neves 2011) screens. Other terms that have also been employed by scholars include "networked screens"

(Fuqua 2012), "composite dispositifs" (Verhoeff 2012), "screen fields" (Verhoeff 2012), "mega screens" (Papastergiadis et al. 2013), "large screens" (Yue 2013; Yue et al. 2014), "public media displays" (Huhtamo 2009, 2010), and "massive media" (Colangelo 2015b), to name a few.

Moreover, the complexities, contradictions, and paradoxes posited by the urbanism implied in the term "*urban* screens" should also not be overlooked. The phrase does not adequately take into account the many iterations of screens found in rural or transitory spaces, such as towns or airplanes. While it can be argued—as Stephen Groening (2013), for example, does—that the placing of screens on airplanes in the forms of inflight entertainment technologies extends the definitions of urban environments both vertically and horizontally, such understandings risk being overly reductive of the workings of both media and urban space. As Anna McCarthy argues, we cannot "come up with a general set of social operations that media always perform regardless of their place" (McCarthy 2001: 4). The mere presence of screens cannot shape the ways places are experienced as either exclusively urban or rural. Instead, media inform the ways we experience places as either urban or rural "but not always in identical ways, producing identical meanings" (McCarthy 2001: 4). This is not to argue that instances of screens on airplanes and in more rural places are not in any way informed by urban cultures, but instead to point to the complexities that are present in the terminology used to describe such screens.

Not one of the terms or phrases listed above fully encompasses the breadth and varieties of moving image media, technologies, cultures, and practices in the diverse spatial scenarios. Unsurprisingly, historians have located urban screens within the long histories of urban cultures, moving image media in public spaces, as well as highlighting the deeply entwined relations between urban screens and other media practices such as spatial design, architecture, billboards, neon, cinema, and television. Media archaeologist Erkki Huhtamo traces the genealogy of urban screens to the signboards of Medieval Europe, advertising billboards and magic lantern shows in the United States throughout the 19th century, and the rise of electric illumination at the turn of the 20th century (Huhtamo 2009). Elsewhere, Huhtamo identifies the uses of fireworks, hot-air balloons, and searchlights as having also contributed to the genealogy of urban screens, or what he terms "public media displays" (Huhtamo 2010). For architectural and planning historian Malcolm McCullough and urban media historian Shannon Mattern, the genealogies of urban screens are more deeply tied to architecture and urban design (McCullough 2013; Mattern 2017). While McCullough argues that "buildings were the first mass communication medium" (McCullough 2013: 140), Mattern likewise adds that urban infrastructures have also always primarily been about the layering of communication throughout the city. In seeing media communication technologies and architecture as having been inextricable from the very beginning, McCullough and Mattern give rather anachronistic meanings to terms such as "media façades", "media architecture", and "media infrastructures". However, such observations also help situate these terms as well as urban screens within the so-called digital age, or what Paul Virilio describes as the "electronic gothic era" of architecture where the architect "has to work with the dominations of global time" and "in fractional dimensions" (Virilio 1998: 61). The designs of buildings and cities thousands of years ago are drastically different from the ones being built today (see Chapter 27, this volume).

Highly influential has also been Scott McQuire's historicization of what he describes as the "media city" or the "electropolis" (McQuire 2008). The "media city", according to McQuire, should be distinguished from the "smart city" in that the former has been in configuration since the end of the 19th century when the electrification of cities first began. Unlike the logics of computation and control that characterize smart cities, according to McQuire, screens along with other electronic media such as mobile computers and wireless connectivity grew out of, and helped perpetuate, a particularly new type of understanding of experience of time and space, one where the landscape is experienced as infinitely and ambivalently dissolving. Electrical illuminations did not help remedy the experience of shock; rather, according to McQuire, they informed an increasingly indecisive and wavering experience of modernity (see also Chapter 1, this volume). In contrast, looking at urban screen culture in Shanghai, Chris Berry argues that a "long but varied local lineage of putting writing into public spaces"—a tradition of furnishing public spaces with logographic Hanzi, as well as magical moving image and illumination technologies—coupled with aspirations to showcase the "lure of consumerism and its myriad pleasures" has strongly informed the aesthetics of outdoor screen cultures in that city (Berry 2013: 111, 122). Rather than an experience and fear of ambivalence, Berry offers a narrative where the intersections between mediation of the built environment have been a part of Shanghai long before LEDs, LCDs, CRTs, or projections existed.

While these scholars tie the histories of urban screens to other media practices, a majority of studies in this area of research—appearing in such diffused disciplines as human–computer interaction, advertising, communication, cinema and media studies, art history, architecture, urban planning, and design—have largely focused on analyzing the technological potentials of outdoor LEDs and digital projections to impact political discourse and social interactions in the city. For example, new media theorist Lev Manovich argues that the "overlaying of dynamic data over the physical space" through screens creates a "new kind of physical space . . . [an] augmented space" (Manovich 2006). Likewise, architecture and design scholars Alexander Wiethoff and Heinrich Hussmann write that media architecture is "a new, smart construction material that can . . . enhance . . . communication and enable a material dialogue between the city and citizens" (Wiethoff and Hussmann 2017: 1). Similarly, in the field of human–computer interactions, Kenton O'Hara et al. argue that the integration of digital displays represents "opportunities for novel forms of communication, coordination and collaboration" (O'Hara et al. 2003: xviii).

If urban screens help create new media environments, these changing environments are also argued to be signaling a shift in spectatorial modes of engagement. Cinema scholar Francesco Casetti sees urban screens as being part and parcel of cinema's "relocation" in the digital age (Casetti 2009). He aligns urban screen spectatorship with the emergence of movies on demand, "cinematic" aesthetics in video games and television shows, ubiquity of the language of movie trailers, screens in the spaces of galleries, as well as the fluidity of sites for movie viewing on mobile screens, in cafes, bars, airplanes, et cetera. Building on a similar notion of relocation, Dave Colangelo argues that the

> techniques and tools drawn from cinema studies (superimposition, montage, and apparatus/dispositif) can be applied to examples of the moving image in public space in order to analyze the ways these techniques evolve in public settings and how they can create new perceptual and creative possibilities for the cinema and the city.
> *(Colangelo 2015a: 113)*

Influenced by Gene Youngblood's ideas of "expanded cinema", Colangelo sees spectators as being able to decode images in terms of a superimposition onto the built environment, adopting an understanding of editing in terms of a "spatial montage"—where panoramic and spatial organization of images asks spectators to make their own connections—as well as recognizing the ways they are sutured into a public environment (Youngblood 1970).

For Annie Dell'Aria, spectators of urban screens are much more mercurially defined and addressed than those of cinema and television: "Unlike the predetermined architecture and seating arrangements of the cinema and domestic television, the body's relationship to the screen in public space is ever-changing and fluid" (2016: 19). Because images and screens "in public space are encountered intentionally, unintentionally, fully, partially, or not at all", Dell'Aria argues, the way "spectators negotiate and construct meaning from a work of public art is contingent on the individual spectator as well as her specific temporal and locational situation" (2016: 19). The inability to arrive at a conceptual model of a captured spectatorial engagement, Dell'Aria argues, demands that we analyze each encounter with urban screens "situationally" as its own distinct event. Zlatan Krajina likewise argues that studies of urban screen spectatorship must be grounded in specific and observed interactions with the "environmental character" of urban screen media—an ambient quality that is shaped by the distance, size, location, and, most importantly, the "glow" of their luminosity (Krajina 2014).

For new media scholar Nanna Verhoeff (2012), the material and technical substances of urban screens give shape to an altogether new kind of space and mode of engagement that she describes as a "visual regime of navigation"—one that is shaped by technologies of augmented reality, wireless communication, mobile computers, and wearable media. She writes that urban screens produce a space that is "layered: at once comprising site-specificity of the screen . . . as well as the surrounding public spaces" (Verhoeff 2016: 125). Within such a configuration, urban screens situate passersby "both as spectators in relation to the screen, and as navigators within and inhabitants of [a] larger, connected space" (Verhoeff 2016: 125). Conversely, Greg Siegel makes a similar argument in his analysis of video screens in sports stadiums, where attendants gain a perceptual agency that allows them to see the event as simultaneously both a live and a mediated event (Siegel 2002).

Such analyses present three related though variable understandings of the relations between urban screen, cinema, and television spectatorship. Whereas for Casetti and Colangelo, urban screens signal the further expansion of cinematic spectatorship, for Dell'Aria and Krajina, they mark its transformation, while for Verhoeff and Siegel, they ultimately mark the breaking away from conventional notions of cinema and television spectatorship. Rather than focusing on the relations between urban screens and cinema or television, Abigail Susik argues that a more productive way of understanding the particular junctures, where a variety of technologies—projections, neon, LED, LCD, and CRT displays—and techniques intersect with architecture, space, and modes of spectatorship, should altogether steer away from making claims about the essences of those media (Susik 2012). When urban surfaces get transformed into information displays, she writes, they also become "keenly contested zone[s] of ideological debate" (Susik 2012: 109). Thus, she poses that a more productive way of analyzing the employment of moving images in outdoor urban settings is by being attentive to "the politics of the 'occupation' of various surfaces by images and the ethics of such an obfuscation of space and place" (Susik 2012: 107). Therefore, she adopts what Rosalind Krauss calls a "post-medium" framework of analysis in order to arrive at more grounded understandings of the political and economic lenses that shape the ownership and control of urban screen media (Krauss 2000).

Not only do scholars see the histories of urban screens as being informed by different discursive frameworks and backgrounds, there are also different views about the material genealogies of these media. Urban screens are defined in terms of the continuations of architecture, urbanism, illumination, street furniture, advertising, cinema, television, computers, and mobile devices. But these histories also illustrate that while the origins of urban screens can be found in different media, it is a particular set of intersections of architecture, moving images, and public space that define the contemporary context of urban screens. As I will argue below, it is anxieties with the hyper-commercialization of public spaces and the idealizations of responsive environments that define a unique blend of material qualities and modes of address as belonging to urban screen media and cultures.

Urban Screens as an Aesthetic Category

Thus far, I have argued that urban screens are broadly defined as the multiplicity of screen technologies that furnish public spaces, but it is important to also note that the term appeared as a way to identify particular kinds of uses of screen technologies in ways that emphasize public and artistic engagements over those strictly tied to commercial-based interests. While shared among many scholars, this employment of the term is perhaps best exemplified by Mirjam Struppek's theorization of "the social potential of urban screens" (Struppek 2006; cf. Clemens et al. 2016 and Cubitt 2016). For Struppek, who initiated the Amsterdam-based *Urban Screens Network* (one of the first research groups devoted to the study of urban screen media), screen media offer new opportunities to challenge the hyper-commercialization of social environments. She asks,

> How can the growing digital display infrastructure appearing in the modern urban landscape contribute to [the] idea of a public space as moderator and as communication medium? . . . How can the currently dominating commercial use of these screens be broadened to display cultural content? Can they become a tool to contribute to a lively urban society involving their audience (inter)actively?
>
> *(Struppek 2006: 173)*

Struppek theorizes urban screens as material and technological assemblages that emerge out of and as reactions to the configurations of cities as systems that are highly tied to the networks and flows of global capitalism—what are also known as "global", "smart", and "creative" cities. Understood as such, urban screens are a fairly recent phenomenon that came about largely in the late stages of post-industrial capitalism, and as a potential remedy to the fears of the weakening of local politics by alienating global forces. She adds:

> Urban Screens can only be understood in the context of the rediscovery of the public sphere and the urban character of cities, based on a well-balanced mix of functions and the idea of the inhabitants as active citizens. Urban Screens combines the function of public space for commerce and trade with a cultural role reflecting the wellbeing of urban society: digital moving displays with a new focus on supporting the idea of urban space as a space for the creation and exchange of culture and the formation of a public sphere using criticism and reflection.
>
> *(Struppek 2006: 174)*

For Struppek, "urban screens" is a category of making use of screen technologies for creative, artistic, social, and communal purposes that defines its audiences not strictly as consumers or law-abiding citizens, but as participants in a cultural event that is mediated by a publicly situated screen (cf. Pop et al. 2012, 2016).

There is an aesthetic and critical tendency to use screens in ways that bring attention to the making of public places more private, commercial, gentrified, and exclusive; that is, to make use of public spaces in more explicitly political, communal, open, accessible, and socially accountable ways. Examples of such uses of screens for artistic and socially conscious goals include works by artists such as Krzysztof Wodiczko, Jenny Holzer, Dara Birnbaum, Pipilotti Rist, Rafael Lozano-Hemmer, Chris Doyle, and Doug Aitken, among others, and through such organizations as Midnight Moment and Public Art Fund (New York City), Quartier des Spectacles (Montréal), Federation Square (Melbourne), Open Sky Gallery (Hong Kong),

SESI-SP Digital Art Gallery (São Paulo), Greeting to the Sun (Zadar), the Medialab-Prado (Madrid), the Media Architecture Institute, the Screen City Biennial, and the Connected Cities network, to name a few. Accordingly, Nikos Papastergiadis et al. argue that "legitimate concerns over commercial dominance of public space should not become an alibi for sweeping and hasty condemnation of public screens" altogether (Papastergiadis et al. 2016: 24). Rather than expecting all uses of screen technologies to achieve the same outcomes, given that vibrant public culture requires much more than the availability of screens, "urban screens" can become instances wherein commercialism is not the only or dominant factor that shapes the organization of public space.

However, it is important to note that urban screens can be problematically tied to other concerns with the uses and control of public spaces. Urban screen media require that their technologies, materials, and spaces be funded, managed, and maintained. Governing bodies that preside over such media in public places can be associated with either the public or private spheres, though they are increasingly also usually tied to pseudo-public or public–private entities such as business improvement districts and public–private partnerships. Examples of such organizations include the Times Square Alliance (Times Square, New York City), the Yonge-Dundas Square Partnership (Yonge-Dundas Square, Toronto), the Quartier des Spectacles Partnership (Quartier des Spectacles, Montréal), and the Fed Square Pty Ltd (Federation Square, Melbourne) (cf. McKim 2012, Halpern 2014, and Yue et al. 2014). Such political and economic organizations can impose significant influence over the uses of screen media and the cultures that accompany them. As Justin Clemens et al. argue,

> the regulatory processes that organize the uses of big screens are tantamount to the inculcation of certain controls on creativity, seeking to capture and canalize aesthetic affects for governmental and corporate ends by, above all, a kind of fiscal moralization of technology.
>
> *(Clemens et al. 2016: 49)*

In other words, although the employment of screens in urban centers can be thought of as a positive strategy for reinvigorating the cultures of cities, the economies of revitalization are also accompanied by the negative consequences of gentrification, privatization, and the reorganization of resources and control of spaces, capital, people, activities, and cultures by neoliberal models of governance.

Still, not all urban screens are organized by public, private, or public–private organizations. Works by artist collectives such as the Dawn of Man, the Illuminator, and the Pixelator are projected without official permission from the owners of the buildings on which the images are displayed, or are not commissioned through any public mandates or authorities. Such guerrilla art-like examples of urban screens test the politics of occupation as well as the saturation of the logics of commercialism and surveillance in public spaces through either unauthorized, disruptive, or explicitly illicit uses of moving image media.

Conclusion

Problems in identifying the constitution of urban screens are not solely attributed to lack of medium specificity or the place of screen media. Rather, such terminological problems are symptomatic of a broad range of historically informed and hegemonic relations that shape the uses of screen media in different spatial, social, political, and cultural scenarios. In their similarities with cinema, television, advertising, architecture, street art, and personal computers, the ubiquity of today's screen cultures points to the appropriation of screen practices, norms, and logics, cultivated in numerous other everyday and historically informed media practices.

Urban screens is both a term used to describe the broad instances of screens in public contexts as well as a category of the uses of screen technologies for specifically public and artistic purposes. It can describe commercial digital billboards, embedded media façades, informational television screens, artistic digital projections, or other combinations of media and uses thereof. It is both as broad a term as cinema, or television, or moving image media, as well as equivalent to the categories of art cinema and digital/video art. Urban screens, in other words, emerge out of the collective histories of other media practices but they also formulate into objects of analyses that are defined by contemporaneous contexts of networked cultures, smart cities, and neoliberal politics, as well as the values that are attributed to public culture, art, creativity, and commerce therein. Papastergiadis et al. remind us that

> as cities across the world are turning en masse to large-scale screens as a popular strategy for "reinvigorating" public space, it is vital to repeat some of the traditional questions about the relationship between media and public culture: Who has access? Who are the "gatekeepers"? How are judgements about content made? What range of voices is heard?
>
> *(Papastergiadis et al. 2016: 24)*

It is important to think often and critically about these questions because it is in the responses to these enquiries that further meanings of urban screens are to be found.

References

Ag4 (2006) *Ag4 Media Facades*, Cologne: Daab.
Berry, C. (2013) "Shanghai's Public Screen Culture: Local and Coeval", in C. Berry et al. (eds.) *Public Space, Media Space*, New York: Palgrave Macmillan, pp. 110–134.
Casetti, F. (2009) "Filmic Experience", *Screen*, 50(1), pp. 56–66.
Clemens, J. et al. (2016) "Big Screens, Little Acts: Transformations in the Structures and Operations of Public Address", in N. Papastergiadis (ed.) *Ambient Screens and Transnational Spaces*, Hong Kong: Hong Kong University Press, pp. 49–58.
Colangelo, D. (2015a) "An Expanded Perceptual Laboratory: Public Art and the Cinematic Techniques of Superimposition, Montage and Apparatus/Dispositif", *Public Art Dialogue*, 5(2), pp. 112–130.
— (2015b) "Curating Massive Media", *Journal of Curatorial Studies*, 4(2), pp. 238–262.
Cubitt, S. (2016) "Defining the Public in Piccadilly Circus", in N. Papastergiadis (ed.) *Ambient Screens and Transnational Public Spaces*, Hong Kong: Hong Kong University Press, pp. 81–94.
Davies, N. et al. (2014) *Pervasive Displays: Understanding the Future of Digital Signage*, San Rafael, CA: Morgan & Claypool.
Dell'Aria, A. (2014) "Cinema-in-the-Round: Doug Aitken's *SONG 1* (2012), the Hirshhorn Museum and the Pleasures of Cinematic Projection", *Moving Image Review & Art Journal*, 3(2), pp. 208–221.
— (2016) "Spectatorship in Public Space: The Moving Image in Public Art", in C. D. Reihnard and C. J. Olson (eds.) *Making Sense of Cinema: Empirical Studies into Film Spectators and Spectatorship*, New York: Bloomsbury Publishing, pp. 17–36.
Fuqua, J. V. (2012) *Prescription TV: Therapeutic Discourse in the Hospital and the Home*, Durham, NC: Duke University Press.
Gehring, S. and Wiethoff, A. (2014) "Interaction with Media Façades", *Informatik Spektrum*, 37(5), pp. 474–482.
Groening, S. (2013) "Aerial Screens", *History and Technology*, 29(3), pp. 281–300.
Haeusler, M. H. (2009) *Media Facades: History, Technology, Content*, Ludwigsburg: Avedition.
Halpern, O. (2014) *Beautiful Data: A History of Vision and Reason since 1945*, Durham, NC: Duke University Press.

Hespanhol, L. et al. (eds.) (2017) *Media Architecture Compendium: Digital Placemaking*, Stuttgart: Avedition.
Huhtamo, E. (2009) "Messages on the Wall: An Archaeology of Public Media Displays", in S. McQuire et al. (eds.) *Urban Screen Reader*, Amsterdam: Institute of Network Cultures, pp. 15–28.
— (2010) "The Sky Is (not) the Limit: Envisioning the Ultimate Public Media Display", *Journal of Visual Culture*, 8(3), pp. 329–348.
Kelsen, K. (2010) *Unleashing the Power of Digital Signage: Content Strategies for the 5th Screen*, Burlington, MA: Focal Press.
Krajina, Z. (2014) *Negotiating the Mediated City: Everyday Encounters with Public Screens*, New York: Routledge.
Krauss, R. (2000) *"A Voyage on the North Sea": Art in the Age of the Post-Medium Condition*, London: Thames & Hudson.
Kronhagel, C. (ed.) (2010) *Mediatecture: The Design of Medially Augmented Spaces*, Berlin: Degruyter.
Manovich, L. (2006) "The Poetics of Urban Media Surfaces", *First Monday*, 11, http://firstmonday.org/ojs/index.php/fm/article/view/1545/1460.
Mattern, S. (2017) *Code and Clay, Data and Dirt: Five Thousand Years of Urban Media*, Minneapolis, MN: University of Minnesota Press.
McCarthy, A. (2001) *Ambient Television: Visual Culture and Public Space*, Durham, NC: Duke University Press.
McCullough, M. (2013) *Ambient Commons: Attention in the Age of Embodied Information*, Cambridge, MA: MIT Press.
McKim, J. (2012) "Spectacular Infrastructure: The Mediatic Space of Montréal's 'Quartier des Spectacles'", *Public*, 45, pp. 128–138.
McQuire, S. (2008) *The Media City: Media, Architecture and Urban Space*, Los Angeles, CA: SAGE.
McQuire, S. et al. (eds.) (2009) *Urban Screen Reader*, Amsterdam: Institute of Network Cultures.
Neves, J. (2011) "Beijing en Abyme: Outside Television in the Olympic Era", *Social Text*, 29(2), pp. 21–46.
O'Hara, K. et al. (2003) "Introduction to Public and Situated Displays", in K. O'Hara et al. (eds.) *Public and Situated Displays: Social and Interactional Aspects of Shared Display Technologies*, Singapore: Springer Science+Business Media, pp. xvii–xxx.
Papastergiadis, N. et al. (2013) "Mega Screens for Mega Cities", *Theory, Culture & Society*, 30(7/8), pp. 325–341.
— (2016) "Introduction: Screen Cultures and Public Spaces", in N. Papastergiadis (ed.) *Ambient Screens and Transnational Spaces*, Hong Kong: Hong Kong University Press, pp. 3–27.
Perrella, S. (ed.) (1998) *Hypersurface Architecture*, London: Academy Press.
Pop, S. et al. (eds.) (2012) *Urban Media Cultures*, Stuttgart: Avedition.
— (2016) *What Urban Media Art Can Do: Why When Where and How?*, Stuttgart: Avedition.
Siegel, G. (2002) "Double Vision: Large-Screen Video Display and Live Sports Spectacle", *Television & New Media*, 3(1), pp. 49–73.
Struppek, M. (2006) "The Social Potential of Urban Screens", *Visual Communication*, 5(2), pp. 173–188.
Susik, A. (2012) "The Screen Politics of Architectural Light Projection", *Public*, 45, pp. 106–119.
Taylor, M. C. (ed.) (1993) *Electrotecture: Architecture and the Electronic Future*, New York: Anyone Corp.
Tomitsch, M. et al. (2015) "The Role of Digital Screens in Urban Life: New Opportunities for Placemaking", in M. Foth et al. (eds.) *Citizen's Right to the Digital City*, Singapore: Springer Science+Business Media, pp. 37–54.
Verhoeff, N. (2012) *Mobile Screens: The Visual Regime of Navigation*, Amsterdam: Amsterdam University Press.
— (2016) "Screens in the City", in D. Chateau and J. Moure (eds.) *Screens: From Materiality to Spectatorship—A Historical and Theoretical Reassessment*, Amsterdam: Amsterdam University Press, pp. 125–139.
Virilio, P. (1998) "We May Be Entering an Electronic Gothic Era", *Architectural Design: Architects in Cyberspace II*, 68(11/12), p. 61.
Wiethoff, A. and Hussmann, H. (eds.) (2017) *Media Architecture: Using Information and Media as Construction Material*, Berlin: De Gruyter.
Youngblood, G. (1970) *Expanded Cinema*, New York: Dutton.
Yue, A. (2013) "New Media: Large Screens in China", in C. Rojas (ed.) *The Oxford Handbook of Chinese Cinemas*, Oxford: Oxford University Press, pp. 359–376.
Yue, Audrey et al. (2014) "Large Screens as Creative Clusters", *City, Culture and Society*, 5, pp. 157–164.

Further Reading

Fortin, C. and Hennessy, K. (2015) "The Appropriation of a Digitally-Augmented Agora: Field Study of the Structuration and Spatialization of an Issue Public in Urban Space", *Canadian Journal of Communication*, 40, pp. 675–693.

Morris, B. (2010) "Un/Wrapping Shibuya: Place, Media, and Punctualization", *Space and Culture*, 13(3), pp. 285–303.

Willis, Holly (2009) "City as Screen / Body as Movie", *Afterimage*, 37(2), pp. 24–28.

4
URBAN CINEMA AND PHOTOGRAPHY
On Cities and "Cityness"

James Donald

Introduction

The opening of Tsai Ming-liang's short film, *The Skywalk Is Gone* (2002), a static shot lasting a minute and a half, elegantly enacts cinema's creative and critical engagement with the changing city. The camera is placed unusually low to the ground so that we see both more pavement and more sky than we might normally expect. The frame is split down the middle by a red banner, with buildings to the right and, on the left, sky, clouds, and a layer of pedestrians toward the bottom the screen (see Figure 4.1). The buildings are plastered with text and brand logos. An advertising LED screen figures prominently on the closest building. We may not immediately recognize which city this is, but we can see that it is obviously of these times. "Junkspace," declares the architect Rem Koolhaas, is "what remains after modernization has run its course, or, more precisely, what coagulates while modernization is in progress." Such remnants and coagulants are conspicuous here: "Superstrings of graphics, transplanted emblems of franchise and sparkling infrastructures of light, LEDs, and video describe an authorless world beyond anyone's claim, always unique, utterly unpredictable, yet intensely familiar" (Koolhaas and Foster 2013: 3, 9).

Observing this urban spectacle, apparently transfixed by the LED screen, is a woman, Chen Shiang-chyi, whom we see from behind and below. As Song Hwee Lim argues in his reading of the sequence, the disjuncture between her immobility and the oblivious hurry and scurry of the pedestrians around her establishes the contrast between "the sound, movement, and speed of new media," as represented by the LED screen and "the silence, stillness, and slowness of old media"—or, more specifically, Tsai's "slow cinema" aesthetic (Lim 2014: 152). However, if we look at the sequence not just through the prism of media ecology, but with the question of how cinema represents "the city" in mind, then it becomes clear that the woman's unmoving presence determines how we register this jumbled and mediatized cityscape not just as contemporary, but also as somehow *typical* of today's cities. However, at the same time, to see any city on screen begs the question of *which* city. Where *is* this?

Unless you have actually been there, or are familiar with the city from other films, there is little in the image as such to indicate that this is Taipei—outside the railway station, to be precise, across from the Shin Kong Mitsukoshi department store. Clues to the location are meta-discursive. Tsai is known as a Taiwan-based director preoccupied by Taipei's constant cycle of

Figure 4.1 The Skywalk Is Gone (Tsai Ming-Liang, 2002) (Screen Grab)

demolition and reconstruction, with an apparent compulsion to create a cinematic archive of its disappearing buildings. *The Skywalk Is Gone* is, effectively, a postscript to his feature from the previous year, *What Time Is It There?* (2001), in which Shiang-chyi bought a watch on the now disappeared "skywalk," or overpass, that had stood in exactly this space, as she prepared for a trip to Paris. Thus, her presence functions to place the film in a way that is both precise and yet, somehow, arbitrary.

In an influential essay on its cinematic mapping in the 1980s Taiwanese "new wave," Fredric Jameson described Taipei as an important Chinese city that possesses neither "the profile or the historical resonance and associations of the great traditional mainland cities" nor "the all-encompassing closed urban space of a virtual city-state like Hong Kong" (Jameson 1992: 120). Taipei is not a city instantly recognizable by its monuments or skyline. An uninitiated spectator of *The Skywalk Is Gone* first observes the typicality of this cityscape, and then has to deduce not just the film's location, but also the significance that Tsai ascribes to it.

This inferential and partially extra-cinematic process of cognition suggests a rejoinder to one worry that repeatedly surfaces in critical work on the city and cinema. Charlotte Brunsdon states it forcefully. Too often, she objects, "city discourse" functions as "a way both of bringing together different objects of study (*different particular cities*) and of making them all the same (*the city in general*)" (Brunsdon 2012: 221; emphasis added). But is an either-or choice between specific actual cities and "'city-ness' in general" really the issue? Watching *The Skywalk Is Gone* demonstrates how a pragmatic intuition of what makes a city into a city is, in practice, a prerequisite for comprehending the uniqueness of every city. We start from our common sense about cities in general to work our way to the particularity of Taipei. "Cityness" implies less homogenization than conceptualization. By the same token, "cityness" as an abstract, inclusive, and salient concept can only be distilled analytically from the experience and representation of actually existing cities.

The creative dynamic between a conceptualization of "cityness," a social and historical interest in the affective reality of living in a modern metropolis, and close attention to the portrayal of different cities on screen has been at the heart of many of the best monographs on the city and cinema—not least Charlotte Brunsdon's own study of postwar London films (2007). Cinematic representations and the declining local film industry were central to Ackbar Abbas's study of the "disappearance" of Hong Kong as the city's sovereignty passed from the United Kingdom to China (Abbas 1997). Edward Dimendberg reimagined the city of American film noir by insisting that *space* and *culture* need to be treated as equally important, and mutually dependent, if the way that the genre "registers and inflects the psychic and cultural manifestations of late modernity" is to be properly understood. The noir city is not merely the expression of "some underlying myth, theme, or vision"; its *spatiality* is "a historical *content*" as significant as the "more commonly studied formal and narrative features" of noir films (Dimendberg 2004: 12, 9). Other monographs have traced the interplay between cinema, space, urbanity, culture, and history in relation to different European or US cities, most notably Berlin (Gleber 1999; Ward 2013), Paris (Phillips 2003), Vienna (Seibel 2017), New York (Sanders 2001; Corkin 2011), Los Angeles (Shiel 2012), and San Francisco (Webb 2014). Beyond a Western frame of reference, Ranjani Mazumdar (2007) has interpreted Bombay cinema as an archive of urban spaces, and Yomi Braester (2010) has shown how Chinese cinema influenced urban developments in Shanghai, Taipei, and Beijing after 1949.

Intellectual Field

Although my own contribution to this tradition, *Imagining the Modern City*, was published in 1999, the way I think about "the city" had been shaped by four remarkable books published in the 1970s. They were the English translation of Walter Benjamin's *Charles Baudelaire: A Lyric Poet in the Era of High Capital* (1971), Raymond Williams's *The Country and the City* (1973), Jonathan Raban's *Soft City* (1975), and Richard Sennett's *The Fall of Public Man* (1977). Although the books differed in style, tone, and focus, and although none was centrally concerned with film or photography, the four authors did all, in their own ways, write about *the city as a medium*. They started from the premise that the city is a symbolic environment, as well as a physical reality, in which the subjectivity of modern citizens was formed and tested, and in which new forms of sociability and new styles of publicness came into being. They showed how citizens learned to interpret the signs, meanings, and spectacle of the city. They conceptualized citizenship as performance, and offered compelling accounts of the *mise-en-scène* of city life. Above all, they sought to capture and articulate the modern city's affective or experiential texture: the interaction between "The Metropolis and Mental Life," to invoke the title of the sociologist Georg Simmel's famous 1903 essay, which Williams had in mind when he referred to Dickens's use of London to "dramatise" a "very complex structure of feeling." Raban simply called it the "city inside the head" (Williams 1973: 158; Raban 1975: 69).

I had first written about urban film and photography in 1992, when I contributed to a sociology course, *Understanding Modern Societies*, being offered by the Open University (OU). The course was chaired by Stuart Hall, whose ecumenical vision of the discipline happily accommodated the topic of the modern metropolis and an approach that drew on film, media, and cultural studies. Even so, I could not assume that the students I was addressing would be familiar with the perspectives and methods of these emerging disciplines. In 1992, no one was talking about "urban media studies," and little had been published on "the city and cinema." I contributed a chapter that laid out different ways in which cities constitute "representational space" (Henri Lefebvre), tracing the historical importance of *metaphors* of "the city as organism" and "the city as machine" for 19th-century reformers and 20th-century architects. Polemically, I called my chapter "Metropolis: City as Text," in order to emphasize the symbolic dimension of all social phenomena and the sensemaking relationship of citizens to urban environments (Donald 1992). To accompany that chapter, I scripted a half-hour OU/BBC television program, *Picturing the Modern City*, which looked at urban photography in the 19th and early 20th century and the "city symphony" films of the 1920s. The program was structured around two interviews. John Tagg, the historian and theorist of photography, explained how photographs were used to create detailed statistical and visual archives about urban populations in the latter part of the 19th century (Tagg 1988; see also Chapter 22, this volume), while Annette Michelson, founding editor of the avant-garde journal *October* and authority on Dziga Vertov, montage, and all things modernist, analyzed cinematic strategies for rendering the fragmentation, diversity, and sheer modernity of the metropolis in two canonical city films, Walter Ruttmann's *Berlin: Symphony of a Great City* (1927) and Vertov's *The Man with the Movie Camera* (1928).

Shortly before embarking on this work for *Understanding Modern Societies*, I had edited a reader for the British Film Institute on *Fantasy and the Cinema* (1989) in which "the uncanny" was a central concept. At the time, I thought of "the city" and "fantasy in cinema" as distinct research interests. Then I read *The Architectural Uncanny*. There, Anthony Vidler tracks a contemporary sensibility, which sees the uncanny erupt in "empty parking lots around abandoned or run-down shopping malls" and in "the wasted margins and surface appearances of post-industrial culture," back to "a feeling of unease first identified in the late eighteenth century" (Vidler 1992: 3). In my chapter and my conversation with John Tagg, I had looked at Victorian reformers who, driven by a fear of darkened spaces and the opacity of the urban populations, had sought to shine a light on those spaces and to enlighten (and so, discipline) those populations. For Vidler, that was only half the story. He saw an "intimate association" between transparency and obscurity as integral to Enlightenment conceptions of urban space from the beginning. From Bentham's Panopticon to Le Corbusier's Ville Radieuse, "all the radiant spaces of modernism" had manifested the same ambiguity: "the presence of death in life, dark space in bright space." Power entailed not "the final triumph of light over dark," but rather "the insistent presence of the one in the other" (Vidler 1992: 17). At the same time, Peter Wollen argued in a *Sight and Sound* article that one aspect of cinema's affinity with the city has been its capacity to give form to the uniquely modern form of the uncanny described by Vidler: "the city is perceived as a kind of dream space, a delirious world of psychic projection rather than sociological projection" (Wollen 1992: 25).

Vidler and Wollen confirmed my misgivings of "city as text" as a rubric. Urban space may be impregnated with multiple meanings and have its own symbolic *texture*, but "city as text" made it sound too language-like by far. "Reading" the city is not like reading words on a page. We negotiate the city's opacity pragmatically, which also means poetically. Working out the relationship between urban experience and a cinematic uncanny led to an article juxtaposing city symphonies against a different modern tradition of fantastic, often dystopian cinematic cities: *Metropolis* (1926), *King Kong* (1933), *Blade Runner* (1982), *Akira* (1988), and *Batman* (1989) (Donald 1995). This new insight also helped to establish the interplay between light and dark, transparency and opacity, and visibility and invisibility that informed *Imagining the Modern City*. I came to understand that, in Simmel's terms, cinema was an important mechanism for translating the external, crystalized structures of "the metropolis" into the subjective, imaginative reality of "mental life."

Modernity

The 1990s saw the appearance of several powerful revisionist histories—influenced by the legacy of Benjamin, Simmel, and Siegfried Kracauer—that set the emergence of cinema against the backdrop of capitalist modernity and a new metropolitan visual culture. Particularly influential were Tom Gunning's argument that a "cinema of attractions," offering the novelty of images that move, hurtling locomotives, and magical transformations, both exemplified "a particularly modern form of aesthetics" and responded to "the specifics of modern and especially urban life," and Miriam Hansen's conceptualization of cinema as "vernacular modernism," an imaginative resource that enabled audiences in capitals around the world to negotiate the disconcerting experience of modernization (Gunning 1995: 126; Hansen 1991). In such histories, the cinematic city functioned as more than an illuminating metaphor for modernity. They told the story of filmmakers and philosophers who believed in the power of film and photography to transform the way that people saw and experienced the city. "I am kino-eye, I am a mechanical eye," wrote Dziga Vertov in 1923. "I, a machine, show you the world as only I can see it. My path leads to the creation of a fresh perception of the world. I decipher in a new way a world unknown to you" (Michelson 1984: 17–18). This assertion of modernity's revolution in human perception draws ultimately on Simmel's ideas about the impact of the metropolis on mental life. Benjamin made the connection to film explicit in the 1930s. The new medium reflected "profound changes in the apperceptive apparatus—changes that are experienced on an individual scale by the man in the street in big-city traffic, on a historical scale by every present-day citizen," he wrote. In cinematic montage, "perception in the form of shocks was established as a formal principle" (Benjamin 1973: 252; 1971: 132). Before film, photography had revealed the existence of an "optical unconscious," comparable to the "instinctual unconscious" discovered through psychoanalysis (Benjamin 1999: 512).

Not everyone was convinced. The film scholar David Bordwell raised two cogent objections to what he called the "modernity thesis" or the "history-of-vision thesis." One concerned the subjective changes supposedly wrought by photography and film. Is it really true, asked Bordwell, that "at some point between 1859 and 1920, perception within European societies changed?" (Bordwell 1997: 141–2). Such an event, he protested, would entail the implausible overthrow of an "intricate mesh of hard-wired anatomical, physiological, optical, and psychological mechanisms produced by millions of years of biological selection" (Bordwell 1997: 142). In defense of the Benjaminian position, it can be pointed out that perception takes place in the mind as much as in the eye, and it has its own grammar whereby sense data are fixed (or *conceptualized*) as intelligible signs by reference to existing experiences and other frameworks of sensemaking. Although an instant rewiring of evolutionary adaptation on the streets of Paris or in the nickelodeons of New York may indeed be improbable, it is entirely conceivable that new frameworks of interpretation emerged (yes, between 1859 and 1920) that influenced how city dwellers came to understand the nature of their being in that modern world. Bordwell's other objection concerned the etiology of film style. Did the fragmentation and tempo of metropolitan life really *determine* the formal principles used in the nascent cinema industry, as Gunning appeared to claim? If they did, then why did not all films of the time exhibit those principles? The legitimate concern underlying the question is that a wide-ranging "modernity thesis" might be pursued at the expense of the detailed historical and aesthetic study of actual changes in film style and film production. But research is not a zero-sum game. An empirical history of film aesthetics can coexist with a social history of cinema, to the benefit of both, if the relationships between cinema, cities, and modernity are conceptualized less as chains of *determination* or *causality* and more in terms closer to the *elective affinity* that the sociologist Max Weber posited between Capitalism and Protestantism. This envisages the possibility that two or more institutions, or mentalities, or sets of beliefs, or modes of cultural production may demonstrate a high degree of formal comparability or compatibility, and can gravitate toward each other in terms of orientations, predispositions, and practices, even when no straightforward causality can be established between them. My point is that cinema and the modern metropolis might have been made for each other.

Surveillance

Coming up to date, what is the relationship between post-digital cinema and the 21st-century city? Is there still an affinity, or has that been lost in the transformations of the world's ever-expanding cities and the emergence of new media technologies and institutions? The confluence of three urban developments is pertinent. First is the rise of "smart cities": the proliferation of cybernetic infrastructures designed to promote the efficient use of resources, ease the flow of traffic, make cities more ecologically sustainable, and, at the same time, monitor the movement and activities of citizens. Second is a renewed sensitivity to the physical fragility of cities. The iconic image remains 9/11, but equally significant has been the devastation caused by "natural" (humanly exacerbated) catastrophes like the sequence of hurricanes since Katrina in 2005, or the Fukushima earthquake-tsunami meltdown in 2011. All that is solid not so much melts into air as risks being pummeled into rubble and dust. And third is the increasing precariousness of city life: less the niggling, press-fanned fear of physical violence than the routine management of urban populations through insecurity and debt. What is touted as unprecedented "freedom of choice" turns out to be an unremitting obligation to take responsibility for individual decisions within overbearing markets. The global recession of 2007 and 2008 and the subsequent years of austerity left citizens with accumulated liabilities, but less often the resources to acquit them. Gone are the supporting disciplinary institutions of the welfare state. The new double-edged "freedom" is controlled through a perennial, fluid, and intimate superintendence that tracks every movement, every transaction, and every interaction through a seamless web of technologies and algorithms (Deleuze 1992). Central to this society of control is "dataveillance," embodied not just in the near-universal and ordinarily unnoticed CCTV, but also in our use of GPS, credit cards, smartphones, social media, and this computer on which I type.

It is as though a hole had opened up in what the science-fiction writer William Gibson called the "meatspace" of the old, modern metropolis, and we ordinary citizens, bodies hunched over our iPhones, stepped through into a cyber-city and became actors in an endless time-coded narrative, perpetually watched by, or at least trackable by, an unseen and not-necessarily-human audience. Vidler's "empty parking lots around abandoned or run-down shopping malls" are now surveilled by CCTV (see also Chapter 14, this volume). (Where is the security camera in *The Skywalk Is Gone*? Look at the top right-hand corner of the casing for the LED screen.) Citizenship "transforms into citizen sensing, embodied through practices undertaken in response to (and communication with) computational environments and technologies" (Gabrys 2014: 34). There is a blurring between the physical city and the represented city as they morph into the digitized and surveilled city, and a merging of citizen with prosthetic technologies: smartphones, social media, GPS, and the rest. To conceptualize "the citizen" of this world, to grasp the nature of being-in-the-contemporary-city, requires an understanding of the relationship between *the city* (urban space and urban infrastructures), *the person* (the human body as well as the human subject), and *the machine* (technologies of control and mediation). That is why the geographer Matthew Gandy talks about the *cyborg city*, rather than the *smart city*: less a parallel virtual space where the human subject is dematerialized than a digitally saturated urban space in which technologically networked but still embodied humans go about their business and are socialized as subjects (Gandy 2005).

Discussing a shot in *Phantom Lady* (Robert Siodmak, 1944), Edward Dimendberg observes, almost as an aside, that, in film noir, the "surveillance of urban space" operates as "the intersection point of the city with the cinematic apparatus" (Dimendberg 2004: 33). The role of surveillance and cinema in mediating *urban space* and managing the *experience of citizenship* persists in contemporary films, from the *Bourne* cycle to *The Wire* on television. Typically, such films take surveillance as a theme, use the city as a setting, and evoke the "look" or sound of surveillance technologies—the grainy black and white of CCTV, the downward zoom of spy satellites, and muffled and distorted telephone taps. Just as pertinent for understanding the relationship between city, cinema, and surveillance is an historical canon of films that reflect on the emergence and discontents of that nexus, registering the growing pervasiveness of media technologies and creating plotlines around the subjective anxieties provoked by their use for surveillance. In these films, the city features as more than a backdrop: it becomes an actor, even a protagonist, in the drama.

As long ago as 1931, Fritz Lang's first sound film, *M*, was given the strapline *A City Searches for a Murderer*. Berlin is portrayed as already comprehensively networked by surveillance and communication technologies. Telephones and teletype messaging allow the police to talk to their political masters, but also connect members of the public to the authorities. Alarm systems in office blocks link directly to the police. Newspapers and wanted posters keep the population constantly informed and updated. Its population of criminals and vagrants is monitored through identity papers, fingerprints, and police checks. As if in anticipation of Deleuze's society of control, "the city" that does the searching in *M* is conjured up in the relentless cross-cutting between the police's deployment of panoptic technologies in their hunt for Peter Lorre's child-murderer and the rather more effective dragnet initiated at street level by Berlin's unperceived but all-seeing underworld of criminals and beggars. Compare this classic modernist surveillance with a much more recent film, Michael Haneke's *Caché* (2005). Here, the strapline might be: *Video Reveals Guilty Secrets*.

Although different districts of Paris, and their hiddenness from each other, have a part to play, it is the invisibly embedded technologies of urban surveillance and their formal integration into its *mise-en-scène* that structure the movement and rhythm of the narrative.

This is evident in *Caché*'s opening shot, which lasts two and a half minutes. For the first minute or so, it appears to be a still image of a house in a bourgeois Paris street, as the credits are slowly typed over it. A passing pedestrian shows that it is in fact a static, time-based recording and off-screen voices discussing where it came from—and a degree of break-up as it is fast-forwarded—finally reveal it to be a videotape being watched by the couple who live in the house and who are coming to realize that they are the subjects of surveillance. As more tapes arrive throughout the film, the need to know who is watching them, and why, becomes more urgent. As in *M*, there is a tension between the stasis of surveillance—the uncertainty about the status and significance of the tapes—and the narrative drive of detection: trawling the city in the search for their source and, along the way, the unravelling of personal guilt and historical denial. The uncertainties continue until the conclusion: a four-minute static long shot of pupils leaving a school at day's end. As in a surveillance tape, the spectator's eye is not directed to the key information: a friendly conversation between the bourgeois couple's son and the son of an Algerian immigrant, who was appallingly wronged in his childhood by the boy's father and whose parents had been among the 200 Algerian protesters killed in the long-disavowed Paris police massacre of October 1961. How does this recording relate to the film's intergenerational and interethnic dynamics and debts? Is this motivated as a point-of-view shot, and if so, whose? Or is this pure surveillance in which we, as audience, are now complicit?

In the 20 years between the mid-1950s and the mid-1970s, an informal but increasingly self-referential cycle of films addressed the vulnerabilities associated with the use of media technologies to observe urban space and so to have some (delusory) mastery over the city. The protagonists are photographers in Alfred Hitchcock's *Rear Window* (1954) and Michelangelo Antonioni's *Blow-Up* (1966), a movie cameraman in Michael Powell's *Peeping Tom* (1960), and a sound engineer in Francis Ford Coppola's *The Conversation* (1974). *Rear Window* is set in New York and, more specifically, one anonymous courtyard in a sweltering Greenwich Village during America's McCarthyite paranoia. *Peeping Tom* and *Blow-Up* are set in London on the cusp of the 1960s and then when the vogue for London was at its height. *The Conversation* is set in San Francisco in the wake of Watergate and the Nixon tapes, and in the early days of major urban redevelopment. Although *Peeping Tom* is primarily concerned with the violence of the voyeuristic gaze—a diffident psychopath using his camera as a murder weapon—London's geography is used to stage his psychodrama. Mark still lives in the house where, as a boy, he was tormented by his sadistic father in the name of science and where he now has his secret cinema. While working as a focus puller at Pinewood Studios, he freelances as a pornographic photographer in the sexualized space of Soho. In the other films, the camera or tape recorder picks up evidence of possible or planned murders, but the emphasis is less on crime and punishment than on the fallibility of mechanical recordings. In *Blow-Up*, the photographer's uncertainty about what truth, if any, can be found in his pictures finally gives way not to plot resolution, but to a mimed game of tennis in a London park that playfully subverts the epistemological authority of cinema through its ambiguity about whether shots are "point-of-view" or not, and whether sound is diegetic or not. *Rear Window* is bookended by two sequences that evoke the urban dynamics of community, density, privacy, loneliness, and being-overlooked-by-strangers. In the opening, the camera leads the audience around James Stewart's apartment like a cat burglar or spy, prying into his stuff before coming to rest on the sleeping photographer, trapped here by a broken leg. Jeff passes the time by using his telephoto lens to snoop on the lives of his neighbors—including a murderer. In the film's climax, the murderer realizes where he is being watched from, breaks into the photographer's apartment, and throws him out of the window—breaking his other leg. Although *The Conversation* ends up in much the same place, with the violation of the hero's home, it begins with a shot that enacts the intersection of urbanism, surveillance, and cinematic apparatus. From an extreme high-angle perspective on Union Square in downtown San Francisco, the camera begins a three-minute zoom down to ground level. With a nod to *Blow-Up*'s ending, it picks out first a white-face mime artist working the lunchtime crowd in the winter sunshine, and then a young couple. A reverse shot reveals the initial perspective to have been that of a surveillance operator on top of a skyscraper, aiming a directional microphone at the couple. Cutting to ground level, the mime is shown irritating a distracted man in a plastic mac—Gene Hackman as Harry Caul, the neurotic sound man—as a prelude to revealing a complex, multi-device surveillance stakeout. The film's conclusion combines the plot echo of *Rear Window* with an elaboration of *Blow-Up*'s cognitive misdirection. In the paranoid privacy of his apartment, Harry improvises on his saxophone to the accompaniment of a jazz record. A call on his off-grid phone, presumably from the corporation that employed him, tells him that "we know you know," runs a tape of the music he has just played, and warns that "we'll be watching you." Shocked at his own vulnerability to surveillance, Harry rips his home apart to find the bug. Thwarted, he slumps on the floor against a ruined wall, despairingly taking up his sax to the accompaniment of a non-diegetic piano. Whereas the intrusive camera at the start of *Rear Window* might be regarded as Hitchcock's authorial signature, here the oscillating camera tauntingly represents the location of the invisible bug. As in *Caché*, surveillance moves "away from the space of the story" and becomes "the condition of the narration itself" (Levin 2010: 583).

Time

In his most famous utterance on cinema and the city, Walter Benjamin celebrated the way that the familiar landmarks and coordinates of everyday metropolitan life—the "prison-world" of taverns and streets, offices and furnished rooms, and railroad stations and factories—had been blown apart by film's "dynamite of the tenth of a second" (Benjamin 1973: 229). Cinematic montage opened up a new way of experiencing the 20th-century city, giving form and expression to its onrush of sensory stimuli, its unprecedented speed, and its syncopated rhythms. Cinema embodied the city's temporality.

One feature of several films discussed here is the presence of unusually long, and often static, shots: the slow pan down from the *dieu voyeur*'s perspective at the start of *The Conversation*, the diegetically ambiguous shots that open and close *Caché*, and the motionless woman in *The Skywalk Is Gone*. That hardly means that the pace of city life has slowed down. On occasion, the static or slowly panning camera seems to mimic the real-time, indiscriminate gaze of electronic urban surveillance. As an ineluctable component of the sociotechnical infrastructure of the city, surveillance, like cinema before it, recalibrates the time-space of the city. This development suggests one last observation. For all that we think about film and photography as visual media, whose principal function *vis-à-vis* the city is to provide visual images of urban spaces and landscapes, could it be that the "cityness" they conjure up is inherently, even preeminently, *temporal*?

In *The Skywalk Is Gone*, Shiang-chyi has returned to the site of the demolished overpass where, a year previously, she had bought a dual-time watch so that she could be synchronized to Taipei time while living in Paris. Even though she has now returned to find the man who sold her the watch, she is so disoriented by the transformation of the place that she fails to recognize him as they pass each other on an underground escalator. Self-consciously, Shiang-chyi is looking for a person and a place. At a more profound level, as Song Hwee Lim explains, she is "in search of lost time" (Lim 2014: 154). Lost time and disappeared places: these are recurrent features not just of Tsai's films, but of all urban film and photography. In the 1930s, Walter Benjamin put his finger on the melancholy resonances of Eugene Atget's photographs of a vanishing Paris: invaluable historical documentation, but also an uncanny archive of evanescence. In 1997, 10 years after making *Wings of Desire* and eight years after the reunification of Berlin, Wim Wenders reflected on cinema, space, and time. "The whole film suddenly turned into an archive for things that aren't around anymore," he said. "Films that don't call themselves documentaries, feature films, do that to an amazing degree" (cit. Brunsdon 2007: 211). It is not just the ephemerality of the city's fabric that is at issue, but the way that cities are haunted by the events that have occurred within them. Cities exist in time as much as in space. Passing time is built into the photographic image; cinema, said Bazin, is "change mummified." Cities have symbolic significance not because of where they are, but because they have histories. Narrative transforms space into place, and photography and film have played their part in that alchemy. They preserve official histories and the passage of time. Their apparently innocent realism and referentiality may be tinged with intimations of loss, but they also free us to imagine the cities we know otherwise than they are.

References

Abbas, A. (1997) *Hong Kong: Culture and the Politics of Disappearance*, Minneapolis, MN: University of Minnesota Press.
Benjamin, W. (1971) *Charles Baudelaire: A Lyric Poet in the Era of High Capital*, London: New Left Books.
— (1973) *Illuminations*, London: Collins/Fontana.
— (1999) "Little History of Photography," in M. W. Jennings, H. Eiland, and G. Smith (eds.) *Selected Writings, 1927–1934*, trans. R. Livingstone, Cambridge MA: Harvard University Press.
Bordwell, D. (1997) *On the History of Film Style*, Cambridge, MA: Harvard University Press.
Braester, Y. (2010) *Painting the City Red: Chinese Cinema and the Urban Contract*, Durham, NC: Duke University Press.
Brunsdon, C. (2007) *London in Cinema: The Cinematic City Since 1945*, London: BFI.
— (2012) "The Attractions of the Cinematic City," *Screen*, 53(3), pp. 209–27.
Corkin, S. (2011) *Starring New York: Filming the Grime and Glamour of the Long 1970s*, New York: Oxford University Press.
Deleuze, G. (1992) "Postscript on the Societies of Control," *October*, 59, pp. 3–7.
Dimendberg, E. (2004) *Film Noir and the Spaces of Modernity*, Cambridge, MA: Harvard University Press.
Donald, J. (ed.) (1989) *Fantasy and the Cinema*, London: BFI.
— (1992) "Metropolis: The City as Text," in R. Bocock and K. Thompson (eds.) *Social and Cultural Forms of Modernity*, Cambridge: Polity/Open University.
— (1995) "The City, the Cinema: Modern Spaces," in C. Jenks (ed.) *Visual Culture*, London: Routledge.
— (1999) *Imagining the Modern City*, Minneapolis, MN: University of Minnesota Press.
Gabrys, J. (2014) "Programming Environments: Environmentality and Citizen Sensing in the Smart City," *Environment and Planning D: Society and Space*, 32(1), pp. 30–48.
Gandy, M. (2005) "Cyborg Urbanization: Complexity and Monstrosity in the Contemporary City," *International Journal of Urban and Regional Research*, 29(1), pp. 26–49.
Gleber, A. (1999) *The Art of Taking a Walk: Flanerie, Literature, and Film in Weimar Culture*, Princeton, NJ: Princeton University Press.
Gunning, T. (1995) "An Aesthetic of Astonishment: Early Film and the (In)Credulous Spectator," in L. Williams (ed.) *Viewing Positions: Ways of Seeing Film*, New Brunswick, NJ: Rutgers University Press, pp. 114–33.
Hansen, M. (1991) *Babel and Babylon: Spectatorship in American Silent Film*, Cambridge, MA: Harvard University Press.
Jameson, F. (1992) "Remapping Taipei," *The Geopolitical Aesthetic*, London: BFI/Bloomington, IN: Indiana University Press, pp. 114–57.
Koolhaas, R. and Foster, H. (2013) *Junkspace* with *Running Room*, Honiton, Devon: Notting Hill Editions.
Levin, T. Y. (2010) "Five Tapes, Four Halls, Two Dreams: Vicissitudes of Surveillance Narration in Michael Haneke's *Caché*," in R. Grundmann (ed.) *A Companion to Michael Haneke*, Chichester: Wiley-Blackwell, pp. 75–90.

Lim, S. H. (2014) *Tsai Ming-liam and a Cinema of Slowness*, Honolulu, HI: University of Hawaii Press.
Mazumdar, R. (2007) *Bombay Cinema: An Archive of the City*, Minneapolis, MN: University of Minnesota Press.
Michelson, A. (ed.) (1984) *Kino-Eye: The Writings of Dziga Vertov*, Berkeley, CA: University of California Press.
Phillips, A. (2003) *City of Darkness, City of Light: Emigré Filmmakers in Paris, 1929–1939*, Amsterdam: Amsterdam University Press.
Raban, J. (1975) *Soft City*, London: Fontana.
Sanders, J. (2001) *Celluloid Skyline: New York and the Movies*, New York: Knopf.
Scott, A. J. (2005) *On Hollywood: The Place, the Industry*, Princeton, NJ: Princeton University Press.
Seibel, A. (2017) *Visions of Vienna: Narrating the Cinema in 1920s and 1930s Cinema*, Amsterdam: Amsterdam University Press.
Sennett, R. (1977) *The Fall of Public Man*, Cambridge: Cambridge University Press.
Shiel, M. (2012) *Hollywood Cinema and the Real Los Angeles*, London: Reaktion.
Simmel, G. (1997) "The Metropolis and Mental Life" [1903], in D. Frisby and M. Featherstone (eds.) *Simmel on Culture*, London: SAGE.
Tagg, J. (1988) "God's Sanitary Law: Slum Clearance and Photography in Late Nineteenth-Century Leeds," in *The Burden of Representation: Essays on Photographies and Histories*, Basingstoke: Macmillan, pp. 117–52.
Vidler, A. (1992) *The Architectural Uncanny: Essays in the Modern Unhomely*, Cambridge, MA: MIT Press.
Ward, S. (2013) *Urban Memory and Visual Culture in Berlin: Framing the Asynchronous City, 1957–2012*, Amsterdam: Amsterdam University Press.
Webb, L. (2014) *The Cinema of Urban Crisis: Seventies Film and the Reinvention of the City*, Amsterdam: Amsterdam University Press.
Williams, R. (1973) *The Country and the City*, London: Chatto & Windus.
Wollen, P. (1992) "Delirious Projections," *Sight and Sound*, 2(4), pp. 24–7.

Further Reading

Clarke, D. B. (1997) *The Cinematic City*, London: Routledge.
Shiel, M. and Fitzmaurice, T. (2001) *Cinema and the City: Film and Urban Societies in a Global Context*, Oxford: Blackwell.
Wilson, E. and Webber, A. (eds.) (2008) *Cities in Transition: The Moving Image and the Metropolis*, London: Wallflower.

5
TELEVISION AND THE CITY

Charlotte Brunsdon

Introduction

Sex and the City (HBO 1998–2004), a successful and long-running television series set and part-filmed in Manhattan, followed the fortunes of four women as they negotiated love lives, careers and shopping in New York. The concern of the four friends with their own romantic, sexual and professional satisfaction and their enjoyment of the opportunities for different kinds of consumption in the city immediately identified the show as a post-feminist text (Arthurs 2003). Within the extensive scholarly discussion, there was some analysis of whether the narrating central character, Carrie, could be seen as a 21st-century flaneuse (Jermyn 2009). Was the television city of *Sex and the City* one in which women could wander, observe and consume? Was the historical masculinity of the *flaneur* being challenged by a television series?

While *Sex and the City* drew attention to the television city in the context of the new modes of television production associated with subscription services like Home Box Office (HBO), it was not until the broadcast of the Baltimore-set *The Wire* (HBO 2002–8) that the television city attracted scholarly attention across the fields of sociology, literature, urban studies and critical race studies (Clandfield 2009; Jameson 2010; Chadda and Wilson 2011; Kennedy and Shapiro 2012). *Sex and the City*, with story-lines and generic inheritances drawing on soap opera melodrama and the women's picture centered on privileged, articulate white women, offered its viewers enticements toward a fantasy participation in a life of cocktails, taxis and high-end shopping. *The Wire*, in contrast, with its first series located within the police investigation of the drug trade within inner-city Baltimore, while still offering the fantasy of access to another world, also offered the promise of the sociological intelligibility of this world to the attentive viewer (Bramall and Pitcher 2013). This show—with its dominantly male, and significantly African American, cast and its concentration on the buying and selling of drugs, not shoes—was taken, in the long tradition of the critical valorizing of realist forms, to be serious television (Turnbull 2014), even though, as Linda Williams (2014) has argued, it too is dependent on the tropes of melodrama.

The narrative architecture of *The Wire*, which proposes a systematic analysis of the policing and propagation of post-industrial Baltimore's drug economy across the institutions of criminal justice, the seaport, city government, education and the press (Corkin 2017), exploits the aesthetic potential of long-form television drama to create emotionally involving, complex and evolving narrative worlds (Creeber 2004; Mittel 2015). These capacities of a time-based medium using a serial structure have been evident throughout television's history, particularly in that most derided of genres, the television soap opera, but the severing of the historical relationship between television drama and national network broadcast schedules has led to the pursuit of more segmented audiences, different patterns of investment and, in some instances, higher production values (Nelson 2007; Bennett and Strange 2011; Newman and Levine 2012). The DVD boxset (so much more portable than VHS), and then digitally enabled streaming capacities across a range of devices, introduced a commodity form for the sale of television fiction to individual audience members rather than networks or national broadcasting corporations. This has led to transformations in the way television is watched, in television drama production and in a concomitant growth in critical attention to the medium as a dramatic forum.

The differing critical reputation of these two programs reveals significant cultural assumptions as well as disciplinary divisions that structure attention to, and scholarship about, television and the city. On the one hand, we have television seen as a feminized and trivial medium, in front of which viewers (housewives, in much of the literature) waste time in fantasy. On the other, we have television with a much more explicitly masculine address somehow redeemed from the history and legacy of television as a medium. As the producing cable company claimed, "This is not television, this is HBO". It is these attitudes, particularly the persistent contempt for television and its female viewers, and this structuring of the disciplinary fields within which television is visible, which explain the relative paucity of research that directly addresses the question of television and the city. Some individual programs, such as *Queer as Folk* (Channel 4, 1998), *Frank's Place* (CBS, 1987–8), *Empire Road* (BBC, 1978–9) and *King of the Ghetto* (BBC, 1986), have attracted commentary on the representation of the city therein, often as a side effect of attention to the representation of particular social groups (Billingham 2000: 119–156; Gray 1995: 113–129; Malik 2009; Newton 2011: 153–160, see also Chapter 43, this volume). However, the general trajectory of scholarship on audiovisual media and the city jumps from cinema to the digital city, relegating television to the suburbs (Brunsdon 2012; Andersson and Webb 2016; Penz and Koeck 2017).

Television, Modernity and the Suburb

The relationship between television and the city can be compared productively with that of cinema to the city. From its beginnings, cinema has had a privileged relation to urban modernity. Early accounts of cinema, fascinated by the shadow play on the screen watched by anonymous crowds, have found in the medium both apprehension of, and metaphor for, urban life (Charney and Schwartz 1995). In addition to providing a series of notable representations of the city, such as the city symphonies of the early 20th century, cinema has been seen as a medium that incites urban feelings, celebrates the anonymity of the crowd and, for Miriam Hansen (1991), provides an alternative, proletarian public sphere, while Jacqueline Najuma Stewart (2005) has shown its formative role in black urban modernity. In contrast, television has been associated with the domestic and the suburbs, particularly in the USA, where the medium—and the suburbs—represent qualities such as conformity, triviality and conservatism. Some of these assumptions about the place of television within US culture were transformed by Lynn Spigel's exploration of the historical arrival of the television set in the living room. Spigel (1992a), writing at the end of the period of the dominance of the US networks, when television still dominated national popular cultures, demonstrated, through archival exploration of sources such as women's magazines, the complexity of the negotiations through which television won its place at the center of domestic arrangements in the post-WWII period. Her later work has continued to explore the relationship between mass-produced housing, ideas of cultural value and "Televisionland" (2001: 15). The role of television in domestic modernity has been traced across many cultures, and some combination of the television, the refrigerator, air conditioning, the washing machine and the automobile has been identified as the symbolic and material icon of achieved 20th-century modernity (Hartley 1999; Mankekar 1999; Yoshimi 1999; Morley 2000).

The exploration of television as a domestic medium has a sometimes contradictory relation to the city and the urban. On the one hand, television is associated with privatization and the retreat from public civic life into the home. The uniformity of the vision of mass-built suburbs is underpinned by a symmetrical glimpse of a family gathered around a TV set, watching fictions that extol the normality and desirability of this life (Medhurst 1997). Spigel has explored the place of television-watching suburban families in notions of "white flight" from urban centers (2001: 107–182). On the other hand, television has been seen as a medium most powerful for its ability to broadcast events worldwide, to make events global and to create media events (Dayan and Katz 1992). Raymond Williams (1984) developed the idea of mobile privatization to describe the contradictory pull in modern societies between the domestic sphere and the wider world. Television is the medium that for him epitomizes this tension, enabling individual families to consume world news, drama and entertainment in their living rooms. When he was writing, the newspaper, the book and the transistor radio were the most portable media forms, but subsequent studies of the Sony Walkman (Du Gay et al. 1997) and the mobile phone (Morley 2017: 159–197) have tracked the transformations in media mobilities. The television, which Williams thought of as confined to the home, is now frequently watched by people themselves on the move, commuting to work. While these changed patterns of use and technological capacity inflect the term "mobile privatization" differently to the way Williams intended, it remains an extremely useful way to think about the modalities and consequences of television viewing in the modern city (Spigel 1992b).

Television Outside the Domestic

The domesticity of television within anglophone scholarship has been challenged by scholars of television viewing practices outside US/European contexts. Thomas Tufte's (2000) ethnography of the viewing of Brazilian telenovelas demonstrated that many viewers in the poorest neighborhoods had televisions positioned so that they could be watched from the street, while Penacchioni (1984) discussed the erection of television screens in public squares in Brazil. Hadj-Moussa's (2010) research into the acquisition of satellite television in Egypt demonstrates once again the complexity of the medium's relationship to, articulation of and sometimes transformation of public and private spaces.

Anna McCarthy's 2001 study of US television in spaces outside the home builds on the cultural studies tradition of the study of the micropolitics of the everyday, exploring the proliferation of TV screens in a range of public and semi-public sites such as airports, bars, shops and health centers. She demonstrates that screens in public places can perform different kinds of site-specific and site-repudiating labor, including transforming the experience of waiting, inviting passersby into particular corporate spaces, commodifying attention and constructing identities such as the regular traveler, guest or patient. The expansion of public screens since her study has been documented by scholars such as Krajina (2014), and the unavoidable presence of large screens in the city in the 21st century, as well as the use of the buildings of the city itself as screen for projection mapping, points to a new coming together of television and the city (McQuire 2008; Georgiou 2013).

This proliferation of digital screens within urban environments, whether enormous or handheld, broadcasting widely varying types of content, can be seen as an example of the digital convergence of different media as it becomes more difficult to distinguish between what were previously separate media such as cinema, television, advertising hoardings and telephones (Casetti 2013). However, even within a convergent 21st century and much talk of virtual cities, television has a particular history in relation to the stories that it has told, and tells, about the city.

The City on Television

For the second half of the 20th century, in which television was the preferred news source for many populations, it was through television that cities were most commonly brought into the home. Bombings, coronations, elections, sporting triumphs, protests, transport trouble: all of these events, if taking place in cities, positioned cities as backdrops to news commentary. Viewers all over the world are familiar with the television grammar in which the reporter stands in front of location-shot footage interpreting what can be seen for people at home (see also Chapter 6, this volume). The ceremonial architecture of individual cities—Tiananmen Square in Beijing, the Arc de Triomphe in Paris, St. Peter's Cathedral in Moscow—is familiar through television. News events such as Hurricane Katrina's ravaging of New Orleans, the Arab Spring—with its new landmark of Tahrir Square—and the bombed destruction of Aleppo bring both the streets and sometimes the inhabitants of distant cities, for viewing in the comfort of television-watching homes.

In addition to these live, broadcast cities, television has produced a vast archive of city-set stories in both fictional and reality/documentary genres. What is most striking is how rarely fictional representations of particular television cities are discussed in comparison to filmic or literary versions. There are three reasons for this neglect. The first is a type of geographical literalism in relation to the presentation of place in audiovisual media that entails the assumption that only film or video filmed in the actual location depicted can be taken to represent it. This idea is particularly common in discussions of film and television by non-film and television scholars (such as architects or cultural geographers) and is indicated by the valuation of audiovisual texts that are location-shot and document actual geographical and architectural sites over those (the vast majority) that use studio spaces, geographical and architectural substitutions (location-shot Baltimore for 19th-century New York) and editing to make audiovisual places. While there is evidently discussion of some importance to be had about the particular qualities of location shooting (Brunsdon 2007), and this geographical literalism is present in relation to both film and television, it leads to the dismissal of most television as, beyond title sequences, location filming was on the whole rare for much of the 20th-century network era. Thus, the New York-set *The Naked City* (ABC, 1958–63), which has ravishing location-shot title sequences, also has very interesting depictions of different New York milieus and social worlds in the body of the program. That most of these scenes are not shot on location in New York does not mean that they do not offer representations of the city that deserve attention. Similarly, the studio-shot interior scenes in the enormously popular sitcom, *The Cosby Show*, are located within New York City by the repeated use of the exterior of the substantial brownstone villa in which the Cosbys live and the types of activity undertaken by characters. Together—these interiors, that exterior—these made a certain kind of upscale New York setting familiar as the Cosby home to audiences all over the globe. If the show was partly innovative for its attention to the everyday life of an economically secure upper-middle-class African American family (Gray 1995: 79–84), it is also significant that this family was shown to live in New York. In each case, the stylistic repertoire of the audiovisual media and, specifically, the use of editing to create and conjoin spaces was employed to create a particular version of New York as a television city.

These televisual New Yorks can usefully be compared to many others across a range of axes: television genre, historical period, changing visibility and characterization of particular areas such as Brooklyn or Harlem, and shifting economies, production methods and sites of the programs and TV companies themselves. The historical portrait of particular television cities that can be documented in this way—and only some can, while many cities remain invisible or only local—enriches and supplements cinematic histories and indicates that it might be more productive to think of the televisual city as more like the literary city than the cinematic city. The comparison with literature challenges assumptions about the transparency of audiovisual media, somehow giving direct access to what is filmed, and thus reminds us that the represented city is always also an imagined city. Nobody dismisses Edith Wharton's New York or Charles Dickens's London because it is evidently an imagined and remembered place created on the page by the novelist. This comparison points to a second reason for the neglect of the television city, and this is the lowly cultural status of the television as a medium, the topic with which this essay commenced. Here, the international success of continuing serials (soap operas) is pertinent, for these have traditionally been regarded with some contempt. In Britain, the Salford of *Coronation Street* (Granada, 1960-), the London of *EastEnders* (BBC, 1985-) and the Liverpool of *Brookside* (Channel 4, 1982–2003) have been among the most significant representations of urban community life, providing long-running narratives about families and neighbors in precisely rendered locales (Geraghty 1991; Newland 2008). While these may be among the most watched of television cities, they are significantly absent from discussion of urban media for reasons that include the cultural status of their audience, the national-ness of their address, the speed of production and, paradoxically, the vastness of the texts, simultaneously ephemeral and persisting in their audience's memories. However, it is these programs that produce a familiarity with the represented city through the rhythms of viewing, the repeated returns to places and people, that are perhaps most illuminating about the particular characteristics of the television city.

The Production of Television in the City: Creative Locales

Michael Curtin (2004) has developed the idea of the "media capital" to approach the analysis of media production in the context of increasingly globalized media flow. Drawing on concepts such as Sassen's "global city" (1991) and Joseph Straubhaar's approach to multicentric media flows (1991), this idea challenges the national assumptions of much television scholarship, instead recognizing the way in which cities like Hong Kong, Bombay and Dubai are positioned at the intersection of complex patterns of economic, social and cultural flows. While Curtin's own work has focused on the continuing significance of Hollywood, the changing status of Hong Kong and the emerging strength of Dubai as media capitals, it has also rendered certain patterns of both national and transnational investment more visible. In particular, Curtin has demonstrated the multiple incentives, internationally, for the development of "new creative locales" (1996: 194). The British government, for example, has offered tax incentives that have supported media industries in post-conflict Belfast where the US series *Game of Thrones* is filmed, while Cardiff, the capital of Wales, has benefitted from the success of *Sherlock* (BBC, 2010-), which is filmed there. The production of long-running series, in particular, can have a significant effect on local urban economies and emerging scholarship offers fascinating case studies, such as those of Helen Morgan Parmett (2012, 2014) about post-Hurricane Katrina New Orleans and the production of *Treme* (HBO, 2010–13) in which she demonstrates the subtle, and not so subtle, consequences of having a production company in town making a series about the rebuilding of that city (Gray 2012). Ipek Celik Rappas and Sezen Kayhan (2018) develop this approach in their analysis of the "entangled relationship between Turkish TV series and the city of Istanbul since the late 1980s", exploring the rapid late 20th-century gentrification of the city, which has proceeded under a neoliberal engagement with globalization.

Drawing partly on the work of Sharon Zukin (1982), Celik Rappas and Kayhan argue that television production "may promote gentrification in less visible yet more subtle and complex ways than other creative industries" (2018: 6). Documenting a range of television series set or made in Istanbul between 1986 and 2014, they identify three different types of production site to explore the ways in which the process of image-making interacts physically with the city space (see also Chapter 23, this volume). Historic neighborhoods like Kuzguncuk, the setting for long-running *mahalle*/neighborhood series, are the sites for the evocation of a past multicultural city to promote modern cosmopolitanism. Post-industrial spaces and working-class neighborhoods, such as Tarlabaşı and Bağcılar, can both house television production studios and provide settings for realist and crime dramas. Business centers and luxury residences, their third type of site, are associated generically with romances and with the depiction of the new, cosmopolitan creative class. This new Istanbul offers the allure of modern living spaces, all glass and bright colors, while the distinctive outlines of a modern city begin to emerge in dramas such as *Binbir Gece* (*1001 Nights*, 2006–9) with an architect hero committed to constructing the signature buildings, which David Harvey (2012: 16) sees as an essential element in the attraction of global tourism and investment.

Celik Rappas and Kayhan succeed in integrating attention to the generic specificity of particular television programs with the processes of urban renovation and gentrification in Istanbul. They argue that TV series production can be instrumental in the marketing of certain neighborhoods either as safe havens or as ripe for redevelopment, while also raising the status of television by depicting positively the new bourgeoisie and its associated lifestyles. The political changes in Turkey under Recep Erdogan (Prime Minister 2003–14; President 2014-), which have been increasingly contested since 2013 (toward the end of their period of study), are likely, if their argument is correct, to have discernible consequences in the depiction of Istanbul in television series and, particularly, the depiction of the creative classes and the aspiration toward a tourist-friendly, secular, cosmopolitan city. The value of this research is that it lays out a schema against which new patterns in television drama production and the imaging of Istanbul can be assessed. In this context, recent reports of substantial increases in visitors to Istanbul from Saudi Arabia, Iraq and Syria (from 35,000 in 2013 to over 200,000 recently (Trade Arabia 2017) can be related to the significant export of Turkish television drama such as *Muhteşem Yüzyıl* (*The Magnificent Century*, 2011–14) across the Arab region. The pattern of expatriate house purchase too seems to be shifting following Erdogan's orientation away from the West, with most house purchases in Istanbul in recent years undertaken by Saudis, Qataris and Kuwaitis (Daily Sabah 2015).

The understanding of contemporary television production and the urban images it produces within complex local and global media ecologies, as found in this research on Istanbul and New Orleans, points to the possibilities for, in Clifford Geertz's terms, "thick description" (2000) of television and the city. The exploitation of particular local histories—such as the interplay of industry, migration, political activism and organized crime in Birmingham, UK—staged in dramas such as the 1970s *Gangsters* (BBC, 1976–8) and the 21st-century *Peaky Blinders* (BBC, 2013-) transforms both the image and the actuality of these cities. Understanding these dramas as both particular texts and specific commodities, with particular conditions of production and circulation, requires an approach attentive to both the symbolic and the material dimensions of culture—even if that culture is primarily available in virtual form on a laptop or a phone. While *Peaky Blinders*, with its heritage aesthetic, dynamic violence and rock soundtrack, has been utilized by the city to market itself as distinctive, simultaneously modern and historical, this 21st-century version of Birmingham did not spring from nowhere. The long history of television production within the city, and particularly the BBC's Pebble Mill Studios (Cooke 2012) and the images it produced, forms an essential part of the history of Birmingham and must be considered alongside other elements of its cultural heritage. Television, the dominant media form of the second half of the 20th century, has more to contribute to ideas of "urban media" than current attitudes and scholarship might seem to suggest.

References

Andersson, J. and Webb, L. (eds.) (2016) *Global Cinematic Cities: New Landscapes of Film and Media*, London: Wallflower.
Arthurs, J. (2003) "*Sex and the City* and Consumer Culture", *Feminist Media Studies*, 3(1), pp. 83–98.
Bennett, J. and Strange, N. (eds.) (2011) *Television as Digital Media*, Durham, NC: Duke University Press.
Billingham, P. (2000) *Sensing the City through Television*, Bristol: Intellect.
Bramall, R. and Pitcher, D. (2013) "Policing the Crisis, or Why We Love *The Wire*", *International Journal of Cultural Studies*, 16(1), pp. 83–97.
Brunsdon, C. (2007) "Towards a History of Empty Spaces", *Journal of British Cinema and Television*, 4(1), pp. 219–234.
Brunsdon, C. (2012) "The Attractions of the Cinematic City", *Screen*, 53(3), pp. 209–227.
Casetti, F. (2013) "What Is a Screen Nowadays?" in C. Berry, J. Harbord and R. O. Moore (eds.) *Public Space, Media Space*, Basingstoke: Palgrave Macmillan, pp. 16–40.
Celik Rappas, I. A. and Kayhan, S. (2018) "TV Series Production and the Urban Restructuring of Istanbul", *Television & New Media*, 19(1), pp. 3–23.
Chadda, A. and Wilson, W. J. (2011) "'Way Down in the Hole': Systemic Urban Inequality and *The Wire*", *Critical Inquiry*, 38(1), pp. 164–188.
Charney, L. and Schwartz, V. R. (eds.) (1995) *Cinema and the Invention of Modern Life*, Berkeley, CA: University of California Press.
Clandfield, P. (2009) "'We Ain't Got No Yard': Crime Development, and Urban Environment", in T. Potter and C. W. Marshall (eds.) *The Wire: Urban Decay and American Television*, New York: Continuum, pp. 37–49.
Cooke, L. (2012) *A Sense of Place: Regional British Television Drama, 1956–62*, Manchester: Manchester University Press.
Corkin, S. (2017) *Connecting* The Wire: *Race, Space, and Post-Industrial Baltimore*, Austin, TX: University of Texas Press.
Creeber, G. (2004) *Serial Television: Big Drama on the Small Screen*, London: British Film Institute.
Curtin, M. (1996) "On Edge: Culture Industries in the Neo-Network Era", in R. Ohmann, M. Curtin, G. Averill, D. Shumway and E. G. Traube (eds.) *Making and Selling Culture*, Hanover, NH: Wesleyan University Press, pp. 181–202.
Curtin, M. (2004) "Media Capitals: Cultural Geographies of Global TV", in L. Spigel and J. Olsson (eds.) *Television After TV: Essays on a Medium in Transition*, Durham, NC: Duke University Press, pp. 270–302.
Daily Sabah (2015) "Arab tourists on the rise in Istanbul", viewed 19 March 2018, www.dailysabah.com.tourism/2015/08/05.
Dayan, D. and Katz, E. (1992) *Media Events: The Live Broadcasting of History*, Cambridge, MA: Harvard University Press.
Du Gay, P. et al. (1997) *Doing Cultural Studies: The Story of the Sony Walkman*, London: SAGE.
Geertz, C. (2000 [1973]) *The Interpretation of Cultures*, New York: Basic Books.
Georgiou, M. (2013) *Media and the City*, Cambridge: Polity.
Geraghty, C. (1991) *Women and Soap Opera*, Cambridge: Polity.
Gray, H. (1995) *Watching Race*, Minneapolis, MN: Minnesota University Press.
Gray, H. (2012) "Recovered, Reinvented, Reimagined: *Treme*, Television Studies and Writing New Orleans", *Television and New Media*, 13(3), pp. 268–278.
Hadj-Moussa, R. (2010) "The Undecidable and the Irreversible: Satellite Television in the Algerian Public Arena", in C. Berry, S. Kim and L. Spigel (eds.), *Electronic Elsewheres: Media, Technology, and the Experience of Social Space*, Minneapolis, MN: University of Minnesota Press, pp. 117–136.
Hansen, M. (1991) *Babel and Babylon*, Cambridge, MA: Harvard University Press.
Hartley, J. (1999) *Uses of Television*, London: Routledge.
Harvey, D. (2012) *Rebel Cities: From the Right to the City to the Urban Revolution*, London: Verso.

Jameson, F. (2010) "Realism and Utopia in *The Wire*", *Criticism*, 52(3–4), pp. 359–372.
Jermyn, D. (2009) *Sex and the City*, Detroit, MI: Wayne State University Press.
Kennedy, L. and Shapiro, S. (eds.) (2012) The Wire: *Race, Class, and Genre*, Ann Arbor, MI: The University of Michigan Press.
Krajina, Z. (2014) *Negotiating the Mediated City: Everyday Encounters with Public Screens*, London: Routledge.
Malik, S. (2009) "'Doing Multicultural London': The Case of *King of the Ghetto*", *Journal of British Cinema and Television*, 6(2), pp. 232–248.
Mankekar, P. (1999) *Screening Culture, Viewing Politics: Am Ethnography of Television, Womanhood, and Nation in Postcolonial India*, Durham, NC: Duke University Press.
McCarthy, A. (2001) *Ambient Television*, Durham, NC: Duke University Press.
McQuire, S. (2008) *The Media City: Media, Architecture and Urban Space*, London: SAGE.
Medhurst, A. (1997) "Negotiating the Gnome Zone: Versions of Suburbia in British Popular Culture", in R. Silverstone (ed.) *Visions of Suburbia*, London: Routledge, pp. 240–268.
Mittel, J. (2015) *Complex TV: The Poetics of Contemporary Television Storytelling*, New York: New York University Press.
Morley, D. (2000) *Home Territories: Media, Mobility and Identity*, London: Routledge.
Morley, D. (2017) *Communications and Mobility: The Migrant, the Mobile Phone, and the Container Box*, Hoboken, NJ: Wiley-Blackwell.
Nelson, R. (2007) *State of Play: Contemporary 'High-End' TV Drama*, Manchester: Manchester University Press.
Newland, P. (2008) "Global Markets and a Market Place: Reading *EastEnders* as the Anti-Docklands", *Journal of British Cinema and Television*, 5(1), pp. 72–85.
Newman, M. Z. and Levine, E. (2012) *Legitimating Television: Media Convergence and Cultural Status*, New York: Routledge.
Newton, D. M. (2011) *Paving the Empire Road: BBC Television and Black Britons*, Manchester: Manchester University Press.
Penacchioni, I. (1984) "The Reception of Popular Television in Northeast Brazil", *Media, Culture and Society*, 6(4), pp. 337–341.
Parmett, H. M. (2012) "Space, Place and New Orleans on Television: From *Frank's Place* to *Treme*", *Television and New Media*, 13(3), pp. 193–212.
Parmett, H. M. (2014) "Media as a Spatial Practice: *Treme* and the Production of the Media Neighbourhood", *Continuum: Journal of Media & Cultural Studies*, 28(3), pp. 286–299.
Penz, F. and Koeck, R. (2017) *Cinematic Urban Geographies*, New York: Palgrave Macmillan.
Sassen, S. (1991) *The Global City: New York, London, Tokyo*, Princeton, NJ: Princeton University Press.
Spigel, L. (1992a) *Make Room for TV: Television and the Family Ideal in Postwar America*, Chicago, IL: The University of Chicago Press.
Spigel, L. (1992b) "Introduction", in R. Williams, *Television: Technology and Cultural Form*, Hanover, NH: Wesleyan University Press, pp. ix–xxxvii.
Spigel, L. (2001) *Welcome to the Dreamhouse: Popular Media and Postwar Suburbs*, Durham, NC: Duke University Press.
Stewart, J. N. (2005) *Migrating to the Movies: Cinema and Black Urban Modernity*, Berkeley, CA: University of California Press.
Straubhaar, J. (1991) "Beyond Media Imperialism: Asymmetrical Interdependence and Cultural Proximity", *Critical Studies in Mass Communication*, 8, pp. 1–11.
Trade Arabia (2017) "Turkish Dramas Continue to Drive Tourism from Arab Region", viewed 16 March 2018, http://tradearabia.com/news/TTN_325663.
Tufte, T. (2000) *Living with the Rubbish Queen: Telenovelas, Culture and Modernity in Brazil*, Luton: University of Luton Press.
Turnbull, S. (2014) *The TV Crime Drama*, Edinburgh: Edinburgh University Press.
Williams, L. (2014) *On The Wire*, Durham, NC: Duke University Press.
Williams, R. (1984) "Drama in a Dramatized Society", *Writing in Society*, London: Verso, pp. 11–21.
Yoshimi, S. (1999) "'Made in Japan': The Cultural Politics of 'Home Electrification' in Postwar Japan", *Media Culture and Society*, 21(2), pp. 149–171.
Zukin, S. (1982) *Loft Living: Culture and Capital in Urban Change*, Baltimore, MD: Johns Hopkins University Press.

Further Reading

Brunsdon, C. (2018) *Television Cities: Paris, London, Baltimore*, Durham, NC: Duke University Press.
Turner, G. and Tay, J. (eds.) (2009) *Television Studies after TV*, London and New York: Routledge.
Williams, R. (1974) *Television, Technology and Cultural Form*, London: Fontana.

6
JOURNALISM
An Urban Affair

Scott Rodgers

Introduction

"London is like a newspaper. Everything is there, and everything is disconnected". These 12 words, which appear in Walter Bagehot's much-discussed 1858 essay on Charles Dickens (Bagehot 1965: 87), preface an evocative, if short, rumination on the relation between 19th-century journalism and the urban. Urban life, Bagehot suggests, involves a mutual estrangement that is precisely the same as the unrelated names listed in newspapers under births, marriages, and deaths. And the reader, moving "from the broad leader to the squalid police-report" (Bagehot 1965: 87)—between stories juxtaposed with seeming abandon in Victorian newspapers—is like the walker turning a city corner and finding one neighborhood abruptly replaced with another. In these observations, Bagehot seems to be inviting us to think about a *formal* relationship of the newspaper and the urban; one in which the urban not only appears through the newspaper, but the newspaper—as a form of journalism—is itself urban.

However, it is also important to put Bagehot's ruminations into context. Reading the essay from beginning to end reveals a critical and occasionally condescending assessment of Dickens' writing. The genius of Dickens, according to Bagehot, is his sublime skills of observation, which bring to life the detail and minutiae of the city. But Dickens' "picturesque imagination" is not complemented by a facility for abstraction (Bagehot 1965: 84–5): "He describes the figs which are sold, but not the talent which sells figs well". For Bagehot, Dickens lacks learned taste; he possesses instead a raw, in-the-moment "creative taste" for describing urban life evocatively (Bagehot 1965: 103). Implying that Dickens owes more to reportage than literature proper, Bagehot's essay not only invokes a relationship of journalism and the urban via its forms (i.e., the newspaper), but also its *norms*: as a model, pattern, or practice for observing and knowing the city.

This formula of forms and norms provides the broad terms of reference for how this chapter will present the specifically urban affair, or situation, of journalism. I am interested not so much in specifying what counts as "urban" journalism or not, but rather how the urban appears through journalism's technical, industrial, architectural, and organizational forms; and also through journalistic norms—that is, its various ways of observing, imagining, and inhabiting the urban. Provided that we think of such forms and norms as always going hand in hand—as being inseparable—then we can reveal the urban affair of journalism as an environmental condition: as something that is never "outside" of the city, but rather is *of* it. A consequence of this deep conception of journalistic urbanity is that our concern will extend beyond the subfield of local journalism. Rather, we will grapple with how nearly all forms of journalism are bound up in different communicative "figurations" in and through cities: that is, various urban constellations of shared relevance, human actors, and practice-technology ensembles (Couldry and Hepp 2017: 66–7). My discussion will be organized around three conceptual lenses (drawing on Morgan Parmett and Rodgers 2018): journalism as a culture of public circulation, journalistic placemaking, and journalistic field spaces.

Journalism as a Culture of Public Circulation

To begin clarifying how journalism might be seen as "of" the urban, I would like to explore the ways that journalism is often considered to be a culture of public circulation. First, let me define what I mean by "public circulation". It is probably uncontroversial to claim that one principal way journalism is bound up with the city is that it makes possible an urban public sphere. The term public itself is a thorny one; once invoked, "public" potentially invites us to take a deep dive into the work of writers such as Habermas, Arendt, or Sennett. But for our present purposes, let us focus on just one feature of journalistic publicness: that, as a practice, it involves recursive acts of urban public *address* (see Iveson 2007: 20–49). Thinking about publicness in terms of address is most associated with literary critic Michael Warner (2002). Addressing a public, for Warner, always already involves a taken-for-granted public sphere, which itself depends on those acts of public address. Therefore, publicness entails a "chicken-and-egg circularity" (Warner 2002: 67). Addressing a public is never a one-way act, since that address always responds to or assumes an existing public. If we accept this, it follows that any model of journalism as a kind of linear urban communication—where journalists send outputs in one direction to urban residents (i.e., their receivers)—is unsustainable. It is in this sense that we might describe journalism as a culture of public circulation. Here, "circulation" is adapted from Lee and LiPuma's (2002) influential critique of globalization research, which argues that cultural forms circulate not by moving in one direction, from point of origin to destination, but by being performed into being by dispersed communities of practice. A journalistic form such as news needs to be recursively enacted by various communities of practice in order to circulate; communities of practice which are simultaneously presupposed by the form (cf. Bødker 2015). And, in circulating news form, journalistic practices are also important in circulating "the imaginary of the city into existence by presupposing its reality as a condition of their own" (LiPuma and Koelble 2005: 175).

One evocative historical illustration of this circularity can be found in David Henkin's (1998) book *City Reading*, an expansive exploration into the material relationships between various forms of written word and city living. Echoing our opening quote from Walter Bagehot, Henkin notices a correspondence between the experience of antebellum New York streets and public spaces and the layout of early printed newspapers. However, this correspondence is not a binary one between urban physical space and its imagination:

> Newspapers were not simply simulacra of primary urban experience or abstract representations of the real spatial contours of the city. Hawked, posted, traded, and read in public view, they had a palpable material presence in the streets, and the symbolic relationship between rectilinear city blocks and rectilinear print columns was reciprocally clarifying.
>
> *(Henkin 1998: 104)*

Fritzsche (1996: 1) makes a similar observation in his study of early 20th-century print culture in Berlin. For Fritzsche, newspapers generated "a second-hand metropolis which gave a narrative to the concrete one and choreographed its encounters"; a kind of enculturation into big city living. Perceiving these dense, interwoven relationships of newspaper and city, Robert E. Park, a leading figure of the Chicago School of urban sociology—and a former journalist (Lindner 1996)—lodged a notable argument against the prevailing, moralistic admonishments newspapers received in the early 20th century. In his provocatively titled essay "The natural history of the newspaper", Park (1923) argues that newspapers should not be judged as purely willful products of their proprietors or journalists. Rather, they were a "natural" ecological emergence of mass urbanization, reproducing "as far as possible, in the city the conditions of life in the village" (1923: 277). Park is not uninterested in politics or power, but he is skeptical of an image of newspapers as a contaminating imposition on urban publics. As an emergent form instilling among their readers an awareness of, interest in, and ability to consume an unprecedented common urban cultural world, newspapers made it possible to mobilize the city as a political body. Newspapers were, in other words, both an urbanized and urbanizing machine, with an unpredictable gravitational push and pull on city life.

A crucial backdrop to such late 19th- and early 20th-century city newspapers, described by Park and others, is the transformation such media forms embodied both economically and in terms of what we call public address. Not only were they unprecedentedly cheap (typically one or two pennies) and therefore accessible to a very wide audience; they were also a secular breakaway from the partisan press (Lindner 1996: 7), addressing their readers not from a particular ideological viewpoint, but as a diverse, differentiated mass urban public (Barth 1982; Kaplan 2002). By the latter half of the 20th century, the descendants of such newspapers grew into larger operations, which, in the North American context at least, began to be described as "metropolitan newspapers". For Phyllis Kaniss (1991), whose Philadelphia-focused study represented an early systematic examination of local news, such newspapers were a significant part of a response to urban sprawl. While taking on the mantle of the historic city center name, such news outlets increasingly engaged in a more abstracted kind of urban public address:

> They have had to come up with a set of institutions, problems, controversies and issues relevant to the entire market. But even more important, they have had to create a regionwide sense of identity that draws their audience together in a psychological if not real form of interdependence.
>
> *(Kaniss 1991: 64)*

However, arguably, television embodies the defining news media environment of postwar American suburbia. Built on the conditions created by radio before it, the rapid domestication of television into homes has led writers such as Silverstone (1994: 52) to name it as the definitively suburban medium, "both historically and sociologically . . . literally of and for the suburb" (see also Chapter 4, this volume). As a journalistic form, television has often been seen to articulate a particular relationship of suburb and inner city: the latter presented as a zone of disorder and criminality, the former a site of televisual spectatorship, with little experience of lived inner city realities (Cottle 1993).

The technical conditions of contemporary journalistic circulation, markedly but not exclusively in the Global North, are of course increasingly defined by digital information and infrastructures, such as websites, mobile apps, desktop computers, feeds, aggregators, streaming, and social media platforms. This is even the case for apparently analog media such as print publications, which are today substantially produced using various software applications and network infrastructures. One notable implication of such transformations is that the previously taken-for-granted dailiness of news has been disrupted by the rise of real-time, streamed, and often interactive news information: "a kind of constantly updated flow of 'news now' . . . simultaneously produced, consumed and re-distributed" (Sheller 2015: 13). Another is that studying "local" news now means contending with a complex, variegated, and rapidly mutating ecology of media practices and forms (Anderson 2013; Coleman et al. 2016).

However, what appears to endure is the urban as a complex object of intentionality for the practice of journalism, or what Edmund Husserl might call its "aboutness". Sometimes, the urban shows up as classificatory scheme for news phenomena or events. Sometimes, the urban is a place identified by a proper name, one invoked to claim shared interests, values, concerns or simply turf; in other words, the urban becomes a collective totality in which "the city" is synonymous with "the public" (Iveson 2007: 40–7). As its forms undulate between analog and digital, old and new, journalism clearly continues to embody a culture of urban public circulation.

Journalistic Placemaking

Journalism is "of" the urban not only via its public address, but also in how it makes urban places. This is perhaps most clearly seen in the ways journalistic organizations make marks on the city through their buildings. As Wallace (2012) shows, for example, early newspaper skyscrapers such as those on Park Row, situated directly across from New York City Hall, not only surpassed in height the city's church spires, but in so doing, signaled their ascendance over organized religion as a new, secular communicative order of the city. More contemporary examples often represent an attempt to incorporate new media practices and technologies into a news organization via architectural or space design. Broadcasting House in London crystalizes the BBC looking toward a digital future, but also back to its broadcasting heritage (see Ericson 2010). Preserved on the original façade, for example, are Prospero and Ariel from Shakespeare's *The Tempest*, the magician and spirit of air who, together, are meant to evoke the magical, enchanting, sublime nature of broadcasting. But inside the redeveloped and expanded facility is a highly efficient input–output operation for a global, multi-platform news operation, with aesthetics taking a (modest) page from the design books of Google or Facebook. The new Axel Springer Campus, designed by Rem Koolhaas, is an immense cube bisected by a diagonal valley across which digital and print employees observe one another, while their productive activities are simultaneously on view to passing Berliners (Gutzmer 2018). Likewise, CCTV Center, also designed by Koolhaas, is a monumental cantilevered loop, which at once routes digital infrastructures, provides spatial organization for CCTV's main departments, and affords a passage for visitors to peer into the production spaces while gaining spectacular views of Beijing (Wallenstein 2010).

These and other buildings are important physical embodiments of journalism's urban places, but they do not exhaust them. As Rose (2012) argues, drawing on Heidegger, the act of building is inherently and reciprocally interwoven with dwelling: that is, with an enduring existential inhabitation of place. If we adapt Rose's terms, journalism might be seen as a form of urban dwelling that marks out and claims a wide range of material objects and environments, including but also going beyond its buildings narrowly defined. So, another way to approach this is to think carefully about what it means to speak of a relationship of journalism and urban place. Pointedly, place*making* has been used to title this section, to underscore that journalism neither encounters pre-existing places, nor affects or impacts place, as if from some external realm. Rather, through its performances, journalism inherently produces urban place.

Early forms of journalistic placemaking were often of the street. As O'Reilly (2017) argues, journalistic observation in mid-19th-century Britain was akin to a more purposeful manifestation of Walter Benjamin's wandering *flaneur*: a writer engaging urban life as embodied, firsthand knowledge. However, late 19th- and early 20th-century British (and American) journalism marked a shift toward increasingly detached reportage; a form of observation that deferred to the scientific conceptions of urban planners and engineers, through which the urban showed up as an abstract spatial imaginary rather than something experienced firsthand. In the process, journalistic observation was largely relocated, from street-treading flanerie to the dedicated, professionalized place of the newsroom.

However, it would be romanticizing the urbanity of the street to conceive of this relocation as somehow leaving the city. Not only are newsrooms sited in urban contexts, but as a locus of media production, they are places through which the urban appears to journalism. While "the newsroom" is associated with professional interiority—so much so that the term has become a synonym for journalistic culture in general—it is also a place fundamentally oriented to its exterior: both the immediate urban milieu of journalistic work and the various public geographies being addressed (Rodgers 2014). It is precisely on the basis of these historically close ties of newsroom and city that contemporary newspaper moves out of city centers, often to cash in on valuable real estate, prompt deep existential questions for journalism. Usher's (2015) ethnographic account of the *Miami Herald*'s relocation from its prominent downtown waterfront building (later demolished) 12 miles west, to a smaller and far more anonymous office park building, previously the headquarters for the US Southern Command, describes a process that was not just disruptive but also ambiguous. While it involved a disruptive departure and new distance from Miami's metropolitan center, journalists finally vacated a newsroom forebodingly strewn with empty desks and the debris of laid-off colleagues; yet only to move to a newsroom that, while lighter and airier, also felt empty and disheartening.

The displacement of major metropolitan newspapers from city centers is in many ways remarkable. But it is also unsurprising, since the journalism taking place through such organizations is not necessarily always at the center of a contemporary, expanding urban news ecology (Anderson 2013; Coleman et al. 2016). Consequentially, the importance of dedicated newsrooms has to some degree eroded. Meanwhile, emergent forms of journalism entail new kinds of journalistic placemaking. Markham (2011), for example, argues that so-called citizen journalism depends on a phenomenological normalization of "third places" such as coffee shops, bedrooms, or converted warehouses as workplaces. This is not to mention that, beyond such amateur and semi-professional activities, news now also emerges from all manner of locales via often ephemeral acts of "witnessing" using mobile media (Sheller 2015).

However, it is important to be cautious of implicitly centering the journalistic experiences of the West or Global North, in which journalism appears to travel from street to newsroom and back again. Cante's (2018) ethnographic study of contemporary community radio practitioners in Abidjan, Côte d'Ivoire, for example, describes a very different trajectory of journalistic placemaking in and through the city. In Abidjan, the work of community or "proximity" radio practitioners is realized as much in the generalized urban milieu as in the radio studio. Whether on the air or off, indeed on or off their jobs, these practitioners—appropriately named *animateurs*—are oriented above all to the enlivening of social situations and events in the city, everything from concerts to weddings (see also Chapter 40, this volume). The work of proximity radio animateurs then entails forms of urban placemaking different from the usual terms of reference seen in the literature on journalism and the city.

Journalistic Field Spaces

Whether the animateurs described by Cante (2018) and their myriad urban placemaking practices—or "citizen journalists" more generally—might be counted as "truly" journalistic is up for debate. And this ambiguity opens up our third and final lens, which is to consider how we might think about the interface of the urban with "journalism" as a dispersed professional field. Recall that Bagehot's essay, discussed in the introduction, is as much a patronizing attack on Dickens's observational style as an appreciation of its formal merits. As Tulloch (2007: 59) argues, in emphasizing Dickens' debt to reportage, Bagehot is signaling "his low status". This is seemingly paradoxical, since Bagehot himself was a journalist. However, Bagehot counted himself part of its higher, more literary order, which essentially disavowed the trade (Campbell 2000). This disavowal is also noticeable in how Robert E. Park, mentioned earlier, accounted for his own journalist provenance. As Lindner (1996) points out in his superb archival study, despite working for more than 10 years as a journalist (between 1887 and 1898) in Detroit, Denver, New York, Chicago, and Minneapolis, Park indebted his urban ecological approach to anthropology, not journalism.

However, for Lindner, the empiricism of Chicago School urban sociology clearly draws from the "new journalism" of the 19th century. New journalism set itself against the moralizing and "civilizing" pretensions of social reformers; it was concerned instead with seeing, knowing, and showing life, rather than stipulating how it should be lived. This shift to a naturalistic "disinterested interest" and later the professional value of objectivity was closely connected to shifts in the economic as well as public model of newspapers. The professionalization of journalism emerged as news organizations shifted toward larger urban regions throughout much of the 20th century, necessitating increasingly complex divisions of labor and specialization. Here, we can again underscore that the relationships of journalism and the urban run deeper than simply local news. As Kramp (2016) argues, in large urban agglomerations there has been historically, and continues to be, a distinctive "metropolitan journalism", which, under certain conditions, has a nucleating potential in relation to journalism's general transformation.

However, these curious disavowals of journalism—by Bagehot, Park, and others—also remind us that journalism involves various genres and positions of relative status, often ordered hierarchically. In this way, we might note that journalism not only encounters the urban through countless, situated acts of seeing, knowing, or showing, but also as a translocal social space. Following others in journalism studies (e.g., Benson and Neveu 2005), in my own work (e.g., Rodgers 2013, 2017) I have adapted Pierre Bourdieu's concept of social field to conceptualize this translocal space. Thinking in terms of field alerts us to the ways in which journalism is a practical game with rules, resources, and relative positions that can transcend specific local instances. The journalistic field is not so much an objective domain abutting subjective urban places as a social space helping constitute the conditions of possibility for concrete or materialized expressions of journalism as situated urban media practice.

If we accept that a significant range of journalistic activities transpire through urban environments, then it soon becomes clear that there is considerable overlap of the journalistic field and urban material spaces. In many ways, the latter are a condition of possibility for journalism in general, not just those forms directed explicitly at phenomena classified, or named in relation to the city. The taken-for-granted notion of a UK national media, for instance, is arguably a myth, considering its notable concentration in London (Tumbler 2011). And, as Archetti (2014) found in her study of foreign reporting networks in London and Oslo, valuations of "good" correspondence are closely tied to how the identities and routines of reporters emerge through the spatial arrangements of the urban contexts to which they are assigned. The urban is both a site for the intensification of practicing journalists and, at the same time, a site for the intensification of events, institutions, places, and other storytelling possibilities for documenting, mapping, and narrating social, political, cultural, and economic affairs, in general.

Yet journalism is also often oriented to the city; it has long been associated with specific ways of narrating urban phenomena and named places (e.g., Parisi and Holcomb 1994). However, within the journalistic field, this kind of orientation is often classified as "local" journalism, a subfield of considerably lower status. This low status is unsurprising: many local newspapers today have undergone a "McDonaldization" process, becoming standardized and packaged titles, produced by overworked and often precariously employed journalists, and owned by multinational media conglomerates (Franklin 2005). Yet at the same time, as Schmitz Weiss (2015) points out, "location"—an historically longstanding focal unit of journalism—has taken on renewed journalistic significance in an era of geographically defined digital information. Locational data, and its close relationships with mobile computational technologies such as smartphones, is beginning to reshape how news is made, distributed, and consumed both spatially (Goggin et al. 2015) and temporally (Sheller 2015). So, in important respects, locality has re-emerged as a central issue for contemporary journalism, notably in what has been described as the nascent news subculture of hyperlocal media (Hess and Waller 2016), as well as new forms of community journalism (Dickens et al. 2015). Not only do such new media production practices appear to offer an antidote to oligopolistic mainstream local media; they may also afford new kinds of voice for disadvantaged urban locales. However, it remains important to question just what kinds of localism, urban or otherwise, are being pursued through such emergent journalistic practices, and why particular technologies are taken for granted as solutions (Rodgers 2018).

Whether an increasingly fragmented urban news environment, mediated by new locative technologies, marks the decline of the citywide journalistic public address that have often characterized print and broadcast media is unclear. It is unlikely that this question can be answered from a purely journalism- or media-centric point of view. Drawing on the Chicago School tradition of urban ecology, as well as humanistic geography, Boyles' (2017) evocative account of post-Katrina New Orleans suggests that journalism is entangled in the urban as a field of care. The urban is more than an object or subject *for* journalism, affording it status, purpose, or intelligibility as a professional field; it is also a complex locus of shared emotional or affective attachment. Here, we can return to the irreducible circularity of urban public address, mentioned earlier: while we might conceptualize journalism as a relatively coherent field space, we should avoid falling back on an image of journalism as an originary site that transduces the urban into certain media forms, which are then outwardly transmitted to its audiences. The journalistic field certainly represents a form of media power, but not necessarily one of public imposition. Rather, it embodies a site of particular norms and forms for attuning with, inheriting, and being affected by urban publics (cf. Rodgers 2014: 80–1).

Conclusion

It seems that in virtually any contemporary discussion of journalism, one must speak in the same breath about its apparent crisis. This crisis, if there is one, is about much more than the evidently unsustainable economic model of newspapers. At a moment where (in principle, at least) anyone can be a media creator, and deference to traditional political institutions is waning, the once near-inimitable cultural position of journalism at the center of public life is clearly in question. Yet in evaluating whether these supposed downward trends also might imply a crisis in mediated urban communication or public life, we might first be mindful of the possibility that the so-called crisis of journalism largely depends on validating an historically specific configuration of journalism. The urban political institution that is or was the city newspaper, for example, might in fact embody an unusually stable configuration of urban public life, one that experienced a kind of peak, or plateau, for perhaps just two or three decades in the postwar period. As Ryfe (2013: 195) concludes in his wide-ranging ethnography of American newsrooms, journalism per se is not dying, but a particular model of journalism is clearly unravelling.

We might also be mindful of the geographical specificities of the apparent crisis of journalism and its urban situation. Scholarly writing that connects journalism and cities (not to mention media and cities more generally) often tends to fall back on Western urban theories. While there may be valid reasons for this, as Robinson (2006) argues, reading all urban situations through the experience of such a small range of cities also seriously hinders our imagination of possible urban futures. Relatively little is known, at least in the English-language literature, about journalistic practice in and through cities in the Global South. Rao's (2010: 45–90) ethnographic work on burgeoning Hindi newspapers in urban India reveals local newsmaking practices quite different from, for example, the well-worn image of professional journalists interacting with city officials. In cities such as Lucknow, journalistic practices often entail brokering among a very wide range of grassroots urban actors, seeking different kinds of voice within a rapidly emerging urban public sphere. So, in studying the futures of journalism and the urban, it is crucial to question what sorts of urban contexts we seek and find journalism in, as well as how cities and their publics are constituted through journalism.

References

Anderson, C. W. (2013) *Rebuilding the news: Metropolitan journalism in the digital age*, Philadelphia, PA: Temple University Press.
Archetti, C. (2014) "Journalism and the city: Redefining the spaces of foreign correspondence", *Journalism Studies*, 15(5), pp. 586–95.
Bagehot, W. (1965 [1858]) "Charles Dickens", in N. St. Jon-Stevas (ed.) *The collected works of Walter Bagehot*, Volume II, London: The Economist, pp. 76–107.
Barth, G. (1982) *City people: The rise of modern city culture in nineteenth-century America*, Oxford: Oxford University Press.
Benson, R. and Neveu, E. (eds.) (2005) *Bourdieu and the journalistic field*, Cambridge: Polity.
Bødker, H. (2015) "Journalism as cultures of circulation", *Digital Journalism*, 3(1), pp. 101–15.
Boyles, J. L. (2017) "Building an audience, bonding a city: Digital news production as a field of care", *Media, Culture and Society*, 39(7), pp. 945–59.
Campbell, K. (2000) "Journalistic discourses and constructions of modern knowledge", in L. Brake, B. Bell, and D. Finkelstein (eds.) *Nineteenth-century media and the construction of identities*, Basingstoke: Palgrave, pp. 40–53.
Cante, F. (2018) "From 'animation' to encounter: Community radio, sociability and urban life in Abidjan, Côte d'Ivoire", *International Journal of Cultural Studies*, 21(1), pp. 12–26.
Coleman, S., Thumim, N., Birchall, C., et al. (2016) *The mediated city: The news in a post-industrial context*, London: Zed Books.
Cottle, S. (1993) *TV news, urban conflict, and the inner city*, Leicester: Leicester University Press.
Couldry, N. and Hepp, A. (2017) *The mediated construction of reality*, Cambridge: Polity.
Dickens, L., Couldry, N., and Fotopoulou, A. (2015) "News in the community? Investigating emerging inter-local spaces of news production/consumption", *Journalism Studies*, 16(1), pp. 97–114.
Ericson, S. (2010) "The interior of the ubiquitous: Broadcasting House, London", in S. Ericson and K. Riegert (eds.) *Media houses: Architecture, media and the production of centrality*, New York: Peter Lang, pp. 19–57.
Franklin, B. (2005) "McJournalism: The local press and the McDonaldization thesis", in S. Allan (ed.) *Journalism: Critical issues*, Maidenhead: Open University Press, pp. 137–50.
Fritzsche, P. (1996) *Reading Berlin 1900*, Cambridge, MA: Harvard University Press.
Goggin, G., Martin, F., and Dwyer, T. (2015) "Locative news: Mobile media, place informatics, and digital news", *Journalism Studies*, 16(1), pp. 41–59.
Gutzmer, A. (2018) "Digital media reflexivities: The Axel Springer Campus in Berlin", *International Journal of Cultural Studies*, 21(1), pp. 57–72.
Henkin, D. M. (1998) *City reading: Written words and public spaces in antebellum New York*, New York: Columbia University Press.

Hess, K. and Waller, L. (2016) "Hip to be hyper: The subculture of excessively local news", *Digital Journalism*, 4(2), pp. 193–210.
Iveson, K. (2007) *Publics and the city*, Oxford: Blackwell
Kaniss, P. (1991) *Making local news*, Chicago, IL: University of Chicago Press.
Kaplan, R. L. (2002) *Politics and the American press: The rise of objectivity, 1865–1920*, Cambridge: Cambridge University Press.
Kramp, L. (2016) "Conceptualizing metropolitan journalism: New approaches, new communicative practices, new perspectives?" in L. Kramp, N. Carpentier, A. Hepp, et al., (eds.) *Politics, civil society and participation: Media and communications in a transforming environment*, Bremen: edition lumière, pp. 151–83.
Lee, B. and LiPuma, E. (2002) "Cultures of circulation: The imaginations of modernity", *Public Culture*, 14(1), pp. 191–213.
Lindner, R. (1996) *The reportage of urban culture: Robert Park and the Chicago School*, Cambridge: Cambridge University Press.
LiPuma, E. and Koelble, T. (2005) "Cultures of circulation and the urban imaginary: Miami as example and exemplar", *Public Culture*, 17(1), pp. 153–80.
Markham, T. (2011) "Hunched over their laptops: Phenomenological perspectives on citizen journalism", *Review of Contemporary Philosophy*, 10, pp. 150–64.
Morgan Parmett, H. and Rodgers, S. (2018) "Space, place and circulation: Three conceptual lenses into the spatialities of media production practices", in K. Fast, A. Jansson, J. Lindell, et al. (eds.) *Geomedia studies: Spaces and mobilities in mediatized worlds*. Oxon: Routledge, pp. 61–78.
O'Reilly, C. A. (2017) "Journalism and the changing act of observation: Writing about cities in the British press 1880–1940", in G. Aiello, M. Tarantino, and K. Oakley (eds.) *Communicating the city: Meanings, practices, interactions*, New York: Peter Lang, pp. 3–15.
Parisi, P. and Holcomb, B. (1994) "Symbolizing place: Journalistic narratives of the city", *Urban Geography*, 15(4), pp. 376–94.
Park, R. E. (1923) "The natural history of the newspaper", *American Journal of Sociology*, 29(3), pp. 273–89.
Rao, U. (2010) *News as culture: Journalistic practices and the remaking of Indian leadership traditions*. Oxford: Berghahn Books.
Robinson, J. (2006) *Ordinary cities: Between modernity and development*, London: Routledge.
Rodgers, S. (2013) "The journalistic field and the city: Some practical and organizational tales about the Toronto Star's New Deal for Cities", *City and Community*, 12(1), pp. 56–77.
Rodgers, S. (2014) "The architectures of media power: Editing, the newsroom, and urban public space", *Space and Culture*, 17(1), pp. 69–84.
Rodgers, S. (2017) "Roots and fields: Excursions through place, space, and local in hyperlocal media", *Media, Culture and Society*, 40(6), pp. 856–74.
Rodgers, S. (2018) "Digitizing localism: Anticipating, assembling and animating a 'space' for UK hyperlocal media production", *International Journal of Cultural Studies*, 21(1), pp. 73–89.
Rose, M. (2012) "Dwelling as marking and claiming", *Environment and Planning D: Society and Space*, 30(5), pp. 757–71.
Ryfe, D. M. (2013) *Can journalism survive? An inside look at American newsrooms*, Cambridge: Polity.
Schmitz Weiss, A. (2015) "Place-based knowledge in the twenty-first century: The creation of spatial journalism", *Digital Journalism*, 3(1), pp. 116–31.
Sheller, M. (2015) "News now: Interface, ambience, flow, and the disruptive spatio-temporalities of mobile news media", *Journalism Studies*, 16(1), pp. 12–26.
Silverstone, R. (1994) *Television and everyday life*, London: Routledge.
Tulloch, J. (2007) "Charles Dickens and the voices of journalism", in R. Keeble and S. Wheeler (eds.) *The journalistic imagination: Literary journalists from Defoe to Capote and Carter*, Oxon: Routledge, pp. 58–73.
Tumbler, H. (2011) "London rules: The myth of a national media", in D. Hutchison and H. O'Donnell (eds.) *Centres and peripheries: Metropolitan and non-metropolitan journalism in the twenty-first century*, Newcastle: Cambridge Scholars Publishing, pp. 161–70.
Usher, N. (2015) "Newsroom moves and the newspaper crisis evaluated: Space, place, and cultural meaning", *Media, Culture and Society*, 37(7), pp. 1005–21.
Wallace, A. (2012) *Media capital: Architecture and communications in New York City*, Urbana, IL: University of Illinois Press.
Wallenstein, S.-O. (2010) "Looping ideology: The CCTV Center in Beijing", in S. Ericson and K. Riegert (eds.) *Media houses: Architecture, media and the production of centrality*, New York: Peter Lang, pp. 163–82.

Further Reading

Kennedy, D. (2013) *The wired city: Reimagining journalism and civic life in the post-newspaper age*, Amherst, MA: University of Massachusetts Press.

Nord, D. P. (2001) *Communities of journalism: A history of American newspapers and their readers*, Urbana, IL: University of Illinois Press.

Schudson, M. (1978) *Discovering the news: A social history of American newspapers*, New York: Basic Books.

Warner, M. (2002) *Publics and counterpublics*, New York: Zone Books.

7

OUTDOOR ADVERTISING AND THE REMEDIATION OF PUBLIC SPACE(S)

Commercialization and Beyond

Cesare Silla

Introduction

Outdoor advertising is a vital part of the marketing system of any advanced economy and was promoted since its early days as a veritable "marketing force" (Outdoor Advertising Association of America 1928) in the economic scheme of any business enterprise. Even though forms of outdoor publicity may be traced far back in time, as shown by media archaeology excavations discussing painted wall inscriptions or signboards to identify services in ancient Rome and during the Middle Ages (Huhtamo 2009; Parikka 2012), it was with the rise of urban consumerism and the shift in focus from information to persuasion in commercial communication that out-of-home advertising gained momentum and led to spectacular progress in its forms and uses, from billboards to signs, from posters to transport advertising (Williams 1982; Silla 2018).

This chapter starts by reviewing the genesis of outdoor advertising and its role in the commercialization of public space; then, it discusses various forms of urban remediation beyond commercialization brought forth by this peculiar medium, and, finally, it addresses major theoretical issues involved in the spread of outdoor advertising, such as questions of gender, ethnicity, class and religion, as well as the debate around the concept of visual pollution and the need for regulation.

Outdoor Advertising in Historical Context

A brief overview of the rise of American consumer capitalism at the turn of the nineteenth into the twentieth century may be used to illuminate the trajectory of the co-emergence of outdoor advertising and urban consumption mentioned above. As shown by cultural and social historians (Lears 1981; Leach 1993), in the space of fifty years from 1880, America went through a dramatic shift from an agrarian, rural economy to an industrial, urban economy. Once the American system of manufacturing achieved unprecedented productive capacity and the system of distribution was implemented through new means of transportation and communication, the institutional basis for the establishment of a consumer society was fairly set. At the same time, the new vision of the good life in "goods", an ideological underpinning of consumer culture, had still to be ingrained into the social imaginary of the American population. The implementation of new business tools like outdoor advertising served the need to place the new "world of goods" (Douglas and Isherwood 1979) into the imaginative center of social life. The larger size and scope of the new economic life demanded a radical alteration in people's relation to material goods if the output of manufacture was to be absorbed and commerce was to flourish (Laermans 1993; Silla 2018).

In turn, the "unproductive" practice of the urban stroller, the *flaneur*, was turned into the "productive" practice of the consumer (Clarke 1997) through a series of marketing strategies and tools, such as inviting attentive interaction through outstanding forms of layout. By the turn of the century in America (Silla 2018), there was a race for outdoor advertising promoted by manufacturers and retailers that reshaped the urban landscape. Billboards and signs were systematically used as the cost of printing and electricity was remarkably reduced. Outdoor publicity found a legitimate place in the promotional campaigns of advertisers once a few business mavericks had the idea of formally leasing space. At the same time, when mass transit moved from the horse-drawn car to the electric-powered vehicle, transport advertising boomed, backed up by the professionalization of lessees and the implementation of technical innovations in cards display. Outdoor advertising of this new kind was established upon a few guiding principles, which are, generally speaking, valid still today: the effectiveness of message and design; a relatively long duration of display for exerting a lasting impression on the public; a careful assessment of location value according to the number of people who were expected to pass the site of display; and the assumed frame of mind of people passing by. Parenthetically, the whole panorama of signs, billboards and posters transformed the city, and even the countryside, sited as they were along highways (Gudis 2004), into a spectacle of commercial imagery, and turned people into an audience whose sight was progressively commanded by this commercialization of public space. Even a cursory glance at its genealogy makes plain how outdoor advertising is worth careful consideration not only as an interdisciplinary academic object or as a recognized business tool, but especially for its broader political, social and cultural significance in the mediated city.

Commercialization and the "Public": Outdoor Advertising as Marketing Medium and Out-of-Home Screens

Outdoor advertising targets all spaces which are freely accessible to the public, whether they are of public or private ownership. Extant literature (Cronin 2010; Stalder 2011; Dekeyser 2018) recognizes the following typology of outdoor advertising: billboards and signs (e.g., on roadsides); posters (e.g., on bus shelters and free-standing panels); transport advertising (e.g., in buses and trains); ambient advertising (e.g., in public toilets, petroleum pumps); and architecture advertising (e.g., murals, media façades, iconic brand architecture). From the viewpoint of the advertising industry, the placement of advertisements is crucial and assessed on the basis of a few spatial parameters that are then considered in close relation with social activity couched in terms of time: working or leisure spaces; travel or dwell spaces; inside or outside spaces. They became more or less profitable in relation to the perceived rhythms of social life (who moves where, why and when).

Besides advertisers, the outdoor advertising industry comprises other key actors who may be variously involved in the advertising circuit: property owners who rent the advertising space; outdoor advertising companies which own and rent physical advertising structures and devices; outdoor advertising agencies which mediate between owners and clients; audiences of outdoor advertising messages; and the public administration acting as the regulator and the alleged guardian of the public interest but usually working in partnership with outdoor advertising companies for the provision of urban infrastructure and services.

Other than being a marketing medium from the viewpoint of the advertising industry, outdoor advertising is also a cultural "medium" which channels various images and ideas into the public scene. Therefore, outdoor advertising can be conceptualized as "public" screens that contribute to the shaping of the visual landscape of the spaces in which we live. In other words, outdoor advertising has become part of the taken-for-granted experience in everyday life (Myers 1999; Cronin 2010; Krajina 2014). This characteristic makes their position in mediated city processes significant beyond their marketing function.

One key issue is when public space is used as a marketing medium by private actors, meaning that the same "public" *space* is imbued with *private* "values" and "images". In the case of advertising, it is first of all the value of commercialism, posing the question of whether it exploits a collective resource and impairs not only the public use of space, but also people's appreciation of urban and natural scenery (Iveson 2012; Portella 2016). For example, in his study on the influence of outdoor advertising on the civic use of different areas in the city of Poznań in Poland, Bonenberg (2015) differentiates between "directing" billboards, defined as the ones that direct potential customers to a different location than the one in which they are placed, and "locating" billboards, defined as those situated in places to which their content refers. He found that the majority of billboards located in the center of the city directed their audiences to the suburbs, possibly undermining the public desire to revitalize the center of Poznań. Increasingly, the diffusion of outdoor advertising is framed as visual pollution, a phenomenon under harsh criticism when it comes to protecting both the natural and urban landscape (Gudis 2008; Chmielewski et al. 2016; Khanal 2018).

The Remediation of Urban Space Beyond Commercialization

The opposition between "private interests" and "public good" implied in the examples above is part of wider transformations (remediations) of public urban spaces that are related to the development and diffusion of outdoor advertising in the mediated city.

Older (printed) forms of outdoor advertising have been supplemented by newer genres, such as digital screens, custom-made advertisement columns, audio-visual installations, quick response code, video walls, media façades and so forth (see also Chapter 27, this volume), deeply affecting the ways in which mobile audiences are addressed in an "integrated" urban media environment. Because of new possibilities offered by interactivity, media-convergence and real-time personalized communication, it is indeed the whole space of the city that is eventually sought to become a marketing environment (Stalder 2011; Iveson 2012; Dekeyser 2018), resembling what Baudrillard (1994: 76) envisioned in terms of a "total functional screen of activities". Following such developments and innovations, when targeting urban audiences marketing practitioners speak of "ambient marketing" as the conceptual evolution of "experience marketing" and "event marketing". It must also be noted that the dissemination of "direct response advertising" (advertisements that ask consumers to take some immediate action) and the movement toward transforming the city into a marketing ambience combine with personal media usage to further advance the stronghold of privatization of "public" places under the guise of interactivity (Mattelart 1991; Crawford 2008; de Souza et al. 2012).

In sum, even if each outdoor advertisement potentially addresses a specific demographic target, the ensemble of outdoor advertising forms an ambience which hardly anybody can escape, notwithstanding the fact that this ambience is usually perceived in distraction (Benjamin 1999). While this condition of distraction may raise doubts about the marketing value of outdoor advertising (disqualifying the assumed causal link between message and behavior), by no means does "distracted" viewing of outdoor advertising debase its social and cultural impact. Even if encounters with outdoor advertisements may happen in a distracted way, they nonetheless mediate the way people experience, sense and remember the spaces they live through. In addition, since the advertising industry frames and quantifies places, especially specific urban sites, in terms of space-time opportunities for interaction, and allocates advertisements accordingly, the study of outdoor advertising is salient with a broader "rhythmanalysis" of social life (Lefebvre 2004; Cronin 2006).

Within this framework, a fine-grained empirical grasp of the form, materiality and "affordances" of each outdoor advertisement in its effect on audiences is not enough to fully appreciate the role outdoor advertising plays in the remediation of space; what is needed is a focus on the co-constitution of space and media-related practices (Graham 2004; Moores 2012; Ridell and Zeller 2013; Tosoni and Ridell 2016). In other words, a focus on the actual "encounters" with advertising screens (Krajina 2014) must be considered as open-ended processes made of a complex interrelation between non-human elements (screens) of spatiality/materiality and human actors (Thrift 2007; Anderson and Harrison 2010).

The implication of this perspective is that the meanings of advertisements may radically diverge from the ones devised by the advertiser. Examples may vary from using billboards as wayfinding devices in navigating urban spaces (Portella 2016; Krajina 2014), up to subversive practices which hijack, debunk or reverse the messages of outdoor advertising, as in the case of anti-billboard movements or various forms of semiotic banditry and "ad busters" (Cronin 2010; De Laure and Fink 2017).

In terms of urban media studies, this focus is able to shed different light on the co-constitution of urban space and media practices, which not only helps us gain an appreciation of the ambiguous and unexpected outcomes of outdoor advertising, but also highlights the power-related nature of the remediation of space (Rodgers et al. 2014). Examples include studies of "captive" audience positions (Tosoni 2015; see also McCarthy 2001) or technologies developed by outdoor advertising companies that react to subversive practices and culture jamming, like anti-graffiti technologies or anti-hacking features of digital screens (Dekeyser 2018).

Issues of Intersectionality

The power-related nature of outdoor advertising is of particular significance when speaking of gendered messages; here, the literature points, in particular, to the "masculine" visual representation of women in posters and billboards, which may be considered as a form of "public" sexual harassment (Rosewarne 2009). Studying outdoor advertisements (billboards) posted in Ukraine from 2005 to 2011, Kis and Bureychak (2015) not only found a prevalent sexist approach through the excessive aestheticization, eroticization and commodification of images of femininity, they also revealed the asymmetry of "face-ism"; that is, the tendency to focus the advertising image on men's faces (related to brain and intelligence) and women's bodies (related to feelings and beauty), reinforcing a stereotyped conception of gender-specific qualities and roles.

However, from a study of three British advertising campaigns of the 1900s targeted to "winning women" in public space, Winship (2000) noted the more complex and ambiguous role played by outdoor advertising in promoting not only new visions of feminine autonomy, gender relations and gender orientation but also "progressive" political stances in terms of class and ethnical relations. In Nigeria, the use of slang and non-standard Swahili in outdoor advertisements helped the anti-HIV-AIDS campaign to address the youth and poorer and marginalized people. As Mutonya (2008: 10) explains, if catchy slogans "provided the youth with the language to discuss abstinence, promiscuity, and pre-marital sex in a manner that is perceived to be 'cool'", the use of non-standard language offered a face-saving tool for the broader community to raise important issues like AIDS prevention, condom use and responsible sexual behavior, which were considered taboo and would have not been discussed in public otherwise. In Brazil, DKT International, a non-profit social marketing enterprise, launched in 2005 a campaign to advertise affordable condoms as a means of STI/HIV prevention for homosexuals. Billboard advertisements generated controversy and debate between people who wanted them removed, because they considered inappropriate the presence of explicit sexual content in a public space, and those who claimed removing those billboards would be a form of discrimination (Darden 2006). In the case of a few sexualized billboards in Manila, the opposition to sexual messages in advertising was based upon religious beliefs and values. Here, the state sought to intervene by defining norms of public morality in opposition to what they had perceived as the "progressive" sensitivity in sexualized imaginary. Moreover, it was the advertising industry that played a "progressive" role when installing new billboards that still had messages revolving around sexuality, but carried out in ways that navigated and even opposed conservative moral norms of religious institutions and the state (Cornelio 2014). It must be noted too that all this happened in an urban region—metropolitan Manila—where the commercialization of public space through the proliferation of outdoor advertising has been advancing at a spectacular pace (Gomez 2013).

In social contexts in which politics and religion are entangled, public representations of bodies, especially female bodies, point also to issues of liberal conception of freedom and self-determination rather than merely to issues of commercialization and commodification. In various cities of Kyrgyzstan, billboards were used as tools for a cultural war between non-Muslims and Muslims over the way women should or should not dress, and women wearing *hijab* and mini-skirts were alternately used negatively to depict the culture of the opposite side (Nasritdinov and Esenamanova 2017). In some Iranian cities, outdoor advertising articulates complex historical-political entanglements. If murals represent the official form of outdoor advertising promoting religious and anti-western values, by portraying male bodies as symbols of martyrdom and veiled females as the embodiment of modesty as a paramount virtue, commercial billboards signal the paradoxical co-existence of political and religious orthodoxy with consumerism. At the same time, graffiti is used by youth subcultures to reclaim urban space and as a means of social expression against financial powers and more subtlety against politics (Khosravi 2013; see also Chapter 37, this volume). Lastly, the analysis by Pype (2012) of the dissemination of portraits of the President of the Democratic Republic of the Congo in billboards demonstrates how outdoor advertising may be used as political propaganda to penetrate daily life and construct an emotional bond between those in power and the people.

Moving the discussion to issues of class and ethnic inequalities, many studies agree on the existence and troubling nature of ethnically and class-targeted outdoor advertising: for example, in American cities, the higher volume of pro-tobacco outdoor advertisements is found in low-income African-American areas (Primack et al. 2007), while the higher volume of food and beverages outdoor advertising is posted outside Hispanic schools (Herrera and Pasch 2017). Given that African-American people are one of the groups most affected by cancer mortality, and Hispanic adolescents are the ethnic group among young people showing one of the highest rates of obesity in the country, it is clear that studies on the impact of outdoor advertising enmeshed with debates on its regulation. As Yancey et al. (2009) claim, the possibility to show empirically, for example, that upper-income audiences remain insulated from "aggressive" outdoor advertising related to food and beverages, regardless of their predominant ethnicity, should advocate in favor of more restrictive legislation on "obesity-promoting" outdoor advertising, such as was made on advertising tobacco and alcohol (Hackbarth et al. 2001).

Conclusion: Regulation and Social Acceptance

The significance of outdoor advertising for urban media debates derives from its contribution to the historical trajectory of the commercialization of public space. It goes further, however, to address issues of public sphere. Indeed, outdoor advertising is related to subtler forms of remediation of public urban spaces, and it also involves the display of messages and images which may enter public debate. At the same time, outdoor advertising disseminates views on some of the most fundamental topics concerning public culture and social life, such as gender, sexuality and ideals of self-realization.

It is for all these reasons that the urban governance of outdoor advertising cannot ignore public debates on the limits to the commercialization of public space, the problem of visual pollution, private land use and the rights of the public. Indeed, as the diffusion of outdoor advertising is accompanied by controversy over its presence, debates about the regulation of outdoor advertising run as long as that of the medium. Going back to the beginning of the twentieth century, besides criticism over the defacing of natural scenery, concerns about moral, health and safety hazards posed by the billboards and signs were used to advocate for a more restrictive legislation (Bogart 1995; Cronin 2010). More recently, a call for regulation comes from academic research studying visual pollution and the "adverse" effects of advertising messages on minorities. However, the governance of outdoor advertising has brought many different solutions. In Venice, the former communist major, Massimo Cacciari, allowed the installation of billboards on historic buildings and sites like Piazza San Marco, in order to gain funds for urban restoration and maintenance. In contrast, in 2006, Sao Paulo became the first city outside the communist world to ban billboards, commercial screens and advertisements on public transport (Iveson 2012; Portella 2016).

It is not surprising, therefore, that the outdoor advertising industry seeks legitimacy not only through self-regulation, but also by means of market research that, while assessing the promotional value of specific outdoor advertisements or campaigns, also promotes the social recognition of outdoor advertising as a necessity for consumer satisfaction and the benefit of any market economy.

References

Anderson, B. and Harrison, P. (2010) *Taking-Place: Non-Representational Theories and Geography*, Farnham: Ashgate.
Baker, Laura E. (2007) "Public sites versus public sights: The progressive response to outdoor advertising and the commercialization of public space", *American Quarterly*, 59(4), pp. 1187–1213.
Banda, F. and Oketch, O. (2011). "Localizing HIV/AIDS discourse in a rural Kenyan community", *Journal of Asian and African Studies*, 46, pp. 19–37.
Baudrillard, J. (1994) *Simulacra and Simulation*, Ann Arbor, MI: The University of Michigan Press.
Benjamin, W. (1999) *The Arcades Project*, Cambridge, MA: Belknap Press of Harvard University Press.
Bogart, M. H. (1995) *Artists, Advertising and the Borders of Art*, London; Chicago, IL: University of Chicago Press.
Bonenberg, A. (2015). "Influence of advertisements on changes in the urban structure of cites on the example of Poznan", *Civil and Environmental Engineering Reports*, 18(3), pp. 5–13.
Chmielewski, S. et al. (2016) "Measuring visual pollution by outdoor advertisements in an urban street using intervisibilty analysis and public surveys", *International Journal of Geographical Information Science*, 30(4), pp. 801–818.
Clarke, D. B. (1997) "Consumption and the city, modern and postmodern", *International Journal of Urban and Regional Research*, (21)2, pp. 218–237.
Cornelio (2014) "Billboard advertising and sexualisation in Metro Manila", *European Journal of East Asian Studies*, 13, pp. 68–92.

Cronin, A. M. (2006) "Advertising and the metabolism of the city: Urban space, commodity rhythms", *Environment and Planning D: Society and Space*, 24, pp. 615–632.

Cronin, A. M. (2010) *Advertising, Commercial Spaces and the Urban*, Houndmills: Palgrave Macmillan.

Crawford A. (2008) "Taking social software to the streets: Mobile cocooning and the (an-)erotic city", *Journal of Urban Technology*, 15(3), pp. 79–97.

Darden, C, (2006) "Promoting condoms in Brazil to men who have sex with men", *Reproductive Health Matters*, 14(28), pp. 63–67.

Dekeyser, T. (2018) "The material geographies of advertising: concrete objects, affective affordance and urban space", *Environment and Planning A: Economy and Space*, 50(7), pp. 1–18.

De Laure, M. and Fink, M. (eds.) (2017) *Culture Jamming: Activism and the Art of Cultural Resistance*, New York: New York University Press.

de Souza e Silva, A. and Frith, J. (2012) *Mobile Interfaces in Public Spaces: Locational Privacy, Control, and Urban Sociability*, New York: Routledge.

Douglas, M. and Isherwood, B. (1979) *The World of Goods*, New York: Basic Books.

Friedberg, A. (1993) *Window Shopping: Cinema and the Postmodern*, Berkeley, CA: University of California Press.

Gomez, J. E. A. (2013) "The billboardization of Metro Manila", *International Journal of Urban and Regional Research*, 37(1), pp. 186–214.

Graham, S. (2004) "Beyond the 'Dazzling Light': From Dreams of Transcendence to the 'Remediation' of Urban Life", *New Media & Society*, 6(1), pp. 16–25.

Gudis, C. (2004) *Buyways: Billboards, Automobiles, and the American Landscape*, New York: Routledge.

Gudis, C. (2008) "The billboard war: Gender, commerce, and public space", in M. S. Shaffer (ed.) *Public Culture: Diversity, Democracy, and Community in the United States*, Philadelphia, PA: University of Pennsylvania Press, pp. 171–198.

Hackbarth, D. P. et al. (2001) "Collaborative research and action to control the geographic placement of outdoor advertising of alcohol and tobacco products in Chicago", *Public Health Reports*, 116, pp. 558–567.

Herrera, A. L. and Pasch, K. E. (2017) "Targeting Hispanic adolescents with outdoor food & beverage advertising around schools", *Ethnicity & Health*, 23(6), pp. 691–702.

Huhtamo, E. (2009) "Messages on the wall: An archaeology of public media displays", in S. McQuire et al. (eds.) *Urban Screens Reader*, Amsterdam: Institute of Network Cultures, pp. 45–64.

Huhtamo, E. and Parikka J. (eds.) (2011) *Media Archaeology: Approaches, Applications, and Implications*, Berkeley, Los Angeles, CA; London: University of California Press.

Iveson, K. (2012) "Branded cities: Outdoor advertising, urban governance, and the outdoor media landscape", *Antipode*, 44(1), pp. 151–174.

Khanal, K. K. (2018) "Visual pollution and eco-dystopia: A study of billboards and signs in Bharatpur metropolitan city", *Research Journal of English Language and Literature*, 6(1), pp. 202–208.

Khosravi, S. (2013) "Graffiti in Tehran", *Anthropology Now*, 5(1), pp. 1–17.

Kis O. and Bureychak, T. (2015) "Gender dreams or sexism? Advertising in post-soviet Ukraine", in M. J. Rubchak (ed.) *New Imaginaries: Youthful Reinvention of Ukraine's Cultural Paradigm*, New York; Oxford: Berghahn Books, pp. 110–140.

Krajina, Z. (2014) *Negotiating the Mediated City: Everyday Encounters with Public Screens*, New York: Routledge.

Laermans, R. (1993) "Learning to consume: Early department stores and the shaping of the modern consumer culture, 1896–1914", *Theory, Culture and Society*, 10, pp. 79–102.

Laird, P. W. (1998) *Advertising Progress: American Business and the Rise of Consumer Marketing*, Baltimore, MD: Johns Hopkins University Press.

Leach, W. R. (1993) *Land of Desire: Merchants, Power, and the Rise of a New American Culture*, New York: Pantheon Books.

Lears, T. J. (1981) *No Place of Grace: Antimodernism and the Transformation of American Culture, 1880–1920*, New York: Pantheon Books.

Lefebvre, H. (2004/1992) *Rhythmanalysis: Space, Time and Everyday Life*, London: Continuum.

Mattelart, A. (1991) *Advertising International: The Privatization of Public Space*, London and New York: Routledge.

McCarthy, A. (2001) *Ambient Television: Visual Culture and Public Space*, Durham, NC: Duke University Press.

McFall, L. (2004) "The language of the walls: Putting promotional saturation in historical context", *Consumption Markets & Culture*, 7(2), pp. 107–128.

McQuire, S. (2008) *The Media City: Media, Architecture and Urban Space*, Los Angeles, CA; London; New Delhi; Singapore: Sage Publications.
Moores, S. (2012) *Media, Place and Mobility*, Houndmills; Basingstoke; New York: Palgrave Macmillan.
Mutonya, M. (2008) "Swahili advertising in Nairobi: Innovation and language shift", *Journal of African Cultural Studies*, 20(1), pp. 3–14.
Myers, G. (1999) *Ad Worlds: Brands, Media, Audiences*, London; New York: Arnold.
Nasritdinov, E. and Esenamanova, N. (2017) "The war of billboards: Hijab, secularism, and public space in Bishkek", *Central Asian Affairs*, 4(2), pp. 217–242.
Outdoor Advertising Association of America (1928) *Outdoor Advertising: The Modern Marketing Force*, Chicago, IL: Outdoor Advertising Association of America, Inc.
Oyebode, O. and Unuabonah, F. O. (2013) "Coping with HIV/AIDS: A multimodal discourse analysis of selected HIV/AIDS posters in south-western Nigeria", *Discourse & Society*, 24(6), pp. 810–827.
Parikka, J. (2012) *What Is Media Archaeology?* Cambridge, UK; Malden, MA: Polity Press.
Portella, A. (2016) *Visual Pollution: Advertising, Signage and Environmental Quality*, Burlington, VT: Ashgate.
Primack, B. A. et al. (2007) "Volume of tobacco advertising in African American markets: Systematic review and meta-analysis", *Public Health Reports*, 122(5), pp. 607–615.
Pype, K. (2012) "Political billboards as contact zones: Reflections on public space, the visual and political affect in Kabila's Kinshasa", in R. Vokes (ed.) *Photography in Africa. Ethnographic Perspectives*, Woodbridge: Boydell & Brewer, pp. 187–204.
Ridell, S. and Zeller, F. (2013) "Mediated urbanism: Navigating an interdisciplinary terrain", *International Communication Gazette*, 75(5–6), pp. 437–451.
Rodgers, S. et al. (2014) "Media practices and urban politics: Conceptualizing the powers of the media-urban nexus", *Environment and Planning D: Society and Space*, 32(6), pp. 1054–1070.
Rosewarne, L. (2009) *Sex in Public: Women, Outdoor Advertising and Public Policy*, Newcastle, UK: Cambridge Scholars Publishing.
Roux, T. (2018) "Industry perspectives on digital out-of-home advertising in South Africa", *Communicare: Journal for Communication Sciences in Southern Africa*, 37(1), pp. 17–37.
Silla, C. (2018) *The Rise of Consumer Capitalism in America, 1880–1930*, London; New York: Routledge.
Stalder, U. (2011) "Digital out-of-home media: Means and effects of digital media in public space", in J. Müller. et al. (eds.) *Pervasive Advertising: Human–Computer Interaction series*, London: Springer, pp. 31–56.
Thrift, N. (2007) *Non-Representational Theory: Space, Politics, Affect*, London; New York: Routledge.
Tosoni, S. (2015) "Addressing 'captive audience positions' in urban space: From a phenomenological to a relational conceptualization of space in urban media studies", *Sociologica*, 3, pp. 1–28.
Tosoni, S. and Ridell, S. (2016) "Decentering media studies, verbing the audience: methodological considerations concerning people's uses of media in urban space", *International Journal of Communication*, 10, pp. 1277–1293.
Williams, R. H. (1982) *Dream Worlds: Mass Consumption in Late Nineteenth-Century France*, Berkeley, CA: University of California Press.
Winship, J. (2000) "Women outdoors: Advertising, controversy and disputing feminism in the 1990s", *International Journal of Cultural Studies*, 3(1), pp. 27–55.
Yancey, A. K., et al. (2009) "A cross-sectional prevalence study of ethnically targeted and general audience outdoor obesity-related advertising", *The Milbank Quarterly*, 87(1), pp. 155–184.

Further Reading

Cronin, A. M. (2010) *Advertising, Commercial Spaces and the Urban*, Houndmills: Palgrave Macmillan.
Koeck, R. and Warnaby, G. (2014) "Outdoor advertising in urban context: Spatiality, temporality and individuality", *Journal of Marketing Management*, 30(13–14), pp. 1402–1422.
Portella, A. (2016) *Visual Pollution: Advertising, Signage and Environmental Quality*, Burlington, VT: Ashgate.

8

CONSUMPTION-CENTERED URBAN RESTRUCTURING AND THE MEDIATION OF URBAN LIFE

From Spaces of Production to the Worlds of Seduction

Erika Nagy

Introduction: The Centrality of Consumption in the Material and Symbolic Transformation of Cities

Historically, cities emerged as places for exchange and consumption, linking production and everyday life. Market places—traditionally, scenes of business and also sociality—were expanding and becoming increasingly specialized, along with the rise of specialized permanent shops and new spaces of exchange (such as seaports and quays) in a number of cities in 16th- to 18th-century Europe. Yet it was the unfolding systems of mass-production together with the separation of production and consumption that produced new spaces (e.g., department stores, shopping arcades) for the latter and induced dramatic changes in cities from the late 19th century, linking unfolding "Western" modernity to consumption. Urban space as a scene of consumption was redefined again in the postwar epoch of massive state interventions providing services for social reproduction that was referred to by Castells as the system of "collective consumption" (Castells 1978). The rise and changes of consumption spaces in cities reflected the transformation of social relations and institutional contexts within and beyond urban spaces across historical epochs, thus offering an analytical ground for scholars to understand the drivers and mechanisms of urban restructuring—profound changes in the economy, social relations, culture, institutions, and their spatial manifestations in cities.

Since the early 1990s, there has been an unfolding academic debate on the material reorganization and the visual transformation of urban space in relation to consumption. The discourse was fed by the rise and spread of new consumption spaces that embodied alternative visuality and aesthetics to the existing structures and produced new socio-spatial practices in this physical-symbolic context, and moreover, along with that, by the transformation of cities themselves into the objects of consumption (Zukin 1998; Miles and Miles 2004). This refiguring of cities as scenes of everyday life organized around social reproduction (work, leisure, family, and community life, etc.) and resorts of collective consumption to include spectacular patchworks of theme parks, festival streets, and mega-projects of property developers became a central issue for scholars in urban, consumption, and media studies (Zukin 1998; Jackson and Thrift 2005; see also Chapter 24, this volume). The latter two fields had their roots in critical cultural theory, inspiring long-lasting debates on the centrality of consumption in organizing and controlling society and on the modalities of making systems of signs and meanings attached to commodities. The debates developed an understanding of consumption as a manifestation of social relations, as a source of subjectivities and identities, and as a site of reproduction of social structures, yet scarcely engaged with the diverse aspects of spatiality of consumption (Ritzer et al. 2001), or did so in abstract terms (e.g., see Benjamin 1969). A new stage was opened up in scholarly work on consumption, relating it to urban change and introducing the concept of space as a social construct; that is, the mutually constitutive nature of society and space (Lefebvre 1991). The "spatial turn" went in at least two directions. In urban and economic geographical studies, the "spatial turn" shifted the focus from space as a neutral background to space as the articulation of social relations, practices, and strategies, while in consumption and media studies, the "turn" raised a concern with materiality and spatiality of social practices (Ritzer et al. 2001; Wrigley and Lowe 2014; see also Chapter 36, this volume). As a result, such fields became interwoven and urban space—a product and mediator of social relations—became a cross-cutting research theme, propelling transdisciplinary debates (Jackson and Thrift 2005).

Theoretical debates on consumption-centered urban restructuring drew dominantly on "core" ("Western" or Anglo-Saxon) economic contexts. Yet a growing body of work revealed a greater diversity of social practices, institutional settings, and their sociocultural contexts, calling for a rethinking of dominant approaches, as well as raising critique of uneven power relations in knowledge production (Timár 2004; Stenning and Hörschelmann 2008). In this process, studies on Central and East European (CEE) "post-socialist" cities were sources of understanding how "Western" concepts of development (i.e., the adoption of the neoliberal scheme in the post-socialist transition process) generated rapid and thorough transformation of social relations, producing new inequalities. Post-socialist transition changed the position of urban dwellers from the subjects of the centrally planned, hierarchical, and production-centered system (as an alternative modernity to capitalism) to the consumer citizen who is under permanent pressure of adaptation to the changing material and symbolic landscapes of cities (Borén and Gentile 2007; Stenning et al. 2010). Yet in the context of the post-Cold War years, CEE cities have been considered rather as "Other" to the Western core of economic power and knowledge production, which should be researched and understood in relation to existing theories and policy schemes of urban restructuring (Grubbauer 2012).

The "spatial turn" in studies of consumption revealed the diversity of socio-spatial practices, turning the status of non-core ("non-Western") fields of academic studies from mere case studies into alternative epistemological grounds and sources of new knowledge. Thus, since CEE urban transitions were shaped by different spatial logics simultaneously (by neoliberal urbanism, the post-socialist production of transient spaces, and the persisting informality of the bazaar), they exhibited multiple dependencies (from capital flows to policy concepts and institutional practices "traveling" from the core economies to the eastern periphery of Europe) as well as continuity and discontinuity in everyday life and its material context. We might draw from such lessons to challenge existing theories on cities and consumption.

In this chapter, I discuss some of the key themes and approaches revolving around consumption, communication, and urban restructuring. I also provide an insight into the case of CEE cities, focusing on various spaces of consumption (the mall, the bazaar, and the street) and hence advocating non-binary (e.g., Western/non-Western) analysis in future urban media debates.

Understanding Cities as Scenes and Objects of Consumption—
Entangling Urban, Consumption, and Media Studies

The emerging centrality of consumption in the (re)production of social relations and everyday life in modernity has been discussed as a powerful process by critical social theorists since the early 20th century. Yet it was the reheated debates on the thorough reorganization of urban life around consumption that challenged existing theories and engaged scholars of media and consumption studies in spatial (urban) research and made meanings and signs subject to urban studies from the early 1990s (Lowe and Wrigley 1996; Ritzer et al. 2001).

One key issue was the definition of *the object of consumption* and its properties (value and meanings) stemming from capitalist social relations. The *critical political economic approach* grew concerned with the ways in which commodities were embedded in industrial production as a material and sociocultural process, as well as the mechanisms operating sign systems that re-contextualized goods and the whole act of buying (Horkheimer and Adorno 1979; Goss 2004). The debates were inspired by early writings on shopping spaces and related social practices that emerged in major cities of Western Europe in the early 20th century (e.g., Benjamin's *Arcades Project* in the 1920s). The process was grasped in the blurred boundaries of stores and the street (i.e., the spread of shop windows and arcades employed to seduce shoppers and offer them protection), in the role of flagship stores in shaping urban architecture, and in hosting or promoting public events, thus making urban and commercial culture inseparable (Ritzer et al. 2001; Wrigley and Lowe 2014). The emerging system of control-through-consumption was a subject of critical theorizations in relation to "cultural industry" and mass consumption (Horkheimer and Adorno 1979; Jackson 1989). After World War II, consumption was re-thought in the context of post-Fordism as a main source of growth through the "democratization of desire," and the incorporation of high and local cultures and lifestyles in the production process to stimulate further innovation and growth (Harvey 1995; Zukin 1998). Meanwhile, *semiotic approaches* placed meanings and the ways commodities operate as signs in focus, highlighting the discursive aspect—the social-semiotic construction of commodities—of consumption and the need for deconstructing meanings that make up our world to understand how/by whom our "reality" (e.g., the values driving the act of buying) is being produced (Clarke 1996; Baudrillard 1998).

Even though both major streams of thinking were critiqued for neglecting either everyday practices and agency or the materiality and the structural contexts of consumption, such debates inspired new research on consumption-related social practices and *the making of subjectivity through consumption*. The latter issue emerged as a key theme along the opposed understandings of agency of the consumer, such as considering her/him as powerless and subject to capitalist exploitation through the system of signs and meanings geared to seduce individuals to consume, vis-à-vis taking the consumer as an autonomous agent for whom choosing and buying goods is a source of freedom and even resistance (Bauman 1998; Goss 2004). Yet scholarly debates on subjectivity were settled mostly between such extreme arguments, considering consumption as a process (a working tension) in which consumer agency meets and interacts with structural conditions shaped by powerful agents' strategies—for example, being seduced by media advertisements of branded producers or carried away by the bustled (yet carefully designated) spaces of the shopping mall. Such argumentations in consumption and media studies helped us understand a lot more about the modalities of organization of the urban society through consumption in the post-1970s era of modernity (the "postmodern"), the scope of individual decisions (Bauman 1998; Miller et al. 1998), and also the multiplicity of social roles and identities (class, family status, age, gender, emerging social/environmental responsibilities, etc.) performed through consumption (Miller 2001). Nevertheless, the ways the objects and subjects of consumption are interrelated remained a contested issue and emerged repeatedly in debates revolving around structure–agency relations (Goss 2004; Morley 2005).

The growing concern with the *material and symbolic context* in which consumption takes place has made *spatiality* a key issue in consumption studies. Space was brought into the analysis as a rationally planned and managed means of constructing alternative realities to enchant and seduce the consumer and dematerialize the act of buying (vis-à-vis Marx's notion of "commodity fetishism") on the one hand, and a scene of consumer agency through which subjectivity could be (re)constituted on the other (Domosh 1996; Ritzer et al. 2001; Benjamin 2008). Moreover, studies that had strong roots in sociology and cultural studies went beyond the immediate context of consumption (e.g., the department store and the mall) by *rescaling the spatial focus* of research and shifting it *toward urban space* as a scene of everyday life reorganized increasingly around consumption. Through this lens, social relations of contemporary (neoliberal) capitalism could be grasped and understood in relation to the changing visuality and new aesthetics of cities. As Zukin put it, deindustrialization and the growth of services, changing employment structures, and the rise of a wealthy service class were underpinning the privatization of urban life (rising owner occupancy, decline of public services, public spaces controlled increasingly by private agents, etc.), gentrification, and proliferation of private consumption spaces (Zukin 1998). Such structural shifts led to the rise of urban symbolic economies—the permanent and interrelated reproduction of things, spaces, and related meanings—that rest on "a collective memory of commercial culture rather than either tolerance or moral solidarity" (Zukin 1998: 834). Urban landscapes, histories, and lifestyles of dwellers were/are being incorporated in this constantly emerging system—for example, through urban regeneration programs driven by property developers with the support of urban planners and policymakers—which connects the transformation of both urban space and culture with wider processes of capital accumulation (Harvey 1995).

This "spatial turn" was interlinked with, and inspired by, the subsequent *re-conceptualizations of space in economic and urban geography*. The critical political economic stream of such studies—relying basically on the Marxist theory of capitalism—considered space inherent in capitalist social relations and related urban restructuring to circulation of capital/its various fractions (Goss 2004; Harvey 2012). Accordingly, consumption-centered urban restructuring (the growth of services, the reorganization and commodification of urban space and culture supported by urban planning such as gentrification and the rise of theme parks, etc.) was explained in relation to the cycles of investment in fixed capital (real estate), consumption as a driver of innovation and growth in the flexible accumulation regime (the creative class, the precariat), and the embedding of retail capital in urban property market processes (Harvey 1995; Wrigley et al. 2005). This stream of studies linked urban consumption spaces to macro-scale processes explicitly. The 2008–2011 global financial crisis further highlighted that financialization processes fueled consumption by spreading mortgage and consumption loans and feeding urban property market bubbles, which finally exploded and led to a colossal debt crisis and rising social polarization in many cities (Aalbers 2008; Harvey 2012; see also Chapter 42, this volume).

Nevertheless, the explanatory power of such macro-focused concepts was limited by their "blindness" to the agency of consumers and the complex role of culture in social relations (Goss 2004). The shifting focus from macro processes toward the micro level of socio-spatial practices and agency in the 1990s was related to the reconceptualization of culture known as the "*cultural turn*" in economic and urban geography. Consumption was made a key issue in the unfolding debates between the political economic and the emerging "culturalist" stream (anchored in cultural and feminist theory). This latter approach was concerned with consumers as agents; that is, their multiple social embedding (gender, age, ethnicity, etc.) practices as sources of identity, and the immediate sociocultural context of shopping (Lowe and Wrigley 1996; Jackson and Thrift 2005). These studies embraced the spatial organization of consumption sites and the related cultural signification processes (Domosh 1996; Goss 2006). "Culturalist" approaches enriched consumption studies, highlighting the entanglement of production and consumption processes by linking agents and places (Wrigley et al. 2005) as well as providing important insight into how the spaces of consumption were relocated subsequently and being extended and transforming the whole urban landscape as a result (Zukin 1998; Harvey 2009).

Thus, from the early 1990s, consumption as a socio-spatial process emerged as a lens through which the cultural logic of contemporary capitalism—the entanglement of culture, space, and economy—and the (re)production of subjectivity in the material and semiotic contexts of buying were researched and re-conceptualized, crossing disciplinary boundaries (Ritzer et al. 2001; Miller 2005). Furthermore, a more recent re-focusing of research on consumption and digital technologies placed the issues of spatiality to the fore to explore the organization of networked (virtual) spaces of consumption, further segmentation of markets, taste, and lifestyle, the necessary sophistication of supporting transport infrastructures, the home as a consumption site, and the changing producer–consumer and capital–labor relations (Wrigley and Lowe 2002; Goss 2006; see also Chapter 15, this volume). Yet all debates have tended to have a strong core economy bias (Timár 2004; Grubbauer 2012) that subsequently shaped research on socio-spatial processes in non-core regions, such as Central and Eastern Europe. From the early 1990s, CEE cities were a scene of policy experimentation—a rapid rollout of the neoliberal capitalist regime—as well as of academic exploration of rapid social restructuring that grew apparent primarily in cities.

Urban Change and the Production of Consumption Spaces in Central and Eastern Europe

Public discourses and policymaking related to urban restructuring were dominated by the neoliberal arguments across CEE cities from the early 1990s (Harloe 1996; Bockman and Eyal 2002). Neoliberalism as an ideology overlooked the socialist legacy (e.g., the lack of institutional culture to drive "marketization" process and urban restructuring, or the environmental problems in CEE cities) and legitimized quick consumption-centered transformation of cities and the institutional practices (such as gaining public consent) supporting this process (Brenner 1999; Timár 2004).

The critique of the neoliberal narrative of CEE urban transition was put forward mostly by critical scholars from outside the region (Timár 2004; Stenning and Hörschelmann 2008), who revealed the interrelatedness of socialism (as an alternative modernity) and post-socialism (e.g., the peripheral/dependent nature and the historically emerged, diverse cultural contexts of institutional transformations) (Harloe 1996; Hirt 2008). Attention turned toward structural changes in urban land markets, their embedding in global capital flows through dependent financialization, and also to the rise of consumption as a central ideology shaping post-socialist identities, which promised better ("Western-like") living standards and wholesale democratization linked intimately to the idea of freedom of choice as individual consumers (Stanilov 2007; Hristova 2010).

From the early 2000s, the research focus shifted to *locally embedded socio-spatial practices and everyday life* in relation to multiscalar institutional restructurings. Such studies helped to outline the "domestication" of the unfolding, consumption-centered neoliberal urbanism in a post-socialist context and the way it produced new polarities, marginalities, and identities. They revealed how everyday life was re-focused from work to consumption, resulting in new mobilities and the shrinkage of life-worlds (Stenning et al. 2010); the ways urban landscapes were transformed by the new, diverse visuality of private developments in contrast to the uniformity of socialist cities

(Borén and Gentile 2007; Hirt 2008); how the boundaries of private/public became blurred in the commodified urban spaces (Bodnar and Molnar 2009; Pastak and Khärik 2016); and how spaces were re-signified by political transition and consumerism appropriating local histories and cultures (Hristova 2010; Poblocki 2012; Sulima 2012).

As changes to social practices were discussed in the context of the unfolding symbolic economies of post-socialist cities, public discourses driving consumer choices and the role of media also emerged as a research issue. Such studies highlighted that the semantic spaces of shopping and their relationship to state socialism and Western modernity were often discussed in terms of binaries: old/new; socialist/post-socialist; modern/obsolete; formal/informal; safe/chaotic; central/marginal. A binary associated with post-socialist cities is that of the mall associated with "Western" consumerism and lifestyle, rationality, and predictability amid permanent change and uncertainty, and the bazaar that is informal and risky, embodying the "Other" to Western consumerism as "normality" (Sik and Wallace 1999; Sulima 2012).

The growing body of studies raised criticism not only of the unfolding new regime itself, but also the ways it was approached and discussed in academic circles. The proponents of rethinking Western-biased urban theories stressed that taking Western modernity as normality—a framework for theorizing socio-spatial processes—leads to historical reductionism and the re-inscription of East/West difference in academic and also political life (Timár 2004; Stenning and Hörschelmann 2008). They argued for re-conceptualizing post-socialism, going beyond its local context, and taking it as a broader epistemic lens through which we can re-theorize urban restructuring in more comprehensive and inclusive (just) ways, relating the post-socialist city to its own history, other post-socialisms, and other capitalist modernities (Stenning and Hörschelmann 2008; Grubbauer 2012).

For transdisciplinary studies focused on consumption spaces beyond CEE cities, such arguments raised new questions and problems to address, such as the diversity of consumption practices (from shopping in malls to growing food for own supply, or being involved in informal/semi-formal networks of exchange in open markets or neighborhoods), the relationships of key agents shaping urban space in dependent economies of neoliberal capitalism, continuity and discontinuity in physical space (spaces and infrastructures inherited from the era of central planning next to new individual buildings of shopping), and the related (re)signification of particular places from one model of modernity to another. In the following subsections, I take a closer look at three types of consumption spaces, the mall, the bazaar, and the street, to highlight the relevance of diverse realities as sources of knowledge about consumption-centered urban restructuring beyond "local" contexts.

Shopping Malls

As a sophisticated toolkit for enchanting consumers through "spectacles produced by simulations, implosions, and manipulation of time and space" (Ritzer et al. 2001: xxii), shopping malls, familiar from the Western context, were put in a new context in post-socialist cities. They embodied the rampant post-1989 financialization process of urban land markets and the power of emerging growth coalitions of property developers, financers, retailers, and urban policymakers across CEE cities. While they fitted the unfolding neoliberal urbanism (e.g., by linking revitalization and creating a new visuality and urban image), they also represented an explicit split from the communist past. Malls spread across cities occupying central, brown-field, and also suburban locations from the mid-1990s, making "other" of the world outside (Nagy 2012; Sykora and Buzarovski 2012).

The consumption-focused regeneration of Smíchov, Prague should be considered as a classical example for this process, as discussed by Temelova (2007). The construction of

Golden Andel was a flagship project to recycle a declining industrial area near the city center for producing high yields in a changing and uncertain institutional context (emerging market economy; redefinition of the role of urban planning) to transform the image of an abandoned socialist industrial space and thus of the whole city. The project was run by an international developer (1996–2000) and taken further by the municipality (traffic calming, greening, face-lifting of public spaces, etc.), by new professional developers, and by small capitalists investing in local housing, forwarding gentrification.

Yet malls were developed as branded spaces across CEE cities rather than places of mass consumption: they emerged as realms of complex visuality, cultural diversity, and safety in contrast to the transient spaces and uncertainties of the emerging post-socialist city (Andrusz 2006) (see Figure 8.1). Nevertheless, because of the sharp contrast with other consumption spaces, the mall had to be developed to embrace collective memories, local culture, and recent discourses by design, housing high culture (art cinemas, theatres, etc.) and organizing events that involved people to whom mall culture might be alien. Such steps toward "domesticating" new local citizens into becoming consumers helped to embed the mall as a space for shopping, leisure, and socializing (Stanilov 2007).

Informal Consumption Practices and Their Spaces

Inherited from state socialism during the post-1989 transition, such spaces were considered parasitic and officially invisible networks of open markets, where things were acquired and re-signified (Verdery 1996). Yet such spaces—*bazaars*—spread, mutated, and transformed in post-socialist cities, representing at once continuity and discontinuity in the new regime, embodying conflicts stemming from the post-socialist transition and emerging capitalisms (Grubbauer 2012). The *bazaars* emerged as increasingly organized, large-scale, contested spaces shaped by strategies of retailers, consumers, producers, the regulative state, urban planners, and local residents. The agents of the bazaar were operating under the pressure of permanent changes and competition (Sik and Wallace 1999). Informality (including smuggling, trafficking, illegal currency exchange) and a dense net of internal social relations were sources of stability and part of the market rationality driving transactions (Sulima 2012). Such spaces emerged as ontological contexts for marginalized consumers, such as being places to emulate the well-off through consumption and also to enjoy the pleasure of bargaining and socializing (Sik and Wallace 1999). The bazaar raised aversion and conflicts reflected by its position in the discursive context of post-socialist urban transition, emerging as the (post-socialist) "other" to new ("Western"/capitalist) spaces of shopping (Sulima 2012). Recently, such places are being brought under stricter institutional (tax, custom, municipal land use) and physical control to domesticate and fit them in CEE neoliberal regimes (see Figure 8.1).

The Street

A central scene of social life, the street embraced diverse interactions historically and thus served the regime of neoliberal urbanism as a stage for reproducing the spectacle of global consumerism (Zukin 1998). Under state socialism, the streetscape displayed state power and order in the semiotic landscape that was transformed rapidly across CEE cities after 1989 by the removal of the visual heritage of former regimes, and the domestication of that legacy by setting up historical sites to re-interpret and also to commodify the past (e.g., see the House of Terror in Budapest) (Rátz et al. 2008; Light and Young 2010). The street was transformed into the realm of regained citizenship and also of diverse consumption practices—the powerful narratives of

Figure 8.1 From Informality to Controlled Spaces of Consumption: Plzen, Czech Republic, 2006 (the market was cleared off two years later)

Source: author

the post-socialist transition (Bodnar and Molnar 2009; Grubbauer and Kusiak 2012). This process was accelerated by shopping mall schemes that "thinned" the street's diversity and public character (Stanilov 2007; Hristova 2010). As a consequence, streets (particularly in historical centers) were emerging as scenes of social selectivity and displacement, disappointment, alienation, and resistance (Nagy and Timár 2012; Pastak and Khärik 2016).

For example, dive bars in Budapest emerged as ephemeral small businesses in inner urban spaces neglected under socialism and awaiting developers up until the early 2000s. They operated in the grey zone of services frequented by locals, students, and less well-off tourists. By reusing courtyards and intruding in the street (e.g., by making noise), they blurred the boundaries between private and public spheres and raised local conflicts. Stimulated by the rapid growth of international tourism in the city, dive bars were growing in number and becoming increasingly professional in management, enacting the neo-bohemian entrepreneurial (hipster) spirit, and effectively transforming the inner part of Districts VI and VII into a party-zone. This shift fitted in the neoliberal concept of urban development and the local state supported the bar owners against residents in the emerging conflicts (Rátz et al. 2008; Keresztély and Scott 2012).

An Outlook for Further Research

Considering *space* beyond the immediate material context of buying and reflections on multiple agencies shaping related socio-spatial practices enriched debates about consumption substantially from the early 1990s and called for a deeper understanding of social restructurings across different regimes of capitalism at the urban scale and beyond. The unfolding of the "spatial turn" in consumption and media studies, along with the "cultural turn" and, more recently, the shifting focus on the "digitalization" of consumption, generated a shared theoretical ground for transdisciplinary debates that might stimulate further research on spatialities and communicative features of consumption.

Reorganization of urban spaces around consumption was also a lens through which CEE urban transformation was researched. As I have shown, the physical and semiotic landscapes of post-socialist cities were transformed radically by the development of new consumption spaces. Although such processes were driven by the cultural and spatial logic of neoliberal capitalism, shifting cities toward visual homogenization and rational organization, CEE urban spaces are still scenes of social relations and practices rooted in state socialism and also in the emerging peripheral capitalisms. This very epistemological context offers topics/spaces for further research on diverse urban modernities of (semi)peripheries. Avenues for comparative analyses have already been opened by earlier studies on Indian, Chinese, and Latin American cities, discussing social restructuring and political discourses that place the middle class (consumer-citizens) at the focus of emerging new modernities (further marginalizing the poor who are not part of global consumer culture); consumption as a vehicle of wider socio-spatial polarization and exclusion; the variety of roles played by the state in such processes; and the development (and socio-spatial diversity) of new social practices and identities related to consumption in such (semi/peripheral) contexts (Fernandes 2004; Sinclair and Pertierra 2012; Tarantino and Cheng 2017).

Acknowledgment

This chapter draws on the results of the project *Institutional and individual responses to state restructuring in different geographical contexts* supported by the Hungarian National Research, Development and Innovation Office (NKFIH, grant no. 109296).

References

Aalbers, M. B. (2008) "The financialization of home and the mortgage market crisis," *Competition & Change*, 12, pp. 148–166.

Andrusz, G. (2006) "Wall the mall: A metaphor for metamorphosis" in S. Tsenkova and Z. Nedović-Budić (eds) *The Urban Mosaic of Post-Socialist Europe*, Heidelberg: Physica-Verlag, pp. 21–42.

Baudrillard, J. (1998) *The Consumer Society: Myths and Structures*, London: SAGE.

Bauman, Z. (1998) *Work, Consumerism and the New Poor*, Milton Keynes: Open University Press.

Benjamin, W. (1969) "Paris: Capital of the nineteenth century," *Perspecta*, 12, pp. 163–172.

Benjamin, W. (2008) "The work of art in the age of mechanical reproduction" in H. Arendt (ed.) *Illuminations*, New York: Schocken Books.

Bockman, J. and Eyal, G. (2002) "Eastern Europe as a laboratory for economic knowledge: The transnational roots of neoliberalism," *American Journal of Sociology*, 108(2), pp. 310–352.

Bodnar, J. and Molnar, V. (2009) "Reconfiguring private and public: State, capital and new housing developments in Berlin and Budapest," *Urban Studies*, 47(2), pp. 789–812.

Borén, T. and Gentile, M. (2007) "Metropolitan processes in post-communist states: An introduction," *Geografiska Annaler*, 89B(2), pp. 95–110.

Brenner, N. (1999) "Globalisation as reterritorialisation: The re-scaling of urban governance in the European Union," *Urban Studies*, 36(3), pp. 431–451.

Castells, M. (1978), *City, Class and Power*, London: Palgrave.

Clarke, D. B. (1996) "The limits to retail capital" in N. Wrigley and M. Lowe (eds) *Retailing, Consumption and Capital*, Harlow: Longman, pp. 284–301.

Domosh, M (1996) "Feminized retail landscape: Gender, ideology and consumer culture in the nineteenth-century New York City" in N. Wrigley and M. Lowe (eds) *Retailing, Consumption and Capital*, Harlow: Longman, pp. 257–270.

Fernandes, L. (2004) "The politics of forgetting: Class, politics, state power and the restructuring of urban space in India," *Urban Studies*, 41(12), pp. 2415–2430.

Goss, J. (2004) "Geography of consumption I," *Progress in Human Geography*, 28(3), pp. 369–380.

Goss, J. (2006) "Geographies of consumption: The work of consumption," *Progress in Human Geography*, 30(2), pp. 237–249.

Grubbauer, M. (2012) "Towards a more comprehensive notion of urban change: Linking post-socialist urbanism and urban theory" in M. Grubbauer and J. Kusiak (eds) *Chasing Warsaw: Socio-Material Dynamics of Urban Change Since 1990*, Frankfurt-New York: Campus Verlag, pp. 35–61.

Grubbauer, M. and Kusiak, J. (eds) (2012) "Introduction: Chasing Warsaw" in *Chasing Warsaw: Socio-Material Dynamics of Urban Change Since 1990*, Frankfurt-New York: Campus Verlag, pp. 9–24.

Harloe, M. (1996) "Cities in the transition" in G. Andrusz, M. Harloe, and I. Szelenyi (eds) *Cities After Socialism*, Oxford: Blackwell, pp. 1–29.

Harvey, D. (1995) *The Condition of Postmodernity: An Enquiry into the Origins of Cultural Change*, Oxford: Blackwell.

Harvey, D. (2009) "The art of rent: Globalization, monopoly rent and the commodification of culture," *Socialist Register*, viewed 21 December 2017, www.socialistregister.com/index.php/srv/article/viewFile/5778/2674.

Harvey, D. (2012) "The urban roots of financial crises: Reclaiming the city for anticapitalist struggle," *Socialist Register*, 48, pp. 1–35.

Hirt, S. (2008) "Landscapes of postmodernity: Changes in the built fabric of Belgrade and Sofia since the end of socialism," *Urban Geography*, 29(8), pp. 785–810.

Horkheimer, M. and Adorno, T. (1979) "The culture industry as mass deception" in G. Durham and D. M. Kellner (eds) *Media and Cultural Studies*, Oxford: Blackwell, pp. 41–72.

Hristova (2010) "Imagining the city as a space for cultural policy," *Sociological Problems*, 42(2), pp. 199–221.

Jackson, P. (1989) *Maps of Meaning*, London: Unwyn Hyman.

Jackson, P. and Thrift, N. (2005) "Geographies of consumption" in D. Miller (ed.) *Acknowledging Consumption*, London: Routledge, pp. 203–236.

Keresztély, K. and Scott, J. (2012) "Urban regeneration in post-socialist context: Budapest and the search for a social dimension," *European Planning Studies*, 20(7), pp. 1111–1134.

Lefebvre, H. (1991) *The Production of Space*, Oxford: Blackwell.

Light, D. and Young, C. (2010) "Reconfiguring socialist urban landscapes: The 'left-over' spaces of state-socialism in Bucharest," *Human Geographies*, 4(1), pp. 5–16.

Lowe, M. and Wrigley, N. M. (eds) (1996) "Toward the new retail geography" in *Retailing, Consumption and Capital*, Harlow: Longman, pp. 116–136.

Miles, S. and Miles, M. (2004) *Consuming Cities*, New York: Palgrave Macmillan.

Miller, D. (2001) *Consumption: Objects, Subjects and Mediations in Consumption*, Oxford: Taylor & Francis.

Miller, D. (ed.) (2005) *Acknowledging Consumption*, London: Routledge.

Miller, D., Jackson, P., Thrift, N., Holbrook, B., and Rowlands, M. (1998) *Shopping, Place and Identity*, London: Routledge.

Morley, D. (2005) "Theories of consumption in media studies" in *Acknowledging Consumption*, London: Routledge, pp. 293–324.

Nagy, E. (2012) "Bargaining, learning and control: Production of consumption spaces in post-socialist context," *Europa Regional*, 20(1), pp. 42–54.

Nagy E. and Timár J. (2012) "Urban restructuring in the grip of capital and politics: Gentrification in East-Central Europe" in T. Csapó and A. Balogh (eds) *Development of the Settlement Network in the Central European Countries: Past, Present, and Future*, Berlin, Heidelberg: Springer Verlag, pp. 121–135.

Pastak, I. and Khärik, A. (2016) "The impacts of culture-led flagship projects on local communities in the context of post-socialist Tallinn," *Czech Sociological Review*, 52(6), pp. 963–990.

Poblocki, K. (2012) "Space, class and the geography of Poland's champagne" in M. Grubbauer and J. Kusiak (eds) *Chasing Warsaw: Socio-Material Dynamics of Urban Change Since 1990*, Frankfurt-New York: Campus Verlag, pp. 269–290.

Rátz, T., Smith, M., and Michalkó, G. (2008) "New places in old spaces: Mapping tourism and regeneration in Budapest," *Tourism Geographies*, 10(4), pp. 429–451.

Ritzer, G., Goodman, D., and Wiedenhoft, W. (2001) "Theories of consumption" in G. Ritzer and B. Smart (eds) *Handbook of Social Theory*, London: SAGE, pp. 410–427.

Sik, E. and Wallace, C. (1999) "The development of open-air markets in East-Central Europe," *International Journal of Urban and Regional Research*, 23(4), pp. 697–714.

Sinclair, J. and Pertierra, A. C. (2012) "Consumer culture in Latin America: An introduction" in J. Sinclair and A. C. Pertierra (eds) *Consumer Culture in Latin America*, Berlin, Heidelberg: Springer Verlag, pp. 1–16.

Stanilov, K. (2007) "Taking stock of post-socialist urban development: A recapitulation" in K. Stanilov (ed.) *The Post-Socialist City*, Berlin: Springer, pp. 3–17.

Stenning, A. and Hörschelmann, K. (2008) "History, geography and difference in the post-socialist world: Or, do we still need post-socialism?" *Antipode*, 40(2), pp. 312–335.

Stenning, A., Smith, A., Rochovská, A., and Swiatek, D. (2010) *Domesticating Neoliberalism: Spaces of Economic Practices and Social Reproduction in Post-Socialist Cities*, Chichester: Wiley-Blackwell.

Sulima, R. (2012) "The laboratory of Polish postmodernity: An ethnographic report from the stadium-bazaar" in M. Grubbauer and J. Kusiak (eds) *Chasing Warsaw: Socio-Material Dynamics of Urban Change Since 1990*, Frankfurt-New York: Campus Verlag, pp. 241–268.

Sykora, L. and Buzarovski, S. (2012) "Multiple transformations: Conceptualising the post-communist urban transition," *Urban Studies*, 49(1), pp. 43–60.

Tarantino, M. and Cheng, C. T. (2017) "Rural spaces, urban textures: Media, leisure, and identity in a Southern China industrial village" in G. Aiello, M. Tarantino, and K. Oakley (eds) *Communicating the City: Meanings, Practices, Interactions*, New York: Peter Lang, pp. 65–79.

Temelova, J. (2007) "Flagship developments and the physical upgrading of post-socialist inner city: The golden Andel project in Prague," *Environment and Planning C. Government and Policy*, 19(1), pp. 45–63.

Timár, J. (2004) "What convergence between what geographies in Europe? A Hungarian perspective," *European Urban and Regional Studies*, 11(4), pp. 371–375.

Verdery, K. (1996) *What Was Socialism, and What Comes Next?* Princeton, NJ: Princeton University Press.

Wrigley, N. and Lowe, M. (2002) *Reading Retail*, London: Arnold.

Wrigley, N. and Lowe, M. (2014) *Reading Retail: A Geographical Perspective on Retailing in Consumption Spaces*, London-New York: Routledge.

Wrigley, N., Coe, N., and Currah, A. (2005) "Globalizing retail: Conceptualizing the distribution-based transnational corporation," *Progress in Urban Geography*, 29(4), pp. 437–457.

Zukin, S. (1998) "Urban lifestyles: Diversity and standardization in spaces of consumption," *Urban Studies*, 35(5–6), pp. 825–839.

Further Reading

Eurasian Geography and Economics, 57(4–5), a special issue on relating post-socialist urban research and urban theory.

Jayne, M. (2005) *Cities and Consumption*, London: Routledge.

Stenning, A. et al. (2010) *Domesticating Neoliberalism: Spaces of Economic Practices and Social Reproduction in Post-Socialist Cities*, Chichester: Wiley-Blackwell.

9
ON THE MOVE
On Mobile Agoras, Networked Selves, and the Contemporary City

Ole B. Jensen

Introduction

The everyday life of contemporary urban dwellers is increasingly defined by mobilities. People are "on the move" in cars, public transport systems, and other infrastructural landscapes and systems such as mobile phones (see also Chapter 15, this volume). However, as we move, we are connected to digital media publics through communication technologies such as mobile devices (phones and computers, but also vehicles such as automatized and computerized cars). A growing amount of software-sorted and algorithmically orchestrated "systems" provide the second nature to the mobile urban dweller. Yet, as we move within and across such complex mediatized landscapes, we are still sensing and experiencing the world through embodied motions. We operate systems; we navigate and "wayfind", and we position ourselves either in face-to-face or mediated interaction through the "thick skin" of vehicles of different sorts. In the midst of this complexity, the materiality of the urban environment plays a vital part. Materiality and spatiality connect us to the digital realm and mediatized systems through the complex dynamics of embodied movement and situational interaction. Often, we seem to think less of the mobilities, landscapes, and systems hosting these mundane practices. We are on the move in order to be elsewhere, and being elsewhere is why we move. The notion of "infrastructure"' even suggests a hidden world or a supportive tissue that lives an inconspicuous and less glorious existence (except when failure, disaster, disruption, and breakdown create vivid testimony to the importance of these hidden urban substrata).

Transportation planners and economists speak of transportation and mobility as a "derived demand" and a "necessary evil". However, this is only a partial truth. As citizens in the more technologically saturated parts of the urban world move, they are not "switched off" as numb billiard balls rolling across a blank surface. Rather, people live their lives (and a growing part actually) in these inconspicuous sites and systems. In line with the "mobilities turn", we may say that mobility is "more than A to B". Increasingly, digital network technology interferes with and affords many of these movements, or occupies us while we are on the move. This chapter discusses some of the social situations where we are "doing mobility" in material settings, with our bodies, relying on multiple sensations, and often in social interaction with co-present fellow passengers, drivers, passersby, et cetera. Following from my earlier work on embodied and situational mobilities, I particularly explore two related concepts. One is the notion of "mobile agoras" as a way of acknowledging the increasing importance (and potential) of rethinking mundane infrastructural sites of mobility in the city as "political". They are "political" in the sense of "being public", but also "bringing publics into being". The other term is the "networked self" and is related to the fact that the mobile subject comes into existence in these overlapping material and digital sites and systems. The ways in which one relates, connects, and reports to digital social networks while on the move are significant to who one is.

I begin by introducing the so-called "mobilities turn" as a particular theoretical framing of contemporary urbanism. Then follows a section about the city as a political space, and this paves the way for a section dedicated to thinking about digital technologies, mobilities, and the city. The chapter then turns to the two concepts of the "mobile agora" and the "networked self" and engages in exploring how they may expand our understanding of contemporary urban media spaces. Finally, I offer some reflections on the future of urban media research from the perspective of mobility.

Mobilities and Moorings: The Contemporary City Understood Through the "Mobilities Turn"

There has been a shift of focus in some quarters of social theory and research over the last two decades or so toward networks, relations, flows, and mobilities. It is beyond the scope of this chapter to present all these new perspectives, so we shall focus on the research explicitly undertaken under the heading of the "new mobilities turn". Here, the work by John Urry (2000, 2007) has been particularly influential in identifying a center of attention. Many other scholars represent the mobilities turn and one may consult a number of anthologies, handbooks, and readers to explore this in more depth (Cresswell and Merriman 2011; Adey et al. 2014; Jensen 2015). The key idea is to "put mobilities first" and problematize static and sedentary ideas of "the social", thus being critical of society "as a thing". Rather, the focus should be on the multiple ways in which the mobility of people, goods, vehicles, ideas, and information reconfigures sociality "beyond society" (Urry 2000). Put simply, the "mobilities turn" demonstrates that mobility is more than simple physical displacement from A to B. Rather, there are social, cultural, and identity-shaping effects of the ways in which mobilities reconfigure cities and vice-versa.

The "mobilities turn" has particularly influenced a redefinition of the city as a place. Emerging literature within human geography in particular suggests alternative ways of "thinking places" in the context of mobility. One such profoundly important element is the relational understanding of place developed by Doreen Massey (1999, 2005). Accordingly, places and sites must always be understood in their relational coupling with or decoupling from other places. Further, the relations between sites, cities, and places are defined by the mobilities and immobilities of people, goods, vehicles, and information (Kolb 2008). Elsewhere this combination has been described as a "relational and mobility-oriented sense of place" (Jensen 2013). The notion of fixed scales (e.g., quarter, city, region, nation) is, moreover, critically being problematized by this thinking. Scales are not "out there" as a static and structural scaffolding for places and societies (Cresswell 2004; Kolb 2008; Herod 2011). The pervasive proliferation of digital technologies is, for example, rendering the strict distinction between the "local" and the "global" obsolete as we seem to be "both in the local and the global" as we move across space "carrying networks" of real-time connectivity. We would not go as far as to argue that we are facing the proverbial "global village" with an extended "central nervous system" as McLuhan (1964) envisioned it. However, there is little left of a world where neighborhoods, cities, regions, and states were thought to be neatly nested in clear and stable hierarchies.

The changed perspectives on place, cities, and mobilities emerging from these developments invite us to rethink the city. In particular, fixed notions of "the urban" become problematized, as do ideas of fixed and sedentary urban institutions and features. One such "classic" theme is the city as a political space.

The City as a Political Space

Since the dawn of urban culture, the hallmark of cities has been a combination of materiality ("urbs", meaning literally the stones of the city) and cultures and social institutions (Simmel 1903; Sennett 1974, 1990, 1994). Aristotle writes in his *Politics* about the ideal size of the city and how the public space of political deliberation among the citizens must be materialized with a square or space that was termed the "Agora" (Aristotle 1995). Numerous urban scholars have discussed the city as the "cradle of public deliberation" and the civic engagements and cultures as the outcome of "civilized society" (Jacobs 1961; Gehl 1971/96; Low 2000). The city became understood in two separate spheres, namely that of the public and the private (some evidence suggest that this line of division may have been more blurred in earlier times than now (Habermas 1962/2009)). The notion of a public sphere and its physical and material dimension was for a long time the prevailing model of deliberation and communication, and the city was where masses congregated as "crowds" and the confrontation of opinion gave way to "publics" (Borch 2012). Some scholars point to the combined emergence of capitalism and book print as the pivotal turning point after which fast communication across vast distances enabled the creation of "imagined communities" (Anderson 1991). However, the key issue in this context is that different media, particularly digital networks, enabled new scales of communication and thus also the construction of larger and more diverse publics. En route to this situation, the notion of a singular public sphere hosting a communal deliberation process (Habermas 1962/2009) has been firmly criticized and substituted by the more accurate description as one of multiple publics and an agonist exchange rather than homogenous consent (e.g., Fraser 1990; Amin and Thrift 2010; Mouffe 2007). Recent debates on the configuration of the public sphere(s) and the institution of democracies have further pointed to the fact that *"Making Things Public"* (Latour and Weibel 2005) is a very material and physical affair. One example hereof is Thelle's analysis of crowds and the formation of political space by instituting the "secret ballot" at a political election in 1901 (Thelle 2016). For the sake of clarification, one should readily discriminate between public space and public domain (Hajer and Reijndorp 2001). Whereas the former is purely a question of open access to a public site, the latter is subtler and requires not only access but also active interaction between socially heterogeneous groups. The forming of public domain through a complex mix of material public spaces and new mediated and digital agoras is what we are concerned with in this chapter.

A number of different examples of the inherent connectivity between the city's public spaces and plazas and ideas of engagement, involvement, and democratic citizenship may be found. Here, we mention the urban scholar and designer Michael Sorkin who in his critique of the privatization of public spaces in predominantly North American cities phrased it rather poignantly: "There are no demonstrations in Disneyland" (Sorkin 1992). In a similar manner, we may think of Benjamin Barber and his account of the so-called "agora coalition" (Barber 2001). This was a protest movement arguing that if malls and other commercial enterprises keep privatizing the public spaces of the city, then publics and citizens must demand the right to exercise their political and democratic voices in these new "semi-public spaces". If the city loses its "old agoras", the new meeting places must allow for political assembly and public gathering (once my urban geography students went "testing" this in a local mall; after playing protest songs and chanting slogans for 10 minutes, a polite mall guard came and escorted them away!). We might argue that from Aristotle over Habermas and Fraser to Latour there has been an ongoing exploration of how democratic institutions and forums will materialize within shifting historical and technological contexts. In this context, the baseline of seeing the city as an inherently "political space" with sites for congregations and voicings may very well be challenged, to say the least. However, this may not need to be a story of decay and erosion only (Sennett 1974; Habermas 1962/2009). Rather, new digital infrastructures and landscapes may implicate new ways of enacting the political and new ways of assembling publics, to which I now turn.

Digital Technology, Mobilities, and the City

It now seems obsolete to point to the fact that contemporary cities are influenced by digital technologies in all sorts of ways (in capturing some of this complexity, see Graham and Marvin 2001; Gordon and Silva 2011; Kitchin and Dodge 2011; Sheller and Urry 2006; Wilken and Goggin 2012). One of the many profound changes affecting the ways we inhabit urban spaces is the omnipresent mobile phone and, in particular, the "smartphone" with its real-time, Internet connectivity. The presence of digital, networked technologies alters the ways we should think of proximity and connectivity. From a cultural and technological context of face-to-face interaction as the condition for "exchange", we have moved toward a reconfiguration of the "proximity-connectivity nexus" (Jensen 2013). Mobile situations are, accordingly, "stretched" across time and space with the effect that we have to think about hybrid relationships between the digital and the physical to such an extent that a strict separation of face-to-face and online interactions has less relevance than before (McCullough 2004). We "carry networks" across time and space in ways that change the way we connect and relate. The digital dimension of urban spaces and transit landscapes thus carries the potential to be understood and appropriated as the digital equivalent of the classic agora.[1] Needless to say, this is only a potential, as multiple digital networks require access codes, log-ons, and passwords, while connectivity is still not universal. The digital realm of the public sphere may or may not become mobilized as the new mobile agoras of the city. The access of people into digital networks and the forming and assembling of publics via these new technologies remains a contested issue.

Apart from the portable devices that people use as personal media, the public space of the city also tends to host a number of public interfaces and interactive screens. Often, we see these technologies being explored by performance artists (Jensen and Thomsen 2008; Brynskov et al. 2012). Public interactive screens may also work to "assemble publics" (Dewey 1927) and facilitate "temporary congregations" (Jensen 2013) and "mobile publics" (Sheller 2004). Again, rights to access and to define the contents of these media platforms are very limited and, thus, in no way trivial. So, both the mobile and the sedentary digital technologies of the city have the potential to "become political". We may think of these infrastructures as "armatures" that could become politicized:

> such armatures may be "rehabilitated" as sites that are more than a necessary evil in getting from point A to point B. Sites hosting mobilities are (potentially) meaningful spaces of social interaction and therefore also the potential new public agoras and sites of political voice.
>
> *(Jensen 2013: 203)*

The "old city" (i.e., the city prior to digital media) with its house façades and billboards already made up a "public sphere of screens". Most often, we have seen these as commercial ads in public spaces and infrastructure (Dorka 2008). Occasionally, this semiotic interpellation of commercial statements to consumer subjects has been challenged by graffiti or critical arts countering these simple messages. The artist Jenny Holzer's anti-commercials from New York in the 1970s are examples hereof. In particular, the movie theatre-type billboard with texts such as "Protect me from what I want" was a compelling illustration of the critical potential in public billboards and screens.

The way in which digital technology works in shaping people's attention to protests and demonstrations is one dimension of this new affordance. From a relatively slow "word-of-mouth mobilization", we are now facing an almost instant mobilization through, for example, social media (as these words are written, the author's Facebook account overflows with bottom-up organizations of anti-Trump protests in American cities). We should be critical and cautious in considering the participatory potentials, as Verhoeff (2012: 169) reminds us:

> The relatively unstable nature of innovative technologies and practices that are changing rapidly, together with the enthusiastic embrace of their possibilities for public engagement, call for a critical interrogation. We must examine not only the possibility of access and the participatory potential of locative, screen-based projects, but also consider the convergence of and conflicts between the ambitions of initiators (i.e., heritage institutions), of media designers, and the media competencies required from the public.

The media, technologies, and "things" of this new digital realm (which is very physical indeed—think of servers, hot spots, devices, etc.) assemble new forms of publics in ways where the material and the digital, the human, and the nonhuman are more than ever entwined realms and ontologies (Latour 2005; Bennett 2010). In the words of Licoppe and Inada: "As soon as people are equipped with handheld connected digital devices, then any kind of public space, be it the street, the museum or the Internet café, becomes a 'hybrid cultural ecology'" (2015: 58). Further, the potential of mobile networked technologies for surveillance and transgression of privacy should not be underestimated (Klauser 2017). The agoras may be policed without our knowing.

The argument is, thus, that the use of mobile devices, interactive screens, Wi-Fi zones, and a large number of different digital networks technologies changes the idea of the agora and the public sphere in the city as a strictly physical and place-bound phenomenon. We are facing the age of mobile agoras, as contingent and technologically mediated realms of interaction.

Mobile Agoras

In my previous work on *Staging Mobilities* (Jensen 2013), I introduced the term "mobile agoras" to understand the linkage between mobility, media, and politics. I argued that networked technologies constitute a field of exploration into broader issues of democracy, multiple publics, privacy issues, forms of segregation, and new mobile (electronic and material) agoras pointing toward a critical re-interpretation of contemporary politics of space and mobilities (Jensen 2013: 125). Diverse engagements with portable and digitally networked technologies during physical travels create situations where we are "linked in motion" and not just passively shuffled across (Jensen 2013: 127). These new mobile and mediated spaces provide new possibilities for existing cities. As Nold (2005: 853) put it:

> Ironically, the city (polis), which is the foundation of politics by gathering people together, today blocks our view of one another. Trapped in streets and hemmed in by tall buildings, it is impossible to get an individual overview of the crowd. Today, this

view of power has been placed in the hands of those with the necessary imaging technology. Fortunately, there is a whole movement of bottom-up media technologists who are developing new communication and representation technologies. Instead of rushing home from a demonstration to have our own subjective experience validated by the mainstream media, these new strains of technology hint at ways to attain our own consensual God's-eye view.

Aristotle's classic notion of the static and fixed agora was challenged before the advent of the networked and mobile technologies. One such challenge came from the British architect Reyner Banham in 1971. Banham went to Los Angeles and described the city in his seminal book *Los Angeles: The Architecture of Four Ecologies* (Banham 1971/2009). One of these "ecologies" was the LA freeway system, which Banham (provocatively) claimed to be a "great public space" and a "state of mind" for the Angelinos (though see Chapters 20 and 42, this volume). There is relevance in Banham's understanding of the freeway system as a potential mobile agora from a pre-digital era. Rather than being a giant "non-place", the freeway system is both an A-to-B movement space and a space of interaction among strangers (Jensen 2014: 189–230). Tokyo, Los Angeles, Mexico City, Beijing, Beirut, Jakarta, and Budapest are among the cities from where reports of potential new agoras and publics are made. In their case study on the Beijing Ring Roads, Yan et al. (in Houben and Calabrese 2003: 197) conclude that:

> The highway has become a public space full of business opportunities. It is inevitable that media gradually infiltrate this space . . . There are plenty of possibilities in which the media can promote the ring road space, with more than commercial intentions. As we drove around the ring roads to shoot the film, we noticed that there were many political slogans and publicity slogans . . . Business, politics and culture are mixed together to produce an urban ramble.

The Beijing project further speculates about the potential for redesigning the highway spaces as a "new carrier of urban information or a new urban media" (Yan et al. in Houben and Calabrese 2003: 206). Here, the discussion of hybridization and connecting digital media with the public space of the ring road precisely touches on the debate of potential mobile agoras. In the words of Hajer and Reijndorp (2001: 14, 16):

> The expanded and mobile city implies a new agenda for the design of public space, not only in relation to the urban centres or in the new residential districts, but especially in the ambiguous in-between areas . . . Furthermore, we seem to think too much about public space in the sense of fixed and permanent physical spaces, and we give insufficient consideration to the way in which public domain comes into being in flux, often extremely temporarily.

The contemporary mobile urban agoras might be found in the "in-between spaces" (from airport lounges to drive-in queues and parking spaces) and they may be hybrid arenas of physical co-presence and digital connectivity, or may in fact come into being literally "everywhere". There are many examples of more technologically afforded publics and agoras and here we can in no way do justice to this fast-moving field (for discussions of how location-based media in particular create new mobile agoras, see for example Doyle 2015; Offenhuber and Ratti 2014; Silva 2017).

The Networked Self

The aforementioned "mobilities turn" has been occupied with exploring the effects of mobility on three different levels. Firstly, how mobility changes the way we engage with the material and physical world. Secondly, how the transforming mobility patterns changes the way we relate to "social others". And finally, how these dynamics influence how we understand our selves. The mobile transformations of contemporary everyday life change the material, social, and psychological dimensions of our existence. The effect on identities (as something constantly "in the making", never entirely fixed and always relational) is, thus, one of the key discussions within this research (for an elaboration of such an identity conception, see Giddens 1991). The "networked self" (Jensen 2013) raises the issue of how the construction of identities on the move becomes a reality. The fact that we are linked in motion and embedded into these mediatized landscapes suggests a new type of self-construction—a networked self, as it were.

In the book *Mobile Lives*, Elliott and Urry (2010: 5–6) developed similar argumentation for the recognition of the intertwined nature of identity, mobility, and media technologies:

> Life "on the move" is one in which "networking" and the "networked" self undertake routine, repetitive operations of connecting and disconnecting, logging on and off ... the use of various miniaturized mobilities involves transformations of self-experience through the storage and subsequent retrieval of affects and emotions in the object world of generalized media communication.

As the notion of a "stretched situation" (Jensen 2013) is helpful to describe the way in which mobile and digital technologies afford new types of interaction across time and space, so do Elliott and Urry argue for a notion of a "stretching of the self", which connotes plasticity, portability, and contingency along the lines of affect and identity (Elliott and Urry 2010: 97). The notion of the "networked self" is a useful framing of a mediated condition not only for communicating but also for experiencing urban mobilities. Further, we very often see and hear in public spaces that checking "where we are" becomes the entry point for much of the networked communication we engage in while on the move. In the adaptation of "airport language" by social media, we "check in" in all sorts of sites and places. Such mobile and mediated network relations create new conditions for the "self" and its ability to "present itself" (Goffman 1959) and will, thus, ultimately change the relations between the "self", mobilities, and the network. Giddens's definition of the Late Modern self as the "capacity to use 'I' in shifting contexts" (Giddens 1991: 53) is further complicated by the networked self. With reference to Goffman, this means that the "self" is becoming what it is, not only in motion individually and collectively, but equally in new networked relations mediated by technologies (Jensen 2013).

As part of these dynamics, the role of place changes. Place may arguably always have been a central dimension of identity and self (e.g., as in notions of belonging). However, with the "constant placing of one's whereabouts" ("*Hi, I am on the bus*"), the place component of identities becomes even more dynamic and mobile. We give real-time accounts of "our place in the world" as well as follow our socially significant others to an unprecedented detail (e.g., through text messages, Snap Chat alerts, or Facebook updates and check-ins). Elliott and Urry speak of "portable personhood" as a process where identity is not only bent toward novel forms of transportation and movement, but more fundamentally recast in terms of capacity for movement. Thus, they speak of a new situation wherein the globalization of mobilities extends into the core of the self (2010: 3). The earlier "place-bound" dimension of identity seems to be challenged and further complicated (Morley 2000).

Concluding Remarks

The complex and mediated relationships between mobile bodies and the infrastructural landscapes of the contemporary city need new descriptions. In this chapter, I discussed the notion of "mobile agoras" and "networked selves" as part of an emerging vocabulary for dealing with understanding contemporary urban developments. The embedding of human bodies into increasingly complex systems of physical and digital mobility demands that we rethink how we "inhabit" these spaces and technologies. If the complex intermingling of digital media and physical spaces with multisensorial human bodies is the foundation for new mediatized spaces and mobile agoras, we are facing a research agenda of some tall order. For now, we see at least four research tasks.

Firstly, we should seek concepts enabling us to grasp such new complexities. Secondly, we need to engage with the empirical realities of these "meetings of entities", as it were, and we should focus on the actual, situational practices wherein publics are coming together, where mobile agoras are being assembled. Thirdly, there is a need for further ethnographic accounts and field studies to account for how different elements (mobile citizens, media practices, virtual and physical spaces) interact in different contexts. Fourth and finally, the research exploring how new networked communication technology affords mobile agoras and networked selves should engage in what Crang and Graham (2007) termed a "politics of visibility". In other words, we need help visualizing (often quite literally) the consequences of the varied uses of the new technologies in urban societies. Here, the agenda is double: we seek creative and dynamic ways to demonstrate the social and political effects of mediated mobilities on the one hand, and on the other hand, we need to creatively explore the unseen and underutilized potentials of technologies to bring about publics and create mobile agoras.

On the latter of these tasks, we may suspect that stronger engagement with the critical design as well as the arts is one important way forward. Posing the speculative "what if?" question in relation to a particular technology might provide impetus to imagining new publics and agoras where we may require "help from outside" the mainstream academia (for an introduction to these ideas, see Jensen 2016, 2017). The exploration of the politics of mobile agoras and networked selves further needs to address the "dark sides" of such developments. Privatized and state-led, undemocratic surveillance practices, social exclusion and filtering through software, and many other critical issues must accompany the exploration of potentials for new publics and civic engagement. So, we may stand before two competing visions: "Digital Deliberation and Mediatized Inclusion" versus "The End of Privacy in Commercial Surveillance Landscapes". Let us end by referencing the now-classic Langdon Winner (1980: 125) paper, "Do Artefacts Have Politics?", thus acknowledging the continued need for understanding technologies as more than simple instrumental artefacts:

> To our accustomed way of thinking, technologies are seen as neutral tools that can be used well or poorly, for good, evil, or something in between . . . If our moral and political language for evaluating technology includes only categories having to do with tools and uses, it does not include attention to the meaning of the designing and arrangements of our artifacts, then we will be blinded to much that is intellectually and practically crucial. We need new research-based vocabularies for understanding the forming of mobile agoras through the emergence of networked selves "on the move" in the changing city.

Note

1 I thank the participants at the Hawke EU Centre Workshop "Innovating European and Australian Mobilities", University of South Australia August 28–29, 2017, for constructive comments on an earlier version of this chapter, which prompted me to clarify the meaning of agora adopted here. The "classic" agora was in no way a space of equality and democracy as women, slaves, foreigners, and children were excluded from this forum (Madanipour 2003: 235). In this chapter, I refer to an idealized or ideal-typical agora as a utopian parable for the discussion. Mobile agoras are, thus, virtual and corrective ideals whose potential for social inclusion and public deliberation needs deeper empirical investigation than this chapter can substantiate.

References

Adey, P., Bissell, D., Hannam, K., Merriman, P., and Sheller, M. (eds.) (2014) *The Routledge Handbook of Mobilities*, London: Routledge.
Amin, A. and Thrift, N. (2010) *Cities: Reimagining the Urban*, Cambridge: Polity.
Anderson, B. (1991) *Imagined Communities. Reflections of the Origin and Spread of Nationalism*, London: Verso.
Aristotle (1995) *Politics*, Oxford: Oxford University Press.
Barber, B.R. (2001) "Malled, Mauled, and Overhauled: Arresting Suburban Sprawl by transforming Suburban Malls into Usable Civic Spaces", in M. Hénaff and T.B. Strong (eds.) *Public Space and Democracy*, Minneapolis, MN: University of Minnesota Press, pp. 201–220.
Banham, R. (1971/2009) *Los Angeles: The Architecture of Four Ecologies*, Berkeley, CA: University of California Press.
Bennett, J. (2010) *Vibrant Matter: A Political Ecology of Things*, Durham, NC: Duke University Press.
Borch, C. (2012) *The Politics of Crowds: An Alternative History of Sociology*, Cambridge: Cambridge University Press.
Brynskov, K., Halskov, K., and Kabel, L. (2012) *Byens Digitale Liv / Digital Urban Living*, Aarhus: Forlaget Ajour.
Crang, M. and Graham, S. (2007) "Sentient Cities: Ambient Intelligence and the Politics of Urban Space", *Information, Communication and Society*, 10(6), pp. 789–817.
Cresswell, T. (2004) *Place: A Short Introduction*, Oxford: Blackwell.
Cresswell, T. (2006) *On the Move: Mobility in the Modern Western World*, London: Routledge.
Cresswell, T. and Merriman, P. (eds.) (2011) *Geographies of Mobilities: Practices, Spaces, Subjects*, Aldershot: Ashgate.
Dewey, J. (1927) *The Public and Its Problems*, New York: Henry Holt.
Dorka, M. (2008) "Design of the Public", in M. Erlhoff, P. Heidkamp, and I. Utikal (eds.) *Designing Public: Perspectives for the Public*, Basel: Birkhäuser, pp. 43–45.
Doyle, M.R. (2015) "Designing for Mobile Activities: WiFi Hotspots, Users, and the Relational Programming of Place", in A.S. Silva and M. Sheller (eds.) *Mobility and Locative Media: Mobile Communication in Hybrid Spaces*, London: Routledge, pp. 188–206.
Elliott, A. and Urry, J. (2010) *Mobile Lives*, London: Routledge.
Fraser, N. (1990) "Rethinking the Public Sphere: A Contribution to the Critique of Actually Existing Democracy", *Social Text*, 25/26, pp. 56–80.
Gehl, J. (1971/96) *Livet mellem husene: Udeaktiviteter og udemiljøer*, Copenhagen: Arkitektens Forlag.
Giddens, A. (1991) *Modernity and Self-Identity: Self and Society in the Late Modern Age*, Cambridge: Polity Press.
Goffman, E. (1959) *The Presentation of Self in Everyday Life*, New York: Doubleday.
Gordon, E. and Silva, A.S. (2011) *Net Locality: Why Location Matters in a Networked World*, Chichester: Wiley-Blackwell.
Graham, S. and Marvin, S. (2001) *Splintering Urbanism: Networked Infrastructures, Technological Mobilities and the Urban Condition*, London: Routledge.
Habermas, J. (1962/2009) *Borgerlig Offentlighed. Offentlighedens strukturændring. Undersøgelser af en kategori i det borgerlige samfund*, København: Informations Forlag.
Hajer, M. and Reijndorp, A. (2001) *In Search of New Public Domain*, Rotterdam: NAi Publishers.
Herod, A. (2011) *Scale*, London: Routledge.
Houben, F. and Calabrese, L.M. (eds.) (2003) *Mobility: A Room with a View*, Rotterdam: NAi Publishers.
Jacobs, J. (1961) *The Death and Life of Great American Cities*, New York: Vintage Books.

Jensen, O.B. (2013) *Staging Mobilities*, London: Routledge.
Jensen, O.B. (2014) *Designing Mobilities*, Aalborg: Aalborg University Press.
Jensen, O.B. (2016) "Of 'Other' Materialities: Why (Mobilities) Design Is Central to the Future of Mobilities Research", *Mobilities*, 11(4), pp. 587–597.
Jensen, O.B. (2017) "Design", in Silva, A.S. (ed.) *Dialogues on Mobile Communication*, London: Routledge, pp. 103–120.
Jensen, O.B. (ed.) (2015) *Mobilities*, London: Routledge, vol. I–IV.
Jensen, O.B. and Thomsen, B.S. (2008) "Performative Urban Environments: Increasing Media Connectivity", in F. Eckardt et al. (eds.) *Mediacity: Situations, Practices and Encounters*, Berlin: Frank and Timme, pp. 407–429.
Kitchin, R. and Dodge, M. (2011) *Code/Space: Software and Everyday Life*, Cambridge, MA: MIT Press.
Klauser, F. (2017) *Surveillance and Space*, London: SAGE.
Kolb, D. (2008) *Sprawling Places*, Athens, GA: University of Georgia Press.
Latour, B. (2005) *Reassembling the Social*, Oxford: Oxford University Press.
Latour, B. and Weibel, P. (eds.) (2005) *Making Things Public: Atmospheres of Democracy*, Cambridge MA: MIT Press.
Licoppe, C. and Inada, Y. (2015) "Mobility and Proximity-Sensitive Digital Urban Ecologies: 'Timid Encounters' and 'Seam-Sensitive Walks'", *Mobilities*, doi: 10.1080/17450101.2014.988530.
Low, S.M. (2000) *On the Plaza: The Politics of Public Space and Culture*, Austin, TX: University of Texas Press.
Madanipour, A. (2003) *Public and Private Spaces of the Cities*, London: Routledge.
Massey, D. (1999) "On Space and the City", in D. Massey, J. Allen, and S. Pile (eds.) *City Worlds*, Milton Keynes: The Open University Press, pp. 157–170.
Massey, D. (2005) *For Space*, London: Sage.
McCullough, M. (2004) *Digital Ground: Architecture, Pervasive Computing, and Environmental Knowing*, Cambridge, MA: MIT Press.
McLuhan, M. (1964) *Understanding Media*, London: Routledge.
Morley, D. (2000) *Home Territories: Media, Mobility and Identity*, London: Routledge.
Mouffe, M. (2007) "Artistic Activism and Agonistic Spaces", *Art and Research: A Journal of Ideas, Contexts and Methods*, 1(2).
Nold, C. (2005) "Legible Mob", in B. Latour and P. Weibel (eds.) *Making Things Public: Atmospheres of Democracy*, Cambridge, MA: MIT Press, pp. 846–854.
Offenhuber, D. and Ratti, C. (eds.) (2014) *De-Coding the City: Urbanism in the Age of Big Data*, Basel: Birkhäuser.
Sennett, R. (1974) *The Fall of Public Man*, New York: W.W. Norton and Company.
Sennett, R. (1990) *The Conscience of the Eye: The Design and Social Life of Cities*, London: Faber and Faber.
Sennett, R. (1994) *Flesh and Stone: The Body and the City in Western Civilization*, New York: W.W. Norton and Company.
Sheller, M. (2004) "Mobile Publics: Beyond the Network Perspective", *Environment and Planning D: Society and Space*, 22, pp. 39–52.
Sheller, M. and Urry, J. (2006) *Mobile Technologies and the City*, London: Routledge.
Silva, A.S. (ed.) (2017) *Dialogues on Mobile Communication*, London: Routledge.
Silva, A.S. and Sheller, M. (eds.) (2015) *Mobility and Locative Media: Mobile Communication in Hybrid Spaces*, London: Routledge.
Simmel, G. (1903) "The Metropolis and Mental Life", in Kasinitz, P. (ed.) (1995) *Metropolis: Center and Symbol of Our Times*, New York: New York University Press, pp. 30–45.
Sorkin, M. (ed.) (1992) *Variations on a Theme Park: The New American City and the End of Public Space*, New York: Hill and Wang.
Thelle, M. (2016) "Crowding as Appropriation: Voting, Violence and Bodies in a Nineteenth-Century Urban Space", *Distinktion*, 17(3), pp. 276–293.
Urry, J. (2000) *Sociology Beyond Societies: Mobilities for the Twenty-First Century*, London: Routledge.
Urry, J. (2007) *Mobilities*, Cambridge: Polity.
Verhoeff, N. (2012) *Mobile Screens: The Visual Regime of Navigation*, Amsterdam: Amsterdam University Press.
Wilken, R. and Goggin, G. (eds.) (2012) *Mobile Technology and Place*, London: Routledge.
Winner, L. (1980) "Do Artifacts Have Politics?", *Daedalus*, 109(1), Modern Technology: Problem or Opportunity? (Winter 1980), pp. 121–136.

Further Reading

Adey, P. (2017) *Mobility* (2nd Edition), London: Routledge
Elliott, A. and Urry, J. (2010) *Mobile Lives*, London: Routledge.
Jensen, O.B. and Lanng, D.B. (2017) *Mobilities Design: Urban Designs for Mobile Situations*, London: Routledge.

10
CITIES OF FEET AND HANDS
Urban Habitations

Shaun Moores

Introduction: Manipulations of Spatial Organization

To help in setting the scene for this chapter, let me start by bringing two quotations, which are drawn from rather different works that appeared many years apart, into close proximity:

> The ordinary practitioners of the city . . . are walkers . . . Their story begins on ground level, with footsteps . . . pedestrian movements . . . intertwined paths . . . walking manipulates spatial organizations.
>
> *(de Certeau 1984: 93, 97, 101)*

> Hands are crucial elements of the life of the city . . . Yet the urban literature is all but silent on what is . . . right in front of its face . . . we forget the city of . . . hands . . . picking their way across keyboards, clicking mice, gripping steering wheels.
>
> *(Amin and Thrift 2002: 86)*

The first of these quoted passages is actually a selection of words that I have made from several pages in Michel de Certeau's analysis of "walking in the city" (see de Certeau 1984: 91–110), offered in the context of his classic book on everyday practices, which has become a key point of reference in what Ash Amin and Nigel Thrift call, in the other passage above, the urban literature (e.g., see Tonkiss 2005; Hubbard 2006). The focus of this French social theorist's analysis is on what might be termed, in the style of Amin and Thrift, a city of feet. He writes there of the significance of the "bustling city" (de Certeau 1984: 93) at ground level, a "mobile city" (de Certeau 1984: 110) which, for him, is constituted by the pedestrian movements and intertwined paths that "create an urban fabric" (de Certeau 1984: 103) of "lived space" (de Certeau 1984: 96). This is "another spatiality" (de Certeau 1984: 93), to be contrasted with the layout of "the planned city" (de Certeau 1984: 110) visible from up high.

Interestingly, though, when de Certeau asserts that walking manipulates spatial organizations, he is clearly employing a metaphor of manual activity. In what follows here, I will say more about his bustling, mobile city of feet, but in pursuing the notion of manipulation, I also want to expand on those brief comments made in passing by Amin and Thrift (2002) in the context of their "reimagining" of the urban, on what they name the city of hands. As these geographers rightly argue, hands, which are involved in the deft, skillful manipulation of things like computer keyboards and car steering wheels, are crucial yet largely forgotten elements of everyday urban living. The main contention of my chapter is that, taken together, such *cities of feet and hands*, of moving, knowledgeable bodies in practical, sensuous, tactile dealings with environments and technologies, are important considerations for urban cultural analysis because they are inextricably linked with matters of dwelling in the city or, in the terms of my subtitle, with *urban habitations*. This is already suggested, of course, by de Certeau's talk of the creation, through practices of walking, of a densely woven fabric of lived space or of "habitable spaces" (de Certeau 1984: 106).

I should add, by way of introduction, that I write as an academic with a background in media studies, but with a commitment to the development of "non-media-centric media studies" (Morley 2007, 2009; Krajina et al. 2014; Moores 2012: 103–10, 2018), which are increasingly informed by "non-representational theories of practice" (Thrift 1996, 2008; Moores 2018), contributing to what I now tend to think of as a more general, cross-disciplinary field of "everyday-life studies" (Moores 2017, 2018: 7, 19, 175–8). Most of my own work in recent years has been concerned with everyday environmental experiences and with the ordinary yet remarkable skills of bodily orientation and, consequently, with processes of dwelling or placemaking. In part, that includes qualitative empirical research on knowing how to get around urban environments, on foot and by various means of mechanized transport, but also, in part, it includes description and analysis of the movement and touch of hands and fingers, or digits, in the uses of new media technologies. This kind of research needs to be understood as a quite explicit departure from what I would regard as the overly media-centered and representation-focused character of much work that has been done, during the past four or five decades, beneath the banner of media studies.

The Street Transformed

At the start of de Certeau's chapter on walking in the city his emphasis is not immediately on the spatiality of ordinary pedestrian movement. It is, rather, on the extraordinary view of a particular city, New York, which he enjoys from an elevated position near to the top of a Manhattan skyscraper. From that tourist vantage point, he reports, the urban landscape is "immobilized before the eyes" (de Certeau 1984: 91), and his experience is one of being "lifted out of the city's grasp . . . looking down like a god" (1984: 92), as if onto a map-like representation of it, at the grid pattern of parallel streets. Only then does he go on to contrast that unusual experience with the everyday practices of walkers who "live 'down below'" (de Certeau 1984: 93), whose interwoven movements are, as he puts it, "other . . . to representations" or "foreign to . . . geometrical . . . space."

This striking juxtaposition of an immobilized city seen from above, looking down from a great height, and the myriad footsteps of the walkers below is discussed further by de Certeau with reference to the discipline of linguistics. In making what I take to be an anti-structuralist argument, which runs throughout his book on the everyday, he seeks to develop a "pragmatics" (de Certeau 1984: 33) of quotidian cultures, pointing out that this is a branch of linguistics concerned with "the use of language . . . the act of speaking. . . in relation to. . . contexts of use," rather than with some supposedly abstract and wholly determining structure or system of language. Applied specifically to situated practices of walking, the perspective of pragmatics leads him to write of "pedestrian speech acts" (de Certeau 1984: 97) and "pedestrian enunciation" (de Certeau 1984: 99) and further, he understands those articulations as uses or appropriations of an "urban system" (de Certeau 1984: 97). They are, in other words, *manipulations of spatial organization*, which involve, for example, the little "shortcuts and detours" (de Certeau 1984: 98) of experienced walkers, but on a grander scale, too, pedestrians who "fill . . . the streets . . . with . . . their desires" (de Certeau 1984: xxi). "Thus the street geometrically defined by urban planning," concludes de Certeau (de Certeau 1984: 117), "is transformed . . . by walkers."

I am broadly sympathetic to de Certeau's cultural analysis, both of walking and, more generally, of a range of practices including talking, reading, shopping, and cooking (see also de Certeau et al. 1998). It certainly has its problems, not least of which is an overly romanticized view that he takes of the tactical, resistant character of everyday activities, perhaps best illustrated by the dedication of his classic book to "a common hero . . . walking in countless thousands on the streets" (de Certeau 1984: v). Still, what I welcome is the attention that he pays there to the often unnoticed, improvisatory, and imaginative aspects of routine, habitual practice or movement, and, relatedly, to the ways in which urban settings are inhabited and made meaningful through skillful bodily "doing" (de Certeau 1984: xi). In turn, as I hope to show, this focus on the ordinary, creative arts of doing suggests the importance of what Thrift (2008: 121), in advocating non-representational theory, calls "practical knowing."

Let me try now to extend this account of a city of feet and of *the street transformed*. Initially, I will do so by considering some work, done many years ago, by two phenomenological geographers, Yi-Fu Tuan (1977) and David Seamon (2015 [1979]), whose interests in environmental experience and the formation of senses of place might be seen to prefigure later non-representational approaches within their discipline, and also, more recently, by anthropologist Tim Ingold (2000, 2007, 2011, 2015), whose evolving concerns with dwelling and with paths or lines of movement make him one of the most compelling non-representational theorists in the social sciences today.

While being unaware, I assume, of de Certeau's analysis of walking in the city, since at the time it was only published in French, Tuan (1977: 199) provides what is in some respects a similar discussion of the appropriation, through movement, of an urban setting:

> We are in a strange part of town . . . unknown space stretches ahead of us. In time we know a few landmarks and the routes connecting them. Eventually what was . . . unknown space . . . lacking significance other than strangeness . . . becomes familiar place . . . filled with meaning . . . We know where we are and we can find our way . . . we are oriented.

Reading Tuan and de Certeau together could give rise to a degree of confusion over terminology. This is because the French social theorist employs the concept of place when writing of "location" (de Certeau 1984: 117), whereas Tuan, as evidenced by the passage quoted here, would contest any notion of place as mere location, preferring to reserve its use for "when space feels thoroughly familiar" (Tuan 1977: 73), filled with meaning and emotion. Therefore, Tuan's definition of place is much closer to what de Certeau names lived space. Nevertheless, they share a fascination with the transformative potential of pedestrian movements for processes of dwelling, as does Seamon (2015 [1979]: 54–6; see also Seamon 1980), who presents valuable research materials on the improvised, interactive, and rhythmic "place choreographies" that are performed in "streets . . . cafes . . . market places" and so on, in which affective attachments can be collaboratively constituted. That particular aspect of Seamon's qualitative research serves to illustrate the multiplicity of intertwined paths and the fabric of lived space, which de Certeau's work points to.[1]

Tuan's notes on urban orientations and habitations add another dimension to the analysis, though, when he writes that: "People who are good at finding their way in the city may be poor at giving street directions to the lost, and hopeless in their attempts to draw maps" (Tuan 1977: 68). With those apparently simple observations, he begins to go beyond de Certeau in appreciating the specific character of the practical knowing that is required in order to get around urban environments on foot. It is typically a pre-reflective knowledge in movement, which may be difficult to convert into symbolic-representational forms, but which enables people to "perform complex acts without the help of mental or material plans" (Tuan 1977: 68).

Ingold (2007: 89) conceptualizes such everyday know-how as "inhabitant knowledge." Inhabitants, he contends, "know as they go, as they journey through the world along paths of travel" (Ingold 2011: 154), so that "moving is knowing" (Ingold 2015: 47) in the "context of journeys previously made" (Ingold 2000: 219). This is an "alongly integrated" (Ingold 2007: 89) knowledge, as opposed to the "upwardly integrated" kind that is produced by surveyors in their construction of "cartographic maps." Indeed, his distinction between alongly and upwardly integrated knowledges reminds me precisely of de Certeau's juxtaposition of mobile and immobilized cities, with that contrast, which I outlined earlier, between walking through the city at ground level and looking down on it from up high, from a position of dramatic vertical elevation. Very much in the spirit of de Certeau (1984: xviii), then, who speaks of the "wandering lines" of quotidian practice, Ingold (2011: 149) thinks of "habitation" as terrestrial and as "lineal." Rather like Seamon, too, he regards places as provisional "knots" (2011: 148–9) of "entwined ... lifelines," which make up part of a wider "meshwork" of "perambulatory movement" or "lines of wayfaring."

Of course, as media theorist Caroline Bassett (2003: 344–5) makes clear in her critical engagement with de Certeau's work, the practices and experiences of urban pedestrians have themselves been transformed these days, since walkers started to carry mobile phone devices and later, I might add, a variety of smartphones and touchscreen tablet computers:

> I still walk in the city. But I am no longer a pedestrian in the old sense because ... city streets are full of virtual doorways ... Countless ways through, ways out and ways in ... are constructed by ... mobile-phone ... use. This change ... means that ... I can walk here in the streets and simultaneously connect with other people ... far away ... I can be reached ... but also ... I can ... reach out ... to move and act in multiple spaces.

A reasonable objection to Bassett's thesis could be that older portable media, such as books, newspapers, and magazines, have also long enabled a sense of connection with elsewhere and yet, as she indicates, there is something historically novel about the current potential for two-way, virtually instantaneous communications with distant others and sites while physically on the move. What digital mobile media technologies offer is, in Bassett's words, "the possibility of remote intervention" (2003: 345).

To pursue that theme of technological and cultural change, and to conclude this section on the transformation of the street through movement, I want to turn next to another sympathetic critique of de Certeau's analysis, which is put forward by Thrift (2008: 75–88; see also Amin and Thrift 2002: 100–1). Although de Certeau (1984: 92) does briefly mention the "New York traffic" in his chapter on walking in the city, Thrift (2008: 75) points to "the practice of driving" as a notable absence in the social theorist's everyday-life studies, arguing for the need to address, alongside perambulatory movement, "the rise of automobility" with its own particular spatiality and its own set of desires and emotions. This geographer wonders whether it is perhaps because de Certeau takes pedestrian activities "as a sign of the human" (2008: 75) that he neglects driving in the city, implicitly regarding it as a technologically mediated mobility that is somehow less human than getting around on foot. For Thrift (2008: 80), however, driving involves "profoundly . . . sensuous experiences." It requires, for instance, the movement and touch of hands on steering wheels and gear sticks, as well as the coordinated movements of feet in operating accelerator, brake, and clutch pedals, and there is, therefore, no reason to exclude it as an example of what de Certeau thinks of, in other contexts, as meaningful, skillful bodily doings. Certainly, as Thrift (2008: 81) acknowledges, the practice of driving constitutes a human–technological hybrid, in which "drivers experience cars as extensions of their bodies," and yet there is a blurring of boundaries, too, between the body and "the technology of footwear . . . boots and shoes" (Ingold 2011: 37) in practices of walking.

Just as the pedestrians in de Certeau's analysis make imaginative shortcuts and detours, so Thrift (2008: 81–2) is interested in such creative manipulations of planned urban space as one element of the everyday doings of drivers. While it is important to understand that walking and driving, and their respective transformations of the street, are frequently in tension or friction with each other, both practices are bound up with processes of urban habitation or dwelling. In the case of driving, "cars . . . inhabit the road" (Amin and Thrift 2002: 101) but they have also become habitable spaces "in themselves," for passengers as well as drivers, partly through the use of media and information technologies including "in-car . . . sound . . . and even video . . . systems" (Thrift 2008: 84–5; see Bull 2001).

Ways of the Hand

I mentioned above, in the preceding discussion of Thrift's account of driving in the city, the movement and touch of hands on steering wheels and gear sticks. In this section of my chapter, I now want to return to Amin and Thrift's related reference to hands picking their way across keyboards (see Amin and Thrift 2002: 86), seeking to develop what they say there in passing. Since those geographers go on to write of clicking on mouse devices, I assume that they must have been thinking specifically of everyday practices of computer keyboard use, and of course, such picking or clicking has been joined, after the publication of their book on cities in the early 2000s, by the deft sliding and tapping of fingers on touchscreens of various sorts, which have become common, taken-for-granted movements in urban quotidian cultures. Before I get to the matter of skilled, mobile hands in the uses of new media technologies, though, it would be helpful for me to reflect on the relevance of previous academic work on keyboards and manual activity.

Phenomenological philosopher Maurice Merleau-Ponty (2002 [1962]: 164–9), in the context of a fascinating set of observations on "the acquisition of habit," including a passage on "the habit of driving a car," offers two examples that feature keyboard users, namely "the typist" and "the organist." Let me discuss each of these in turn.

In the case of typing on a mechanical typewriter, which might be seen, at least in some ways, as a "more muscular . . . forerunner of" (Tomlinson 2007: 109) contemporary computer keyboard use, Merleau-Ponty (2002 [1962]: 166) notes that: "It is possible to know how to type without being able to say where the letters . . . are to be found on the banks of keys." This is precisely because the kind of knowing involved in the practice of typing is an integrated, pre-reflective knowledge in movement, "a knowledge bred of familiarity . . . knowledge in the hands, which is forthcoming . . . when bodily effort is made" (Merleau-Ponty 2002 [1962]: 166). The typist's fast-moving fingers or digits know as they go, and the complex hand movements are, rather like the footsteps of the walkers in de Certeau's work on the city, other to representations.

Similarly, in Merleau-Ponty's account of an experienced organist who, in preparation for a musical performance, is faced with an instrument which is not the one "he is used to playing" (2002 [1962]: 168), the philosopher asks: "Are we to maintain that the organist analyses the organ, that he conjures up and retains a representation of the stops, pedals and manuals and their relation to each other?" Merleau-Ponty (2002 [1962]: 168) provides the following answer:

> During the . . . rehearsal preceding the concert, he does not act like a person about to draw up a plan. He sits on the seat, pulls out the stops, gets the measure of the instrument with his body, incorporates . . . the relevant directions and dimensions, settles into the organ as one settles into a house.

Three things need to be stressed here, with regard to this particular example. First, as Merleau-Ponty himself is at pains to stress, the musician has no map-like mental plan of the instrument, which is then operationalized in the concert performance. Secondly, it seems to me that the philosopher's main purpose, in introducing the quite unusual case of organ playing, is to make a point about the adaptability or generative capacity of the performer's practical, sensuous, tactile engagement with the technology. Merleau-Ponty (2002 [1962]: 169) realizes that routine, habitual practices are caught up with the formation of "stable dispositional tendencies," and yet the example of the organist is employed to show how acquired bodily dispositions also have a significant degree of flexibility and a certain improvisational quality. Indeed, a further link between Merleau-Ponty's philosophy and de Certeau's social theory can be made at this juncture, given the latter's interest, too, in the improvisatory aspects of everyday acts. Lastly, and crucially from my perspective, in comparing the process of finding ways about on the instrument with that of settling into a house, Merleau-Ponty's words suggest a strong connection between matters of orientation and habitation, which is the central theme of my chapter and one that I will continue to explore below.

Other relevant literature on manual activity includes a remarkable book by sociologist David Sudnow (2001), which tells the story of his learning to play jazz on the piano, and which was directly influenced by Merleau-Ponty's observations on habit acquisition, keyboard use, and knowledgeable hands. At the outset, then, Sudnow (2001: 12) recalls the "substantial initial awkwardness" of his "beginning pianist" hands, and how he gradually developed "an embodied way of accomplishing distance" (2001: 15) in his early dealings with the keyboard, handling chords and playing chord progressions competently. In Merleau-Ponty's terms, Sudnow was starting to get the measure of the instrument with his body.

At a later stage in Sudnow's narrative, he goes on to describe the considerable difficulties he faced in figuring out how to do jazz improvisation, noting his puzzlement on witnessing the "interweaving intricacies" (2001: 28) of his piano teacher's hand movements. After a lengthy period of frustration, though, Sudnow (2001: 51–2, 55) reports that:

> A hand was developing that was possessed of mobile ways . . . generative ways of knowing how to be at home in a setting of keys . . . a hand that had its bearings . . . a hand at home on the keyboard . . . able to do all sorts of things.

These things included the emergence of "up-a-little-down-a-little ways, rocking ways and every-other-finger ways . . . skipping ways, hopping ways, rippling ways . . . and more" (Sudnow 2001: 59). Sudnow's hands were becoming "wayfully oriented" (2001: 69), until eventually "the hand knew its ways" (2001: 114). "My hands make it up as they go along" (2001: 125), he writes.

Sudnow (2001: 125–7) concludes that it is this going along or journeying "in a terrain nexus of hands and keyboard . . . over myriad varieties of paths" that has enabled him to feel at home there, and he refers explicitly to pianists' relationships to their instruments as a dwelling. The keyboard space comes to be experienced, in the practice of playing or the creative manipulation of that space, as familiar place, filled with meaning and emotion. It is inhabited as the relevant directions and dimensions are incorporated, as the hand gets its bearings and is able to "reach for the music" (Dreyfus 2001: x). To borrow the words from the title of Sudnow's book, *ways of the hand* are established over time.

Improvising jazz on the piano is, as Sudnow (2001: 2) states right at the beginning of that book, "an extraordinary domain of action," a rare skill, but, following in Merleau-Ponty's footsteps, he nevertheless wants his detailed descriptions of keyboard use to serve as a model "for the closer study of the body and its works in general." Indeed, in the book's foreword, philosopher Hubert Dreyfus (2001: ix) encourages readers to regard the description and analysis of piano playing there as "a phenomenology of how we come to find our way about in the world . . . of how our bodies gain their grasp of the world." It is a case study of the kind of habitation processes that are evident, too, in those ordinary arts of doing which feature in de Certeau's writing on the city and the everyday.

I wonder if it might be possible, by drawing on such previous approaches to manual activity, and on the views of pedestrian movement and automobility discussed earlier in my chapter, to imagine future investigations of media use in urban contexts that could focus on wayfully oriented practices and on the inhabiting of environments or the weaving of a fabric of lived space? Investigations of this type would benefit from the adoption of Sudnow's descriptive method, and, in fact, he is the author of another remarkable book (Sudnow 1983) that tells the story of his learning to play basic video games many years ago. While the descriptions of hand movement in that study are not so detailed, he does refer promisingly to how his fingers gained an "electronically enhanced . . . territory for action" (1983: 22) and to how "hands now create sights" (1983: 24) on the screen. Gaming, rather like the practice of driving in the city that interests Thrift, constitutes a human-technological hybrid.

As I have argued elsewhere, it is now necessary for media studies to assert "the primacy of practice or movement" (Moores 2018: x), thereby questioning "particular foundational positions" in the field, inherited from old structuralist-semiotic influences, "where there has been a tendency . . . to make assumptions about the primacy of representation." My non-media-centric perspective, with its non-representational theoretical emphasis, involves a strong commitment not only to the de-centering of media, "so as to understand better the ways in which media . . . and everyday life are interwoven with each other" (Morley 2007: 200), but also as an important aspect of that shift to the exploration of *habitation as lineal*.

Of course, as David Morley (2007: 1) acknowledges when he first calls for "a non-media-centric analytical framework," it is important to remember that media have their own specific affordances, their "particularities," which distinguish them from a range of other technologies in quotidian cultures. For example, a piano and a smartphone or tablet computer clearly have different capacities for their users, and one of the distinctive characteristics of contemporary mobile media is that facilitation of live dialogue and remote intervention while on the move, mentioned above in my brief account of Bassett's work. I accepted there that the transformation of city streets today has to do partly with the ability of digital mobile media users to be reached from, and to reach out beyond, an immediate physical setting.

Conclusion: Habitation as Lineal

The challenge for non-media-centric media studies or for everyday-life studies that are inspired by non-representational theories broadly conceived, including by phenomenological approaches in geography, philosophy, and sociology, is to hold together, within a common analytical framework, several dimensions of movement and dwelling or placemaking that are often simultaneously in play. In digital mobile media use, for instance, there can be a wandering on foot and an inhabiting of urban environments, the gripping and skilled manipulating of a new media technology with which the hands and fingers have come to feel at home, and corresponding lineal travel through a variety of online settings, some of which are experienced as thoroughly familiar while others are flexibly adapted to on the basis of previous "digital orientations" (Moores 2018). Although Ingold would be unlikely, I think, to concur with this conclusion, my sense is that those multiple interweaving intricacies, in cities of feet and hands, are best summed up in Ingoldian terms as a meshwork of the lines of wayfaring (see also Pink 2012).[2]

Notes

1 There is a further story to be told about phenomenological geography, alongside the one I have just outlined regarding its helpful conceptualizations of place and placemaking, and, although I do not have room to tell it at any length now, my feeling is that this other, more problematic aspect of the approach should at least be indicated. I am thinking of its assumptions to do with a growing "placelessness" (see especially Relph 2008 [1976]; Seamon 2015 [1979]: 91, 141–2) brought by modern communications, including mechanized transportation. Indeed, similarly pessimistic accounts of social and spatial change can be found elsewhere too, as in Joshua Meyrowitz's second-generation medium theory (Meyrowitz 1985), with its no-sense-of-place thesis, and in anthropologist Marc Augé's arguments (Augé 2009 [1995]) concerning what he calls "non-places." For readers wishing to pursue these debates about place and placelessness, I have previously offered detailed critical discussions of all the writings that are cited in this note (see Moores 2012; see also Chapters 35 and 36, this volume).
2 I say here that Tim Ingold would be unlikely to agree with this application of his concepts because he is another theorist who tends to take a pessimistic view of the consequences of contemporary media and information technologies. For Ingold (2007: 144), then, even the use of an old-fashioned mechanical typewriter is compared negatively with the practice of handwriting, since, in his words, the typist's fingers "dance on ... the keyboard, not on ... the page." See my fuller engagement with Ingold's non-representational theory (Moores 2015, 2018: 121–40).

References

Amin, A. and Thrift, N. (2002) *Cities: Reimagining the Urban*, Cambridge: Polity.
Augé, M. (2009 [1995]) *Non-Places*, London: Verso.
Bassett, C. (2003) "How Many Movements?", in M. Bull and L. Back (eds) *The Auditory Culture Reader*, Oxford: Berg, pp. 343–55.
Bull, M. (2001) "Soundscapes of the Car: A Critical Study of Automobile Habitation," in D. Miller (ed.) *Car Cultures*, Oxford: Berg, pp. 185–202.
de Certeau, M. (1984) *The Practice of Everyday Life*, Berkeley, CA: University of California Press.
—, Giard, L., and Mayol, P. (1998) *The Practice of Everyday Life, Volume 2: Living and Cooking*, Minneapolis, MN: University of Minnesota Press.
Dreyfus, H. (2001) "Foreword," in D. Sudnow, *Ways of the Hand: A Rewritten Account*, Cambridge, MA: MIT Press, pp. ix–xiii.
Hubbard, P. (2006) *City*, London: Routledge.
Ingold, T. (2000) *The Perception of the Environment: Essays on Livelihood, Dwelling and Skill*, London: Routledge.
— (2007) *Lines: A Brief History*, London: Routledge.
— (2011) *Being Alive: Essays on Movement, Knowledge and Description*, London: Routledge.
— (2015) *The Life of Lines*, London: Routledge.
Krajina, Z., Moores, S., and Morley, D. (2014) "Non-Media-Centric Media Studies: A Cross-Generational Conversation," *European Journal of Cultural Studies*, 17(6), pp. 682–700.
Merleau-Ponty, M. (2002 [1962]) *Phenomenology of Perception*, London: Routledge.

Meyrowitz, J. (1985) *No Sense of Place: The Impact of Electronic Media on Social Behavior*, New York: Oxford University Press.
Moores, S. (2012) *Media, Place and Mobility*, Basingstoke: Palgrave Macmillan.
— (2015) "We Find Our Way About: Everyday Media Use and 'Inhabitant Knowledge,'" *Mobilities*, 10(1), pp. 17–35.
— (2017) "For Everyday-Life Studies," in P. Adams, J. Cupples, K. Glynn, A. Jansson, and S. Moores, *Communications/Media/Geographies*, New York: Routledge, pp. 183–8.
— (2018) *Digital Orientations: Non-Media-Centric Media Studies and Non-Representational Theories of Practice*, New York: Peter Lang.
Morley, D. (2007) *Media, Modernity and Technology: The Geography of the New*, London: Routledge.
— (2009) "For a Materialist, Non-Media-Centric Media Studies," *Television and New Media*, 10(1), pp. 114–16.
Pink, S. (2012) *Situating Everyday Life: Practices and Places*, London: SAGE.
Relph, E. (2008 [1976]) *Place and Placelessness*, London: Pion.
Seamon, D. (1980) "Body-Subject, Time-Space Routines and Place-Ballets," in A. Buttimer and D. Seamon (eds) *The Human Experience of Space and Place*, London: Croom Helm, pp. 148–65.
— (2015 [1979]) *A Geography of the Lifeworld: Movement, Rest and Encounter*, London: Routledge.
Sudnow, D. (1983) *Pilgrim in the Microworld*, New York: Warner Books.
— (2001) *Ways of the Hand: A Rewritten Account*, Cambridge, MA: MIT Press.
Thrift, N. (1996) *Spatial Formations*, London: SAGE.
— (2008) *Non-Representational Theory: Space/Politics/Affect*, London: Routledge.
Tomlinson, J. (2007) *The Culture of Speed: The Coming of Immediacy*, London: SAGE.
Tonkiss, F. (2005) *Space, the City and Social Theory: Social Relations and Urban Forms*, Cambridge: Polity.
Tuan, Y. (1977) *Space and Place: The Perspective of Experience*, Minneapolis, MN: University of Minnesota Press.

Further Reading

Brown, E. and Shortell, T. (eds) (2016) *Walking in Cities: Quotidian Mobility as Urban Theory, Method, and Practice*, Philadelphia, PA: Temple University Press.
Ingold, T. and Vergunst, J. L. (eds) (2008) *Ways of Walking: Ethnography and Practice on Foot*, Aldershot: Ashgate.
McGinn, C. (2015) *Prehension: The Hand and the Emergence of Humanity*, Cambridge, MA: MIT Press.
Pink, S. et al. (2016) "Tactile Digital Ethnography: Researching Mobile Media Through the Hand," *Mobile Media and Communication*, 4(2), pp. 237–51.

11

SUBJECTIVITY IN THE MEDIA CITY

The Media Life and Representation of the Cosmopolitan Stranger

Myria Georgiou and Jun Yu

Introduction

This chapter focuses on constructions and imaginings of urban subjectivity in the media city. For increasing numbers of urban dwellers, everyday life is mediated life: many individuals depend on apps to navigate the city's spatial, cultural, and economic interfaces; urban sociality relies on social media networks; and imaginings of urban life are mediated by representations on smartphone and television screens (see also Chapters 5 and 35, this volume). The growing, but unequal, mediation of urban lives raises important questions about the ways urban subjects are constituted in and through the media: who and how is seen, heard, and recognized in the media city? The discussion in this chapter identifies "the stranger" as the par excellence subject of the media city, a city that is both cosmopolitan and deeply divided. As shown, the stranger of the media city has different incarnations, being produced through cosmopolitanism, othering, and flanerie. Strangeness, *flanerie*, and cosmopolitanism are anything but new dimensions of city life, as the seminal works of Simmel, Baudelaire, Benjamin, and Sennett remind us. Yet, as argued, they are reconfigured in the context of intense mediation. Learning from these works, the chapter examines how city life makes the stranger, but also how the media shape the different strangers' representations, subjectivities, and values.

The present analysis of urban subjectivity starts from a double premise. First, in the media city, the fundamentals of urban life—from the economy and finance to cultural production and consumption, education and policing—are largely organized and ordered through communication infrastructures. Second, the city is a space of convergent and coexisting differences, as it has always been: in the city, people live next to each other and constantly have to negotiate and compete with other strangers for access to physical and symbolic resources. As a permanent condition of urban life, difference is ever-present, but takes particular meanings through its mediation. With this double premise—mediation and difference—as starting point, the chapter delves into an exploration of the media city and its subjectivities.

The discussion offers a three-step analysis. It starts with a definition of the media city as the city that, more than any other, is lived, imagined, and represented through mediations of encounters on the street and on the screen. Second, it defines urban subjectivities in the media city as being conditioned to the immediate, yet mediated, experience of urban difference;

difference is the way to live and consume in the city. By outlining the most fundamental dimensions of subjectivity—strangeness, cosmopolitanism, *flanerie*—the discussion shows that in the media city, struggles for visibility, voice, and recognition are less about the divide between cosmopolitanism and parochialism, and increasingly about cosmopolitanism's internal and incorporated divides. The discussion concludes by highlighting the ethical challenges presented by the mediated hypervisibility of strangers in the media city.

The Media City as a Site of Mediation and Difference

The media city is shaped through many synergies between the media and all elements of urban life—cultural, economic, social, and political. This is the city that is recognized through its powerful representations in the media, such as cinematic screens, advertising, and tourism; it is also the city that is deeply connected internally and externally through communication infrastructures mediating interactions among individuals and between institutions and individuals. The media city is defined as much through its exchanges in global cultural markets as through everyday mediated experiences: the ways in which friends connect on social media and urban dwellers make and consume urban music and use apps to navigate desirable and undesirable places for leisure, work, and consumption.

The media city geography—with the likes of London, New York, and Los Angeles at the top of its global order, but also with Berlin, Mumbai, Hong Kong, and many more cities included in its architecture—is linked to regional and global systems of longstanding power. The media city's symbolic power is acquired through histories of imperialism and colonialism that privilege certain locations with investment and concentration of infrastructures and cultural industries (McQuire 2008; Georgiou 2013). Thus, as a location, it has long attracted newcomers, through waves of internal and cross-border migration associated with imperialism and globalization. While representing the ultimately connected and globally recognizable urban media location, the media city is not an exception, but rather an exemplification of the growing organization of urban life through mediated connections and representations. Infrastructures and forms of mediation are unequally distributed and controlled, but they demarcate who is seen, heard, and recognized in the urban world. Representing an exemplary case of connectivity and intense mediation, the media city constitutes a powerful example for studying how urban subjects see and hear each other through communication infrastructures, and how they are not only represented by the media, but also represent themselves in their everyday mediated lives on screens and streets. Paradoxically, media bring urban strangers closer together by, at the same time keeping them distant and apart.

This paradoxical negotiation of proximity and distance becomes apparent in the ways strangers are always present on screens, or in the ways social media increasingly organize the communication geography of the city. During a fieldwork interview, for example, an interviewee noted that he became friends with neighbors, not by meeting them on the street, but by encountering them on "Nextdoor"—the hyperlocal medium available to many urbanites across the USA, connecting them only to those in close proximity. In this case, like many others, strangers across the street become mentally proximate first through digital geography, and only secondarily through physical geography; their proximity becomes subject to the filtering that the media allow, or even enforce—to select, to block, to contain subjectivities and encounters. This condition raises a number of questions. What kind of encounters do media enable and restrict? What kinds of urban subjects do they bring closer and who do they keep at a distance? And do the media order the ways in which urban dwellers see each other as proximate, yet controlled, strangers?

These questions have long preoccupied social scientists, especially those lamenting the urban alienation and anomie resulting from technological change in the city. More recently, digital media have become a particular target of this critique. American sociologist Sudhir Venkatesh noted the absence of protests despite the much-bruited "populist rage" amid the financial crisis of the time in a *New York Times* article (2009):

> Our cities are no longer dense, overcrowded industrial centers where unionized laborers and disgruntled strikers might take a public stand . . . in today's cities, even when we share intimate spaces, we tend to be quite distant from one another . . . [T]hese days, technology separates us and makes more of our communication indirect, impersonal and emotionally flat. With headsets on and our hands busily texting, we are less aware of one another's behavior in public space. Count the number of people with cellphones and personal entertainment devices when you walk down a street. Self-involved bloggers, readers of niche news, all of us listening to our personal playlists: we narrowly miss each other.

Venkatesh identifies a contrast between the engaging urban encounters of the past and present encounters, which, as argued, are filtered through the self-absorbed mediation that mentally detaches and isolates urban dwellers from proximate others. Venkatesh's lamentation over the death of solidarity builds on a long tradition of critique of technological change, especially its brutal incorporation in neoliberal politics and economics (Sennett 1976, 2006; Zukin 1998, 2010). In much of this scholarship, urban dwellers' experience presents a critical domain for understanding how the city is lived and ordered. Directly or indirectly building on the ecological approach to the city by the Chicago School of Sociology (e.g., Wirth 1938; Park et al. 1967), such scholarship identifies communication as a core dimension of urban solidarity and community.

More particularly, the Chicago School of Sociology emphasized that the city is more than a static composition of infrastructures and institutions; rather, it is a system made through emotions, customs, and traditions—the people it hosts and constitutes. As Park et al. powerfully put it: "The city is not, in other words, merely a physical mechanism and an artificial construction. It is involved in the vital process of the people who compose it" (1967: 1). By putting urban subjectivities at the core of the analysis of the city, the Chicago School's ecological approach, alongside Simmel (1950a, 1950b), Baudelaire (1964), Benjamin (1973), and Jacobs (1964), sets the cornerstone for a humanist urban scholarship; within it, urban subjectivities are not mere outcomes of larger processes associated with capitalism and urbanization. Rather, large-scale processes, forms of sociality, and urban subjectivities are dialogically constituted (Zukin 2010).

In fact, it is in the process of gathering together and pushing apart different actors, objects, and discourses that urban dwellers put their mark on the city while, at the same time, being constituted through the same process. Massey (2005) emphasizes that the city is a place of "throwntogetherness"—a space where people who have different histories and trajectories come together, largely as a result of wider processes associated with global capitalism and migration. These are processes that turn the city into *a difference machine*, as Isin puts it:

> The city is a difference machine because groups are not formed outside the machine and encounter each within the city, but the city assembles, generates, distributes and differentiates these differences, incorporates them within strategies and technologies, and elicits, interpellates, adjures and incites them . . . Such differences are generated and assembled *in* and *through* the city.
>
> *(2007: 223; italics in original)*

Today, the strategies and technologies of making subjects and for orienting themselves toward or against others (Isin 2007) are increasingly mediated. For Lefebvre (1996), communication and information make the urban what it always has been: a "place of desire, permanent disequilibrium, seat of the dissolution of normalities and constraints, the moment of play and the unpredictable" (Lefebvre 1996: 129). Communication and information organized on media and in the media city order desire and playfulness as much as freedom and the "permanent disequilibrium" (Lefebvre 1996: 129) of urban inequalities. Not least, making the city desirable, sellable, and consumable as a site of unpredictability and openness turns it into a site where strangers might find a destination and where *flaneurs* might become exposed to endless stimulation. For example, as Massey (2007) notes in relation to London, certain world cities have a reputation that is not explained through economic activity alone. Symbolic forms, she argues (2007), produce and reproduce meanings of the place as unique and global; these symbolic forms include iconic media imagery of city skylines, cinematic plots emerging out from city life, as well as digital abundance of information on countless culinary, nightlife, and dating opportunities. Within these systems of mediation, urban difference, as reflected in cultural, ethnic, racial, and social diversity, is routed and re-routed through the media feeding into contemporary imaginings of the city. In the neoliberal context especially, (unthreatening) difference has become a valuable asset that can generate reputation and wealth, even if such symbolic and monetary benefits are far from equally distributed.

The ever-presence of difference that makes certain cities both desirable and intensely mediated is directly linked to the condition of cosmopolitanization, best captured by Beck (2009). Beck (2009) argues that most people experience the involuntary confrontation with others resulting from the erosion of clear borders separating markets, states, civilizations, cultures, and life-worlds: "This may influence human identity construction, which needs no longer to be shaped in opposition to others, as in the negative, confrontational dichotomy of 'we' and 'them'" (Beck 2009: xi-xii). In the media city, we can observe precisely those conditions of cosmopolitanization, not least in musical, cinematic, and culinary cultures. Cosmopolitanization is fundamental to understanding the ordinariness of encounters with difference in the city, beyond theorizations of cosmopolitanism as a strict set of moral norms. However, while useful in recording the ordinariness of encounters with difference, Beck's conceptualization still underestimates the persistent, and often growing, symbolic and material inequalities that come with cosmopolitanization and largely ignores the moral challenges it presents. Against Beck's analysis, which emphasizes reflexive individualism and the retreat of class antagonism within cosmopolitanization, the present discussion recognizes the conflicting incarnations of urban cosmopolitanism and the plurality of its moral trajectories (Georgiou 2017; Gilbert 2017). Thus, the discussion challenges the vision of urban dwellers' singular cosmopolitan vision and instead identifies the complex and antagonistic cosmopolitan subjects of the media city as strangers and as *flaneurs*.

Subjectivities of the Media City

Urban subjectivities in the media city are shaped within an overstimulating environment, where difference is always proximate but also commodified in the context of neoliberal circulation of symbolic and material cultural commodities. The celebration of difference in popular media culture, alongside the readiness of digital media tools to navigate new places and experiences, have largely normalized cultural and social diversity, making it less threatening and extraordinary. In fact, the mediation of difference in representations and experiences of the city has revived, expanded, and redefined the relevance of the ultimate subjectivity of modernity: "the stranger."

The urban strangers are constantly present and exposed to other strangers, as films, advertising, and popular culture reproduce their hypervisibility on the city's mediascapes and soundscapes. Such hypervisibility has turned the stranger into the ultimate urban icon: to be feared and to be desired. But strangers are more than a representation: they are urban subjects, the ultimate urban dwellers. As subjects of the media city, they represent an almost all-encompassing category: "strangers" refer to people who have different cultural, social, and geographical origins and trajectories, but who presently converge in the city and who have no choice but to live among other strangers. These are strangers who use the media to make their one's own stories of the city, successfully or unsuccessfully: from navigating its streets on apps and consuming the city on film, to making the city through sociality organized on social media. Strangers on screens and on streets remind us that the media city is simultaneously a representation, a lived place, and a space where struggles for voice and recognition remain unresolved. How do the strangers of the media city manage difference, and which strangers find recognition and which do not? Following an introduction to the concept of "the stranger," two different incarnations of this figure and their differential and hierarchical recognition in the media city are outlined below.

For Simmel, who originally put forward the concept of "the stranger," the city provides constant exposure to others and their diverse orientations and desires. In this intense environment, and in response to it, a particular mode of subjectivity emerges: the stranger (Simmel 1950b). Strangers are *tenuously* committed to each other through proper distance (Silverstone 2007), adopting what Simmel calls a *blasé* attitude of interaction (Simmel 1950a). Strangers are members of a social system, yet not strongly attached to that system, and therefore they can more easily deviate from its norms. In Simmel's words: "Distance means that he, who is close by, is far, and strangeness means that he, who is also far, is actually near" (Simmel 1950b: 402). Even though individuals often seem to insulate themselves from the city life and others, not least as lamented in critiques of mediated life discussed above, for Simmel, negotiation of proximity does not necessarily constitute alienation. Rather, the stranger has become a form of identity that needs to be considered in its own right. The *blasé* attitude symbolizes a withdrawal of emotional responses from social interactions and an emphasis on the dispassionate reason as a face presented to self and others (Gerlac and Hamilton 2004: 124). It is in this very reserve—the mutual strangeness of the metropolis—that Simmel finds the potential for personal freedom, independence, and creativity, and an opportunity to preserve individual personality (Jacobs 2002). It is also this same strangeness that constitutes cosmopolitan subjectivities, according to Sennett (1976). As Sennett argues in his early work, the structural conditions of modern urban life, in which people from different backgrounds mingle in a shared space, are in favor of cosmopolitanism, producing a cosmopolitan being with "a right to be left alone" (1976: 27)—the "perfect public man" (1976: 17).

Simmel's and Sennett's starting point assumes a somewhat ideal moment in early modernity, where urban dwellers managed the challenges of city life by sustaining proper distance. However, as Sennett (1976, 2006) admits, the urban stranger takes on a new meaning within the context of neoliberal capitalism and the rise of individualism, a condition whereby strangeness might become a valuable commodity, but not a value for recognition. Then, even though strangeness is a condition of urban modernity, some strangers have long enjoyed more freedom and independence and greater recognition than others. This longstanding differential and hierarchical order of/within strangeness in the city is analyzed further in other scholarly works. As critical urban scholarship has repeatedly argued, the figure of the stranger is deeply ordered. Alexander (2004) highlights that it is the representational construction by the society's core groups of difference, not commonality, that makes certain groups appear dangerous and strange. Indeed, the different incarnations of the stranger in the media—as desired or feared—reveal the discursive construction of strangeness. As Tonkiss (2005) notes, urban encounters with difference have been replaced by consumption of difference in neoliberal contexts, advancing distrust and alienation. This argument is echoed by Zukin, who notes that the material conditions, such as gentrification, set by powerful actors in the city—developers, bankers—delimit the possibilities of encounters that advance recognition of certain strangers (1989, 2010).

The hierarchical order of strangeness as an inherent characteristic of capitalist urban modernity is amplified in neoliberal contexts and in contexts of intense mediation in three ways. First, the abundance of representations of difference, on the street and on the screen, means that urban dwellers are constantly reminded of the presence of others. Second, the commodification of difference in a cultural economy of unprecedented scale means that certain voices are more widely heard, for example through music, fashion, and other forms of creativity. And third, the immediacy and simultaneity of mediated communication redefines relations of proximity and distance in the city: the stranger is never quite that far but, at the same time, she is always remote, as mediated filtering of encounters enhances proximity in the media, but increases physical distance in the material city. Resulting from these conditions, the stranger is always present and visible in the city. But do all strangers make the city in the same way? And do they all have the same kind of right to the city (Lefebvre 1968)? Two incarnations of the stranger in the media city—the subaltern stranger and the elite stranger—suggest otherwise.

Two Strangers: The Subaltern and the Elite

Migrants and ethnic minorities represent one kind of the ultimate urban stranger. More than any other urban subjects, they carry the city's histories of difference through travels and cultural practices that are both incorporated and marginalized in urban cultural life. These are the urban dwellers who make the city a home through strangeness; being outsiders but also insiders in their presence, they remind citizens and consumers of the inherent openness of the city. In the media city, this presence has expanded in two ways: through increased representations in film, television, and the press; and through migrants' and minorities' own use of digital media. Thus, it can be argued that the visible presence of migrants and ethnic minorities in media representations and on the street enhances their voice and their right to the city. Most prominently, this claim could be made in relation to music: urban music often comes from the city's margins and through minority subjects' own creative uses of digital technologies; the outcome of such creativity is then embraced by cultural industries and consumers. In this way, arguably, the ethnic minority stranger finds recognition as a creative and internal subject of the city; a subject that is made in the city and through its mediation.

Yet, and while heard and amplified in the media, these voices are usually heard under strict conditions; conditions that reaffirm their marginality and the safe distance between their urban experience and the experience of those who consume it. The migrant, minority strangers are more visible than ever in the media city, but when it comes to media representations almost always they appear to speak through exceptionality: urban music speaks of the hopeless or violent lives of the urban poor; televisual representations put those same subjects' marginality at the core of urban imaginaries—the cop, the drug dealer, the exceptionally moral subject who comes out of poverty to confirm her exceptionality, and the immorality and impurity of others around her. These representations strictly identify the limits of the minority stranger's voice, depriving the subaltern subject of the right to speak in different voices.

Ironically, in the case of the subaltern stranger, digital media uses become subject to the same dominant representational frames. While subaltern strangers use digital media in many different and complex ways, their uses, unlike those of the digital *flaneurs* discussed later, are often pathologized. The conditionality of the agentic digital user is evident in media and middle-class imaginaries that attribute labels such as "Blackberry rioters" and "chavs" (Leurs and Georgiou 2016) to subaltern digital media users. Such labels are constant reminders of the ordered strangeness that contests practices that do not conform to the commodification of difference (e.g., political protest, struggles against structural inequalities). Thus while the migrant, minority strangers might be interior to the city, their experiences and identities are often subject to frames that delimit them as exterior and often inferior (Levinas 1969) to the city's norms. While powerful and narrow media representations do not erase the diversity of media experiences among subaltern strangers, they play a fundamental role in creating powerful frames within which subaltern subjectivities are perceived, legitimized, or delegitimized in the city. Thus, as certain subaltern subjectivities find recognition (e.g., through creativity), others become misrecognized and invisible (e.g., through experience of deprivation). The commodification, normalization, and reaffirmation of certain kinds of strangeness acts as a performative form of power (Butler 2015). As certain forms of recognition become extended, others become unrecognizable and not worthy of recognition, argues Butler (2015): in a narrow set of representations of the stranger, she is left with membership without inclusion. On the other hand, it is the media city that opens up spaces for vernacular cosmopolitanism to be seen and to be heard, perhaps more than anywhere else. A condition that still begs the question is then: can the mediation of the ordinary go beyond the re-articulation of existing order? Can the media city open up spaces for the subaltern stranger to speak and be seen beyond Otherness?

Alongside the subaltern urban strangers who are *seen* but not necessarily *recognized*, there is a growing range of elite strangers whose experiences find recognition in the media city: most typically, the white male jetsetter torn by his rootlessness while enjoying the cosmopolitan urban lifestyle across borders; or, the socially and physically gifted white woman who moves across spaces and experiences, but who challenges the dominant moral order and societal expectations. These are mere examples of many incarnations of elite subjects, who, precisely by projecting a cosmopolitan strangeness, find voice in the media and become targeted as ideal consumers for many digital products. Elite urban subjects' cosmopolitanism is best captured in Hannerz's definition of cosmopolitanism: "an orientation, a willingness to engage with the Other . . . an intellectual and aesthetic stance toward divergent cultural experiences, a search of contrasts rather than uniformity" (1996: 103). A celebratory incorporation of strangeness, this subjectivity is enhanced in the media city, not least as it depends on a consumption-driven aesthetic (often referred to as aesthetic cosmopolitanism, Walkowitz 2006) and on (controlled) encounters with difference. This kind of cosmopolitanism becomes most evident in the digital practices of elite strangers. As for Simmel's ideal stranger, for the elite stranger, (digital) technologies sustain safe distance from others (who the elite stranger can choose to engage with or avoid, after having all relevant information at hand). But unlike the subaltern subjects whose strangeness is defined through alterity (which media stereotype through representations and selective celebration of digital agency), for elite urban subjects, strangeness is freedom. Like Baudelaire's curious explorer and Benjamin's reflexive explorer, the elite stranger is also a digital *flaneur*.

The convergence of the stranger and the *flaneur* is a consequence of mediated lives. In its original articulation, the subjectivity of the *flaneur* was oppositional to the stranger. Simmel's stranger withdraws from others, while the *flaneur* is drawn to others' differences. The *flaneur* was an observer in the crowd for Baudelaire (1964), and a reflexive and engaged explorer of city life for Benjamin (1973). In the media city, the *flaneur* returns as an explorer and an observer equipped with digital tools and digital capital to navigate locations old and new as a curious, aware, and cosmopolitan subject. In the media city and in the experience of the elite subject, the identity of the stranger and the *flaneur* amalgamate, creating a paradoxical relation of distance and proximity. While desiring to consume others' "strange" media and cultural products, not least music, cinema, and culinary cultures, elite strangers use sophisticated systems of communication—apps, CCTV, exclusive social networks that are digitally organized—to keep "undesired strangers" away (see also Chapter 18, this volume). Thus, the *flaneurs* are not just any kind of digital users. They are the users who are equipped with symbolic and material tools to manage proximity and distance playfully, but not necessarily responsibly toward other strangers. They are the strangers who reflect most vividly the urban formulation of neoliberal subjectivity: the individualistic subjects affectively experiencing the city as observers and as consumers, well equipped with technologies and knowledge of navigation, to playfully and eagerly negotiate the city's openness and unpredictability.

In playfully negotiating proximity and distance from other strangers, elite strangers remind us of some of the fundamental challenges of urban life, as already identified by Simmel (1950b) and Sennett (1976): as both Simmel and Sennett emphasized, tenuous commitment and proper distance between strangers set the conditions for freedom and cosmopolitanism in the city. If the media, which elite strangers enjoy and consume constantly and playfully, challenge proper distance (Silverstone 2007), what commitment and what ethics are at stake?

Conclusions: The Ethical Predicament of the Media City

As this chapter has shown, the contemporary challenges to urban subjectivity emerge partially with media increasingly setting conditions for strangers' appearance and voice in the media city. For elite strangers—who are often targeted as ideal consumers in the cosmopolitan media city, and who are also capable of taking advantage of digital media products—strangeness is often a quality for reflexively navigating the media city while keeping undesired strangeness apart. Conversely, within the enhanced yet selective visibility and proximity mediated by the contemporary communication infrastructures and media representations, subaltern strangers often lose their voice; their recognition becomes strictly delimited and contained, or, at best, hinges on the way they are represented on media, even though it is paradoxically the presented difference of subaltern strangers that contributes to making the media city a space of lived cosmopolitanism.

From this vantage point, it becomes clear that the question for the media city at stake—whether the city allows for voice, recognition, and proper distance between individuals within the context of its apparent cosmopolitan nature—concerns not only the immediate *and* mediated presence of the stranger. It also (and perhaps more importantly) concerns the ethics of media in terms of not only what media represent, but also more fundamentally how media can allow for the possibility of being recognized. Paraphrasing Lefebvre, this is the ethics that can address an equitable "right to the media city." Or, as Silverstone puts it, to share the space of the mediapolis with "all parties accepting the obligation to open their space to the stranger irrespective of their position in the media hierarchy" (2007: 143). This is a major challenge urban subjects are presented with—the need to not only accept the commodified co-presence with other strangers, but also to build the conditions of mutual responsibility in the media city.

Returning to the starting point of this chapter, the hypervisibility and overrepresentation of strangers on the media city's streets and screens, in conjunction with the media representations of the city, have generated conditions for imagining and living the city as a cosmopolitan space—a city made by and of strangers who live next to each other and who acknowledge each other's presence. These conditions bring to life both opportunities and challenges for shaping cities that are both diverse and inclusive, and relate to narrating the story of the city through its long history of alterity. But there have also emerged new challenges, with strangeness taking a new contour within transition to the media city in which urban dwellers' experiences and subjectivity are increasingly mediated and managed by media. It is hoped that this chapter contributes to comprehending today's media city as a site of mediation and difference, marked by an ordered form of cosmopolitanism, while opening up further debates on the media ethics that are essential for discussing the right of urban strangers to the media city.

References

Alexander, J. (2004) "Rethinking Strangeness," *Thesis Eleven*, 79(1), pp. 87–104.
Baudelaire, C. (1964) *The Painter of Modern Life and Other Essays*, London: Phaidon.
Beck, U. (2009) "Foreword," in M. Nowicka and M. Rovisco (eds.) *Cosmopolitanism in Practice*, Farnham: Ashgate, pp. xi–xiii.
Benjamin, W. (1973) *Charles Baudelaire*, London: Verso.
Butler, J. (2015) *Notes Toward a Performative Theory of Assembly*, Cambridge, MA: Harvard University Press.
Georgiou, M. (2013) *Media and the City*, Cambridge: Polity.
— (2017) "Is London Open? Mediating and Ordering Cosmopolitanism in Crisis," *International Communication Gazette*, 79(6–7), pp. 636–655.
Gerlac, N. and Hamilton, S. (2004) "Preserving Self in the City of the Imagination," *Canadian Review of American Studies*, 34(2), pp. 115–134.
Gilbert, J. (2017) "The Crisis of Cosmopolitanism", *Stuart Hall Foundation*, http://stuarthallfoundation.org/library/the-crisis-of-cosmopolitanism.
Hannerz, U. (1996) *Transnational Connections*, London: Routledge.
Isin, E. (2007) "City. State," *Citizenship Studies*, 11(2), pp. 211–228.
Jacobs, J. (1964) *The Death and Life of Great American Cities*, Harmondsworth: Penguin.
Jacobs, K. (2002) "Subjectivity and the Transformation of Urban Spatial Experience," *Housing, Theory and Society*, 19(2), pp. 102–111.
Lefebvre, H. (1968) *The Right to the City*, Oxford: Blackwell.
— (1996) *Writings on Cities*, Oxford: Blackwell.
Leurs, K. and Georgiou, M. (2016) "Digital Makings of the City? Young People's Imaginaries of London," *International Journal of Communication*, 10, pp. 3689–3709.
Levinas, E. (1969) *Totality and Infinity*, Pittsburgh, PA: Duquesne University Press.
Massey, D. (2005) *For Space*, London: SAGE.
— (2007) *World City*, Cambridge: Polity.
McQuire, S. (2008) *The Media City*, London: SAGE.
Park, R., Burgess, E., and McKenzie, R. (1967) *The City*, Chicago, IL: University of Chicago Press.
Sennett, R. (1976) *The Fall of Public Man*, Cambridge: Cambridge University Press.
— (2006) *The Culture of the New Capitalism*, New Haven, CT: Yale University Press.
Silverstone, R. (2003) "Proper Distance: Toward an Ethics for Cyberspace," in G. Liestol, A. Morrison, and R. Terje (eds.) *Digital Media Revisited*, Cambridge, MA: MIT Press, pp. 469–490.
— (2007) *Media and Morality*, Cambridge: Polity.
Simmel, G. (1950a) "The Metropolis and Modern Life," in K. Wolff (ed.) *The Sociology of Georg Simmel*, New York: Free Press, pp. 409–424.
— (1950b) "The Stranger," in K. Wolff (ed.) *The Sociology of Georg Simmel*, New York: Free Press, pp. 402–408.
Tonkiss, F. (2005) *Space, the City and Social Theory*, Cambridge: Polity.
Venkatesh, S. (2009) "Feeling Too Down to Rise Up," *New York Times*, March 28, www.nytimes.com/2009/03/29/opinion/29venkatesh.html?mcubz=1.
Walkowitz, R. (2006) *Cosmopolitan Style*, New York: Columbia University Press.
Wirth, L. (1938) "Urbanism as a Way of Life," *American Journal of Sociology*, 44(1), pp. 1–24.
Zukin, S. (1989) *Loft Living*, New Brunswick, NJ: Rutgers University Press.
— (1998) "Urban Lifestyles," *Urban Studies*, 35(5–6), pp. 825–839.
— (2010) *Naked City*, Oxford: Oxford University Press.

Further Reading

McQuire, S. (2016) *Networked Cities and the Future of Public Space*, Cambridge: Polity Press.
Simmel, G. (1950) "The Stranger," in K. Wolff (ed.) *The Sociology of Georg Simmel*, New York: Free Press, pp. 402–408.
Trimikliniotis, N., Pasnanoglou, D., and Tsianos, V. S. (2015) *Mobile Commons, Migrant Digitalities and the Right to the City*, Basingstoke: Palgrave.

# PART II

Media as Urban Infrastructure; City Spaces as Media

INTRODUCTION TO PART II
Media as Urban Infrastructure; City Spaces as Media

Deborah Stevenson and Zlatan Krajina

It is difficult to exaggerate the centrality of the urban for thinking about a wide array of issues. As Bell and Haddour (2000: 1) put it, "'(t)he city' has come to be a symbol—maybe even a symptom—of almost every social and cultural process". Or, in Bauman's words, "city and social change are almost synonymous" (2003: 5). In probing the interlinking of the media, communication and the city as dialogical sites of change, a key task of this collection has been to examine the extent to which cities are not simply inert conduits for the flow of information, or sites within which media and communication forms and practices are located. Rather, city spaces, including urban parks, roadways and public squares, are themselves a dynamic medium of, and channel for, communication. At the same time, many procedures, technologies and practices of communication, from traffic monitoring to the lighting of public space, are forms of urban infrastructure. There is also overlap in ways of thinking about and knowing the media and the urban, with theories of both now routinely engaging with, and seeking to explain, this entanglement and its consequences (Matsaganis et al. 2013; Ridell and Zeller 2013). These themes, connections and possibilities are the focus of the chapters in this Part of the book, which begins with Shannon Mattern's exploration of city-as-computer scenarios. A central concern for Mattern is first to trace powerful narratives that understand the city through computing metaphors that are detached from lived urban experience and subjectivity. Mattern challenges this view, arguing that planning, building and knowing cities require more than computation. Drawing from diverse urban contexts, including contemporary New York and the renaissance Florence, Mattern shows that cities must encompass and engage with the complex and diverse intelligences embedded in cities and urban space. The concerns traversed by Vjeran Pavlaković and Gruia Bădescu in their chapter are a long way from metaphors of the city as computer; nevertheless, a theme in common is the enshrining of knowledge and experience, in this case those of the past, in the built form of the city. Pavlaković and Bădescu point to the role of place names, monuments and memorial sites in particular in transmitting powerful ideologies of the nation. As repositories of officially sanctioned memory, exemplified by an array of cases, and particularly Vukovar, Astana and Washington DC, the chapter demonstrates that the spaces of cities are shaped and reshaped by military defeat and victory, by national myths and political ambition. Pavlaković and Bădescu conclude the chapter by posing the question of whether the nationalist appropriation of public space may be challenged by the emergence of landscapes of consumption and cosmopolitanism, which, they suggest, eschew grand political narratives and speak instead to themes of affluence, fragmentation and the moment.

As the city of the day becomes the city of the night, the familiar spaces of work and leisure take on very different forms and functions. Spaces that may be vibrant and safe by day become abandoned and forbidding as the light moves from the "natural" to the "artificial" and street lighting demarcates the spaces of fear and desire from spaces of withdrawal and safety. In examining such issues and their antecedents, Robert Shaw suggests in Chapter 14 that it is possible to understand the history of the artificially lit city through "three key moments": the night spectacle produced by the introduction of gas and electric lighting; the emergence of the discourses of fear and safety associated with the presence and absence of urban illumination, alongside the acceptance of urban light as mundane; and third, the new lighting technologies that are creating new urban challenges including those associated with pollution, climate change and inequities of access to illumination. Tracing the institutionalization of artificial light across several dozen cities across the globe, Shaw demonstrates that urban illumination is best understood as simultaneously social, urban and environmental, a form of infrastructure inseparable from the ways in which city space is formed, lived and imagined. Just as the elevator propelled the development of skyscrapers, which underpinned the presence of many citizens in city centers, technologies such as the telephone helped businesses spread across the city and beyond niche quarters (De Sola Pool 1981). Ways in which the social and the technological combine to produce the urban are also a focus of Aaron Shapiro's chapter which is concerned with geographical and historical interconnections between telecommunication and transportation infrastructure. The chapter explores these concerns through a consideration of house numbering and street addresses (proxies, he says, for race and socio-economic status), utilities poles, telecommunication cables and radio dispatch (a technology that is implicated in the "logistical coordination" that maintains the spatial boundaries between privilege and exclusion).

From the very local and the urban space of infrastructure, the book then moves to the global, but it does this not via a traditional examination of global cities and their role as infrastructural hubs for global networks of information, financial capital and elites, but by commencing from the premise that it is necessary to understand all cities as formed through the often contradictory forces of the local and the global (see also Burdett and Sudjic 2011). In prosecuting this argument in Chapter 16, Paul James problematizes the view that global cities are a 20th-century phenomenon pointing to the impact on cities over time of various and changing modes of communications. The media, he says, both mediates and communicates; it brings people together as it abstracts social relations across time and space. Perhaps the space where social relations are at their most personal and immediate is the space of the home, which is also a space, and a set of gender and interpersonal relations, that are being reshaped and often reinforced through a complex of media forms and engagements. Not only are houses, as Chris Chesher and Justine Humphry point out in Chapter 17, physically organized to support the consumption of media, but they are also integral elements of the "fabric and constitution" of the increasingly mediated city. The authors focus their discussion on the phenomenon of the smart house, suggesting that it is (remains) a highly masculinized digital space which is both permeated and protected by forms of media, including robotics. From the comfort of their lounge rooms and often via their smart televisions, people now surveil their homes and barricade themselves electronically from external threats both real and imagined. As Bauman (2003: 33) reminds us, any city "prompts *mixophilia*"—that is, inclination to interact with strangers—"as much as, and simultaneously with, *mixophobia*" or fear of the other, which leads him to emphasize that "(c)ity life is an intrinsically and irreparably *ambivalent* affair". Indeed, Roy Coleman argues in Chapter 18 that public and private surveillance has become an/the "urban way of life". Coleman traces contemporary practices and technologies of surveillance and the "mediated" city, from their roots in the cities of the 19th century with their links to significant social, economic and political as well as urban change and the associated struggles. He makes the very important point that technology is never neutral. Rather it is deeply embedded in, and articulates, cities, as well as structuring the particular ways (usually stereotypical) in which people, groups of citizens, are viewed. At the same time, however, technology can provide alternative ways of seeing, and disrupt established discourses and structures of power. Coleman concludes with a challenge, which is to imagine the ways in which alternative forms of surveillance might contribute to social change and the rethinking and reshaping of cities.

The intersection of urban media and social change is the focus of Chapter 19 where Naomi Schiller provides a compelling account of the ways in which people in the cities of the Global South use media to effect social change. The starting point for Schiller is the premise that media—as a form of infrastructure—is fundamental to the organization and governance of cities. In other words, Schiller, like other contributors to this collection, is keen to stress that media technology is embedded in, and must be understood in terms of, the social, and as central to the struggles of urban life. She explores these issues and interconnections through an examination of community media in Caracas, Venezuela, highlighting how what she describes as "intertwining infrastructures" are negotiated and engaged with "in ways that allow people to cope, oppress, struggle, and make meaning". A central theme again is struggle—the struggle to manage and influence change (both urban and social); the struggle over meaning; the struggles of those who lack power. Struggle is also explored in Matteo Tarantino's chapter but this time the focus is the struggle associated with communicating the environmental risks of urban pollution to city dwellers (see also Hjorth et al. 2016).

With a focus on air pollution, Tarantino approaches his subject matter from three directions: the impact of pollution on cities; the forms of pollution that are communicated to citizens including the role of media discourse in defining pollutants; and finally, he traces how the communicated information is received. A key argument is that with increasing information about pollution, those with the resources to do so will choose to live in areas where the pollution levels are low. Of course, class-based urban segregation is not new—poorer residential areas have long been located close to polluting industries and major transport thoroughfares (Savage, Warde and Ward 2002); what is new is the role of the urban environmental media, such as smartphone apps, in providing fine-grained information on pollution at levels that were not available when the key indicators were the senses. Not only does digital and networked technology facilitate greater access to information about a local area and its environmental conditions, but it is also providing people with important platforms through which to participate in, or influence, the governance of their city or locality. It can, for instance, be a space for responding to environmental issues in ways that promote change. Governments, too, are increasingly seeking to use media technology as a tool for civic participation and "e-governance" as well as to gain information about the city and, by extension, to manage resources and services. These are complex relationships and, as Kristin Erickson argues in Chapter 21, all digital platforms produce pitfalls and challenges as well as participatory possibilities. Rather than opening up channels for dialogue and communication as a virtual public sphere, the outcome can be misinformation and ideological fragmentation. The rise of contemporary forms of populist nationalism can, the chapter argues, be linked very directly to social media and the siloing of ideas and political discourse.

Having tracked the media, communication and/as urban infrastructure from computing to governance, the starting point for the final chapter in this Part of the book is the intersection of urban planning and city visioning. Sarah Barns identifies key moments when innovations in media technologies have created the circumstances for the transformation of urban design, planning and management, and been influential in informing new ways of knowing and imagining the city. Utopian visions of the city permeate the history of urban planning (Harvey 2000). From the order, cleanliness and abundance of nature that are features of Thomas More's vision of the ideal city, to the dream of the Garden City that was influential in the formation of the town planning movement in Britain, to the new urban visions informed by the computational intensification of the city, techniques of imagination and visualization have long influenced the way in which cities are built and rebuilt. As Barns points out, with each technological innovation come new ways of seeing and knowing the city. Not all of these, however, have improved the urban condition or created new (emancipatory) possibilities for urban life.

References

Bauman, Z. (2003) *City of Fears, City of Hopes*, London: Goldsmiths College.
Bell, D. and Haddour, A. (2000) "What we talk about when we talk about the city", in Bell, D. and Haddour, A. (eds.) *City Visions*, Harlow: Pearson Education, pp. 1–11.
Burdett, R. and Sudjic, D. (eds.) (2011) *Living in the Endless City*, London: Phaidon.
De Sola Pool, I. (1981) *The Social Impact of the Telephone*, Cambridge, MA: MIT Press.
Harvey, D. (2000) *Spaces of Hope*, Edinburgh: Edinburgh University Press.
Hjorth, L., Pink, S., Sharp, K. and Williams, L. (2016) *Screen Ecologies: Art, Media, and the Environment in the Asia-Pacific Region*, Cambridge, MA and London: MIT Press.
Matsaganis, M. D., Gallagher, V. J. and Drucker, S. J. (eds.) (2013) *Communicative Cities in the 21st Century: The Urban Communication Reader III*, London: Peter Lang.
Ridell, S. and Zeller, F. (2013) "Mediated urbanism: Navigating an interdisciplinary terrain", *International Communication Gazette*, 75(5–6), pp. 437–451.
Savage, M., Warde, A. and Ward, K. (2002) *Urban Sociology, Capitalism and Modernity* (Second Edition), Houndmills, UK: Macmillan.

12

THE CITY IS NOT A COMPUTER

On Museums, Libraries, and Archives

Shannon Mattern

Introduction

Y Combinator, the formidable tech accelerator, has launched a thousand tech startups, from Airbnb and Dropbox to robotic greenhouses and wine-by-the-glass delivery services. In summer 2016, it announced a new research agenda: building cities from scratch (Cheung and Altman 2016). Cities, after all, were not so different from the company's other technical ventures. "There's no shortage of space to build new cities," project co-leader Ben Huh (2016) effervesced, and "technology can seed fertile starting conditions across nations and geographies." Huh aimed to "create an open, repeatable system for rapid *cityforming* that maximize[s] human potential."

Meanwhile, Alphabet (formerly Google) had begun moving forward with plans to build its own optimized cities (see Brown 2016; Mattern 2016c; Weinberg 2016). Its urban-tech division, Sidewalk Labs, had installed public Wi-Fi kiosks on New York City streets; these infrastructural nodes (known as "Links") may someday exchange data with autonomous vehicles, public transit, and other urban systems (see also Chapter 15, this volume). The company was also partnering with the US Department of Transportation on efforts like the "Smart City Challenge," and implementing Flow, its transportation data analytics platform, in several other cities (Transportation for America 2016). Revealing much greater ambitions, Dan Doctoroff (2016), the Michael Bloomberg associate who founded Sidewalk Labs, wondered: "What would a city look like if you started from scratch in the Internet era—if you built a city 'from the Internet up'?" In November 2016, the company took another step in that direction, launching four new "labs" that would work on housing affordability, healthcare and social services, municipal processes, and community collaboration. The company planned to run pilot projects in select urban districts, then scale up and, ultimately, "accelerate the process of urban innovation" (Doctoroff 2016).

Unlike their Industrial Age predecessors, who assembled "company towns" around their manufacturing operations, today's tech titans rarely have the luxury of building on a blank slate (Green 2010). Yet companies such as Alphabet and Uber have dramatically reshaped the cities where their boardrooms and research labs reside (Hollister 2014; Cagle 2015; Morris-Lent 2015; Kang 2017). And elsewhere in the world, particularly in Asia and the Middle East, Cisco, Siemens, and IBM have partnered with real estate developers and governments to build "smart cities" *tabula rasa*. Their marketing materials portray an urban future in which embedded sensors, ubiquitous cameras and beacons, networked smartphones, and the operating systems that link them all together will produce unprecedented efficiency, connectivity, and social harmony.

These various developments aim to transform the idealized topology of the open web and Internet of Things into urban form. They liken urban planning to tech development, and the city itself to an information processor. Programmer and tech writer Paul McFedries (2014: 36) explains this thinking:

> The city is a computer, the streetscape is the interface, you are the cursor, and your smartphone is the input device. This is the user-based, bottom-up version of the city-as-computer idea, but there's also a top-down version, which is systems-based. It looks at urban systems such as transit, garbage, and water and wonders whether the city could be more efficient and better organized if these systems were "smart."

What becomes of urban experience when our subjectivity is reduced to that of a cursor? Do all urban systems lend themselves to efficiency-oriented programming? What urban "input" cannot be filtered through a smartphone?

In this chapter, I will explore the longevity and limitations of such city-as-computer scenarios. While McFedries spins his tale around contemporary technical references, and Sidewalk Labs's and Y Combinator's visions reveal their origins in an age of big data and cloud computing, these algorithmic dreams are rooted in earlier reveries. I begin by tracing the history of urban metaphors, particularly that of the city-as-information-processor. Then, moving beyond "information" and its "processing" in creating more generous, inclusive maps of urban information ecologies, I look to other sites and collections—archives, libraries, museums, and repertoires of embodied culture—where urban intelligence is generated, organized, preserved, distributed, and activated. Finally, I reassess the power of these urban metaphors to condition urban design, planning, and administration, and consider alternative epistemological models that are better equipped to encompass the breadth of intelligences embodied in cities.

A History of Informatic Metaphors

Ever since the Internet was little more than a few linked nodes, urbanists, technologists, and sci-fi writers have envisioned cybercities and e-topias built "from the 'net up'" (Gibson 1984; Castells 1989; Mitchell 1995; Boyer 1996). Modernist designers and futurists saw morphological parallels between urban forms and circuit boards. Just as new modes of telecommunication have always reshaped physical terrains and political economies, new computational methods have informed urban planning, modeling, and administration (Graham and Marvin 1996; Light 2004; Vallianatos 2015).

Modernity is good at renewing metaphors, from the city as machine, to the city as organism or ecology, to the city as cyborgian merger of the technological and the organic (and some argue that the city-as-machine has a much deeper history, as evidenced by use of grid layouts, linear patterns, and regular geometric forms since ancient times, and by the use of standardized patterns for colonial urban development; see Lynch 1981: 81–88; Gandy 2005; Solesbury 2014; Nientied 2016; Verebes 2016). The current paradigm, the *city as computer*, appeals because it frames the messiness of urban life as programmable and subject to rational order. Anthropologist Hannah Knox explains: "As technical solutions to social problems, information and communications technologies encapsulate the promise of order over disarray . . . as a path to an emancipatory politics of modernity" (2010: 187–188). And there are echoes of the pre-modern, too. The computational city draws power from an urban imaginary that goes back millennia, to the city as an apparatus for record-keeping and information management.

We have long conceived of cities as knowledge repositories and data processors, and they have always functioned as such. Lewis Mumford observed that when the wandering rulers of the European Middle Ages settled in capital cities, they installed a "regiment of clerks and permanent officials" and established all manner of paperwork and policies (deeds, tax records, passports, fines, regulations), which necessitated a new urban apparatus, the office building, to house its bureaus and bureaucracy (1961: 344). The classic example is the Uffizi (Offices) in Florence, designed by Giorgio Vasari in the mid-16th century, which provided an architectural template copied in cities around the world. "The repetitions and regimentations of the bureaucratic system"—the work of data processing, formatting, and storage—left a "deep mark," as Mumford put it, on the early modern city (see also Kittler 1996).

Yet the city's informational role began even earlier than that. Writing and urbanization developed concurrently in the ancient world, and those early scripts—on clay tablets, mud-brick walls, and landforms of various types—were used to record transactions, mark territory, celebrate ritual, and embed contextual information in landscape (Mattern 2016b). Mumford described the city as a fundamentally communicative space, rich in information:

> Through its concentration of physical and cultural power, the city heightened the tempo of human intercourse and translated its products into forms that could be stored and reproduced. Through its monuments, written records, and orderly habits of association, the city enlarged the scope of all human activities, extending them backwards and forwards in time. By means of its storage facilities (buildings, vaults, archives, monuments, tablets, books), the city became capable of transmitting a complex culture from generation to generation, for it marshaled together not only the physical means but the human agents needed to pass on and enlarge this heritage. That remains the greatest of the city's gifts. As compared with the complex human order of the city, our present ingenious electronic mechanisms for storing and transmitting information are crude and limited.
>
> *(1961: 569)*

Mumford's city is an assemblage of media forms (vaults, archives, monuments, physical and electronic records, oral histories, lived cultural heritage); agents (architectures, institutions, media technologies, people); and functions (storage, processing, transmission, reproduction, contextualization, operationalization).[1] It is a large, complex, and varied epistemological and bureaucratic apparatus. It is an information processor, to be sure, but it is also more than that.

Were he alive today, Mumford would likely reject the creeping notion that the city is simply the Internet writ large. He would remind us that the processes of city-making are more complicated than writing parameters for rapid spatial optimization. He would inject history and happenstance. *The city is not a computer.* This seems an obvious truth, but it is being challenged now (again) by technologists (and political actors) who speak as if they could reduce urban planning to algorithms (see also Mazzotti 2017).

It is important to debunk obviously false metaphors because they give rise to technical models, which inform design processes that in turn shape knowledge and politics, not to mention material cities. The sites and systems where the city's informational functions are located—the places where it is possible to see information processing, storage, and transmission "happening" in the urban landscape—shape larger understandings of urban intelligence.

Informational Ecologies of the City

The idea of the city as an information-processing machine has in recent years manifested as a cultural obsession with urban sites of data storage and transmission. Scholars, artists, and designers write books, conduct walking tours, and make maps of Internet infrastructures. Some people take pleasure in pointing at nondescript buildings that hold thousands of whirring servers, at surveillance cameras, camouflaged antennae, and hovering drones: "the city's computation happens here" (see Blum 2012; Mattern 2013, 2016a; Burrington 2015–17).

Yet such work runs the risk of reifying and essentializing information, even depoliticizing it. When we treat data as a "given" (which is, in fact, the etymology of the word), we see it in the abstract, as an urban fixture like traffic or crowds (Rosenberg 2013: 18). It is necessary to shift attention and look at data in context, at the lifecycle of urban information, distributed within a varied ecology of urban sites and subjects who interact with it in multiple ways. We need to see data's human, institutional, and technological creators, its curators, its preservers, its owners and brokers, its "users," its hackers and critics. As Mumford understood, there is more than information *processing* going on here. Urban information is *made*, commodified, accessed, secreted, politicized, and operationalized.

But where? Can we point to the chips and drives, cables and warehouses—the specific urban architectures and infrastructures—where this expanded ecology of information management resides and operates? I have written about the challenges of reducing complicated technical and intellectual structures to their material, geographic manifestations; that is, mapping "where the data live" (Mattern 2016a; see also Amoore 2016). Yet such exercises can be useful in identifying points of entry to the larger system—a system composed of personnel and paperwork and protocols, machines and management practices, conduits and cultural variables. Mapping the informational ecology offers an escape from the totalizing metaphor of the *city as computer*, and an opportunity to recognize the countless other forms of data and sites of intelligence-generation in the city: municipal agencies and departments, universities, hospitals, laboratories, corporations. Each of these sites has a distinctive orientation toward urban intelligence. Let us consider a few of the more public ones.

First, the municipal archive. Most cities today have archives that contain records of administrative activity, finances, land ownership and taxes, legislation, and labor. The archives of ancient Mesopotamian and Egyptian cities held similar material, although historians debate whether ancient record-keeping practices served similar documentary functions (O'Toole 2004). Archives ensure financial accountability, symbolically legitimize governing bodies and colonial rulers, and sometimes serve to erase the heritage of previous regimes and conquered populations. They monumentalize a culture's historical consciousness and intellectual riches. In the modern age, they also support scholarship (Walsham 2016). Thus, the "information" inherent in the archive resides not solely in the content of its documents, but also in their very existence, their provenance and organization (there's much to be learned about the ideals of a culture by examining its archival forms), and even in the archive's omissions and erasures (Stoler 2010).

Of course, not all archives are ideologically equal. Community archives validate the personal histories and intellectual contributions of diverse publics (Caswell, Harter, and Jules 2017). Meanwhile, law enforcement agencies and customs and immigration offices are networked with geographically distributed National Security Agency repositories and other "black boxed" federal or corporate data banks. And many cities have open data repositories (which do not always adhere to archival standards) that encourage civic engagement and promote government transparency, but simultaneously reify data as "raw," "neutral" representations of urban operations and sometimes promote "private sector models of governance" that, Morgan Currie argues, "parse complex urban troubles as post-political, instrumental problems that technology can solve" (2016: 8; see also Lauriault 2017). These archives are not of the same species, nor do they "process" "data" in the same fashion, nor are their politics and practical applications clearly defined.

Practices and politics of curation and access have historically distinguished archives from another key site of urban information: libraries. Whereas archives collect unpublished materials and attend primarily to their preservation and security, libraries collect published materials and aim to make them intelligible and accessible to patrons (Besser 2004). In practice, such distinctions are fuzzy and contested, especially today, as many archives seek to be more public-facing. Nevertheless, these two institutions embody different knowledge regimes and ideologies.

Modern libraries and librarians have sought to empower patrons to access information across platforms and formats, and to critically assess bias, privacy, and other issues under the rubric of "information literacy" (Mattern 2016d). They build a critical framework around their resources, often in partnership with local schools and other urban educational and cultural institutions. Libraries also perform vital symbolic functions, embodying a city's commitment to its intellectual heritage and its epistemological politics. And public libraries serve as critical social infrastructures—as urban "community centers," "public squares," platforms for the disconnected, harbors for the marginalized (Mattern 2014). In the wake of recent urban unrest and natural disasters, many American libraries—including those in Ferguson, MO, and Baltimore, MD—have kept their doors open to serve as safe havens, information exchanges, and, when those communities begin to heal, as platforms for civic discourse (Cottrell 2015).

Some city museums are likewise committed to civic engagement and "social practice"; for example, the Queens Museum of Art in New York has been celebrated for reaching out to local immigrant populations, including especially seniors and youth, and to other local civic organizations in creating "community development" programs that exploit the Museum's "core competencies as an arts institution" (Reddy 2015: 30). In fostering such exchanges of local intelligence, the museum's collection can play a critical role: it can reflect a city's commitment to knowledge in embodied form, to its artifacts and material culture. An institution that synthesizes masterworks and art by local creators—or that integrates canonical historical artifacts with community-harvested antiques—makes a statement about the intellectual and creative legacies and (possible futures) of its urban communities. Acquisition policies, display practices, and access protocols are immediate and tangible, and they reflect particular cultural and intellectual politics.

Just as important as the data stored and accessed on city servers, in archival boxes, on library shelves, and on museum walls are the forms of urban intelligence that cannot be easily contained, framed, and catalogued. What place-based "information" does not fit on a shelf or in a database? What are the non-textual, un-recordable forms of cultural memory? These questions are especially relevant for marginalized populations, indigenous cultures, and developing nations. Performance studies scholar Diana Taylor (2003) calls for an acknowledgment of the ephemeral, performative forms of knowledge, such as dance, ritual, cooking, sports, and speech. These forms cannot be reduced to "information," nor can they be "processed," stored, or transmitted via fiber-optic cable. Yet they are vital urban intelligences that "live" within bodies, minds, and communities. Oral historians, folklorists, linguists, and anthropologists have developed conceptual and methodological tools for acknowledging, and honoring, these embodied forms of knowledge.

Finally, consider data of the environmental, ambient, "immanent" kind. Malcolm McCullough has shown that cities are full of fixed architectures, persistent terrains, and reliable environmental patterns that anchor all the unstructured data and image streams that float on top (2013: 36, 42). It is necessary to ask what can be learned from the "nonsemantic information" inherent in shadows, wind, rust, signs of wear on a well-trodden staircase, and the creaks of a battered bridge—all the indexical messages of our material environments. The intellectual value of this ambient, immanent information exceeds its function as stable ground for the city's digital flux. Environmental data are just as much figure as they are ground. They remind us of necessary truths: that urban intelligence comes in multiple forms; that it is produced within environmental as well as cultural contexts; that it is reshaped over the *longue durée* by elemental exposure and urban development; and that it can be lost or forgotten. It is important to think on a climatic scale, a geologic scale, as opposed to the scale of financial markets, transit patterns, and news cycles.

The Case Against "Information Processing"

We can extract such geologic insight from T. S. Eliot's 1934 poem "The Rock":

> Where is the Life we have lost in living?
> Where is the wisdom we have lost in knowledge?
> Where is the knowledge we have lost in the information?

Management theorist Russell Ackoff took Eliot's idea one step further, proposing the now-famous (and widely debated) hierarchy: data < information < knowledge < wisdom (Sharma 2008; Weinberger 2010). Each level of processing implies an extraction of utility from the level before. Thus, contextualized or patterned data can be called information. Or, to quote philosopher and computer scientist Frederick Thompson (1968), information is "a product that results from applying the processes of organization to the raw material of experience, much like steel is obtained from iron ore." Swapping the industrial metaphor for an artistic one, he writes, "data are to the scientist like the colors on the palette of the painter. It is by the artistry of his theories that we are informed. It is the organization that is the information" (quoted in Bates 2010; see also Capurro and Hjørland 2003). Thompson's mixed metaphors suggest that there are multiple ways of turning data into information and knowledge into wisdom.

Yet the term "information processing," whether employed within computer science, cognitive psychology, or urban design, typically refers to *computational* methods. As Manzotti and Parks (2016) explain, when neuroscientists adopt the metaphor of the *brain as computer*, they imply that information is a "mental, non-physical stuff" that's "processed," which sets up a false, "subtle dualism, as if the brain contained organic matter on the one hand and this mysterious, immaterial 'information' on the other." The metaphor survives because it makes an irresistible claim about "how marvelously complex we are and how clever scientists have become." Psychologist Robert Epstein (2016) laments that "some of the world's most influential thinkers have made grand predictions about humanity's future that depend on the validity of the metaphor." But the appeal of analogy is nothing new. Throughout history, the brain (like the city) has been subjected to faulty metaphors derived from the technologies of the time. According to Epstein, we've imagined ourselves as lumps of clay infused with spirits, as hydraulic or electrochemical systems, as automata. The *brain as computer* is just the latest link in a long chain of metaphors that powerfully shape scientific endeavor in their own images.

The *city as computer* model likewise conditions urban design, planning, policy, and administration—even residents' everyday experience—in ways that hinder the development of healthy, just, and resilient cities. Applying Manzotti's and Epstein's critiques at the city scale shows that urban ecologies "process" data by means that are not strictly algorithmic, and not all urban intelligence can be called "information." One cannot "process" the local cultural and economic effects of long-term weather patterns, for example, or derive insights from the generational evolution of a neighborhood without a degree of sensitivity that exceeds mere computation. Urban intelligence of this kind involves site-based experience, participant observation, sensory engagement, and oral history.

Urbanists need new (or old) models for thinking about cities that *do not compute*. Contemporary urban discourses, where "data" rhetoric is often frothy and fetishistic, seem to have lost a critical perspective on how urban data become meaningful spatial information or translate into place-based knowledge. Those who think about and design cities need an expanded *repertoire* (to borrow a term from Diana Taylor) of urban intelligences, to draw upon the wisdom of information scientists and theorists, archivists, librarians, intellectual historians, cognitive scientists, philosophers, and others who think about the management of information and the production of knowledge (see also Foth, Odendaal, and Hearn 2007). They can foster greater understanding of the breadth of intelligences that are integrated within cities, which would be greatly impoverished if they were to be rebuilt, or built anew, with computational logic as their prevailing epistemology.

Scholars could also be better attuned to the lifecycles of urban information resources—to their creation, curation, provision, preservation, and destruction—and to the assemblages of urban sites and subjects that make up a city's intellectual ecologies. "If we think of the city as a long-term construct, with more complex behaviors and processes of formation, feedback, and processing," architect Tom Verebes (2016) proposes, then it is possible to imagine it as an organization, or even an organism, that can learn. Urbanists and designers are already drawing on concepts and methods from artificial intelligence research: neural nets, cellular processes, evolutionary algorithms, and mutation (see, for instance, the work of Michael Batty). Perhaps quantum entanglement and other computer science breakthroughs could reshape the way we think about urban information, too. Yet we must be cautious to avoid translating this interdisciplinary intelligence into a new urban formalism.

Instead of more gratuitous parametric modeling, urbanists need urban epistemologies that embrace memory and history; that recognize spatial intelligence as sensory and experiential; that consider other species' ways of knowing; that appreciate the wisdom of local crowds and communities; that acknowledge the information embedded in the city's façades, flora, statuary, and stairways; and that aim to integrate forms of distributed cognition paralleling our brains' own distributed cognitive processes.

Scholars and designers and administrators must also recognize the shortcomings in models that presume the objectivity of urban data and conveniently delegate critical, often ethical decisions to the machine. Humans *make* urban information by various means: through sensory experience, through long-term exposure to a place, and, yes, by systematically filtering data. It is essential to make space in our cities for those diverse methods of knowledge production. And we have to grapple with the political and ethical implications of our methods and models, embedded in all acts of planning and design. *City-making* is always, simultaneously, an enactment of *city-knowing*, which is more than computation.

Note

1 Marcus Foth's conception of "urban informatics" is similarly capacious: it encompasses "the collection, classification, storage, retrieval, and dissemination of recorded knowledge," either (1) in a city or (2) "of, relating to, characteristic of, or constituting a city" (2009: xxiii). Such a definition acknowledges a wide variety of informational functions, contents, and contexts. Yet his focus on *recorded* knowledge, and on informatics' reputation as a "science" of data processing, still limits our understanding of the city's epistemological functions.

Acknowledgment

This chapter is a modified version of "A City Is Not a Computer," which first appeared in *Places Journal* in February 2017, https://placesjournal.org/article/a-city-is-not-a-computer.

References

Amoore, A. (2016) "Cloud Geographies: Computing, Data, Sovereignty," *Progress in Human Geography* (August), http://journals.sagepub.com/doi/10.1177/0309132516662147.

Bates, M. J. (2010) "Information," in M. J. Bates and M. N. Maac (eds.), *Encyclopedia of Library and Information Sciences*, 3rd ed. New York: CRC Press, pp. 2347–2360.

Batty, M. (n.d.) *A Science of Cities*, blog, www.complexcity.info.

Besser, H. (2004) "The Museum-Library-Archive," Report to Canadian Heritage Information Network, www.nyu.edu/tisch/preservation/program/04spring/chin-libraries.html.

Blum, A. (2012) *Tubes: A Journey to the Center of the Internet*, New York: HarperCollins.

Boyer, M. C. (1996) *CyberCities: Visual Perception in the Age of Electronic Communication*, New York: Princeton Architectural Press.

Brown, E. (2016) "Alphabet's Next Big Thing: Building a 'Smart' City," *Wall Street Journal*, 27 April, www.wsj.com/articles/alphabets-next-big-thing-building-a-smart-city-1461688156.

Burrington, I. (2015–17) All columns for *The Atlantic*. www.theatlantic.com/author/ingrid-burrington.

Cagle, S. (2015) "Why One Silicon Valley City Said 'No' to Google," *Next City*, May 11, https://nextcity.org/features/view/why-one-silicon-valley-city-said-no-to-google.

Capurro R. and Hjørland, B. (2003) "The Concept of Information," in B. Cronin (ed.), *The Annual Review of Information Science and Technology*, 37, pp. 343–411, www.capurro.de/infoconcept.html.

Castells, M. (1989) *The Informational City: Information Technology, Economic Restructuring, and the Urban-Regional Process*, Oxford: Basil Blackwell.

Caswell, M., Harter, C., and Jules, B. (2017) "Diversifying the Historical Record: Integrating Community Archives in National Strategies for Access to Digital Cultural Heritage," *D-Lib Magazine* 23 (5/6), www.dlib.org/dlib/may17/caswell/05caswell.html.

Cheung, A. and Altman, S. (2016) "New Cities," *Y Combinator Blog*, June 27, https://blog.ycombinator.com/new-cities.

Cottrell, M. (2015) "Libraries Respond to Community Needs in Times of Crisis," *American Libraries*, 15 May, https://americanlibrariesmagazine.org/2015/05/15/libraries-respond-to-community-needs-in-times-of-crisis.

Currie, M. (2016) *The Data-Fiction of Openness: The Practices and Policies of Open Government Data in Los Angeles*. Dissertation, University of California Los Angeles.

Doctoroff, D. L. (2016) "Reimagining Cities from the Internet Up," *Medium*, 30 November, https://medium.com/sidewalk-talk/reimagining-cities-from-the-internet-up-5923d6be63ba#.w14z5q5jf.

Epstein, R. (2016) "The Empty Brain," *Aeon*, 18 May, https://aeon.co/essays/your-brain-does-not-process-information-and-it-is-not-a-computer.

Foth, M. (ed.) (2009) *Handbook of Research on Urban Informatics: The Practice and Promise of the Real-Time City*, Hershey, PA: Information Science Reference.

Foth, M., Odendaal, N., and Hearn, G. N. (2007) "The View from Everywhere: Towards an Epistemology for Urbanites," in *Proceedings of the 4th International Conference on Intellectual Capital, Knowledge Management and Organizational Learning*, Cape Town, South Africa.

Gandy, M. (2005) "Cyborg Urbanization: Complexity and Monstrosity in the Contemporary City," *International Journal of Urban and Regional Research*, 29, pp. 26–49.

Gibson, W. (1984) *Neuromancer*, New York: Ace Books.

Graham, S. and Marvin, S. (1996) *Telecommunications and the City: Electronic Spaces, Urban Places*, New York: Routledge.

Green, H. (2010) *The Company Town: The Industrial Edens and Satanic Mills that Shaped the American Economy*, New York: Basic Books.

Hollister, S. (2014) "Welcome to Googletown," *The Verge*, 26 February, www.theverge.com/2014/2/26/5444030/company-town-how-google-is-taking-over-mountain-view.

Huh, B. (2016) "Should I Pursue My Passion or Business?" *Medium*, 25 October, https://medium.com/@benhuh/should-i-pursue-my-passion-or-business-76187b6b83fb#.f43ipmeb3.

Kang, J. (2017) "Pittsburgh Welcomed Uber's Driverless Car Experiment. Not Anymore," *New York Times*, 21 May, www.nytimes.com/2017/05/21/technology/pittsburgh-ubers-driverless-car-experiment.html?mcubz=0&_r=0.

Kittler, F. A. (1996) "The City Is a Medium," *New Literary History*, 27(4), pp. 717–729.

Knox, H. (2010) "Cities and Organisation: The Information City and Urban Form," *Culture and Organization*, 16(3), pp. 185–195.

Lauriault, T. P. (2017) "Open Spatial Data," in R. Kitchin, T. P. Lauriault, and M. W. Milson (eds.), *Understanding Spatial Media*, Thousand Oaks, CA: SAGE.

Light, J. (2004) *From Warfare to Welfare: Defense Intellectuals and Urban Problems in Cold War America*, Baltimore, MD: Johns Hopkins University Press.

Lynch, K. (1981) *Good City Form*, Cambridge, MA: MIT Press.

Manzotti R. and Parks, T. (2016) "Does Information Smell?" *New York Review of Books*, 30 December, www.nybooks.com/daily/2016/12/30/consciousness-does-information-smell.

Mattern, S. (2013) "Infrastructural Tourism," *Places Journal* (July), https://placesjournal.org/article/infrastructural-tourism.

— (2014) "Library as Infrastructure," *Places Journal* (June), https://placesjournal.org/article/library-as-infrastructure.

— (2016a) "Cloud and Field," *Places Journal* (August), https://placesjournal.org/article/cloud-and-field.

— (2016b) "Instrumental City: The View from Hudson Yards, Circa 2019," *Places Journal* (April), https://placesjournal.org/article/instrumental-city-new-york-hudson-yards.

— (2016c) "Of Mud, Media, and the Metropolis: Aggregating Histories of Writing and Urbanization," *Cultural Politics*, 12(3), pp. 310–331.

— (2016d) "Public In/Formation," *Places Journal* (November), https://placesjournal.org/article/public-information.

Mazzotti, M. (2017) "Algorithmic Life," *Los Angeles Review of Books*, 22 January, https://lareviewofbooks.org/article/algorithmic-life.

McCullough, M. (2013) *Ambient Commons: Attention in the Age of Embodied Information*, Cambridge, MA: MIT Press.

McFedries, P. (2014) "The City as System [Technically Speaking]," *IEEE Spectrum*, 51(4), p. 36, http://ieeexplore.ieee.org/document/6776302.

Mitchell, W. J. (1995) *City of Bits: Space, Place, and the Infobahn*, Cambridge, MA: MIT Press.

Morris-Lent, C. (2015) "How Amazon Swallowed Seattle," *Gawker*, 18 August, http://gawker.com/how-amazon-swallowed-seattle-1724795265.

Mumford, L. (1961) *The City in History: Its Origins, Its Transformations, and Its Prospects*, New York: Harcourt.

Nientied, P. (2016) "Metaphor and Urban Studies: A Crossover, Theory and a Case Study of SS Rotterdam," *City, Territory and Architecture*, 3(21), http://cityterritoryarchitecture.springeropen.com/articles/10.1186/s40410-016-0051-z.

O'Toole, J. J. (2004) "Back to the Future: Ernst Posner's *Archives in the Ancient World*," *The American Archivist*, 67, pp. 161–175.

Reddy, P. (2015) "Being a Good Neighbor: Queens Museum's Experiments in Community Engagement," in D. Agapova (ed.), *Participatory Culture: Museum as a Forum for Dialogue and Collaboration*, St. Petersburg: CEC ArtsLink, St. Petersburg Centre for Museum Development.

Rosenberg, D. (2013) "Data Before the Fact," in L. Gitelman (ed.), *Raw Data Is an Oxymoron*, Cambridge, MA: MIT Press, pp. 15–40.

Sharma, N. (2008) "The Origin of the Data Information Knowledge Wisdom (DIKW) Hierarchy," February, www.researchgate.net/publication/292335202_The_Origin_of_Data_Information_Knowledge_Wisdom_DIKW_Hierarchy.

Solesbury, W. (2014) "How Metaphors Help Us Understand Cities," *Geography*, 99(3), pp. 139–142.

Stoler, A. (2010) *Against the Archival Grain: Epistemic Anxieties and Colonial Common Sense*, Princeton, NJ: Princeton University Press.

Taylor, D. (2003) *The Archive and the Repertoire: Performing Cultural Memory in the Americas*, Durham, NC: Duke University Press.

Thompson, F. B. (1968) "The Organization Is the Information," *Journal of the Association for Information Science and Technology*, 19(3), pp. 305–308.

Transportation for America (2016) "16 Cities Join T4America's Smart Cities Collaborative to Tackle Urban Mobility Challenges Together," press release, 18 October, http://t4america.org/2016/10/18/16-cities-join-t4americas-smart-cities-collaborative-to-tackle-urban-mobility-challenges-together.

Vallianatos, M. (2015) "Uncovering the Early History of 'Big Data' and 'Smart City' in Los Angeles," *Boom California*, June, https://boomcalifornia.com/2015/06/16/uncovering-the-early-history-of-big-data-and-the-smart-city-in-la.

Verebes, T. (2016) "The Interactive Urban Model: Histories and Legacies Related to Prototyping the Twenty-First Century City," *Frontiers in Digital Humanities*, 3 (February), http://journal.frontiersin.org/article/10.3389/fdigh.2016.00001/full.

Walsham, A. (2016) "The Social History of the Archive: Record-Keeping in Early Modern Europe," *Past & Present*, 230(11), pp. 9–48.

Weinberg, C. (2016) "Is Alphabet Going to Build a City?" *The Information*, 5 April, www.theinformation.com/is-alphabet-going-to-build-a-city.

Weinberger, D. (2010) "The Problem with the Data-Information-Knowledge-Wisdom Hierarchy," *Harvard Business Review*, 2 February, https://hbr.org/2010/02/data-is-to-info-as-info-is-not.

Further Reading

Klinenberg, E. (2018) *Palaces for the People: How Social Infrastructure Can Help Fight Inequality, Polarization, and the Decline of Civic Life*, New York: Penguin Random House.

Mattern, S. (2017) *Code and Clay, Data and Dirt: 5000 Years of Urban Media*, Minneapolis, MN: University of Minnesota Press.

Sauter M. (2018) "Google's Guinea-Pig City," *The Atlantic*, 13 February, www.theatlantic.com/technology/archive/2018/02/googles-guinea-pig-city/552932.

13
URBAN MONUMENTS AND THE SPATIALIZATION OF NATIONAL IDEOLOGIES

Vjeran Pavlaković and Gruia Bădescu

Introduction

Cities have been arenas of political display, with architecture embodying messages of power or ideology, from the medieval castle and cathedral communicating a sense of control, to obelisks and arches, monuments and memorials employed to narrate the nation. The materiality of built space has often been used as a powerful urban medium to convey power and express political visions. In *Architecture, Power, and National Identity*, Lawrence Vale (2014) shows how political regimes have often reshaped urban space in capital cities to convey a particular national vision. From Washington DC, designed as a capital for the budding American democracy, to Ankara's message of Turkey's secular republicanism after the collapse of the Ottoman Empire, and to Brasilia's sense of expansive modernism embodying Brazil's "order and progress" motto, Vale highlighted how through architecture, urban design, and monument projects, political regimes communicated their version of national ideology, the built environment becoming an urban media of power and identity alike.

Capital cities, in particular, embody a national narrative, but urban space more broadly can express ideology, which can be defined as a "form of social, symbolic and imaginary production of ideas, values, and beliefs" (Šuvaković 2014: 4). Such urban interventions appear at multiple scales—from erecting, from scratch, entire new capital cities to reconfiguring segments or discrete points—and from the large-scale urban plan to the single monument. For instance, Paris' Triumphal Arch conveyed the power of the French state and had echoes as diverse as Bucharest's *Arc de Triumf*, dedicated to the 1918 union of Romanian provinces, or the arch in Mexico City, dedicated to the Mexican Revolution, the tallest in the world. By the late 19th century, Washington DC superseded Baltimore as "the monumental city," with statues, memorial sites, and national museums filling Pierre L'Enfant's urban plan of the capital of the United States. The totalitarian regimes of the 20th century, such as Mussolini's Italy, Hitler's Germany, and Stalin's Soviet Union, dedicated considerable resources to designing urban spaces to reflect the respective ideological foundations of each state. Albert Speer, Hitler's favorite architect, designed a new, monumental capital called Germania, which was supposed to feature the largest triumphal arch in the world (Kitchen 2015) and highlight the regime's achievements. The EUR quarter of Rome signals Mussolini's dream for a fascist Italy, responding to its Roman roots while expressing a form of modernity (Lasansky 2004). In the Soviet Union under Stalin, socialist-realist architecture aimed to reshape housing, while monumental structures and large squares provided space for parades and the display of the regime's power (Hudson Jr 2015).

The apartments, office buildings, factories, roadways, and other infrastructural aspects of any urban center serve as a palimpsest for each ruling ideology, whether fascist, communist, or neoliberal, upon which to inscribe the visual signifiers of the dominant values and beliefs. Less transformative in the long run, yet perhaps more visible to the citizens who live and work in urban spaces, are the monuments, memorial plaques, and place names that fill the streets, squares, and walls of each city. Most of the time, these are physical structures or signs, but they can also be mediated and reproduced in many ways. Not only do symbols fill the cityscape, cities themselves become symbols that are replicated in the press, art and commemorative performances. A pedestrian, whether a local hurrying to work or a visitor strolling through an unknown landscape, is confronted with a visual barrage and physical objects that are negotiated on a daily basis. Architecture communicates differently (Vesely 2004): often monuments are invisible, blending into the background noise of steel, concrete, glass, and neon lights, while at other times, they overpower all other structures, becoming the defining object that demands the absolute attention of passersby. Liberal democracies in the capitalist West tend to fill urban spaces with public art, shopping centers, and, occasionally, memorials that in recent years push the boundaries of abstraction (so-called *Gegendenkmal*, or counter-memorials) (Stevens and Franck 2016: 50). Authoritarian, nationalist, or recently independent states create urban spaces that more explicitly emphasize ideology, drawing upon mythical pasts or recent traumas to imbue historical narratives into everyday life.

Although the postmodern era introduced a pastiche of architectural styles that blurred distinct national and temporal references in the world's leading metropolises (Jencks 1991), articulating the postmodern alleged demise of grand historical narratives, the collapse of communism in Eastern Europe, and the disintegration of multinational states such as the Soviet Union and Yugoslavia, resulted in a new wave of nationalist spatialization from the Adriatic Sea to Central Asia (Diener and Hagen 2013). The periods of dramatic political and socio-economic transition that were observed in the 1990s reveal that newly minted national narratives are heavily mediated through monuments, street names, public space, and urban infrastructure, particularly in capitals, which are thought to be of crucial importance in those nations' search for a place in the history of "great nations" and the battle against self-perceived invisibility in wider geopolitics. While these rapid transformations after 1989 predictably resulted in heated polemics over which traces of the past to remove and which new monumental objects to erect, especially in the former Yugoslavia where the wars in the early 1990s added another layer of violence to the traumas of World War II and communist dictatorship, racial tension in the United States shows that debates about a society's monumental heritage can flare up and result in passionate calls for reshaping the ideological landscape (Upton 2015; see also Chapter 41, this volume). The capital of Kazakhstan, Astana, provides an example of radical post-socialist transition but without the violence that characterized Yugoslavia's disintegration (see also Chapter 24, this volume).

While this chapter broadly looks at the spatialization of national ideologies, it also focuses on several case studies that are particularly relevant to understanding how the past, especially a contested and traumatic one, is mediated in urban space. The wars accompanying Yugoslavia's dissolution in the 1990s remain a focal point of memory politics, geopolitics, and socio-economic debates, and urban spaces frequently reflect the contested memories of the recent past (Pavlaković and Pauković, forthcoming). Not only are the cityscapes of the former Yugoslavia dominated by the legacies of fallen empires and the ambitious socialist modernist architecture from the Titoist era after 1945, they have also been shaped by new conflicts and nationalist imaginations. While many cities in Bosnia and Herzegovina, like the state itself, remain physically divided (such as Mostar or Sarajevo), cities in Serbia reflect the selective memory of Serb involvement in those conflicts (Bădescu 2016), while those in Macedonia have turned to the distant past with kitschy projects such as Skopje 2014, which included grandiose antimodernist constructions such as the Warrior on the Horse, a triumphal arch (Porta Macedonia), and numerous historicist ornamentations and fountains (Graan 2013). Similar to cities in Bosnia and Herzegovina, Croatian cities have been most systematic in imbuing the narrative of the country's war of independence, referred to as the Homeland War (*Domovinski rat*, 1991–1995), in the urban landscape. The dual narratives of the war, with Croatia simultaneously both a victim and victor, are mediated not in the urban space of the capital city, Zagreb, but in cities that have come to embody and symbolize the Homeland War, such as Vukovar. Vukovar, destroyed during a siege and reconstructed during an atmosphere of victorious nation-building, functions as the key *lieux de memoire* of the Homeland War, with elaborate memorials, museums, iconic images, commemorative practices, and educational initiatives to ensure the official narrative of the war is transmitted to the next generations. As this chapter will show, the intersection of cities and nations, as overlapping rather than discrete levels of political action, makes monuments, street names, graffiti, and other forms of memorialization types of urban media, which negotiate the recent past.

Postwar/Post-Socialist Transition

In *The Language of Cities*, Deyan Sudjic observes how "cities measure out their histories in multiple identities, throwing light on to the varying political and cultural agendas of their leaders" (2017: 44). Cities that have undergone dramatic political change, or have suffered massive destruction due to natural catastrophes or wars, are more likely to be shaped by nationalist or other ideological goals than those cities that undergo growth mainly due to economic or demographic booms. After 1945, Warsaw, leveled by the Nazis, was rebuilt as a double communicative gesture: the Old Town was rebuilt in its pre-war image to convey continuity of the nation by the new communist government fearful of being seen as outsiders, while the rest was rebuilt with wide avenues, socialist-realist, and later modernist buildings to convey communism's urban transformation (Elżanowski 2010). Skopje (Macedonia) was leveled by a powerful earthquake in 1963, which resulted in an international rebuilding effort most known for the work of brutalist Japanese architect Kenzo Tange and symbolizing solidarity and collaboration as transgression from Cold War politics (Tolic and Cohen 2011). In the aftermath of the Spanish Civil War, Francisco Franco encouraged a top-down reconstruction effort throughout the country that focused on a return to traditional, Castilian architecture, while preserving some towns, such as Belchite, in a state of ruin to serve as a reminder of the war that his regime openly blamed on the defeated Republican side (Viejo-Rose 2011).

Post-catastrophic reconstructions and the connection with ideologies have been addressed by work in recent historiography (Kohlrausch and Hoffmann 2011), but also in urban studies (Bădescu 2017). Beyond conflict and reconstruction, the relationship of urban space in "ordinary cities" (Robinson 2006) and commemorative practices has been discussed in particular by heritage studies, where concepts of "dissonant heritage" (Tunbridge and Ashworth 1996) and "difficult heritage" (Macdonald 2010) have marked a discussion of the importance of the built environment in narrating the nation, embodying ideology and providing both a prompt and a challenge for memory practices. An attention to the increase in memorial architecture and museums, seen as an outburst of a "politics of regret" (Olick 2007) of various states, has emerged in disciplines as varied as geography (Mitchell 2003) and the emerging field of memory studies (Sodaro 2018). As such, the relationship of urban space and commemorative practices is a dynamic, interdisciplinary pursuit, evocative of both the "memory turn" and the "spatial turn" in the humanities and the social sciences. Yet it is in the discussions of the nationalizing regimes of the post-socialist world (Diener and Hagen 2013) that the tropes of nation-building and national ideologies feature more prominently; as such, a more in-depth discussion of the former Yugoslavia, which experienced both war and nation-building processes after 1991, is illustrative of the relationship between urban space and national ideologies.

After the Partisan victory in World War II, the Yugoslav regime embarked on a vast modernization project that included the expansion of capital cities full of new socialist workers, such as New Zagreb and New Belgrade (Le Normand 2014). In seeking "socialist monumentality, translated into the language of architecture," Yugoslav architects based their "identity in the negation of both the functional approach of Western European modernism and the eclecticism of the Soviet model," yet drew from a complex mixture of global influences (Kulić et al. 2012). In addition to architectural interventions—which have received increasing attention in the West, such as the 2018 exhibition at the Museum of Modern Art in New York City—the Yugoslav regime, as well as numerous local Partisan veteran organizations, erected thousands of monuments, memorial plaques, and memorial parks dedicated to the People's Liberation War (Kirn and Burghardt 2012). Most of the massive, epic memorials were located in the suburban or rural wilderness and rough terrain where the Partisan's guerrilla war was fought, but many city centers also featured monumental complexes commemorating the founding myths of socialist Yugoslavia (such as Užice, Velenje, and Mostar).

During the socialist period, Zagreb noticeably lacked massive memorialization of the People's Liberation War. The city remained dominated by its Austro-Hungarian heritage, and occasional reference to medieval rulers such as the statue King Tomislav were modified with plaques referencing Yugoslavism (Kolar Dimitrijević 1998). The post-1945 communist authorities quickly erased all symbols of the earlier fascist Ustaša regime (1941–1945), including gravestones of those considered to have been enemies of the people (Pavlaković 2012).

The disintegration of both state socialism and the common Yugoslav state unleashed a backlash of suppressed memories and urban transformations. While the fall of the Berlin Wall sparked nationalist reinterpretations of urban space across Central and Eastern Europe as well as the successor states of the Soviet Union (Radović 2013; see also Chapter 33, this volume), the wars that raged in Yugoslavia during the early 1990s not only destroyed the socialist memorials, but also created new traumatic memories and nationalist narratives that began transfiguring urban spaces before the guns even fell silent. Between 1990 and 2000, nearly all institutions' and street names formerly carrying reference to antifascist struggles or socialism were changed and about half of Croatia's 6,000 antifascist monuments were destroyed, removed, damaged, or defaced, although a number of them have been restored, while other Yugoslav successor states experienced greater or lesser destruction of their monumental heritage (Hrženjak 2002: xii). In countries such as Hungary, Lithuania, Estonia, and Bulgaria, some memorials were relocated from the center of cities to special "memory parks" while others remained in public spaces, occasionally defaced or left to deteriorate (Czaplicka et al. 2009). Central Asian cities underwent dramatic changes that accompanied the nation-building projects, resulting in megalomaniacal monuments in Turkmenistan and a postmodern capital city, Astana, in Kazakhstan (Diener and Hagen 2013). In Ukraine, the conflict with Russia since 2014 provoked the widespread removal of Lenin statues, although other memorials to fallen soldiers from World War II remained untouched.

Urban Commemorations of the "Homeland" War

Over 25 years after independence, the Homeland War plays a central role in Croatian political discourse, commemorative practices, and relations with neighboring countries. The decade after

Yugoslav autocrat Josip Broz Tito's death in 1980 was characterized by the rise of nationalist politicians who challenged the stagnant communist establishment during a period of economic crises. As ethnic tensions between Serbs and Croats increased in Croatia, the so-called "Log Revolution" (*balvan revolucija*) erupted in the area around Knin in August 1990. Croatian Serbs established autonomous regions that eventually formed the parastate Republic of Serbian Krajina, with Knin as its capital (Pavlaković 2013). After Slovenia and Croatia declared independence on June 25, 1991, the conflict exploded as the increasingly Serb-dominated Yugoslav People's Army intervened and tried to forcibly prevent the dissolution of the federation. Whereas the fighting in Slovenia lasted 10 days, the war in Croatia became considerably bloodier (and eventually spread to Bosnia-Herzegovina in 1992) when the rebel Croatian Serbs and the Yugoslav People's Army tried to carve out as much territory as possible once it became clear that saving Yugoslavia was impossible (Marijan 2016). While numerous cities, towns, and villages were damaged or destroyed during the fighting in 1991, the three-month siege and eventual fall of the town of Vukovar in eastern Croatia was represented as the greatest symbol of suffering during the war, as was the case of the siege of Sarajevo and massacre in Srebrenica (Marijan 2013).

Thus, the wars accompanying Yugoslavia's dissolution undeniably left deep traumas in the post-Yugoslav societies that are reflected in the landscapes and urban plastic in each of successor states. While Slovenia, Macedonia, and Montenegro suffered relatively little in the Yugoslav wars and this part of the past is barely visible in public memory, Bosnia-Herzegovina's cultural memory remains deeply divided and fragmented, just like the state (Moll 2013; Bădescu 2015), while Serbia, in addition to a new wave of nostalgia for its medieval kingdom, commemorates its suffering at the hands of NATO bombing in 1999 while denying accountability or even involvement in the conflicts in neighboring countries (Gordy 2013). Kosovo, the most recent of the ex-Yugoslav states to declare independence, remains divided between a Serb-majority northern enclave and the Albanian majority rest of the country that is visually defined by images related to the armed independence struggle against Serbia (Ermolin 2015). Croatia, as mentioned earlier, not only has a single official narrative of the war codified in the constitution and parliamentary declarations, but commemorates it both as a victim and celebrates it as a victor.

Even as Croatian society seems increasingly divided over the legacy of World War II, there appears to be a relative consensus over the Homeland War, especially after all Croatian Army officers indicted by the International Criminal Tribunal for the former Yugoslavia were acquitted. Unlike the capital cities of Serbia (Belgrade) and Bosnia-Herzegovina (Sarajevo), Croatia's capital Zagreb has very few traces of the war in its cityscape. As was the case of the People's Liberation War memorials during socialism, the city administration in Zagreb placed most of the memorials to the Homeland War on the periphery of the city.

Remembering Vukovar

Vukovar, once a vibrant multi-ethnic city on the banks of the Danube River known for its manufacturing and industry (Cvek et al. 2015), became one of the most powerful images of destruction, ethnic cleansing, and war crimes in the Homeland War. Travel guides such as *Lonely Planet* summon idyllic pre-war descriptions of this formerly wealthy agricultural and industrial center, telling readers that "its streets were once rimmed with elegant Baroque mansions, art galleries and museums, but all that changed with the siege of 1991, which destroyed its economy, culture, infrastructure, civic harmony and soul" (2018). Not only were hundreds of people killed during the three-month siege, but the entire non-Serb population was expelled, the city was essentially completely destroyed, and valuable cultural heritage was pillaged or even burnt to the ground, such as the Eltz manor, a Baroque castle housing the Vukovar City Museum. For years, the city's shattered buildings, bullet-riddled façades, and piles of rubble were a constant reminder of the war and the divided ethnic communities. Slowly, the Croatian authorities rebuilt the city and invested in its infrastructure, but the wounds of the war remain even though a visitor today will find it harder to find the level of destruction seen on news reports in the 1990s.

Nevertheless, even though the whole region is facing a massive demographic decline as the jobless young and educated have been migrating to Western Europe seeking a more fortunate future for themselves, Vukovar is a city that still narrates the history of the Homeland War and thus Croatian national identity, at practically every street corner, even though approximately 30% of its remaining population are ethnic Serbs. The city not only functions as a narrator of the war within Croatia, but has also expanded in recent years to offer war tourism for an increasingly international audience arriving on tour boats traveling down the Danube (Šuligoj 2017). The most dominant symbol of Vukovar is the 50-meter-tall Water Tower, built in 1968 and heavily damaged during the siege. The tower survived over 600 direct hits from shells and bullets, and became a symbol of the Croatian resistance (see Figure 13.1).

The image of the Vukovar Water Tower can be found on many souvenirs, t-shirts, media reports about Vukovar, and other items dealing with the battle for Vukovar or the Homeland War more generally. The ongoing reconstruction would leave the damage visible but enable visitors to go to the top and see a memorial center inside the structure. Thus, the most recognizable symbol of Vukovar will be transformed into a memorial site as part of the broader Memorial Centre of the Homeland War—Vukovar, headquartered in a former Yugoslav People's Army military base.

In addition to the domineering Water Tower, the rest of Vukovar is a prime example of nationalist spatialization from one end of the city to the other. At the north entrance to the city, at the so-called "Tank Graveyard" on Trpinja Road, a massive tank stands guard next to the Memorial Room of Croatian Defenders (*Spomen soba hrvatskih branitelja*) and a bust of Blago Zadro, one of the Croatian commanders of an anti-tank unit killed in 1991. One of the central monuments, dedicated to "Victims who fell for a free Croatia," is a large white cross on the bank of the Vuka River where it flows into the Danube. Smaller monuments throughout the city are dedicated to former Croatian wartime President Tuđman, fallen Croatian soldiers, foreign volunteers, and the victims of the Ovčara massacre. The Vukovar Memorial Cemetery, the Vukovar City Museum, the Vukovar Memorial Hospital Site of Memory, and the Ovčara Memorial Museum all narrate the conflict through exhibits, objects, video materials, publications, and memorial plaques incorporated into the sites. Although Croatian citizens of Serb ethnicity were also killed during the siege or murdered by Croatian paramilitaries, the cityscape has no room for memorialization of the those from the "other" side.

Once a year, the victimization of the city is reenacted through commemorative practices within this landscape of national symbols and monumental plastic. The central event of the Vukovar commemoration, held annually on November 18, is the symbolic Procession of Memory (*Kolona sjećanja*), which follows the 5.5-kilometer route from the Vukovar hospital, from which patients were taken away and later killed, to the Memorial Cemetery of the Homeland War Victims. The procession symbolizes the expulsion of Vukovar's Croats (Kardov 2007), and the participatory nature of this commemoration, in which tens of thousands of people from all over Croatia take part, creates an exceptional affect unlike any other commemoration of the Homeland War. Erika Doss notes the importance of "affect as a fundamental element in contemporary commemoration," and the performed reenactment of expulsion and loss during the procession in Vukovar contributes to the feelings of victimization, especially since the final destination is the Memorial Cemetery (2010: 15).

The Spatialization of National Ideologies

Figure 13.1 Vukovar Water Tower

The narrative of Vukovar is also transmitted in public space throughout Croatia, both officially through street names and monuments, and more subversively (yet equally visibly) through graffiti, often produced by football fan groups (Brentin 2019). Every major city and most towns in Croatia have a Vukovar Street, which is often the site of commemorative events on November 18, often with messages of "Never Forget" or references to volunteers who lost their lives defending the city. While the urban spaces of Vukovar represent the ultimate symbols of both victim and victor in the Homeland War, their narratives are mediated both formally and informally throughout Croatia. Beginning in 2014, the Croatian Ministry of Veteran Affairs initiated a program for a two-day visit to Vukovar by all Croatian eighth-graders to learn about the Homeland War as well as other cultural sites in Eastern Slavonia. The pupils stay in renovated barracks at the Memorial Centre of the Homeland War and visit key sites of memory related to the siege. Although the atmosphere of the Memorial Centre is one that is focused on military equipment and battles, the official website states that the program ends with a lecture about peace that enables the pupils to return home with "a message of peace, nonviolence, and tolerance upon which to build a future."

A major controversy exploded in 2013 when the left-wing national government tried to implement a law on minority rights that would have allowed Serbs in Vukovar, estimated at over 33% in the 2011 census, to use the Cyrillic alphabet on municipal buildings. Veteran organizations, supported by the nationalist opposition, organized a Headquarters for the Defense of Croatian Vukovar (*Stožer za obranu hrvatskog Vukovara*) to protest the use of Cyrillic in public space, since many of them considered the script to be a symbol of Serb aggression and occupation. Several signs were destroyed by veterans wielding hammers, and a massive demonstration in Zagreb against introducing Cyrillic into the Vukovar cityscape was followed by a scandal at the 2013 commemoration, when veteran groups blocked the president, prime minister, and other members of the government and diplomatic corps from participating in the Procession of Memory. Local elections brought a right-wing mayor to power, who succeeded in preventing the implementation of any further Cyrillic signs, declaring the city to be a place of "special piety" and thus exempt from certain regulations, such as the Constitutional Act on the Rights of National Minorities in the Republic of Croatia, enacted in 2002. While incidents of interethnic violence are rare, many Croats and Serbs frequent separate cafes, and the school system is segregated despite civic efforts to create unified schools with a single curriculum. The controversy over Cyrillic revealed how sensitive and sacred to victimization narrative Vukovar remains, and although it is not a divided city in the sense of Mostar (Bosnia-Herzegovina), Skopje (Macedonia), or Mitrovica (Kosovo), nationalist symbols continue to be divisive in this town once famed for its multinational character (see Figure 13.2). The dynamics of memory and the heritage of war in Vukovar have led heritage scholars like Britt Baillie (2013) to call for an understanding of "conflict-time" rather than "post-conflict" in the depiction of contemporary dynamics of memorialization in urban space.

Capital Building: Astana

Kazakhstan's new capital city of Astana further highlights how interventions in urban space can articulate national ideology. While in the post-Yugoslav cases, the interventions discussed signal a reconfiguration of urban space at a small scale focused on the memorial dimension of nation-building mobilized through war, Kazakhstan, which split peacefully, and some say unwillingly, from the Soviet Union (Anacker 2004), highlights the case of advancing a fluid identity to build the future.

In December 1997, the capital of Kazakhstan was relocated by presidential decree from southern Almaty to the small provincial city of Akmola, renamed Astana, which in Kazakh means simply "capital city". Eight billion dollars were spent on the makeover of Soviet Akmola and the construction of new Astana (Köppen 2013). Studies on Astana examined the power dimension of the politics of its relocation (Anacker 2004). The old capital was described in

Figure 13.2 Bilice Vukovar Graffiti

the official media as plagued by its remote location and environmental challenges, but also its meaning as a center of the Soviet administration. The reasons invoked for the move remind us of similar scenarios in several African countries, which embarked on new capital city building (Schatz 2004). While in many of these cases, the relocation implied the move from the former colonial center of power to the geographical center of the country or to the new regime's regional stronghold, Astana was located in the northern extremity and was seen as a way to pacify the opposition in the region to President Nursultan Nazarbayev, who hailed from the south. Linking the architectural with the political, Köppen (2013) discussed the reshaping of urban space in Astana as an expression of the national ideology of Eurasianism, while Bekus and Medeuova (2017) pointed to the fuzziness of this national ideology in urban space.

The architectural transformation of Astana had two pillars. The first, sustainability, came through the work of Japanese architect Kisho Kurokawa, and was to legitimize the state's desire that the city would be a showcase of contemporary best practices in urbanism. Yet the focus on architectural expression related to the pillar of Nazarbayev's national ideology centered on the concept of Eurasianism: the new Astana was supposed to represent a bridge between East and West, while embodying Kazakhness. Nazarbayev was well embedded in the power structure of the Soviet system prior to independence, and also shared the general view in Kazakhstan of the Soviet period as one of modernization (Köppen 2013), as opposed to the occupation and oppression narrative existing in other (Western) Soviet republics (Račevskis 2002). As such, while Nazarbayev emphasized the preeminence of Kazakhs in the new nation state, he was careful not to express a narrative of exclusive ethno-based nationalism to avoid destabilizing the young state (Anacker 2004). Instead, he emphasized that all people of Kazakhstan, including the Kazakhs, the significant number of Russians, and others, are all Eurasians, and the country's future lies in its regional geography.

While Astana's urban plan was seen as a bridge between East and West, the emphasis in architectural references was focused on the Kazakh people, using a repertoire related to nomadism and pastoralism, such as circles, and the *shanyrak*, the round opening on top of a yurt (Köppen 2013). In the center, an iconic tower references Kazakh motifs, such as the egg that symbolizes Kazakh fertility and continuity. It stands 97 meters high so that it refers to 1997 as a year of birth. On the other hand, the Triumph of Astana skyscraper references Soviet buildings of the 1930s and is read by Köppen (2013) as a reference to the Russian ethnicity present in the country, as well as to the importance of the Soviet past. Above all stands the presence of Nazarbayev: his handprint is located at the top of the Baiterek Tower, symbolizing the president as creator of the capital and father of the nation. However, the presidential palace resembles the US Capitol building in Washington DC, as a reference to the democratic nature of the new Kazakhstan.

The official narrative portrays Astana as a successful embodiment of the new Kazakhstan's success and modernity. Criticism of the makeover, in which new façades were just placed in front of old Soviet-era buildings, similar to the practice in Skopje (with a different makeover, one of modernity here versus one of invented tradition in the Macedonian case), nevertheless led to Astana being called a Potemkin village of modernity and national ideology by some (Köppen 2013). It presents the story of capital city space being used to project national ideology for a long time, while its architectural expression is often that of a postmodern gesture, of multiple references, and of fluidity.

Concluding Remarks

Architecture, monuments, names of public spaces, and other memorial sites are the most visible transmitters of national ideologies in the cityscape, especially in those urban environments where dramatic political transformations have resulted in systematic intervention into the fabric of cities. Capital cities traditionally showcase the national narrative, whether a city like Washington DC, which was practically designed as a platform for monumental collective remembrance, or Astana (Kazakhstan), which embraces the creation of a new postmodern vision of the nation. The cities in the various Yugoslav successor states were not only transformed by the processes of post-socialist transition, but also by the traumatic consequences of the wars of the 1990s. Each country deals with the past differently, some preserving the damage to remind future generations of the destruction (Belgrade, Sarajevo), while others rebuild rapidly to hide the scars of war (Zagreb, Dubrovnik).

Throughout the Yugoslav successor states, ruling elites continue to imbue the landscape with national ideologies that reinforce the nation state and overshadow the multinational and common narratives of the Partisan struggle. Although it is difficult to predict future impacts, the migrant crises increasingly affecting Europe and the rise of populism could inspire a new cycle of nationalist appropriations of public space to reaffirm national identities that are perceived to be under threat. On the other hand, the rise of mega-cities underpins the development of a pastiche of symbols, influences, and images, creating postmodern (whether cosmopolitan or consumption-led) landscapes that might challenge narrow nationalist interpretations of urban space.

Acknowledgment

This chapter was made possible by generous funding from the Croatian Science Foundation (HRZZ—Hrvatska zaklada za znanost) through the project "Framing the Nation and Collective Identity in Croatia: Political Rituals and Cultural Memory of 20th Century Traumas."

References

Anacker, S. (2004) "Geographies of Power in Nazarbayev's Astana," *Eurasian Geography and Economics*, 45(7), pp. 515–533.
Bădescu, G. (2015) "Dwelling in the Post-War City Urban Reconstruction and Home-Making in Sarajevo," *Revue d'études Comparatives Est-Ouest*, 46(4), pp. 35–60.
— (2016) "'Achieved without Ambiguity?' Memorializing Victimhood in Belgrade after the 1999 NATO Bombing," *Südosteuropa*, 64(4), pp. 500–519.
— (2017) "Post-War Reconstruction in Contested Cities: Comparing Urban Outcomes in Sarajevo and Beirut," in J. Rokem and C. Boano (eds.) *Urban Geopolitics*, London: Routledge, pp. 17–31.
Baillie, B. (2013) "Capturing Facades in 'Conflict-Time': Structural Violence and the (Re) Construction Vukovar's Churches," *Space and Polity*, 17(3), pp. 300–319.
Bekus, N. and Medeuova, K. (2017) "Re-Interpreting National Ideology in the Contemporary Urban Space of Astana," *Urbanities: Journal of Urban Ethnography*, 7(2), pp. 10–21.
Brentin, D. (2019) "Ambassadors of Memory: 'Honouring the Homeland War' in Croatian Sport," in V. Pavlaković & D. Pauković (eds.) *Framing the Nation and Collective Identities: Political Rituals and Cultural Memory of the Twentieth-Century Traumas in Croatia*, London: Routledge, pp. 160–176.
Cvek, S. et al. (2015) "Jugoslavensko radništvo u tranziciji: 'Borovo' 1989," *Politička misao*, 52(2), pp. 7–34.
Czaplicka, J. et al. (eds.) (2009) *Cities after the Fall of Communism: Reshaping Cultural Landscapes and European Identity*, Washington, DC: Woodrow Wilson Center Press.
Diener, A. and Hagen, J. (2013) "From Socialist to Post-Socialist Elites: Narrating the Nation through Urban Space," *Nationalities Papers*, 41(4), pp. 487–514.
Doss, E. (2010) *Memorial Mania: Public Feeling in America*, Chicago, IL: Chicago University Press.
Elżanowski, J. (2010) "Manufacturing Ruins: Architecture and Representation in Post-Catastrophic Warsaw," *The Journal of Architecture*, 15(1), pp. 71–86.
Ermolin, D. (2015) "When Skanderbeg Meets Clinton: Cultural Landscape and Commemorative Strategies in Postwar Kosovo," *Politička misao*, 51(5), pp. 157–173.

Gordy, E. (2013) *Guilt, Responsibility, and Denial: The Past at Stake in Post-Milošević Serbia*, Philadelphia, PA: University of Pennsylvania Press.

Graan, A. (2013) "Counterfeiting the Nation? Skopje 2014 and the Politics of Nation Branding in Macedonia," *Cultural Anthropology*, 28(1), pp. 161–179.

Hrženjak, J. (ed.) (2002) *Rušenje antifašističkih spomenika u Hrvatskoj, 1990–2000*, Zagreb: Savez antifašističkih boraca hrvatske.

Hudson Jr, H. D. (2015) *Blueprints and Blood: The Stalinization of Soviet Architecture, 1917–1937*, Princeton, NJ: Princeton University Press.

Jencks, C. (1991) *The Language of Post-Modern Architecture*, London: Academy Editions.

Kardov, K. (2007) "Remember Vukovar: Memory, Sense of Place, and the National Tradition in Croatia," in S. P. Ramet and D. Matić (eds.) *Democratic Transition in Croatia: Value Transformation, Education and Media*, College Station, TX: Texas A&M University Press.

Kirn, G. and Burghardt, R. (2012) "Jugoslovenski partizanski spomenici: Između revolucionarne politike i apstraktnog modernizma," *Jugolink*, 2(1), pp. 7–20.

Kitchen, M. (2015) *Speer: Hitler's Architect*, New Haven, CT: Yale University Press.

Kohlrausch, M. and Hoffmann, S. (2011) "Introduction: Post-Catastrophic Cities," *Journal of Modern European History*, 9(3), pp. 308–313.

Kolar Dimitrijević, M. (1998) "Povijest gradnje spomenika kralju Tomislavu u Zagrebu 1924. do 1947. Godine," *Povjesni prilozi*, 16, pp. 243–307.

Köppen, B. (2013) "The Production of a New Eurasian Capital on the Kazakh Steppe: Architecture, Urban Design, and Identity in Astana," *Nationalities Papers*, 41(4), pp. 590–605.

Kulić, V. et al. (2012) *Modernism In-Between: The Mediatory Architectures of Socialist Yugoslavia*, Berlin: Jovis Verlag.

Lasansky, D. M. (2004) *The Renaissance Perfected: Architecture, Spectacle, and Tourism in Fascist Italy*, vol. 4, University Park, PA: Penn State Press.

Le Normand, B. (2014) *Designing Tito's Capital: Urban Planning, Modernism, and Socialism in Belgrade*, Pittsburgh, PA: University of Pittsburgh Press.

Lonely Planet (2018) viewed June 15, 2018, www.lonelyplanet.com/croatia/vukovar.

Macdonald, S. (2010) *Difficult Heritage: Negotiating the Nazi Past in Nuremberg and Beyond*, New York: Routledge.

Marijan, D. (2013) *Obrana i pada Vukovara*, Zagreb: Hrvatski institut za povijest.

— (2016) *Domovinski rat*, Zagreb: Hrvatski institut za povijest.

Mitchell, K. (2003) "Monuments, Memorials, and the Politics of Memory," *Urban Geography*, 24(5), pp. 442–459.

Moll, N. (2013) "Fragmented Memories in a Fragmented Country: Memory Competition and Political Identity-Building in Today's Bosnia and Herzegovina," *Nationalities Papers*, 41(6), pp. 910–935.

Olick, J. K. (2007) *The Politics of Regret: On Collective Memory and Historical Responsibility*, New York: Routledge.

Pavlaković, V. (2012) "Conflict, Commemorations, and Changing Meanings: The Meštrović Pavilion as a Contested Site of Memory," in D. Pauković, V. Pavlaković, and V. Raoš (eds.) *Confronting the Past: European Experiences*, Zagreb: CPI.

— (2013) "Symbols and the Culture of Memory in the Republika Srpska Krajina," *Nationalities Papers*, 41(6), pp. 893–909.

— (2014) "Fulfilling the Thousand-Year-Old Dream: Strategies of Symbolic Nation-Building in Croatia," in P. Kolstø (ed.) *Strategies of Symbolic Nation-Building in Southeastern Europe*, Farnham: Ashgate.

— (2018) "Sukobljena jasenovačka kultura sjećanja: postkomunistički memorijalni muzej u Jasenovcu u doba povijesnog revizionizma," in A. Benčić, S. Odak, and D. Lucić (eds.) *Jasenovac: manipulacije, kontroverze i povijesni revizionizam*, Jasenovac: Spomen područje Jasenovac.

Pavlaković, V. and Pauković, D. (eds.) (forthcoming) *Framing the Nation and Collective Identities: Political Rituals and Cultural Memory of the Twentieth Century Traumas in Croatia*, New York: Routledge.

Račevskis, K. (2002) "Toward a Postcolonial Perspective on the Baltic States," *Journal of Baltic Studies*, 33(1), pp. 37–56.

Radović, S. (2013) *Grad kao tekst*, Belgrade: XX vek.

Robinson, J. (2006) *Ordinary Cities: Between Modernity and Development*, vol. 4, London: Psychology Press.

Schatz, E. (2004) *Modern Clan Politics: The Power of "Blood" in Kazakhstan and Beyond*, Seattle, WA: University of Washington Press.

Sodaro, A. (2018) *Exhibiting Atrocity: Memorial Museums and the Politics of Past Violence*, New Brunswick, NJ: Rutgers University Press.
Stevens, Q. and Franck, K. A. (2016) *Memorials as Spaces of Engagement: Design, Use and Meaning*, New York: Routledge.
Sudjic, D. (2017) *The Language of Cities*, London: Penguin.
Šuligoj, M. (2017) "Warfare Tourism: An Opportunity for Croatia?" *Economic Research-Ekonomska Istraživanja*, 30(1), pp. 439–452.
Šuvakovic, M. (2014) "General Theory of Ideology and Architecture," in V. Mako, M. Roter Blagojević, and M. Vukotić Lazar (eds.) *Architecture and Ideology*, Newcastle on Tyne: Cambridge Scholars Publishing.
Tolic, I. and Cohen, J.-L. (2011) *Dopo Il Terremoto: La Politica Della Ricostruzione Negli Anni Della Guerra Fredda a Skopje*, Parma: Diabasis.
Tunbridge, J. E. and Ashworth, G. J. (1996) *Dissonant Heritage: The Management of the Past as a Resource in Conflict*, Chichester: John Wiley & Sons.
Upton, D. (2015) *What Can and Can't Be Said: Race, Uplift, and Monument Building in the Contemporary South*, New Haven, CT: Yale University Press.
Vale, L. (2014) *Architecture, Power and National Identity*, New York: Routledge.
Vesely, D. (2004) *Architecture in the Age of Divided Representation the Question of Creativity in the Shadow of Production*, Cambridge, MA: MIT Press.
Viejo-Rose, D. (2011) *Reconstructing Spain: Cultural Heritage and Memory after Civil War*, Brighton: Sussex Academic Press.

Further Reading

Hatherley, O. (2016) *Landscapes of Communism: A History through Buildings*, London: Penguin Books.
Langer, B. and Lechler, J. (2010). *Reading the City: Urban Space and Memory in Skopje*, Berlin: Universitätsverlag der TU Berlin.
Schatz, E. (2004) "What Capital Cities Say About State and Nation Building," *Nationalism and Ethnic Politics*, 9(4), pp. 111–140.

14
ARTIFICIAL LIGHT AND THE MODERNIST REDEFINITION OF URBAN SPACE
Reading the "Electropolis"

Robert Shaw

Introduction

When English novelist Fanny Trollope visited the USA in the late 1820s, she was struck by the lack of street lighting in most cities. She complained, "this darkness, this stillness is so great that I almost felt it awful" (in Baldwin 2012: 1). By contrast, European cities had already begun to use artificial light to transform their nights, breaking the shackles of one of the most fundamental limitations that human society had always faced, namely the reduced capacity for activity in the dark. It is perhaps unsurprising that for many 19th-century writers, this transformation of the night-time city was nothing short of miraculous. Lit city streets, illuminated shop windows, lighting in the home, and 24-hour factory operations all had transformative effects on different spheres of urban life.

However, lighting quickly fell into the urban background. As Trollope's quote suggests, people who have become used to artificial light in cities come to expect its presence and to fear or dislike darkened cities. However, over the last 20 years artificial lighting has once again become a topic of contestation and debate. This contestation has occurred in the context of concerns about light pollution, energy use, and in the rise of new technologies of "smart" artificial lighting, including outdoor LED lighting. As such, many of the debates surrounding lighting, which disappeared in the 19th century, have returned. This chapter seeks to illuminate (sorry) the history of the artificially lit city through three key moments. First, it will explore how through gas and then electricity the "night spectacular" of the 19th century was produced. Second, it will take the 20th-century night and its representations to show how artificial lighting has contributed to contradictory discourses of the night as an open space of change and opportunity, and as a dangerous space of fear and darkness. Third, it will move to the 21st century and the reworking of the "electropolis" through new lighting technologies. The wider argument in this chapter is that while the production of an "electropolis" fundamentally changed urban life, these changes quickly became accepted as a normal part of urban living. Further, the outcome of such changes is not a homogenous illuminated city, but a complex and layered tapestry of unequally accessed artificial lighting.

Nineteenth Century: The Night Spectacular

The history of artificial lighting might begin with the invention of fire and later the candle and oil lamp, but public lighting technologies did not move beyond these until the late 18th century. Fireworks and other spectacular festival lighting have a longer history in multiple cultures, notably China, but these were still fundamentally "fire"-based (Huang 1991). The first public street lighting appeared in Europe in the 1660s: first in Paris and Amsterdam and by the early 1700s across many European capitals and provincial cities in France. This lighting was initially limited to areas around royal courts (Koslofsky 2002) or in the districts inhabited by the growing urban bourgeois (Schivelbusch 1988). Early lighting was provided by lanterns, fueled either by candles or by oil. Typically, lights were installed outside properties and funded on a private basis: London's first lighting was provided by Edward Heming on a license from the City of London, for which he charged householders six shillings per year (Alvarez 1996). Similar schemes operated in multiple cities, with lights lit and snuffed out by "lamplighters," a job that continued to exist in many cities until the full rollout of electric lighting in the mid-20th century (Shakhmatova 2012). This early lighting, which adapted longstanding technologies, was limited in both distribution and strength: the technologies did not spread beyond major European city centers, and the light provided was gloomy and unreliable. It was followed by technological innovation: first improvements to candle- and oil-based lighting (Schivelbusch 1988), before the invention of gas lighting in the early 1800s.

Gas lighting differed from previous technologies in the need for the provision of a new scale of public infrastructure As Schivelbusch argues, "with a public gas supply . . . lighting entered its industrial—and dependent—stage" (1988: 28). Lighting shifted from small-scale and individual, to a collective endeavor connecting home and state. The connection of the home to these public infrastructures mixed public and private space in new ways, contributing to what Schlör calls the "internal urbanization" of citizens (1998: 16). By this, Schlör argues that the material "external" changes to urban life that occurred in the 19th century, such as the introduction of street lighting, contributed to "internal" changes in how people imagine themselves and inhabit the city. He argues that new infrastructures helped the "formation of urban behaviors necessary for survival in the city . . . changes in the city night form an important chapter in the ensemble of new challenges to behavior, perception and attitudes" (1998: 16). In other words, gas street lighting was part of the production of urban modernity, and it disseminated at a speed and following pathways similar to other technologies of modernity such as sewerage and paved roads. European cities such as Istanbul and Moscow were lit in the 1850s (Buckler 2015), while Shanghai and Tokyo both received artificial lighting around the same time (Lu 1999). A small number of then colonial centers—Mumbai, for example—were also lit with gaslights by the 1860s (Woods 2015), but the need for extensive infrastructural work stopped the development of artificial lighting in the gas-era in many cities, with dimmer oil lighting dominating instead.

On city streets, gas lighting felt qualitatively different from the previous baby-steps toward illumination, offering the ability to provide widespread, comparatively cheap and simple lighting across cities. As Trollope's quote at the opening of this chapter illustrates, by the late 1820s—just 20 years after the first gas lighting in London—the non-gas-lit city could seem dangerous and "backward" at night for those used to living in well-lit cities (Baldwin 2012). Histories of lighting abound with accounts of how commentators at the time were awestruck by the brightness of night-time lighting. Schlör cites the *Vossische Zeitung*'s report of new lighting on the central Under den Linden street in Berlin in 1826:

> A great crowd of curious onlookers were attracted by this spectacle, and all of them were surprised: for we have never seen the Linden more brightly lit by the most splendid illuminations. Not in meagre little gleams but as broad as a hand the dazzling light shoots forth, so pure that one can perfectly well read a letter at a distance of 20–25 paces.
>
> *(1998: 59)*

Beamish reports similar enthusiasm in Boston where an 1816 exhibition of gas lighting was reported as providing "brilliant illumination" attracting "a large concourse of people, who appeared delighted with the scenery" (Beamish 2015: 13). In London, too, the *Monthly Magazine* reported in 1807 that new gas lighting on The Mall was "beautifully white and brilliant" (Schivelbusch 1988: 115).

The astonishment of gas lighting and new infrastructure quickly produced new ways of engaging with the city. Speaking of the earliest stages of public lighting, Koslofsky argues that it contributed to "a fundamental shift in the rhythms of daily life in early modern cities and courts, where the hours after sunset slowly entered the respectable part of daily life" (2002: 744). Gas lighting enhanced this, with entrepreneurs quick to recognize the possibility for new retail and leisure opportunities. An author taking the name "Photophilos" enthused about the possibility of lighting festivals as early as 1801 (Barnaby 2015), and both through events and on a day-to-day basis, new forms of commerce and nightlife emerged with urban lighting. Perhaps the most striking example of this in the gaslight era was the Thames Tunnel, an ambitious project constructed between 1827 and 1843. The Thames Tunnel was a pedestrian tunnel in East London, designed by the engineer Isambard Kingdom Brunel. Lined with stalls and lit entirely by gas, the intention of the tunnel was to replicate the famous arcades of Paris (Pike 2005). While the tunnel largely failed as an enterprise—it was converted to a railway tunnel in 1869—it nonetheless illustrated the new entertainment possibilities created by public gas lighting and, for Pike, "functioned as a key threshold space for a modern London coming to terms with radical changes in its cityscape and social dynamics" (2005: 351). Thus, the newly illuminated city intersected with developing urban modernity and capitalism to facilitate a range of leisure activities.

Electric lighting followed closely behind gas and had the same revolutionary effect, quickly making the gas-lit cities appear dark in comparison to the bright white light of electricity (Schivelbusch 1988: 118). Early artificial electric lighting was provided by "arc lights": mini suns, effectively, placed at a height that illuminated all below them. Arc lighting produced an effect akin to daylight: the first arc lighting appeared in the 1870s America in Cleveland, Ohio, bringing "the light of noon" which, according to the *Cleveland Herald* at the time, "turned every gas light within half a dozen squares green and yellow with envy" (Baldwin 2012: 157). While spectacular, arc lighting was not ideal for most uses: the light produced was dazzling and as such had to be placed high, at a level where trees and fog could interfere with lighting quality. The areas below the lights would be brightly and indiscriminately lit, with dark and gloomy gaps surrounding them. City authorities attempted to counter this with ever more impressive arc light towers. New and growing towns had the space to develop them: the boomtown of Kimberley in South Africa became the first electrified city in the Southern Hemisphere in 1880, and they were popular in American cities in particular: Detroit, where the system was most extensive, was illuminated by 122 arc lamps set at 175 feet (53 meters) above street level (Baldwin 2012: 158).

However, it was with the invention of the incandescent light bulb that electric lighting finally took off on a major scale. The invention of the incandescent bulb was a contested one, as the technology was not invented in one single move but emerged out of the work of multiple inventors. In the UK, Joseph Swan led the development of public electrical lighting in the city of Newcastle-upon-Tyne. A rapidly growing industrial city, much of central Newcastle was rebuilt between 1824 and 1841, with wide boulevards and neoclassical architecture providing a clear sense of what a modern city ought to look like. In 1879, Swan provided the first public lighting with incandescent lightbulbs in Moseley Street, Newcastle, and the following year he helped to make industrialist William Armstrong's manor of Cragside near Newcastle the world's first fully electrified home. Innovation continued as two electricity companies (Newcastle and District Electric Lighting Company and Newcastle-upon-Tyne Electric Supply Company) were founded in 1889 to provide electricity to the city. Charles Merz, who inherited the latter from his father in 1899, saw Newcastle as an opportunity to prove the advantages of the full electrification of a city, as a city-sized "proof of concept test" (Hughes 1983). By the mid-1900s, Newcastle was fully lit with incandescent electrical lights, which formed part of a wider grid that electrified the full city. The innovations in Newcastle occurred because it was a major industrial and engineering city, bringing together scientific innovation with finance. In the production of the first urban electricity grid, lighting also moves away from being a singular system independent of other urban technologies and becomes more closely integrated into wider networks of electrification.

Elsewhere, the spread of lighting technologies emerged in a more patchwork fashion. As electrical lighting could be installed alongside the wider rolling out of the electrical network, many cities outside of Europe, North America, and East Asia bypassed the "gas stage" of lighting, with electrical lighting installed as the first artificial lighting in the early 20th century (Feld 2015; Lee 2015). Zanzibar, for example, had oil lights with the first electrical lighting installed in royal buildings in the 1880s and in street lights by 1906 (Royer 2006). However, in both the dominant centers of global power and in peripheries, the different lighting technologies began to overlap much more. Baldwin (2012) describes the nocturnal streetscape of American cities in the early 20th century as "a crazy quilt of different forms of illumination: arc light towers, arc light gloves near street level, incandescent lights, gaslights with and without mantles, lamps burning gasoline or kerosene" (2012: 159). In some ways, Baldwin's description continues to describe the reality of street lighting in cities to the present day. In areas with advanced lighting networks, cities are likely to be lit by a mixture of: the "SON" sodium gas-based orange lighting that dominated for much of the 20th century; new LED lighting from streetlights and screens; and from light that spills over from advertisements, car headlamps, and a variety of domestic or business lighting. In areas with less extensive infrastructure, we will find all of these forms of lighting, as well as continued use of gas and kerosene in homes and informal settlements.

This brief overview of the introduction of artificial lighting reveals a process that, once it began, quickly started to transform urban life. Technologies that seemed new, bright, and innovative were old, dull, and mundane within 30 years. The spectacular quickly gave way to the ordinary. Moving into the 20th century, I want to connect more clearly to questions of modernity and media: how did the newly electrified city produce new ways of urban living, and new imaginations of what the city meant?

Twentieth Century: Modernity and the Lit City

In 1903, the sociologist Georg Simmel wrote that:

> to the extent that the metropolis creates these psychological conditions—with every crossing of the street, with the tempo and multiplicity of economic, occupational and

social life—it creates in the sensory foundations of mental life, and in the degree of awareness necessitated by our organization as creatures dependent on differences, a deep contrast with the slower, more habitual, more smoothly flowing rhythm of the sensory-mental phase of small town and rural existence.

(Simmel 1903: 11–12)

In other words, by the start of the 20th century, writers were already realizing that new forms of urbanity were fundamentally altering mentalities, changing how we experienced the city. This awareness was also the recognition of "modernity"—the period marked by the promise that technology and capitalism might annihilate problems common to pre-industrial societies, at the cost of producing an increased pace of lifestyle and associated psychosocial stresses and inequalities. The effects were both the creation of spaces and discourses of hope and optimism, but also despair and alienation. The introduction of electric lighting was part of this story, enabling, as it did, a shift in lifestyles so that everyday urban life could cover ever-longer periods, irrespective of changing seasonal levels of light and dark.

In the electric city, a range of new practices and economic spaces became accessible. In many cities, the electrification of everyday urban life has come alongside the proliferation of light, through advertisements and screens (McQuire 2005). As Baldwin (2012) notes, night-time entertainment districts were some of the first to grow: "electricity represented energetic modernity and signaled the city was a forward-looking, prosperous place" (2012: 159). These districts became a key symbol of urban life, as did another phenomenon that arrived with electric lighting, the brightly lit city advert. The first electrically lit adverts appeared on Broadway in New York in the 1890s and, by 1910, these and the lights on Times Square had become tourist attractions in their own right (Baldwin 2012). Electrification also brought the possibility for spectacular urban lighting festivals and events. The coastal resort of Blackpool in the UK pioneered a tourist-oriented illuminations festival in 1879, scheduling it for the autumn to extend the tourist season: the annual festival continues to this day as a touchstone of working-class culture in Northern England (Edensor and Millington 2013). In Lyon, the traditional *Fête des lumières* evolved into a lighting festival, which has in recent years been used as a site of technological innovation as part of a wider resurgence in lighting festivals (Edensor 2015). Other contemporary lighting spectacles include Singapore's city center night-time Formula 1 race and New Year's Eve celebrations, both of which "cast the city in a spectacle of light and sound that serves as an exuberant exhibition of nationalism, cosmopolitanism and globalism" (Yeo and Heng 2014: 714). Thus, night-time entertainment and festivals are now used as evidence of a city's modern, international, and cosmopolitan nature.

This connection between the electropolis and modernity can be seen in representations of the night as well. In film noir cinema, for example, the partial lighting that electricity brings has been used to emphasize the interplay of light and dark morals. Like the city backdrop cast in shadows, characters in film noir often have to cope with limited information and ambiguous moral choices. Bronfen (2013) argues that in film noir, "the night emerges as the privileged site for a discussion of how infatuation and self-delusion can lead to criminal transgression" (2013: 278). The genre uses lighting carefully, such that the low-key lighting "visually corresponds to the nocturnal attitude espoused" (Bronfen 2013: 278) in the films. A contemporary example can be found in the 2014 film, *Nightcrawler*. Set in Los Angeles, the film's lead character "Lou Bloom" encounters a night-time road traffic accident and discovers the role of "stringers," freelance photojournalists who listen in to emergency service radio signals in order to get to crime scenes before the police, so that they can record exclusive footage to sell to local television news networks. Bloom becomes increasingly skilled in this role and starts to concoct or incite criminal behavior in order to create scenes to film. Like many film noir movies, the lead character in *Nightcrawler* is drawn into the night's seedier elements and the main action of the film takes place in the darkened night-time city, amid occasional flashes of artificial light, including from Bloom's camera (see also Chapter 3, this volume). Artificial lighting in the night-time city has also appeared in literary depictions of urban life. A common feature has been the nocturnal *flaneur*, a position taken by writers such as Dickens (Hollington 1981), Baudelaire (Bronfen 2013: 245), and, more recently, Will Self (Beaumont 2015). Such writers have again used the interplay of light, shadow, and dark that the night-time city creates to depict lifestyles that are lived on the urban periphery.

Representations and experiences of the 20th-century night reflect the alienation identified with the modernist city, but also the opportunities for new ways of living that were created within it. But as images of the world at night help illustrate (Pritchard 2017), there are many gaps and unlit areas across the planet. Sub-Saharan Africa and much of non-coastal South America remain largely unlit, for example. In many other areas, suburbs or small towns remain quite dark. So, while the city of the 20th century saw artificial lighting reach a new peak, the energy and infrastructure cost of lighting meant that many places remained in the dark.

Twenty-First Century: LEDs and the Retreat of Light?

In the modernist city, artificial lighting was understood to be a public good; there was a period of technological stability and shared political will for more and brighter lighting. But today, urban lighting is possibly at its most dynamic since the innovations of the 19th century. The first change was the invention of outdoor LED lighting in the late 1990s, which became suitable for use as street lighting by the mid-2000s (Taguchi 2008). LEDs require less energy to provide the same levels of illumination, can be instantly turned on and off, and can be set to light with different (or indeed varying) colors. These capacities have created opportunities for various new lighting practices. The second change was the recognition of the role of artificial lighting in generating fossil fuel emissions, and as such contributing to climate change. Since the turn of the century, cities have become increasingly responsible for both mitigating and adapting to climate change (Bulkeley 2010) and, as such, street lighting—a major component of many urban authority's carbon footprint—has received increased attention. Third, since 2008, cities in Europe and North America, the locations that are most extensively lit, have undergone extensive periods of austerity. Most famously, Detroit suffered a bankruptcy, and the effects that this had on street lighting were quickly recognized (Peck 2012). Thus, many of the most brightly lit cities in the world have been looking for ways to reduce the costs of street lighting without removing services. Fourth, the world has continued to see urbanization on a global scale and, in particular, the emergence of mega-cities in Asia and Africa has produced new challenges for lighting. Cities are becoming larger, wealthier, increasingly complex, and better connected (Bishop and Phillips 2013). This growth means that more and more cities are requiring artificial lighting in more and more places, and these expanding cities have been on the lookout for ways of rolling out artificial lighting, but clearly are interested in keeping costs low (see also Chapter 16, this volume).

These prompts have combined to generate a "policy window" for new lighting practices (Verbong and Geels 2007). In particular, local authorities have moved toward various practices that bring an end to constant through-night lighting. These practices can be categorized in three ways (Shaw 2014). The first are practices of "dimming." Using the capacities of LEDs to change lighting level quickly, dimming can be set to make lights brighter during peak hours and darker during off-peak hours. By dimming lights after most pedestrians have used urban spaces, planners can save energy, cutting both carbon footprints and energy bills. The second set of practices is the logical extension of "part-night lighting." Part-night lighting was once common with gas and oil lanterns, but the compressed sodium-based lights of the 20th century, which burn efficiently and brightly but require a lot of energy to be ignited, were more suitable for a constant lighting provision. With LEDs and their quick and easy startups, part-night lighting has returned in a remarkable shift away from the "modernity'" of the 21st-century city. Typically, lighting will be programmed for the early evening until pedestrian and vehicle levels drop off and will, if needed, be resumed for the early morning commuter. Third, and perhaps most interestingly, are practices of smart lighting. Smart lighting technologies refer to the use of sensors, real-time data, and monitoring to create lighting that is responsive to urban conditions (Castro et al. 2013). Examples might include lighting that responds directly to passing traffic or changes brightness levels according to busyness. Smart lighting can be controlled from control centers or managed directly by appropriate authorities (e.g., emergency services).

In the Global South, where many cities were previously unlit or partially lit, LEDs have spread quickly. In tropical or sub-tropical locations, many have been able to take advantage of the fact that LED lights require less power to produce the same level of illumination, which means that in locations with reliable sunlight, they can run off rechargeable batteries that use solar energy (Pode 2010). A 2015 survey into the solar LED industry, for example, found distributors whose major countries of operation were Ethiopia, Haiti, India, Kenya, Malawi, Tanzania, and Zambia, revealing the use of this technology for cities in poor and rapidly urbanizing countries (Mills 2016). Perhaps the biggest uptake of LEDs has been in China, which has also seen extremely fast urbanization, producing a series of challenges for sustainability. The cost of lighting China's cities has been estimated at over US$1 billion a year, using more than 2 million tons of coal (Liu et al. 2010). Perhaps unsurprisingly, LEDs have been widely accepted in China, which has used its manufacturing capacities to produce LEDs at a low cost (Mills 2016). The bright lights of LED lighting have been appealing for China too, allowing for ambitious and high-profile urban lighting projects that present Chinese cities as technologically innovative (Lin 2015). Solar LED lighting has been used to avoid reliance on fuels, with the city of Lin'an in the Zhejiang Province lit entirely by solar LED lights (Liu et al. 2010), while with different motivations, this technology has been used in China's rural hinterland to provide off-grid lighting. Chinese cities are continuing to lead innovation in street lighting, with 2015 seeing the introduction of car charging portals into electric street lights (Li 2015).

The story of LED lighting technologies is one of a changing, perhaps "postmodern" move in which lighting is both spreading more rapidly across the globe as well as becoming more partially present in the cities where it is installed. During the time in which this chapter was written, researchers have been able to draw from newly available satellite data, using for the first time observations of artificial lighting on a neighborhood level at a global scale (Kyba et al. 2017). This data has shown that globally light pollution rose by 2.2% a year between 2012 and 2016, driven by new lighting being installed in previously unlit rural and urban areas. At the same time, a reduction in lighting in city centers in the brightest-lit cities was also observed (Kyba et al. 2017: 3–4). This may support the thesis of an inversion of a "modernist" brightly lit city surrounded by darker environments, but perhaps most importantly, reveals that the outcomes of new LED technologies and how they will be used in cities in the future remain contested and uncertain.

Conclusion

In putting urban lighting in the context of debates about urban communication, we need to remember that with the electrification of cities beginning in the second half of the 19th century, artificial lighting transformed the way that we perceive city streets, creating new expectations as to visibility, sociability, and access. This chapter has attempted to tell this story of the ways in which lighting emerged first as spectacular, but subsequently became mundane: a common or essential part of urban life, taken for granted as part of what urban living should be. As such, to be a modern city is to be a brightly lit city. However, this chapter has also shown that all lit spaces also have their dark corners, spaces into which a shadow is cast. Like all infrastructural developments, artificial lighting and electricity have spread unevenly, with a wide mixture of quality of artificial lighting across the globe, including many unlit spaces. Into the 21st century, the technological innovation of lighting has returned to the pace of the 19th century, resulting in the proliferation of multiple new forms of urban lighting alongside one another. Future trends are likely to be driven by ongoing concerns about the economic and environmental impact of urban lighting, such that the (impossible) modernist goal of the constantly lit electropolis seems to be being replaced by the more modest aim of getting the right lighting, in the right place, at the right time.

References

Alvarez, A. (1996) *Night*, London: Vintage.
Baldwin, C. (2012) *In the Watches of the Night*, Chicago, IL: University of Chicago Press.
Barnaby, A. (2015) "London," in S. Isenstadt, M. Maile-Petty, and D. Neumann (eds.) *Cities of Light: Two Centuries of Urban Illumination*, London: Routledge, pp. 20–27.
Beamish, A. (2015) "Boston," in S. Isenstadt, M. Maile-Petty, and D. Neumann (eds.) *Cities of Light: Two Centuries of Urban Illumination*, London: Routledge, pp. 10–19.
Beaumont, M. (2015) *Nightwalking: A Nocturnal History of London*, London: Verso Books.
Bishop, R. and Phillips, J. W. (2013) "The Urban Problematic," *Theory, Culture & Society*, 30(7–8), pp. 221–241.
Bronfen, E. (2013) *Night Passages: Philosophy, Literature, and Film*, New York: Columbia University Press.
Buckler, J. (2015) "Moscow," in S. Isenstadt, M. Maile-Petty, and D. Neumann (eds.) *Cities of Light: Two Centuries of Urban Illumination*, London: Routledge, pp. 123–129.
Bulkeley, H. (2010) "Cities and the Governing of Climate Change," *Annual Review of Environment and Resources*, 35(1), pp. 229–253.
Castro, M., Jara, A. J., and Skarmeta, A. F. G. (2013) *Advanced Information Networking and Applications Workshops (WAINA), 2013 27th International Conference*, 25–28 March 2013.
Edensor, T. (2015) "Light Art, Perception, and Sensation," *The Senses and Society*, pp. 1–20.
Edensor, T. and Millington, S. (2013) "Blackpool Illuminations: Revaluing Local Cultural Production, Situated Creativity and Working-Class Values," *International Journal of Cultural Policy*, 19(2), pp. 145–161.
Feld, G. (2015) "Buenos Aires," in S. Isenstadt, M. Maile-Petty, and D. Neumann (eds.) *Cities of Light: Two Centuries of Urban Illumination*, London: Routledge, pp. 92–95.
Hollington, M. (1981) "Dickens the Flaneur," *Dickensian*, 77(394), p. 71.
Huang, S. (1991) "Chinese Traditional Festivals," *The Journal of Popular Culture*, 25(3), pp. 163–180.
Hughes, T. (1983) *Networks of Power: Electrification in Western Society, 1880–1930*, Baltimore, MD: Johns Hopkins University Press.
Koslofsky, C. (2002) "Court Culture and Street Lighting in Seventeenth-Century Europe," *Journal of Urban History*, 28(6), pp. 743–768.
Kyba, C. C. M. et al. (2017) "Artificially Lit Surface of Earth at Night Increasing in Radiance and Extent," *Science Advances*, 3(11).
Lee, C. (2015) "Johannesburg," in S. Isenstadt, M. Maile-Petty, and D. Neumann (eds.) *Cities of Light: Two Centuries of Urban Illumination*, London: Routledge, pp. 96–100.
Li, X. (2015) "Intelligent Street Lamps Installed in Shanghai," *China Daily*, viewed 12 March 2017, www.chinadaily.com.cn/china/2015-10/29/content_22304349.htm.
Lin, J. (2015) "Shanghai," in S. Isenstadt, M. Maile-Petty, and D. Neumann (eds.) *Cities of Light: Two Centuries of Urban Illumination*, London: Routledge, pp. 115–122.
Liu, L.-Q. et al. (2010) "Solar Energy Development in China: A Review,"" *Renewable and Sustainable Energy Reviews*, 14(1), pp. 301–311.

Lu, H. (1999) *Beyond the Neon Lights: Everyday Shanghai in the Early Twentieth Century*. Berkeley, CA: University of California Press.
McQuire, S. (2005) "Immaterial Architectures: Urban Space and Electric Light," *Space and Culture*, 8(2), pp. 126–140.
Mills, E. (2016) "Job Creation and Energy Savings through a Transition to Modern Off-Grid Lighting," *Energy for Sustainable Development*, 33, pp. 155–166.
Peck, J. (2012) "Austerity Urbanism," *City*, 16(6), pp. 626–655.
Pike, D. L. (2005) "'The Greatest Wonder of the World': Brunel's Tunnel and the Meanings of Underground London," *Victorian Literature and Culture*, 33(2), pp. 341–367.
Pode, R. (2010) "Solution to Enhance the Acceptability of Solar-Powered LED Lighting Technology," *Renewable and Sustainable Energy Reviews*, 14(3), pp. 1096–1103.
Pritchard, S. B. (2017) "The Trouble with Darkness: NASA's Suomi Satellite Images of Earth at Night," *Environmental History*, 22(1), pp. 312–330.
Royer, T. (2006) *Lights of Zanzibar*, viewed 23 February 2017, www.zanzibarhistory.org/lights_of_zanzibar.htm.
Schivelbusch, W. (1988) *Disenchanted Night*, Oxford: Berg Publishers.
Schlör, J. (1998) *Nights in the Big City: Paris, Berlin, London 1840–1930*, London: Reaktion.
Shakhmatova, S. (2012) *A History of Street Lighting in the Old and New Towns of Edinburgh World Heritage Site*, Edinburgh: Edinburgh World Heritage City viewed 20 February 2017, www.ewht.org.uk/what-we-do/project-portfolio/historic-street-.
Shaw, R. (2014) "Streetlighting in England and Wales: New Technologies and Uncertainty in the Assemblage of Streetlighting Infrastructure," *Environment and Planning A*, 46(9), pp. 2228–2242.
Simmel, G. (1903) *The Metropolis and Mental Life*, Oxford: Blackwell.
Taguchi, T. (2008) "Present Status of Energy Saving Technologies and Future Prospect in White LED Lighting," *IEEJ Transactions on Electrical and Electronic Engineering*, 3(1), pp. 21–26.
Verbong, G. and Geels, F. (2007) "The Ongoing Energy Transition: Lessons from a Socio-Technical, Multi-Level Analysis of the Dutch Electricity System (1960–2004)," *Energy Policy*, 35(2), pp. 1025–1037.
Woods, M. N. (2015) "Mumbai," in S. Isenstadt, M. Maile-Petty, and D. Neumann (eds.) *Cities of Light: Two Centuries of Urban Illumination*, London: Routledge, pp. 37–44.
Yeo, S.-J. and Heng, C. K. (2014) "An (Extra)ordinary Night Out: Urban Informality, Social Sustainability and the Night-Time Economy," *Urban Studies*, 51(4), pp. 712–726.

Further Reading

Edensor, T. (2017) *From Light to Dark: Daylight, Illumination, and Gloom*, Minneapolis, MN: University of Minnesota Press.
Isenstadt, S., Petty, M. M. and Neumann, D. (2014) *Cities of Light: Two Centuries of Urban Illumination*, London: Routledge.
Schivelbusch, W. (1995) *Disenchanted Night: The Industrialization of Light in the Nineteenth Century*, Berkeley, CA: University of California Press.

15
URBAN TRANSPORT AND TELECOMMUNICATIONS

Dual Forms of the Communicative Skeleton of the City

Aaron Shapiro

Introduction

"It is not an infrequent experience," wrote James Carey (1989: 202), "to be driving along an interstate highway and to become aware that the highway is paralleled by a river, a canal, a railroad track, or telegraph and telephone wires." This palimpsest-like overlaying of transportation and telecommunications infrastructures—readily visible but often overlooked—provides a glimpse of the historic and geographic connections between two seemingly disparate types of system: one for the movement of goods and people, the other for the movement of signals, information, and messages. Today, we tend to treat these infrastructures as distinct. But as many have noted (e.g., Carey 1989; Morley 2011), this was not always the case. Prior to the development of the telegraph and railroad networks in the 19th century, "communication" referred to both transportation and message transmittal—"for the simple reason that the movement of messages was dependent on their being carried on foot or horseback or by rail" (Carey 1989: 203). It was only after the telegraph lines hugged the railroad tracks, stretching from city to city, coast to coast, that we began to understand communication as distinct from transport, as freed from the constraints of geography. Thus do those geographic palimpsests along the interstate seem so striking to keen observers today.

Much research has studied the interrelated expansions of transport and telecommunications infrastructures, querying the role they've played as constitutive elements of modern, capitalist social relations (Harvey 1989; Giddens 1990; Morley 2011). For instance, in the essay on the telegraph quoted above, Carey goes on to detail how the telegraph facilitated the standardization of time across national territories. But the relationship has also been considered for its role in colonialism and imperialism (Mattelart 1994; Larkin 2008), in the development of national- and global-scale political economies of manufacture, distribution, and finance (Chandler 1977; Beniger 1986; Sassen 1991), and in the creation of diasporic communities, of both subalterns and elites (Appadurai 1996; Sharma 2009).

These varied literatures have tended to focus on the socio-geographic relationships between and within urban nodes at the national or international scale. But this has left aside questions about the role that transport and telecommunications play in producing the *internal fabric* of the city—as an ideal-type construct, as lived experience, and as a material space (Lefebvre 1992). This chapter explores the possibility that how we imagine the city abstractly, and how we navigate its public and private spaces concretely, are profoundly shaped by the "stacking" of telecommunications and transportation infrastructures in urban environments (Shapiro 2018). Of course, in the "smart city," this stacking is becoming increasingly apparent as mobile, Internet-, and location-enabled devices proliferate across the urban landscape, generating a renewed awareness of the interconnectedness between transport and telecommunication infrastructures in the "Internet of Things." But focusing too intently on these more recent technological overtures would miss the historical depth of transport and telecommunications' dynamically interrelated operations. How have these infrastructures conspired to produce and reproduce spaces as *urban*—as negotiations of interiority and exteriority, inclusion and exclusion, public and private, of legibility and anonymity (Osborne and Rose 2004)? What capabilities and constraints do these infrastructural intersections afford? This chapter considers these questions through a discussion of three technologies and technological affordances, examining how transportation and telecommunications have been "infrastructured" together to function as a communicative skeleton for the modern capitalist city (Hughes 1989). The first section considers the relationship between rational address or house numbering systems and rational spatial orderings; the second examines the utility pole as a technology of extensibility and urban expansion in the 20th century; and the third considers the role of mobile dispatch as a technology of coordination in the maintenance of uneven urban geographies.

Locatability and Navigability: Rational Address Systems

Opening Google Maps on an Internet browser or smartphone today, one could be forgiven for imagining that cities were always organized rationally: businesses pop up on the map with all of their information available—address, telephone number, website, etc.—and users can get real-time instructions on how to get there. However, this rational ordering of geographic and communications information is actually a relatively recent phenomenon. Prior to the 1860s, buildings in US cities were numbered haphazardly. Their addresses were "static" in the sense that existing structures were simply objects to be enumerated without orientation to the city grid. As cities continued to grow in size and complexity, and as national postal systems expanded and matured (e.g., Henkin 2007), their lack of systematic addressing made them increasingly difficult to navigate. Visitors found it difficult to locate destinations. Markets developed for pocket-sized guides and business directories, which included detailed directions for finding places (Rose-Redwood 2006). For example, in a directory of brothels (i.e., "houses of ill-fame") in Philadelphia (Anonymous 1849), building locations were described as "No. 4 Wood Street, Near Eleventh" or "No. 341 Lombard Street, Above Tenth." Addresses bore no relation to a structure's position within the city grid. No. 4 Wood St. might sit in between No. 27 and No. 13, as determined by the order in which the structures were erected or replaced.

The Philadelphia address system, developed in 1860–1, sought to bring order to house numbering and ameliorate the growing confusion of static address systems (Rose-Redwood 2006). When implemented in US cities, haphazard addresses were replaced by a decimal schema, with building locations corresponding to their position within the Cartesian grid of the city. A "house of ill-fame," then, would be renumbered from No. 4 Wood St. to, say, 1034 Wood St., to reflect its location between 10th and 11th Streets (and, being an even number, its position on the south side of Wood St.). In fact, street signs in Philadelphia today are labeled with their "block hundred number"—1000 Wood St., for example—such that the address can serve as a practical coordinate within the textually demarcated grid.

Geographer Reuben S. Rose-Redwood (2006: 481) argues that the Philadelphia system exemplifies how "governmentalization" at the local, urban level was essentially a spatial-infrastructural endeavor, "a process whereby municipal officials increasingly took on the responsibility of devising a spatial regime of inscriptions that facilitated the individualization of the population." Of particular interest for the present discussion are the dual dynamics of individualization and aggregation—locatability and navigability (Elmer 2010)—that this "spatial regime of inscriptions" allows for. Individualization and aggregation, together, rationalize the organization of urban space. In fact, spatial "legibility," in James Scott's (1998) sense of the term, might best be understood as the twinning of these affordances: individualized units that can be located within navigable, aggregate systems. Rational address systems render urban geographies legible: physical structures become informatically stable—"events" within the organized system of the textually inscribed landscape (Malik 2005)—allowing increasingly complex cities to become navigable, even to outsiders. With such a system in place, individual units, buildings, and whole districts could be located much more easily through an interplay between cartographic representations and the series of textual indicators that local governments ensure are distributed throughout physical spaces (cf. Lefebvre 1992). From this point of view, navigation apps like Google Maps would be simply the partial computerization of this locatability and navigability; autonomous or "self-driving" vehicles would be their complete automation.

However, at a more fundamental level, rational address schema like the Philadelphia system could be said to provide the epistemological template upon which all contemporary telecommunications and transportation infrastructures operate. With its functions of navigability and locatability, aggregation and individuation, the Philadelphia system provided a spatial rubric that would facilitate a much smoother surface for the movement of goods and people and for the movement of symbols, images, and messages—across both urban and rural landscapes as well as public and private spheres. But rational address schema have also played a more essential role as a prototype for nearly every information infrastructure to come afterwards (Bowker et al. 2010). In other words, we are talking not just about home addresses, but also *IP addresses* and the *email addresses*. Such prototypic prowess may owe to the fact that although addresses, being numeric, are *symbols* in Peircean semiotics, they are also *indices*. They connect objects, places, and things to one another within informatically stable, organized systems. More precisely, addresses are made to *stand in* for whatever subject or object that they index. "From the national postal service to the public telephone to the license plate on every registered vehicle, media are at work replacing people with their addresses" (Kittler 1996: 725). It is this standing-in that enables infrastructural movement, both in terms of transport and telecommunications. A passenger in a taxi does not need to direct the driver to her home; she can simply state her address. When making a phone call, a telephone number now connects you directly to a person or business on the other end of the line. An IP address identifies individual computers on web traffic, signaling where responses to requests should be sent.

To grasp the centrality of these and other forms of address to infrastructural systems, consider Friedrich Kittler's (1996: 725) quip that "addresses are data which allow other data to appear." The standing-in of the address for its indexically connected subject or object links physical matter to its informatic double, calling forth the relationality of the informatic system in which the address is situated. These dynamics make the *infrastructuring* of transport and telecommunications possible (Hughes 1989). Addresses yield productive partitions and generative divisions. "They separate mountain streams from waterways, people from subjects, cities from capitals" (Kittler 1996: 725). They classify at the level of both genre (i.e., aggregation) and specimen (i.e., individual).

All of these affordances have become increasingly important as cities came to be understood by urban managers not just as sites for economic exchange or as concentrations of political power, but also as concrete milieus for the extraction of value from mobile populations (cf. Osborne and Rose 1999; Shapiro 2018). By rendering urban spaces legible and informatic, navigable, and locatable, addresses also produced an informatics of population. The street address was not only useful for the postal service, but also, later, for marketing firms, who used postal address and neighborhoods as a proxy for race and socio-economic status, producing audiences as consumer blocks of households and demographic segments, as commodities to be sold to advertisers (cf. McGuigan and Manzerolle 2014; Dalton and Thatcher 2015). Rational address systems create the rubrics according to which new forms of data and new formats of informatic standing-in proliferate and circulate.

Extensibility: The Utility Pole and the Grid

Rational address systems render urban landscapes legible—an *intellectual* rather than material technology (Miller and Rose 2008). Intellectual technologies are epistemic in nature. They deal with how the world is organized and understood. Nevertheless, intellectual technologies have profound material effects. Changing the way that we come to know and navigate the urban landscape, intellectual technologies also shape the material organization of cities. This section considers one material technology that has become essential to urban spatialization in the 20th century: the utility pole.

The first utility poles were erected by telegraph companies in the mid-19th century as a cheaper and quicker alternative to laying wire underground (Mulqueen and Zafar 2014). Their initial expansion hugged the emergent railroad lines in the United States, the United Kingdom, and Europe, linking telecommunications infrastructure with transportation (see Hu 2015: chapter 1). In addition to being cheap and quick to erect, poles had other advantages for private and public utilities: connections could be expanded seemingly without limit, as could the number of lines that hung from the poles. By the time that electricity became common for urban households in the early 20th century, followed soon after by the telephone, telegraph poles had already become commonplace along urban corridors. From the late 1970s and early 1980s, cable television providers began adding their lines to the poles. Today the standard utility pole stands 35 feet high and is compartmentalized into as many as four sections. The primary level, the highest section of the utility pole, houses high-voltage electricity wires (which carry more than 600 volts); the secondary level, located just below, houses electrical currents that have been "stepped down" from the primary wires through a transformer; the third-tier communication level, some 40 inches below the secondary level, is where telecommunication cables are attached, including telephone, television cable, fiber-optic cable, and, in some cities, wireless Internet hubs; finally, at the base is the "public level," with no apparent functionality (Siegel 1984; Mulqueen and Zafar 2014).

Throughout the 20th century, with radio, telephone, and television becoming standard in households, telecommunications infrastructure connected individuals to one another and to centrally controlled mass media outlets, fundamentally restructuring the domestic sphere (Spigel 2001; Hartley 2002). The exterior world was brought into the interior home in new ways, buttressing the solidity of domestic space as a coherent realm distinct from the outside. Interior spaces were, in turn, flipped inside out and objectified as media companies amassed subscribers and ratings companies like Nielsen aggregated family-consumers into audience blocks, which could then be bought and sold to advertisers. More recently, the widespread availability of high-speed Internet has laid the ground for the rise of a network structure that threatens to destabilize the broadcast system's hegemony. New modes of collectivization and surveillance have emerged to fill the gaps of the waning broadcast model (McGuigan and Manzerolle 2014).

However, remaining constant through these transformations was the spatializing function of these infrastructures. The network of telecommunications connections overlays the grids of cities like Philadelphia, New York, and Chicago. And like the city grid, the "grid" of telecommunications connectivity is entirely extensible thanks to the utility pole. And this extensibility works both vertically (as in the addition of new lines to the utility pole) and horizontally or spatially, owing to the pole's ability to expand connections across distances inexpensively. Further, as AbdouMaliq Simone (2004: 426) has argued, the public emplacement of utility poles is co-opted communally (and quite invisibly) by those living on the urban fringes of Johannesburg and other cities, with clandestine electrical and telecommunications riggings lighting and connecting "ten times as many households as there are official connections" (see also Chapter 19, this volume).

Concurrent with these developments was a radical rescaling of the urban landscape via suburbanization. As David Harvey (2008) has argued, the suburbanization of the US provided a means to absorb postwar surplus capital. But to do so required new, extensible infrastructures—both of transport (as in automobility and interstate highway systems) and telecommunications infrastructure. The technique of extensibility, baked into the utility pole as a technology, prefigures a new scale of urbanization—suburbanization, the age of the automobile, the age of the commuter. The point is not merely that the utility pole, upon which extensible networks of telecommunications infrastructures are built, lines transportation corridors, but rather that the rescaling of the urban required new means of connection and collectivization for which the utility pole played a key role. As several scholars have shown, urban geographies were profoundly reshaped to accommodate suburban development by (literally) paving the way for the automobile, often leaving out or intently excluding racial minorities and lower-class communities (Winner 1980; Sheller and Urry 2000; Harvey 2008). However, left out of these discussions is the role that telecommunications infrastructures played in connecting previously rural, suburbanizing areas with the urban center—in folding urban peripheries into the core of expanding urban regions. While the utility pole first linked the grid of city streets to the grid of communications connectivity, it later became central to the rescaling of the entire urban project. Entire regions were able to be linked together as a metropolis—with car commuting, yes, but also statistically, as in designations used in censuses such as "metropolitan statistical area," and commercially, as in media markets that incorporate metro and tri-state areas. The work of the utility pole is to facilitate these types of mundane collectivizations, even as—or, more precisely, *especially* as—communal life was increasingly atomized according to the imperatives of capital and its often-oppressive norms (for instance, of the white, heteronormative middle-class variety; see Spigel 2001). In short, the connectivity afforded by the utility pole's extensible grid made possible distinctly suburban forms of alienated collectivization and an entire rescaling of the urban project.

Coordination: Mobile Dispatch

In the US, the postwar prosperity gospel that made suburbs so attractive to white, middle-class populations was underwritten by social unrest and violent clashes between urban African American communities and the police in the cities that suburban white populations were leaving behind. "White flight," enabled by the extensibility of transportations and telecommunications infrastructures, forged vast new spatial disparities and uneven geographies in what amounted to the urban crises of the 1970s (Katznelson 1982; Sugrue 2014). However, the accepted narrative of "urban decline" tends to overlook the fact that spatial disparities and uneven geographies are not just made by the evacuation of wealth and capital from city centers, but rather require constant reproduction and perpetuation—not just whites and their wealth leaving the city or certain neighborhoods, but active *dis*investment in those spaces (cf. Smith 1996). At the same time that suburbanization was gutting city budgets, new, highly localized investments in city centers were ramping up, often in exchange for massive tax benefits (Harvey 1989). The globalization of capital that began in earnest in the 1980s created what Saskia Sassen (1991) has called "global cities," centers of high technology and high finance, to serve as infrastructural hubs for the movement of finance capital, information, and elites (see also Chapter 16, this volume). Thus, cities came to be divided between spaces of privilege, where participants in the elite economy of finance, insurance, and real estate operate, and exclusion, where those populations thrust out of the new economy live. Peter Marcuse (1997) describes these two types of spaces—the *citadel* and the *outcast ghetto*—as being key components of the contemporary city.

Crucially, the maintenance of boundaries between the spaces of privilege and exclusion, the citadel and the outcast ghetto, requires logistical coordination, and logistical coordination requires both the movement of goods and people as well as the movement of information—the conjunction of transportation and telecommunications infrastructures (see also Chapter 9, this volume). One such coordinative technology that has been central to the maintenance of urban boundaries is *radio dispatch*—enacted through the pairing of two-way radio with automobility. Dispatch is a coordinative technology. It connects individual mobile units to centralized command and control centers. Communications over the radio allow dispatchers (emergency call centers, for example) to mobilize units in response to events happening in real time. The outcome is the networking together of individual units, making them a responsive, mobile fleet.

In spaces of exclusion, dispatch is used to coordinate the surveillance of outcast populations—the "lumpenized" urban poor and minority communities most often viewed as a threat to the prosperity of the city (Wacquant 2009). In carceral states like the US (Simon 2007), lower-class and racial and ethnic minority communities are controlled through an increasingly militarized mode of police patrol (Graham 2011; see also Chapter 18, this volume), for which dispatch remains a crucial, if understated, function. The installation of two-way radios in police squad cars began in the 1930s and fundamentally altered the nature of police patrol, "increasing the *speed* of transport for both criminals and police, extending the *territory* over which police patrols were distributed and creating new demands and capacities for police *communication*" (Reeves and Packer 2013: 372, emphasis mine). Of course, today, squad cars are outfitted not only with a two-way radio, but also with onboard computers that can be used to connect the mobile unit with criminal and suspect databases (Ferguson 2017). However, like the rational address system discussed above, dispatch also serves as a template for these broader coordinative functions. Dispatch provides an overarching structure—the mobile fleet of individual units and the central command and control—that depends, at a fundamental level, on the nexus between transportation and telecommunications. An officer pulls a minority community member over for suspicious driving; the officer obtains the driver's license and insurance information and runs it through his onboard computer, radioing in to dispatch; the driver's name yields a bench warrant for unpaid traffic violations, likely issued under similar circumstances; the officer calls in backup and arrests the driver upon their arrival. While benign enough at an abstract level, this coordinative capacity intersects with the increasing isolation and exclusion of marginalized groups (low-income communities of color) and military-style police logics (police as occupying forces in cities' expanding outcast ghettos). And these intersections result in insidious feedback loops of criminalization, in which low-income and minority groups who are already subject to intensive surveillance are subject to further police scrutiny and intervention. Dispatch as a coordinative technology is essential to this regime of police patrol.

In contrast, in spaces of privilege—the techno-citadels of the world's finance capitals—the coordinative functions of dispatch must be tuned to the global scale. Whereas the coordination of outcast ghettos looks inward, to the maintenance of exclusion and isolation, the citadel looks outward, toward the global networks of mobile capital. This is true of the information and communications technologies that facilitate capital flows (i.e., "fintech") (cf. Sassen 1991), but also of the more mundane infrastructural accommodations that must be made for mobile populations of global elites who pass through the "non-places" of airports and business centers. As Sarah Sharma (2008) shows in her research on taxi drivers in Toronto, the medium of taxi cab dispatch is integral to the tuning of global time, synchronizing the movement of people on the ground with global transportation infrastructures. Like the squad car, taxis operate as both individual units and as components of a fleet through their dispatching. But unlike the police patrol, their dispatch function is not to coordinate a surveillant mesh over the city's "dangerous" zones, but rather to *synchronize* the movement of passengers to "external forces beyond the driver's control" (Sharma 2008: 459). "The space of the cab," Sharma writes,

> is layered with multiple and competing temporal demands that the driver has no choice but to negotiate . . . the tempo of the fares, airline schedules, the time-management demands of the dispatchers, and the multiple rhythms of the spaces they traverse.
>
> *(2008: 459)*

Ride-hailing apps like Uber and Lyft simply automate this dispatching function, using algorithms to match customers with nearby drivers.

That spaces of privilege and spaces of exclusion both entail mobile dispatching suggests that coordination is a crucial component to milieus of differentiation, of social sorting, between populations. Valuations of social worth are assigned to specific areas. Large swaths of the urban landscape are relegated to those populations deemed unproductive and disposable, seen as requiring constant surveillance and control through police patrol. In contrast, spaces of value are reserved for the exchange and circulation of capital, for the pure consumer—desiring and desirable, deserving of corporate investment (Sharma 2009). Reflecting on the role of dispatch in this differentiation should give us pause generally, and good reason, specifically, to question the uneven distribution of investment and control across urban spaces.

Conclusion

Urban geographies are made and remade, constituting cities as spaces of exchange, circulation, and communication. The sets of technologies and technological affordances considered here demonstrate how the infrastructuring of transport and telecommunications fundamentally altered the social landscape of urban geographies. Rational address systems reorganize urban geographies, rendering them legible, while simultaneously providing an epistemological template for countless other information infrastructures. Utility poles enable the expansion of municipalities into 20th-century suburbanized metropolises, folding peripheral spaces into the center through infrastructural connection and collectivization. The mobile dispatch facilitates the coordinative maintenance of boundaries between zones of inclusion and exclusion. These technologies and their affordances illustrate how the infrastructuring of transport and telecommunications has fundamentally shaped how we come to know, navigate, and live in cities. But the examples also demonstrate the complex ethical dynamics at play in urban spatial production, as each technology considered here is as responsible for the production of new forms of exclusion as it is for bringing progressive and egalitarian improvements to the urban landscape. As intersections between transport and telecommunications are again made evident to observers through the "smart city" and the "Internet of Things," urban media scholars need to stay vigilant of these exclusions and consider that the infrastructuring of transport and telecommunications is never an entirely innocent endeavor.

References

Anonymous (1849) *A Guide to the Stranger, or Pocket Companion for the Fancy, Containing a List of the Gay Houses and Ladies of Pleasure in the City of Brotherly Love and Sisterly Affection*, www.librarycompany.org/shadoweconomy/section4_5.htm.

Appadurai, A. (1996) *Modernity at Large: Cultural Dimensions of Globalization*, Minneapolis, MN: University of Minnesota Press.

Beniger, J. R. (1986) *The Control Revolution: Technological and Economic Origins of the Information Society*, Cambridge, MA: Harvard University Press.

Bowker, G. C. et al. (2010) "Toward Information Infrastructure Studies: Ways of Knowing in a Networked Environment," in J. Hunsinger, L. Klastrup, and M. Allen (eds.) *International Handbook of Internet Research*, Dordrecht: Springer Science and Business Media B.V., pp. 97–117.

Carey, J. W. (1989) "Technology and Ideology: The Case of the Telegraph," in *Communication as Culture: Essays on Media and Society*, New York: Psychology Press, pp. 201–229.

Chandler, A. D. (1977) *The Visible Hand: The Managerial Revolution in American Business*, Cambridge, MA: Harvard University Press.

Dalton, C. M. and Thatcher, J. (2015) "Inflated Granularity: Spatial 'Big Data' and Geodemographics," *Big Data & Society*, 2(2), pp. 1–15.

Elmer, G. (2010) "Locative Networking: Finding and Being Found," *Aether: The Journal of Media Geography*, V.A. (March), pp. 18–26.

Ferguson, A. G. (2017) *The Rise of Big Data Policing: Surveillance, Race, and the Future of Law Enforcement*, New York City: NYU Press.

Giddens, A. (1990) *The Consequences of Modernity*, Cambridge: Polity Press.

Graham, S. (2011) *Cities Under Siege: The New Military Urbanism*, New York: Verso.

Hartley, J. (2002) *Uses of Television*, New York: Routledge.

Harvey, D. (1989) "From Managerialism to Entrepreneurialism: The Transformation in Urban Governance in Late Capitalism," *Geografiska Annaler. Series B. Human Geography*, pp. 3–17.

— (2008) "The Right to the City," *New Left Review*, 53, pp. 23–40.

Henkin, D. M. (2007) *The Postal Age: The Emergence of Modern Communications in Nineteenth-Century America*, Chicago, IL: University of Chicago Press.

Hu, T.-H. (2015) *A Prehistory of the Cloud*, Cambridge, MA: MIT Press.

Hughes, T. P. (1989) "Evolution of Large Technological Systems," in W. E. Bijker and T. J. Pinch (eds.) *The Social Construction of Technological Systems: New Directions in the Sociology and History of Technology*, Cambridge, MA: MIT Press, pp. 51–82.

Katznelson, I. (1982) *City Trenches: Urban Politics and the Patterning of Class in the United States*, Chicago, IL: University of Chicago Press.

Kittler, F. A. (1996) "The City Is a Medium," *New Literary History*, 27(4), pp. 717–729.

Larkin, B. (2008) *Signal and Noise: Media, Infrastructure, and Urban Culture in Nigeria*, Durham, NC: Duke University Press.

Lefebvre, H. (1992) *The Production of Space*, Malden, MA: Blackwell.

Malik, S. (2005) "Information and Knowledge," *Theory, Culture & Society*, 22(1), pp. 29–49.

Marcuse, P. (1997) "The Enclave, the Citadel, and the Ghetto: What Has Changed in the Post-Fordist US City," *Urban Affairs Review*, 33(2), pp. 228–264.

Mattelart, A. (1994) *Mapping World Communication: War, Progress, Culture*, Minneapolis, MN: University of Minnesota Press.

McGuigan, L. and Manzerolle, V. (eds.) (2014) *The Audience Commodity in a Digital Age: Revisiting a Critical Theory of Commercial Media*, New York: Peter Lang.

Miller, P. and Rose, N. (2008) *Governing the Present*, Malden, MA: Polity Press.

Morley, D. (2011) "Communications and Transport: The Mobility of Information, People and Commodities," *Media, Culture & Society*, 33(5), pp. 743–759.

Mulqueen, A. and Zafar, M. (2014) "A Brief Introduction to Utility Poles. California Public Utilities Commission, Policy & Planning Division," www.cpuc.ca.gov/uploadedFiles/CPUC_Public_Website/Content/About_Us/Organization/Divisions/Policy_and_Planning/PPD_Work/PPDUtilityPole.pdf.

Osborne, T. and Rose, N. (1999) "Governing Cities: Notes on the Spatialisation of Virtue," *Environment & Planning D*, 17, pp. 737–760.

— (2004) "Spatial Phenomenotechnics: Making Space with Charles Booth and Patrick Geddes," *Environment & Planning D: Society and Space*, 22, pp. 209–228.

Reeves, J. and Packer, J. (2013) "Police Media: The Governance of Territory, Speed, and Communication," *Communication & Critical/Cultural Studies*, 10(4), pp. 359–384.

Rose-Redwood, R. S. (2006) "Governmentality, Geography, and the Geo-Coded World," *Progress in Human Geography*, 30(4), pp. 469–486.

Sassen, S. (1991) *The Global City: New York, London, Tokyo*, Princeton, NJ: Princeton University Press.

Scott, J. C. (1998) *Seeing Like a State*, New Haven, CT: Yale University Press.

Shapiro, A. (2016) "The Mezzanine," *Space & Culture*, 19(4), pp. 292–307.

— (2018) "The Urban Stack: A Topology for Urban Data Infrastructures," *Tecnoscienza: The Italian Journal of Science & Technology Studies*, 8(1), pp. 5–21.

Sharma, S. (2008) "Taxis as Media: A Temporal Materialist Reading of the Taxi-Cab," *Social Identities*, 14(4), pp. 457–464.

— (2009) "Baring Life and Lifestyle in the Non-Place," *Cultural Studies*, 23(1), pp. 129–148.

Sheller, M. and Urry, J. (2000) "The City and the Car," *International Journal of Urban and Regional Research*, 24(4), pp. 737–757.

Siegel, A. J. (1984) "The History of Cable Television Pole Attachment Regulation," *Communications and the Law*, 6.

Simon, J. (2007) "Rise of the Carceral State," *Social Research*, 74(2), pp. 471–508.

Simone, A. (2004) "People as Infrastructure: Intersecting Fragments in Johannesburg," *Public Culture*, 16(3), pp. 407–429.

Smith, N. (1996) *The New Urban Frontier: Gentrification and the Revanchist City*, New York: Routledge.

Spigel, L. (2001) *Welcome to the Dreamhouse: Popular Media and Postwar Suburbs*, Durham, NC: Duke University Press.

Sugrue, T. J. (2014) *The Origins of the Urban Crisis: Race and Inequality in Postwar Detroit*, Princeton, NJ: Princeton University Press.

Wacquant, L. (2009) *Punishing the Poor: The Neoliberal Government of Social Insecurity*, Durham, NC: Duke University Press.

Winner, L. (1980) "Do Artifacts Have Politics?" *Daedalus*, 109(1), pp. 121–136.

Further Reading

Martin, R. (2016) *The Urban Apparatus: Mediapolitics and the City*, Minneapolis, MN: University of Minnesota Press.

Morley, D. (2018) *Communications and Mobility: The Migrant, the Mobile Phone, and the Container Box*, Oxford: Wiley.

Sheller, M. (2018) *Mobility Justice: The Politics of Movement in an Age of Anxiety*, New York: Verso.

16
GLOBAL CITIES AS MEDIATED SPACES

The Role of Media in Forming Contradictory Places

Paul James

Introduction

Cities have always been mediated spaces. One image of the city provides what was perhaps the first enduring metaphor for understanding the tensions of extended communications. In the Biblical story of a city divided, possibly the city of Babylon, perhaps connected to the Sumerian myth of Enmerkar, humans had tried to build a physical connection to heaven. The God of the Old Testament responded adversely, fracturing their previous unity of communication into a babel of different voices spread across the world. Visualizations of the Tower of Babel reverberate across history, and the city has subsequently remained a contested trope of communicative connection and fracturing. This tension is basic to understanding the phenomenology of global cities as mediated spaces.

To the extent that the story of Babel focused attention on two comfortably understood processes—the way that embodied communication has across human history been divided by languages; and the contribution cities make as the locus of a world-historical process bringing strangers together across such communicative divides—it has, however, also contributed to stopping us seeking to understand the *contradictory* relationship between media and the city. Media mediate—they abstract relations over extensions of space. They also provide the means for mutually interactive connections (see also Chapters 1 and 16, this volume). What does it mean, for example, that the media, both in content *and* form, divides citizens of a global city, even as it brings them together? What does it mean that cities are intensely local places but the same media that represents citizens to each other also connects them globally? These two questions weave through this chapter, which explores how global and local forces coalesce in mediated urban spaces.

Before responding to those questions, we need first to define the use of the concept of "global cities" in this chapter: precisely because it goes against the mainstream deployment of the term. Evoking different kinds of cities at different times in world history—cities as diverse as Babylon, Rome, Florence, Havana, Los Angeles, Boston and Dili—provides touchpoints throughout the chapter for suggesting that the way in which much of the contemporary literature defines global cities is reductive, modern-centric and economistic. The chapter suggests that the so-called "global cities", New York, Paris, London and Tokyo (Sassen 2001), need to be de-centred from contemporary theorizing. Further, the impressions that "global cities" are a twentieth-century phenomenon and that the movement of finance capital predominantly defines their global status also need to be thoroughly rethought. The globalization of all cities has been a long-term process intensifying across a very long history. Like the nature of communications, the dominant forms of globalization have changed significantly, and their effects have been increasingly intensified and extended. However, globalization processes did not begin with abstracted finance capital exchange over the past couple of decades. And it cannot be reduced to questions of financial flows. Accordingly, the concept of "global cities" cannot be reduced to economic exchange, or even economics plus a few other extras such as communication lines. In summary, we need a different approach both to the phenomenon of global cities and the question of media connectivity. This chapter begins to set out an alternative.

Exploring the Contradictory Role of the Media in the Formation of Cities

The role of different media in contributing to changing urban form, including the way in which different media link the global and the local, is discussed occasionally in the literature. Harold Innis argues that "The monarchies of Egypt and Persia, the Roman empire, and the city-states were essentially products of writing. Extension of activities in more densely populated regions created the need for written records" (1950: 8). He describes how writing on portable papyrus, rather than on relatively immobile stone, allowed the city-state of Rome to become a globalizing, empire. That is, the city-as-empire used written communications to manage power relations with others far beyond its immediate walls. Innis, however, is an evocative writer rather than a deeply documenting one. Even the passage quoted above leaves the determinative relations confused. Did the media make the city, or the city create the need for extensive media?

There is no equivalent in the urban studies space to books such as Benedict Anderson's *Imagined Communities* (1991) in nationalism studies. There we read the now-classic analysis of the way in which the intersection of a particular mode of mediated communications—print—and a particular mode of production—capitalism—was critical to the transition from the absolutist state to nation-state. Print-capitalism ushered in a world of temporal simultaneity across extended distances. According to Anderson, a community of people, otherwise abstracted strangers to each other living in different parts of the country, relive daily the sense of national connection to each other as they recognize themselves as members of a single reading community. Each daily newspaper reader "is well aware that the ceremony he performs is being replicated simultaneously by thousands (or millions) of others of whose existence he is confident, yet of whose identity he has not the slightest notion" (1991: 35). For all of the limits of his analysis here, Anderson is onto something. It is not only the *content* of the media that was critical but also its mediating *form*.

Unfortunately, he does not have an adequate theoretical framework for handling his pathbreaking intuitions. It would certainly have helped us in relation to understanding how cities give strangers a sense of deep connection. Why, we could ask, cannot the same thing be said of cities as for nations? Why does not reading the *New York Times*, the *Boston Globe*, the *London Evening Standard*, the *Moskovskiy Komsomolets* and the *Sydney Morning Herald* remind the newspaper reader, "observing exact replicas of his own paper being consumed by his subway, barbershop, or residential neighbours", in Anderson's words, "that the imagined world [of New York, Boston, London, Moscow and Sydney] is visibly rooted in everyday life" (1991: 35–36)? It just seems too obvious. After all, newspapers tend to be named after cities, not nations (see also Chapter 6, this volume).

Cities have always been mediated spaces, and different forms of media have always acted to give urban communities a common sense of location-bound fate. Perhaps it is because of the obviousness of this point that it is rarely explored in relation to the nature or form of social relations in the city. Across the century, since Park and Burgess wrote of the urban disruption of face-to-face relations, with the newspaper acting as "the great medium of communication within the city" (1922: 39), there has been little sustained attention given to this issue of mediated urban form. Rather, the focus of analysis shifted firmly to the media as providing representational *content*—that is, as representing the drama and "immediacy" of notable events beyond the immediate neighbourhood, and the everyday patterns of urban life (e.g. Koch and Latham 2014).

The central argument of this chapter is that the subjective-objective power of cities has been built substantially upon the contradictory nature of mediated communications, stretching between face-to-face relations and differently abstracted levels of communication. At least three contradictory processes can be lifted out for discussion here. Firstly, different media, used in different ways, simultaneously integrate and differentiate people. Secondly, media both contribute to abstracting cities from place (and time) and, at the same time, reflect back to local places a representational immediacy that enhances the local and its sense of "now". And thirdly, media simultaneously provide an infrastructure for the globalization of cities, and, ironically by transcending space, they bring the world back to the city—again enhancing its localness. This complexity arguably contributes to the lack of sustained analysis. It also suggests that we might need to engage with, rather than put aside, the implicit tension between the *content* and *form* of media.

The elusiveness of the issue that the outcomes of communicative mediation are contradictory has left many urban commentators perplexed. This problem is bound up with the dominant sense that communications equals connectivity. Just as with the Tower of Babel example, the usual orientation towards all urban communicative acts is to treat them as flat extensions of embodied communication. Communications media in the city thus become means of connection-at-a-distance in much the same way as orality is a means of connection when in the presence of other persons. This dominant way of apprehending the media misses the contradictory abstracting processes that all media entail. With the predominance of the concept of "connectivity" in this space of media theory (e.g. Tomlinson 1999), the idea that a social-relational phenomenon can have impact at a distance without connecting people together seems to have been overlooked (James and Steger 2016). For example, the Cold War, reinforced by ideological contestation through different media systems, constituted a global system that at once drew cities into a common imaginary, and at the same time led to decreasing or demarcated connectivity between many cities on different sides of the Iron Curtain. Havana, for example, which earlier had deep historical connections to London, Madrid and New York, was effectively isolated. Even relations with its new metropole, Moscow, were limited by distance and cultural difference.

Before we embark upon a discussion of the three contradictions lifted out for attention, we need to outline the different forms of media in relation to different ontological formations and different formations of cities. This will help to clarify the changing forms of mediation and their different and contradictory impact on the nature of cities, and global cities in particular. The conventional distinction made in the literature is between oral, written and electronic communication. This distinction is still useful in the hands of subtle writers (e.g. Goody 1987). However, because of the tendency to either turn the difference into a Great Divide between the modern (print) and pre-modern (orality), or to conclude that communicative forms are all the same, there is a need for more elaborate and layered schema.

The present approach works with four formations rather than a single divide or epochal sequence: customary, traditional, modern and postmodern formations of practice and meaning (James 2006). And the major forms of communication map across these formations. There are at least six clear distinguishable dominant forms of communicative interchange and mediation across world history, and at this level of generality it is possible to make some broader but defensible claims about urban mediation. The following modes are discussed from the least abstracted to the most abstracted. Paradoxically, the more abstracted the way of encoding meaning, the more it provides a mimesis of the multisensory possibilities of embodied communications of which orality is a part (see Figure 16.1).

Forms of Communication Across Human History in Relation to Urban Change

Orality

Oral communication is dominant in early *customary* formations but continues to be foundational for all human communication. This simple point makes it possible to trace a complex intertwined lineage from oral-symbolic communication to electronic communication without setting up epochal divides. In this point, the important recognition that orality continues to be foundational to all intentional communication between humans is carefully qualified by the argument that power is layered and contextual. By the same logic, orality continues to be foundational to all city life, but in modern globalizing cities its integrative consequences are qualified by the extensive power of media communications and, more recently, social media and automated algorithmic communication. This is one source of many of the contradictions of urban media. With this in mind, a further dramatic point becomes clear. Orality as a mode of communication was not sufficient for cities to form. Elaborate and dense locales for living, together with complex transactions effected over time, required, for example, a mode of communication that abstracted meaning from embodied memory. By the same argument, communities formed in the dominance of oral communications are only globalizing in one respect: the slow embodied colonization of the planet by oral communities as they gradually spread over the entire globe, first by walking and later using pack animals.

Figurative Symbolism

Based initially on analogical meaning dominant in customary formations, but abstracted for both cosmological expression and life-sustaining utility in societies with a more extensive reach, *figurative and list-based symbolism* spanned practices of body- and object-inscription to became central to the emerging dominance of *traditional* formations. Most relevant here, such symbolism (which gradually changed into writing: for example, cuneiform) was important to the possibility of forming post-subsistence urban conglomerations. Cities required the organization of resources at a distance to do basic things such as feed people. This means of communication was then later rationalized for data-keeping under conditions of urban commercial life, for example in the form of double-entry booking keeping. It became a key condition for the power of globalizing medieval European trading cities such as Florence and Amsterdam and obviously is still relevant today. In short, figurative symbolism, transforming into writing, was a necessary condition of *traditional* urban formation, but it was not sufficient for supporting extensive processes of globalization.

Writing

Writing in scripted form (sometimes with vestiges of the figurative) makes a more dramatic difference to urban formation than figurative symbolism. It became dominant in established traditional societies and was fundamental to the basic constitution of city-states and cities-as-empires, particularly as they began to accommodate strangers and develop more extended political connections. Script encoded law and lore. It made possible extensive and complex trade beyond the city walls that sustained large urban populations. Here written communication moved between being framed as sacred text and being used for organizing the poiesis of the polis. It moved between relating the "City of Man" to the "City of God" and organizing such activities as urban commerce and diplomacy. The emerging dominance of this mode of communication was from the early Middle Ages to around the sixteenth century, and beginning earlier in some key globalizing cities such as Athens, Rome and Xianyang. It is interesting that the city of Canterbury, for example, could be said to be more powerful during this time than London.

One of the basic contradictions during this period was founded on the fact that most people could not read. Orality mediated script. Nevertheless, writing contributed to the possibility of globalizing urban relations through top-down imperial extension. Rome was exemplary here. Writing in the first century, Ovid is credited with the well-known aphorism: "To all other peoples, fixed boundaries are set in the world; for Rome, the bounds of city and globe are one" (*urbis et orbis idem*). The Roman sense of the global in the first century was very different from that of Boston or Tokyo in the twenty-first century, but the Roman orb was certainly not the flat-earth extension sometimes attributed to those who lived prior to the "Copernican revolution".

Print

The mechanical reproduction of text—print—was critical to the coming dominance of the *modern* (Eisenstein 1983), including an emergent mode of production-exchange such as globalizing capitalism. It carried forward the abstracting possibilities of writing to cross time and territory, but gave it a new generality that gradually drew a once largely non-literate population into the communicative nexus. Print gave us newspapers. And in the nineteenth century, the press almightily enhanced the representational life of cities, just as it was important to the formation of nation-states.

Analogue Coding

Analogue-encoded communication, exemplified in telegraphy, was writing encoded communication. It was part of complex web of developments, later linked to sound-encoded and image-encoded communication, that become part of the web of *modern* communications, exemplified by telephony and analogue television. Here the image and practice of watching the world on television screens sitting in one's family lounge room—what Raymond Williams (1974) called "mobile privatization"—began to compete with the street as the heartland of urban experience. This process also globalized cities through a new layer of social relations.

Digital Coding

Digitally encoded communication extended the possibility for multi-modal encoding, part of a more recent set of developments linked to computerization and satellite transmission, for example the Internet and social media, email, digital-mobile telephony, and digital television. At a certain point, not entirely dissimilar to the transformation from figurative symbolism and writing, multi-modal relativized communication emerged as a new *postmodern* layer of communications in the late twentieth century. It was characterized by meaning being encoded digitally and automated for variously machine-to-machine, many-to-many and one-to-select-others transmission, with each instance of interchange relativized in terms of who or what is the subject of the transmission (Van Dijck 2013). In Liam Magee's words, automated media refabricated the city (Magee 2016).

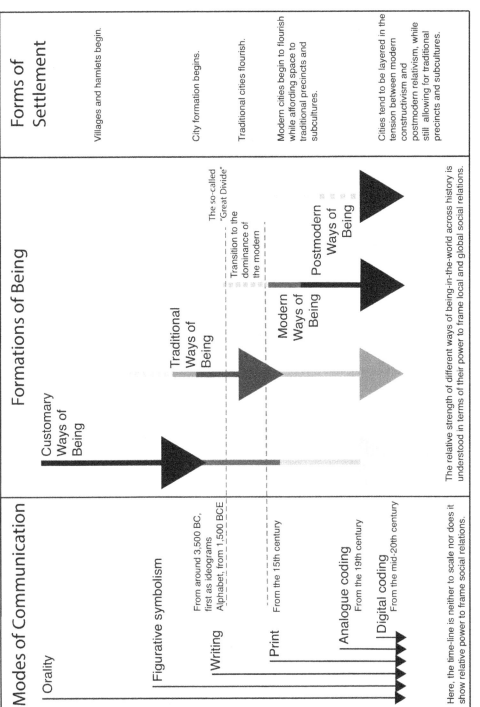

Figure 16.1 Forms of Communication in Relation to Ways of Being and Forms of Urban Settlement

Source: author.

These different modes of communication represented graphically in Figure 16.1, each working at different levels of material abstraction from the embodied to the disembodied, have fundamental consequences for the nature of basic processes such as urbanization and globalization. Keeping in mind these different forms of mediation, we can now turn to elaborating the nature of the contradictions introduced earlier.

Media as Contradictory Forces in the Process of Urban Formation

The Patterned Use of Communications Media Simultaneously Integrates and Differentiates People

Our argument then is that cities have always been formed in the contradictory layering of communication from the direct face-to-face engagement of orality to more abstracted, technologically mediated communications. At the same time, different categories and classes of citizens and denizens have also been both divided objectively and made subjectively aware of these divisions through media practices (Morley 2000). Here the concept of "citizen" tells its own story. It is derived from the Latin *civitas*, "city", and linked to the changing meaning of *denizen*, originally meaning the person who dwells *within*. The concept quickly came to denote just an inhabitant with variable rights.

Examples of this contradictory civic connection and urban division can be found across history. Going back to the classical period, SPQR, originally an abbreviation for Senatus Populusque Romanus, was regularly inscribed onto city walls, a communicative process linking figurative symbolism and writing. It named the supposedly deep relationship between the seat of power and "the people of the city"—citizens. However, even in its original use, the inscription crisscrossed the connection–division divide. Rome was deeply class-divided and gender-divided. SPQR was inscribed on the Arch of Constantine in 315 CE, and spread across urban Europe from London to Vienna as a symbol of urban civic engagement and republican "democracy"—with the last name changed to accommodate different cities. However, this spread also accentuated the lack of generalized popular will in each of these imperial cities, including republican and contemporary Rome. The political nadir of this contradictory symbolism was perhaps Mussolini's Rome in the 1930s, when SPQR was inscribed next to fascist symbols into street-furniture from lamp-posts to street-drainage covers.

Coming forward to the present, social media—a form of digital coding that abstracts presence but at the same time presents data in a very personal way—provides a parallel but very different example of bringing people together *and* dividing them. For a time, in mainstream accounts responding to the 2011 events in Tahrir City Square in Cairo, Marjeh Square, Damascus, and Taksim Square, Istanbul, the social media itself came to be treated as the "fourth actor" in the squared relationship between authoritarian regimes, city-squares and protest-movements. Social media was projected as bringing people together in an "Arab Spring" that would usher in a new period of democracy. During this time, almost every mainstream commentator was arguing that social media provided the scaffolding for the uprising. However, we now know that at the very same time as Facebook was being used to schedule events, pro-regime agents were also using social media to mitigate the effect of protesting voices (Moss 2018). And it is pertinent that most of the protestors described the media as a tool—not as a reason or a cause of their actions (see also Chapter 39, this volume).

Since then the hype about so-called "Facebook revolutions" has waned. Academic and journalist writing has made very little of the use of social media to organize massive urban rallies, for example in Sanaa's Sabeen Square, Yerevan's central Republic Square, Syntagma Square in

Athens and in Trafalgar Square, London, where 250,000 people gathered in 2018 to protest against the US president Donald Trump's visit.

Media Both Abstract from Place (and Time) and Reflect Back to Local Places a Representational Immediacy That Enhances the Local (and Its Sense of "Now")

Enduring and emergent modes of communication within global cities and their complex layering do not lend themselves to a singular argument about the relational importance of different media to urban life. The mainstream agenda of media studies still tends to focus on one or the other of these modalities in themselves rather than in relation to either what it means to live in a city or how they affect the form of the city. However, we can say that across history, aural and visual communications—church bells, ballad-singers, town-criers, advertising billboards, newspapers, television, mobile phones, electronic screens and tweeting—have all been important in different ways to giving cities a sense of local place. As David Garrioch (2003) documents, for early modern Europe, soundscapes afforded urban spaces an intense sense of localized rhythm. One of those sounds, the voice of the town crier, shows how this contradiction works. In late Medieval to Renaissance Florence, the communal *banditore* were an important (dialogical) oral presence, carriers of communal identification, and at the same time they were agents of the city contracted to deliver written texts as articles of top-down governance (Milner 2013: 110).

By the mid-sixteenth century, dialogical orality gave way to the scripted form. A century later, town-criers had most disappeared and edicts were written in stone or embedded as plaques in city walls, thus returning to either figurative symbolism or writing—but from a more abstract standpoint. Fast-forwarding this process, completely abstracted corporate logos beginning with a red triangle, trade-marked in 1876 for the Bass Brewery, became part of the streetscape from the late nineteenth century, and they were quickly joined by "everywhere" images that contradictorily contrived to reclaim an embodied place in the urban landscape: globes, apples, arches, mountains, pumas, bulls and targets. Urban iconography, constructed around this tension between abstraction and representational immediacy, thus changed dramatically across the twentieth century. Digital coding combined with electronic billboards and live broadcasting screens added a new intensity to the sense of "nowness" and "being there". Standing in Times Square or Piccadilly Circus now affords an extraordinary sense of immediateness through global-to-local live-streaming. In response, some media theorists began to treat these multiplying urban screens as providing possible platforms for a building of a new kind of "glocal" participatory engagement (Papastergiadis 2016). However, with notable exceptions, public screens transcend places all too easily. They have remained prime spaces for addressing citizens as "audiences" rather than dialogical participants. Notwithstanding the multiple ways in people respond to public screens (Krajina 2014), the communication of transnational corporate culture or global sporting extravaganzas continues to prevail in much public screen content.

As the lives of denizens have become increasingly mediated both privately and publicly, a long lineage of scholars including Jane Jacobs (1961), Richard Sennett (1994) and Sharon Zukin (2010) have argued that denizens in contemporary large cities have lost the immediacy of meaningful connection. Mediated life has taken over. They argue that contemporary cities, rather than becoming just spaces of abstract connectivity, need to be built in such a way as to encourage enriching forms of embodied friction between different peoples. Social life needs to return to the streets as more than simulated or commodified authenticity. Locals and strangers should rub shoulders—sometimes uncomfortably—as they move through locally defined places.

The problem with this argument is that people are now increasingly drawn into the street to rub shoulders with others through the lure of big screens and big spectacles such as fireworks and sporting events that, while designed for the specificities of the local, tend to be framed by the variable content of global/local consumer capitalism.

Media Are Simultaneously a Means of the Globalization of Cities, and, by Transcending Space, They Bring the World Back to the City, Enhancing Its Sense of Localness

For two millennia, cities have been the crucible of globalization, and the different kinds of media that had their origins in cities were simultaneously part of these dual processes of globalization and representing the world locally to those cities. Classical Rome epitomized the *traditional* globalizing city, while still being centred on the meaning carried by the stones of the streets and bodies of its citizens (Sennett 1994). There, the media included figurative symbolism and writing, which came together in disciplines such as cartography and geography, with the signs of connection inscribed in the local landscape. From the time of Ancient Rome, and perhaps before, cities have consistently been the sites of globalizing communication and exchange. Cities were the locus for both the embodied encounter of peoples and the mediated communications that transcended city-boundaries. Dominant cultural groupings continuously came into relation with outsiders—including peoples that they called "barbarians". Thus, processes of globalization, defined as the extension and intensification of social relations across world space, simultaneously changed the way in which people lived in cities, at least going back to the period when the Romans declared *urbis et orbis*—the City of Rome and the Orb of the World are one. This also means that cities, multiculturalism and globalization have been intimately linked together across human history.

Processes of globalization intensified greatly in the transition from traditional cities to modernizing cities across the period of the sixteenth century into the present. Again, it was agents of empire who were key carriers of global connection, along with literate-trained clerics, cartographers, merchants and poets, stretching their influence across the globe in uneven but increasingly significant ways. Renaissance Florence was a globalizing city with written credit bills and promissory notes adding to the dominant lines of urban communication. But, as with Rome, the sense of the city continued to be captured by the immediacy of stone and inscription. And to add a further example, twentieth-century Los Angeles was a pre-eminent global city. There, the dominant media of connectivity moved from analogue celluloid to digital encoding, as Hollywood stretched a particular approach to the moving-image across the globe. At same time, the word "Hollywood", originally a local real estate sign from 1923, continues to provide a daily reminder to drivers on the 101 Freeway that the city and the globe are "visibly rooted in everyday life".

It was not just powerful European cities that experienced the push and pull of globalization or found themselves at the crossroads of multicultural interchange. The capital of Timor Leste, Dili, was established as an administrative town by the Portuguese in October 1769, a year before the English explorer Captain Cook "discovered" Australia and two decades before the French Revolution centred on the City of Paris. Apart from global relations with competing outside traders and colonialists—English, Dutch, Portuguese and Chinese—the global and the local mingled within Dili. The extensive writings of naturalist Henry Forbes in the 1880s confirm the plural origins of peoples there. This included descriptions of Dili which suggest the form of multiculturalism that was developing there was paralleled in the most cosmopolitan of the European cities such as London, Lisbon and Madrid:

Tall, erect indigenes mingled with Negroes from the Portuguese possessions of Mozambique and the coasts of Africa; tall, lithe East Indians from Goa and its neighbourhood; Chinese and Bugis of Macassar, with Arabs and Malays and natives from Allor, Savu, Roti, and Flores; besides a crowd in whose veins the degree of cominglement of blood of all these races would defy the neatest computation.

(Forbes 1883: 418)

This was the period in which the Polish-British novelist Joseph Conrad travelled the region. His writings, like the communications of many others, carried images across the globe for an expanding readership. "Cominglement", hybridity and ethnic complexity notwithstanding, anthropologists and ethnographers would soon arrive on the island of Timor to begin mapping the genotypes based on the "neatest computation" possible. They were part of a process that began to divide humanity into demarcated races and language (the new Gods of Babel), and began to treat multiculturalism as either anathema or something to be carefully managed.

Conclusion

While the dominant modes of mediation and communication have been changing across history, they have in their different ways been foundational to gathering strangers into extended built-places of local condensation—cities. The effect of those changing media on the nature of the city has been largely taken for granted. In other words, while there are many different studies of particular forms of media *in* the city, mediation appears so obvious in cities that it has not sufficiently been explored by a comparative or long-term enquiry into its consequence *for* the city. This chapter lays out the various and changing modes of communications across human history, linking them to their important impact on the nature of the urban form. The central argument is that different media, from the most embodied to the most abstracting, have had a contradictory relationship to the urban form. At the centre of this argument are two inter-related contentions that are so basic that their inter-relation is often overlooked: firstly, media mediate—they abstract social relations across time and space. Secondly, media communicate—they bring people together around the interchange of meaning. These two contentions are not logically or philosophically contradictory, but they are founded on material contradictions that have profound consequences for how we live in cities. And the practical contradictions that follow are easy to say and hard to fathom: media are simultaneously used to integrate and to differentiate people. Media both abstract from place and reflect back to local places with renewed intensity. And media are concurrently a key infrastructure for the simultaneous and competing processes of globalization and localization. Nevertheless, by exploring these contradictions across questions of both form and content, the possibility is opened for addressing issues of urban media and communications and their mutual influence together rather than separately. To remake our cities, we need to attend closely to the contradictory, manipulative, co-opting, democratizing and revolutionary consequences of all these developments.

References

Anderson, B. (1991) *Imagined Communities: Reflections on the Origin and Spread of Nations* (2nd edn), London: Verso Publications.

Appadurai, A. (1996) *Modernity at Large: Cultural Dimensions of Globalization*, Minneapolis, MN: University of Minnesota Press.

Castells, M. (2010) *The Rise of the Network Society* (2nd edn), Cambridge: Blackwell Publishing.
Eisenstein, E. (1983) *The Printing Revolution in Early Modern Europe*, Cambridge: Cambridge University Press.
Forbes, H. (1883) "On Some Tribes of the Island of Timor", *Journal of the Anthropological Institute of Great Britain and Ireland*, 13, pp. 402–430.
Garrioch, D. (2003) "Sounds of the City: The Soundscape of Early Modern European Towns", *Urban History*, 30(1), pp. 5–25.
Goody, J. (1987) *The Interface between the Oral and the Written*, Cambridge: Cambridge University Press.
Innis, H.A. (1950) *Empire and Communications* (1986 edn), Vancouver: Press Porcepic.
Jacobs, J.M. (1961) *The Death and Life of Great American Cities*, New York: Random House.
James, P. (2006) *Globalism, Nationalism, Tribalism: Bringing Theory Back In*, London: Sage Publications.
— and Steger, M.B. (2016) "Globalization and Global Consciousness: Levels of Connectivity", in R. Robertson and D. Buhari (eds) *Global Culture: Consciousness and Connectivity*, Farnham: Ashgate, pp. 21–39.
Koch, R. and Latham, A. (2014) "Representing and Imagining the City", in R. Padison and E. McCann (eds), *Cities and Social Change: Encounters with Contemporary Urbanism*, Los Angeles, CA: Sage Publications.
Krajina, Z. (2014) *Negotiating the Mediated City: Everyday Encounters with Public Screens*, New York: Routledge.
Magee, L. (2016) *Interwoven Cities*, Basingstoke: Palgrave Macmillan.
Milner, S.J. (2013) "'Fanno bandire, notificare, et expressamente comandare': Town Criers and the Information Economy of Renaissance Florence", *I Tatti Studies in the Italian Renaissance*, 16(1/2), pp. 107–151.
Morley, D. (2000) *Home Territories: Media, Mobility and Identity*, London: Routledge.
Moss, Dana M. (2018) "The Ties That Bind: Internet Communication Technologies, Networked Authoritarianism, and 'Voice' in the Syrian Diaspora", *Globalizations*, 15(2), pp. 265–282.
Papastergiadis, P. (ed.) (2016) *Ambient Screens and Transnational Public Places*, Hong Kong: Hong Kong University Press.
Park, R.E. and Burgess, E.W. (1922) *The City: Suggestions for Investigation of Human Behavior in the Urban Environment*, Chicago, IL: University of Chicago Press.
Sassen, S. (2001) *The Global City: New York, London, Tokyo* (2nd edn), Princeton, NJ: Princeton University Press.
Sennett, R. (1994) *Flesh and Stone: The Body and the City in Western Civilization*, London: Faber and Faber.
Tomlinson, J. (1999) *Globalization and Culture*, Cambridge: Polity Press.
Van Dijck, J. (2013) *The Culture of Connectivity: A Critical History of the Social Media*, Oxford: Oxford University Press.
Williams, R. (1974) *Television: Technology and Cultural Form*, London: Fontana.
Zukin, S. (2010) *Naked City: The Death and Life of Authentic Urban Places*, Oxford: Oxford University Press.

Further Reading

James, P. (2006) *Globalism, Nationalism, Tribalism: Bringing Theory Back In*, London: Sage Publications.
Magee, L. (2016) *Interwoven Cities*, Basingstoke: Palgrave Macmillan.
Sennett, R. (1994) *Flesh and Stone: The Body and the City in Western Civilization*, London: Faber and Faber.

17
OUR OWN DEVICES
Living in the Smart Home

Chris Chesher and Justine Humphry

Introduction

Even before the advent of the "smart home", urban infrastructures and mass media alike were structured around the interfaces between the interiorities and exteriorities of the modern home, connecting the household with its region, suburbs, and cities. The newspaper is delivered at the threshold, bringing localized news and advertising. The fixed-line phone connects domestic spaces with addressable spaces outside. Broadcast signals penetrate the walls, enveloping the household in a media environment of entertainment and information. The space of the contemporary home—whether house or apartment—is largely configured around media consumption: book shelves, lounge chairs, television stands, desks, and so on.

Urban media scholars place media at the forefront for understanding contemporary social life and the constitution of our urban environment. McQuire (2008) in his *The Media City* argues that media, traditionally studied as separate to urban processes, must be seen as thoroughly interconnected and transformative within the city itself. He points to the array of new mobile and GPS-enabled media devices and screens that shape experiences of urban spaces and contexts. Homes, as material sites of shelter and habitation, as well as giving a sense of belonging and comfort, are part of the fabric and constitution of our increasingly mediated cities.

Digital technologies complicate the domestic media ecology. The personal computer emerged as a device for media production as well as consumption. Connected to the Internet, it communicated beyond the home. Mobile and automobile devices moved smoothly between domestic and public spaces. More recently, smart home devices have allowed householders to regulate the environment—light, climate, and security—and to make the home remotely accessible. While not exclusively an urban phenomenon, the smart home as currently envisaged and implemented is premised on the infrastructural capacities typically available only in largely urbanized and well-connected settings. In this way, the smart home is very much tied up in its material as well as social and economic conditions of possibility.

In this chapter, we explore and map the meanings of the smart home from an urban media perspective. We canvas literature on the smart home and analyze a range of smart consumables, including their representation in advertisements, YouTube videos, online forums, and exhibition sites. We ask what these say and do to understandings of the home, how they reconfigure the space and time of home, how they express the home as "smart", and what their role is in the larger process of smartification of domestic life and the post-industrial transformation of suburban living. Our examination shows that the home is "hypermediated"—it is the site of its constitution through the proliferation, interconnection, and interaction of a vast number of digital media devices, sensors, and screens. However, we also recognize the smart home as a site or platform for creating what Gabrys (2016: 183) has called new "modalities, materialities, and environments of computation". The smart home builds on the possibilities and desires for accumulation and control set in motion in previous home automation movements. It creates new interfaces to the home and methods for programming and controlling its operations. It also opens up the home to new kinds of public and networked performances and forms of play. We demonstrate these transformations by mapping what we see as the four main processes of domestic smartification: automation, command, mediation of exteriorities, and play.

On the "Smart" Home

Academic literature on the smart home builds on a long history of studying the meanings and practices of home, particularly in a European, Western context. Saunders and Williams (1988) argue that the contemporary Anglo-Saxon home has seen multiple imperatives toward privacy, privatism, and privatization. First, while values of privacy are as old as industrial cities, there is a growing belief that the home should be free of state surveillance and external influence. Second, there has been an increasing orientation toward privatism—home-centeredness and withdrawal from the surrounding community. Third, there are tendencies toward privatization, with previously collective practices subject to private consumption, such as policing, public transport, healthcare, entertainment, and streetscaping.

An important contribution to our understanding of the modeling of the home in terms of privatization derives from the studies of domestic media as they come into the home and are domesticated into its spaces and times (Morley and Silverstone 1990; Silverstone and Hirsch 1992; Silverstone and Haddon 1996; Lally 2002). Home is a key site for the personalization and appropriation of mass-produced commodities like televisions, cars, furnishings, toys, and computers. Lally (2002), for example, tells the story of early personal computers crossing the home's threshold and becoming a point of articulation between the inside and outside worlds.

The house and the organization and display of domestic life have been closely tied to the historical construction of gender and class, as evidenced by a fascination with the interiors of homes in Western European culture since the Renaissance (Rybczynski 1986; Aynsley and Grant 2006). Silverstone (1997) explained the rise of the 20th-century suburban home in terms of the long-term development of what he calls "middle space": "to create for middle classes middle cultures in middle spaces in middle America, Britain or Australia" (1997: 4). The suburban home, and suburbia more broadly, according to Silverstone, is a bourgeois project designed as a defense against urban modernity and the "threat" of difference, perceived as the key problem, rather than advantage, of inner-city life.

Drawing on Giddens' work on the importance of "locale" in reproducing social action, Saunders and Williams (1988: 83) point out that the home's surroundings is one of the determinants of the meaning and constitution of home: "We 'belong' and 'place ourselves' spatially just as we do socially". The home performs as a space and surface for signifying meaning to those outside, such as political posters at the front of homes during election campaigns. Similarly, home is shaped by particular neighborhood, suburban, and municipal contexts and politics, as exposed in the Grenfell Towers fire in 2017, in which at least 79 people died, largely as a result of a lack of basic fire ordinances. Safety and security are not straightforward results of being at home, whether through negligence, or the more common risk of violence within the home (Mallett 2004).

What we can learn from the rich literature on the home is that meanings and materialities of the home are contested and socially constructed (Lloyd and Vasta 2017). How we think about and express home is bound up in a complex set of claims, categorizations, mediations, and boundary-making exercises. Many of these claims are rehearsed through idealizations of the home in visions of the home of tomorrow in popular culture, such as *The Jetsons, Futurama*, and *Lost in Space*. The home of the future has long been represented in art, architecture, and world fairs and exhibitions. The Chicago World Fair introduced the idea of "Homes of Tomorrow" in 1933. Disneyland's 1957 "House of the Future" sponsored by plastics company, Monsanto, imagined home life in 1986. For Spigel (2001), postwar American visions of the "Home of Tomorrow" presented the suburban home in futuristic terms, yet their impulse was backwards, preserving social structures and dichotomies from the past.

While the futuristic promise of the imminent arrival of the smart home has been made for some time, the question of what a smart home can actually be has not been fully answered. The smart home itself is the latest in a long line of descriptors for the idealized home of the future (Harper 2011; Chambers 2016). Smart home marketing makes a clear distinction between earlier electronic home automation movements and the digital smart home. However, we suggest that more recent smart domestic technologies and visions play into a number of tendencies identified as part of the long-term construction of home in a westernized context: securing privacy, establishing a controlled, comfortable, and entertaining interior space, and displacing collective practices through ubiquitous connectivity and home-delivered consumption.

Smartification

Homes are undergoing a process of being re-envisaged as smart, propelled by the intrusion of digital media into everyday life, with expectations that the $14.6 billion smart home market in the US in 2017 will grow to $32.2 billion by 2021 (Gartner 2017). Smart homes are also a subset of the Internet of Things, a vision of ubiquitous connection to and between everyday objects via the Internet, providing the foundation for "smart cities". We have identified four processes at play in the construction of the smart home, each of which is associated with commodified and gendered relations of affect, labor, and ideology. Moreover, just as media domestication involves the process of bringing things home, crossing and negotiating a variety of physical and social boundaries such as public/private, formal/informal, inside/outside, and leisure/work, so too does *smartification* involve a re-articulation of the temporality and territory of the home.

Automation

Home automation emerges in the context of longer-standing patterns in defining and imposing control over the private sphere. Many technologies of industrial-era domestic automation promised to relieve householders of mental and physical labor. Devices introduced during the 20th century are now almost ubiquitous in the developed world: washing machines, vacuum cleaners, blenders, food processors, dishwashers, and so on. These typically displaced other means of domestic work (including household servants), but did not necessarily reduce the overall load for the predominantly female and unpaid workers (Wajcman 1991).

Many of these artifacts allegedly operate autonomously: once set in motion, they perform the task of cleaning clothes or preparing food with minimal intervention. The work is delegated to a nonhuman actor. However, this delegation is always a transformation of these practices: they have their own properties, and require new human competencies and rituals (Johnson 1988). The washing machine might tangle or damage clothes, or the colors in the fabrics might run.

While the devices themselves may be almost autonomous, they each operate as a sociotechnical ensemble (Bijker 1995). Even with autonomous appliances, human physical and mental labor remains part of these ensembles (such as mastering dishwasher stacking, separating clothes for machine washing, or programming devices using complex instruction manuals).

Therefore, an aspiration for advocates of domotics is that it sutures together sociotechnical relations to reduce labor even further, and to compress everyday activities in time and space. Many smart home devices allow users to program events for particular times, or to respond to changes in the environment—turning lights on and off, starting up coffee pots, turning on water sprinklers, triggering appliances, or programming media recordings. Robotic vacuum cleaners can clean the house while the inhabitants are out. These programmed set-and-forget operations can follow or establish routines in the home, mirroring the daily rhythms of night and day, working and leisure time, and even cultural beliefs. However, critics observe that few smart devices are actually designed to replace domestic labor, other than the autonomous vacuum cleaner (Chambers 2016). Moreover, the extension of automated control to the home serves as an intrusive form of regimentation. Nicholas Carr criticizes its tendency to impose an institutional order and "Taylorist mentality" onto domestic life: "They subtly encourage people to adapt themselves to established routines and schedules, making homes more like workplaces" (Carr 2014: 126).

Another form of automation is in the domestic artifacts that automatically maintain the environment such as refrigerators, ovens, room heaters, and air conditioners. These usually have an informational dimension in the thermostatic control that regulates their operation. Digital thermostats gave much greater control over heating and cooling, making it possible to program the operation of devices or systems over time with great precision. Thermostats operate according to what philosopher of technology Don Ihde (1990) refers to as "background relations". That is, for the most part, they don't require the focal attention of users, and the technology recedes into the background of everyday activity, unless they malfunction.

One of the aspirations and justifications for smart home services is to use resources better, such as minimizing power consumption, lowering water use, reducing greenhouse gas emissions, and interfacing with smart cities. Ironically, smart technologies do not always achieve these ends, as consumer electronics are approaching being responsible for half of households' electricity consumption (Røpke et al. 2009). Strengers argues that the introduction of smart meters, which measure power consumption in real time over a network, has been accompanied by a vision of a "Smart Utopia" (2013: 2) ruled by rational power use. Smart meter advocates claim such technologies will result in cleaner, cheaper, and more secure energy supply. In practice, energy use is subject to the messy dynamics of everyday life (Strengers 2013). The "dumb and disorderly behaviour" (Strengers 2013: 54) of householders doesn't respond to the imperatives expected of rational energy consumers. There are many ways that compulsory smart metering is being resisted (Hess 2014). Many people are concerned about the security of these infrastructures (Komninos et al. 2014). Others consider smart metering as a form of surveillance, and others still believe their radio frequencies are a health risk.

The discourse of the smart home—as a singular entity—has set an expectation that all the operations of automation should be managed centrally through a single hub, with integrated and remotely accessible interfaces. The dream is for a total control system. In practice, most homes currently have many standalone devices with little integration. Even if they have connectable devices, as a consequence of market competition, there is a plethora of incompatible home automation standards: X10 (1975), C-Bus (1994), Bluetooth (1994), Wi-Fi (1997), ZigBee (2004), Insteon (2005), Z-Wave (2008), Thread (2014), Apple Homekit (2014), and Bluetooth 5 (2017). While some platforms support multiple standards, consumers have no easy choices, and getting the smart home to work takes considerable dedication and labor.

Command

If systems of automation are said to eliminate human agency, apparatuses of command are designed to enhance it by putting devices in the home on call. The householder can trigger simple or complex events, even from a distance. In the industrial home, the light switch is the emblematic apparatus that summons light into a space. In the smart home, the householder might use gestures, voice, sound, remote controls, or a smartphone to trigger environmental effects such as turning on, dimming, or changing the color of lights. Enthusiast Dan Thyer (2014) posted a YouTube clip in which he delights in demonstrating gestures that control devices in his home. He points at a Christmas tree, moves his hand across his face, and the tree's lights switch on.

The capacities that smart home systems offer to householders go beyond instrumentalism and into the domain of affect by creating new moods and sensations in the home. Such non-representational events are sold as promoting a sense of empowerment by making perceptible changes to the domestic space. The lights dim to mark seduction or sleep. The lights fade up to mark the beginning of a new day. The smart home offers magical invocations of buttons, voice, or gesture to produce changes in the mediated space.

Intelligent voice assistants such as Amazon's Alexa, Google's Assistant, and Apple's Siri constitute a distinctive new medium characterized by asymmetrical conversations between machines and users. The user is positioned as being in command, while the servile simulated character waits quietly for commands: "Alexa", "OK Google", or "Hey Siri". Communicating by voice brings a certain interpersonal intimacy in spite of the synthesized speech. Most of these devices default to gentle, female voices, appropriating "the housewife" by exhibiting behaviors of subservience, constant presence, and care. They take the place of the wife or the domestic servant (Kennedy and Strengers 2017), purportedly fulfilling the problem referred to by Crabb (2014) as "the wife drought". Yet, in the family, the actual performance of housework continues to be largely carried out by women, even if working full-time (Ruppaner 2017). This command relationship also has a racialized history, privileging the figure of the white middle-class mother over the exploited, domestic servant of color (Phan 2017).

The invocation of a caring, sexy housewife is even more apparent in the Japanese rival virtual assistant, Gatebox (Morris 2016). The character Azumi Hikari appears as a glowing female anime 3D "hologram communication robot". In the product trailer, the virtual assistant doubles as a chatbot sending encouraging check-ins and care texts throughout the day to her young male professional owner such as "Come home early" and "Don't forget your umbrella". When he returns from work, she wriggles in delight as he approaches.

While the constant presence of virtual assistants may be desired, it may simultaneously be feared. As voice command systems use cloud-based services to interpret users' statements, speakers are subjecting themselves to new forms of data surveillance. Google assures users that the audio captured is encrypted and confidential, but uses this data to improve the voice recognition performance, and for consumer profiling. There are also anxieties that users will become habituated to using voice assistants to the point that it replaces social interaction (Hui and Leong 2017).

Controlling devices using smartphones, tablets, or dedicated panels, unlike voice control, presents users with diagrams of the current or possible state of affairs across the interactive screen space. This quasi-commodification of media space maps the home for consumption. In Apple's Homekit iPhone app, each connected device and its status is available as an icon on the screen. Users can command devices individually or define whole scenes that correspond to particular routine activities, such as getting up in the morning, leaving home, or going to bed at night. In practice, the command relationship between users and their devices is capricious. Online forums are populated by male-sounding users reporting a gamut of difficulties associated with incompatible devices, standards, and operating systems compromising the ideal of seamless command. One such user posted: "when I launch the app it just gets stuck on this white screen that says Loading Home . . ." (App Developer Forums 2016).

Mediating Exteriorities

The home has long been bounded by physical barriers, legal abstractions, and symbolic meanings, and in many ways, smart home devices serve to reinforce and extend these. In legal terms, a property is defined by a property line, established by a professional surveyor, and documented in land titles registries. But this line is associated with other meanings, as it marks the threshold of the inside and the outside. On the outside is the neighboring private and public space: extension, danger, neighborhood, and community. On the inside are the private domains of the household, with associations of family, reproduction, and security. As previously noted, the industrial-era home was constructed as a space of security, familiarity, and comfort of the idealized nuclear family, a site of refuge from and entry to the public sphere (Lloyd and Vasta 2017). However, the home's boundary has always been permeable. The home has been conditionally open to face-to-face entry of outsiders such as guests, salespeople, government officials, and police (with a search warrant). Traditional media such as newspapers, radio, television, and particularly the telephone brought the outside into the home. In each case, from phone calls to the front door, there are rituals and protocols that need to be followed in recognition of crossing the threshold to the private domain.

In the smart home, technologies and practices protecting the boundaries of the home, such as walls, locks, and front doors, have been supplemented by digital technologies. A Gartner survey (2017) found that nearly twice as many homes had installed alarm systems than other connected home applications, such as home monitoring, automation, and health. Security systems attempt to solve the problem of the empty home, a function of the long-term organization of paid labor outside the (unpaid) domestic realm. Despite the increasing ability to work from home, many inhabitants are absent for work and travel. Alarm systems typically feature sensors such as door and window alarms, motion detectors, and cameras to sense breaches of exterior boundaries. The more advanced systems such as the Lighthouse (2017) use machine learning and AI to differentiate the appearances (face recognition) and movements (action recognition) of legitimate (pets, family members) and illegitimate (intruders) presences inside the home.

Beyond their instrumental effectiveness, these technologies of security are succors for the anxiety of householders about the integrity of their home and property. Security is a subjective feeling as much as a material state of affairs. Paradoxically, though, some of the very technologies that make the home "smart" make it potentially open to unwanted corporate, government, and criminal surveillance. Everyday uses of networked technologies make cyberstalking possible (King-Ries 2011). Wi-Fi, Bluetooth, and Z-Wave signals bleed across into surrounding homes and streets, making them open to hacking, particularly if they are inadvertently left open to access. Images and sounds of the household are increasingly revealed by householders through smart speakers, webcams, connected toys, and multiplayer games. Even paying security companies to monitor the sensors and cameras inside the home represents a conditional opening to surveillance.

Home monitoring practices also reflect power dynamics within the home. One application for home monitoring is the surreptitious observation of babysitters, cleaners, domestic workers, and other members of the family. Access to the administrator privileges of surveillance systems can reinforce differential and gendered relationships of visibility. Domotics tend to sit in the purview of males, as mastering technology has historically been associated with learning to be a man (Horowitz 2011). The "head" of the family is in a position to monopolize access and impose arbitrary surveillance and control over others.

Play

The attraction of much actual smart home technology is also about play: turning the smart lights in the living room to disco mode, or starting up the home theatre with a voice command. IFTTT (If This Then That) is a cloud service that integrates home automation devices and other cloud services through applets. Some of these are nerdy and playful, such as playing music from Star Wars when wearers of the Star Wars Forceband move their arms, or flashing lights when the international space station goes past. Google Home Assistant tells jokes and hosts a quiz show. Even Barbie now has a US$300 smart home. The house can be voice controlled with over a hundred commands. Saying "Hello Dreamhouse: let's have a dance party!" will turn the house into party mode: the lights flash, music plays, and the stairs convert into a slide.

These devices can playfully transform the space of the home. Huizinga (1950) famously argues that play takes place within a magic circle, such as the tennis court, the playground, or even the court of law. Many home automation applications define a magic circle of influence within range of sensors and controlled devices. In one YouTube clip, Facebook founder Mark Zuckerberg shows off his smart home, which features a small cannon in his cupboard that throws him a T-shirt. Programmable smart robotic toys such as Sphero and Cozmo move around the home autonomously or by remote control within a designated wireless field. The magic circle of play in the context of the smart house is technologically enabled.

Internet-connected and wirelessly networked devices also enable new forms of networked public exhibition. For example, the camgirls phenomenon between 1998 and 2003 saw young women such as Jennifer Ringley and Teri Senft installing webcams on their computers, opening up their homes to a wider public. In the 2010s, vloggers began producing short videos of their everyday experiences to very large audiences. Unlike traditional cinema celebrities, whose private lives were only revealed in very staged ways, microcelebrities (Senft 2008) provide more intimate and regular access to the private sphere to establish and maintain their authentic status (Jerslev 2016).

Future Trajectories of the Smart Home

Despite the massive transformation and destabilization of ideas and practices of home from the latter half of the 20th century, and the impossibility of home ownership for many, some trajectories of the home appear to be restabilized through the smart home. Smartification tends to preserve and shore up the value of the home as a private space, standing against the tensions and contradictions of contemporary urban life. It defines and controls the space and time of the home. Privatization is premised on technological control, provided by more efficient and automated technologies that free up leisure time. Ironically, competition between smart tech manufacturers creates more work for householders negotiating devices and standards, and this requires a high level of literacy and interest.

New systems of command provide an array of new ways of interfacing with home automation systems, with consoles, voice, smartphone, and gestures, which support affective rather than purely instrumental relationships to the home. At the same time, smartified command remains premised on gendered control. The home's expanded media space becomes a masculinized digital space. While there are opportunities for different family members to appropriate smart home technologies (e.g., microcelebrities), the re-negotiation of domestic work and roles involves a far wider set of external as well as internal changes. This is evidenced by the fact that earlier generation domestic technologies did not radically change the roles of domestic labor: women continue to do more of the non-digital mundane chores of cleaning, washing, and cooking. Smart technology only makes this old problem less visible through design strategies such as making buttons fewer and less visible (cf. Morley 2006).

Trends in the sales of smart home technologies suggest that security and remote monitoring will continue to be the mainstay of this market. Even as the home's boundary expands and becomes increasingly permeable through networked and mobile digital technologies, investment in smart homes has been in technologies that secure its borders. Recent adoption of the term "smart living" (Solaimani et al. 2015) suggests a more convincing shift in focus toward technologies premised on health, education, and assistive living goals. Nevertheless, home remains an essential site of shelter as well as a powerful symbol for anticipating and shaping the future of urban living. Rather than being a refuge from post-industrial urbanization, the home might better be conceived as at the very center of these larger social structural transformations (Honeywill 2017). Ultimately, play might have the most potential to disrupt established paradigms of the smart home. Thinking playfully about the home, we can foreground contemporary structures of feeling associated with domestic media that embrace, negotiate, resist, and reject particular sociotechnical paradigms, proposing alternative trajectories. What remains to be seen is whether these are able to overcome the cost, limited functionality, and unimaginative framing of smart home technologies.

References

App Developer Forums (2016) "Home app stuck on Loading Home . . . screen", https://forums.developer.apple.com/thread/48718.
Aynsley, J. and Grant, C. (2006) *Imagined Interiors: Representing the Domestic Interior Since the Renaissance*, London: V & A Publications.
Bijker, W. E. (1995) *Of Bicycles, Bakelites, and Bulbs: Toward a Theory of Sociotechnical Change*, Cambridge, MA: MIT Press.
Carr, N. (2014) *The Glass Cage: Automation and Us*, New York: W.W. Norton & Company.
Chambers, D. (2016) *Changing Media, Homes and Households: Cultures, Technologies and Meanings*, New York: Routledge.
Crabb, A. (2014) *The Wife Drought*, London: Ebery.
Gabrys, J. (2016) "Rethingifying the internet of things", in N. Starosielski and J. Walker (eds.) *Sustainable Media: Critical Approaches to Media and Environment*, New York: Routledge.
Gartner (2017) "Gartner survey shows connected home solutions adoption remains limited to early adopters", Press release, www.gartner.com/newsroom/id/3629117.
Harper, R. (2011) *The Connected Home: The Future of Domestic Life*, London: Springer.
Hess, D. J. (2014) "Smart meters and public acceptance: Comparative analysis and governance implications", *Health, Risk & Society*, 16(3), pp. 243–258.
Honeywill, E. (2017) "The coming home of postindustrial society", in A. Vasta and J. Lloyd (eds.) *Reimagining Home in the 21st Century*, Cheltenham, UK: Edward Elgar, pp. 150–164.
Horowitz, R. (2011) *Boys and Their Toys: Masculinity, Class and Technology in America*, New York: Routledge.
Hui, J. Y. and Leong, D. (2017) "The era of ubiquitous listening: Living in a world of speech-activated devices", Lee Kuan Yew School of Public Policy Research Paper No. 17–21, https://ssrn.com/abstract=3021623.
Huizinga, J. (1950) *Homo Ludens: A Study of the Play Element in Culture*, Boston, MA: Beacon.
Ihde, D. (1990) *Technology and the Lifeworld: From Garden to Earth* (No. 560), Indianapolis, IN: Indiana University Press.
Jerslev, A. (2016) "In the time of the microcelebrity: Celebrification and the YouTuber Zoella", *International Journal of Communication (Online)*, October, pp. 5233-5252.
Johnson, J. (1988) "Mixing humans and nonhumans together: The sociology of a door-closer", *Social Problems*, 35(3), pp. 298–310.

Kennedy, J. and Strengers, Y. (2017) "Addressing the wife drought: Gendered visions of voice-activated assistants in the smart home", At Home with Digital Media Symposium, November 2-3, QUT.

King-Ries, A. (2011) "Teens, technology, and cyberstalking: The domestic violence wave of the future", *Texas Journal of Women & the Law*, 20(2), pp. 131–164.

Komninos, N., Philippou, E., and Pitsillides, A. (2014) "Survey in smart grid and smart home security: Issues, challenges and countermeasures", *IEEE Communications Surveys and Tutorials*, 16(4).

Lally, E. (2002) *At Home with Computers*, Oxford: Berg Publishers.

Lighthouse (2017) "Lighthouse: Technology", www.light.house/technology.

Lloyd, J. and Vasta, E. (eds.) (2017) *Reimagining Home in the 21st Century*, Cheltenham, UK: Edward Elgar.

Mallett, S. (2004) "Understanding home: A critical review of the literature", *The Sociological Review*, 52(1), pp. 62–89.

McQuire, S. (2008) *The Media City: Media, Architecture and Urban Space*, London: SAGE.

Morley, D. (2006) *Media, Modernity, and Technology: The Geography of the New*, London: Routledge.

Morley, D. and Silverstone, R. (1990) "Domestic communication: Technologies and meanings", *Media, Culture & Society*, 12(1), pp. 31–55.

Morris, D. Z. (2016) "The creepy virtual assistant that embodies Japan's biggest problems", *Fortune*, December 18, http://fortune.com/2016/12/18/gatebox-virtual-assistant-japan.

Phan, T. (2017) "Nostalgia, class privilege, and domestic labor: A discourse analysis of the Amazon Echo's promotional material", At Home with Digital Media Symposium, November 2-3, QUT.

Røpke, I., Christensen, T. K., and Jensen, O.J. (2009) "Information and communication technologies: A new round of household electrification", *Energy Policy*, 38(4), pp. 1764-1773.

Ruppaner, L. (2017) "Census 2016: Women are still disadvantaged by the amount of housework they do", *The Conversation*, April 11, https://theconversation.com/census-2016-women-are-still-disadvantaged-by-the-amount-of-unpaid-housework-they-do-76008.

Rybczynski, W. (1986) *Home: A Short History of an Idea*, New York: Penguin Books.

Saunders, P. and Williams, P. (1988) "The constitution of the home: Towards a research agenda", *Housing Studies*, 3(2), pp. 81–93.

Senft, T. M. (2008) *Camgirls: Celebrity and Community in the Age of Social Networks*, New York: Peter Lang Publishing.

Silverstone, R. (ed.) (1997) *Visions of Suburbia*, London: Psychology Press.

Silverstone, R. and Haddon, L. (1996) "Design and the Domestication of Information and Communication Technologies: Technical Change and Everyday Life", in R. Silverstone and R. Mansell (eds.) *Communication by Design: The Politics of Information and Communication Technologies*, Oxford: Oxford University Press, pp. 44–74, http://eprints.lse.ac.uk—/64821.

Silverstone, R. and Hirsch, E. (1992) *Consuming Technologies: Media and Information in Domestic Spaces*, London and New York: Routledge.

Solaimani, S., Keijzer-Broers, W., and Bouwman, H. (2015) "What we do—and don't—know about the Smart Home: An analysis of the Smart Home literature", *Indoor and Built Environment*, 24(3), pp. 370–383.

Spigel, L. (2001) *Welcome to the Dreamhouse: Popular Media and Postwar Suburbs*, Durham, NC: Duke University Press.

Strengers, Y. (2013) *Smart Energy Technologies in Everyday Life: Smart Utopia?*, London: Springer.

Thyer, D. (2014) "Kinect Living: Control lights with gestures and speech recognition" [YouTube video], https://youtu.be/g92MtCEgYSs.

Wajcman, J. (1991) *Feminism Confronts Technology*, University Park, PA: Pennsylvania University Press.

Further Reading

Chambers, D. (2016) *Changing Media, Homes and Households: Cultures, Technologies and Meanings*, London: Routledge.

Hargreaves, T. and Wilson, C. (2017) *Smart Homes and Their Users*, New York: Springer International Publishing.

Strengers, Y. (2013) *Smart Energy Technologies in Everyday Life: Smart Utopia?*, London: Springer.

18
SURVEILLANCE AS AN URBAN WAY OF LIFE

Roy Coleman

Introduction

This chapter provides insight into the main theoretical tools developed to think about surveillance and its relationship to socio-spatial identities, divisions, and justice. Some might assume that surveillance is a seamless gaze of control and transparency. On the contrary, it is uneven and partial in practice. The kind of information and knowledge that surveillance accumulates reflects, reinforces, and sometimes challenges the interests and priorities of powerful ways of seeing the city and the people in it. At the heart of media technologies, surveillance involves watching and being watched in ubiquitous and semi-visible ways. Surveillance is connected to the right to visibility and invisibility as well as the right to urban habitation and belongingness in the city.

What Is Surveillance?

Surveillance is ubiquitous to modern urban living and most of us are daily subjects, producers, and targets of surveillance. Fundamentally, surveillance expresses the modern quest for a form of life that is amenable to categorization so that agents can shape and control people in (largely) urbanized life. Urban life is based on information gathered with and without our consent. In this sense, surveillance is about continuous examination of selves and spaces at particular times with a view to managing idealized identities, norms, and values consistent with modern urban living. Surveillance plays a key role in allowing access to, and exclusion from, urban life.

We as individuals collect and provide information to be used by corporate giants such as Facebook and Google who can pass this information elsewhere (e.g., to national policing agencies). Our desires, favored locations, political opinions, romantic connections, and consuming habits are all given over as we leisurely communicate and "share" identities and experiences online (Fuchs 2017).

But surveillance favors hard boundaries and seeks categorical identities using human observation, metrics, and algorithms. The production of surveillance data is bound up with identity formation (identities constructed *for us* and those we construct *for ourselves*). Identity is central to the functioning of cities to establish "who we are" and to register and authenticate our identity to move through a given space. Surveillant identity ascertains our location in space (electronic or physical) and our reasons for being there; it may seek to ascertain our motives, both short- and long-term, as citizens, travelers, consumers, or workers; it may inquire about our social status as credit-worthy—"deserving" or "undeserving" of goods and services. Surveillance renders aspects of our social lives visible for the purposes of managing flow and stability within and across socio-spatial borders in an era characterized as fearful and mistrusting (Coleman 2009).

Surveillance orders and sorts people in that it "obtains personal and group data to classify people and populations according to variable criteria, to determine who should be targeted for special treatment, suspicion, eligibility, inclusion, access and so on" (Lyon 2003: 20). Surveillance reflects and reinforces normative judgments concerning cultural assumptions that delineate categories such as the "deserving" poor, "respectable" womanhood, "responsible" youth, or "legitimate" victim. Even when no human appears present in automated surveillance, cultural judgments are the impulses driving surveillance practice and make it a human exercise. As such, it is important to focus on the cultures of surveillance as interrelated but not entirely synchronized processes that facilitate the production and maintenance of socio-spatial order consistent with the divisions of gender, class, or race. In this sense, it facilitates cultural assumptions, messages, and meanings relating to preferred and idealized readings of the city: its identity, its inhabitants, and its spatial utility (Coleman 2004).

For some, surveillance is organized and perceived in a way that is non-burdensome or beneficial; for others it is bound up with a system of "detection, judgement . . . and punishment, aimed at limiting freedom and channelling behaviour" (Gilliom 2006: 125). Therefore, as already noted, surveillance is uneven and differentially experienced depending on overlapping identities as mothers, convicts, students, or middle-class experts who move through divergent surveillance contexts.

Surveillance is neither neutral nor uniform: it is experienced and responded to differently depending on location, gender, profession, age, and race. The surveillance we see around us today has its roots in urban, cultural, political, and economic change initiated in the 19th-century city. Therefore, we need to be mindful of continuities and discontinuities in surveillance and the city. Indeed, today's surveillance is a development of struggles, cultural contestation, and political developments that make up our history of the present.

Panoptic Cities

Many writers have attested to the idea that "the rise of surveillance society may be traced to modernity's impetus to coordinate or control" (Lyon 2001: 49) and for Foucault, this is initially found in the power of a few (prison guards, police, criminologists) being able to observe, control, and coordinate the many (the urban masses). The 19th-century prison is where this kind of surveillance began and led to new ways of identifying, controlling, and predicting individuals—to self-police and discipline their own conduct, under conditions of constant, yet unverifiable, watching (Foucault 1977: 206). Throughout the 20th century to the present, the power of panoptic surveillance has dispersed into all manner of spaces, bringing forth the dream "of the perfectly governed city" (Foucault 1977: 198). Thus, schools, hospitals, workplaces, shopping centers, and online spaces are replete with technologies of watching, categorization, and norm enforcement. Foucault implies that this kind of society *is* premised on fine-graded surveillance involving each individual's internalization of the gaze. In other words, we watch, train, correct, and "punish" ourselves when we "fail" to live up to dominant norms and values (see later in the chapter in relation to women).

For Cohen (1979, 1985), modern urbanism is characterized by the *net-widening* of formal surveillance bringing about increases in numbers of deviants communing under surveillance in the first place. An increase in private and communal surveillance leads to a "thinning of the mesh" with "old and new deviants being subject to levels of intervention (including traditional institutionalization) which they might not have previously received" (Cohen 1985: 44). This dispersal of surveillant power blurs the boundaries between formal/informal and public/private forms of control, resulting in "more people [getting] involved in the 'control problem' [and] more rather than less attention . . . given to the deviance question" (Cohen 1985: 231). For Cohen, widening surveillance does not replace older methods of control and monitoring, such as the prison and police, but supplements their targeted and discriminatory nature. In the last quarter of the 20th century to the present, the increases in the use of stop-and-search, street camera surveillance, and imprisonment in the UK, USA, and France, disproportionately targeted at young, poor, black men, demonstrate this (Coleman and McCahill 2011).

Surveillance not only continues to grow into the minutia of social life, but also brings with it new forms of expertise and control (or secondary controls), which we encounter and even come to depend upon (as parents, workers, travelers, consumers, workers). This is far removed from Jacobs's (1961) plea for informal, less distant, and face-to-face contact-based surveillance whereby the city is "policed" by its inhabitants who must be encouraged to embrace difference and rub shoulders with inequality. The "death" of the American city, as Jacobs saw it, was in its elevation of secondary surveillance controls that technologized policing alongside increasing fear and mistrust within urban communities themselves. Her ideal of "public responsibility" whereby urban inhabitants look out for "each other even if they have no ties to each other" (1961: 82) is marginal to the growth in formal corporate and state-organized CCTV surveillance systems, private security patrols, gated communities, and the further militarization of city life over the last 50 years. We can also include the growth of Facebook and other social media giants who routinely define and police "community standards" in the digital realm (Fuchs 2017). In the last three decades, a whole range of institutions and individuals have been encouraged into taking responsibility for "crime", urban "safety", surveillance, and "policing". In this sense, we are increasingly governed through particular images and ideas about "crime", which have consolidated commonsense assumptions about *who* commits crime, against *whom*, and *where* (Coleman 2004). These scenarios point to a collapse of the boundaries between formal and informal surveillance and an increase in those being labeled "risky", "troublesome", or "deviant".

As indicated, these developments in expanding surveillance have not led to a broadening definition of deviance or criminality. According to one writer,

> entrusting members of the public with surveillance technology will encourage them to internalize the norms of state surveillance and policing: they will identify the problem the same way the police do, thanks, at least in part, to having been accorded the role of an agent of the state.
>
> *(Andrejevic 2007: 176)*

The technologies of surveillance may be ever more available and sophisticated but the cultural assumptions underpinning their uses and applicability remain relatively static. For example, definitions of crime remain focused on the streets and under the rubric of state- and corporate-defined "public order". Violence against women—in public and private space and relative invisibility—remains a significant social problem yet is under-surveilled and under-policed compared to other crimes (Coleman and McCahill 2011). The surveillance of "criminality" and "deviance" in the city is uneven and differentially targeted based on powerful vested interests and associated spatial-cultural assumptions. Of course, these assumptions are subject to contestation and change.

Surveillance in the City: The Visible

The development of surveillance in the 19th century targeted particular groups and spaces. Historians of the early modern city have shown how the culture of the urban poor was problematized by politicians, factory owners, and men of property in an era when thriftiness, sobriety, and discipline were required by the emerging capitalist factory system (Coleman and McCahill 2011). Typical in an emerging modern city was the need for authorities to render visible the streets as a forerunner to their control. For example, between 1836 and 1910, the policing mandate in the second city of the British Empire, Liverpool, aimed to "to divide off, to map out, the lower-class areas" (Brogden 1982: 52). The subjects of police work penalized the sources of capitalist mercantile economics—"disorderly boys", "children trundling hoops", "rough characters", "prostitutes", and "street hawkers", all subject to police surveillance, categorization, and control (Brogden 1982: 63).

Then as now, it was the economically and politically powerful who were able to influence surveillance authorities in what was targeted, and street order and monitoring remain contemporary priorities. Early police surveillance amounted to a form of street cleansing in which officers operated as uniformed garbagemen, arresting for minor misdemeanors. These early surveillance efforts increased visibility of the street and working-class life, whilst leaving unseen other spaces such as the injurious factories, mines, and fraudulent corporate offices where law and social censure have been relatively absent up until the contemporary period.

Intriguingly, the cultural targeting and demonization characteristic of early urban surveillance has intensified in the contemporary city. The gaze of both police- and privately operated CCTV control rooms of the late 20th and early 21st centuries continues to fall disproportionately on young, working-class males. Similar findings have been reported in relation to the use of CCTV surveillance systems (in shopping malls, gated communities, city center plazas) that has focused on "street nuisances". Empirical research has also shown that the language used by private security officers in urban spaces is often the same as the police officers' description of police property. CCTV operators in two shopping malls in a Northern City, for example, targeted young working-class males who were described as "scumbags", "shit", "druggies", and "G heads" (i.e., "glue sniffers"). In practice, the gaze of CCTV cameras in both "public" and "private" space is mediated by the selective concerns of the operators who tend to disproportionately target young working-class males. There is a correspondence of interests among a range of policing bodies about *who* constitutes the property of surveillance and who the *proper* objects of surveillance power are. Often, the property of panoptic surveillance is the poor, most vulnerable, and powerless in urban space past and present (see Coleman and McCahill 2011 for a review of research on these themes).

Indeed, the development of public-private surveillance networks has emerged within a wider political and economic restructuring of the late 20th-century city characterized as "entrepreneurial" or "neoliberal". Moreover, in these newly "revitalized" cities, it is the blurring of public and private policing practices that is producing "fortress cities, brutally divided between fortified cells of affluent society and . . . the criminalized poor" (Davis 1990: 224). The rise of "defensive" urban spaces in the form of gated communities, access control points, alcohol-free zones, business improvement zones, and privately owned and secured leisure and consumption areas attests to the continuing interrelationship between policing and surveillance and the control of working-class activity and space (Coleman 2009).

In terms of contemporary entrepreneurial city building, some scholars have observed how the need to maintain competitiveness in local urban economies has dovetailed with security and surveillance partnerships geared toward controlling petty offences and clearing city streets of human detritus and related "obstructions" to the idealized image of a crisis-free urban order. This is an extension of the 19th-century push to secure the cultural and economic viability of emerging modern cities, their workforces, and emergent political structures. The management of "visibility", both then and now, demonstrates the importance of rendering certain forms of information that is deemed helpful to the smooth running and ordering of the capitalist city. This is no less true today in the neoliberal or entrepreneurial city where youth cultures, signs of poverty (e.g., in the presence of the homeless), and behaviors associated with non-consumption have been singled out for surveillance attention by networks of "new urban primary definers" (Coleman 2009). These powerful coalitions of economic, political, and cultural interests—including property developers and business leaders—have joined with more established surveillance experts (the police and local authorities) to both reconstitute the local state and demarcate "new" visions of culture and behavior in increasingly commercialized urban space. Here, the centrality of image management in promoting cities as "desirable destinations" has underpinned local elite concern to "reclaim the streets" and place restrictions on movement in cities increasingly defined through heritage, tourism, and service economies. In this context, contemporary street surveillance has reflected and reinforced order-maintenance or zero-tolerance approaches to crime control, as witnessed in the networked policing of "petty nuisances" associated with vagrancy, skateboarding, and street trading (Coleman 2004).

The culture of 21st-century surveillance has a resentful element (Monahan 2017). Tendentious surveillance targeting has supported ruthless street cleansing and "purification" of the "public" realm under governing ideals that speak of "renaissance", "cleanliness", and cultural "diversity" (Coleman 2004). In this context, forms of punitive surveillance have also heralded a "return" to aggressive and heavy-handed policing and surveillance of poor and disadvantaged groups. This is crucial in that panoptic surveillance strategies have always been patchy, and it cannot be said that we all experience the same surveillance regime. However, at the punitive end of the spectrum, a re-emphasis on public-order policing has raised questions concerning "public belonging" and the right to the city in relation to poor and racialized minorities (Wacquant 2009). This has also led to increases in complaints against police corruption and violence (Coleman and McCahill 2011). Surveillance sites, nets, and spaces have widened control, as Cohen predicted, but the ideological and cultural definitions of crime, deviance, and the "dangerous" have remained broadly the same, reinforcing an idea of harm "emanating solely from powerless and disaffected people" (Coleman 2004: 227). Are streets and public spaces the most dangerous places to be in a modern city?

. . . And the Relatively Invisible

Cities can certainly be dangerous places. But *where* is that danger located—*who* are the "dangerous" and is surveillance targeted at them appropriately? Again, we need to approach question like this by looking at powerful, taken-for-granted assumptions and the embedded institutional urban forms that have come to define how we perceive "crime", "danger", and "risk".

Thinking about the visibility of dangerousness forces consideration of how powerful actors and institutions are mediated, perceived, and received in urban communications. In the 21st century, we have witnessed intensification in the celebration of business and a merging of business interests and mainstream politics (Tombs 2017). Within *entrepreneurial cities*, surveillance technologies continue *not* to be targeted at the most harmful and dangerous practices that emanate from business. It is "the great unwatched" who nevertheless generate urban social harms with the greatest financial and environmental costs (Coleman and McCahill 2011: 156). These harms take on global proportions whether in environmental destruction or financial loss, but these costs have been evaluated as dwarfing those incurred by conventional crime and met predominantly, not by corporations themselves, but by the population at large (Reiman and Leighton 2016). Such harms include urban/environmental devastation, loss of savings and income, and deaths and injuries at work. Regarding this latter form of harm, even the officially compiled statistics in developed countries tell us that one is more likely to be a victim of lethal harm and non-lethal injury related to work than one is to be a victim of conventional crime—and that most of these harms are related to violations of law (Tombs 2017). For example, in the UK today, occupation-related fatality rates are estimated at around 50,000 (including industrial illness and exposure). Homicide rates (as indicative of "serious conventional crime") are recorded at around 1,000 per year (Tombs 2017).

Surveillance of the most dangerous city spaces is under-resourced in the entrepreneurial or "business-friendly" city. In the UK, there are fewer than 1,000 inspectors employed by the Environment Agency and similar numbers in the Health and Safety Executive (HSE), compared to over 16,000 community support officers—as adjuncts to the police—involved in the regulation and surveillance of street crime and other petty offences or nuisances (Tombs 2017). Consequently, in terms of health and safety at work, on average, workplaces in the UK can anticipate an inspection from the HSE once every 20 years.

The visibility of work-based harm, compared to what we think of as conventional crime, is limited. In general terms, there is a dearth of time spent on, and resources allocated to, surveillance in this area, together with the accruement of "knowledge" about such harms that surveillance may help bring into the public and political domain. Harmful corporate actions scarcely figure as prominently as other less harmful activities. For Reiman and Leighton (2016), knowledge produced by the surveillance and categorization work of criminal justice systems operates like a carnival mirror with distorting images of what threatens us. It might seem, for example, that state servants such as police officers represent quintessential victims of violence sustained during their duty. In fact, it is far more dangerous—from the point of view of serious injury and loss of life—to be a construction worker than a police officer. The killing of a police officer "represents a profound, symbolic moment in the culture and politics of a society", whereas the comparatively high death rate of workers remains invisible and silenced by a discourse of the "routine costs—literally mere occupational hazards—of a certain set of social relations in a society in which 'risk' and 'entrepreneurialism' are increasingly validated" (Sim and Tombs 2008: 99). The carnival mirror presents to us the "typical" criminal or purveyor of harm (young, male, poor, disproportionately black) but also filters out the more socially costly and dangerous activities associated with powerful actors (middle-class, affluent individuals engaged in corporate misdemeanors, embezzlement, and fraud).

Past and Future City

Although these trends in surveillance silences are being challenged (see the Conclusion), the future urban landscape will display many continuities with past practices. Surveillance in the 21st century has an automated pre-crime logic, promising a trouble-free future in which risks and anticipated disruptions (to consuming, tourism, and leisure) are "nipped in the bud"—pre-seen and dealt with prior to any evidence of wrongdoing! House arrests, detention without trial, and curfews are already in force in many cities around the world as "precautionary" measures against young (black) youths, religious minorities, and potential (terrorist) threats. Although pre-crime-type surveillance is extensively *forward looking*—imagined future scenarios are elevated and *not* past criminal events or activities—it represents a shift to preemption or the anticipation and removal of undesirable behavior. Algorithms (such as facial recognition technology) are programmed to automatically identify "suspects", "wrong-space/face", "wrong-time" behaviors, and "suspicious speeds and interactions". But, as Cohen and Foucault forecast, teachers, social workers, and doctors are being encouraged into this preemptive effort against potential future criminality and nuisance behavior.

Twenty-first-century cities are places of production and consumption with competitive service economies built mainly around tourism, culture, and heritage. In service-based cities, surveillance retains its street order function, as already discussed, but at the same time, it has a micro-managing function in assessing the efficiency, economic and cultural worth, and productivity of individual citizens as they move around a city. Both modes of surveillance have an exclusion/inclusion logic. Our phones, banking, and Internet usage leave trails of data used to monitor and judge us as credit-worthy or valuable customers. Some might experience this as enhancing mobility (less laborious security airport check-ins, faster highways, and easier access to public or private services in health, banking, and education). Others, on the margins of economic and political life, face welfare and consumer exclusions, and slow or no mobility, because of punitive surveillance. The targeting of "suspect communities" (Irish, Aboriginal, Black, "unfeminine" women) has not abated with predictive surveillance and, for some, banishment from "civilized life" is achieved by surveillance, both old and new. Indeed, for Greenfield (2017: 233), automated surveillance technologies are not neutral and have racial-, class-, and gender-based cultural assumptions programmed into them, distilling "the way we chose to order our societies in the past".

Mediated Cities, Synoptic Cities

If 21st-century cities are mediated, they are synoptic cities. They are spaces in which we are all encouraged to view (via text and screen) and participate (through social media engagement) in shared understandings of what the city is, its meaning, and its uses (Coleman 2018). Some see this as a democratizing force, in that everyone (including the powerful) find it increasingly hard to preserve their anonymity as viewing technologies become ubiquitous and enhance visibility (Haggerty and Ericson 2006). Therefore, cities are not only panoptic but also synoptic in allowing *the many to observe the few*. However, the fact that we do observe the "few" (notorious criminals, celebrities, politicians) and we do possess surveillance devices ourselves does not mean that old hierarchies of power are breaking down. Indeed, synoptic viewing does not represent a complete break with "older" sociocultural divisions and prejudices.

Watching the "Criminal"

The power of synopticism (where the many see the few) can be explored with respect to how it encourages particular understandings and perceptions of crime, harm, and violence. Here, the viewing public is encouraged to watch the few in a way that arouses collective cultural assumptions and emotions relating to "crime", power, and order.

Reality TV shows about crime (such as *Crimewatch, America's Most Wanted, Cops Camera Action*) offer an example. Within the fabric of cities, one can see screens and posters containing mug shots of known or suspected offenders: for example, Chicago's Hit List—a police-inspired public messaging system that announces the neighborhood's top 50 most wanted felons. Surveillance produces knowledge in the form of categorical cultural messages that inform understanding of social problems. What kind of knowledge do these screens and TV serials offer about the "the problem of crime", who commits it, and where? What kinds of emotive messages do such screenings relay about the powerful—in this case, the police and forces of law and order? What do these synoptics stay silent about?

The proliferation of synoptic surveillance exemplified in the growth of crime-related reality TV typically draws upon accredited surveillance experts (police, security personnel, and crime profilers) and camera footage with the result that crime is depicted from a particular vantage point. This is usually a depiction of atypical and murderous events, or interpersonal violence and petty street offences. Such mass encoding represents events and people in ways that ascribe supposedly commonly held social values. This is achieved through over-typifying and over-emphasizing some behaviors and activities as the source of socially harmful behavior whilst underplaying other social harms. This raises questions about how we are encouraged to "see" (in emotional-cultural terms) different segments of the population through powerful definitions of "crime", "order", and "disorder" circulated in the mass media. This can encourage the identification and monitoring of others (e.g., in drawing attention to longstanding "enemies" or folk devils in the form of deviants around whom the possibility exists to mobilize social forces for order maintenance). In this sense, we can understand synoptic and panoptic forms of surveillance as interconnected. But, as already suggested, they are also differential in the way they are connected, targeted, and received among the wider population. Surveillance does not merely reflect or "find" difference or deviation from commonly defined social norms, but actively shapes and reinforces specific cultural values and ways of feeling or thinking about what or who is "different". This encourages the pursuit and punishment of pre-categorized and defined social harms: the gruesome murderer or the street nuisance as "typical" modes of harm or criminality (see also Chapter 42, this volume). In this sense, synoptic media provide an arena for the public (as viewers and listeners) to "contemplate" the few: whether celebrities, politicians, or notorious criminals.

Synoptic cities appear to prioritize the "personal and the individual, the deviant, the shuddering, the titillating" (Mathiesen 1997: 230). Further, fear-inducing tales of criminality and terror are often the basis for expanding real-world panoptic surveillance, unintentionally endorsing calls for more street cameras, militarized environments, bigger prisons, more data checks, and police powers. The repetitive image-driven reportage of the events of 9/11 in the USA and the subsequent terrors in Madrid, London, and Paris has had its impact upon extending surveillance, pre-crime initiatives, street curfews, and DNA datasets in advanced societies (Coleman and McCahill 2011).

Surveillance contributes as much to our understanding of, and exposure to, events in the world as it does to creating "a spiral of silence" over what we do not see and are not informed about (Mathiesen 2004: 103). In synopticism, corporate wrongdoing, committed in pursuit of legitimate goals, along with the negative consequences of a range of corporate action hardly features. Further, in the world of the private domestic sphere, where two women are murdered per week in the UK and where feminist writers would argue gendered violence is endemic, relatively little or no attention is apparent.

Surveillance silences are created when economically, culturally, and politically powerful actors influence their own surveillance and direct how, and under what circumstances, they are "seen" (in panoptic and synoptic forms). The ability to influence surveillance regimes is never total, but can refer to the power of celebrities, politicians, and business people to influence how we see them and how they are monitored (by law, media, and regulatory agencies).

Watching Women

Historically, women's presence in urban spaces has been problematized and women's presence on the streets has been criminalized and sexualized, and has provoked physical and emotional violence from state officials and men. In short, and to varying degrees in history and location, women have been, and still are, subject to a condition of being "public property" in urban areas, and this is illustrated with reference to their formal and informal surveillance as well as the continued use of women's bodies in advertising (Coleman and McCahill 2011).

Today, information (i.e., images) produced by new surveillance technologies such as the smartphone allows images, location, and identities to be "stored" in electronic spaces (on a computer file or videotape), ready to be disseminated at some future time and place. This applies to so-called "upskirting": a term used to describe men taking photographs underneath an unsuspecting woman's skirt using a mobile phone camera. The informal use of surveillance technology to sexually harass and intimidate women (posting these photos on social media with typical comments of "slut" attached) is a little-discussed area in surveillance studies, yet it highlights a relatively invisible and informal panopticon. Upskirting is a current urban phenomenon that extends the idea of women as sexual objects and reinforces a cultural assumption that women's bodies are public (men's) property (alongside the growth in pornography) (Saner 2009). This has continuities with the 19th-century sexualization of women's bodies in masculinized cities (e.g., through prostitution) and the routine policing enacted against the unaccompanied female urban presence (BBC 2018). Plan International's (2017) survey criticizes digital social media as scoping an informal surveillance world that is sometimes exclusionary for women: posing a threatening, sexually abusive, and predatory "public" space.

Conclusion: Surveillance, Power, City

Surveillance reflects and reinforces economic, political, and cultural divisions of urban life. It is not a neutral technology: it reflects and reinforces the struggles, conflicts, and tensions found in any city. Surveillance denotes ways of seeing and thinking (about, for instance, "crime" and "womanhood") and it also leaves silences in understandings and what can be made visible in the city, particularly in regard to the harms of the city. Surveillance is about making cities and urban lives visible (at least to some extent), but it also has a role in leaving silences and leaving some behaviors and spaces unseen.

However, what about surveillance undertaken that challenges power relations and silencing? Forms of counter-surveillance propagate dissent and resistance to oppressive forms of government and harmful corporate conduct. These are important forms of surveillance that break the silence in the fields of work or corporate decision-making. *Hazards.org*, a web-based magazine, aims to get "behind the company safety hype, and give answers . . . to workplace problems" in using "a global network of union safety correspondents" to provide information that corporations either hide or deny (see: www.hazards.org/abouthazards/index.htm). No2iD is a site focused on "the threat to liberty and privacy posed by the rapid growth of the database state" (see: www.no2id.net).

Similarly, there are websites devoted to citizen surveillance of the police, breaking the official silence on issues such as police brutality, racism, and sexist practice (e.g., see https://blacklivesmatter.com). Such forms of counter-surveillance may be fairly localized, but all stand outside of, and in opposition to, official surveillance. For those involved in these monitoring initiatives, the goals of surveillance are characterized as socially progressive in relation *to the kinds of visibility* they promote for workers, those fighting injustice, and consumers.

Surveillance can be, and is, used to present alternative knowledge and experiences of the city: ones that will not be found in powerful official narratives. How successful such relatively under-resourced, technologically unsophisticated, and localized surveillance can be in rethinking what cities are for, and who can legitimately belong in them, is an ongoing debate concerning the right to the city.

References

Andrejevic, M. (2007) *iSPY: Surveillance and Power in the Interactive Era*, Lawrence, KS: University Press of Kansas.
BBC (2018) "Public sexual harassment to be investigated by MPs", BBC News, viewed May 15, 2018, www.bbc.co.uk/news/uk-42684820.
Black Lives Matter, viewed July 16, 2018, https://blacklivesmatter.com.
Brogden, M. (1982) *The Police: Autonomy and Consent*, London: Academic Press.
— (1991) *On the Mersey Beat: Policing Liverpool Between the Wars*, New York: Oxford University Press.
Cohen, S. (1979) "The punitive city: Notes on the dispersal of social control", *Contemporary Crises*, 3(4), pp. 339–363.
— (1985) *Visions of Social Control*, Cambridge: Polity Press.
Coleman, R. (2004) *Reclaiming the Streets: Surveillance, Social Control and the City*, Cullompton: Willan.
— (2009) "Policing the working class in the city of renewal: the state and social surveillance", in R. Coleman, J. Sim, S. Tombs, and D. Whyte (eds.) *State, Power, Crime*, London: SAGE, pp. 60–75.
— (2018) "The synoptic city: state, 'place' and power", *Space and Culture*, January, pp. 1–15.
Coleman, R. and McCahill, M. (2011) *Surveillance and Crime*, London: Sage.
Davis, M (1990) *City of Quartz*, London: Verso.
Foucault, M. (1977) *Discipline and Punish*, London: Allen Lane.
Fuchs, C. (2017) *Social Media: A Critical Introduction*, 2nd edition, London: SAGE.
Gilliom, J. (2006) "Struggling with surveillance: resistance, consciousness and identity", in D. K. Haggerty and R. V. Ericson (eds.) *The New Politics of Surveillance and Visibility*, Toronto: University of Toronto Press, pp. 111–139.
Greenfield, A. (2017) *Radical Technologies: The Design of Everyday Life*, London: Verso.
Haggerty, D. K. and Ericson, R. V. (eds.) (2006) "Introduction", *The New Politics of Surveillance and Visibility*, Toronto: University of Toronto Press.
Hazards, viewed July 16, 2018, www.hazards.org/abouthazards/index.htm.
Jacobs, J. (2016 [1961]) *The Life and Death of Great American Cities*, New York: Vintage Books.
Jeffreys, S. (2005) *Beauty and Misogyny: Harmful Cultural Practices in the West*, London: Routledge.
Lyon, D. (2001). *Surveillance Society: Monitoring Everyday Life*, London: Open University Press.
— (ed.) (2003) "Surveillance as social sorting", *Surveillance as Social Sorting: Privacy, Risk and Digital Discrimination*, New York: Routledge, pp. 13–30.
Mathiesen, T. (1997) "The viewer society: Michael Foucault's panopticon revisited", *Theoretical Criminology*, 1(2), pp. 215–234.
— (2004) *Silently Silenced*, Hook, UK: Waterside Press.
Monahan, T. (2017) "Regulating belonging: Surveillance, inequality, and the cultural production of abjection", *Journal of Cultural Economy*, 10(2), pp. 191–206.
No2iD, viewed July 16, 2018, https://www.no2id.net.
Plan International (2017) "Unlock the digital power of girls", viewed July 16, 2018, https://plan-international.org/education/unlock-digital-power-of-girls.
Reiman, J. and Leighton, P. (2016) *The Rich Get Rich and the Poor Get Prison: Ideology, Class and Criminal Justice*, London: Routledge.
Saner, L. (2009) "I feel completely violated", *The Guardian*, February 25.
Sim, J. and Tombs, S. (2008) "State talk, state silence: work and 'violence' in the UK", in L. Panitch and C. Lees (eds.) *Violence Today: Actually Existing Barbarism*, London: Merlin Press, pp. 88–104.
Tombs, S. (2017) *Social Protection After the Crisis: Regulation Without Enforcement*, Bristol: Policy Press.
Wacquant, L. (2009) *Punishing the Poor: The Neoliberal Government of Social Insecurity*, Durham, NC: Duke University Press.

Further Reading

Coleman, R. and McCahill, M. (2011) *Surveillance and Crime*, London: SAGE.
Lyon, D. (2007) *Surveillance Studies: An Overview*, Cambridge: Polity Press.
Monahan, T. (2017) "Regulating belonging: surveillance, inequality, and the cultural production of abjection", *Journal of Cultural Economy*, 10(2), pp. 191–206.

19
URBAN MEDIA AS INFRASTRUCTURE FOR SOCIAL CHANGE

Naomi Schiller

Introduction

The aim of this chapter is to explore the ways that people in the Global South engage media in ways that foster social change. More than simply a metaphor for the groundwork that makes possible sociocultural transformation, I explore media as a form of infrastructure entangled with other forms of infrastructure. I draw attention to how media infrastructure—with its complex materialities, poetics, and content—is central to the constitution and governance of cities. This approach to media as urban infrastructure, I argue, allows us not only to theorize the way that media and cities are inextricably linked, but also to identify and better understand the embeddedness of media in the processes of exchange, relationality, and power. Through engagements with and demands for infrastructure, people struggle over continuity and change in the city and, by extension, the broader society (Ginsburg et al. 2002; Appel et al. 2018).

My approach embraces recent efforts to challenge sub-disciplinary thinking that tends to separate media from other forms of social mediation. This chapter heeds recent calls to shift anthropological attention from "media anthropology" to "anthropology of mediation" (Boyer 2012) and, at the same time, to rethink local studies of *media in cities* to instead theorize urban media as part of broader processes of *city-making* (Ćaglar and Glick Schiller 2018). This framework dovetails with the recent scholarly turn to examine infrastructures as a particularly helpful heuristic to understand the paradoxes, promises, and perils of the contemporary period (Howe et al. 2016).

I briefly review urban media as infrastructure for social change in different historical periods, with a focus on colonial, postcolonial, and neoliberal cities. I highlight how change is not an outcome of the invention or adoption of a particular technology. Rather, people create, embrace, reject, engage, and tinker with the intertwining urban infrastructures as part of an effort to reproduce and transform their cities and their broader social, political, economic, and cultural worlds. I explore the tensions between the egalitarian promise of infrastructure accessible to all and its threat of top-down organization of social life. Communications media are taken up at times in unexpected ways to advance social struggle for basic rights to resources and to participate in urban governance.

To ground my claims about the interconnections between cities, communications infrastructure, and social change, I explore efforts to make community media in Caracas,

Venezuela during the first decade of the 21st century. The case of community media in Caracas reveals a struggle for access to media infrastructure as part and parcel of a struggle for the "right to the city" (Lefebvre 1996).

Media and Social Change

Various methodological and theoretical approaches have emerged in the past decade in contemporary anthropology, communications, and geography that provide an excellent foundation to understand the co-constitutive character of media, cities, and infrastructure.

Beginning in the 1990s, "media worlds" became a central area of inquiry for anthropologists and other ethnographers (Ginsburg et al. 2002). This research emphasizes the importance of understanding media as a practice embedded within webs of human sociality. In opposition to technological or media determinism, an ethnographically grounded perspective underscores that media does not catalyze social change, but rather that engagement with media—including its messages and materialities—is a *process* and a cultural *practice* of negotiating social relationships (Ginsburg 1994; Star 1999; Boyer 2007). Ethnographic studies of media practices challenge the ethnocentrism that characterizes much of the study of mainstream media, with its historically narrow focus on North America and Western Europe (Ganti 2014). Ethnographic work on diverse media practices serves as an important counterpoint to dominant theories of social change, development, and modernization, which characterize technology as the linchpin in the story of how "man" moves from pre-modern to modern. In this fantasy, technology is supposed to grant "man" power over nature so that he may untether himself from a traditional state of being. Anthropologists reject this narrative. They approach development and modernization not as a neutral process of change, but rather as discourses of capitalism first developed in the post-World War II period that have produced knowledge about and power over the Global South (Escobar 1995).

Ethnography of media, as Lila Abu-Lughod argues, is particularly useful to upend the "tradition/modernity dichotomy" (2005: 25) that continues to organize many scholarly and popular visions of world populations and urban life. This binary of tradition and modernity characterizes some people and places as stuck in the past, unequal, and disconnected, particularly those in remote and rural areas. The study of media practices and infrastructures can provide a vivid avenue to counter the misperception that any group is isolated, timeless, bounded, or disconnected from global forces of exchange and distribution. Tradition and modernity; the rural and urban; and development and underdevelopment are not dichotomous but intertwining and interdependent processes. The persistence of dichotomous thinking and facile assumptions about development as an apolitical path to progress is demonstrated through the rehashing of these ideas through the categories of "the digital age" and "the digital divide" (Ginsburg 2008). These categories speciously divide contemporary living people into different time periods and spaces of modernity or non-modernity.

Despite the onslaught of claims that our "network society" represents a rupture with the past (Castells 1996), most scholars agree that "the presumption that digital technologies are the basis of planetary transformations is widespread, but unfounded" (Coleman 2010: 489). Efforts to make claims about the specific causal relation between a discrete technology and an event or broader social shift often do so by delineating arbitrarily a starting point and ending point of social transformation and excising the social messiness of life, its interconnections, and non-linear changes.

From early scholarly debates about indigenous people's uptake of video (Turner 1991; Faris 1992; Ginsburg 1994) to more recent efforts to understand online sociality, the underlying question for many anthropologists who study media is how people use novel representational and communicational technologies in contexts of specific constraints in ways that create social change or, for some scholars, how people are remade by these technologies in ways that precipitate transformations. At the root of these debates is the question about the relationship between the technical power of media and the power of human agency (Boyer 2006). A dialectical Marxist approach shifts attention away from form or a reified understanding of culture and technology to instead emphasize unfolding human action, activism, and experience in particular sociopolitical contexts (Mahon 2000). This work underscores how people from social groups and social classes with differential access to power use media technology alongside other forms of social mediation to make meaning and negotiate power. Media technologies are not in themselves either revolutionary or reactionary.

Increasingly, scholars approach media as a social practice that shapes and is shaped by broader dynamics of power, rather than an autonomous force that determines life. Yet, notwithstanding this approach, marking something as "media" is an intellectual act that works to categorize a set of practices and things as separate and distinct from other human forms of knowledge production, construction of sociocultural worlds, and exchange (Boyer 2012: 389). Instead, we might better place media engagement within the broader context of *social mediation*—the study of the social transaction of "images, discourses, persons, and things" (Mazzarella 2004; Boyer 2012: 383). The provocation to abandon the sub-disciplinary silo of "media anthropology" (or "media sociology") to embrace, instead, a more holistic approach to social mediation (Boyer 2012) is one that urges scholars to recognize that bounding something off something as "media" can discourage the integration of analyses of communication systems and infrastructures into studies of all areas of life.

Infrastructure, Media, and Cities

Infrastructures distribute resources. Infrastructures are the pathways through which goods, ideas, energy, water, and people move (Larkin 2013). As a central "terrain of power and contestation" (Appel et al. 2018: 2), all infrastructure is deeply social and political, not simply technical (see also Chapters 15 and 41, this volume). Infrastructure is what is necessary to extract wealth and to extend domination, but it is also indispensable to challenge inequality and dispossession. Scholars have begun to approach media technologies as infrastructure, while at the same time characterizing that which we traditionally might think of as infrastructure—roads, sewage lines, power generators, and wind parks—as forms of mediation (Howe and Boyer 2016).

Why is it useful to approach media *as* infrastructure? Like bridges, sewer systems, runways, and power lines, communicational media form a critical component of the sociocultural and material grid that supports (and can undermine) human life. Approaching communications media as infrastructure allows us to understand that communicational forms of exchange are embedded within and negotiated alongside other exchange of matter, people, and discourse. Rather than viewing "the media" as separate or unique catalysts of change, people practice media technologies in contexts of a layered history of uneven access to multiple kinds of infrastructure.

As "assemblies of infrastructures," cities are central nodes of movement of capital, energy, water, signal traffic, and people (Appel et al. 2018: 11). As cities are built and rebuilt, different forms of infrastructure are layered on top of one another and often follow existing pathways: telephone lines have been installed along railway lines and cell phone towers are perched on water towers (Parks and Starosielski 2015: 40). The substrata of our cities are layered, interpenetrating, and interdependent material of pipes, wires, roads, and tunnels. These entanglements suggest that delineating the object of study—where an infrastructure begins and ends—is in some senses an arbitrary act, but also that the materiality and meaning of media and of other processes that make up cities cannot be separated. Infrastructure and urbanism are inseparable.

Recent scholarship urges us to move beyond a "container approach" to cities that focuses on what people do *in* cities to instead "envision more daringly the wider cultural political economy of urbanization processes" (Ćaglar and Glick Schiller 2018). While many scholars study media production, consumption, and circulation *in* urban settings, anthropologists and others have recently begun to explore how city-making and media-making are co-constitutive processes. Contemporary analyses of urban media attempts to think through communications media, alongside other forms of infrastructure, as part of the cultural political economy of urbanization, with a focus on how people have engaged with media in their efforts to advance social change.

A focus on infrastructures allows us to think through how cities develop and are funded, governed, and maintained through multiscalar connections (Glick Schiller 2014). Cities have their own infrastructures, leaders, and regulatory systems, while at the same time they are embedded within and produce broader systems of governance and infrastructure (Glick Schiller and Ćaglar 2009). The study of urban infrastructure—a category that includes communications media—allows us to think about how particular urban sites, materials, and peoples are connected and disconnected across "interpenetrating scales of relationality" (Glick Schiller 2014: 291), which include the "corporal, local, urban, regional, national, international, and global" (Mattern 2015: 107).

As material things themselves and as a relation between things, infrastructures are notoriously "conceptually unruly" (Larkin 2013: 329). We necessarily limit ourselves to study particular places, people, and processes. We recognize that a community television station is not the same as a sewer. But when we identify how these different forms of social mediation share similarities and are interrelated, we can better understand the city, its inhabitants, and processes of social change (Star 1999).

I focus my attention on three intertwined dimensions of infrastructure: the content, the material, and the poetic. The content is the stuff that travels through infrastructure; in the context of communications media this includes the words, images, and sounds, which Parks and Starosielski call the "audio visual signal traffic" (2015). The materiality of infrastructure includes the fiber-optic cables, asphalt roads, and sewers. The poetics of infrastructure, as Brian Larkin explains, refers to the aesthetics and meaning that people grant infrastructure; the ways that "form is loosened from technical function" (2013: 335). For example, the experience of going to the cinema (Larkin 2008) or the process of making a television program (Schiller 2018) can be more locally significant as a political performance of modern subjectivity than the audience's engagement with the messages embedded in film or television representations. Engagement with infrastructure is generative in ways that often exceed its supposed purpose or the impact of its content.

The content, material, and poetic aspects of infrastructure are overlapping and provisional categories, given that there is "no materiality that is not mediated by discourse, and there is no discourse that is unrelated to materialities" (Escobar 1995: 130). Attention to these interrelated aspects of infrastructure and the labor required to produce, maintain, demolish, or retrofit is vital to efforts to analyze social hierarchy and modes of rule. While leaders sometimes draw explicit attention to infrastructure to bolster the legitimacy of their rule, infrastructures are often hidden. As a result, they are little understood by the public and vulnerable to control by private interests (Parks and Starosielski 2015: 6). In many places, infrastructures remain invisible until they break down (Graham and Marvin 2001; Larkin 2008). Exposing the materiality of media infrastructures and the labor and maintenance they require can work to "locate media distribution within systems of power" (Parks and Starosielski 2015: 5).

Before moving on to an ethnographic example of urban media as infrastructure for social change, I turn now to trace briefly the historical links between the creation and negotiation of urban media infrastructure and the exercise of power.

Media and Social Change in Colonial, Postcolonial, and Neoliberal Infrastructures of Rule

The creation and use of infrastructure have been central to processes of urbanization throughout human history, from ancient, precolonial, colonial, postcolonial, to the contemporary neoliberal period. Rulers have used the content, material, and poetics of infrastructure to create and alter modes of governance, subject formation, and ownership. Infrastructures are often ideally imagined to unite cities into coherent, governable, and livable urban spaces under the purview of public planning and oversight (Graham and Marvin 2001: 9). In fact, in pre-modern periods where cities were planned to manage populations and create zones of exclusion through more recent neoliberal shifts to privatize infrastructures and services, access to infrastructure has been unequal across time-space.

From the initial growth of cities in most places in the world to the present, urban infrastructure has largely been built for the extraction of wealth by the few from the many. Scholars who draw on a historical-materialist perspective emphasize that the process of urbanization takes place "through geographical and social concentrations of a surplus product" (Harvey 2003a: 24). Others highlight how communication and ceremony have been equally important as economics in the creation of cities (Mattern 2015). The processes of extraction, exchange, and circulation have relied on infrastructure of roads and aqueducts as far back as the cities of ancient Rome in the eighth century BC. Mattern argues that the materiality of the built environment of ancient Rome and Greece—the "urban surfaces, volumes, and voids"—provided the acoustic infrastructure for speech and vocality, which was central to governance and sociality (2015: 98).

From 16th-century Iberian colonial projects in the Americas (Mundy 1996; Kagan 2000) to Europe's 19th-century projects to "enframe" a colonial city's inhabitants, people have used infrastructure to shape new subjectivities, extract labor power, and instantiate hierarchies (Mitchell 1988). Colonizers relied on enslaved and oppressed peoples to build infrastructure that could assert their mastery and legitimize their power. As elsewhere, British colonial discourse and the production of knowledge about the colonized—distributed in print starting in the 15th and 16th centuries and later in audiovisual media—were profoundly connected to the operation of colonial power (Said 1978). Larkin highlights the relation between "infrastructural technologies" and "modes of rule" (2013: 3) in British Colonial Nigeria in the 19th century. For example, across Africa, commercial cinemas served as "powerful instances of modernity, along with electric lighting, amplified popular music, factory wages, and motorized vehicles" (Haynes 2011: 68). In addition to serving as conduits for representations and the flow of ideas, colonial communications infrastructures had important poetic dimensions. Infrastructure provokes the imagination, instills hope, and fuels fantasies of progress (Spitulnik 1998–99).

In many developing postcolonial cities, urban media were part of the broader effort to remake societies according to a vision of Western modernity as an "unalloyed good" (Abu-Lughod 2005: 132). Radio, railway, and electricity grids encouraged what James Ferguson calls "expectations of modernity" (1999). Postcolonial elites in Cairo used cinema and television, alongside other infrastructural projects in agriculture, education, and social welfare, as didactic tools to educate, uplift, and reform—an ideology known as "developmentalism" (Abu-Lughod 2005). In Caracas, infrastructure projects have been used by leaders to display personalized power or the broader "magic" of the state (Coronil 1997). The materiality, the content, and the poetics of communications infrastructure have been used by rulers as mechanisms of governance.

Neoliberal restructuring of the global capitalist economy has exacerbated the racialized, gendered, and class projects of dispossession, labor exploitation, and environmental destruction (Maskovsky and Brash 2014; Williams 2014). Neoliberal privatization of public resources, the increasing precarity of everyday life, and the imposition of particular ideas about the relationship between the self and the social have produced varied responses in cities (see also Chapter 42, this volume). For example, the neoliberalization of urban Nigeria and the state's concomitant retreat from supporting the development of cinema created an absence that Nigerian video filmmakers rushed to fill. The rise of the Nigerian film industry—often referred to as Nollywood—offers producers and viewers ways to respond to the intense insecurity of the neoliberal city (Larkin 2008: 173). The Nigerian film industry is not only based in Lagos, but it also helps produce the city through its material informal economy and through its circulation of ideas about the city (Haynes 2007). In response to privatization and enclosure in Caracas, a different kind of non-professional media industry developed: barrio-based community television. Urban activists turned to media projects as part of a broader social movement to reject neoliberalism and, instead, construct participatory democracy and socialism.

While centralizing infrastructure has connected subjects to oppressive colonial, postcolonial, and neoliberal states and has shared affinities with authoritarian and exploitative modes of rule, we should not dismiss the egalitarian possibilities of infrastructure (Larkin 2008: 245). To ground this discussion of the relationship between infrastructure, media, social change, and the city and to explore efforts to construct and extend infrastructures in the interest of social justice and equality, I turn to explore the work of community television producers in Caracas.

Urban Media as Infrastructure for Social Change in Caracas

Between 2003 and 2008, I conducted 14 months of ethnographic research with community media activists in Caracas. I observed how people from very poor neighborhoods embraced community television as a tool for social change often in unanticipated ways. The social and political shifts that I observed during this period did not emerge principally from the impact of the television production they created, but rather from their material engagement and the poetic dimensions of their work to make media in poor neighborhoods and inside central state institutions. The many gains that community media activists in Caracas made during the period of my research have been sharply eroded by 2018, as the country faces deep political and economic turmoil. This crisis emerged with the collapse in oil prices, ongoing efforts at home and from abroad to undermine projects aimed at redistribution, as well as government corruption and mismanagement. Despite these developments, we have much to learn about how urban media has been taken up at particular historical conjunctures in the struggle for the right to the city.

Since the early 20th century, Venezuela has been a central node of the global oil economy as a major exporter. Over this time, social struggles have focused on efforts to gain access and channel the wealth from the sale of oil, much of which has been taken out of the country. The infrastructure of oil—a vast collection of extraction, distribution, and processing technologies that include pipelines, shipping systems, and refineries across multiple states—and the politics of who will control and benefit from this infrastructure are intertwined with almost every other form of infrastructure in Venezuela, including communications technologies.

With the shift from an agricultural to an oil-based economy in the early 20th century, Venezuela rapidly urbanized. For many urban poor communities, the experience of being connected to infrastructure involved being submitted to top-down regulation of daily life. The authoritarian government of Pérez Jiménez first pushed forward urban renewal projects in the 1950s in the name of modernizing the city and its inhabitants (Velasco 2015). Demands for infrastructure and claims for resources were met with discourse and instruction that revealed how elites approached infrastructure as a method to civilize the barbarous and unruly masses (Kingsbury 2017). After a period of economic growth and massive public spending on infrastructure from 1958 through 1978, the dramatic decline in world oil prices pushed the government to turn to international borrowing. The imposition of neoliberal austerity measures as a condition of loans to bail out the country in the late 1980s led to massive urban upheaval that revealed longstanding social divides in access to basic infrastructure along class and race.

The urban social movements that came together to bring Hugo Chávez to power in 1998 first began to demand the right to the city in the late 1980s and 1990s in response to neoliberal visions of individual rights and privatized resources. By the late 1990s, Caracas, a city of more than five million people, was starkly divided between formally planned neighborhoods of middle-class and luxury housing and extensive densely packed and informally constructed poor neighborhoods. This geography is racialized (Ciccariello-Maher 2016); the descendants of African and indigenous populations inhabit the most unstable and historically state-neglected land. The formal utility infrastructure of piped water, a closed sewage system, and electric power has long been out of reach of large sectors of the urban population who live in shantytowns. At the same time, the formal infrastructure of mass communication production—the headquarters of the most powerful stations and the media-makers who work there—has historically had little presence in poor regions of the city. The urban poor were the objects and consumers of mass media but not its producers.

In the first decade of the anti-neoliberal Bolivarian movement led by Chávez, the government used windfall oil revenues from the latest boom to develop a vast network of social welfare projects, including the expansion of public transportation, housing, electrification, and sewer lines and social projects in education and media (Torres et al. 2017). Demands for access to basic urban infrastructure were intertwined with projects to develop barrio-based media outlets. With new legal protections and funding from the Chávez government, Caracas's community media organizations expanded from informal groups of activists to licensed broadcasters.

The interrelationship between media infrastructures and other forms of urban infrastructure emerged with stark clarity in my research with Catia TVe, Venezuela's most prominent community media organization. Catia TVe's founders, like their community video counterparts elsewhere in the region, were convinced that without direct control of images and narratives about their own lives and struggles, broader efforts to challenge inequality and upend the social order were impossible. Their goal was not simply to provide a voice to the voiceless—to transform the content—but also to use the process of media production to transform Caracas, the Venezuelan state, and beyond. In short, their community media-making was a demand to the right to the city. As Harvey notes, "the right to the city is not merely a right of access to what already exists, but a right to change it" (2003b: 939). For Catia TVe producers, this entailed demanding access not simply to resources for the poor and working class, but also to a right to participate in the process of design, construction, and decision-making about this infrastructure, be it roads or television stations.

With funding from the state-owned oil company, Catia TVe began broadcasting in 2002. At the time of my research in 2007, Catia TVe had 30 full-time paid staff members and around 100 volunteers. Catia TVe's 14 hours of daily programming were filled with local news segments, complaints about government programs, political debates, and musical performances. Catia TVe producers used their status as media-makers to gain access to elite spaces, such as presidential press conferences and television studios, where they challenged traditional barriers shaped by race, class, and gender. Access to the means of media production connected people from poor neighborhoods to the managerial middle class as partners rather than only as clients, as well as supported alliances with global social movements. Poor people's movements for paved streets, electricity, housing, community-based media, and water developed through community action and in dialogue with state officials and institutions to use state resources to develop initiatives to challenge inequality.

Through access to the means of media production, I documented how poor people in Caracas participated in shaping the process of state formation (Schiller 2018), which in its most immediate form involved the process of urbanization—the work to create and manage electric lines, television transmitters, sewers, and housing. Catia TVe producers struggled every day to negotiate the tension inherent in working to produce and maintain infrastructure in collaboration with actors in central state institutions; they faced both the egalitarian promise and threat of top-down control. They used media in anticipated and unanticipated ways to claim access to housing, clean water, safety, and the right to shape the process of urbanization itself. Through their participation in poor neighborhoods and central state institutions, Catia TVe taught basic media literacy and analysis but also demystified media production as an everyday time-consuming labor. Their work to participate in media production alongside their allies in state institutions allowed my interlocutors to see state institutions as penetrable and ad hoc human constructions. This knowledge encouraged broader participation in everyday forms of city and state formation.

The interconnectivity of urban infrastructures of oil, electricity, media, and waste disposal; the intertwining threads of media (content, form, and poetics); and the tension between equality and subordination were particularly visible one Sunday afternoon when I accompanied a 19-year-old Catia TVe staff member named Nestor to document a meeting in a poor neighborhood of west Caracas. We took the metro and then a four-wheel-drive Jeep to reach the neighborhood, nestled high on the hilltop overlooking downtown Caracas. We found a street blocked off with rope. Three-story houses of concrete and terracotta blocks were situated incongruously between massive steel lattice towers that supported electric cables. Inhabitants had built the neighborhood in the 1980s on land that the Ministry of Energy had cleared for electricity towers. Two decades later, these former squatters were self-organizing for better regularized access to the electric grid, waste management, and water.

We were there that afternoon on the invitation of a local activist who was part of a group trying to promote the construction of a communal council, a local governance organ written into law in 2006. A community council brought together several hundred families from the same neighborhood to formulate proposals for funding from state institutions and oversee the budgeting and implementation of community development projects in health, housing, communications, and water. Some councils fulfilled their mandate to democratize participation and reorder power, while others reproduced traditional forms of top-down administration.

Our host, Douglas, took us on a quick tour of the street, pointing out problems that he hoped the communal council would one day address. The boys needed a place to play basketball. The garbage was rarely collected and contributed to flooding when it rained. Part of the street was crumbling. As we slowly made our way down the street, Nestor's camera and microphone drew considerable notice. A group of small girls tugged at Nestor's pant leg, wanting to know what television station he was from. A group of young men around Nestor's age with his same brown complexion, baggy jeans, and sneakers studied him with more guarded enthusiasm. Douglas seemed quite pleased at the attention Nestor attracted. Although few people we encountered had heard of Catia TVe, as the signal did not reach that neighborhood, the presence of a local media outlet bolstered Douglas's prestige in the community. Nestor's act of media-making validated not only Douglas's aspirations to local leadership, but also the legitimacy of his community's initiative. Given how technology is the privileged sign of progress, poor and brown people making television carried significant weight as a sign of broad social change and possibility. The status of media-maker granted Nestor and his colleagues the ability to enter diverse communities to work with other poor people all over the city to participate in projects aimed at local governance.

As I would learn many times throughout my research, it was the process and poetics of media production, rather than through the effects of the content of their programs on audiences, that Catia TVe staff and volunteers had the most impact in encouraging their interlocutors to actively embrace political participation in shaping the city. Although Catia TVe had a high profile among activists and government officials, few people watched the station's broadcasts. The station's motto, "Don't Watch Television, Make it!", articulated their primary interest in producing media-makers, not viewers. Indeed, the primary impact of their media work was the face-to-face political organizing they conducted with the people they filmed, the volunteers they trained to understand the materiality of media production, and the government officials with whom they created complex relationships. They engaged community media-making as a tool of city- and state-making.

Conclusion

This chapter heeds a call to decenter media as a separate and distinct form and practice from other forms of meaning-making and negotiations for power. In this integrative approach to urban media as infrastructure for social change, I have focused on how people in Caracas and elsewhere have struggled to negotiate and engage intertwining infrastructures—the things in themselves, the things they carry, the things they are made to represent—in ways that allow people to cope, oppress, struggle, and make meaning. My approach suggests that we explore the ways in which urban media make up the fabric of the city materially and as a collection of beliefs, ideas, and aspirations. Rather than attributing political or social outcomes to the special and unique properties of any particular pathway for the distribution of resources and ideas, such as sewage lines or mobile-phone texting, we hone our attention to understanding the city as part of broad social fields with different kinds of connections shaped by forces of exchange, knowledge production, domination, struggle, and capital accumulation (Appel et al. 2018).

The process of making media by and for historically disenfranchised populations in Caracas, as in many cities, involves teaching and learning about local needs, approaches, and problems and solutions for urban infrastructure. The work of city-making shaped, and was shaped by, the ways that Caracas—as the capital of an oil state—was positioned in broad fields of power. Placing media alongside other critical infrastructure that connect and disconnect people and things encourages us to avoid technological determinist erasure of human action, organizing, and decision-making. We see media as one of a number of complex conduits for resources that involve material and immaterial processes of city-making.

References

Abu-Lughod, L. (2005) *Dramas of Nationhood*, Chicago, IL: University of Chicago Press.
Appel, H., Anand, N., and Gupta, A. (eds.) (2018) "Temporality, Affect, and the Promise of Infrastructure," in *The Promise of Infrastructure*, Durham, NC: Duke University Press, pp. 1–40.
Boyer, D. (2006) "Turner's Anthropology of Media and Its Legacies," *Critique of Anthropology*, 26(1), pp. 47–60.
— (2007) *Understanding Media: A Popular Philosophy*, Chicago, IL: Prickly Paradigm Press.
— (2012) "From Media Anthropology and the Anthropology of Mediation," in R. Fardon (ed.) *The ASA Handbook of Social Anthropology*, Thousand Oaks, CA: SAGE, pp. 383–392.
Çaglar, A. and Glick Schiller, N. (2018) *Migrants and City-Making: Dispossession, Displacement, and Urban Regeneration*, Durham, NC: Duke University Press.
Castells, M. (1996) *The Rise of the Network Society*, Cambridge, MA: Blackwell.
Ciccariello-Maher, G. (2016) *Building the Commune: Radical Democracy in Venezuela*, London: Verso.

Coleman, G. (2010) "Ethnographic Approaches to Digital Media," *Annual Review of Anthropology*, 39, pp. 487–505.

Coronil, F. (1997) *The Magical State*, Chicago, IL: University of Chicago Press.

Escobar, A. (1995) *Encountering Development: The Making and Unmaking of the Third World*, Princeton, NJ: Princeton University Press.

Faris, J. (1992) "Anthropological Transparency, Film, Representation and Politics," in P. Crawford and D. Turton (eds.) *Film as Ethnography*, Manchester: University of Manchester Press, pp. 171–189.

Ferguson, J. (1999) *Expectations of Modernity: Myths and Meanings of Urban Life on the Zambian Copperbelt*, Berkeley, CA: University of California Press.

Ganti, T. (2014) "The Value of Ethnography," *Media Industries*, 1(1), pp. 16–20.

Ginsburg, F. (1991) "Indigenous Media: Faustian Contract or Global Village?" *Cultural Anthropology*, 6(1), pp. 92–112.

— (1994) "Culture/Media: A (Mild) Polemic," *Anthropology Today*, 10(2), pp. 5–15.

— (2008) "Rethinking the Digital Age," in D. Hesmondhaigh and J. Toynbee (eds.) *The Media and Social Theory*, London: Routledge, pp. 127–144.

Ginsburg, F., Abu-Lughod, L., and Larkin, B. (eds.) (2002) "Introduction," in *Media Worlds: Anthropology on New Terrain*, Berkeley, CA: University of California Press, pp. 1–36.

Glick Schiller, N. (2014) "Transnationality: Transnationality and the City," in D. M. Nonini (ed.) *A Companion to Urban Anthropology*, Medford, MA: Wiley, pp. 291–305.

Glick Schiller, N. and A. Ćaglar (2009) "Towards a Comparative Theory of Locality in Migration," *Journal of Ethnic and Migration Studies*, 35(2), pp. 177–202.

Graham, S. and Marvin, S. (2001). *Splintering Urbanism*, London: Routledge.

Harvey, D. (1989) *The Condition of Postmodernity*, Hoboken, NJ: Wiley-Blackwell.

— (2003a) "The Right to the City," *New Left Review*, 53, pp. 23–40.

— (2003b) "The Right to the City," *International Journal of Urban and Regional Research*, 27(4), pp. 939–941.

Haynes, J. (2007) "Nollywood in Lagos, Lagos in Nollywood Films," *Africa Today*, 54(2), pp. 131–150.

— (2011) "African Cinema and Nollywood: Contradictions," *Situations*, 4(1), pp. 67–90.

Howe, C. and Boyer, D. (2016) "Aeolian Extractivism and Community Wind in Southern Mexico," *Public Culture*, 28(2), pp. 215–235.

Howe, C., Lockrem, J., Appel, H., Hackett, E., Boyer, D., Hall, R., Schneider-Mayerson, M., Pope, A., Gupta, A., Rodwell, E., Ballestero, A., Durbin, T., el-Dahdah, F., Long, E., and Mody, C. (2016) "Paradoxical Infrastructures: Ruins, Retrofit, and Risk," *Science, Technology, and Human Values*, 41(3), pp. 547–565.

Kagan, R. (2000) *Urban Images of the Hispanic World*, New Haven, CT: Yale University Press.

Kingsbury, D. (2017) "Infrastructure and Insurrection: The Caracas Metro and the Right to the City in Venezuela," *Latin American Research Review*, 52(5), pp. 775–791.

Larkin, B. (2008) *Signal and Noise: Media, Infrastructure, and Urban Culture in Nigeria*, Durham, NC: Duke University Press.

— (2013) "The Politics and Poetics of Infrastructure," *Annual Review of Anthropology*, 42, pp. 327–343.

Lefebvre, H. (1996) *Writings on Cities*, trans. E. Kofman and E. Lebas (eds.), Cambridge, MA: John Wiley and Sons.

Mahon, M. (2000) "The Visible Evidence of Cultural Producers," *Annual Review of Anthropology*, 29, pp. 467–492.

Maskovsky, J. and Brash, J. (2014) "Governance: Beyond the Neoliberal City," in D. Nonino (ed.) *A Companion to Urban Anthropology*, Medford, MA: Wiley, pp. 255–270.

Mattern, S. (2015) "Deep Time of Media Infrastructure," in L. Parks and N. Starosielski (eds.), *Signal Traffic: Critical Studies of Media Infrastructures*, Urbana, IL: University of Illinois, pp. 94–114.

Mazzarella, W. (2004) "Culture, Globalization, Mediation," *Annual Review of Anthropology*, 33, pp. 345–367.

Mitchell, T. (1988) *Colonizing Egypt*, London: Cambridge University Press.

Mundy, B. (1996) *The Mapping of New Spain*, Chicago, IL: University of Chicago Press.

Parks, L. and Starosielski, N. (eds.) (2015) *Signal Traffic: Critical Studies of Media Infrastructures*, Urbana, IL: University of Illinois Press.

Said, E. W. (1978) *Orientalism*, New York: Pantheon Books.

Schiller, N. (2018) *Channeling the State: Community Media and Popular Politics in Venezuela*, Durham, NC: Duke University Press.

Spitulnik, D. (1998–99). "Mediated Modernities: Encounters with the Electronic in Zambia," *Visual Anthropology Review*, 14(2), pp. 63–84.

Star, S. L. (1999) "The Ethnography of Infrastructure," *American Behavioral Scientist*, 43(3), pp. 377–391.
Torres, A., Pineda, V., and Rey, E. (2017) "Las disputas urbanas en la Caracas del siglo XXI: retos y potencialidades en la producción social del suelo," *Territorios*, 36, pp. 47–68.
Turner, T. (1991) "The Social Dynamics of Video Media in an Indigenous Society," *Visual Anthropology Review*, 7(2), pp. 68–76.
Velasco, A. (2015) *Barrio Rising: Urban Popular Politics and the Making of Modern Venezuela*, Oakland, CA: University of California Press.
Williams, B. (2014) "Race," in D. M. Nonini (ed.), *A Companion to Urban Anthropology*, Malden, MA: John Wiley & Sons, pp. 210–222.

Further Reading

Anand, N., Appel, H., and Gupta, A. (eds.) (2018) *The Promise of Infrastructure*, Durham, NC: Duke University Press.
Boyer, D. (2012) "From Media Anthropology and the Anthropology of Mediation," in R. Fardon (ed.) *The ASA Handbook of Social Anthropology*, Thousand Oaks, CA: SAGE, pp. 383–392.
Glick Schiller, N. (2014) "Transnationality: Transnationality and the City," in D. M. Nonini (ed.) *A Companion to Urban Anthropology*, Medford, MA: Wiley, pp. 291–305.

20

IN THE AIR TONIGHT

The Struggles of Communicating About
Urban Environmental Quality

Matteo Tarantino

Introduction

With the majority of the world's inhabitants living in cities, the environmental risks related to urban pollution have become a key concern for citizens and urban authorities. At the same time, cities have become key nexuses of a wider (post-Carbon) transition toward sustainability, which most commentators consider crucial to the future of the planet. However, the ways in which this issue is communicated to city users are fraught with controversy: as we will see, differences large and small invest how to measure, package, circulate, and react to urban pollution information.

Melosi (1993) argues that environmental communication has always struggled with finding a place for cities, due to a deep-seated tendency to equate the environment with the nonhuman: the city was seen as the quintessentially human construct and thus antithetical with the "environment." At the same time, cities have historically been the initial site for organized environmental struggles (Taylor 2009), which have largely concentrated on air, water, waste, and noise pollution.

Communication about pollution can be seen as a sub-class of environmental risk communication. In his work, Slovic (1999) stressed the political dimension of such communication, famously stating "danger is real but risk is socially constructed" and that "whoever controls the definition of risk controls the rational solution to the problem at hand." For this reason, pollution measurements have always been controversial, even more so the communication of such, and doubly so in cities, where financial and political interests tend to be concentrated.

This chapter will deal with three aspects of urban environmental communication: first, it will situate the object of communication, discussing how pollution impacts the city; subsequently, it will discuss the forms of pollution communicated, stressing, in particular, issues of controversy, lack of standardization, and efficacy; finally, it will discuss the question of the reception of the information—that is, the struggle related to governing pollution awareness. The chapter will assume air pollution as a paradigmatic case of urban environmental communication. My choice is motivated by the fact that air pollution communication can be considered the earliest, largest, most systematic, and most extensively studied attempt to communicate urban environmental quality. At the same time, I hold that many of the critical junctures concerning environment, cities, and media, which I discuss later, are applicable to other kinds of pollution.

Smoke-Shaped Space: The Relevance of Air Pollution for Social Production of Space

Pollution exerts considerable influence on processes of social production of space, especially when high urbanization is followed by high pollution. To understand this influence, we can turn to human geography. The discipline has progressively de-abstracted issues of urban space and re-incarnated it into everyday life by exploring how space emerges from (or is "socially produced" through) the continuous interplay between the material, the symbolic, and the practical. This attempt has relied extensively upon Lefebvre's (1991) famous argument that space is simultaneously produced by social actors through a trialectics of conceived (maps), lived (imaginations), and practiced (used) space (for a possible use of the concept of "translation" to describe the relationship between the three levels, see Tosoni and Tarantino 2013). Once we conceptualize space as above, we can consider how the three levels of spatial production are impacted by air pollution.

At the material level, air pollution "can corrode metal and stone, discolor and dirty buildings outside and in, and in general make a neighborhood look shabby" (Ridker and Henning 1967: 1). Moreover, it physically encumbers space, reducing visibility. Air pollution impacts urban development: most of the research accumulated since Ridker and Henning's seminal work on hedonic theory and air pollution applied to the residential market (Ridker and Henning 1967) tends to agree that such an impact is significant, albeit the exact determinants vary among different authors (Chay and Greenstone 1998; Kim, Phipps, and Anselin 2003). However, everyone seems to agree that people are willing to pay a premium to live away from polluted air (Chattopadhyay 1999; for similar correlations found for water see Poor, Pessagno, and Paul 2007, and for noise, see P. Nelson 2004; J. P. Nelson 2008).

At the symbolic level, air pollution can transform urban social spaces into "pollution landscapes"; that is, spaces in which "environmental pollution occurs in such a way that the consequences of change become the dominant feature of the landscape" (Broto et al. 2007). Some cities have risen to such a role, including London in the postwar period, Los Angeles in the 1970s and 1980s, and Beijing since the late 1990s. However, the relationship between pollution and its *negative* representations is not necessarily univocal. Bickerstaff and Walker speak of a "localized understanding of pollution," dependent on personal and contextual features (Bickerstaff and Walker 2003; Bickerstaff 2004). For instance, literature has shown multiple cases in which residents of a particular urban area tend to underestimate or downplay the amount of local air pollution (called the "neighborhood halo effect"), albeit this seems to be more the case of cities in developed countries (Howel et al. 2002; Lyytimäki et al. 2012) than of those in developing ones (Egondi et al. 2013), in which place attachment seems to be weaker. Values attached to a polluter, for example a purveyor of wealth or jobs (either directly as an employer or indirectly in the form of services), can also reduce the perceived threat posed by its pollution.

At the practice level, air pollution impacts city users' practices by reducing available options for daily activities through the hazards it entails. For instance, studies found evidence that estimations of health hazards factored heavily on choices such as spending time outdoors and adopting and using air conditioners, and more in general on adapting daily routines (Bresnahan et al. 1997). Changes in air quality also impact, for example, on mobility practices. Air pollution levels not only motivate policymakers to restrict the use of automotive transportation, discouraging the use of private cars, but also driving styles themselves change because of the limited visibility: for instance, Knittel et al. (2016) found a correlation between pollution levels and fatal car accidents in California. Strong air quality levels may lead policymakers to impose urban road pricing schemes in attempts to limit inward automotive flows. All of the described impacts on the material, symbolic, and practice levels are contingent on the degree to which social actors *perceive* and are *aware* of the pollution. This leads us to our second section: the struggle to define the means to communicate air pollution.

The Controversial Communication of Air Pollution

How do we become aware of pollution? Air pollution may be primarily experienced through the senses and the body, but since the 19th century at least, it has been variously synthesized and repackaged in arbitrary measurements for purposes of mass communication. The objective has always been to communicate to citizens the health and security risks that pollutants in the air exposed them to. Since their beginnings, the connection between the expert communities designing the measurements, the policymakers applying them, and the public receiving them has been problematic.

The earliest systematic attempts to measure air pollution focused on particulate matter residue and date back to the 19th century, as coal combustion became prominent in the rapidly industrialized parts of the urban world. The most popular ones used visual estimations, comparing emission from chimneys against scales of gray in order to estimate smoke density: for instance, the Ringelmann Smoke Chart (Uekoetter 2005), which remained popular until the mid-20th century. Such measurements already produced indexes (albeit not known as such) from one to four, and were instrumental in the first pollution-abatement policies, and to their ends, in the construction of what the chief investigator of the Mellon Institute's Smoke Investigation of Pittsburgh of 1912–1914 called "an enlightened public opinion upon the smoke problem" (Benner 1912). In other words, these indexes were designed to rally public pressure against polluters. However, since the beginning, the value of these kinds of measurement encountered issues of mistrust, as direct experience of pollution was instinctively privileged against hard data (Uekoetter quotes sources of the period with the examples of "the housewife struggling to keep her home clean or a businessman incurring losses for soiled goods" to whom "knowing the precise weight of sootfall must have appeared somewhat redundant" [2005: 13]). On the other hand, albeit scientifically debated from the start, these early visual measurements proved popular and were instrumental to setting the first legal thresholds (such as when the smoke one could see matched the "60% black" image on the chart) and were even printed in mass media, for example by the *Baltimore Sun* in 1945 (Uekoetter 2005: 19–20) for the lay public to use. However, they remained measures of emission density, more intended to put pressure on polluters than to assess air quality (albeit they could be used to roughly estimate the total amount of sootfall, as was done as early as 1912–1913 in Pittsburgh). Measurement of urban air quality was significantly improved in the 1960s, at the onset of the "environmental era." Along with better measurements of pollutants in the air (epitomized by dedicated automatic monitoring stations) came innovations in their communication.

Among the most used products of this evolution have been air quality indexes (AQIs). AQIs are synthetic indicators of the risk run by the proximate population due to the degree of air pollution on the basis of the concentration of selected substances, chiefly particle matters (PM), sulfur oxides, nitrogen oxides, ozone, and carbon dioxide. AQIs take discrete measures of the concentration of these various air pollutants and produce a single figure through discretionary formulas, which vary at the national and sub-national levels. AQIs originated in the 1960s in the USA to convey to the public the data flows enabled by the nascent practice of automatic or semiautomatic air quality monitoring (Longhurst 2005; Shooter and Brimblecombe 2008). Because of their (actual or potential) impacts on city economics and on citizens' sense of place, AQIs have, from the very beginning, been contested measures; and because of the lack of consensus on their definition and application, they are often marked by high variance between countries, and sometimes also between cities or regions within the same countries. Media and communication play important roles across all stages of the indexes' establishment, namely the selection of pollutants, the indexes' monitoring networks, and the final form through which the index reaches the public.

A first area relates to how communication impacts the definition of air pollution at the chemical level. Most frequently, the pollutants included in AQIs are the ones with the strongest assessed short-term effects on health; in fewer indices, long-term effect pollutants are also included, and even fewer account for cumulative and interactional effects. However, the exact extents of health impacts are in themselves controversial, which complicates factoring them into quantitative evaluations. Overall, the choice of pollutants correlates also with the cost of monitoring operations, with a rough direct correlation between number of pollutants, complexity of the monitoring stations, and final cost. Typically, the final AQI corresponds to the normalized measurement of the pollutant with the highest concentration (so-called "single-pollutant AQIs"); more rarely, multiple concentrations are taken into account. The resulting number is then measured against scale-matching intervals in AQI with health effects, going usually from "safe" to "hazardous" (or analogous expressions) and thus producing an easily communicable estimate of air quality. A chromatic scale usually accompanies these expressions for even easier communication (see Figure 20.1). The kinds of pollutants included in an AQI for a specific city depend on a number of factors, including the state of monitoring technology, resources available, and the city's political and economic structure. Media discourse can play an important role in defining the list of pollutants. For example, in many countries the nanoparticles PM2.5 are typically not measured or disclosed, whereas most disclose only the larger particles PM10. China was one notable example of this development, until the AQI was revised in 2012 to include, among other changes, PM2.5. This change came on the heels of an intense campaign involving both traditional media and social media campaigns (Huang 2015).

A second issue concerns how information and communication technologies (ICTs) can impact on the measurement methods. This relationship concerns the networks that deliver the measurements. In many countries (e.g., the US and China), environmental agencies and bureaus at different levels (state, regional, municipal, etc.) each have their own monitoring network. These networks may not be communicating with each other, and may even follow different measuring procedures. This situation leads to considerable consequences: users need to peruse different sources to collect comprehensive information. Another important implication is that each of these networks has its monitoring stations located in different parts of the city. Location is very important for air quality measurement: a sensor placed over a highly trafficked road will return a much higher concentration of some pollutants than one placed over a quiet alley. The number and positioning of sensors (along with the timing of sampling and the averaging techniques applied) are important strategic choices in which accuracy in measurement must be balanced against representational politics. Different positioning results in different measurements and different final numbers. In the last decade, experimentation has been attempted regarding crowdsourcing air quality measurements by way of using citizens' mobile phones connected with portable or wearable sensors and transmitting measurements to a common database (Devarakonda et al. 2013). These ICT-based solutions to the issues related to the positioning of monitoring networks have multiple barriers to overcome, the primary of which is users' motivation (Tarantino and Tosoni 2014), scientific reliability and data credibility (Castell et al. 2017; Lewis and Edwards 2016), and political opportunity. In the same vein, other solutions have tried to employ nonhuman city users as sensors, most notably its fauna: experiments

Air Quality Index (AQI) Values	Levels of Health Concern	Colors
0 to 50	Good	Green
51 to 100	Moderate	Yellow
101 to 150	Unhealthy for Sensitive Groups	Orange
151 to 200	Unhealthy	Red
201 to 300	Very Unhealthy	Purple
301 to 500	Hazardous	Maroon

Figure 20.1 A Table Representation of United States EPA AQI, Using Numbers, Levels, and Colors to Express Risk
Source of data: US-EPA. Elaboration by the author.

with pigeon dissection to gauge exposure to pollutants have been going on since the late 1960s (Tansy and Roth 1970; Schilderman et al. 1997) and in 2016, the volatiles have been (more humanly) equipped with strap-on sensing technology for a three-day experiment over London (Vaughan 2016).

A third area of controversy relates directly to communication; that is, choices about how to repackage the discrete readings into understandable AQIs. Also, in this respect, the spectrum is characterized by high variance among cities. In theory, the WHO specifies an AQI that is intended as a global benchmark. In practice, different territorial units may measure and communicate AQIs in different ways, according to the specifics of each urban context. For example, the US AQI has 10 levels grouped in five tiers, whereas Canada has four ranging from "Low" to "Very High" risk; each Spanish region has its own AQI with a number of levels ranging from three to six; the city of Geneva (Switzerland) uses only three (bad, average, and good), and so on. Intuitively, this means that citizens in two cities with the same AQI number may be breathing air of very different quality. For this reason, projects attempting to build world atlases of air quality, such as the website airqn.cn, generally choose not to present all the various local AQIs but rather to recalculate all values according to a unique AQI formula, usually that of the US. This operation is possible because disclosure through the Internet lowered, for cities, the cost of disclosing the whole hourly set of measurements of each station, across all of the measured pollutants (something that would have been impossible with the press and extremely costly with television). This choice is of high political relevance, as it prioritizes and, to some extent, naturalizes one AQI model over the others: through the accessibility of Internet media and because of the choice of a single private actor, one city becomes the model through which all the others are evaluated. Within cities, AQI ranges are periodically revised with significant political effects: Longhurst (2005: 35) cites the case of Pittsburgh introducing a "satisfactory" range in its AQI in 1973 with the effect (very positive for policymakers) of halving the yearly percentage of time residents would be breathing "unsatisfactory" air from 90% to 45%, without anything changing in the quality of the air itself. In other cases, such as the mentioned example of China, urban AQIs have been renegotiated, making them stricter in order to support, through heightened public pressure, various policies aimed at curbing urban pollution.

Still concerning the form of AQIs, there is the question of what kind of information must come along with the numerical index. Shooter and Brimblecombe point out how citizens are interested in "what should our outdoor activities be today" (2008: 309). In contexts such as China, we are currently observing a trend toward including (along with numbers, colors, and broad indications) specific advice about daily activities (such as whether or not to wash one's car, perform outdoor exercise, wear masks, etc.). Again, this is made convenient by the portability of ICTs: users can receive such recommendations through mobile apps, in some cases tailored to their own needs and preferences, as specified in one's profile (e.g., the *Weilan Ditu* app in China, produced by the Institute of Public and Environmental Affairs [Tarantino and Zimmermann 2017]).

Further, widespread reliance on Internet-based disclosure platforms has driven more and more cities to increase the resolution of data over both the spatial and time axes. On the spatial axis, more and more cities now offer disaggregated readings for each monitoring station, something made possible by the availability of Internet-based maps, which make such representations easy and convenient. Concerning the time axis, we have witnessed a considerable increase in the frequency of disclosure: from monthly averages to daily averages to hourly data for each single monitoring station, to forecasting. This acceleration in time has important impacts on the quality of data disclosed. Releasing unvalidated hourly data in real time means accepting a significant error. Indeed, real-time data are mostly released as "provisional"; validated historical series (released after days or weeks) represent, from a scientific point of view, the "true" picture of air quality in a city. However, they are deemed not as capable of driving behavioral change as real-time data, however imprecise. Most authors concur that forecasting and frequent release of data are key to seize city users' attention (Shooter and Brimblecombe 2008). This leads us to the last part of our discussion: what are the objectives of this kind of communication?

Gain Trust, Fight Apathy

However controversial the measure, the key problem of air quality communication is to overcome what was already identified in the 1969 Ranking as "apathy" of city users with respect to air pollution:

> the average citizen, while recognizing the problem, was unfamiliar with what could be done, or what has been done, and appeared apathetic or pessimistic regarding his own role and the likelihood of control. These findings are of some concern, but hardly surprising. For the typical city-dweller, air pollution exists as a kind of shapeless and impersonal force—at best a nuisance and at worst a serious threat to health and property.
> *(Rankin 1969: 578–569)*

This detached attitude hinders both the acceptance of behavioral changes to curb pollution and the enactment of collective action to pressure polluters. Air quality communication has historically attempted to reverse this attitude. Studies have stressed the role played by "media alerts" concerning AQIs in sensitizing citizens and driving temporary changes in daily routines (Wen, Balluz, and Mokdad 2009). However, the success of this mediated information in actually changing people's behavior is controversial. Many studies indicate that *bodily experience*—be it through senses (see Chapters 10 and 34, this volume) or adverse health effects—is the core precursor of pollution awareness and subsequent behavioral change and indicate widespread mistrust in official information on air quality, along with lack of understanding of the measurements and the phenomena (Bailey, Yearley, and Forrester 1999; Bickerstaff and Walker 1999). Often, this mistrust is related to the damage that such information does to one's assets, especially in terms of real estate value, social prestige, and attachment to place. As Shooter and Brimblecombe summarize:

> Public understandings tend to be localised within their immediate physical, social and cultural landscape, which is often far more localized than the spacing of individual monitoring sites. Trust in data is more likely to derive from personal experiences of local air quality than the accuracy of validated numerical data. Air quality data and information requires links to personal or health interests of individuals to meet public expectations.
> *(2008: 306)*

The media can further exacerbate this mistrust, when the information released is incoherent. Such has been the case of Beijing, where the presence of an alternative AQI circulated since 2009 by the US Embassy and widely re-circulated through websites, social media, and then mobile apps may have problematized trust in the official AQI produced by the Beijing Environmental Protection Bureau (EPB). This was acknowledged by the Chinese Ministry of Foreign Affairs itself and led to a diplomatic incident in 2009.[1] This discredit pivoted on the fact that the US air quality readings, calculated through the US standard, were considerably higher (i.e., they depicted a worse situation of air quality) than the Beijing EPB's ones. This was irrespective of the fact that the former was a single-point measurement and the latter was based on a wider network of stations. Some commentators argue that the circulation of the US AQI was instrumental in accelerating the 2012 revision of the index by the Chinese Ministry of Environmental Protection toward a stricter model, which also included PM2.5, hitherto excluded by the AQI calculation (Huang 2015; Sheng and Tang 2016).

Sensitizing citizens to air quality is particularly important in post-industrial contexts where the source of a significant percentage of urban air pollution has transitioned from industrial sources to citizens' behaviors, such as driving and heating. On the one hand, therefore, institutions are interested in increasing citizens' awareness of the issue so that citizens start changing their habits. On the other hand, communication of environmental data and the presence of environmental policies can also contribute to *creating* social issues: social amplification of risk can be rapid (van den Elshout, Léger, van Paassen, and Heich 2014).

Inter-city comparisons can help increase awareness, but are complicated by the variability of AQIs. Already in the mid-1970s, Ott and Thorn pointed out such concerns, referring to the US case:

> Because many different index types have come into routine use, a citizen who travels to different cities will receive a confusing picture of air pollution levels in each city. Further, existing indices, because of their diversity, cannot be used to assemble a national picture of air pollution levels or trends.
>
> *(1976: 460)*

Efforts have been made toward unifying and standardizing, at least internally, countries' AQI communication, with varying results. A number of agreements, drawing from the Aarhus convention of 1995, stipulate that public authorities must guarantee accessible environmental information—what has come to be known as the "right-to-know"—but tend not to specify guidelines about the concrete forms of environmental communication (van den Elshout et al. 2014). As a result, single countries or sub-national entities perform disclosure according to their own will, resources, and necessities. As such, many projects aiming at providing global pictures of air quality are operated not by consortia of state authorities but by nongovernmental organizations, which take care of all the re-standardization, bypassing the intricacies of interstate negotiations.

Conclusion

This chapter examined the relationship between the perception of urban pollution and sociospatial production. The mediatization of this process intensifies, albeit with issues of trust and urban justice. According to the hedonic model, visualization and easy online availability of urban pollution data render air quality easier to factor into one's choice of urban dwelling, which brings about questions of risk distribution. What, until now, required physical perception (physical discomfort, blackened walls) can now be increasingly abstracted from experience. All else being equal, the market will put a premium on a house in the better-AQI neighborhood, much like it does with better-scoring schools, which many never experienced. This factor might contribute to further spatial segregation of urban environmental risk settings along class or census lines. Therefore, sensor placement and choice of pollutants acquire high political value, whereas much of the current reflection is on the effectiveness of the means of disclosure. In the struggle for developing fair environmental urban politics, urban environmental communication can play a central role only by taking into account the infrastructural and technical elements *along* with the linguistic ones.

Note

1 See the US diplomatic cable 09BEIJNG1945 from 7/10/2009 on the encounter between US Embassy staff and Chinese representatives of MFA and Beijing EPB.

Acknowledgment

This chapter was elaborated within the frame of the CHIPOMAP project funded by SNF grant #153291 and by the Confucius Institute of the University of Geneva, directed by Prof. Basile Zimmermann. The author declares no conflict of interest.

References

Bailey, P., Yearley, S., and Forrester, J. (1999) "Involving the public in local air pollution assessment: a citizen participation case study," *International Journal of Environment and Pollution*, 11(3), pp. 290–303.
Benner, R. C. (1912) "The smoke investigation of the Industrial Research Department of the University of Pittsburgh," *Ind. World*, 46, pp. 1270–1273.
Bickerstaff, K. (2004) "Risk perception research: socio-cultural perspectives on the public experience of air pollution," *Environment International*, 30(6), pp. 827–840.
Bickerstaff, K. and Walker, G. (1999) "Clearing the smog? Public responses to air-quality information," *Local Environment*, 4(3), pp. 279–294.
— (2003) "The place(s) of matter: matter out of place—public understandings of air pollution," *Progress in Human Geography*, 27(1), pp. 45–67.
Bresnahan, B. W., Dickie, M., and Gerking, S. (1997) "Averting behavior and urban air pollution," *Land Economics*, 73(3), pp. 340–357.
Brody, S. D., Peck, B. M., and Highfield, W. E. (2004) "Examining localized patterns of air quality perception in Texas: a spatial and statistical analysis," *Risk Analysis*, 24(6), pp. 1561–1574.
Broto, V. C. et al. (2007) "Coal ash and risk: four social interpretations of a pollution landscape," *Landscape Research*, 32(4), pp. 481–497.
Castell, N. et al. (2017) "Can commercial low-cost sensor platforms contribute to air quality monitoring and exposure estimates?" *Environment International*, 99, pp. 293–302.
Chattopadhyay, S. (1999) "Estimating the demand for air quality: new evidence based on the Chicago housing market," *Land Economics*, 75(1), pp. 22–38.
Chay, K. Y. and Greenstone, M. (1998) *Does air quality matter? Evidence from the housing market*, Washington DC: National Bureau of Economic Research.
Devarakonda, S. et al. (2013) "Real-time air quality monitoring through mobile sensing in metropolitan areas," paper presented at the Proceedings of the 2nd ACM SIGKDD International Workshop on Urban Computing.
Egondi, T. et al. (2013) "Community perceptions of air pollution and related health risks in Nairobi Slums," *International Journal of Environmental Research and Public Health*, 10, pp. 4851–4868.
Howel, D. et al. (2002) "Urban air quality in North-East England: exploring the influences on local views and perceptions," *Risk Analysis*, 22(1), pp. 121–130.
Huang, G. (2015) "PM2.5 opened a door to public participation addressing environmental challenges in China," *Environmental Pollution*, 197, pp. 313–315.
Kim, C. W., Phipps, T. T., and Anselin, L. (2003) "Measuring the benefits of air quality improvement: a spatial hedonic approach," *Journal of Environmental Economics and Management*, 45(1), pp. 24–39.
Knittel, C. R., Miller, D. L., and Sanders, N. J. (2016) "Caution, drivers! Children present: traffic, pollution, and infant health," *Review of Economics and Statistics*, 98(2), pp. 350–366.
Lefebvre, H. (1991) *The production of space*, Oxford: Blackwell.
Lewis, A. and Edwards, P. (2016) "Validate personal air-pollution sensors," *Nature*, 535(7610), pp. 29–31.
Longhurst, J. (2005) "1 to 100: creating an air quality index in Pittsburgh," *Environmental Monitoring and Assessment*, 106(1), pp. 27–42.
Lyytimäki, J., Tapio, P., and Assmuth, T. (2012) "Unawareness in environmental protection: the case of light pollution from traffic," *Land Use Policy*, 29(3), pp. 598–604.
Melosi, M. V. (1993) "The place of the city in environmental history," *Environmental History Review*, 17(1), pp. 1–23.

Nelson, J. P. (2008) "Hedonic property value studies of transportation noise: aircraft and road traffic," in Baranzini A. et al. (eds.) *Hedonic methods in housing markets*, New York, NY: Springer.

Nelson, P. (2004) "Meta-analysis of airport noise and hedonic property values: problems and prospects," *Journal of Transport Economics and Policy*, 38(1), pp. 1–27.

Ott, W. R. and Thorn, G. C. (1976) "Air pollution index systems in the United States and Canada," *Journal of the Air Pollution Control Association*, 26(5), pp. 460–470.

Poor, P. J. et al. (2007) "Exploring the hedonic value of ambient water quality: A local watershed-based study," *Ecological Economics*, 60(4), pp. 797–806.

Rankin, R. E. (1969) "Air pollution control and public apathy," *Journal of the Air Pollution Control Association*, 19(8), pp. 565–569.

Ridker, R. G. and Henning, J. A. (1967) "The determinants of residential property values with special reference to air pollution," *The Review of Economics and Statistics*, pp. 246–257.

Schilderman, P. A. E. L. et al. (1997) "Possible relevance of pigeons as an indicator species for monitoring air pollution," *Environmental health perspectives*, 105(3), pp. 322–330.

Sheng, N. and Tang, U. W. (2016) "The first official city ranking by air quality in China: a review and analysis," *Cities*, 51, pp. 139–149.

Shooter, D. and Brimblecombe, P. (2008) "Air quality indexing," *International Journal of Environment and Pollution*, 36(1–3), pp. 305–323.

Slovic, P. (1999) "Trust, emotion, sex, politics, and science: surveying the risk-assessment battlefield," *Risk Analysis*, 19(4), pp. 689–701.

Tansy, M. F. and Roth, R. P. (1970) "Pigeons: a new role in air pollution," *Journal of the Air Pollution Control Association*, 20(5), pp. 307–309.

Tarantino, M. and Tosoni, S. (2014) "Spatial annotation for the improvement of urban space: a learning-by-doing approach," *The Electronic Journal of Communication/La Revue Electronique de la Communication*, 24(1 and 2).

Tarantino, M. and Zimmermann, B. (2017) "Database green: software, environmentalism and data flows in China," *The China Quarterly*, 217(3).

Taylor, D. E. (2009) *The environment and the people in American Cities, 1600s–1900s: disorder, inequality, and social change*, Durham, NC: Duke University Press.

Tosoni, S. and Tarantino, M. (2013) "Media territories and urban conflict: exploring symbolic tactics and audience activities in the conflict over Paolo Sarpi, Milan," *International Communication Gazette*, 75(5–6), pp. 573–594.

Uekoetter, F. (2005) "The strange career of the Ringelmann smoke chart," *Environmental Monitoring and Assessment*, 106(1–3), pp. 11–26.

van den Elshout, S., Léger, K., van Paassen, A., and Heich, H. (2014) "Communicating air quality," *Environmental Software Systems*, 7, pp. 324–335.

Vaughan, A. (2016) "Pigeon patrol takes flight to tackle London's air pollution crisis," *The Guardian*, March 14, www.theguardian.com/environment/2016/mar/14/pigeon-patrol-takes-flight-to-tackle-londons-air-pollution-crisis.

Wen, X. J., Balluz, L., and Mokdad, A. (2009) "Association between media alerts of air quality index and change of outdoor activity among adult asthma in six states, BRFSS, 2005," *Journal of Community Health*, 34(1), pp. 40–46.

Further Reading

Fenger, J. (2009) "Air pollution in the last 50 years: from local to global," *Atmospheric Environment*, 43(1), pp. 13–22.

Graham, S. (2015) "Life support: the political ecology of urban air," *City*, 19(2–3), pp. 192–215.

Hyslop, N. P. (2009) "Impaired visibility: the air pollution people see," *Atmospheric Environment*, 43(1), pp. 182–195.

21
THE PROMISES AND PITFALLS OF CYBER URBANISM
Governance and Participation

Kristin Erickson

Introduction

The past two decades have brought forth an intensification of both urbanization and Internet usage around the globe. In 2016, the United Nations estimated that over 54% of the world's population lived in cities and predicted that this percentage would rise to 70% by 2050 (United Nations Department of Economic and Social Affairs 2017). Meanwhile, global Internet penetration, a term used to describe the portion of the world's population that has access to the Internet, was at 46.1% at the end of 2016 (Internet Users 2017). But while over half of the world's urban residents lack broadband Internet access, almost 90% of urbanites are connected to 3G mobile networks (International Telecommunication Union 2015). With greater access to mobile technologies, democratic and egalitarian ideals tend to thrive; people are led to believe that they are better informed and have greater opportunities to participate in larger sociopolitical processes, and that digital participation helps level the playing field. But as the Internet continues to transform urban spaces of communication, it also functions to transform political processes. Manuel Castells (2011: 98) suggests that the Internet is "not a neutral space," but is rather "conditioned by the economic and political interests of the media companies and governments."

As cities continue to grow at unprecedented rates, governments are turning to digital technologies to more efficiently manage the strains of growing populations on urban infrastructure, city resources, and services. But as digital networks are almost imperceptibly woven into the urban landscape, and certain elements of cyber urbanism become increasingly complex and globalized, so do the challenges of e-governance and online civic participation. As Greg Keeffe (2014: para. 10) wittily remarked, "We need a new generation of poly-math cyber-urbanists to scatter-bomb our way through the urban/technological minefield." To better understand digital governance and participation in everyday urban life, this chapter explores both the possibilities and challenges that become characteristic of today's cyber urbanism.

The Intersections of Urban Space, Cyberspace, and Democratic Potential

Historically, cities and cyberspace have been described in both utopian and dystopian terms, as either diverse, pluralized spaces of social, political, and economic progress or as dangerous and dense fields of subversion, alienation, and concentrated hyper-capitalism (Scott 2016: 18).

Also, within cities and cyberspace, anonymity, autonomy, connection, and community have become simultaneously competing and complementary key features. However, ultimately, our experiences of and practices within both urban spaces and online, and the intersections thereof, become co-constitutive, fluid, flexible, and inextricably intertwined with current social, cultural, and political contexts.

In the mid-1990s, William Mitchell (1995: 115) advanced the rather utopian position that the virtual city, in its interconnected spaces of information, had the potential to free us from our corporeal world and the "constraints of physical space." Digitally mediated environments, he argued, would be crucial in helping to establish the lives we imagine for ourselves and within urban communities of our own making (Mitchell 1995). In this post-geographical environment, Mitchell (1995: 5) argued, we would finally overcome the "tyranny of distance" through increasing cyberspace connectivity. Mitchell (1995: 17) also suggested that with the "digital telecommunications revolution," urban civic infrastructures could thrive and profoundly improve not only economic opportunities, but also the quality and effectiveness of public discourse and therefore locate greater democratic potential within urban cyber-networks. However, Robins and Webster (1999) rejected these and similar optimistic visions of cyberspace or the virtual city. They instead argued that the then-emerging virtual city was losing touch with reality, becoming a sort of cyberspace equivalent to the Tower of Babel, and detrimentally homogenizing the global conversation. Even more concerning, Robins and Webster suggested (1999), was that cyberspace, as a mediator of urban life, led not to democratic potential, but rather neutralized space, politics, and autonomy.

Despite these and other debates, the potential for democratic governance is still often located in the intersections between the city and cyberspace. Just as Michael Warner (2002) located political potential in the urban public sphere as necessitating conversations between strangers for more effective political discourse, Peter Shane (2004: 136) argues that online anonymity, as it places more emphasis on content rather than the person, often allows people to "avoid persecution" and "speak their conscience freely," which then allows for more honest public discussion. However, as Shane (2004) also suggests, anonymity can have a detrimental effect, allowing some to avoid accountability and the consequences of public speech. Echoing these concerns, Sherry Turkle (2011) argues that our sense of community is often illusory, resulting in great part from an over-reliance on digital technologies; we are, she insists, often "alone together," increasingly absorbed in personal digital networks, while publicly en masse. With digital isolation, as it often ironically stems from incessant and meaningless online or text communication, a greater potential for conversational atrophy exists, which then threatens empathy and encourages a sort of talking *at*—rather than *with*—one another. This phenomenon is perhaps most clearly evident in recent years, as hate speech and political divisiveness becomes increasingly visible, prompting Amnesty International (2017: 12) to identify a "global trend towards angrier and more divisive politics" brought about in great part by unfettered online hate speech.

While some have argued that cyberspace and our experiences within it have become increasingly disconnected from the particulars of time and space (Giddens 1990), allowing us greater access to others around the world, the accessibility and availability of mobile devices also have transformed the ways we come together and interact in physical urban space (Humphreys 2010). Anthony Townsend (2000), for instance, suggests that mobile technology changes the urban metabolism by accelerating the exchange of information to the point that it can bring about a "real-time" city. But with the increasing decentralization that results from ubiquitous mobile communications, he contends, "the complexity of these systems becomes greater and therefore less predictable," making digital governance and participation more challenging (Townsend 2000: 66). Lee Humphreys (2010: 6) underscores this concept when she suggests that our use of mobile social networks helps to turn public spaces, of primarily strangers, into "parochial realms," wherein people find commonalities with acquaintances. As communication is shared about a particular area through mobile networks, for example, these urban public spaces become characterized by a stronger sense of community and personal networks (Humphreys 2010).

On the other hand, a growing number of citizens, journalists, and scholars not only have questioned the effectiveness of the digital public sphere in an already information-saturated environment, but also have expressed concern over governmental use of digital technologies and social media platforms for purposes of tracking and monitoring citizens, surveillance, spreading propaganda, or in other ways using these technologies against citizens. First, because digital flows of information cannot be disarticulated from flows of capital, these same technologies can also function to obscure and solidify existing networks of power. Second, the recent insidiousness of Twitter bots, fake news, and search engine bias, for example, has many asking whether social media now functions to strengthen or destroy democratic political processes.

However, the emerging power of the global, networked city to transcend or challenge the sovereignty of nation-states and geographical borders is remarkable. With greater communicative mobility, perhaps, comes increased territorial fragmentation. At the intersection of the Internet/city nexus, a hybrid space seems to have emerged, in which digital devices and practices are now built into and help to construct the logic and organization of the city, as well as its sociopolitical ecosystem. Adriana de Souza e Silva (2006: 2) argues that these hybrid spaces arise when virtual communities "migrate to physical spaces due to the use of mobile technologies as interfaces." Thus, these hybrid spaces are, necessarily, also often mobile spaces. Successful contemporary political movements, for instance, often arise in cyberspace, but necessarily inhabit city streets with on-the-ground activism and mobile phones in hand. And it is this straddling of cyberspace with urban space, as Manual Castells (2011) suggests, that characterizes this era of civic participation, though not always to the benefit of either the people or the political public sphere.

Urban Cyber-Infrastructures

Crang, Crosbie, and Graham (2006: 2552) argue that existing urban digital divides were not just created through unequal access to the Internet, but that "different styles and speeds of technologically mediated life" often function to underscore existing urban "sociospatial inequalities." In other words, how we use the Internet is as important as where we use the Internet. This happens in two ways, according to the authors. The pervasive and continuous use of the Internet by affluent residents helps to either construct or support a privileged infrastructure, they argue, while more marginalized communities exhibit more "episodic" Internet usage and are often characterized by prevailing neighborhood connections (Crang, Crosbie, and Graham 2006). The authors refer to this phenomenon as "multispeed urbanism," wherein some neighborhoods are in the fast lane (higher speeds and more frequent usage), while others are "stuck in an urban 'slow' lane," a divide that no doubt will become even more pronounced with the erosion of net neutrality and as access to the Internet becomes increasingly privatized (Crang, Crosbie, and Graham 2006).

Further, the uneven acceleration of multispeed urbanism has challenged previous notions of binary spatial divisions between the haves and the have-nots. The increased usage of smartphones and mobile phones, additionally, characterizes rather different patterns of access and further complicates attempts to quantify or map urban digital divides. However, as the authors predicted, mobile Internet usage has now enabled users to convert dead spaces into ones of active communication with others that are not physically present (Crang, Crosbie, and Graham 2006).

In an attempt to respond to recent architectural design challenges to incorporate interactive, networked environments into physical spaces, Malcolm McCullough (2004) argues that embedded network infrastructures can function to extend urban architecture, rather than replace them. While the ubiquity of technological networks does not preclude people's need for actual physical space, McCullough (2004) suggests that future architects will need to better understand how pervasive computing intersects with built space. Alberto Jiménez (2014: 342), as he examines how residential use of digital devices and networks is increasingly built into the logic and organization of urban public spaces, describes the rise of "open source urbanism" as having a unique destabilizing power. Challenging traditional public and commercial forms of digital spaces and infrastructure, citizen-driven open source urbanism helps shape a new political landscape, as urban residents are "wiring the landscape of their communities" with the digital devices and networks that are important to their local social and political life (Jiménez 2014: 343). Using Madrid as a case study, Jiménez (2014) demonstrates how such infrastructures are making urban governance more accountable and giving more voice to the people.

Jiménez (2014: 358) also argues for the "right to infrastructure," echoing Lefebvre's "right to the city," as it articulates the most promising "avenues for political governance and action in urban settings." However, while Lefebvre's theory focused on the possibility for a future city as yet unestablished, Jiménez (2014) rather underscores the ways in which urban citizens might reimagine or reconstruct existing infrastructures. Ignacio Farías and Anders Blok (2016: 539), as they explore the relationship between urban environments and "technical democracy," elaborate on Jiménez's (2014) theory of the right to infrastructure by drawing a parallel to the notion of "hacking the city." Urban residents, they suggest, increasingly enact more "subtle yet consequential subversions" by inhabiting urban digital networks (Farías and Blok 2016: 542).

Digital Governance and Citizensourcing

Pierre Lévy (1999) was one of the first to argue for the increasing potential for virtual communities to harvest "collective intelligence," or the free exchange of ideas in cyberspace, for digitally mediated governance. Howard Rheingold (2000) similarly suggested that online forums enable radical re-imaginations of the public sphere and the potential to revitalize participatory democracy. Today, one of the ways in which urban officials are deploying digital technologies for governance includes the use of crowdsourcing techniques to engage citizens in urban projects, solicit feedback on city plans, and assist officials in acquiring important information that then helps to inform policy decisions. Typically, with crowdsourcing, a call is sent out to a general, non-specific public, asking for voluntary assistance in the completion of a specific task or project. And governmental practice of crowdsourcing techniques is often now referred to as "citizensourcing" (Scott 2016: 48). Since citizen participation is one of the greatest hallmarks of the democratic process, opening digital channels for residents to have a voice in city planning and policies perhaps offers tremendous potential for civic engagement.

Certainly, when combined with assumptions that the Internet is an inherently democratizing space, some urban officials consider the practice of citizensourcing to be an innovative opportunity for governance and urban planning efforts. However, Thapa et al. (2015) are more hesitant to adopt the practice, concerned that urban citizens are unable to understand the complexities of governing, or that opening up decision-making processes to citizens may not only slow down an already laborious process, but also create more confusion. For example, the former New York City mayor, Michael Bloomberg, was reported as saying that using social media makes governance more difficult and that, as a result, government officials are essentially "having a referendum on every single thing that we do every day" (O'Shea 2012: para. 2). Despite these kinds of concerns, the practice of citizensourcing has been gaining traction worldwide, as urban governments struggle to manage growing populations.

In most cities, for example, and in great part due to rapid population growth, access to and maintenance of public spaces pose a persistent challenge. Therefore, cities are using virtual citizensourcing techniques to leverage the collective power and intelligence of urban residents to not only help officials govern, but also collectively solve urban problems and assist in the redevelopment or enhancement of physical public space. In the Columbian city Medellín, for instance, city officials have built a website to solicit citizen ideas to help solve some of the city's most pressing problems, from how to deal with a lack of parking and traffic problems to how to improve air quality in the city; after collecting responses, new urban policies and development plans are put into place (Medellín 2017). As Juan Restrepo (2014: para. 3) remarks, "reclamation of public space" is happening in "cities all around the world," and in great part through citizensourcing projects, such as Okuplaza in Santiago, which solicited citizens' suggestions for the redevelopment of a parking lot into a plaza. And in Reykjavik, Iceland, the online ideas collected from residents led to the creation of over 200 urban projects to enhance the city (Restrepo 2014). Iceland was also the first in the world to use crowdsourcing techniques to help draft a new constitution by soliciting feedback from citizens on social media; this method garnered 3,600 comments and a total of 360 unique suggestions for changes to constitutional drafts (Restrepo 2014).

Supporters of citizensourcing often suggest that such techniques can greatly enhance the efficiency and quality of governmental services. In Islamabad, Pakistan, for instance, city officials launched an initiative to receive direct feedback from more than 3 million mobile users of public services to help government officials track the effectiveness of public services, as well as work to prevent corruption (Van Ransbeeck 2015). Shortly after receiving a government service, the user receives a text message asking for feedback; responses are collected, data are aggregated and analyzed, and action is taken. Data are also gathered from mobile users to help inform policy decisions, such as when the Punjab Information Technology Board gave smartphones to city workers to track dengue outbreaks by uploading geotagged photos, which then helped the city to better manage the health crisis; and within the first year, dengue virus cases dropped dramatically (The World Bank 2013). In New York City, citizens can report city service needs, upload photos, and file non-emergency complaints to their smartphone NYC311 apps, and later receive updates from the city. And other cities around the world are tapping into social media to update users about municipal services (such as bus or train delays) or solicit citizen input on local initiatives.

A thriving political sphere, of course, depends on citizen engagement with multiple viewpoints. When we consider that 77% of the world's megacity inhabitants are located in the "Global South," and yet only account for approximately 35% or less of the world's Internet users, there exist significant socio-economic disparities, and a large number of people are left out of the governance and decision-making processes of their digital political landscapes (Miniwatts Marketing Group 2017). Additionally, a thriving democracy and effective civic engagement cannot depend on the Internet alone; not only is the Internet inherently unreliable, as earlier discussed, but social movements and activism also need to transpire in physical space in order to have significant effects. In the case of social media or digitally driven protests that fail, such as those that erupted in capital cities against the alleged fraudulent elections of President Aleksandr Lukashenko of Belarus in 2006 (Citizen Lab 2013) and Mahmoud Ahmadinejad in 2009 (Dabashi 2013), or the Red Shirt protesters in Thailand calling for early elections in 2010 to remove Abhisit Vejjajiva from office (Horn 2010), the results—in all three cases—were even greater social media control, violent and fatal governmental crackdowns, and increased censorship. But the reason they failed, many believe, is in great part due to the disconnect between online protests and those in physical urban space.

Fast, reliable connection to urban residents is also considered crucial, and many major cities are set up to send SMS text notifications in the event of an emergency. In the United States, all mobile users are automatically connected to the Wireless Emergency Alerts system, which sends geographically targeted text alerts to those within a certain vicinity. According to the rules set by the Federal Communications Commission, only three kinds of alerts can be sent: those involving imminent threats to safety, Amber Alerts (missing person), and those issued by the president of the United States—a fact that has recently provided fodder for sarcastic humor under the current Trump administration, given the president's propensity for unabashed Twitter tantrums (Searingen 2016). While most text alerts send important emergency information, some text notifications have been called into question, such as in the case of an alert sent out one September morning in 2016 to all smartphones in New York City. After a trash dumpster bombing occurred in one of the city's neighborhoods, an emergency text was sent out the next morning that read: "Wanted: Ahmad Khan Rahami, 28-yr-old male. See media for pic. Call 9-1-1 if seen" (Feldman 2016). Although the suspect was identified, apprehended, and arrested after the alert went out, concerns were raised about the use of emergency text messaging for this purpose, suggesting that not only was there was no imminent threat to safety, but these kinds of texts also open the doors to digitalized public racial and ethnic profiling in a country in which Muslims already are regularly harassed and attacked.

Therefore, the practice of citizensourcing also has its critics who often suggest that the custom is just a more appealing way of describing how urban governments shift their responsibilities onto the tax-paying citizen, as residents are enlisted to do the job of government or solve problems that government has unsuccessfully addressed (Scott 2016: 48–49). The use of the term citizensourcing also raises questions about the nature of citizenship, particularly in cities in which many that are being crowdsourced (either directly or indirectly through data gathering) are not receiving citizen benefits because of their legal status; and so the same governmental services that they are helping to develop and sustain are inaccessible to them, as undocumented residents.

As Florian Schmidt suggests, "the term [crowdsourcing] has a lineage of cheap [and free] labor and globalized exploitation written into its DNA" (Schmidt 2013: para. 1), as crowdsourcing is built almost imperceptibly into the fabric of the urban information economy. While crowdsourcing can certainly have benefits to contributors, such as in the case of Wikipedia, as the site allows for anyone with an Internet connection to retrieve and edit all the compiled information, it is also a technique that has been used by various entities to simply acquire free or inexpensive labor. Critics of crowdsourcing and citizensourcing have suggested that this new "low-wage virtual labor phenomenon" has created an unregulated and exploited workforce (Marvit 2014: para. 3). Additionally, as citizensourcing becomes normalized in the digital age to achieve various governance goals through massive online participation, the collection of information also is increasingly taking place without the contributor's knowledge, such as in the case of data mining through one's daily Internet habits.

In some instances, the collection of data through unpaid user-producer labor becomes useful information for urban governance and planning, but also represents a new trend in "digitalized human capital" (Scott 2016: 107). Whereas human capital represents the practice of active and intentional labor production, digitalized human capital materializes, in great part, through the monitoring, tracking, recording, and collection of data by everyday citizens going about their daily lives (Scott 2016: 107). Such data, once collected and aggregated, can not only inform urban policy and development decisions, but also generate income or financial benefit for the city and its corporate partners. This practice of urban sensing, which includes the use of sensors, cameras, and GPS built into mobile phones, is often described as a way of "listening" in on the digital undercurrents of the urban environment, purportedly for the purposes of urban sustainability efforts (Estrin 2011; see also Chapter 34, this volume). Take, for example, the "Real Time Rome" project, which obtains and aggregates data from mobile phones to create maps that visualize activities and connectivity, informs urban planning efforts, and helps reduce contemporary inefficiencies of city systems (Calabrese et al. 2011). On the one hand, governments and urban planners can learn a lot about the dynamics of their city and increased stress on urban infrastructures through the collection of data about activities such as urban flow of both traffic and people, concentrations of workers versus residents in certain areas of the city, social interactions, and geographical cell phone usage patterns (Becker et al. 2011). However, concerns also have been raised about surveillance, the collection of personally sensitive data (Lane et al. 2008), and the unpaid labor that contributes to the wealth of cities and the urban financial investors or corporations with whom they partner (Levien 2011). There have also been concerns over the accuracy of such data, as well as data interpretations and subsequent applications of aggregated data.

The Online Public Sphere: Algorithm Bias and Search Engine Manipulation

Increasingly, cities are collecting and then leveraging the power of aggregated data to make decisions about how to enhance urban operations and identify opportunities for interventions. Computer programs that are designed to solve problems by compiling and analyzing collected data, or data algorithms, have offered government officials insight into how to address various urban issues. For example, in 2016, Singapore launched a website/mobile phone app for commuters to help create new commuter routes, based on crowdsourced data that indicates gaps in effective transportation options (Soon 2016). Proponents of the use of data algorithms and data-generated mobile applications also have suggested such practices can be used for the benefit of the larger public. In 2016, for example, Tinder, a popular US dating app, launched a new feature called "swipe the Vote," which matched young voters with their dream political candidates using user-targeted data algorithms (Porcaro 2016). In the 2013 Kenyan elections, users could upload real-time data and reports of election tampering to the mobile app, Ushahidi; patterns were then calculated and helped to inform others about ongoing election issues (Ross 2016). And in Cambridge, UK, the city council published collected data about pedestrian and bicycle traffic over a certain bridge, proposed plans for enhancements to that bridge based on the aggregated data, and then solicited citizens to offer further improvement suggestions online (Cambridge City Council 2015). Whether for large or small urban projects, the use of data to inform and generate a democratic process of citizen feedback in urban government decisions is well documented.

While data ideally are objective, data are often biased. Because algorithm results originate from a variety of data collection processes and compute a variety of (often selective) factors, data are rarely neutral. When one considers how data are obtained, what data are chosen as important, what data are left out, and how data are categorized, the collection and analysis of such data can create hidden biases. Critics, such as Kristin Scott (2016) and George Joseph (2016), have argued that algorithm bias can have particularly detrimental effects on already socially and economically disadvantaged groups of people (see also Chapter 41, this volume). Take, for example, the recent adoption of risk and threat assessment tools by criminal justice systems, courts, and criminologists in major US cities to determine levels of risk of violence, repeat offenders, and the probability of future criminal acts occurring. In Baltimore, Maryland, for example, courts are using a risk assessment software to help them make decisions about whether to allow defendants out of jail on bail, while awaiting trial dates (Joseph 2016). NYC is also adopting a similar algorithm-driven pre-trial risk assessment tool to determine who should be allowed bail and who can be sent home (Leonard 2017). In the state of Pennsylvania, recent legislation mandates the development of a risk assessment tool that can be used to determine criminal sentences; not only can a sentence potentially be based on the crime one has committed, but also on what crime that defendant may be deemed likely to commit in the future (DeMichele and Laskorunsky 2014). And in London, the open data available from the London's Metropolitan Police of every incident and arrest that is publicly logged are fed into an algorithm that now not only predicts, but also visualizes, future crime (Burgess 2017).

While such data may have some benefits in crime control, others have argued that the benefits are far outweighed by adverse effects on racial minorities, who are disproportionally targeted as criminal risks (Skeem and Lowenkamp 2016). *Pro Publica*, a non-profit investigative journalism organization in the US, conducted a study in 2016 that suggests that such software is biased against blacks, because it is based on already prejudiced data (such as data about poverty, geographical markers, and employment statuses) that are often correlated with race (Angwin et al. 2016). Despite the recent criticisms, many cities are nevertheless moving forward with similar risk assessment tools in an effort to curb urban crime. Unfortunately, the visualization of urban crime, along with search engine bias, can also have deleterious effects on underdeveloped or already-marginalized city neighborhoods, as these tools help to construct perceptions of safe or unsafe urban spaces and influence where we visit, spend money, and purchase homes.

Conclusion

While the intersections of cyberspace and urban governance certainly have the potential to be globalizing, decentralizing, and democratically empowering, some of the greatest threats to governance and digital democratic participation may now lie within those very same digital platforms and practices. Eli Noam (2001: para. 4) predicted that "far from helping democracy, [the Internet would be] a threat to it." Noam (2001: para. 15) also argued that as the quantity of published information increased, information clutter would lead to distortions and misinformation; additionally, he suggested that the Internet "disconnects as much as it connects," through self-imposed stratification. In other words, we tend to align ourselves online with those who have similar views and therefore tend to search for news sources or political pieces that already support our perspectives.

Further, the importance of locality and space cannot be underestimated, no matter how digitally inclined our lives become. Nor can we afford to miscalculate the power of digital governance. To some degree, particularly as of late, the ability of some to govern by tweet has reached absurd proportions. And while the use of social media for governing and civic engagement makes sense in many ways, as cities successfully have been utilizing these practices for years, such intersecting practices have not been devoid of major problems. And perhaps this is the key to thinking about the role of cities and digital governance moving forward. In an era of populist nationalism, increased border controls, and cyber-surveillance, the threats to Internet freedom abound. In response, major cities around the world necessarily are creating digital networks that transcend national boundaries and open space for a multiplicity of public spheres and communicative potential. Political progressiveness, perhaps, then lies in a new form of cyber-transurbanism that functions to defy or at least challenge growing nation-state isolationism.

References

"57 percent of the global urban population lacks internet access: Study," *Tech2*, http://tech.firstpost.com/news-analysis/57-percent-of-the-global-urban-population-lacks-internet-access-study-321541.html.

Amnesty International (2017) *Amnesty International Report 2016/17: The State of the World's Human Rights*, www.amnesty.org.uk/files/2017-02/POL1048002017ENGLISH.PDF?xMHdSpNaJBUNbiuvtMCJvJrnGuLiZnFU.

Angwin, J., Larson, J., Mattu, S., and Kirchner, L. (2016) "Machine Bias," *ProPublica*, www.propublica.org/article/machine-bias-risk-assessments-in-criminal-sentencing.

Becker, R.A., et al. (2011) "A Tale of One City: Using Cellular Network Data for Urban Planning," *IEEE Pervasive Computing*, 10(4), pp. 18–26.

Burgess, M. (2017) "This Map Claims It Can Predict Crimes Across London Before They Happen," *Wired*, www.wired.co.uk/article/london-crime-predict-police-2017.

Calabrese, F., Colonna, M., Lovisolo, P., Parata, D., and Ratti, C. (2011) "Real-Time Urban Monitoring Using Cell Phones: A Case Study in Rome," *IEEE Transactions on Intelligent Transportation Systems*, 12(1).

Cambridge City Council (2015) *Green Dragon Bridge: Footway and Cycling Improvements*, www.cambridge.gov.uk/sites/default/files/documents/Green-dragon-bridge-consultation-2015.pdf.

Castells, M. (2011) "Democracy in the Age of the Internet," *Transfer: Journal of Contemporary Culture*, 6(1).

Citizen Lab (2013) *After the Green Movement: Internet Controls in Iran, 2009–2012*, https://opennet.net/sites/opennet.net/files/iranreport.pdf.

Crang, M., Crosbie, T., and Graham, S. (2006) "Variable Geometries of Connection: Urban Digital Divides and the Uses of Information Technology," *Urban Studies*, 43(13), pp. 2551–2570.

Dabashi, H. (2013) "What Happened to the Green Movement in Iran?" *Aljazeera*, www.aljazeera.com/indepth/opinion/2013/05/201351661225981675.html.

DeMichele, M. and Laskorunsky, J. (2014) *Sentencing Risk Assessment: A Follow-Up Study of the Occurrence and Timing of Re-Arrest among Serious Offenders in Pennsylvania*, http://justicecenter.psu.edu/research/projects/files/PCS%20_Risk%20Assessment_Tool.pdf.

De Souza e Silva, A. (2006) "From Cyber to Hybrid: Mobile Technologies as Interfaces of Hybrid Spaces," *Space and Culture*, 9(3), pp. 261–278.

England, P. (2015) "Iceland's 'Pots and Pans Revolution': Lessons from a Nation That People Power Helped to Emerge from Its 2008 Crisis All the Stronger," *Independent*, www.independent.co.uk/news/world/europe/icelands-pots-and-pans-revolution-lessons-from-a-nation-that-people-power-helped-to-emerge-from-its-10351095.html.

Estrin, D. (2011) "Participatory Urban Sensing," *Scientific American*. www.scientificamerican.com/citizen-science/participatory-urban-sensing-ucla.

Farías, I. and Blok, A. (2016) "Technical Democracy as a Challenge to Urban Studies," *City*, 20(4), pp. 539–548.

Federal Communications Commission (2017) *Wireless Emergency Alerts (WEA)*, www.fcc.gov/consumers/guides/wireless-emergency-alerts-wea.

Feldman, B. (2016) "New Yorkers Just Received a Terrible Emergency Alert," *New York Magazine*, http://nymag.com/selectall/2016/09/new-yorkers-just-received-a-terrible-emergency-alert.html.

Giddens, A. (1990) *The Consequences of Modernity*, Stanford, CA: Stanford University Press.

Horn, R. (2010) "On Bangkok's Bloody Streets, a Crackdown Breaks Protests," *Time Magazine*, http://content.time.com/time/world/article/0,8599,1990184,00.html.

Humphreys, L. (2010) "Mobile Social Networks and Urban Public Space," *New Media and Society*, 12(5), pp. 763–778.

International Telecommunication Union (2015) "ICT Facts and Figures: The World in 2015," www.itu.int/en/ITU-D/Statistics/Documents/facts/ICTFactsFigures2015.pdf.

"Internet Users" (2017) *Internet Lives Stats*, www.internetlivestats.com/internet-users.

Jiménez, A. (2014) "The Right to Infrastructure: A Prototype for Open Source Urbanism," *Environment and Planning D: Society and Space*, 32, pp. 342–362.

Joseph, G. (2016) "Justice by Algorithm," *CityLab*, www.citylab.com/crime/2016/12/justice-by-algorithm/505514.

Keeffe, G. (2014) "The Future Is Unwritten: Cyber Urbanism," *The Technoscape*, February 24, www.gregkeeffe.co.uk/technoscape/The_Technoscape/Entries/2014/2/24_Cyber_Urbanism.html.

Lane, N.D., Eisenman, S.B., Musolesi, M., Miluzzo, E., and Campbell, A.T. (2008) "Urban Sensing Systems: Opportunistic or Participatory?" in *Proceedings of the 9th Workshop on Mobile Computing Systems and Applications*, pp. 11–16, ACM.

Leonard, M. (2017) "NY to Try Algorithm-Driven Pretrial Risk Assessments," *Government Cloud Insider*, https://gcn.com/articles/2017/01/13/justice-analytics.aspx.

Levien, M. (2011) "Special Economic Zones and Accumulation by Dispossession in India," *Journal of Agrarian Change*, 11, pp. 454–483.

Lévy, P. (1999) *Collective Intelligence: Mankind's Emerging World in Cyberspace*, New York: Basic Books.

Marvit, M.Z. (2014) "How Crowdworkers Became the Ghosts in the Digital Machine," *The Nation*, www.thenation.com/article/how-crowdworkers-became-ghosts-digital-machine.

McCullough, M. (2004) *Digital Ground*, Cambridge, MA: MIT Press.

Medellín (2017) *Medellín: Co-Creación Ciudadana* (2017), www.mimedellin.org.

Miniwatts Marketing Group (2017) *Internet World Stats: Usage and Population Statistics*, www.internetworldstats.com.

Mitchell, W.J. (1995) *City of Bits*, Cambridge, MA: MIT Press.

Noam, E. (2001) *Will the Internet Be Bad for Democracy?*, www.citi.columbia.edu/elinoam/articles/int_bad_dem.htm.

O'Shea, C. (2012) "Bloomberg Is Wary of the Siren Song of Social Media," *Adweek*, www.adweek.com/digital/bloomberg-is-wary-of-the-siren-song-of-social-media.

Porcaro, G. (2016) "Democracy in the Age of the Internet of Things," *TechCrunch*.

Restrepo, J.M. (2014) "Let's Empower Citizens to Recreate Cities," *NewCities*, www.newcitiesfoundation.org/lets-empower-citizens-recreate-cities.

Rheingold, H. (2000) *The Virtual Community: Homesteading on the Electric Frontier*, Cambridge, MA: MIT Press.

Robins, K. and Webster, F. (1999) *Times of the Technoculture: From the Information Society to the Virtual Life*, London: Routledge.

Ross, E. (2016) "Apps for Democracy: Open Data and the Future of Politics," *The Guardian*, www.theguardian.com/media-network/2016/aug/19/apps-for-democracy-open-data-and-the-future-of-politics.

Schmidt, F.A. (2013) *Why Crowdsourcing Needs Ethics*, www.researchgate.net/profile/Florian_Schmidt12/publication/261126823_The_Good_The_Bad_and_the_Ugly_Why_Crowdsourcing_Needs_Ethics/links/02e7e537c5e2662206000000.pdf.

Scott, K. (2016) *The Digital City and Mediated Urban Ecologies*, Basingstoke: Palgrave Macmillan.

Searingen, J. (2016) "Starting January 20, Donald Trump Can Send Unblockable Mass Text Messages to the Entire Nation," *NYMag.com*, http://nymag.com/selectall/2016/11/president-trump-can-send-emergency-alerts-to-everyone.html.

Shane, P.M. (2004) *Democracy Online: The Prospects for Political Renewal Through the Internet*, New York: Routledge.

Skeem, J.L. and Lowenkamp, C.T. (2016) "Risk, Race, and Recidivism: Predictive Bias and Disparate Impact," *SSRN*, http://dx.doi.org/10.2139/ssrn.2687339.

Soon, L. (2016) "Big Data: A Solution for Urban Problems?" *Future Ready Singapore*, www.futurereadysingapore.com/2016/big-data-a-solution-for-urban-problems.html.

Thapa, B.E., Niehaves, B., Seidel, C.E., and Plattfaut, R. (2015) "Citizen Involvement in Public Sector Innovation: Government and Citizen Perspectives," *Information Polity: The International Journal of Government and Democracy in The Information Age*, 20(1), pp. 3–17.

The World Bank (2013) "Leveraging Mobile Phones for Innovative Governance Solutions in Pakistan," www.worldbank.org/en/news/feature/2013/12/11/leveraging-mobile-phones-for-innovative-governance-solutions-in-Pakistan.

Townsend, A. (2000) "Life in the Real-Time City: Mobile Telephones and Urban Metabolism," *Journal of Urban Technology*, 7, pp. 85–104.

— (n.d.) "Mobile Communications in the 21st Century City," www.anthonymobile.com/wp-content/uploads/Townsend-TheWirelessWorld-BookChapter.pdf.

Turkle, S. (2011) *Alone Together: Why We Expect More from Technology and Less from Each Other*, New York: Basic Books.

United Nations Department of Economic and Social Affairs (2017) *The World's Cities in 2016*, www.un.org/en/development/desa/population/publications/pdf/urbanization/the_worlds_cities_in_2016_data_booklet.pdf.

Van Ransbeeck, W. (2015) "What Is Citizensourcing?" *CitizenLab*, www.citizenlab.co/blog/civic-engagement/what-is-citizensourcing.
Warner, M. (2002) "Publics and Counterpublics," *Public Culture*, 14(1), pp. 49–90.

Further Reading

Goldsmith, S. and Kleiman, N. (2017) *A New City O/S: The Power of Open, Collaborative, and Distributed Governance*, Washington, DC: Brookings Institution Press.
Tufekci, Z. (2017) *Twitter and Tear Gas: The Power and Fragility of Networked Protest*, New Haven, CT: Yale University Press.
Willis, K. and Aurigi, A. (2017) *Digital and Smart Cities*, New York: Routledge.

22

TOOLS OF THE TRADE

Urban Planning, Urban Media and the Refashioning of Urban Space

Sarah Barns

Introduction

Cities are becoming more and more dense with information, as distributed sensors and glowing rectangle screens become part of the minute details and experiences of everyday urban lives. Emerging data-rich urban landscapes are inspiring a new wave of thinking about the nature of the urban, and the possibilities of "data-driven" urban planning. Cities are being reimagined as complex, hybrid entanglements of data and dirt, flesh and stone and software. Data-driven urban science is in the ascendant, with new techniques of visualization used to analyze large urban data sets, celebrated for their capacity to deliver new insights into the conditions of our cities, from levels of air pollution to the conditions of ageing bridges (see also Chapter 20, this volume). With vast new streams of information now being emitted, seemingly from every footpath, many celebrate our new-found capacity to understand the nature of the city as a complex urban system, and to better organize the myriad interactions that take place within cities, enabling our city leaders, governors and planners to improve the way we design and manage the complex requirements of an increasingly urbanized planet.

The field of "smart cities" is one of the key domains of urban planning that clearly demonstrates how much interest there is in the potential for advanced data visualization to improve the workings of our cities. Smart cities apply new information and communication technologies (ICTs) to the day-to-day management of the city, using big data, machine learning, distributed sensors and algorithms to support more "responsive" interactions between disparate urban infrastructures, utilities, public services and urban citizens. The growing amount of interest and investment in the benefits of smart city technologies reflects the widespread belief that new media technologies are able to better represent, and by extension, better respond to, the complex challenges of urban life. As I discuss in this chapter, this belief is by no means unique to the contemporary era, but is consistent throughout the history of urban planning.

Urban planning as a profession has historically relied on innovations in visual media to capture the urban condition, to make sense of its messy complexity and to offer aspirational urban forms. Through its entanglements with the evolution of urban planning, we can see the role of urban media as not simply representing the diverse conditions of urban transformation, but as helping to constitute the very production of urban space. This history sheds a different light on the nature of urban media technologies, suggesting it is not so much that urban media—whether those of historical eras or the smart technologies of more recent times—finally capture the true complexity of cities, but rather that they recalibrate urban knowledge and expertise in their own image.

This chapter offers a series of sojourns to key moments in the history of planning: moments that illustrate the connections between different idealized visions of the city, the tools used to produce them and their role in the reorganization of urban space. This account offers a perspective on how particular technological media innovations have created the conditions for historical transformations in the realm of design, planning and management of cities, as well as informing new ways of knowing cities. In this way, the space of the urban is understood as a site that is not only documented, but also refashioned and reconstituted, in ways that privilege the expectations and conventions of emerging urban media.

Part One: Visions of the City

The ideal of the city has attracted the imaginations of social reformers since ancient times. Indeed, the very notion that there *might be* an ideal condition of the city is often linked to the potent historical image of the Athenian agora, integral to the functioning of Greek democracy, where goods and ideas could be disseminated freely. But the notion of an ideal city—whether Augustine's City of God, a kingdom existing in a realm out of time or the concept of utopia as Thomas More first imagined it in the 16th century—has also, historically, been completely out of our reach. More's utopia was at once an ideal place ("*Eutopia*") and a "no-place" ("*Utopia*"), as in nowhere present in the world. Diffusing the eschatological hopes of Christianity, the city came to symbolize both the promise of what could be, but also the messy realities of our (fallen) human world (Fishman 1982; Hall 1988; Coleman 2005; Pinder 2005: 21).

Historians of urban planning emphasize the importance of idealized notions of the city to the early development of the trade. Planning historians such as Hall (1988) and Benevolo (1967) underscore the importance of utopian thinkers, among them Saint Simon, Fourier and Robert Owen, to the work of late 19th-century urban reformers such as Patrick Geddes and Ebenezer Howard. These early planners saw the need for unique spatial solutions to the problems of social and industrial disorder they saw overwhelming their cities. Issues relating to public health, social dislocation and even moral decline needed to be addressed, they argued, by considering the design of human settlements *as a whole*—and not only by reforms to specific infrastructures, whether they be transportation, lighting, water or sewerage (Fishman 1982: 21–28; Batty and Marshall 2009; Sennett 2018). In their reformist zeal, pioneers of planning were driven by a desire to reclaim the city as a space of political hope—Geddes' called his particular designs a "civics" of cities (2004 [1904]). Ebenezer Howard, who led the Garden City movement, himself explicitly noted the influence of Thomas More's conception of utopia on his own urban designs, arguing that More had only narrowly failed to give expression to the idea of the Garden City that he was proposing. Howard's concept of the Garden City (1902), set out during the late 19th century, sought to connect individualism and socialism through a new kind of urban form that would reintegrate people living in cities with the countryside (see Figure 22.1). Howard produced simple diagrams of the ideal urban form to communicate his vision, which would ultimately prove highly influential in shaping the design of many modern towns, even if his political ideas did not. To Howard, utopianism was central to enabling urban and social change: "It is essential to have an ideal showing us the direction in which we should move" (Pinder 2005: 40).

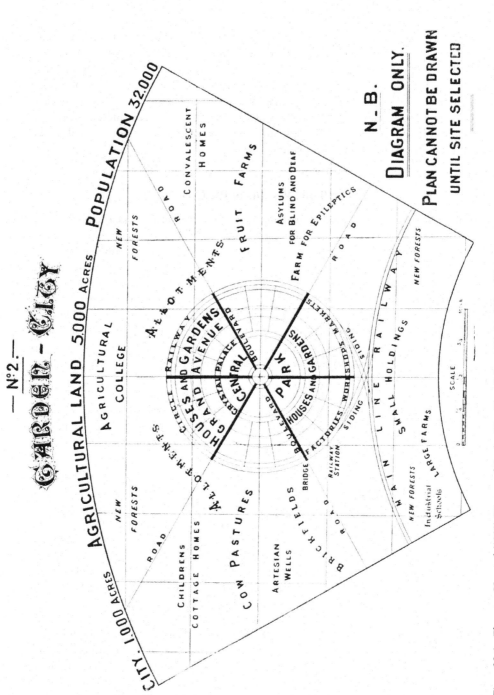

Figure 22.1 Ebenezer Howard (1902) *Diagram of Garden City*. Plate 2 from *Garden Cities of Tomorrow*. Public domain image.

Resonant with its utopian promise, the city served at this time as a visual leitmotif of the utopian impulse (Leach 2002: 2). But the reality of urban life was far from ideal. Aghast at the seemingly unstoppable rise of cities racked by huge social tensions, disease and political ferment, late 19th-century reformers set about constructing unitary spatial designs that might reconstitute the space of the city as an "ideal worth fighting for" (Hall 1988: 7). Described by Harvey (2000: 175) as "utopias of spatial form", the plans devised by early town planners were not only original and wide-sweeping in an urban design sense, but were also concerned to bring about fundamental social change as well. As the architectural historian M. Christine Boyer has argued, "by following the path of scientific methodology and assuming their role to be that of social engineering, [early planners] sought an absolute correspondence between the exterior city reality and its truthful and purified representation" (1996a: 19–21).

Scientific methods of classification were integral to the work of these reformers, assisting them to introduce greater "legibility" to urban space. The influential Scottish planner Patrick Geddes was originally trained under biologist Thomas Huxley, a prominent defender of Darwin's radical evolutionary theories, and used the emerging principles and classificatory schemas of evolutionary thought as a means to control the disorders of industrialization (Batty and Marshall 2009). He saw the industrial city as "a sorry aggregate of ill-constructed houses, mean or showy without, unhealthy within, and containing little of permanent value" (Geddes 1885, quoted in Welter 2002: 17). By coming to view the city as a biological system subject to states of equilibrium and decay, Geddes established new principles for a more contained and controllable urban spatial form (Geddes 1915).

Resistant to the seemingly unstoppable forces of growth and expansion, Geddes' vision of the city was one that more efficiently captured resources from its wider region, a position that came to be known as "regionalism" (Welter 2002; Batty and Marshall 2009). Underpinning this vision were theoretical expositions about different urban social structures, which were graphically rendered as "thinking machines" and represented through various matrices and diagonal components abstracted as "Place", "Folk" and "Work" (Geddes 1915). By visually abstracting the core elements of otherwise chaotic urban spaces, Geddes asserted the need for cities to be organized as unified, classifiable and contained entities, whose unruly and unhealthy natures could be effectively tamed through improved spatial organization (Hall 1988; Welter 2003: 30).

Geddes' radical ideas about urban space informed the urban planning strategies he produced for some 50 cities across India during the first decades of the 20th century, and were to prove influential to the work of numerous urban reformers during the following decades and beyond. In particular, the idea that a city could and should be comprehensively ordered according to objective classificatory schemas would help propel the use of city-wide mapping techniques adopting the most advanced scientific methods of the time. While committed to decentralization of power, Geddes' concepts and techniques of urban abstraction would, ironically, pave the way for the state's disciplined management of urban space over the coming century (Hall 1988).

In the city of Paris, the role of urban media in the refashioning urban space by planners is most radically apparent during the tumultuous decades of the mid-19th century. Both celebrated and castigated as one of the most notorious city planners in history, the figure of Baron Georges-Eugène Haussmann is synonymous with the modernization of Paris, and the introduction of comprehensive planning techniques. Haussmann used the concept of the geometric grid as a central organizational principle through which to rebuild the city (Cosgrove 2006: 148). The need for a newly fashioned visual order resulted in the razing of some 12,000 buildings, creating widened boulevards, known as "arteries", running east and west, north and south. This new design at once expanded and divided medieval Paris into equal sections or *arrondissements*, and rid the city of its radical communes, obliterating the strategic routes of its revolutionaries. Out of the rubble emerged a modern city of light and air.

Removed of its alleyways and tenement slums, the modern city of Paris was rebuilt as a space of scenic composition. Demolition was a process of "disencumbering" particularly focused on clearing the spaces adjacent to monumental historic buildings and major new civic structures. By clearing away the detritus that surrounded a major public building, Haussmann saw that the meaning and significance of that building could be more easily discerned and thus promote greater civil obedience (see Hamer 2000: 174). In this way, the act of disencumbering imposed a vision of the city as a unified space in which the relation between local parts was to be subordinated to the coordination of the whole (McQuire 2008: 35). Paris after Haussmann "ceased to be a conglomeration of small towns, each with its distinctive physiognomy and way of life" (Dubech and d'Espezel, cited in Benjamin 1999: 129). As Boyer has written, the monumental and iconographical gestures of Haussmann's *boulevards* and *Place de la Concorde* cemented an idealized image of the city as a space of harmonious arrangement and scenic composition, which was in turn used to highlight the civilizing role of the modern bourgeois state (Boyer 1996a: 185).

In Paris, the rapidly changing city was a testing ground for new visualization technologies, among them cartographic maps, bird's-eye perspectives and, not least, photography. Indeed, in places like Paris, photography not only emerged as a media technology used to document the city, but also played a symbiotic role in its symbolic and material transformation (Jones 2013: 2). Some of the most celebrated photographs of "Old Paris" were taken by photographer Charles Marville, employed by Haussmann to capture large-format images of areas about to undergo *percements* or "piercings" (demolition). Through the photographer's lens, Haussmann sought to document that which would forever be lost, but following the reconstruction of Paris he also found a new use for the photographer (see Figure 22.2). Presenting a series of Marville's "before and after" images of Paris at the Universal Exhibition of 1878, Haussmann found the photographs acted as compelling evidence of rational progress and justification of the modernist urbanization project. Thus, Marville's photographs provided visually persuasive evidence of Haussmann's belief that Old Paris was indeed a sick city that needed "surgery" in the form of demolition (Kennell 2013; Tormey 2013: 41).

Haussmann's 1853 clearance of the alleyways and tenement slums of Paris is widely recognized as the first decisive act against the perceived disorderly nature of the 19th century (Berman 1982: 151; Boyer 1996a: 38; Harvey 2003). This mass reconstruction of the city of Paris presented a new visual typology of urban spaces that helped reinforce the city's permanent, eternal existence—and became a benchmark against which other cities compared themselves. In this approach, as Welter writes, "the typical became more important than specific historic circumstances" (2002: 86). As cluttered slums of pestilence gave way to composed spaces of civilized order and scientifically calculated construction patterns, the city could be revealed as a "work of art" (Boyer 1996b), projecting an aestheticized vision of industrial modernity to the world as efficient, safe and prosperous. "Haussmann" in turn became an exemplary practice, described by Engels as "the practice which has now become general, of making breaches in the working-class neighborhoods of our big cities, particularly those that are centrally situated" (Engles, cited in Benjamin 1999: 145).

Architectural historians now recognize Haussmann's intervention as one that reconstituted the modern metropolis through "memory maps", whereby the city is reconstructed through a memorialized version of itself (Vidler 2000: 179). But in the act of imposing a unified, memorialized spatial order within an otherwise inchoate and disorderly terrain, Haussmann's intervention also embodied industrialization's creative destruction, epitomizing the scale and speed of modernity as it utterly transformed everyday spaces, in turn reinforcing a terrifying

Figure 22.2 Charles Marville, *Rue de Glatigny*, 1865
Image out of copyright.

sense of sociospatial dislocation. Mourning the loss of his "Old Paris", the photographer Eugene Atget took up a large-format bellows camera and set about documenting his city in exhaustive and comprehensive detail. Beginning in 1898 and continuing throughout the early decades of the 20th century, Atget's images of Paris would go on to inspire generations of documentary street photographers (see Chapter 4, this volume). Determined to capture all that was being lost before him, Atget's photographs were at once realism unadorned and a celebration of a city quickly vanishing.

Visual surveys of the city, such as those established by Patrick Geddes, were to prove highly influential during the postwar period. British planner Patrick Abercrombie, whose Greater London Plans of 1943/4 were commissioned by the City of London as part of its postwar reconstruction, was strongly influenced by Geddes' ideas, and would go on to become the inspiration for countless other major postwar urban plans, including the City of Sydney's *County of Cumberland Planning Scheme* (1945), among others. These plans would establish coordinated and large-scale categorizations of land uses across a metropolitan area as the basis for developing long-term strategies for transportation, open space and designated public services. While Abercrombie's Greater London Plan was not as successful as he had wished for, public acceptance of these large-scale visual typologies of the city was achieved through the provision of bird's-eye perspectives on London's "horribly confused" condition, along with notable films such as *The Proud City* (van Roosmalen 1997: 259). Abercrombie's sketch was accompanied by hand-drawn sketches of Greater London, organized as a series of concentric rings with different functional and spatial requirements. Such classificatory schemas would continue to guide the regulatory basis for planning decisions for decades to come.

Dreaming *the Rational City*, Boyer's (1987) study of the rise of planning as a professional discipline of urban improvement in America, describes how important the abstraction of the city has been to what she calls the effective "disciplinary order" of planning. Drawing on the work of Foucault, Boyer recounts:

> [D]isciplinary order . . . begins with a fear of darkened places in the city, the shadowy spaces where light and vision are blocked . . . Discipline proceeds from the distribution of individuals in space, it requires an enclosed area, a space divided into intricate partitions where everything has its place, and every place in the order of things.
>
> *(Boyer 1987: 33)*

As Boyer describes, from the early 20th century, the spatial organization of the city was employed as a material element in the production and circulation of goods (1987: 62). The planning mentality here is "as much a utopian disciplinary order . . . as the city of Olympian design" (1987: 69–70). In Boyer's account, emergent technologies of visualization in the early 20th century—across cartographic, photographic or filmic forms—were central to this disciplining of urban space. Through recourse to scientific method, urban knowledge would come to be associated with the city as represented through these media (Boyer 1996a: 21).

Just as Haussmann had used the art of photography to both meticulously document the city and project new, scenically composed visions, so the experience of flight would also unleash a wave of new thinking about the most appropriate forms of the urban (Campanella 2001). Early uses of the aerial photograph to depict urban settlement patterns were met with wonder and fear: Tafuri saw a "new Acropolis", where "the battle of technology against nature is grasped with a sense of vertigo" (Vidler 2000: 39). Vidler (2000) has called this a "photourbanism" afforded by the aerial view, which empowered Le Corbusier to diagnose the disorders of the city from a fresh perspective. Ecstatic with enthusiasm about how flight could aid the work of city-makers, Le Corbusier (1935: 5) extolled its diagnostic potential, exclaiming: "The airplane eye . . . now looks with alarm at the places where we live, the cities where it is our lot to be. And the spectacle is frightening, overwhelming. The airplane eye reveals a spectacle of collapse".

To Le Corbusier, flying over Manhattan for the first time in the 1930s, the aerial view ratified a conviction that the architectural past was bankrupt: the city needed a new form.

Ultimately, the panoramic perspective that Le Corbusier offered through his architectural accomplishments depended on his capacity to set himself apart, to view from above the disorderly spaces of the old city and to advocate the need for a new urban consciousness (Boyer 1996a: 43; Sennett 1990: 173–174; Pinder 2005: 71–72). As he exclaimed in *Aircraft: The New Vision*:

> It is as an architect and town planner—and therefore as a man essentially occupied with the welfare of his species—that I let myself be carried off on the wings of an airplane, make use of the bird's eye view, of the view from the air, to which end I directed the pilot to steer over cities . . . The airplane indicts.
>
> *(Le Corbusier 1935: 5)*

Like Geddes and Haussmann before him, Le Corbusier was influenced by new technologies of vision to see the city in more biological terms, and the urban planner as a kind of surgeon restoring good health to his patient. The vision of *La Ville Radieuse* ("The Radiant City") born of the architect's flight over Moscow created space for "machines of circulation" (the automobile) that could create fluidity and reduce stagnation. Like other urban blueprints that came before, the Radiant City was both a plan for the city—one designed to sustain attack from their air—and also a project of radical social reform. By the 1940s, after the hostilities of World War II had come to a close, the aerial view became institutionalized as a central tool of the planning profession (Vidler 2000: 40). And yet, the city in its spiraling complexity continued to confound.

Part Two: Fragmented Views

The drive to systematically rationalize urban space by urban planners and reformers confronted new limits during the volatile period of the 1960s and 1970s. American geographer Ed Soja has described this period as one that saw a breakdown in abstracted, "systems-level" analyses of city life, which were unable to account for the citizen unrest and disorder taking place across the cities of the Western world (1996: 96–97). Invigorated by increasingly sophisticated cybernetic technology, a new breed of urbanists would also question totalizing visions of the city espoused from the vantage of a bird's-eye "zenith view". Founders of the Chicago School of urban sociology were criticized for their overemphasis on the internal coherence of the city in a search for a kind of moral order. Urban activists such as Jane Jacobs (1965) would lead activist campaigns that proclaimed the ignorance of the master planner in favor of street-level smarts and "unexpected treasure hunts" capable of understanding the wisdom of the "street ballet". To this new breed of urbanists, the city, still the major site for cultural and political action, could no longer be left to the planners to be saved.

Inspired by the emerging logics of cybernetics, architects and urbanists such as Archigram would seek new conceptual renderings of the city as a "kit of parts", which could be "playfully deployed according to the dictates of individual desires" (Scott 2007: 262). Also inspired by cybernetics, the novelist Italo Calvino imagined the city as a kind of hypertext, one in which the reader can imagine a multiplicity of routes concurrently (Calvino 1974; Boyer 1996b: 142). This way of rendering the city resisted the notion of linear, spatial sequences and the rational ordering of space associated with more traditional, Euclidian geometry. For Calvino, cybernetics was destabilizing because it reordered the very nature of our cognitive reasoning, by presenting the world as "discrete", in a mathematical sense, no longer continuous in form but operating as separate, divisible parts that were, by nature, interchangeable (Boyer 1996b: 141).

The French Situationists, appalled by the banality of the reconstructed, postwar city, turned to "psycho-geographic" maps of the city created not through totalizing visual abstractions, but through aimless *derives* (drifts) designed to disrupt the disciplinary control associated with spatial and administrative order (see also Chapter 38, this volume). Surrealism, rather than reductive scientific reasoning, was to offer the visual motifs for a more emancipatory mode of urban representation, one that allowed space for the unconscious, the experiential and the dream-state (Debord 1958). Also opposed to the unitary construct of the city, Marxist geographer Manuel Castells (1977) would criticize ideas of the city being bounded in a territorial, arguing for greater attention to the globalized conditions of urbanization. Castells would later consider the implications of a network society as one in which "spaces of flow" come to substitute "the space of places" through a placeless structural logic (2000: 33). At the other end of the scale, Marxist sociologist Lefebvre advocated the need to critically engage the conditions of spatial production and experience in ways that were grounded in the reality of everyday urban existence. Meanwhile, media theorist Marshall McLuhan, responding to the rise of globalized media and communications, saw the coming of a "global village" that would spell the demise of the city as a coherent dimension of social life. It must, he wrote, "inevitably dissolve like the fading shot in a movie" (McLuhan 1964: 366).

In this way—as "cultures of time and space" (Kern 1983) embraced the urban mediations generated by an increasingly globalized visual culture, alive to the promises of cybernetics and, later, networked technologies—totalizing visions of the city were politicized. By century's end, students of urban planning would be taught of the tragedy of modernist planning, and the geographies of single-use enclaves and far-flung highways they had spawned. A new urban planning consensus, informed by postmodern and Marxist influences, recognized the limits of spatial ordering as a means of social reform, while still embracing the vitality of urban space as a locus for progressive reform. From this crisis emerged a critical re-evaluation of the idea of the city as it had previously been conceived.

As Crary argues, urbanism at this time "collided with that moment in capitalism when the rationalization of built space became secondary to problems of speed and the maximisation of circulation" (cited in Scott 2007: 261). The legibility of the (Western) city, it seemed, amidst the acceleration of global media technologies, had reached "the threshold of oblivion" (2007: 261). The specific spatial form of the city had given way to notions of circuits and networks and feedback loops, no longer containable as a spatially legible order (Castells 1977). But as the city was reimagined once again, recast as a site for radical politics, its utopian promise was reaffirmed—if not as the well-ordered space imagined by Thomas More, then as a space resonant with political and speculative possibility nevertheless.

In more recent years, the computational intensification of the city has given rise to new visions of the city, this time empowered by big data and the techniques of machine learning, data visualization and algorithmic intelligence (Kitchin 2014). A new "science of cities" is in the ascendant (Townsend 2015). Data mining, sensing and analytics are tools used to understand cities as complex sites of interaction: in the quest to build "smarter" cities, big data is used to expose the relationships between discrete realms of urban management and planning, with a view to integrating the management and provision of utilities, transportation and housing in more "responsive" ways (Crawford and Goldsmith 2014). The granular insights afforded by big data have seen analyses of urban forms return to biological or evolutionary metaphors (Batty 2013; Townsend 2015) and the universal laws of physics (West 2018). The computational power now distributed through the hands of smartphone-enabled urban citizens has unleashed a new wave of urban disruption, as geo-specific data harvesting, combined with mass social media, is being leveraged by data-driven platform companies to disrupt major urban industries across transport, tourism, real estate, energy and city governance (Barns et al. 2017). Cities are again being "disrupted" and reshaped, this time in accordance with the data sciences, and the conditions of platform-based "gig economy" services, as they facilitate data-driven, on-demand and algorithmically managed ways of interacting with the city.

These transformations are not without controversy, despite the appeals of a more objective, data-driven urban science. Critics argue we are now returning to an era of (data) behaviorism, with a resurgent, yet mistaken, belief that the challenges of cities can be solved through recourse to scientific methods (Townsend 2015). For Mattern, we are forgetting the lessons of the past: by uncritically linking external behaviors, in this case visual manipulations of data, with causality (Mattern 2013). To Eisenmann, digital visions of the city are representative of a new "virulent breed of formalism—more virulent because they are posed under the banner of a neo-avant garde technological determinism" (in Vidler 2000: vii). Some fear planning itself is losing ground to the global influence of platform companies such as Google, whose forays into urban planning through sister company Sidewalk Labs point to the potential for city precincts to be managed as proprietary data ecosystems (Barns 2017; Sadowski 2017).

Conclusion

A journey to different historical points in the development of urban planning provides insights into the constitutive role played by urban media in shaping the way the city has come to be known, planned, governed and experienced. Technologies of visualization and abstraction, of connectivity and flow, have a habit of unleashing not only new perspectives but also new diagnoses of the city—used by urban planners and reformers to decipher and, in turn, reform the urban condition. Each new vision, ennobled by new tools of the trade, sees the city as a space to be resolved into its own image, achieving widespread urban disruption, whether through demolition or redesign, or, more surreally, radical *detournement*. "By spreading out like a magma into reality, technology—or its image—subsumes it", wrote Tafuri of Le Corbusier's "Plan Obus" for Algiers (cited in Vidler 2000: 39).

And if this story has been told before, it will no doubt need to be told again as we look ahead to an era of smart cities, emboldened by the possibilities of advanced visualization technologies and data-rich urban analytics. New challenges are emerging, accompanied by widespread debate over the limits of data-driven knowledge and algorithmic urban management. As both site and symbol of our love affair with technology and modernity, the city continues to confound, repel, disrupt and inspire.

References

Barns, S. (2017) "Can a tech company build a city? Ask Google", *The Conversation*, viewed July 1, 2018, https://theconversation.com/can-a-tech-company-build-a-city-ask-google-86402.
Barns, S., Cosgrave E., Acuto M., et al. (2017) "Digital infrastructures and urban governance", *Urban Policy and Research*, 35, pp. 20–31.
Batty, M. (2013) *The New Science of Cities*, Cambridge, MA: MIT Press.
Batty, M, and Marshall, S. (2009) "Centenary paper: The evolution of cities: Geddes, Abercrombie and the new physicalism", *Town Planning Review*, 80, pp. 551–574.
Benevolo, L. (1967) *The Origins of Modern Town Planning*, London: Routledge.
Benjamin, W. (1999) *The Arcades Project*, trans. Eiland, H. and McLaughlin, K., Cambridge, MA: Harvard University Press.
Berman, M. (1982) *All That Is Solid Melts into Air: The Experience of Modernity*, New York: Simon and Schuster.
Boyer, M. C. (1987) *Dreaming the Rational City: The Myth of American City Planning*, Cambridge, MA: MIT Press.
— (1996a) *The City of Collective Memory*, Cambridge, MA: MIT Press.

—— (1996b) *Cyber Cities: Visual Perception in the Age of Electronic Communication*, New York: Princeton Architectural Press.
Calvino, I. (1974) *Invisible Cities*, trans. W. Weaver, New York: Harcourt Brace Jovanovich.
Campanella, T. (2001) *Cities from the Sky: An Aerial Portrait of America*, New York: Princeton University Press.
Castells, M. (1977) *The Urban Question: A Marxist Approach*, trans. A. Sheridan, London: Edward Arnold.
—— (2000) *The Rise of the Network Society*, Oxford: Blackwell.
Coleman, N. (2005) *Utopias and Architecture*, London: Routledge.
Corbusier, L. (1935) *Aircraft: The New Vision*, Paris: The Studio.
Cosgrove, D. (2006) "Carto-city", in Hall, P. and Abrams, J. (eds.) *Else/Where Mapping: New Cartographies of Networks and Territories*, Minneapolis, MN: University of Minnesota Design Institute, pp. 148–157.
Crawford, S. and Goldsmith, S. (2014) *The Responsive City: Engaging Communities Through Data-Smart Governance*, New York: Wiley.
Debord, G. (1958) "Theory of the *Derive*", *Internationale Situationiste No. 2*, trans. K. Knabb, viewed July 1, 2018, http://library.nothingness/.org/articles/SI/en/display/314.
Fishman, R. (1982) *Urban Utopias in the Twentieth Century: Ebenezer Howard, Frank Lloyd Wright and Le Corbusier*, Cambridge, MA: MIT Press.
Geddes, P. (1915) *Cities in Evolution: An Introduction to the Town Planning Movement and to the Study of Civics*, London: Williams and Norgate.
—— (2004 [1904]) *Civics as Applied Sociology*. Project Gutenberg, www.gutenberg.org/ebooks/13205.
Hall, P. (1988) *Cities of Tomorrow: An Intellectual History of Planning and Design in the Twentieth Century*, Oxford: Blackwell.
Hamer, D. (2000) "Planning and Heritage: Towards Integration", in Freestone, R. (ed.) *Urban Planning in a Changing World*, New York: Routledge, pp. 194–208.
Harvey, D. (2000) *Spaces of Hope*, Berkeley, CA: University of California Press.
—— (2003) *Paris: Capital of Modernity*, New York and London: Routledge.
Howard, E. (1902) *Garden Cities of To-Morrow*, London: Swan Sonnenschein and Co Ltd.
Jacobs, J. (1965) *The Death and Life of Great American Cities*, New York: Random House.
Jones, P. (2013) "Picturing Urban Regeneration: A Study of Photographers in Liverpool, UK", *Sociological Research Online*, 18, pp. 1–11.
Kennell, S. (2013) *Charles Marville: Photographer of Paris*, Chicago, IL: University of Chicago Press.
Kern, S. (1983) *The Culture of Time and Space: 1880–1918*, Cambridge, MA: Harvard University Press.
Kitchin, R. (2014) *The Data Revolution: Big Data, Open Data and Their Consequences*, London: SAGE.
Leach, N. (2002) *The Hieroglyphics of Space: Reading and Experiencing the Modern Metropolis*, London: Routledge.
Le Corbusier (1935) *Aircraft: The New Vision*, London and New York: The Studio, viewed July 1, 2018, www.bl.uk/collection-items/aircraft-by-le-corbusier.
Mattern, S. (2013) "Methodolatry and the Art of Measure: The New Wave of Urban Science", *Places*, November.
McLuhan, M. (1964) *Understanding Media: The Extensions of Man*, Cambridge, MA: MIT Press.
McQuire, S. (2008) *The Media City: Media Architecture and Urban Space*, London: SAGE.
Pinder, D. (2005) *Visions of the City*, Edinburgh: Edinburgh University Press.
Sadowski, J. (2017) "Google wants to run cities without being elected. Don't let it", *The Guardian*, viewed July 1, 2018, www.theguardian.com/commentisfree/2017/oct/24/google-alphabet-sidewalk-labs-toronto.
Scott, F. (2007) *Architecture or Techno-Utopia: Politics After Modernism*, Cambridge, MA: MIT Press.
Sennett, R. (1990) *The Conscience of the Eye: The Design and Social Life of Cities*, New York and London: Knopf.
Sennett, R. (2018) *Building and Dwelling: Ethics for the City*, London: Allen Lane/Penguin.
Soja, E. (1996) *Postmodern Geographies: The Reassertion of Space in Critical Social Theory*, London: Verso.
Tormey, J. (2013) *Cities and Photography: Routledge Critical Introductions to Urbanism and the City*, London: Routledge.
Townsend, A. (2015) "Cities of data: Examining the new urban science", *Public Culture*, 27(2), pp. 201–212.
van Roosmalen, P. K. M. (1997) "London 1944: Greater London Plan", in Bosma, K. and Hellinga, H. (eds.) *Mastering the City: North-European Town Planning 1900–2000*, Rotterdam: NAi Publishers/EFL Publications.
Vidler, A. (2000) "Photourbanism: Planning the city from above and below", in Bridge, G. and Watson, S. (eds.) *A Companion to the City*, Oxford: Blackwell.

Welter, V. M. (2002) *Biopolis: Patrick Geddes and the City of Life*, Cambridge, MA: MIT Press.
West, G. (2018) *Scale: The Universal Laws of Life and Death in Organisms, Cities and Companies*, London and New York: Penguin.

Further Reading

Boyer, M. C. (1996) *The City of Collective Memory: Its Historical Imagery and Architectural Entertainments*, Cambridge, MA: MIT Press.
McQuire, S. (2008) *The Media City: Media Architecture and Urban Space*, London: SAGE.
Scott, F. (2007) *Architecture or Techno-Utopia: Politics After Modernism*, Cambridge, MA: MIT Press.

PART III

Media Cities as Sites of Creative Industries and Post-Industrial Urbanism

INTRODUCTION TO PART III
Media Cities as Sites of Creative Industries and Post-Industrial Urbanism

Deborah Stevenson and Zlatan Krajina

The media in all its guises makes it possible to know and experience aspects of a city without ever physically going there. Such experiences can be immersive, for instance via virtual and augmented reality, or a reader can be transported through the evocative words of a novel. As well as being the subject of media framing, cities are also the sites in which media in all its forms are made, displayed and consumed. The contemporary cultural and creative industries are almost by definition products of urban environments and commodities mobilized in the service of selected urban populations. Concerted efforts are made to attract the "creative class" (Florida 2003) who is imagined as cosmopolitan, affluent and urban. Terms such as "cultural clusters", "creative precincts", "media zones" and "creative cities" have entered the lexicon of planners, politicians and city boosters alike. City visions, centered on creativity, are thus not merely located in, but are also articulated through, urban space, while spatial design is increasingly bound up in conversing with multiple stakeholders. If, as El-Khoury and Robbins (2013: 3) argue, the urban is "an amalgam of different realities . . . (d)esigners and planners today, in ways that are new and unique, face not the design of a city singular, but the realities of similarity and difference". Creativity, formerly a reflective dimension of industrial production, has now through media and culture assumed a prominent place on the post-industrial urban policy and city reimaging agendas of cities around the world. As Hall (2000: 640, cited in Jayne 2006: 173) put it, "culture is now seen as a magic substitute for all the lost factories and warehouses and as a device that will create new urban image, making the city more attractive to mobile capital". Indeed, strategies focused on fostering cultural activity and the creative industries in order to "animate space" have emerged to be amongst the most important local policy initiatives of recent decades. Initiatives can range from the oft-called "Europeanization" of the city centers through the establishment of cultural, education or entertainment precincts, to the high-profile "cultural capitals" schemes of a number of national and supra-state bodies, including UNESCO. In this Part of the book, chapter contributors engage with the contours of these trends and the associated debates to highlight challenges and complexities that are often ignored in treatises overly concerned with quick-fix cultural strategies for complex urban environments and societies.

In Chapter 23, the first chapter of this Part, Xin Gu highlights the globalized nature of creative cities policies with reference to moves by the cities of Manchester and Shanghai to establish designated media clusters in two very different social and urban contexts even though neither city had a prior reputation as a center for media production. As the chapter points out, both these cities initially adopted broader creative industries/creative city-informed redevelopment and re-imagining strategies before shifting their focus to media production which was regarded as high-growth and high-value. The chapter shows how while Manchester developed a strong profile as a center for creative activity before being positioned as a media city, Shanghai embraced the media very quickly. In both cases, reimaging involved the spatial clustering of media industries, the redevelopment of former industrial spaces and the concentration of resources away from other cultural forms, spaces and practices. City branding and global positioning are clear aims of strategies such as these along with attracting global capital. Attracting tourists may also be a byproduct, but many cultural industry-focused city imaging strategies have tourism as their primary aim as places are being made and remade for the consumption of tourists. As Deborah Stevenson explains in Chapter 24, these tourists, in turn, produce and consume media texts that variously reinforce and reinterpret place. Indeed, it is almost impossible to separate contemporary tourist places and experiences from a range of media representations. The media is central to the promotion of cities as tourism destinations at the same time as it frames the context of travel and the expectations of tourists. In addition, travel experiences and tourist encounters with, and in, place are mediated through a range of media practices such as travelers' feedback, which can disrupt established parameters and discourses of travel.

International bodies, such as the European Union, have increasingly become enmeshed in local attempts to use the cultural and creative industries to rebrand and market cities. Such bodies have pursued a range of policies that directly focus on the city, with Capital of Culture schemes standing out as emblematic (Stevenson 2017). What is particularly interesting is the way in which such schemes have become attractive to post-industrial cities, notably (and emblematically) the Scottish city of Glasgow. With reference to the European Capital of Culture program, Peter Campbell and Dave O'Brien examine this interrelationship, highlighting the ways in which being afforded the title mediates the normative idea of "the city". They examine the role the European Capital of Culture scheme plays in supplementing already-existing discourses and practices associated with urban culture not only in a specific city, but also more broadly in the particular EU's visions of cities in general. The intersection of the global and the local are themes evident also in the chapter by David Rowe and Brett Hutchins which probes the shaping of urban events by the technologies and practices of their representation. The authors argue that media communication is now integral to major urban sporting events, such as the Summer Olympics and the FIFA World Cup, because these events are highly dependent on a multitude of screen devices situated in public and private spaces across the city. This interdependency, however, raises important questions of inclusion and exclusion that may play out spatially but go to social structures of power and inequality.

Screens may now be central to the experience of contemporary urban events, but Hank Haeusler, in Chapter 27, seeks to move beyond the screen to ponder the phenomenon of urban media façades as an emerging interface between the physical and the digital. Haeusler also probes the potential consequences that new technological interfaces might have for the urban landscapes, including streetscapes and public space. He investigates these ideas with reference to two interdisciplinary design projects intended to address the challenges posed by new forms of education, and partnerships between the researchers and industry. Jennifer Craik, in her chapter, takes a very different approach to the subject of urban media by focusing on fashion, which she describes as the cultural industry that most "typifies" the mediated cities of the present and those of the imagined future, because of its ability to communicate the signs and symbols of social status and action. Craik's argument rests on the observation that the features of the mediated city—displaying connections and intersections between material (physical presence, urban form and spatial layout) and symbolic (image, communicated branding and social networks) formations—fit the archetype of global fashion capitals. Indeed, she argues that not only did fashion define the cities of modernity, but as "the mediated city evolved, the fashion industry re-invented itself to match postmodern cities themselves".

In Chapter 29, Martin Zebracki addresses the issue of the mediated city through a consideration of uses of art in urban space. In particular, he is interested in examining how the digital reconfigures engagement with art in public space and, from this consideration, to probe whether the urban condition is also reconfigured through the engagement of art in digitally networked space. He is concerned, however, that because of a range of social and spatial factors, many people are excluded from participating in digital urban culture. The chapter thus concludes with a call for policy interventions capable of addressing this digital divide and to provide support for digital public art practices that have the potential to advance more inclusive urban futures and uses of public space. Exclusion from public space is also a concern for Irina van Aalst whose chapter scrutinizes the urban night-time economy and the cultures and forms of governance that are produced in the mediated city at night. In particular, van Aalst highlights how a fear of crime shapes women's use of the city after dark and sets up barriers to their participation in the night-time economy. Along with gender, the chapter also considers "soft" surveillance strategies which highlight the integral role of the technologies and practices of communication. She points to examples drawn from around the world including the UK, Asia, Europe and the United States to illustrate what are ubiquitous trends and practices.

The urban night-time economy might be a place of play for some, but as Ingrid Richardson demonstrates in Chapter 31, the intersection of urban space and everyday play can, if not defy, then disrupt temporality. Taking the example of *Pokémon GO* (described as a significant "moment" in the history of urban media), the chapter probes the entanglement of games, mobile media use and playful imaginaries in everyday urban life, suggesting that the results are changes to the ways in which "being" and "doing" are experienced in mediated urban space. For Richardson, unplanned and location-based gaming demonstrate how the media pervades the everyday city and reshapes ways of being and interacting in urban space. The premise that the media plays a fundamental role in affecting how certain social forms take shape in urban space and vice versa underpins the examination of scenes and subcultures undertaken in Chapter 32. In this chapter, Geoff Stahl considers both "subcultures" and "scenes" in terms of the intersection of urban media, cultural space and collective life. He also traces the shift within social science from a concern with urban subcultures, which he describes as cohesiveness and homogeneous, to instead talking about scenes which, according to Stahl, are more informal and heterogeneous social gatherings than subcultures.

A recurring theme throughout this collection is that cities are more than physical spaces. Indeed, cities and urban life can only fully be understood if there is a consideration also of the structures and rhythms of meaning and emotion that are embedded in the concept and experience of place. People identify individually and collectively with where they live, with a particular house, in a particular street, in a particular neighborhood, town, city or region (Urry 1985; Kwon 2002). And they use a range of media to represent and connect with these spaces and their memories and histories of place. Such initiatives are especially poignant at times of profound social and urban change, including that which occurs when familiar and meaningful landmarks are destroyed, and communities dislocated. It is fitting, therefore, that the final chapter in this Part of the book is an examination of mediated remembrance in the context of urban change. Anita Bakshi is particularly interested in the ways in which people living in urban areas that are undergoing substantial change engage with this transformation and recount stories and memories of their neighborhoods. Situating her examination in the context of the rich literature on the city and collective memory, Bakshi highlights the relationship between the past, a sense of identity and place-based memories. She draws on the rich examples of two collaborative projects she developed including one in the Cypriot city of Nicosia, which is the contested capital of both the Greek-Cypriot Republic of Cyprus and the Turkish Republic of North Cyprus. Demonstrating the ways in which multi-faceted and multi-media projects can engage with community memories and histories, Bakshi recounts how the past can be linked with the present through thoughtfully designed initiatives that also serve as instruments for dynamic and meaningful transformation.

References

El-Khoury, R. and Robbins, E. (2013) "Introduction", in R. El-Khoury and E. Robbins (eds.) *Shaping the City, 2nd Edition: Studies in History, Theory and Urban Design*, London and New York: Routledge, pp. 1–5.

Florida, R. (2003) *The Rise of the Creative Class: And How It's Transforming Work, Leisure, Community and Everyday Life*, North Melbourne: Pluto Press.

Hall, P. (2000) "Creative cities and economic development", *Urban Studies*, 37(4), pp. 639–649.

Jayne, M. (2006) *Cities and Consumption*, London: Routledge.

Kwon, M. (2002) *One Place After Another: Site-Specific Art and Locational Identity*, Cambridge, MA: MIT Press.

Stevenson, D. (2017) *Cities of Culture: A Global Perspective*, London and New York: Routledge.

Urry, J. (1985) "Social relations, space and time", in D. Gregory and J. Urry (eds.) *Social Relations and Spatial Structures*, Houndmills, UK: Macmillan.

23
FROM "CREATIVE CITIES" TO "MEDIA CITIES"
The Cases of Manchester and Shanghai

Xin Gu

The media industry's predominant business activities entail the production and distribution of "symbolic goods," which place high value on originality, innovation, and creativity with low costs for reproduction and distribution (Hesmondhalgh 2013). The complex nature of media products (film, TV, music, etc.) makes media firms highly dependent on globally networked labor markets (Hesmondhalgh and Baker 2013) and resources, which reflects the diversity of global cultural markets (Pratt 2002; Scott 2004). The globalization strategy implemented by media firms has explicit local implications. Media cities where global media firms are located serve as nodal points in the global networks of cities (Hoyler and Watson 2013). Thus, the list of top world cities based on concentration and connectivity of global corporate service centers matches well with the list of cities as hubs for global media industry, with New York, London, and Paris at the top of the list (Krätke and Taylor 2004). From this basis, inter-city competition has started to be measured by the ability to attract global media firms.

Meanwhile, the centrality of the cultural industries—of which media is a key element—in the rejuvenation of post-industrial cities has attracted significant attention from policymakers and scholars. Advocates of the "creative city" emphasize new forms of softer, human-centered planning, breaking with top-down development models and looking to the integration of arts and culture into the everyday life and landscape of the city (Jacobs 1969). The development of the "creative city" includes using large-scale flagship cultural institutions to improve the image/brand of the city and its sense of identity, and to enhance the immediate and adjacent built environment for commercial, cultural, and recreational purposes (Landry and Bianchini 1995).

Significant problems present in the implementation of creative city policies result in diverse and sometimes contradictory approaches. Drawing from the UK's experience, Pratt (2008) categorized four main "creative city" policy approaches, all of which have to be carried out through cross-departmental collaboration. During this process, the departments in charge of local economic development became increasingly important in shaping and defining creative city policies through their ability to align "creative" funding with capital spending on hard infrastructure.

Media industries are among the most desirable in this developmental paradigm shift toward the knowledge economy, combining production and consumption, and the global circulation of capital and local economic development. Richard Florida's notion of "creative class" further substantiated the media city approach as his imagined "creative class" shares many common characteristics with media workers; those who are active networkers, favor "tolerant" and diverse locales, and profess a strong entrepreneurial spirit (Florida 2002). Just as the museums, art galleries, and other upmarket cultural consumption venues all contribute to a particular instrumental vision of the creative city, large-scale media cluster developments reveal an equally instrumental approach to urban cultural politics. Nevertheless, what media cities policies often incorporate—digital infrastructure, real estate development, business services, and collective branding—stands in stark contrast to the somewhat vague or abstract notion of the "creative city" as a cultural policy agenda (Mould 2014).

In this chapter, I will analyze the paradigm shift from creative cities to media cities in Manchester (UK) and Shanghai (China) with a focus on media clusters. Both cities are not traditionally known as global centers for media production. Creative city and media city models in both cases are about the redevelopment of de-industrialized areas in cities. Manchester was one of the first to embrace creative city policies and did so with particular zeal—from investment in cultural infrastructure and the adaptive use of post-industrial zones, to the development of new kinds of cultural policy agencies (the establishment of the Creative Industries Development Service). A decade after the first DCMS (1998) mapping of the UK creative industries (CIs) was released, Manchester has been successfully transformed into one of the most recognized faces of the creative city. Today, Manchester is undergoing a dramatic transformation, one that has seen the rise of the MediaCityUK in Salford, built on the relocation of parts of the BBC to the city and the building of offices and apartment blocks serving the media workers from outside of Manchester. This particular media city vision has been challenged by local CIs who have very different visions about the kinds of infrastructure and investment needed by the city.

I will argue that the gradual replacement of the creative city vision by the media city illuminates some of the challenges of culture-led urban regeneration policy. In Manchester, the folding of the creative city into the media city highlights that the sustainability of such creative strategies is heavily dependent upon such policy's capital investment needs. The media city, heavily laden with infrastructure development needs, resonates better with local policymaking concerned with attracting inward investment.

The case of Shanghai raises another crucial aspect of the sustainability of creative city strategies. Shanghai was the first Chinese city to develop a comprehensive creative city agenda in response to the national restructuring of its manufacturing economy. As policymakers were forced to grapple with a new and fluid post-industrial identity, the notion of the creative city provided a practical solution. The initial focus on culture was very quickly replaced by media, and used to attract global media corporations and footloose knowledge workers. The media city gained momentum in Shanghai by appealing to a respected group of social actors—international media executives and knowledge workers—who were more powerful in influencing policy settings than artists and local residents. However, this lack of connection with social actors beyond these powerful groups ultimately limits the effectiveness of the media city. The displacement of the creative city and the rise of the media city in both Manchester and Shanghai allow us to understand some of the dynamics underpinning those media city strategies that are now a rising global trend.

Media Clusters and Local Creative Milieus

The media city agenda is frequently applied in second-tier cities in relation to the short-term enhancement of ICT connectivity and foreign direct investment (Dugmore and Mavhungu 2011). Media firms produce "non-physical goods and services." The traditional clustering benefits, especially lower transportation cost associated with co-location, do not apply. Emerging media cities can become attractive by providing the technological facilities such as audiovisual equipment, recording studios, and editing suites that are necessary for media firms but are expensive to buy and maintain by smaller firms (Cook and Johns 2011). Large media complexes are now emerging on a global scale, for example *Dubai Media City* (Quinn et al. 2003), the *Tomorrow City* in Songdong (Seoul), *Digital Corridors* (Malaysia), and *NDSM* (Amsterdam). Evans suggests that the recent embracing of media clusters is driven by a globalized "digital city" utopia, which has emerged out of the "lack of alternative strategies and sustainable growth options" in these cities (Evans 2009: 1032). Thus, the "media city" emphasizing corporatization and the global flow of capital becomes the only option for many aspiring global cities willing to sacrifice their local development context for a globalized vision (Cooke and Lazzeretti 2008). The shift from creative city to media city, in other words, reflects a much deeper transition toward a neoliberal approach to the restructuring of the inner-city economy, one based not on culture as national identity building or expanded citizenship, but culture as an important segment of local economic sector.

Media clusters are based on a particular cultural economy model designed to accommodate a range of media production activities, including broadcasting, publishing, film, and digital media. The policy interest in developing media clusters is largely driven by innovation in local economic development agendas. Hence, there is a strong tendency for these to emerge in cities with a rapid growth of ICT technologies (Karlsson and Picard 2011).

There are three important characteristics of media industries which inform a significantly different cluster strategy compared to traditional industrial clusters. The first is media convergence. One of its most important features is its reliance on the convergence of multiple platforms/devices/and networks. Henry Jenkins (2006) defines convergence media as those companies involved in providing interactive media service enabled by a combination of computing, communications, and media content. These companies are now well-known global media empires—Google and Facebook, to name a couple—but also work a huge number of small and micro firms specializing in services that would be too expensive to produce in-house by the former. Media cluster development focuses on attracting anchor tenants in the form of global media corporations, which are then expected to bring trickle-down effects to smaller specialized firms in their nearby vicinity (Scott 2006). The second characteristic is project-based work. As these small firms form multiple temporary sub-contractual relationships with the big players through loosely bounded projects (Grabher 2002), face-to-face communication is essential in communicating the complex and intangible qualities involved in the work. Co-location provides the necessary condition for contextualizing inter-firm communication beyond the level of business transaction (Gu 2010). Third, despite the globalization of media production, creative conception is taking place increasingly at the local level. Examples of this include the co-production of films or the local production of global format television programs. Co-production based on the need for idea scouting happens not only in advanced media production cities (e.g., Vancouver's media clusters) (Barnes and Coe 2011) but also in media markets where understanding local tastes plays a significant role in marketing the product (such as global platform TV production in China).

Because of the highly complex nature of media production, media clusters tend to locate in major media markets with a well-established creative milieu, such as film in Hollywood, newspaper publishing in New York (Scott 2000), and advertising and other CIs in Soho, London (Pratt 2004). These clusters tend not to have clear geographical boundaries, and the ownership of property in the area is dispersed, though sometimes collectively managed by a diverse range of public and private stakeholders. Although media cluster identity in this case is shaped by the concentration of particular economic activities, "soft" values deriving from the broader creative milieu such as "cool," "creativity," and "bohemianism" are important too.

These "spontaneous" media clusters can only be found in global cities like London, New York, and Tokyo, demonstrating media's preference for specific nodal positions in the global market (Sassen 1991).

In the last decade, we have seen the emergence of top-down developed media clusters in second-tier cities. These initiatives range from agglomerations of smaller media companies in high-end refurbished industrial buildings (Ultimo, Sydney), through to highly capitalized regional initiatives (MediaCityUK). These media clusters seek to house large media conglomerates and to capitalize on a "core–peripheral" media industry ecosystem. These media cities may or may not have a concentration of media industries already in place. They try to start by directing investment into digital infrastructure with the aim of cultivating agglomeration. It is this top-down planned media cluster model that will be examined in the remainder of this chapter. In particular, I will look at Manchester and Shanghai, which, though very different in scale and history, represent similar approaches to the media city. The first represents a second-tier city struggling to acquire post-manufacturing industries and pinning its hopes on the CIs. The second represents a large de-industrializing city with an old-style, second-tier state media infrastructure, now positioned by a powerful local and national state to become a new global media capital.

A key issue concerning these planned media clusters is whether their primary aim is to attract global talent or create local jobs. Though some have suggested positive interaction between local labor markets and global media industries (e.g., Coe 2001), there is no guarantee that the presence of global media industries will lead to a specialized and diversified local market (Oakley 2006). Media industries present substantial differences in terms of their sociospatial preferences to other forms of locally based creative sectors. Markusen (2006) observed the very different needs of artists groups in comparison to the other occupational groups included in Florida's "creative class." Artist spaces are shaped in particular by a set of urban politics, including a strong policy commitment to artistic development within a community development context. Although many artist-creatives work for local media industries and tend to co-locate with these employing firms, their decision to remain often involves not only economic considerations but also the potential to engage in aesthetic and political urban transformations.

In contrast, media clusters may be less responsive to local creative milieus than other CIs (Montgomery 2005). Local CIs thrive in milieus that are about long-term trust and shared values between a large number of very small companies and freelancers; these values may not be shared by media industries operating on short-term contracts and across temporarily linked extra-local media markets (Oakley 2006). Thus, we cannot assume that globally integrated media industries can be easily translated into localities. Media industries are operating increasingly outside of national boundaries and are frequently more sensitive to changes in the global marketplace than they are to domestic conditions (Deuze 2007). Top-down planned media clusters in cities without the immediate connection to the global creative labor market face some serious challenges in attracting talent. Media clusters tend to concentrate in cities where there is already a well-formed creative milieu from which it can draw skilled workers. The success of media clusters is highly dependent upon existing labor market environment, without which the sustainability of the media cluster is highly questionable (Pratt 2008).

Nevertheless, media clusters are having an increasing impact on the local creative milieu as they come with high levels of investment and political-institutional heft. Given the significant size of the investment required to attract such global companies and their requisite personnel, cities may spare investments on the broad creative milieu and focus on flagship media cluster projects. Thus, there is a close correlation between media clusters and gentrification, one that works at much greater speeds and with higher levels of economic and political capital than those traditionally associated with arts-led gentrification (Novy and Colomb 2013). Media clusters, with their ability to produce compelling metrics around innovation, jobs, and wealth generation, and a whole range of real estate developers, technology vendors, global recruitment agencies, and security firms, are highly attractive politically. They are capable of creating new kinds of "creative tech" growth coalitions, through which gentrification moves up a few more notches.

MediaCityUK

MediaCityUK exemplifies three common media city characteristics. First, it has invested heavily in cutting-edge media technologies. The fast broadband connection, for example, gave frictionless connection between London and Manchester, allowing data-laden procedures such as CGI to be done online in real time. Cloud computing is another example of the technological facilities required of media clusters. Not only does this take up huge physical space on site, it costs a lot to maintain physical facilities, such as cooling systems. The spatial design of MediaCityUK was from the beginning shaped by a particular media sector—broadcasting in the form of the BBC. Since 2010, the BBC has moved half of its production from London to MediaCityUK. The TV studios, editing suites, and radio studios were all equipped based on the production needs of broadcasting firms, including large urban screens simultaneously broadcasting programs made in the Salford studio. Broadcasting plays such an important role in the country's CIs landscape that the media clusters tend to prioritize the needs of broadcasting industry over the rest of the CIs (Mould 2014).

The choice and development of MediaCityUK in Salford Quays was a textbook case of Florida's "creative class" vision, with the luxury waterfront apartments attracting those media professionals who like to mix "play" with "work." There are hotels, bars, and cafes catering to the social networking needs of those working here. The perception is very much that the auxiliary services required by the media industry need to be different from those offered by and for locals—from a Salford whose very name is a byword for social deprivation. Thus, these social amenities are provided on site as part of the real estate development. Peel Holdings, who own MediaCityUK, have sanitized the entire site by removing all mobile vendors from its precincts and employing security guards to patrol "public" areas in the media cluster in the manner of a shopping mall. Even without this enforced "exclusivity," the art installations, large urban screens, and landscapes send a clear message to the public that this is no place for cultural trespassers.

Manchester is not new to the idea of creative clusters. The Northern Quarter (NQ), located next to Manchester city center, is one of the first creative clusters in UK, developed organically over time. It gained a critical mass of small and micro-sized creative firms in its many redundant textile factories and warehouses and has been central to Manchester's regeneration narrative. The Creative Industries Development Service, operating as an intermediary between the creative sector and local government, was the first of its kind in the country (O'Connor and Gu 2010). The NQ is a vibrant creative milieu mainly because it is affordable and adaptable. The local cafes and restaurants contribute further to the buzz and help sustain a shared identity of creative firms nearby. There is a shared sense among these creative businesses that they need to give something back to the urban community as a whole.

MediaCityUK, in contrast, conveys an entirely different story. It feels like a business park rather than a creative cluster. Media firms' choice of relocation to MediaCityUK is predominantly based on commercial considerations—sub-contracting, projects, and social networking opportunities through co-location with global media firms like the BBC and ITV. There have been some attempts at generating synergies between the MediaCityUK and local CIs. The Greenhouse, for example, is an incubator aimed at attracting smaller firms in order to address the local talent issue.

However, rents (except the Greenhouse) are much higher in MediaCityUK than those at NQ. And the promises of local job creation by the MediaCityUK project have not been delivered, with only a fraction of new jobs (16 out of over 2000) going to the locals. A 2012 report found that the public-private partnership model has left the local council short of cash in maintaining other public services (Hollingshead 2012).

The development of MediaCityUK is driven clearly by the rhetoric of the BBC's relocation of some of its services from London to the North and has since attracted a disproportionate number of creative professionals to Manchester. Sheffield, Birmingham, and Cardiff have all since invested in media clusters copying Manchester. To sustain its competitiveness, Manchester has to prove that MediaCityUK has access to a local creative talent pool that is capable of supporting the kinds of media production required by organizations like the BBC. But the connections between project-based media employment and the spatially dispersed production networks on which these projects draw do not necessarily run through the immediate locality of the cluster. It is entirely possible that firms like the BBC may still prefer to use their off-site contractors in London rather than choosing partners nearby. These preferences arise less from spatial proximity than the trust across project-based networks, which takes a long time to build. In short, the geographical concentration of media production remains highly uncertain in its outcomes for local employment.

Even if there are synergies between local creative SMEs and those in MediaCityUK, the possibility of translating this into the shared urban regeneration agenda is questionable. The SMEs and freelancers thrive in the NQ because the creative cluster offers not only business opportunities but also protection from the financial pressure of the global economy. Local know-how is an essential survival strategy for these SMEs. The NQ, for them, represents a shared social and cultural set of aspirations and values, in which their commitment to maintaining a local presence is not based on purely commercial calculations. These values drove the sector in its earlier attempts to rejuvenate the derelict city center of Manchester and the wider image of the city. It was the success of these efforts that allowed the city to attract the BBC in the first place. The overly economic arguments for the MediaCityUK represent an abandonment of any wider cultural political agenda.

Media Clusters in Shanghai

Shanghai has the highest concentration of digital media production activities in China. It contributes to an annual growth of over 30% per annum, three times more than the rest of the CIs sectors. Key activities, including animation, game design, and digital publishing, are supported by a plethora of large global media corporations such as Alibaba and Tencent and tens of thousands of SMEs. Shanghai has over 10,000 firms registered under this category, leading the national average.

But the city lacks the affordable inner-city space to house large media complexes. Large media technology companies tend to cluster in government-run science and technology parks at the edge of the city. Media clusters like Zhangjiang Multimedia Park are almost cities on their own, with dedicated bus services, hospitals, and other public services. Homogenous provision of high-end technological facilities and incubators is aimed specifically at encouraging innovation in the digital media sector, entirely assessed on the number of patents it generates. Three of the largest gaming firms are based there, contributing to the 10 billion USD worth of revenue of the entire sector in 2007. These media clusters also tend to offer various "one-stop shop" facilities for media firms. In Zhangjiang, the co-location of the National Digital Publishing Centre and the Copyright Centre offers specialized advice to the firms within.

Media clusters can often be found around university campuses at the edge of the city. KIC is one of the largest, located in Yangpu district adjacent to the two elite universities—Tongji and Fudan University. These projects are large-scale top-down planned real estate developments with a specific urban imaginary—to become the next Silicon Valley with a focus on tech start-ups and entrepreneurship. These projects flourished in China under the national "mass innovation" policy. To copy Silicon Valley's media cluster model, residential buildings in KIC were named "lofts" with typically one-bedroom flats for young graduates starting businesses from their own bedrooms. Big media businesses such as Oracle have relocated near KIC to take advantage of the local talent pool.

In recent years, media clusters have mushroomed in the inner-city areas of Jing'an, Changning, and Xuhui District. The clusters in these more built-up areas tend to be smaller in scale but have a more significant impact on the geographies of cultural economy than the others. They may not have clearly defined boundaries, characterized by dispersed buildings composed of both purpose-built areas and adaptive uses. *Bridge8* in Luwan District was redeveloped from an old automobile manufacturing plant to be a creative cluster of seven buildings spread across both sides of Jianguo middle road. Because of the constraints of space, they are ideal for smaller creative firms through adaptive use. *Bridge8* initially targeted artists, fashion designers, and architecture design firms. But after just a few years in operation, the domination by digital media firms—including animation, advertising, digital publishing, and PR—became pronounced and started to have a definitive effect on its neighborhood.

The spatially transformative power of media clusters is telling of the significant role they play in shaping the new cultural economy in Shanghai. Here, the generative processes of media cluster can be summarized as, first, the emergence of new amenities based on the needs of those working in the media industry; second, the investment in real estate development exploiting the image capital of media cluster; third, the gradual replacement of cultural production activities by media specific production activities; and fourth, spiraling out of gentrification effects from the media cluster to the neighboring area.

The rise of property values in the area since the development of *Bridge8* has been significant. The rental price for a 10-sqm ground-floor shop/studio space in *Tianzifang*, a nearby creative cluster, has risen from 1,000 RMB per month in 2005 to about 50,000 per month in 2012. That's an increase of 50 times in 7 years! This growth is driven by the amenity service needs of media firms. These are mediated via expats working for global media corporations. Cafes and restaurants are given names such as "Asia Corner," "Kommune," and "Bohemia" to convey a sense of global cosmopolitanism. From "flat white" to "New York Burger," the imagined Soho media executive can find comfort in this "authentic" downtown media cluster.

The clustering of media businesses in *Bridge8* has further attracted smaller media firms to relocate in its neighborhood, including *Tianzifang*. Since as early as 1998, some residential buildings and small factories here have been used by artists as studios and exhibition spaces. The artists' conscious preservation of local lifestyle (including heritage-built forms) contributed to the experiential value of the area. The arrival of media firms attracted by this "cool" image of *Tianzifang* pushed up rents significantly, pricing out many art studios. And for gentrifiers, this presented a perfect opportunity for the adaptive use of heritage buildings. Art does not contribute sufficient direct income (in the form of tax and rental). Media, on the other hand, are much more desirable because of their "conventional" business activities and higher rental contributions.

The gradual emptying out of non-media cultural businesses in the area since as early as 2008 is one of many impacts of Shanghai's new media city policy. It confirms the geographical marginalization of less market-oriented creative activities in the formation of the new inner-city cultural economy. This could have a detrimental effect on the wider cultural economy upon which the media industry is dependent for new ideas and talent.

For other Chinese cities wanting to copy the media cluster model, some lessons can be learnt. Shanghai has one of the highest concentrations of digital media industries within China, one that is capable of sustaining the local real estate market growth. Many of the newly built media clusters elsewhere in China are mega real estate investment projects, mostly standing in isolation from the livelihood of the city. Suzhou, for instance, is building a mega media cluster worth over AUD 1.4 billion. The success of Shanghai's media cluster demonstrates the importance of a creative milieu in the feasibility of creating a media cluster, including the sense of place, culture, and history this milieu can bring. At the same time, the very existence of this local creative milieu is challenged by the dynamics of this highly capitalized global media economy. The gentrification process brought by media clusters bears unique Chinese modernization characteristics but can also be read generically as indicative of the problems around the popularization of media clusters globally.

Conclusion

From Manchester to Shanghai, the stories of media clusters are diverse but increasingly interconnected. Media is seen to be a high-growth, high-value sector of the CIs, and one with close connections to the wider digital economy and advanced business services. Thus, attracting these media industries is high on the local economic development agenda in post-industrial cities that see themselves as competing on a global playfield. It is a risky business, as the media industry is highly dependent on global media conglomerates; attracting these industries involves high capital costs but high returns for the winners.

Both Manchester and Shanghai are trying to promote media industries as components of the new inner-city cultural economy, linking both to global city competition and local economic development agendas. They have invested heavily in digital infrastructures in order to attract global media industries. Manchester has secured major players in the BBC, whilst Shanghai has China's largest concentration of digital media firms. As for local economic development, Manchester has a diverse local media creative industry that Shanghai does not but is keen to develop.

The animating vision of a creative city has clearly motivated these cities in their development of media clusters, but the demands involved in setting up such clusters frequently set them apart from, and can be disruptive of, the wider creative infrastructure and milieu. Investing in media clusters and their digital infrastructure can seem a direct route to successful creative city branding, but often diverts attention from the importance of the wider local creative milieu.

Manchester's grassroots CIs have much to contribute to the success of MediaCityUK. However, diverting investment from the broader CIs toward the narrow focus on "media" has had a powerful and negative impact on the local creative milieu. Similarly, Shanghai is recalibrating the city's many creative clusters to attract media firms and thus pushing less profitable cultural activities to the edge of the city. In summary, media clusters have contributed to a new round of urban gentrification, making the already fragile creative ecosystem even more unlikely to be sustained in the inner city.

Compared to other creative city approaches, it seems that the media cluster is tokenistic in addressing the role of culture in local economic development, the purported essence of the creative city approach. It demonstrates how the economic aspect often leads to a suppression rather than flourishing of the cultural value underpinning "creative cities." Support for networks of cultural producers which do not seem to promise immediate economic benefit is slipping down the agenda as the city conforms to a competitive global vision. Under such circumstances the difficult balance between the language of "creative" and "media," and between the cultural and the economic, disappears under "media cluster" development policy, which sees the language of the "creative city" as a remnant of cultural policies past.

References

Barnes, T. and N. Coe (2011) "Vancouver as Media Cluster: The Case of Video Games and Film/TV," in C. Karlsson and R. Picard (eds.) *Media Clusters: Spatial Agglomeration and Content Capabilities*, Cheltenham: Edward Elgar Publishing Inc., pp. 251–280.

Coe, N. (2001) "A Hybrid Agglomeration? The Development of a Satellite-Marshallian Industrial District in Vancouver's Film Industry," *Urban Studies*, 38(10), pp. 1753–1775.

Cook, G. and J. Johns (2011) "The Transformation of Broadcasting and Film in Manchester and Liverpool," in C. Karlsson and R. Picard (eds.) *Media Clusters: Spatial Agglomeration and Content Capabilities*, Cheltenham: Edward Elgar Publishing, pp. 161–198.

Cooke, P. and L. Lazzeretti (eds.) (2008) *Creative Cities, Cultural Clusters and Local Economic Development*, Cheltenham: Edward Elgar Publishing.

DCMS (1998) *Creative Industries: Mapping Document*, London: DCMS.

Deuze, M. (2007) *Media Work*, Cambridge, Malden, MA: Polity.

Dugmore, H. and J. Mavhungu (2011) "Media Industry Clustering in South Africa: Prospects for Economic Development and Spatial Reconfiguration," in C. Karlsson and R. Picard (eds.) *Media Clusters: Spatial Agglomeration and Content Capabilities*, Cheltenham: Edward Elgar Publishing, pp. 326–327.

Evans, G. (2009) "Creative Cities, Creative Spaces and Urban Policy," *Urban Studies*, 46(5–6), pp. 1003–1040.

Florida, R. (2002) *The Rise of the Creative Class*, New York: Basic Books.

Grabher, G. (2002) "Cool Projects, Boring Institutions: Temporary Collaboration in Social Context," *Regional Studies*, 36(3), pp. 205–214.

Gu, X. (2010) "Social Networks and Aesthetic Reflexivity in the Creative Industries," *Journal of International Communication*, 16(2), pp. 55–66.

Hesmondhalgh, D. (2013) *The Cultural Industries*, 3rd Edition, London: SAGE.

Hesmondhalgh, D. and S. Baker (2013) *Creative Labour: Media Work in Three Cultural Industries*, London: Routledge.

Hollingshead, I. (2012) "Media City: Can the BBC Save Salford?" *The Telegraph*, viewed June 1, 2017, www.telegraph.co.uk/culture/tvandradio/bbc/9031837/Media-City-Can-the-BBC-save-Salford.html.

Hoyler, M. and A. Watson, A. (2013) "Global Media Cities in Transnational Media Networks," *Tijdschrift Voor Economische en Sociale Geografie*, 104(1), pp. 90–108.

Jacobs, J. (1969) *The Economy of Cities*, New York: Vintage.

Jenkins, H. (2006) *Convergence Culture: Where Old and New Media Collide*, New York: NYU Press.

Karlsson, C. and R. Picard (eds.) (2011) *Media Clusters: Spatial Agglomeration and Content Capabilities*, Cheltenham: Edward Elgar Publishing.

Krätke, S. and Taylor, P. (2004) "A World Geography of Global Media Cities," *European Planning Studies*, 12(4), pp. 459–477.

Landry, C. and F. Bianchini (1995) *The Creative City*, London: Demos.

Markusen, A. (2006) "Urban Development and the Politics of a Creative Class: Evidence from a Study of Artists," *Environment and Planning A*, 38(10), pp. 1921–1940.

Montgomery, J. (2005) "Beware 'the Creative Class': Creativity and Wealth Creation Revisited," *Local Economy*, 20(4), pp. 337–343.

Mould, O. (2014) "Mediating the City: The Role of Planned Media Cities in the Geographies of Creative Industry Activity," in S. Conventz et al. (eds.) *Hub Cities in the Knowledge Economy: Seaports, Airports, Brainports*, London: Routledge, pp. 163–180.

Novy, J. and C. Colomb (2013) "Struggling for the Right to the (Creative) City in Berlin and Hamburg: New Urban Social Movements, New 'Spaces of Hope'?" *International Journal of Urban and Regional Research*, 37(5), pp. 1816–1838.

Oakley, K. (2006) "Include Us Out: Economic Development and Social Policy in the Creative Industries," *Cultural Trends*, 14(4), pp. 283–302.

O'Connor, J. and X. Gu (2010) "Developing a Creative Cluster in a Postindustrial City: CIDS and Manchester," *The Information Society*, 26(2), pp. 124–136.

Pratt, A. (2002) "Hot Jobs in Cool Places: The Material Cultures of New Media Product Spaces—The Case of South of the Market, San Francisco," *Information, Communication and Society*, 5(1), pp. 27–50.
— (2004) "Creative Clusters: Towards the Governance of the Creative Industries Production System?" *Media International Australia Incorporating Culture and Policy*, 112(1), pp. 50–66.
— (2008) "Creative Cities: The Cultural Industries and the Creative Class," *Geografiska annaler: Series B Human Geography*, 90(2), pp. 107–117.
Quinn, S. et al. (2003) "Tale of Three (Media) Cities," *Australian Studies in Journalism*, 12, pp. 129–149.
Sassen, S. (1991) *The Global City: New York, London, Tokyo*, Princeton, NJ: Princeton University Press.
Scott, A. J. (2000) *The Cultural Economy of Cities: Essays on the Geography of Image-Producing Industries*, London: SAGE.
— (2004) "Cultural-Products Industries and Urban Economic Development: Prospects for Growth and Market Contestation in Global Context," *Urban Affairs Review*, 39(4), pp. 461–490.
— (2006) "Creative Cities: Conceptual Issues and Policy Questions," *Journal of Urban Affairs*, 28(1), pp. 1–17.

Further Reading

Hoyler, M. and A. Watson (2013) "Global Media Cities in Transnational Media Networks," *Journal of Economic and Social Geography*, 104, pp. 90–108.
McQuire, S. (2017). *Geomedia: Networked Cities and the Future of Public Space*, Hoboken, NJ: John Wiley and Sons.
O'Connor, J. and X. Gu (2012) "Creative Industry Clusters in Shanghai: A Success Story?" *International Journal of Cultural Policy*, 20(1).

24
BRANDING, PROMOTION, AND THE TOURIST CITY

Deborah Stevenson

Introduction

Writing in the Australian daily newspaper, *The Sydney Morning Herald*, journalist Amy Croffey (2017) asked, "If you don't boast about your trip to Europe with carefully curated, incessant Instagram posts, are you even in Europe?" Indeed, it has become increasingly difficult to separate the experience and physicality of place—the "being there" of travel—from its representation. It is unsurprising, therefore, that tourism promoters use a range of media to brand and market their tourism "products", including the tourist city. From guidebooks to Instagram, photography to virtual reality, media imagery is central to tourism, prominent elements not only of specific tourism campaigns whereby selected images and stories of place are packaged for markets around the world, but also of everyday tourism experiences and expectations. With this entwining of image, space, and experience has come the redevelopment and reimaging of urban landscapes in ways specifically intended to attract tourists. The term urban tourism was coined originally to refer to the repackaging and promotion of deindustrializing cities but, increasingly, it has come to mean any concerted effort to brand a city as a tourist destination. Even "world cities', such as New York and London, are routinely marketed as places to visit. Importantly, what is being sold in city reimaging and promotion strategies are not just the physical spaces of the city, but also its symbolic spaces, including how the city feels and what it means (Ashworth and Voogd 1990).

The focus of this chapter is the interrelationship between cities, media, and tourism. It commences with a discussion of the image as a central element of tourism before considering the more recent forms of media and, in particular, social media which construct the tourist space and its experience. It then moves on to examine urban tourism and the features and elements that mark it as a specific form of tourism; important here are the practices and processes of city branding. Following Wearing et al. (2010: 111), the chapter assumes that travel and tourism (including that which is associated with the urban) are "mediated as much through the spaces of representation and imagination as it is through 'real' encounters and [. . .] co-presence in 'real' tourist space".

Image, Tourism, and Space

In his ground-breaking book *The Tourist Gaze* (1990), the British sociologist John Urry drew on Foucault's (1976) influential work on the "gaze" to trace the shifting relationship between the objects that tourists gaze upon and broader social and cultural processes. He argues that the consumption of sights is as important to the tourist experience as encounters with "real" places and people in "real" time. In this context, he suggests that images play a key role in the anticipation of travel and the selection of tourist destinations, as well as being potent memory triggers in the post-travel period, central elements of the construction of traveler recollections. The image encompasses the ephemeral, fleeting, and voyeuristic aspects of the tourist gaze as well as pointing to a predictable, commodified mass tourism experience (Wearing et al. 2010). In a subsequent work, co-authored with Carol Crawshaw, Urry further argues that not only are photographs shared with friends and family and serve as key markers (evidence) of having "been there", but images are part of the "language by which we learn to describe and appreciate the environment" (Crawshaw and Urry 1997: 183). They explain the travel/image nexus as follows:

> It is the visual images of places that give shape and meaning to the anticipation, experience and memories of travelling . . . Photographs provide evidence—that you have been away, that the mountains were that high, that the weather was so good. At home, afterwards, the visual images are interwoven with the verbal commentary to remember the experience and to tell others about it.
>
> *(1997: 179)*

In the decades since these works were published, the centrality of the image to the tourism experience as well as to tourism promotion and the discourses of place has intensified at the same time as becoming increasingly fragmented. And in this fragmentation and intensification, the notion and significance of the "at home" referred to in the passage above have been reconfigured.

Contemporary tourism and travel may continue to be framed through imagery, but the nature of this imagery and the ways in which it is consumed have considerably changed. Tourist experiences are now recounted and interpreted via a range of media, including journals, diaries, emails, blogs, and social media. Social media is particularly noteworthy because it is in this space, and utilizing a combination of words (spoken and written), images, and explanation, that the tourist simultaneously shares, and reflects on, the travel experience and the visited place. Through processes of sharing and reflection, the traveler interacts with both traveling and non-traveling others whilst in the travel space—they can "be socially present while physically absent" (White and White 2007: 89). In addition, travel destinations and experiences are filtered/mediated through an ongoing engagement with "home" during travel, and "away" whilst at home.

Media and communications spaces and technologies have thus reshaped the relationship between home and away, disrupting the established notions of space and time, presence and absence, that historically have been at the heart of travel and tourism. It is now increasingly difficult to find travel experiences and destinations that are untouched by media. Even those travelers, such as backpackers, who are often very assertive in demonstrating their difference/distance from mainstream tourism, routinely rely on tourism media, whether the more conventional guidebooks or locative apps and websites with users' reviews and recommendations (such as "Trip Advisor"), as they plan and negotiate their journeys and travel experiences (Rowe 2006). Tourism is no longer only about materiality and presence, but also about the consumption of signs and images, and mediated experiences that do not necessarily involve physical travel. Indeed, the departures that occur can be located in the imaginary, and the destination encountered as a space of the image/imagination rather than geography. The internet is not only "an indispensable source of travel-related information and phantasmagoria" as André Jansson (2018: 101) puts it, but, as he goes on to say, there has been:

a formidable explosion of social media platforms and mobile applications for navigation, accommodation (finding, rating and sharing), and the creation and circulation of images and other types of content.

The centrality of media and the technologies of communication to the experiences and processes of tourism and to shaping people's virtual experiences of travel led Scott Lash and John Urry in 1994 to canvass the "end of tourism", while others have talked about having entered a period of "post-tourism". According to Maxine Feifer (1985), post-tourism has three key dimensions:

1. The presence of technologies that make it is possible to "gaze" on, or consume, places without physically having to travel;
2. A surfeit of possible tourism experiences and available destinations resulting from the fragmentation of tourism;
3. An absence of "authentic" travel experiences which means the post-tourist is knowingly playing a game.

According to this schema, the post-tourist is mindful of the inauthenticity of travel destinations and their own travel experiences within these destinations (Feifer 1985)—they are "self distanced and conscious" (Arellano 2004: 70). Similarly, Chris Rojek (1993: 177) describes post-tourism as a game that is characterized by the commodification and consumption of signs, suggesting that the post-tourist is knowingly enthused by the intertextuality of the tourist space which is a playful mosaic of discourses where experience is valued as "an end in itself".

For many, the term post-tourism has become meaningless as even the most routine of travel experiences is now a highly mediated assemblage of places, people, and spaces. The virtual is not a space apart and the imaginary cannot be separated from the "real" (Wearing et al. 2010). But others, such as Jansson (2018: 1–3), suggest that the notion continues to be useful not as an empirical category, but as a conceptual tool for examining the "socio-cultural mechanisms through which the boundaries of tourism are challenged and re-negotiated". In seeking to trace these reconfigurations and the ways in which technology is shaping spatial practices and modes of spatial consumption under conditions of post-tourism, Jansson (2018) considers the phenomenon of "urban exploration" (UE), which is concerned with the hidden, off-limits parts of the city including derelict buildings and abandoned factories—the interstitial spaces of the city. He argues that urban exploration is particularly revealing because it is a set of tourism practices that is heavy reliant on media and, connecting with modes of social and cultural distinction, what emerges as important are the processes of negotiation that accompany decisions not about what to photograph, but about what images to share. UE is also a form of urban tourism that operates both physically and symbolically in opposition to the dominant form of contemporary urban tourism where representation, promotion, branding, and reimaging meld with curated experiences and the rehabilitation and reshaping of abandoned city space. In both cases, however, imagery and image sharing are central to framing the tourist city.

Tourism and the City

Cities are amongst the most visited places on earth. They are attractions and destinations in their own right as well as key entry and exit points for people in transit to other places. For many cities, tourism makes an almost incidental contribution to the local economy but, for others, particularly those second, often regional, cities that are struggling with the economic consequences of deindustrialization and depopulation, tourism is regarded as the key to economic recovery. To this end, local politicians and business interests in cities around the world are engaged in finding ways of raising the profile of their particular city in what has become a crowded global urban tourism marketplace. Indeed, there has been a proliferation of reimaging strategies that, attempting to mark (and market) cities as different, are designed to attract tourists, investment, and residents. The arts and culture are prominent in such strategies, along with special events, and the knowledge and innovation "industries". Often also involved is the wholesale redevelopment of rundown or abandoned city precincts (the hidden or "dark" spaces of urban exploration) and the building of leisure, cultural, and recreational facilities intended to attract visitors (Wearing et al. 2010). Sharing many spatial and representational features, urban tourism developments often adopt similar styles of architecture and are the sites of a predictable suite of facilities and commercial outlets. The result is that instead of making places that are unique and grounded in the local and idiosyncratic, too often these sites are anonymous, placeless, and serial—everywhere becomes anywhere.

Also central to many urban tourism strategies are special events and festivals. These events can be high profile and global in their scope, such as the Olympic Games or Football World Cup, but usually they are much smaller scale, including local music or community festivals. When discussing the use of a mega-event to transform a city's landscape and image, it is Barcelona and its staging of the Olympic Games in 1992 that is often cited as exemplary. Held in the context of considerable industrial decline and economic crisis, the Barcelona Olympics is credited with increasing local employment, improving public transport, opening the city up to the coast, and providing new and redeveloped urban facilities and infrastructure (Horne and Manzenreiter 2006). The Games also played a major part in establishing Barcelona as a leading tourism and conference destination and its experience influenced many non-"world" cities to bid to host the Olympics, although few host cities have successfully managed to be repositioned in quite the same way. Nevertheless, the Olympic Games is a brand and the Olympic City is branded through the staging of the event.

A consequence—indeed, often an overt aim—of the renewal associated with urban tourism is gentrification. Usually understood as the movement of the middle class into traditional working-class areas, gentrification occurs when property values rise and original (poorer) residents are forced to move to cheaper residential areas often on the fringes of the city. The rebuilding associated with urban renewal and reimaging routinely includes purpose-built up-market high-density housing alongside a suite of cultural and leisure facilities and, although these redevelopments are frequently on abandoned former industrial sites rather than in existing residential areas, the effects are often the same, with regeneration leading to increased property values and the gentrification of neighboring suburbs. In textbook processes of gentrification, artists (as the "vanguard of gentrification") are often the first to move into a low-income area because of the availability of affordable studio and residential spaces. Ironically, though, it is the presence of artists that makes the place desirable to the middle class and, in turn, leads to an increase in property values that means the area becomes unaffordable to the artists. This process is evident also in tourism-focused precinct redevelopments whereby artists often occupy the warehouses and former industrial buildings that become the objects of redevelopment. But with redevelopment, the artists are forced to move out and, although the cultural and creative industries are routinely included in such redevelopments, the focus is routinely on sanitized cultural spaces such as galleries, art and craft retail outlets, or the studios of architects and designers, for instance, rather than the (messy) spaces of traditional creative work and production (Stevenson 2018). In other words, artists will be physically displaced, but their work remains important. And of course, it is artists and creative workers who produce the imagery that is used to market the rebranded, reimagined city. Indeed, city "branding" and "visioning" are two highly significant inclusions in the vocabulary of contemporary urban tourism, along with the creation of a range of image-focused place-marketing exercises intended to "brand" the city as a specific destination.

Brands in the Landscape

An important element of place-marketing and urban tourism is city branding which is a complex of advertising, visions, and narratives, as well as catchy (official and unofficial) city slogans and mottos (Kavaratzis 2004), with "Glasgow's Miles Better", "I ♥ New York", "The City that Never Sleeps", and "City of Angels" being four city slogans, developed for very different purposes, that come readily to mind. A brand is both a statement and a promise. It is intended to be an instantly recognizable sign or marker of place and the experience of being in that place—to move reimagining beyond the functional to the imaginative and representational. A city brand(s) can be crafted to speak variously and sometimes simultaneously to a city's past, present, and future and is usually designed to highlight—summarize—those features and qualities of the city that supposedly are unique or special. Not surprisingly, developing a resonant city brand can be a fraught and often highly contentious process. Donald and Gammack (2007: 45) argue, for instance:

> that branding has entered . . . debates in an attempt to capture and shape the city as a product and knowable entity for residents and visitors. While brand creation and brand maintenance for goods and services have become an immensely sophisticated industry and set of practices, "destination" and—especially—"city" branding pose a yet more complex layer of challenge, identifications, and contradictions.

City branding is a process of inclusion and exclusion that privileges and highlights some aspects and ways of understanding a city at the same time as marginalizing others. Not only do some interests stand to benefit from city imaging and place-marketing at the expense of other interests, but various interests have different, often-incompatible, perceptions of "their city". The brand as well as the process and rationale for determining it are thus the outcomes of relative power. Even branding processes that are seemingly designed to engage with a broad range of local interests inevitably prioritize limited agenda and ways of seeing (Stevenson 1999). The emergence of city branding can be traced to the rise of neoliberalism and specifically to what has been called the "entrepreneurial city" (Hall and Hubbard 1998), whereby cities are increasingly run as businesses and the practices of business are applied to the processes of urban governance. It was the entrepreneurial approach to city governance that led to the techniques and methods of product marketing being applied to the promotion of the city. Indeed, Hubbard and Hall (1998: 8) acknowledge that:

> the manipulation of city images, cultures and experiences has become probably the most important part of the political armoury of urban governors and their coalition partners in the entrepreneurial era.

They go on to outline the contours of the generic model of entrepreneurial governance as being focused on city marketing, urban redevelopment, staging mega-events, the use of the arts and cultural industries, and of public–private partnerships (involving governments entering into an alliance with the private sector) as ways of attracting external investment and funding the infrastructure that (it is believed) will foster local economic development. With somewhat different emphasis, urban entrepreneurialism is also examined by David Harvey (1989) who foregrounds, in particular, the importance of (global) inter-urban competition for capital investment in city redevelopment and reimaging, and the reshaping of urban governance (Stevenson 2013).

The notion of city branding points to the manipulation of place image and city marketing strategies and the power of urban interests, as well as, increasingly, to the presence of brands in the landscape, and the term "brandscape" has been coined to refer to this proliferation of city brands and brand-related products (Sherry 1987). The brandscape is a highly interactive, three-dimensional space that simultaneously advertises products and marks/creates cityspace. Times Square in New York City is emblematic. It is awash with neon signs, billboards, and video screens which bombard the senses with advertisements for a raft of products and brands, such as Samsung, Coca Cola, Disney, and HSBC, as well as promotions for movie screenings, sporting events, and the latest Broadway shows. Times Square even advertises nations—for instance, in January 2011, to coincide with the visit of its President Hu Jintao to the United States, China arranged the high-repetition screening of a sixty-second promotional video on a series of billboard-size screens on Times Square. Described as a "public diplomacy campaign", the videos ran 300 times a day for about a month (Barron 2011). Street advertising is more important in marking and making this particular urban space than the buildings, roads, and footpaths which are rendered almost to the status of backdrop. Times Square is also an instantly recognizable marker of New York City and the focal point for many of the city's public celebrations including, most notably, the New Year's Eve countdown when the now-famous "New Year's Eve Ball" descends the flagpole at One Times Square.

For Anna Klingmann (2010), brandscapes are more than the proliferation of advertising signs and architecture is not simply a backdrop to the branding process. Signature buildings, for instance, are important elements of the branded landscape and frequently highly visible markers of corporate power. Klingmann explains that with the emergence of the "experience economy" in the 1990s, architecture moved away from being simply functional to being an expression of the identity of the building owner and, in turn, frequently a marker more broadly—as icon—of the city. Architecture, she suggests, spatializes the brand. Klingmann points to the importance of themed "brand" and "flagship brand" stores to this restructuring of the brand. She suggests that flagship stores, such as Niketown and Prada Epicenter, took the idea of the brand and translated it quite literally into an all-enveloping experience. People go to a flagship store for the experience as much as for the products on offer. They are destinations in their own right. The geography of the brandscape thus moves beyond function to being highly immersive. Brands mold ideas and experience; they can confer prestige or a particular type of status on both the consumer and the space.

So, as a central element of the branded landscape, the flagship store is not the neutral backdrop to, or support for, billboards and signs; rather, it is a sign in itself. While flagship stores can be explicitly branded with company logos or names, in many cases, such as the Prada Epicenters, the branded environment that is the flagship store does not actually involve the overt use of signs at all but relies instead on often subtle architectural and style codes. Such stores speak to the elegance, exclusivity, and sophistication of both the product and the consumer. The central notion here is that of the insider—those consumers with the cultural capital required to "read" the embedded codes and the economic capital to be able to shop there. According to Kozinets et al. (2002: 17), flagship brand stores have three distinguishing characteristics:

> First, they carry a single (usually established) brand of product. Second, that brand's manufacturer owns them. Finally, they are operated—at least in part—with the intention of building or reinforcing the image of the brand rather than operating to sell product at a profit.

They go on to suggest that with the flagship store, manufacturers are entering not only the retailing industry but also the "entertainment business". The contemporary brandscape, suggests Klingmann (2010), also includes the hotel industry. For instance, the W hotel chain uses architecture and design as part of a strategy to mark each of its hotels as unique—different in form and image from the generic "international" hotel. As explained on the hotel website:

> W was born and raised among the chaos and culture of NYC. Today W takes that 24/7 energy worldwide, bringing the best of Music, Fashion, Design and Fuel to coveted destinations around the globe.
>
> *(www.starwoodhotels.com/whotels/about/index.html, accessed November 2018)*

The performance of brandscaping combined with the global competitions that now exist between cities have been influential also in prompting the emergence of the celebrity architect. People, including Frank Gehry, Renzo Piano, and Zaha Hadid, among others, are serially engaged to produce signature, landmark buildings in cities around the world. Significant here is what has come to be known as the "Bilbao effect" or "Bilbao factor", which refer to the international trend that followed the opening in 1997 of the Frank Gehry-designed Guggenheim Museum in the provincial Spanish city of Bilbao. Built on a rundown former industrial site, the museum brought considerable prestige and economic benefits to the city, including an increase in tourism. It also led to the routine inclusion of a celebrity architect commission in many city branding and reimaging strategies. The rationale was that while very few cities will be selected as locations for a Guggenheim Museum, any city can have a signature building that has been designed by a "starchitect" (McNeill 2008). The cities of the Middle East, and Dubai in particular, stand out as emblematic of this trend but there are others. For instance, since becoming the capital of the post-Soviet nation of Kazakhstan in 1997, Astana has been the object of a highly ambitious program of city building and branding which includes the construction of a number of landmark buildings designed by leading architects, notably Norman Foster.

Celebrity architects bring to the brandscape recognizable built icons, something which is not in itself a new phenomenon, of course—the landmark Guggenheim Museum in New York City, for instance, which opened in 1959, was designed by renowned architect Frank Lloyd Wright—but the context in which signature architecture and the "starchitect" has emerged is very different. Architecture in the age of celebrity and the entrepreneurial tourist city is intended to put a signature to the brand as part of broader global processes of city imaging and inter-urban competition. With brandscaping, however, also comes the risk of seriality and predictability. Twenty-first-century signature buildings may eventually homogenize cityscapes, just as Starbucks or McDonalds and other brand and flagship stores have done. There is a risk that replication will also adversely affect local business, economies, and cultures. Many have noted, for instance, the sameness of British High Streets which have come to be dominated by chain brand stores. Also important in this context is the staging of mega-events involving large-scale urban redevelopment, and the building of themed landscapes, such as waterfront developments, shopping malls, and landmark buildings intended to be central aspects of the built legacy of the event—and soundly enmeshed in the making of tourism space and the tourist experience.

Conclusion

The media are pivotal to shaping the ways in which people, including tourists, know and imagine the city. Images of cities are encountered in all forms of media including films, magazines, and newspapers as well as in literature, art, and maps. City life is frequently both celebrated and berated in the lyrics of popular songs from Gershwin to Rap. The media provides people who have never been to the "great" cities of the world, like New York, London, and Paris, with strong impressions of their physical and symbolic form. Cultural texts define the symbolic parameters of what is meant by the term "urban" and frame imagined urbanism and, in the context of travel, urban tourism as it is experienced, imagined, anticipated, and remembered. The media is now central to the promotion of the city as tourism destination. People know, engage with, and imagine the city through a range of media, just as tourism promotion and city branding are media phenomena.

Through a range of media forms and communication technologies, including the internet and mobile phones, tourists are able to remain in contact with people outside the tourism space. They also use technology to narrate and receive feedback on their experience and interpretation of travel. The travel narrative that was once assembled through the writing of a personal journal over the course of a journey away from home is for many now framed in the immediacy of the virtual. Images, too, which are central to the construction of the identity of both the traveler and the destination, are shared instantaneously with those "at home" not as *aides-mémoires* for the telling of travel stories or as part of an overarching reflection on a journey, but as interactive commentaries on the "now" of the tourism moment. For some, emerging technologies are framing the contemporary traveler as "post-tourist". For others, they are the latest influence in the negotiation of travel and the experiences of place and identity that construct and define it. What are being challenged and reconfigured are the time-honored dichotomies or dualisms of tourism discourse—home/away, tourist/traveler, self/other, host/guest, being there/getting there, real/imagined. It is in this context that urban tourism must be understood. It is a space of image and imagination, of experiences and places that are mediated and remediated, and of cultures that speak to themes and expectations that are global.

Acknowledgment

An earlier version of sections of this chapter was published in D. Stevenson (2013) *The City*, Cambridge, UK and Malden, MA: Polity.

References

Arellano, A. (2004) "Bodies, Spirits, and Incas: Performing Machu Picchu", in M. Sheller and J. Urry (eds.) *Tourism Mobilities: Place to Place, Places in Play*, London and New York: Routledge, pp. 67–77.

Ashworth, G. and Voogd, H. (1990) *Selling the City: Marketing Approaches in Public Sector Urban Planning*, London: Belhaven.

Barron, J. (2011) "China's Publicity Ads Arrive in Times Square", in *The New York Times*, 18 January, http://cityroom.blogs.nytimes.com/2011/01/18/chinas-publicity-ads-arrive-in-times-square (accessed April 2011).

Crawshaw, C. and Urry, J. (1997) "Tourism and the Photographic Eye", in C. Rojek and J. Urry (eds.) *Touring Cultures: Transformations of Travel and Theory*, London: Routledge.

Croffey, A. (2017) "If You Don't Boast About Your Trip on Instagram, Are You Even in Europe?", in *The Sydney Morning Herald*, 23 July, www.smh.com.au/lifestyle/celebrity/yes-we-know-you-are-in-europe-20170717-gxcwbc.html (accessed 23 July 2017).

Feifer, M. (1985) *Tourism in History: From Imperial Rome to the Present*, New York: Stern and Day.

Foucault, M. (1976) *The Birth of the Clinic*, London: Tavistock.

Donald, S. and Gammack, J. (2007) *Tourism and the Branded City: Film and Identity on the Pacific Rim*, Aldershot, UK: Ashgate.

Harvey, D. (1989) "From Managerialism to Entrepreneurialism: The Transformation in Urban Governance in Late Capitalism", *Geografiska Annaler. Series B, Human Geography*, 71(1), pp. 3–17.

Horne, J. and Manzenreiter, W. (2006) "An Introduction to the Sociology of Sports Mega-Events", *The Sociological Review*, 54(s2), pp. 1–24.
Hubbard, P. and Hall, T. (1998) "The Entrepreneurial City and the 'New Urban Politics'", in T. Hall and P. Hubbard (eds.) *The Entrepreneurial City: Geographies of Politics, Regime and Representation*, Chichester: John Wiley and Sons.
Jansson, A. (2018) "Rethinking Post-Tourism in the Age of Social Media", *Annals of Tourism Research*, 69, pp. 101–110.
Kavaratzis, M. (2004) "From City Marketing to City Branding: Towards a Theoretical Framework for Developing City Brands", *Place Branding*, 1(1), pp. 58–73.
Klingmann, A. (2010) *Brandscapes: Architecture in the Experience Economy*, Cambridge, MA: MIT Press.
Kozinets, R., Sherry, J., DeBerry-Spence, B., Duhachek, A., Nuttavuthisit, K. and Storm, D. (2002) "Themed Flagship Brand Stores in the New Millennium: Theory, Practice, Prospects", *Journal of Retailing*, 78(1), pp. 17–29.
Lash, S. and Urry, J. (1994) *Economies of Signs and Space*, London: Sage.
Law, C. (1992) "Urban Tourism and Its Contribution to Economic Regeneration", *Urban Studies*, 29, pp. 599–618.
McNeill, D. (2008) *The Global Architect: Firms, Fame and Urban Form*, New York: Routledge.
Rojek, C. (1993) *Ways of Escape: Modern Transformations in Leisure and Travel*, London: Macmillan.
Rowe, D. (2006) "Leisure, Mass Communications and Media", in C. Rojek, S. Shaw, and A. Veal (eds.) *A Handbook of Leisure Studies*, Houndmills, UK and New York: Palgrave Macmillan, pp. 317–331.
Sherry, J. (1987) "Cereal Monogamy: Brand Loyalty as Secular Ritual in Consumer Culture", paper presented at 17th Annual Conference of the Association for Consumer Research, Toronto, Canada.
Stevenson, D. (1999) "Reflections of a 'Great Port City': The Case of Newcastle, Australia", *Environment and Planning D: Society and Space*, 17(1), pp. 105–121.
Stevenson, D. (2013) *The City*, Cambridge, UK and Malden, MA: Polity.
Stevenson, D. (2018) "The Unfashionable Cultural Worker: Considering the Demography and Practice of Artists in Greater Western Sydney', *The International Journal of Cultural Policy*, www.tandfonline.com/doi/abs/10.1080/10286632.2018.1436168?journalCode=gcul20.
Urry, J. (1990) *The Tourist Gaze*, London: Sage.
Wearing, S., Stevenson, D. and Young, T. (2010) *Tourist Cultures: Identity, Place and the Traveller*, London: Sage.
White, N. and White, P. (2007) "Home and Away: Tourists in a Connected World", *Annals of Tourism Research*, 31(1), pp. 834–851.

Further Reading

Law, C. (1992) "Urban Tourism and Its Contribution to Economic Regeneration", *Urban Studies*, 29, pp. 599–618.
Rojek, C. and Urry, J. (eds.) (2002) *Touring Cultures: Transformations of Travel and Theory*, London; New York: Routledge.
Rowe, D. and Stevenson, D. (1994) "'Provincial Paradise': Urban Tourism and City Imaging Outside the Metropolis", *Australian and New Zealand Journal of Sociology*, 30(2), pp. 178–194.

25
"EUROPEAN CAPITAL OF CULTURE" AND THE PRIMACY OF CULTURAL INFRASTRUCTURE IN POST-INDUSTRIAL URBANISM

Peter Campbell and Dave O'Brien

Introduction

In the final quarter of the 20th century, theorizing around the emergence and importance of a "new economy," central to "post-industrial" cities and regions, flourished. In many versions of this theorizing, an emphasis was placed on the key role that cultural, artistic practice could play in creating value in these new economic times. Although the urban environment has long functioned as a catalyst for myriad forms of cultural activity, the idea that culture has come to occupy a place "at the very centre of urban development" (García 2004: 313) has become ever more prominent. It is increasingly held that the successful city of the 21st century is one that employs policies that explicitly work toward providing a strong cultural offering, and one that values and promotes "creativity" in some form.

This chapter examines how one example of a cross-national political project, the European Capital of Culture (formerly "City of Culture," henceforth "ECoC") competition, emerges and develops in this time period. This competition is perhaps the most prominent and successful of the now global "capitals of culture" movement, which has proliferated in recent years (Green 2017: 7). Currently, there are two ECoC host nations each year, with a selection panel judging potentially successful locations within these nations against criteria including artistic content, capacity to deliver, and the "European dimension" of their prospective cultural program (Green 2017: 29). Subject to assessment during the planning phase, the EU will award hosts €1.5m, but recent host cities generally see total program budgets over €20m, with some budgets in excess of €100m (Green 2017: 32). The ECoC is used here as an example of the shifting position of cultural policy within the contemporary city, which develops alongside transformations in the meaning and uses of culture within cities. In order to substantiate these contentions, the chapter considers both the development of the manner in which this program narrates and mediates the role for culture within the city, and how the program exists as a technology to implement this role. As the "capital of culture" model has been adopted in some form across the globe, the title is considered here as the most prominent example of an international trend toward cultural policies that aim to leverage artistic and/or "creative" practice to deal in part with the challenges presented by post-industrial cities. These challenges, to which we refer throughout the chapter, refer to, since the late 1960s, the rise of unemployment and the relocation of industry away from Western cities; urban inequalities associated with social policy questions of housing, education, health, and crime; and depopulation. Although Western cities have reversed trends such as depopulation, the other challenges we note have remained. There has yet to be a single urban policy to fix these issues, and this is the context in which to understand the turn to culture-led approaches.

Although cultural investment such as the ECoC has become a somewhat common tool in attempts to achieve urban transformation in recent decades (and continues to be so), it should be noted that as the urban environment changes, so too does the role which such investment is deemed to play. We can, therefore, trace the development of contrasting "models" for the ECoC title and as such, a change in the outcomes expected from such interventions. Thus, it is necessary to examine how the title serves to mediate not only *specific* cities, but also the idea of "the city" itself and, in so doing, how the ECoC plays a part in augmenting a range of discourses and practices regarding the nature of culture within specific cities, and "the city." By setting out the possibilities that have been attached to the ECoC, we outline the emerging dominance of a narrative around the primacy of cultural infrastructure in post-industrial urbanism. In particular, we consider the developing role of creative and media industries within these emergent ECoC models.

Using the ECoC to exemplify the way in which narratives aligning cultural festivals with post-industrial urban success emerge and proliferate, with a focus on the juncture between creative, communicative activity, and the cultural festival, allows us to conclude with some notes of caution on the potential success of cultural program such as the ECoC. This is particularly the case if they are too readily understood in terms of the role culture may play in "the city," generally speaking, as opposed to specific cities with specific histories and locations, and caution too about the all-too-easy possibility of confusing evidence of a successful *narrative* around the role of culture with evidence of success in the actual *outcomes* from such cultural interventions.

From European Identity to Urban Regeneration

Interestingly, given its later implementation, dominant accounts of the "pre-history" of the ECoC narrate an underlying intention to formulate a program that could augment and counterbalance a European community (EC) excessively focused on economic matters. Gold and Gold note "no specific provision for culture" in the 1957 Treaty of Rome, which established the European Economic Community, followed later by an emphasis at the 1969 Hague Summit, which agreed on the enlargement of the Community, on Europe's "exceptional culture" that "needed preserving" (2005: 221). Mittag (2012: 40) notes how such a position was built on during the 1970s in the Document on European Identity and the Tindemans report considering the nature of European integration, arguing that at this point in time, culture was increasingly considered at the European level as a means of fostering and strengthening a common European identity, and broader support for transnational integration. In the prevailing climate of economic recession and stagnation, Mittag also notes a tendency toward negative perceptions of the EC by the early 1980s, and the proposal for the ECoC comes at this point as part of an overall push toward "relaunching" the European project (Gold and Gold 2005: 222), conceived by many as a means of giving it a "human face" (Bullen 2013: 19). At this time, then, the foundations for the ECoC are broadly based around communicating and strengthening a common European identity and, thus, providing a counterpoint to the often-problematic economic relations between European nations; at the same time as the ECoC is being proposed, contemporaneous discussion can be seen to be questioning the future of the EC (as was), and its ability to deal effectively with fundamental social and economic issues in member states. After the failure of the 1983 Athens Summit, for instance, the EC is seen by some to be "in a blind alley" (Hrbek 1984: 3).

Broadly speaking, the use of culture as a tool for communication within and between cities at an international level is a thread that runs through the justification for the ECoC award since this point of its inception in the early 1980s, with the variety of cities and cultures to be celebrated reflecting the subsequent European Union motto of *"In Varietate Concordia"* ("United in Diversity") (Although initially an EC initiative in the 1980s, the ECoC was formally adopted as an EU program in the 1990s [Green 2017: 29]). However, the means by which the particular unifying character of the ECoC title is understood have changed over time, and achievements of the title have similarly been understood in varying ways. Thus, it is important to separate the multiple meanings and uses of this cultural program as it coincides, or otherwise, with post-industrial urban policy. In the initial stages of the competition, for instance, the influence of the "pre-history" traced briefly above can clearly be seen. The first cities to host the ECoC program, beginning with Athens in 1985, were all prominent cultural centers, with international reputations in the field of culture, and so this initial phase can be seen as something of a "celebration" of European culture (cf. Connolly 2013: 168), with an underlying theme of attempting to communicate a unifying sense of "European-ness" beyond the specific cities and nations hosting the title. In these early stages, cities were tasked with acting as a "beacon" to communicate what a "European" city is, could, or should be. Whilst this project was aligned to the wider European project of economic and political integration, and whilst investment was made by the initial host cities, these cities all had significant and visible existing cultural reputations and associated tourist infrastructures outside of the ECoC competition; indeed Gold and Gold note the low budget for the 1989 Paris ECoC and also the fact that as it was "subsumed into the bicentennial celebrations of the French Revolution," it lacked significant visibility as a European event (2005: 225).

However, as has now become an often-told story, as the ECoC arrived in the UK for the first time in 1990, the selection of the city of Glasgow as host in an internal national competition marked a new era for the ECoC. Glasgow's tenure sees the emergence of a persistent discourse around a new "model"—the "Glasgow model"—for using culture to "regenerate" a city facing significant challenges in the post-industrial era. García (2004: 320) notes the *dual* aspects of this model in terms of the issues at hand here: "Glasgow 1990 transformed perceptions not only of the city but also of the ECoC programme." This transformation takes a number of forms, but its legacy clearly persists in the operation of the ECoC from this point on, in a turn toward a focus on city marketing, image transformation, the promotion of tourism, attracting external investment, the renewal of cultural infrastructure, and so on (cf. García 2004; Mittag 2012). The official European Commission assessment of this turning point in the ECoC program and the effects it is said to have had is worth considering at length:

> Glasgow 1990 is deemed to have rejuvenated a city suffering from urban decay, heavy unemployment and a reputation for street crime, with many positive after-effects on the creative scene and a radical boost to its international image. Not only do cafés fill its streets on sunny days, but it is now considered a major cultural tourism destination. Antwerp 1993, too, had interesting after-shocks: it helped to challenge some of the extremist political tendencies that were emerging there. Key restoration projects were initiated, cultural projects launched and the city has now become synonymous with creativity.
>
> *(European Commission 2009: 5)*

By a position such as the above, the uses to which cultural programs can be put in dealing with the difficulties of post-industrial urban transformation are varied indeed. What is certainly true is that there is a shift here from celebrating established cultural centers to promoting the development of cultural capacity, with a clear focus on the potential economic results this may have (albeit not *exclusively* on such economic factors). This model is increasingly in evidence throughout the 1990s (Labrianidis and Deffner 2000: 32).

Work reflecting on the role the ECoC is deemed to play in the early 21st century continues to focus on factors aligned with urban "regeneration," conceived in myriad ways, with many noting the interplay between cultural, social, and economic goals (e.g., Bergsgard and Vassenden 2011; Bullen 2013; Connolly 2013). In a report on the preparation for the country's second hosting of the ECoC, for instance, the UK government's Department for Culture, Media and Sport explains that:

> The purpose of the title is not simply to highlight existing cultural excellence, but to encourage cities to develop and innovate in the cultural field. It will be an opportunity to show that culture is central to the life of a city, and demonstrate its contribution to regeneration, social inclusion, education and business. In addition, the European Capitals of Culture scheme aims to foster European cultural co-operation and understanding.
>
> *(2003: 2)*

However, it should be noted that whilst the notion is of the communication of a shared European identity, and, thus, some emphasis on the international links of the cities hosting the award, the reality "on the ground" is often one in which such communication becomes somewhat opaque. Sassatelli (2002: 444) notes how, even in 2000 when nine cities held the title simultaneously and such linkages could be made more explicitly and directly across nations, "Europe is not so much an issue, the real focus of attention is on the specificity of the city itself and on big events, regardless of their having a European dimension or not." This "falling away" of initial aims of augmenting the non-economic side of European integration in favor of a consideration of local practice in the host city and how the desired "regenerative" outcomes of cultural practice, European or not, can be leveraged seemingly intensifies as the 2000s continue. Lähdesmäki (2014: 193) emphasizes the wide range of scholarship which identifies an absence of the "European dimension" to cultural programs and, specifically, that evaluations of the 2007 and 2008 programs note this as "the least emphasized aim," a point emphasized in Bullen's work considering the place of communication between cultures in the 2008 case:

> In Liverpool much rhetoric was initially linked to a model of multiculturalism and intercultural dialogue. But this was soon deemed not to fit with the "world-class" aspirations of the city elite. We see a shift to a more mainstream understanding of culture, with cultural policy positioned as subject to the economic regeneration policies of the city.
>
> *(2013: 84)*

Creative Industries in Creative Cities?

As we move toward the 2010s, then, in concert with broader economic regeneration theories and policies, we can see cities bidding for and hosting the ECoC being more explicit about the ways in which they expect the program to be of specifically economic benefit, and, more precisely, to assist in the development of the "creative industries," seen by many to be central to economic prosperity in post-industrial cities. Thus, in this period, we see references to the ECoC being "used as a shaper of creative economies" (Comunian et al. 2010: 7).

The success of Liverpool's bid for hosting mentioned above, for instance, was in part justified on the benefit to these creative industries (albeit unusually defined, cf. Connolly 2013), and the subsequent expansion within the UK of a *national* City of Culture competition was partly justified using a narrative of a successful impact on creative industries being achieved (Campbell 2011), with other ECoCs also expressing a desire to replicate a "Liverpool model." This desire to use the ECoC to diversify and develop the urban economy can also be seen in the other 2008 host city of Stavanger (Bergsgard and Vassenden 2011) and, although focused more on a region than a single city, we see claims subsequent to this that RUHR.2010 was to be "the first European Capital of Culture to integrate the creative industries in its overall concept" and a focus on creative industries persisted in the bid documents for subsequent cities such as Riga 2014, San Sebastián 2016, and Valletta 2018 (García and Cox 2013: 60–61).

This represents the current iteration of policy orientation toward both ECoC specifically, and urban cultural interventions more generally. Whilst much of the fever associated with creative industries can be traced to the influence of narratives of the need to attract or retain a "creative class" within post-industrial cities (Florida 2002), the engagement with creative industries as a new economic driver is motivated by a wider set of factors. Whilst the UK was the site of a new "model" for utilizing the ECoC, the UK has also been influential in its position and policies regarding creative industries. As these have spread, so too has a conflation and confusion between the sorts of urban spaces governmental cultural policy is capable of creating and supporting (e.g., the gallery or the museum); the vision of the uses of these spaces to attract and retain a specific demographic of artist, performer, and cultural worker; and the actual location of a major part of the economic growth associated with "creative industries" in those subsets of IT and computer services workers that are less interested in traditional cultural venues and practices than are the rest of the cultural workforce (O'Brien et al. 2016; Campbell et al. 2018). The conception of the ECoC as a catalyst or driver for creative industries sits within a broader trend toward the development of "creative cities," and can be used to reinforce the same conflation that underpins this trend.

Despite these tensions and conflations, by the mid-noughties, Schlesinger (2007: 377) had identified creativity as a hegemonic term "in an increasingly elaborated framework of policy ideas," and in work toward the end of the decade, identified how the creativity game leveraged by competitions such as ECoC was increasingly one that cities were compelled to play regardless of the problems it presented:

> the terms of the discourse may become so compelling that *not* to buy into these is tantamount to self-exclusion . . . This is demonstrably the case in the debate over "creativity" that has dominated thinking about the cultural industries for more than a decade in the United Kingdom and that has increasingly been exported elsewhere by its exponents.
>
> *(Schlesinger 2009: 5)*

Thus, culture and creativity in the post-industrial city become almost "compulsory." The hegemonic status of creativity is not just concerned with bidding to stage festivals or improve or develop creative industries. Rather, cities are now tasked with narrating themselves as creative in a broad-ranging, generalized sense to attract a creative class to live, work, and pay taxes in the creative places and spaces constituting the contemporary European urban settlement. In theory, as Schlesinger (2007) and many others (e.g., Garnham 2005; Oakley 2014; O'Brien 2014) have pointed out, creativity can in theory be open to all, applicable in any site. This perhaps accounts in part for its continuation. Many aspects of our lives, and many aspects of any city, could conceivably be framed as "creative" ones. However, what this apparent universality hides is the inevitable hierarchies in the practices with which creativity is most often aligned; for instance, culture and the arts, with the inevitable hierarchies and contestations over value and worth; or urban regeneration, with explicit winners and losers in terms of property, capital, and residents.

Just as the ECoC mediates specific cities as well as the idea of "the city" in the abstract, so it is useful to consider how the role for such festivals and culture more broadly is itself mediated. The rise of creative industries has been closely aligned with specific modes of evidence-making. Models constructed and developed by social science assist in sustaining the hegemonic discourse aligning cultural festivals with urban regeneration interventions and creative industry policy noted above. Again, this issue in part returns to Florida (2002), with his urban economics argument as to the benefits of a "creative class" for a city. It is also underpinned by narratives of economic success of ECoCs in Glasgow and Liverpool that have jumbled the economic impact of a specific set of regeneration plans, property development, EU structural and regional support funds, and a pre-financial crash moment of public sector investment. In Liverpool, this moment was buttressed by the cultural and sporting infrastructure, which provided a strong tourist offer as well as an attraction to potential investors. The "£800m" case created from Liverpool (Campbell and O'Brien 2017), reliant as it was on an almost unique confluence of circumstances, was wrapped up with creative industries policy so as to be both the blueprint, along with the evidence-based policy case, for ECoC interventions elsewhere. However, the ability of current research practices to demonstrate the effects of cultural programs such as this remains open to question (Campbell et al. 2017).

ECoC—A Cultural Policy for the Creative City?

The "evidence bases" collected around the ECoC assist in the conflation of the cultural festival with urban regeneration interventions with creative industry policies. In the post-industrial society, there is, thus, a core tension between the most recent "creative industry" strands of the ECoC and the broader "cultural" focus of the initial driver of pan-European community building. This tension, and the concurrent conflation, is mediated by both the faith in the economic benefits of creative industries for economic growth and employment, alongside the research data, taken out of context, to support this belief. The latter is the "£800m" case that has now embedded itself in British discourses of cultural festivals and is likely to move beyond that context in conjunction with the UK's export of creative industries discourse (O'Brien 2015; Campbell et al. 2017; Campbell and O'Brien 2017). Indeed, although subsequent ECoC host cities have tended to be more cautious in assertions recording the economic benefits likely to accrue from the award, the stress on new forms of urban economy, particularly through creative industries, remains.

There is a particular irony at the current point in time. As the above account attests, it seems that key changes in the operation or understanding of the ECoC have been driven, or intensified, by the two occasions on which the program has been held in the UK. The UK, or at least large sections of British politics and media, now seeks to turn its back on a common European identity by leaving the European Union and repudiating the European narrative associated with the EU (May 2017). Two of the cities bidding to host ECoC 2023, Milton Keynes and Nottingham, are home to populations of which a majority voted for leaving the EU. Ironic, given the explicit European community-building elements of the original ECoC iteration, but also in keeping with previous uses of the event where the "European" elements have been side-lined in favor of more local celebration and the inevitable economic dimensions. Thus, this ECoC risks being starkly detached from lived experience in these cities. We may well look at patterns of cultural engagement, though, and ask to what extent a cultural festival such as the ECoC is inherently susceptible to being an elite project, at a distance from those making everyday cultures, whether as consumers or producers, in European cities.

Whilst the creativity discourse may be framed as a way to break apart such cultural hierarchies, similar social hierarchies are reflected in the reality of work in the creative industries. In particular, the mode of organization of many creative labor forces still privileges the same middle-origin, white, well-educated men who are a core audience for "elite" or "high" culture (O'Brien et al. 2016; Oakley et al. 2017). This structure is underpinned by working conditions, commissioning assumptions, and broader forms of firm and institutional organization that act to exclude those from outside of the cultural sector's "somatic norm" (Saha 2013; Conor et al. 2015; Yuen 2016; O'Brien and Friedman 2017).

Despite the potential for a form of cultural democracy (Hanquinet 2017) to come via creative industries' broader understanding of culture, then, the structure of these areas of economic and social life mitigates against a truly transformative impact on a host city without any activity in this area being part of a broader-reaching set of interventions or transformations. The economic growth associated with creativity is primarily evidenced through activities that have little "cultural" connotations, for example via the design of databases or through software consultancy (Campbell 2014). Even those sectors with large economic benefits that do draw on cultural activity are either not the type of sector a city would base a bid or a festival upon, for example advertising, marketing, and PR, or have specific cluster effects that are hard to replicate outside of existing centers, for example the film and television industries. *Development* of, and through, creative industries is, thus, a very tricky prospect for those places unable or unwilling to celebrate a creative city of advertising executives, or get into competition with Holly-, Nolly-, and Bolly-wood. Once the advantages of many of these industries have been established, the first movers have moved, and the centrifugal force of successful clusters results in unbalanced geographies of economic growth that are not easily rebalanced. The dominance of London over cultural production in Britain is the obvious example (Oakley et al. 2017).

Conclusion

What then is the place of an ECoC in a new Europe of mediated cities? As we have demonstrated, the ECoC has moved through various iterations, with equally varied forms and impacts on host cities. It may be appropriate to view it as a constructed and contested idea with a "social life" (Campbell et al. 2017). This social life has gone with the grain of other transformations in culture and cultural policy across Europe, notably the challenge to cultural hierarchy; the rise of urban regeneration; and, for now, the triumph of creative industries discourses.

To move to a conclusion, it is worth reflecting on the ironies of ECoC's pre-eminence within Europe's "second-order" urban settings. The project of a pan-European identity faces several strains, from the British decision to attempt to leave the EU, via the refugee crisis and post-crash economic problems, to the rise of far-right, explicitly anti-European, political movements in France and Germany. It is uncertain how an urban intervention designed to use culture to boost creative industries would speak to any of these issues. Indeed, the danger, given the inequalities associated with creative industries, would be the exacerbation of the social divisions reflected in the challenges confronting the EU.

This danger then is the test set for the future of ECoC, of how to build a festival in the mediated city that is open to all. Indeed, this is a particularly difficult problem as fragmented and mediated *cultures* in cities create (entirely justified) cosmopolitan demands for recognition and resources. If the original vision of ECoC was reflective of an elite narrative of culture, and the urban regeneration and creative industry approaches were open to similar critiques for their distance from host populations, an ECoC that lived up to the promise of such a cultural intervention would be one placing democracy—urban, cultural, and creative—at the center of its practice. However, at present, the policy imagination for such an intervention has yet to be realized. Here, perhaps, is also the place for future academic practice.

References

Bergsgard, N. A. and Vassenden, A. (2011) "The Legacy of Stavanger as Capital of Culture in Europe 2008: Watershed or Puff of Wind?" *International Journal of Cultural Policy*, 17(3), pp. 301–320.

Bullen, C. (2013) *European Capitals of Culture and Everyday Cultural Diversity: A Comparison of Liverpool (UK) and Marseille (France)*, Amsterdam: European Cultural Foundation.

Campbell, P. (2011) "Creative Industries in a European Capital of Culture," *International Journal of Cultural Policy*, 7(5), pp. 510–522.

Campbell, P. (2014) "Imaginary Success? The Contentious Ascendance of Creativity," *European Planning Studies*, 22(5), pp. 995–1009.

Campbell, P. and O'Brien, D. (2017) "Whatever Happened to the Liverpool Model? Urban Cultural Policy in the Era After Urban Regeneration" in M. Bevir, K. McKee, and P. Matthews (eds.) (2017) *Decentering Urban Governance*, London: Routledge, pp. 139–157.

Campbell, P., Cox, T., and O'Brien, D. (2017) "The Social Life of Measurement: How Methods Have Shaped the Idea of Culture in Urban Regeneration," *Journal of Cultural Economy*, 10(1), pp. 49–62.

Campbell, P., O'Brien, D., and Taylor, M. (2018) "Cultural Engagement and the Economic Performance of the Cultural and Creative Industries: An Occupational Critique," *Sociology*, 53(2), pp. 347–367.

Comunian, R., Chapain, C., and Clifton, N. (2010) "Location, Location, Location: Exploring the Complex Relationship between Creative Industries and Place," *Creative Industries Journal*, 3(1), pp. 5–10.

Connolly, M. G. (2013) "The 'Liverpool Model(s)': Cultural Planning, Liverpool and Capital of Culture 2008," *International Journal of Cultural Policy*, 19(2), pp. 162–181.

Conor, B., Gill, R., and Taylor, S. (2015) *Gender and Creative Labour*, London: Wiley-Blackwell.

Department for Culture, Media and Sport (2003) *Report on the Short-Listed Applications for the UK Nomination for European Capital of Culture 2008*, London: DCMS.

European Commission (2009) *European Capitals of Culture: The Road to Success. From 1985 to 2010*, Luxembourg: Office for Official Publications of the European Communities.

Florida, R. (2002) *The Rise of the Creative Class*, New York: Basic Books.

García, B. (2004) "Cultural Policy and Urban Regeneration in Western European Cities: Lessons from Experience, Prospects for the Future," *Local Economy*, 19(4), pp. 312–326.

García, B. and Cox, T. (2013) *European Capitals of Culture: Success Strategies and Long-Term Effects*, www.europarl.europa.eu/RegData/etudes/etudes/join/2013/513985/IPOL-CULT_ET(2013)513985_EN.pdf.

Garnham, N. (2005) "From Cultural to Creative Industries," *International Journal of Cultural Policy*, 11(1), pp. 15–29.

Gold, J. R. and Gold, M. M. (2005) *Cities of Culture: Staging International Festivals and the Urban Agenda, 1851–2000*, Aldershot: Ashgate.

Green, S. (2017) *Capitals of Culture: An Introductory Survey of a Worldwide Activity*, www.racines.ma/sites/default/files/Capitals%20of%20Culture%20An%20introductory%20survey%20%20Steve%20Green%20October%202017.pdf.

Hanquinet, L. (2017) "Inequalities: When Culture Becomes a Capital" in V. Durrer, T. Miller and D. O'Brien (eds.) *The Routledge Handbook of Global Cultural Policy*, London: Routledge, pp. 327–340.

Hrbek, R. (1984) "The Community of Ten after the Athens Summit," *Intereconomics*, 19(1), pp. 3–9.

KEA European Affairs (2006) *The Economy of Culture in Europe*, www.keanet.eu/ecoculture/studynew.pdf.

Labrianidis, L. and Deffner, A. (2000) "European Cities of Culture: Impacts in Economy, Culture and Theory" in P. Delladetsimas, V. Hastaoglou, C. Hatzimihalis, M. Mantouvalou, and D. Vaiou (eds.) *Towards a Radical Cultural Agenda for European Cities and Regions*, Thessaloniki: Kyriakidis.

Lähdesmäki, T. (2014) "Discourses of Europeanness in the Reception of the European Capital of Culture Events: The Case of Pécs 2010," *European Urban and Regional Studies*, 21(2), pp. 191–205.

Mittag, J. (2012) "The Changing Concept of the European Capitals of Culture: Between the Endorsement of European Identity and City Advertising" in K. K. Patel (ed.) *The Cultural Politics of Europe: European Capitals of Culture and European Union since the 1980s*, London: Routledge.

Oakley, K. (2014) "'Creativity Is for People—Arts for Posh People': Popular Culture and the UK's New Labour Government" in T. Miller (ed.) *Routledge Companion to Popular Culture*, New York: Routledge.

Oakley, K., Laurison, D., O'Brien, D. and Friedman, S. (2017) "Cultural Capital: Arts Graduates, Spatial Inequality, and London's Impact on Cultural Labor Markets," *American Behavioral Scientist*, 61(12), pp. 1510–1531.

O'Brien, D. (2014) *Cultural Policy*, London: Routledge.

— (2015) "Business as Usual: Creative Industries and the Specificity of the British state" in K. Oakley and J. O'Connor (eds.) *The Routledge Companion to the Cultural Industries*, London: Routledge, pp. 452–463.

O'Brien, D. and Friedman, S. (2017) "Resistance and Resignation: Responses to Typecasting in British Acting," *Cultural Sociology*, 11(3), pp. 359–376.

O'Brien, D., Laurison, D., Friedman, S., and Miles, A. (2016) "Are the Creative Industries Meritocratic?" *Cultural Trends*, 25(2), pp. 116–131.

Saha, A. (2013) "'Curry Tales': The Production of Race and Ethnicity in the Cultural Industries," *Ethnicities*, 13(6), pp. 818–837.

Sassatelli, M. (2002) "Imagined Europe: The Shaping of European Cultural Identity Through EU Cultural Policy," *European Journal of Social Theory*, 5(4), pp. 435–451.

Schlesinger, P. (2007) "Creativity: From Discourse to Doctrine?" *Screen*, 48(3), pp. 377–387.

— (2009) "Creativity and the Experts: New Labour, Think Tanks and the Policy Process," *The International Journal of Press/Politics*, 14(1), pp. 3–20.

Steiner, L., Frey, B. S., and Hotz, S. (2013) *European Capitals of Culture and Life Satisfaction*, www.crema-research.ch/papers/2013-07.pdf.

Yuen, N. (2016) *Reel Inequality: Hollywood Actors and Racism*, London: Rutgers University Press.

Further Reading

Campbell, P., Cox, T., and O'Brien, D. (2017) "The Social Life of Measurement: How Methods Have Shaped the Idea of Culture in Urban Regeneration," *Journal of Cultural Economy*, 10(1), pp. 49–62.

Frank, J. (2018) *Regenerating Regional Culture: A Study of the International Book Town Movement*, London: Palgrave Macmillan.

Mould, O. (2013) *Urban Subversion and the Creative City*, London: Routledge.

26
THE MEDIAT(IZAT)ION OF URBAN LEISURE

Screening the Event

David Rowe and Brett Hutchins

Introduction: Watching, Being, and Making the Event

Live events (meaning those involving co-present performers and audiences for specified periods) have long been an important feature of urban leisure. In modernity, cities developed specific enclosed spaces (such as concert halls, theatres, and sport stadia) in which performances could take place in response to the development of the culture and entertainment industries that "produced" leisure practiced by professionals before paying crowds, supplemented by ancillary commercial practices involving gambling, hospitality, and merchandising (Sayre and King 2003). Industrialism and capitalism, in creating the conditions for the precise calculation of labor time, also brought into being the notions of leisure and recreation as means of reproducing labor power (Clarke and Critcher 1985; Rojek 1985). These arrangements involved the rationing of real-time presence: crowds would assemble for special moments, enjoying the pleasures of the unique event and relishing the collective experience of "having been there" which could, in turn, be "traded" as the cultural capital associated with the aura of a never-to-be-repeated temporal-spatial-performative conjunction. This imperative of physical presence was especially powerful before the invention of electronic media, especially television, that could reproduce and transmit the experience (Rowe 2004). A specific mode of fan-based sociality emerged in which spectators self-consciously participated in the spectacles to which they were witnesses. In the case of sporting events, a particular kind of fandom was created. Their competitive framework created two or more "sides," meaning that the audience was interested not only in seeing their preferred sportspeople win, but also in active dialogue with their opposition within the audience, often leading to their segregation on grounds of public order.

This experience was very different from, for example, that of attending an event with a reproducible text, notably entailing exposure to already-prepared films or newsreels. The action was three- rather than two-dimensional, and the watched shared space with the watchers. However, the subsequent development of real-time mediation established an intimate relationship between the enclosed venue and the world beyond. The viewing at a distance made possible by live broadcasting, which brought the sights and sounds of the concert hall or stadium into the home, gave new, expanded access to the "action." Increasingly, mediation enhanced the viewing experience in ways that, via various angles, multispeed replays, close-ups, and so on, became in various ways superior to that of the in-venue spectator confined to a single viewing position and often with restricted sightlines (Dayan and Katz 1992). As a result, large screens were brought into the live venue as, ironically, compensation for being co-present in real-time and space (although, crucially, co-presence was still a source of "bragging rights"). Therefore, the history of live event broadcasting has involved the progressive refinement of mediated experience across and between cities, insinuating itself into the stadium, spillover areas, remote live sites, licensed premises, and private homes (Levy 2017).

This development, though, has been followed by another that is less dependent on fans being exposed to ever more sophisticated live broadcast texts. Just as fans created spectacles inside enclosed venues and, especially in sport, in moving to and from them, they have also come to possess the means of making their own live media texts. Continuing advances in hardware and software technologies position the smartphone as a key screen in the presentation and consumption of live and on-demand entertainment content (Goggin 2012). But sophisticated mobile cameras and computational photography and video recording applications (apps) also mean that live events are sites where mobile users can informally live stream or distribute content (Palmer 2014). In other words, the same devices that can receive professionally produced texts are also used by "amateurs" to make and disseminate them. These new practices of making media texts in and around live events by the people attending or, more precisely, attending *to* them have had significant consequences for urban leisure. It is now possible to engage in an unprecedented, real-time mass activity of "sharing." The few-to-many broadcast model still thrives (arguably, it is substantially responsible for the commercial survival of free-to-air and subscription television), but it is accompanied by peer-to-peer communication (fans sending messages to their significant others and friendship networks) and the many-to-many communication of uploading fan-generated texts made available to anyone via the Internet. This communicative apparatus enables whole, multi-point narratives of the fan experience to be created at, around, and at various distances from the event location (Hutchins and Rowe 2012).

This chapter analyzes the ways in which, in the 21st century, event-based urban leisure has developed into a set of multiply mediated practices that is highly dependent on access to a multitude of screen devices and uses. It is argued that mediation has evolved into a progressive *mediatization* whereby the event is shaped by the technologies and practices of its own representation (Hjarvard 2013). Therefore, media communication must now be understood not as a secondary process of relaying a primary event, but as an integral element of the urban event itself. Although any live performance is affected by these developments, we argue that they are most advanced in sporting contests, and several of the examples that we use draw on the experiences of sport in urban environments.

Event Mobilities

Live events necessarily involve high levels of mobility (Salazar et al. 2017). They require audiences of various sizes to assemble at a particular venue, where they will encounter performers who have also traveled there. In order to make the event possible, others will have to travel to the same place—the workers who service the event, police and security staff to control and monitor those attending, and the specialist media who are engaged in recording and covering it for a wider audience, most of whom cannot be present. The degree of mobility has expanded with the development of a global leisure and entertainment industry. Rock and pop musicians and athletes, especially, engage in global tours and tournaments, taking advantage of technological developments in travel—especially the jet airplane—to traverse the globe each year, stopping briefly in one city and country before moving on to the next. Elite performers have the largest supporting entourage, drawing in their wake a substantial media contingent supplemented by local journalists. This rolling cycle of mobile events requires sophisticated organization, and also has significant environmental consequences—for example, Toby Miller (2018) noted the vast expenditure of carbon-intensive energy on travel involved in global events like the FIFA World Cup, Formula 1, and the Olympic Games, while saturation media coverage demands a massive and largely hidden consumption of materials and electricity (Maxwell and Miller 2012).

A key aspect of live events is that they are rigorously scheduled. There is little or no opportunity for variation of agreed place and time. This strict limitation means that substantial live events are newsworthy in themselves because they have the potential to disrupt the orderly routines of cities (*International Journal of Cultural Policy* 2008; Sam and Hughson 2011). Large numbers of people pass along public and private transport corridors, patronize local establishments, and occupy public space. The subsequent creation of spectacle lends itself to formal media coverage—a standard component of broadcast news bulletins, for example, entails showing sport fans in bars and city squares, often performing by invitation for the cameras to express their impressions and sporting allegiances in the "costumes" of their various teams. In some cases, especially when involving association football, media coverage addresses the possibility and transpiration of disorder, usually involving physical confrontations between rival fan "firms" (Redhead 2015). Audiovisual footage of, and commentary on, these conflicts provides newsworthy material (often much replayed and frequently out of context as stock footage), sometimes verging on the exaggerated representation and projection of "moral panic" (Critcher 2003).

However, the subjects of these representations are not passive recipients of the media gaze. In the pre-digital era, they photographed and videoed each other and contributed to "fanzines" that often defiantly discussed their experiences and accused the authorities, media organizations, and "moral entrepreneurs" of bias, exaggeration, and misrepresentation (Haynes 1995). In Britain during the last century, this reaction to media coverage—and what was regarded as the demonization of football fans—even produced a "hit and tell" literary genre (Redhead 2015), while one notable academic work (among many dealing with the subject of football hooliganism) took its title from a chant by Millwall FC fans in response to being called "animals" by the press—"We Hate Humans" (Robins 1984). In the digital and mobile era, though, sport fans do not have to wait to print their views and images on paper fanzines. The arrival of the Internet made it possible for them to post content to proliferating fan-based websites, although until the widespread availability of smartphones and Wi-Fi networks there were inevitable delays in uploading via desktop and laptop computers. Now, just as the institutional media cover the arrival of visiting sport fans and their passage to and from the stadium, the fans themselves can communicate their own experiences, freely posting messages, images, and sounds via mobile social media. In some cases, they may be in a position to challenge mainstream media accounts of widespread fan disorder by demonstrating that they are selective and exaggerated, or that the violence was initiated by rival fans or by the authorities. They can also use the same privately held media technologies to celebrate legal, joyous expressions of fandom on the streets or to arrange fights and provide graphic footage of violence and disorder. This process of collective mediation can continue all the way to the venue or stadium—but it does not stop there.

In and Outside the Venue

The economic imperatives of commercial popular culture, which involve the increased expense of transporting performers across ever-greater distances, have increasingly demanded larger venues to accommodate bigger crowds. Smaller venues in inner-city and suburban neighborhoods have in many cases been supplanted by large stadia in both "brown-" and "green-field" sites. To a substantial degree these changes have been caused by urban developments, including gentrification, that have imposed intense pressure to relocate sport spaces in densely populated working-class suburbs with rising land values (Bramham and Wagg 2009). The historical parallels between popular music and sport (Rowe 1995) became spatially accentuated when large sport stadia were temporarily repurposed as venues for major pop and rock concerts. Such "massification" of large events, in the context of the increasingly lavish provision of live sound and vision for audiences in their homes via high-definition television, created the paradox that "being there" might, as noted above, be an inferior experience to watching at a distance but also in camera-facilitated close-up. The *auratic* pleasure of sharing the unique moment in real-time and space might seem like inadequate compensation for having to watch, from uncomfortable, expensive "nose bleed" seats, performers who appear to be in miniature, while not having the advantage of replays and alternative points of view. It is for this reason that, as noted, vast screens were brought into the stadium to enable co-present spectators to see the action (in the case of rock music, this also meant the use of enormous stacks of speakers).

The large screens being viewed are vastly outnumbered by the small, handheld screens that are being used to communicate text and image beyond the venue. Indeed, it is not unusual to see sport crowd photographs in which many of those people present are looking at screens rather than directly at the physical spectacle for which they have paid. In turning themselves into media communicators, especially when using live streaming applications like Periscope, WeChat, Instagram Live Stories, and Facebook Live, they may also find themselves in conflict with the event's broadcast rights holders. Another material effect of the process of mediatization is clearly exposed here—it has shaped the sensory expectations of audiences and altered the structure and look of live venues. Seating has been removed to accommodate screens and the visual appearance of stadia adjusted to appeal to the televisual eye. Indeed, during global sport mega events, the location of the stadium may actually be determined by the visual touristic appeal of the establishment shot, as the camera pans across the telegenic sites of the city and its physical setting to the stadium (Weed 2008). This was, for example, the media logic that, at the 2010 FIFA World Cup, led to the placement of a stadium in Cape Town in an inappropriate, socially disruptive location (Broudehoux 2017). Further, inside the latest stadia are state-of-the-art media facilities designed both to give distant audiences the best view of proceedings and co-present audiences optimal opportunities to communicate their experiences to the same faraway audiences. It should be noted, though, that injudiciously built venues for mega events may become "white elephants," abandoned and allowed to fall into neglected disrepair once the global media gaze has found new sporting spaces on which to fix (Street, Frawley, and Cobourn 2014).

The developments described in this section hint at two important consequences of how media practices, devices, and infrastructures are increasingly integrated into the planning and experience of live events. Perhaps counter-intuitively, the first involves attempts to limit the widespread use of mobile media devices in venues by controlling where and/or when users can access their smartphones, thereby limiting the sharing of audiovisual content via services such as YouTube, live.ly, and Facebook. Such attempts to regulate mobile usage complicate the evolving expectations of many users, who now routinely engage in "mass self-communication" of their social experiences via social media and video-on-demand platforms (Castells 2009). The second effect highlights the formalized spatial expansion of events through the creation of live sites operated in conjunction with the in-stadium or venue action, which is a development linked to the promotion of particular urban agglomerations as "sporting cities" (e.g., Melbourne and London) or "music cities" (e.g., Austin, Texas, and Berlin) (Sam and Hughson 2011; Homan et al. 2016).

The diffusion of mobile broadband networks and smartphones continues to challenge and alter social norms of co-present interaction and communication at a distance by citizens (Ling 2008). The visible contestation of these norms is apparent in the staging of various cultural events concentrated in sizable urban markets, including live comedy, music, and sport. For instance, those people who purchased tickets for shows during the 2017 international tour of US comedian Chris Rock entered a phone-free event, with anyone caught contravening this condition of entry threatened with ejection from the venue. Underpinned by both experiential and intellectual property concerns, Rock's stance is shared by other comedians such as Dave Chappelle and (the now disgraced) Louis CK, and popular musicians including Alicia Keys, The Lumineers, and Guns N' Roses (Hutchins 2016a). Common to many of these examples is the use of a branded lockable pouch, Yondr, in which each attendee's smartphone is placed upon entry to the venue, carried with them during the event, and then unlocked again upon exit. Mobile phone recording has also been banned by a Melbourne live music venue and by the city's Comedy Festival, principally on the grounds of spoiling the experience of both performers and audiences (Harrison 2018). In the case of live sport, the owner of the National Basketball Association's (NBA) Dallas Mavericks, celebrity entrepreneur Mark Cuban, opts for persuasion over confiscation in relation to mobile device use. He argues publicly that live NBA matches are events where spectators can experience the pleasure of looking up from their mobile screens to focus instead on the physical spectacle and excitement. Indeed, he contends, in an echo of Jonathan Crary's (1999) analysis of Western modernity's demand for close attention to particular forms of spectacle and text, that the constant distractions prompted by mobile screens in everyday life see people attend live matches so that they can "just stop staring" at their smartphones and get "away from all that" for a period (cited in Hutchins 2016b: 429).

The motives of the performers and event promoters detailed here vary. Nonetheless, their actions and arguments all speak to the contested character of *auratic* pleasure and individual and collective experiences. Overlaid on an image of a live music venue, the online sales pitch for the Yondr (2017) pouch mentioned above is a reflection of this contestation:

> We think smartphones have incredible utility, but not in every setting. In some situations, they have become a distraction and a crutch—cutting people off from each other and their immediate surroundings.
>
> Yondr has a simple purpose: to show people how powerful a moment can be when we aren't focused on documenting or broadcasting it.

This branded pouch is a profit-seeking material response to the ongoing "embedding" of mobile communications across a range of social settings and the differential effects produced by this process (Ling 2012). It is but one example of how different orders of "non-mediatized and mediatized modes of contact and sharing" are created and balanced in the course of live events, thereby going to pressing questions about how best to organize social life in heavily mediated and mediatized environments (Hutchins 2016b: 428; Couldry 2012). It should be noted in passing, though, that attention and distraction have long been concerns for intellectuals as diverse as Walter Benjamin, Henri Bergson, Guy Debord, Edmund Husserl, Siegfried Kracauer, and Gustave Le Bon (Crary 1999).

Judging by the available contemporary news reports and their reader comments, reactions to the likes of Rock, Keys, and Cuban range between enthusiastic embrace, muted acceptance, and open frustration. The experience of a phone-free event appears to have been a pleasurable novelty for some attendees, allowing them to concentrate on the performance and enjoy the shared focus of the audience. However, for others, the need to put away their phone is an unwanted interference with, and intervention in, their leisure activities, breaking the promise of "perpetual contact" made possible by far-reaching telecommunications networks and smartphone-based telephony, messaging, and content sharing (Katz and Aakhus 2002).

Debates over appropriate degrees of mobile media use and non-use highlight why live events are culturally significant features of urban life. They are sites at which the production of sociality is observable through the deliberate arrangement of people, spectacle, media, technology, and infrastructure. This development recalls and re-contextualizes the arguments of Karin van Es (2017) and Paddy Scannell (2001, 2014) about television and the social experiences produced by live broadcasts, as well as bearing on debates about differential interpretations on global media events according to national, cultural, and spatial context (de Moragas Spà, Rivenburgh, and Larson 1995; Couldry, Hepp, and Krotz 2010). The organization of live events is conditioned by expectations of a specific experience or range of experiences for the audience; that is, "the possibilities of participation" and "effects of being there" (Scannell 2001: 409; van Es 2017: 6). The rise of the smartphone and its seeming ubiquity have, therefore, changed and problematized the anticipated "communicative entitlements" (Scannell 2014: 207) attached to attendance at live events. For selected performers and attendees, a temporary suspension of mobile media use affords access to an experience that privileges sensory engagement and focused attention on the performance and/or spectacle. The right to be free of distractions caused by the mobile media use of others is, in effect, an entitlement in the course of live events that is dependent on collective effervescence, as conceived by Emile Durkheim (1964), for their success (Couldry 2003). However, for those people who want to share and upload, an inability to connect and bear witness to a live event via their smartphone inhibits an entitlement that they are able to exercise in many other domains, including assorted work, home, and leisure activities. For them, to be disconnected is to lose access to the commercial platforms and services (e.g., Instagram, Snapchat, and Twitter) that, justifiably or otherwise, function as repositories of "the social" for the multitudes of users who regularly share messages, as well as audio and/or visual content, in negotiating the competing meanings of their daily lives (Couldry and van Dijck 2015), including of the live performances that they have witnessed. Yet, despite the differences between these contending communicative entitlements, each leads back to the same objective—connection with a wider social world through the experience of live events.

The second consequence of mediatization sees our focus move back to sport and the expanding scale of media events and spaces. Despite the increasing size of sport stadia, they still cannot accommodate all who would like to attend major events. Even huge venues have limited capacity, and mediatization has meant that many in the host and other cities believe, especially if they are in the same country and the national government has underwritten the event, that they have rights as cultural citizens to see them live through the media (Scherer and Rowe 2014). As a result, live sites have emerged as an essential feature of major sport events. They can be positioned across host and other cities, and may be in the shadow of the host stadium, in city squares and parks, and in other stadia. They have the advantage of offering, at little direct cost to the participant, a screen- and crowd-based sense of "being there" that is unavailable in the more atomized experience of "mobile privatisation" in the home (Williams 1974: 26). While licensed outlets and restaurants can also provide screens for live collective viewing, the sociality of the live site is a closer simulation of being co-present. In so doing, it spreads and clusters the experience across the urban landscape, with crowds supporting rival teams and athletes expressing their affiliations through positioning in the available space, dress and conduct, and communicating with the live screen as if they could be seen and heard by the performers and spectators at the actual event site (Rowe and Baker 2012a, b). The live site, as it grows in scale and frequency of use, also confronts the same matters of organization and practice as the "main event," including securitization and commercialization (Fussey et al. 2011; Baker and Rowe 2014). Therefore, the once-freewheeling ability of sports fans and curious bystanders to move easily between live sites and other venues connected to sport events is increasingly curtailed by bag searches for dangerous objects and goods that breach the exclusive intellectual property rights of the host sponsors.

Despite these impediments to mobility, during a long tournament such as the Summer Olympics and FIFA World Cup, in particular, host cities become the equivalent of giant film sets or television studios. The "outside broadcasts" that once were dedicated to capturing and relaying the sporting action are, in the digital age, overwhelmed by the constant downloading and uploading of material by professionals and non-professionals alike. This "dance" of representation is conducted across whole cities—the very presence of residents and visitors in large numbers in urban spaces for reasons linked with the sport event is grist for broadcast news bulletins and newspaper editions. Those same media subjects are constantly (perhaps compulsively) self-imaging and making images of all that is around them—of other people both familiar and unknown, of the landmarks that signify place, and even of the media that are watching them. In turn, they receive responses to the messages that they generate and to which they, in turn respond, in a hyperactive and hyper-mediated feedback loop. Maintaining such busy rhythms of media-oriented urban leisure, it can be observed, requires regular, rapid-fire, and often exhausting communicative work.

Conclusion: Splintered Urban Experiences?

The discussion presented in this chapter reveals that live events exemplify a deepening interpenetration of urban life, mediatized sociality, physical infrastructure, screen-based technologies, telecommunications networks, and professional labor (involving sophisticated engineering know-how and international time-space coordination). It is essential to recognize the patterns and outcomes flowing from this process, especially given their connections to the global tourism, hospitality, leisure, and culture industries, international sporting and cultural associations, gentrification, community groups, governments at multiple levels, and technology, telecommunications, and media markets. Yet, left unstated in much of this chapter are the emerging differential impacts of the outlined events and processes on the urban fabric, which require further systematic investigation.

Another layer is being added to familiar forms of social inequality organized along the lines of income, education, gender, sexuality, race, and/or disability. Sitting within and alongside each of these overlapping categories is, according to Jordan Frith (2012), the "splintering" of access to events, media technologies, and the infrastructures of urban areas. Such concerns are often sublimated or overwhelmed by marketing messages, the popular excitement triggered by major events, the novelty of high-resolution screens of all sizes, and the "hyping" of new mobile software such as augmented reality mobile apps designed for use during live events. This splintering is about more than the already-steep price of admission to stadia, venues, or live sites, or the exorbitant cost and dubious quality of food, drink, and merchandise once inside (Parry et al. 2018). Additional imposts are created by the capacity to afford and upgrade mobile devices, purchase broadband subscription plans linked to reliable telecommunications services, download and pay for "freemium" and premium apps, and maintain a series of user profiles on services that encourage the constant posting of content. Full access to media-based sociability in urban spaces is a costly affair for many citizens, introducing new forms of differentiated consumption, access, and exclusion in the experience of leisure. Ironically, even attendance at a phone-free event involves an additional cost embedded in the overall ticket price to cover the provision of yet another branded smartphone accessory, a Yondr pouch. This is a requirement that further complicates the theme introduced at the outset this chapter, that of "watching, being, and making the event." A new analytical imperative is to investigate who is able to watch and in what ways, who has the capacity to communicate meaningfully their experience of being at events, and to grasp the nature of the emerging zones of inclusion and exclusion that construct live events in mediatized urban environments. These are questions of structure, agency, and power that even the shiniest new handheld device cannot conceal or delete.

References

Baker, S. A. and Rowe, D. (2014) "Mediating Mega Events and Manufacturing Multiculturalism: The Cultural Politics of the World Game in Australia," *Journal of Sociology*, 50(3), pp. 299–314.
Bramham, P. and Wagg, S. (eds.) (2009) *Sport, Leisure and Culture in the Postmodern City*, Aldershot: Ashgate.
Broudehoux, A.-M. (2017) *Mega-Events and Urban Image Construction: Beijing and Rio de Janeiro*, New York, NY and Abingdon, UK: Routledge.
Castells, M. (2009) *Communication Power*, Oxford, UK: Oxford University Press.
Clarke, J. and Critcher, C. (1985) *The Devil Makes Work: Leisure in Capitalist Britain*, London: Macmillan.
Couldry, N. (2003) *Media Rituals: A Critical Approach*, London and New York: Routledge.
— (2012) *Media, Society, World*, Cambridge, UK: Polity Press.
Couldry, N. and van Dijck, J. (2015) "Researching Social Media as if the Social Mattered," *Social Media and Society*, 1(2), pp. 1–7.
Couldry, N., Hepp, A., and Krotz, F. (2010) *Media Events in a Global Age*, London and New York: Routledge.
Crary, J. (1999) *Suspensions of Perception: Attention, Spectacle, and Modern Culture*, Cambridge, MA: MIT Press.
Critcher, C. (2003) *Moral Panics and the Media*, Buckingham, UK: Open University Press.
Dayan, D. and Katz, E. (1992) *Media Events: The Live Broadcasting of History*, Cambridge, MA: Harvard University Press.
de Moragas Spà, M., Rivenburgh, N. K., and Larson, J. F. (1995) *Television in the Olympics*, London: John Libbey.
Durkheim, E. (1964) [1915] *The Elementary Forms of the Religious Life*, London, UK: George Allen and Unwin.
Frith, S. (2012) "Splintered Space: Hybrid Spaces and Differential Mobility," *Mobilities*, 7(1), pp. 131–149.
Fussey, P., Coaffee, J., Armstrong, G., and Hobbs, D. (2011) *Securing and Sustaining the Olympic City: Reconfiguring London for 2012 and Beyond*, Aldershot: Ashgate.
Goggin, G. (2012) "The Eccentric Career of Mobile Television," *International Journal of Digital Television*, 3(2), pp. 119–140.
Harrison, D. (2018) "Melbourne's Cherry Bar Introduces Mobile Phone Ban for Live Music Events," *ABC News*, February 21, www.abc.net.au/news/2018-02-21/cherry-bar-mobile-phone-ban-live-music/9469310.
Haynes, R. (1995) *The Football Imagination: The Rise of Football Fanzine Culture*, Aldershot: Ashgate.
Hjarvard, S. (2013) *The Mediatization of Culture and Society*, London, UK: Routledge.
Homan, S., Cloonan, M., and Cattermole, J. (2016) *Popular Music Industries and the State: Policy Notes*, New York: Routledge.
Hutchins, B. (2016a) "There's a Time to Put Down the Smartphone—Seriously!" *The Conversation*, July 25, https://theconversation.com/theres-a-time-to-put-down-the-smartphone-seriously-62699.
— (2016b) "'We Don't Need No Stinking Smartphones!' Live Stadium Sports Events, Mediatization and the Non-Use of Mobile Media," *Media, Culture and Society*, 38(3), pp. 420–436.
Hutchins, B. and Rowe, D. (2012) *Sport Beyond Television: The Internet, Digital Media and the Rise of Networked Media Sport*, New York, NY and Abingdon, UK: Routledge.
International Journal of Cultural Policy (2008) "Sport and Cultural Policy in the Re-imaged City," J. Hughson (ed.), 14(4), pp. 355–477.
Katz, J. E. and Aakhus, M. (eds.) (2002) *Perpetual Contact: Mobile Communication, Private Talk, Public Performance*, New York, NY: Cambridge University Press.
Levy, D. (2017) "Is Watching Sports on TV Actually Better than Being at the Game?" *Bleacher Report*, January 10, http://bleacherreport.com/articles/923563-is-watching-sports-on-tv-actually-better-than-being-at-the-game.
Ling, R. (2008) *New Tech, New Ties: How Mobile Communication is Reshaping Social Cohesion*, Cambridge, MA: The MIT Press.

— (2012) *Taken for Grantedness: The Embedding of Mobile Communication into Society*, Cambridge, MA: The MIT Press.
Maxwell, R. and Miller, T. (2012) *Greening the Media*, New York, NY: Oxford University Press.
Miller, T. (2018) *Greenwashing Sport*, Abingdon, Oxon and New York, NY: Routledge.
Palmer, D. (2014) "Mobile Media Photography," in G. Goggin and L. Hjorth (eds.) *The Routledge Companion to Mobile Media*, New York, NY: Routledge, pp. 245–255.
Parry, K., George, E., Hall, T., and Rowe, D. (2018) "Healthy Fandom: Moving Away from Pies and Beer," in D. Parnell and P. Krustrup (eds.) *Sport and Health: Exploring the Current State of Play* (International Council of Sport Science and Physical Education Perspectives), London and New York: Routledge, pp. 219–237.
Redhead, S. (2015) *Football and Accelerated Culture: This Modern Sporting Life*, Abingdon, Oxon and New York, NY: Routledge.
Robins, D. (1984) *We Hate Humans*, Harmondsworth: Penguin.
Rojek, C. (1985) *Capitalism and Leisure Theory*, London: Tavistock.
Rowe, D. (1995) *Popular Cultures: Rock Music, Sport and the Politics of Pleasure*, London: SAGE.
— (2004) *Sport, Culture and the Media: The Unruly Trinity*, 2nd Edition, Maidenhead, UK: Open University Press.
Rowe, D. and Baker, S. A. (2012a) "Live Sites in an Age of Media Reproduction: Mega Events and Transcontinental Experience in Public Space," *Global Media Journal—Australian Edition*, www.hca.westernsydney.edu.au/gmjau/archive/v6_2012_1/pdf/rowe_and_baker_RA_6_1_2012.pdf, 6(1), pp. 1–10.
— (2012b) "The 'Fall' of What? FIFA's Public Viewing Areas and the Quality of Public Life," *Space and Culture*, 15(4), pp. 395–407.
Salazar, N. B., Timmerman, C., Wets, J., Gama Gato, L., and Van den Broucke, S. (eds.) (2017) *Mega-Event Mobilities: A Critical Analysis*, Abingdon, Oxon and New York, NY: Routledge.
Sam, M. P. and Hughson, J. E. (eds.) (2011) *Sport in the City: Cultural Connections*, Abingdon, Oxon and New York, NY: Routledge.
Sayre, S. and King, C. (2003) *Entertainment and Society: Audiences, Trends and Impacts*, Thousand Oaks, CA: SAGE.
Scannell, P. (2001) "Authenticity and Experience," *Discourse Studies*, 3(4), pp. 405–411.
— (2014) *Television and the Meaning of "Live": An Enquiry into the Human Situation*, Cambridge, UK: Polity Press.
Scherer, J. and Rowe, D. (eds.) (2014) *Sport, Public Broadcasting, and Cultural Citizenship: Signal Lost?* London and New York: Routledge.
Street, L., Frawley, S., and Cobourn, S. (2014) "World Cup Stadium Development and Sustainability," in S. Frawley and D. Adair (eds.) *Managing the Football World Cup*, Basingstoke, UK: Palgrave Macmillan, pp. 104–132.
van Es, K. (2017) "Liveness Redux: On Media and Their Claim to Be Live," *Media, Culture and Society*, 39(8), pp. 1245–1256.
Weed, M. (2008) *Olympic Tourism*, Oxford, UK: Elsevier.
Williams, R. (1974) *Television: Technology and Cultural Form*, Glasgow: Fontana.
Yondr (2017) "Our Vision," http://overyondr.com.

Further Reading

Hutchins, B. and Rowe, D. (eds.) (2013) *Digital Media Sport: Technology, Power and Culture in the Network Society*, New York: Routledge.
Rowe, D. (2011) *Global Media Sport: Flows, Forms and Futures*, London, UK: Bloomsbury Academic.
van Es, K. (2016) *The Future of Live*, Cambridge, UK: Polity Press.

27

MEDIA ARCHITECTURE

Post Screens, Ante [Insert Here]

Hank Haeusler

Introduction

In this chapter, I discuss the transition of media architecture parallel to a transition in architectural design from planar to spline-based and data-driven. This transition is argued for by presenting the theoretical context as well as discussing a series of prototypes and installations that were designed between 2009 and 2016 by the author and collaborators. This chapter will introduce the reader to media façades, an urban media phenomenon, by discussing key aspects and existing knowledge from an architectural and façade technology. The chapter will also outline a transformation of architecture that has happened in parallel to transformations in technology and present in detail two case studies, *Orkhēstra* and *ParticipationPlus*, that showcase ways in which media façades have an explicit connection to the architectural discourse, in particular computational architecture or design. Finally, this entry will look into relevant trends in other related fields so as to better understand new developing interface(s) between the physical and the digital in a potentially post-screen era, as well as pondering the potential consequences these new interfaces might have for the urban fabric such as streets and public spaces (see also Chapter 3, this volume). The chapter concludes with observations and suggestions for research toward digital infrastructure at the scale of the hybrid city.

The history of media façades, as a façade technology, reaches further back in time than one might expect, given that most media façades only started dominating global cities like New York, Tokyo or Shanghai in the last two decades. As the field of media façade research is a very young, I would like to provide readers with a brief preamble concerning the technological development of media façades before outlining the historical development and current experimentations.

The technological development is relevant and was discussed in earlier publications (Haeusler 2009a, 2017). The title of my earlier work on the subject, *History, Technology, Content* (2009a), implied a causality—understood as a relation between cause and effect—that accorded technology as the first event that is responsible for content. Media façade technologies are found in the following two main areas of production: mechanical and electronic media façades. I will focus on the second category, electronic media façades, which are to be found in most contemporary built examples. The communication of an image via an electronic medium can be further sub-classified to reflect the range of technologies available. There are essentially three kinds of electronic media technology that can be used to transport a text, graphic or image: projector technology (e.g., CRT, LCD, DLP projectors); illuminant technology (e.g., fluorescent lamps, halogen lamps); display technology (e.g., LED, TFT, LCD plasma). How then are these three sub-categories of electronic media technology and mechanical technology used in a media façade context? I suggested that projection façade technology uses a façade as a projection screen, with the projector mounted onto another building (2009a). Rear projection façades technology uses a projector behind a translucent projection surface to project images. The illuminant form uses two kinds of technology. Window raster animation technology uses existing window grids on buildings. When animated with a lamp, each window functions as a single pixel. Low-resolution messages or animations reminiscent of early computer games are possible. The second form of the illuminated façade technology uses dimmable neon tubes or light bulbs to display low-resolution black and white moving images. Lastly, the display technology is based on a pixel-based display technology that uses LED technology or other screen technologies such as TFT or LCD plasma. With this technology, the façade can function as a large display screen. There are several systems available produced by various companies. Voxel façades technology uses a 3D matrix of LEDs to allow a 3D representation of media content.

Some of these groups can again be separated into smaller subgroups to reflect the specific variants offered by the technology. Display technology, for instance, uses several different systems, all based on LED technology. The way the LEDs are used to build a display façade, however, varies from one system to another. To give a ready example, a LED curtain consisting of embedded LEDs allows the same kind of presentation of content as does the OLite system which assembles LEDs into a block. Although they both use the same technology, the way they can be used as a building material differs.

With this sketch of media façade technology in mind, how did media façades develop historically? Again, the discussion here limits itself to technological milestones as points in time when a technology, such as projection in cinemas or TV as common household technology matured and architects started thinking about integrating these new technologies in their design (see also Chapters 1 and 5, this volume). In the 1920s and 1930s, when cinema became commonplace in cities, it was only a matter of time until a designer or architect came up with the idea to take the projection screen from an indoor wall to an exterior façade. Consequently, in the 1930s Oskar Nietschke presented a proposal for a building, "Maison de Publicité", in Paris with an exterior projection façade, via a "collage" or "montage" (Tomitsch et al. 2015), which could be considered as one of the first media façades, when understanding media façade as a building surface that is able to communicate dynamic text, graphic or image via an electronic or mechanical medium (Haeusler 2009a). Thirty years later, similar collages or montages were developed by Cedric Price for the Fun Palace Project, amongst others (Hardingham 2015), outlining the idea that a façade could become a screen. Arguably Price influenced Richard Rogers and Renzo Piano with his work toward their successful competition entry for the Centre Pompidou in Paris in 1971 (Silver 1994). Even while taken in serious considerations and detailed studies by the project team to realize the Centre Pompidou with a media façade, the constraints on budget did not recognize the potentials of available technology of the time and hence the media façade was never realized. From the mid-1980s onwards, large videos displays found their way around the urban world into transport infrastructure projects, as outlined by Simpson's publication (1991) about video walls. The next "cycle" of architecture's engagement with the media façade technology started again in the mid-1990s with a theoretical discourse on Hypersurface Architecture Theory (Perrella 1998, 2000) with the exemplary projects like Salt and Freshwater Pavilion by Nox, Lars Spuybroek and Kas Oosterhuis, respectively. By the early 2000s, media façades matured to the point at which different categories, based on the kind of technology used to present content, were recognized (Haeusler 2009a).

Still at this time, arguably up to approximately 2007,[1] the main challenge for media façades was technical, such as controlling LEDs, cable management of LEDs, projection mapping and lumen (brightness) issues when using projectors, all in order to realize the ideas and concepts that have been presented through the collages and montages in earlier decades. With the proliferation of media façades and their long history of iconic presence in places such as Times Square, New York and Shibuya Crossing in Tokyo, one could consider how the transformation of technology—from florescent tubes to video screens to LED screens—initiated a transformation of space (Haeusler 2009a).

My own engagement with media façades took a similar path. In a student project during my architectural degree in 2002, I designed an office/hotel complex with a media façade facing the adjacent plaza in order to activate the place with temporary events like showing soccer games and represented this concept via a collage. Only a year later, I had to learn that designing and building a media façade is actually a complicated undertaking and struggled with the building of the media façade for the Mercedes-Benz 2004 Car Booth in Geneva, Switzerland (Kauffmann et al. 2017).

By 2012, it was widely understood that media façades are a global phenomenon, built at nearly each corner of the earth (Haeusler et al. 2012) and recognized as an "element" of architecture (Zaera-Polo et al. 2014). Current discussions have moved away from seeing media façades as an issue of an individual building to matters of placemaking and urban design as discussed at the Media Architecture Biennale 2016 in Sydney (MAB16 2016; Hespanhol et al. 2017) and therefore related more to urban design and landscape architecture as responsive landscapes (Cantrell and Holzman, 2016). At events such as the 2018 Media Architecture Biennale in Beijing (MAB18 2018), possibilities were even raised for a further move away from lights and screens as main medium to other and new forms of digital infrastructures in the hybrid city.

In order to understand the above observations, we first need to examine the direction in which architecture, in particular digital architecture, is moving and how this trajectory can be related to media façades. For this examination, a brief review of literature in contemporary digital architecture discourse, in particular discussions in computational design, is necessary. A presentation and discussion of two case studies, *Orkhēstra* and *ParticipationPlus*, will further help to clarify the present discussions in computational design. These case studies are projects designed and developed by the author and an international team of collaborators as "litmus test" to determine whether media façades can keep up with contemporary digital architecture discourse or needs to stay in the realm of a 2D planar screen.

Brynjolfsson and McAfee describe in their 2015 book *The Second Machine Age* contemporary General Purpose Technologies (GPTs) such as exponential growth of computing power with Moore's law, Internet of Things (IoT), digitalized information (Big Data), user-generated data, social media and Artificial Intelligence that are sometimes perceived to be at the core of all current societal changes. It is argued that these second machine-age GPTs have played and will continue to play an important role in the transformation of our built environment and cities. From a perspective of the architectural practitioner, an investigation into these technologies will help us better understand how "Second Machine-Age Architecture" could look and outline the opportunities media architecture can have in helping us define upcoming urban infrastructures.

Screens as Part of Architecture

Historical developments of media façade architecture have been summoned persuasively by Mario Carpo in his 2012 book *The Digital Turn in Architecture*, which saw a fundamental shift in architecture toward the digital in the 1990s, while his further, 2017, book *The Second Digital Turn* recognized contemporary echoes of the avant-garde in digital architecture. This chapter does not allow a full explanation but only a short summary of Carpo's arguments concerning the first digital and second digital turn. Carpo described the first digital turn as a new architectural form enabled through the spline. A spline is a numerical function that is piecewise defined by polynomial functions, and which possesses a high degree of smoothness at the places where the polynomial pieces connect (Wikipedia 2018). CAD software such as Maya and Rhino allowed architects to design with splines via the computer and certain construction advancements to build such projects. Exemplary here are projects like those of Zaha Hadid or Frank Gehry, to name but two prominent architects who designed with splines. Carpo argued that this form of digital architecture is a thing of the past and would be superseded by new digital design that makes use of larger amounts of data, the ability of computers to handle the data and their capacity to generate a data-based physical output enabled through a "digital trial and error" process. Hence, the digital design of future architecture, according to Carpo, will no longer be generated by humans, but by software (designed by humans). The software will generate design outcomes out of the input variables (data) and the rules defined within the software, or hundreds or thousands of potential design outcomes from which a human can then select a suitable or preferred one.

Neither "digital"/"non-standard" nor "non-planar" media architecture have become mainstream yet, but there is an opportunity for exploration through experimentation as presented in the following two case studies, *Orkhēstra* and *ParticipationPlus*.

Orkhēstra was designed and developed in 2013 and presented at the Frankfurt Light and Building Festival (Luminale) in 2014 (MAI Orkhēstra 2018), which represents media façades at the first digital turn, and *ParticipationPlus* was designed and developed through a series of workshops in Beijing and Sydney from 2014 onwards and presented at the Vivid Sydney Festival in 2016, which represents media architecture in the second digital turn.

Orkhēstra

The first case study presents a project that merged current developments in architecture and computational design, engineering and digital technology, and science and interaction design to an amalgam that pushed further the existing boundaries in designing responsive environments. The project is the result of bringing specialists from different disciplines together. The international design team comprised the University of New South Wales/Computational Design Undergraduate Degree and staff and students of the discipline, Sydney; The Städelschule—University of Applied Arts, Architecture Class (SAC), Frankfurt; Media Architecture Institute; Ludwig Maximillian University, Munich; and the LED manufacturing company Media Façades LED, Shenzhen. The project was developed in phases through meetings, workshops and testing iterations across the above institutions.

Orkhēstra consisted of a double-curved polypropylene skin that infolds and exfolds in numerous, differentially scaled perforations (see Figure 27.1). The installation was developed using state-of-the-art computer modeling technology and delivered an organic form that challenged the conventional use of orthogonal surfaces for building components and LED placement. The 1.2-mm-thick polypropylene sheets were laser-cut to generate 7732 unique pieces, which were assembled with a finger joint system to form a thick, double-layered outer skin.

The installation used customized software that supported what passers-by usually tend to do at light installations in public—pull out their cameras and take a picture, often with the flashlight set automatically. The flash would trigger a response in the installation's sensor and the LED lights would start to blink across the structure. The blinking would start soon after the flash was triggered and would dissolve slowly. This set-up mimics the natural

Figure 27.1 Orkhēstra Installation in Frankfurt, 2014
© Wolf Leeb.

reflexions of the light, hence orchestrates the depth of light. The light movement was made possible via the custom-made software that breaks down the complex curved surface into smaller screen components allowing a media content, like the wandering light points, to display in a controlled manner on the surface.

The team had to overcome various issues. The digital fabrication of the installation as a design required a complex numbering system to allow a later assembly of several thousand individual parts. LEDs required energy and data and thus several hundred meters of cables had to be positioned inside the structure. The LEDs as such needed to be fixed to the structure and hence a custom-made fixing system was developed with the LED manufacturer. All these issues could only be solved by a nexus of architecture and design with engineering and science and through a profound understanding of computing and computation. The project recognized that urban media needs to cover a large variety of fields of expertise in order to design and build a media façade. With computational design and digital fabrication being a prominent area of investigation and investment of global architecture firms, construction firms and developers, the expectation on media façades will increase and a planar screen might no longer be desired by clients. Thus, an investigation on an installation scale on how to design and fabricate a curved surface and combine spline-based form with LED technology might support new ways of thinking on urban media via a built example.

ParticipationPlus

ParticipationPlus is a second investigation into adopting and testing the "second digital turn", as outlined by Carpo (2017), where computation allows for form finding by simulation and optimization (see Figure 27.2). The design process started with a workshop run by the Media Architecture Institute in 2013 with students at China Central Academy of Fine Arts (CAFA), Beijing. Students were asked to design and develop a physical component with an embedded LED which would function as a "digital brick" one can stack on various ways to form a media façade. The workshop resulted in a series of speculative media façade prototypes that challenged conventional understandings of media façades as planar screens facing only in one direction. One design prototype designed by CAFA students was chosen for a further design development. It used the concept from Ray and Charles Eames' project "House of Cards", where one card can be connected to another card to generate a 3D object. The UNSW students further optimized the "card" as a flat object into a physical component (Pixel) in the shape of a "+" made out of white polypropylene with four embedded StrongLED™ RGB LEDs and a connection mechanism that allowed connection of one Pixel to another in 90-degree variations using a set of "M"-shaped connectors.

The Pixel was manufactured via rotation molding and digital fabrication techniques. For the team, these Pixels were effectively a form of "LEGO" bricks with LEDs, to the extent that LEGO allows one to design endless designs using the one and the same brick. What one needs is a plan of what to build with LEGO bricks. At this point we were no longer interested in the design of the construction or the Pixel as an object but in *Objectile*—defining a script that takes the object Pixel and builds something out of it. Objectile, outlined first by Deleuze (1993), is a function that contains an infinite number of objects. In design terms, the interest in the object (whether in industrial, architectural or urban design) shifts as the object no longer has an essential or definite (digital) form. When design variables are fed into an algorithm, they become part of a mathematical function and hence can take on an infinitive number of forms. A two-tiered design object therefore compromises or involves two levels, one the mathematical function that defines the infinitive number of forms and a second one resulting object that will be produced (a decision a designer need to make when examining the produced outcomes).

Figure 27.2 ParticipationPlus Installation in Sydney, 2016
© UNSW Built Environment.

Adopted and applied in our design exploration and in Computational Design in general (Carpo 2011, 2012, 2017; Terzidis 2006), a function (in the form of a script or software) was developed which can generate infinitive amounts of objectiles (in our case installations with LEDs able to interact). Variables in our case were conditions of a site (size, access, surroundings, etc.); number of available Pixels and variables that are directly related to data management (DMX) and power supply; and civil engineering constraints. With the help of the script, the design team could alter the number of available Pixels and the position of the installation. In a few minutes the computer generated a design. Through this method we were able to produce with the minimum of effort an unlimited amount of iterations. Yet which version corresponded with our vision? Computers are versatile machines but they cannot—yet—articulate aesthetic preferences. Here an early definition of media façades helped. For a media façade to be classified as media architecture and not as light architecture, it needs to be able to communicate a dynamic text, graphic or image (Haeusler 2009a). Based on this understanding, the design team could examine the results and assess if one can read either text, graphic or image on the generated design. If not, the designed outcome is possible from a technical level but would not fulfill the requirements of a media façade and hence would not meet aesthetic preferences of humans. *ParticipationPlus* offered a first step toward a new direction where machines offer design options, which humans can evaluate.

The case studies have demonstrated that media façades do not need to stay in the realm of planar screens but can deliver the promises of digital ("intelligent") architecture envisioned in the 1990s by achieving smooth curvature enabled through the spline as shown with *Orkhēstra* or newer developments with *ParticipationPlus*. Media façades industry can keep up with the digital architecture discourse. But façade design as well as screen design is more than complex curvature or computational concepts. Façades usually have opening for windows and doors and are made of different materials such as glass or concrete. Screens, on the other hand, assume a different aspect ratio and resolutions, which can impact on their visibility at certain positions and distances. Thus, more research has been done on merging façades and screens since the early 2000s. Commercial and design research projects have investigated and developed media façades which:

- can have opening like windows as in the *Mercedes-Benz, Maybach, DaimlerChrysler Salon de l'Automobile Geneva 2004* car booth (Kauffmann et al. 2017);
- can be a mixed medium combining architectural materials such as concrete with LEDs (Haeusler 2009b);
- can be complex curved as shown with *Orkhēstra* 2014 or with the *Janus Screen* project in Sydney 2009 (Haeusler et al. 2012);
- can be a screen made out of autonomous pixels that are independent from power and data supply (Haeusler 2009c);
- can alter media façades from being a screen only to a responsive skin that can sense, compute and communicate content (Haeusler 2012)
- can have various screen resolutions in the same screen as shown in *Hypersurface Architecture [Redux]* 2012 (Haeusler 2013).

Consequently, one can argue that media façades respond to the promises of digital/intelligent architecture rhetoric of the 1990s, to a considerable degree, by using a spline-based media façade, and an evolutionary algorithm. Further to the above list, media façades can still be taken up all kinds of forms and functions as a more conventional architectural element too (e.g., ornament/decoration, narration/sign).

Post Screens—Ante [Insert Here]

One can argue that urban screens primarily function as an interface between the physical and digital spaces. Digital processes, ranging from Big Data (any form of data), to information gathered via social networks (Facebook, Twitter, etc.), to Internet of Things (all the sensors around us), and user-generated content (YouTube), are only useful as long as we can make sense of them and we do so primarily via screens.

For Mihye, half a century ago, at the end of the first machine age, infrastructure

> was confined to material, and by contrast digital infrastructure is no longer confined to material but is in formation and operates between different dimensions, systems, people and abstractions: image to sound, gesture to function, 2D to 3D, algorithm to capital, event to signal.
>
> *(2016: 21)*

We might have not seen the full extent of this transformation but let us consider its possibilities by looking at how architecture has been transformed through General Purpose Technologies (GPTs) such as combustion engine or electricity. Both GPTs introduced in the first machine age, in the late 19th and beginning of the 20th century, enabled typologies such as high-rise buildings (only possible because of elevators—hence engines were either combustion or electric), transformations from medieval urban settings to the "car-friendly city" (combustion engine) or spatial design (greater building depth only possible through electric light). Hence, one can argue that second machine-age GPTs will transform our built environment in a similar way as combustion engine or electricity had in the past. But what are these new interfaces made of, what GPTs do they use and how do they impact public space?

One can argue that present examples of these new interfaces are bike-sharing platforms such as OFO, Mobike, Rydo, Reddy Go and the like. Bicycles have been around for a long time and are physical objects that appear in public space, but that their location can be identified, booked and paid for is only possible because of Second Machine-Age General Purpose Technologies such as smartphones, Internet of Things (GPS, Bluetooth, WiFi) and digitalized payment systems. Do they change the built environment? Arguably so. In cities such as Beijing, bike-sharing platforms and bicycles are situated in their thousands and compete for floor space with other functions in the public domain. Arguably, they require more space than media façades as an interface between the physical and digital (see also Chapter 39, this volume).

Another example are drones as part of delivery systems involving a physical object (miniature helicopter) that is coupled with digital technology. Amazon is actively working on what the logistic industry is calling "the last mile to the consumer", via drone delivery, and has demonstrated its functionality via various case studies. Still, what the promotion videos show is a drone landing on a backyard lawn and delivering the parcel (Amazon 2018). This does not consider the fact that residents in inner-city areas do not have a back yard where a drone could land, or that a balcony would not be able to accommodate a drone with the necessary size to carry a standard parcel. Thus, if drone-enabled delivery of goods is to happen in inner-city areas, one needs space for them to land—a landing platform of approximately 4 square meters and potentially in front of every residential high rise where the drone can land and where more than one parcel can be stored for a period of time as the "delivery station" will cater for potentially several dozens to hundreds of customers.

Conclusion

This chapter has introduced the reader to media façades, a fast-developing urban media phenomenon, by discussing key historic milestones outlining the related transformation of architecture as well as presenting two case studies, *Orkhēstra* and *ParticipationPlus*. Beyond demonstrating that media façades can adopt architectural functions, namely window openings, material integration and form variations from planar to complex curved, the chapter has speculated that the second machine-age architecture is likely to go beyond screens and create new interface(s) between the physical and the digital (e.g., bicycle-sharing system and drone landing platforms). But what are the consequences for the urban fabric such as streets and public spaces when new interfaces between the physical and the digital appear?

More floor space is required and most likely the density of public space use will increase. Density, on an urban scale, has been widely discussed as a method to improve transport issues (dependency on private vehicles, making public transport infrastructure investments more economical, etc.); housing affordability (costs of land, economy of scales, etc.); or livability (access to amenities, vibrancy of areas, etc.). New physical/digital interfaces will add another dimension: density in public spaces. Cities developed at times when horses and carriages were the main mode of transport and have already sacrificed most space between buildings for cars, leaving only little space for sidewalks. Because of increased population size in cities, sidewalks are already heavily utilized by citizens walking from and to work, social engagements, shopping and other day-to-day activities. Hence public space is already highly contested and, arguably, ongoing debates in global cities about responsive environments, digital placemaking, urban interaction design, smart cities and similar developments indicate that density in public space is co-created by the uses of physical/digital interfaces.

The two design projects outlined above addressed the challenges of new forms of education and new partnerships in research and industry. The Media Architecture Institute is a useful example in this sense. Both projects were initiated by the Institute and were developed by a multidisciplinary team of social scientists, computer scientists, interaction designers, architects and several other specialists working together.

This chapter offered a new design field that researchers and designers in urban planning and landscape architecture together with engineers and scientists might use to develop new interfaces between the physical and digital. This may happen again via collages and montages, and similar to what previous designers and scholars like Oskar Nietschke, Cedric Price or Renzo Piano and Richard Rogers have done earlier. But this investigation is timely. While Nietschke's collages from the 1930s took 70 years to become reality (e.g., the media-saturated environments in Tokyo, New York or Shanghai), new interfaces between the physical and the digital might not need so long to populate our cities and public spaces. Second machine-age technologies develop exponentially (e.g., smartphones became widespread only within a decade) and the challenge is how to design new interfaces between the physical and digital realms and create new mediated urban publics (see also Chapter 36, this volume).

Acknowledgment

The ideas presented in this chapter were first developed and presented in my inaugural professorial appointment keynote at the China Central Academy of Fine Arts in Beijing, China at their EAST (Education Art Science Technology) Conference in November 2017.

Note

1 This definition of this year as a turning point was the result of discussions with LED manufacturers, designers and architects who were involved in the design and realization of media façades from the early 2000s, as well as participating in the 2007 Media Architecture Conference at Central Saint Martins, London (see www.mediaarchitecture.com).

References

Amazon (2018) "Amazon Testing Drone Delivery System", available on: www.youtube.com/watch?v=Le46ERPMlWU (accessed June 2018).
Brynjolfsson, E. and McAfee, A. (2016) *The Second Machine Age: Work, Progress, and Prosperity in a Time of Brilliant Technologies*, W. W. Norton & Company, New York.
Cantrell, B. and Holzman, J. (2016) *Responsive Landscapes: Strategies for Responsive Technologies in Landscape Architecture*, New York: Routledge.
Carpo, M. (2011) *The Alphabet and the Algorithm*, Cambridge, MA: MIT Press.
Carpo, M. (2012) *The Digital Turn in Architecture*, Hoboken, NJ: Wiley & Sons.
Carpo, M. (2017) *The Second Digital Turn in Architecture*, Hoboken, NJ: Wiley & Sons.
Deleuze, G. (1993) *Le pli: Leibniz et le baroque* (Paris: Éditions de Minuit, 1988); *The Fold: Leibniz and the Baroque*, trans. Tom Conley (Minneapolis, MN: University of Minnesota Press, 1993).
Haeusler, M. (2009a) *Media Façades: History, Technology, Content*, Ludwigsburg: Avedition.
Haeusler, M. (2009b) "Media-Augmented Surfaces: Embedding Media Technology into Architectural Surface to Allow a Constant Shift between Static Architectural Surface and Dynamic Digital Display", in *Computation: The New Realm of Architectural Design*, 27th eCAADe Conference Proceedings Istanbul (Turkey) 16–19 September 2009, pp. 483–490.
Haeusler, M. (2009c) "Autonomous Pixel", in S. McQuire, et al. (eds.) *Urban Screens Reader*, Amsterdam: INC, pp. 83–96.
Haeusler, M. (2012) "Media Façades: Quo Vadis?" in Pop, S. et al. (eds.) *Urban Media Cultures*, Ludwigsburg: Avedition, pp. 180–185.
Haeusler, M. (2013) "Hypersurface [Redux]", in A. Chatterjee (ed.), *Surface and Deep Histories Critiques and Practice in Art, Architecture and Design*, Cambridge: Cambridge Scholar Publishing, pp. 64–73.
Haeusler, M. (2017) "From Allopoietic Content to Autopoietic Content for Media Architecture through a Better Understanding of Architectural Typologies", in Wiethoff, A; Hussmann, H (eds.), *Media Architecture in the Public Domain*, Munich: De Gruyter, pp. 65–74.
Haeusler, M. et al. (2012) *New Media Façades: A Global Survey*, Ludwigsburg: Avedition.
Hardingham, S. (ed.) (2015) *Cedric Price Works 1952–2003: A Forward-Minded Retrospective*, London: Architectural Association.
Hespanhol, L et al. (2017) *Media Architecture Compendium: Digital Placemaking*, Ludwigsburg: Avedition.
Kauffmann, D. B. et al. (2017) "Mercedes-Benz 2004 Car Booth in Geneva, Switzerland", available on: www.ktp-architekten.de (accessed 15 August 2017).
Media Architecture Biennale 2016 (2016) available on: http://mab16.org (accessed: 24 January 2018).
Media Architecture Biennale 2018 (2018) available on: http://mab18.org (accessed: 30 January 2018).
Mihye, A (2016) *Atlas of Fantastic Infrastructures: An Intimate Look at Media Architecture*, Basel: Birkhaeuser.
Orkhēstra (2018) Media Architecture Institute Project, available on: www.mediaarchitecture.org/orchestrating-the-depth-of-light (accessed 10 January 2018).
Perrella, S. (ed.) (1998) *Hypersurface Architecture*, AD Magazine, Hoboken, NJ: John Wiley & Sons.
Perrella, S. (ed.) (2000) *Hypersurface Architecture II*, AD Magazine, Hoboken, NJ: John Wiley & Sons.
Silver, N. (1994) *The Making of Beaubourg: A Building Biography of the Centre Pompidou Paris*, Cambridge, MA: MIT Press.
Simpson, R. (1991) *Videowalls: The Book of the Big Electronic Image*, Oxford: Focal Press.
Terzidis, K. (2006) *Algorithmic Architecture*, Amsterdam and London: Architectural Press.
Tomitsch, M. et al. (2015) "The Role of Digital Screens in Urban Life: New Opportunities for Placemaking", in M. Foth et al. (eds.), *Citizen's Right to the Digital City: Urban Interfaces, Activism, and Placemaking*, Singapore: Springer Press, pp. 37–54.
Wikipedia (2018) "Spline (Mathematics)", available on: https://en.wikipedia.org/wiki/Spline_(mathematics) (accessed 18 December 2017).
Zaera-Polo, A. et al. (2014) *Elements of Architecture: Façade*, Venice: Marsilio, pp. 160–169.

Further Reading

Brynjolfsson, E. and McAfee, A. (2016) *The Second Machine Age: Work, Progress, and Prosperity in a Time of Brilliant Technologies*, New York: W. W. Norton & Company.
Carpo, M. (2017) *The Second Digital Turn in Architecture*, Hoboken, NJ: Wiley & Sons.
Hespanhol, L. et al. (2017) *Media Architecture Compendium: Digital Placemaking*, Ludwigsburg: Avedition.

28
FASHION
An Urban Industry of Style

Jennifer Craik

Introduction: Fashioning the City Then and Now

Fashion is arguably the cultural industry that most typifies the mediated city, both historically and contemporaneously, because of its ability to communicate signs and symbols of social status and actions. Since the 19th century, fashion has developed a distinctive form related to the parallel emergence of consumerism and spaces of consumption, spectacle, leisure, and pleasure (Wilson 1985, 2006). These institutions and places were able to emerge with the increased mobility of people and migration to cities from peripheral locations. Fashion was a vital social and cultural formation of the period, especially the phenomenon of the *flaneur*—a citizen who organized their public life around being seen and seeing in spaces of public participation and consumption.

The characteristics of the mediated city as simultaneously exhibiting linkages and cross-hatching between material (physical presence, urban form, and spatial layout) and symbolic (image, communicated branding, and social networks) formations fit the archetype of global fashion capitals. Within this context, fashion is also a form of communication especially in everyday dress. That is, clothing embodies and conveys signs about the meaning of garments and details that constitute a symbolic language (Barthes 2006; Barnard 2008). Fashion is a social practice that embodies the dialectic between the materiality of the city: on the one hand, in the material form of apparel and accessories; production and manufacture; fashion businesses and organizations; and retail spaces and shopping/consumption habits; while, on the other, the symbolic way in which fashion communicates messages in the form of style, taste, and image; as well as the many types of fashion communication such as fashion shows; shop window displays; fashion media, publishing, and advertising.

At another level, fashion involves a constant tension between the desire to belong to a group (as a class, demographic group, style niche, or subculture) and the impulse to project an individual sense of self and unique identity. These characteristics were explored by Georg Simmel (1957) who observed the tension between a person's desire to fit in (imitation) at the same time expressing selfhood (differentiation). He argued that these oppositional tendencies were evident both in fashion as a social practice and in the city as a technique of civility; that is, as citizens balanced both tendencies as fundamental human needs. The city constrains the individual to fit into instrumental and organized ways of life that produce superficial, one-dimensional, and alienating blandness, yet at the same time, liberates people from the parochialism of small communities by providing space and opportunities for individual expression of self.

Although fashion defines popular modes of dress and symbolizes the meaning of particular garments in many cultures, the modern fashion industry developed in response to industrialization and mass production. This occurred alongside the establishment of shopping in new palaces of consumerism such as arcades and department stores, as argued by Walter Benjamin (Benson 1979; Howard 2015). New techniques of selling and promoting goods through visual forms of communication, such as advertising using new communication channels, store windows, mannequin displays, catwalk parades, and sales personnel, were central to embedding fashion in urban spaces. While the city and the fashion industry have been transformed since Simmel wrote, contemporary theorists still observe the tension between group belonging and individual projection as the defining feature of fashion in the mediated city (Craik 2009).

In the 20th century, fashion in the city became synonymous with the iconic fashion capitals of London, Paris, New York, Milan, and Tokyo, although equally important was the democratization of ready-to-wear fashion in department stores and clothing for everyday consumers in urban centers across the globe (Gilbert 2006). Fashion has been an early adopter of new techniques of communication to sell goods via new media platforms. This has increased with the advent of digital media and communication technologies and postmodern urban forms and spaces. The term "lifestyle shopping" describes the centrality of consumer desire and acquisition of consumer goods to achieve happiness in the postmodern city (Shields 1992).

Another feature of fashion in the city is hierarchies of value and worth. Fashion creates hierarchies in all aspects of the industry, including tiers of fashion cities (Breward and Gilbert 2006). Possessing and promoting a fashion industry has become an essential element of creating the mediated city as a symbol of postmodernity. With the rise of the online and virtual media, fashion has embraced creative collaborations alongside conventional consumption spaces in favor of cultural and design precincts.

Symbolically, fashion has become the leitmotif of travel, tourism, urban development, and regeneration strategies and thus has cemented the role of fashion in placemaking and urban identities. As the geographic axis shifts from north to south and west to east, fashion's fortunes are competing with European and North American taste-making via the rapid emergence of fashion cities in polycentric locations (Niessen, Leshkovich, and Jones 2003). Emerging fashion cities and regions include Greater China (including Hong Kong and Taiwan), South America (including Buenos Aires, Rio de Janeiro, and São Paolo), and Africa (Lagos, Dakar, Johannesburg). A successful fashion city is a symbol of a future-oriented, innovative, dynamic, livable place that offers citizens and visitors alike a plethora of experiences, human interactions, and opportunities.

Despite the proliferation of fashion cities, the iconic four—Paris, London, New York, and Milan—remain the epitome of fashion capitals with Paris at the center of the fashion universe. Histories of the Paris and London fashion industries explore the dynamics of how these fashion cities developed: industrialization (mass production of apparel), new employment opportunities (factories, artisan crafts, retailing, advertising, media), migration (to cities), mercantile and consumerism (retail facilities and shopping, expenditure on goods), and world trade (import, export, outsourcing of production, travel, and tourism) (Steele 1988; Breward 2003; Rocamora 2006). Modern cities attracted large numbers of people for work and to live taking advantage of urban infrastructure, services, and facilities. Accompanying these physical elements was the development of a distinctive sense of city identity. Fashion provided an immediately visible and tangible signpost of identity through distinctive modes of dress and style (Breward and Gilbert 2006). Fashion defined the city of modernity. As the mediated city evolved, the fashion industry re-invented itself to match postmodern cities themselves (Crewe 2017).

Fashion in the Mediated City

While the status of the early fashion capitals has persisted, the nature of the fashion industry has changed significantly as the materiality of the city has absorbed new symbolic and virtual forms of communication and interaction. In the case of the fashion industry, this has created a dispersed global industry, shifting "from a localized and craft-based trade, to one of the industries where a global division of labour is most pronounced" (Hauge, Malmberg, and Power 2009: 529). While Europe and North America remain the dominant fashion centers in terms of top designers, brands, and labels, the majority of production occurs where labor is cheaper.

One example is Swedish fashion brand Hennes and Mauritz (HandM), which has penetrated the global fashion marketplace. HandM has crafted highly successful promotional campaigns that appeal to young urban "cool" consumers across the globe. But while HandM epitomizes fast fashion, Sweden also owns small and medium brands like Acme, Eton, Gant, and Nudie Jeans. The distinctive feature of the Swedish fashion industry is its investment in knowledge and innovation in "design, brand value, efficient marketing channels, logistics and distribution" rather than on the material production of apparel that occurs in "low-cost locations" (Hauge et al. 2009: 530). For Swedish fashion firms, material production is little more than a specialized input. Instead, it is "the production and management of ideas (fashion) that is the core product" (Hauge et al. 2009: 530). This global shift in production arrangements has become the norm for large-scale fashion manufacture in many countries.

By outsourcing the material production of fashion, the crucial elements of the contemporary fashion industry are design, innovation, management, and quality control. Fashion industries develop an entrepreneurial spirit thrives. Key to success is the cultural capital that a fashion city creates. In Sweden, other brands and new fashion companies benefit from the rub-off effect of the global success of the Made in Sweden branding and status that makes their own promotion easier and more effective to consumers already knowledgeable and positive about "Swedish" fashion. Similarly, successful fashion industries have been established in Denmark, Belgium, Holland, and Germany (Anna and Gronbach 2006; Smelik 2017).

Networking and Placemaking Through Fashion

Another feature of the fashion industry in the mediated city is the centrality of networking and communication between players in the industry. At its heart, rivalry and competition abound in fashion industries but at the same time, everyone is mutually dependent on everyone else to maintain the image of a coherent and viable industry. To this end, the fashion community relies on socializing, monitoring, and networking with the aim of seeking enhanced market position. The combination of "reputation spillover" and export success is bolstered by the endorsement of fashion bedfellows (muses, celebrities, photographers, models, stylists, fashion bloggers, fashion editors, forecasters, and buyers) who create a "groupthink" consensus of trends and styles within fashion cities (Hauge et al. 2009: 541).

Fashion retailers and shop assistants are also important because they "exhibit an interesting mix of fashion high-status with financial low-pay/low-status" yet "embody the image by wearing the products they sell" and are selected and trained to reflect the brand DNA (Hauge et al. 2009: 540). Their detailed knowledge of fashion (past and present) as well as looking the part is acknowledged by buyers and journalists who, for example, cite the ubiquitous air kiss as "part of the culture of the field, allowing for performative enactments necessary to the continued presence in the field and field participants" (Entwistle and Rocamora 2006: 746–747).

The spillover effect of a fashion identity flows to and from the cities in which they are located. Cities with a strong symbolic brand and set of values can capitalize on their distinctive sense of place as a crucial ingredient in promoting a fashion culture: "the brand infuses products (and firms) with the 'feel' of the city: for example, cool clothes come from cool places" (Jansson and Power 2010: 892). Products become associated with places and places with particular products (Scott 1996, 2010).

One example is the fashion icon of Milan. The transformation of postwar Milan from de-industrialization to become simultaneously a football city, a fashion city, and a finance center began in the 1970s (Bovone 2005; Jansson and Power 2010: 892). Now, Milan is renowned as an innovative city of excellence for fashion and design, and the city's "brand" (White 2000; Steele 2003; Segre Reinach 2006, 2014). Milan has usurped Florence as Italy's fashion capital by collaborations with allied design sectors, vertical integration from design to production, specialized in product innovation, and transformed distribution strategies. At a symbolic level, Milan has re-invented the previously elitism of fashion events by creating a party-like atmosphere and less exclusive guest list (Segre Reinach 2014). Milan specializes in prêt-à-porter fashion that appeals to a broader market share and in recent years has added fast fashion as a specialty that rests on:

> the power to define the symbols of fashion and design, and function as switching points where ideas and values are negotiated . . . [and] central to fashion-based industries innovation and value-creation processes.
>
> *(Lees-Maffei and Fallan 2014)*

It is achieved through four brand channels:

- promotional events largely focused on prêt-à-porter and high-end designer brands;
- high-profile spokespersons such as designers, brand advocates and patrons;
- exclusive flagship stores and showrooms that showcase brand values; and
- different types of retail districts (for example, exclusive, "boho," vintage and, design hubs) that target distinct consumer groups (Jansson and Power 2010: 895–900).

Fashion and design industries in Milan compete to "appropriate the symbolic landscape" through billboards, branded businesses, and promotional events (Jansson and Power 2010: 899). Like Sweden, Milan fashion focuses on export, although cultivating a fashion-conscious local clientele. Unlike Sweden, Milan has benefitted from local manufacturing and artisanal hubs that justify the Made in Italy tag, even when in Prato's case, the labor force is largely immigrant Chinese (Dallabona 2014; Dei Ottati 2014).

Fashion in mediated cities reflects the shift from craftsmanship to factories to post-Fordist dispersal of design studios and offshore production. Investment is in product development, contracting, quality control, merchandising, and distribution. Above all, promotional and marketing strategies are crucial to success as innovative design and sellable products:

> Global cities in cultural industries—where competitiveness rests upon differentiation—are important as switching centres and especially productive crucibles for forging immaterial value and knowledge.
>
> *(Jansson and Power 2010: 902)*

Design in the City and the Labor of Design and Fashion

The result is that design and designers have become critical to the contemporary branding of fashion cities (Rantisi 2004; cf. Florida 2012). Rantisi has explored the symbiotic relationship between the designer and the city. On the one hand, designers seek inspiration in the place or city in which they reside as well as travel experiences, other cultures, and historical references. Designers also tweak previous styles and aesthetic eras and the work of other designers; mainstream and niche retail stock, stores and enclaves; forecasting and trend sites; fashion/design-centered blogs and publications; and autobiographical and personal preoccupations. Despite this plethora of inspiration, Rantisi found that over 80% of responses by New York designers cited references that were "specific to the New York cultural economy" as their creative inspiration revealing "a strong and positive relation between the city and the creative process" (Rantisi 2004).

On the other hand, cities draw on the images and symbolism created by fashion and design industries to feed into the ways in which the distinctive attributes of a city are curated and projected. Well-known designers have become celebrities, fêted as "creative geniuses" (Santagata 2004: 78). They are frequently employed to promote the image of cities desired by governments. While iconic fashion designers are associated with Paris, a growing number of iconic fashion designers reflect the culture of other cities: for example, Ralph Lauren or Donna Karan and New York; Armani or Versace and Milan; Alexander McQueen or Vivienne Westwood and London; Issey Miyake or Rei Kawakubo and Tokyo. The status of designers is associated with wealth, which in turn has become the image of the fashion industry in general.

The reality is that many designers have precarious career paths while the industry as a whole is composed of precarious labor, including apparel-making factory workers, retail assistants, craft artisans, and aspiring models. While there is an increasing diversity of careers in the fashion industry as it transforms into an image industry, employment depends on the success of the last collection, so peaks and troughs chart career paths as fashion workers chase the magic ingredient that popularizes a "look." Yet, perceptions of the fashion industry focus either on the celebrity and glamorous designer, at one end, or the exploited and unskilled manufacturing labor, at the other; in other words, Karl Lagerfeld versus the Rana Plaza victims. These polarized pictures piggyback on fashion's wicked problem, namely the disjunction between the impulse to produce new fashion for a voracious market while creating unsustainable and environmentally damaging side-effects, including massive problems of waste (Brown 2010; Fletcher 2014).

Many workers in the fashion industry make only part of their income from their fashion-related work, supplementing incomes with part-time or casual jobs such as barista, retail, or teaching. Most fashion careers are not at the "pointy" ends of design or consumption but in the immaterial and symbolic interstices such as technical specializations, forecasting, buying, merchandising, media, PR, and styling (Jackson and Shaw 2006). Where fashion is the primary occupation, incomes vary enormously. For example, the annual 2016 *Fashionista* survey found that average salaries in the area of Design ranged from $36,000 for an Assistant Technical Director to $163,000 for a Design Director; while in the area of Creative, an Assistant Graphic Designer earned $33,000, while a Creative Director earned $206,000 (Indvik 2016).

In the USA, the fashion industry in New York City is arguably "the fashion capital of the world ahead of Paris, Milan, and London," being home to over 900 fashion companies and the largest retail market in the country, generating more than $15 billion in annual sales (Maloney 2015: 4; see also Rantisi 2003, 2004; Curid 2007). Although manufacturing jobs have largely gone offshore, high-value jobs have replaced these in R&D, design, and marketing. While New York City and Los Angeles remain the largest fashion cities in the USA, other cities are developing fashion industries including San Francisco, Nashville, Columbus, Seattle, and Dallas (Maloney 2015). Like fashion in other cities, the investment centers on specialized knowledge and innovation, along with industry collaborations, government support, education and training, and specialized production. Frequently, fashion-related industries are located in creative clusters interacting with other design professions as collaborations and innovation crucibles.

As in Europe, there is evidence of "reshoring" as companies shift to quicker design-market timeframes, shorter supply chains, and smaller product runs monitored by RFID systems (Maloney 2015). In addition, the rise of the "handmade" (bespoke and customized products) that are deemed to be "eco"-friendly and sustainable (Black 2008; Brown 2010) is creating opportunities for skilled craftspeople and artisans by revitalizing skills like embroidery, beading, metal-work, accessory design, leatherwork, pleating, and hand-dyeing (Scott 1996). The development of 3D printing has created fashion-related specialist jobs. These trends are packaged as emotionally durable design that slows the pace of fashion, modifies consumerism, and reduces waste (Cramer 2011).

Creating Fashion Capitals and Animating Cities Through Fashion Weeks

Visibility of the global fashion industry is the proliferation of fashion weeks around the world. Once confined to Paris, London, New York, and Milan, fashion trends and innovations are unveiled in a multitude of cities across continents (Breward and Gilbert 2006). The traditional two fashion week periods for spring/summer and autumn/winter collections have many competitors including specialist fashions (such as lingerie or accessories), trans-seasonal collections, and designer-specific events. The aims of fashion shows and fashion weeks are multifaceted (Skov 2006). At a business level, they are trade shows, designed to show off the latest collections to buyers and the media, leaving time for stock to go into production for the next season. Success often depends on celebrity guests and endorsement whose presence contributes to taste-making and popularizing fashions. Fashion weeks are sponsored by governments to promote a city image and fashion-conscious sensibility, alongside private sponsorship such as cosmetic companies, fashion brands, and retail behemoths. Fashion weeks are an essential element of a fashion capital. Urbanity, communication, cultural intermediation, and fashionability are the key markers of the city of the future in a centrifugal process that draws people into the city.

Fashion weeks have adapted to the impact of fast fashion (shorter and shorter design-to-market timelines), just-in-time schedules, and frequent new drops to satisfy the consumer appetite for immediacy. Knock-offs and counterfeit add a further element to the changing role of fashion weeks. The spread of fashion weeks reflects the shifting geographic focus of fashion from Western Europe and North America to cities in Asia, Eastern Europe, South America, and Africa/Middle East. Overall, fashion flows are shifting from north to south and west to east, as cities in emerging markets dominate midmarket and luxury fashion consumption over mature markets (Remy, Schmidt, Werner, and Lu 2014; Maloney 2015). Fashion weeks also kickstart the creative industries as part of economic restructuring around consumption-based activities.

New cities promote themselves as fashion cities by fashion weeks and other events, fashion exhibitions, trade shows, and industry expos. Although the fashion industry is now global, it has paradoxically created opportunities for local fashion to market itself as distinctive and unique point of difference. Despite the dominance of iconic Western fashion labels and brands, fashion in the city still revolves around local designers, labels, and retailers who offer fashions that resonate with local urban culture.

Diversification of Fashion Media

Another factor in the development of Parisian fashion and other fashion cities was innovations in reproduction techniques and the growth of media fashion promotion. Hand-painted fashion plates gave way to fashion illustrations, fashion advertisements, fashion reportage, and features on designers and labels. A succession of media platforms enthusiastically incorporated fashion content. However, the tension between exclusivity and accessibility of fashion has persisted. Copying, counterfeiting, poaching, adaptation, and serendipity have plagued the industry, defying regulation. The luxury fashion sector is especially affected with French luxury brands accounting for 70% of counterfeit (Stewart 2005: 122). By the 1930s, couturiers addressed counterfeit by creating affordable ready-to-wear lines for the everyday consumer, suggesting that:

> Haute couture was beginning to accept that fashion was about emulation and hence democratization, but it was also learning how to distinguish haute couture from copies—in short, how to disseminate haute couture and sustain its elitist nature.
> *(Stewart 2005: 130)*

Disseminating information about fashion inevitably meant democratizing fashion and making it available to consumers across the globe became the central preoccupation of 20th- and 21st-century fashion. Nonetheless, fashion promotion has retained its hierarchy that sets apart exclusivity from other market levels (Entwistle and Rocamora 2006: 738). There are hierarchies within designers, models on the catwalk, journalists and fashion editors, buyers from stores, fashion stylists, exclusive clients, and celebrities, which are actualized spatially at fashion shows via seating arrangements and differential access (Entwistle and Rocamora 2006: 736).

These hierarchies establish status in the self-referential fashion "community" of fashion weeks; that is, "the importance of seeing and being seen on the front row" (Entwistle and Rocamora 2006: 737). As well as a ticketing system and discretionary invitations creating spatial divisions between participants, social and cultural hierarchies are established on the basis of personal friendships and professional recognition. The pantomime of performing the hierarchy of fashion capital at fashion shows reinforces the status quo. Bodily performances including choice of outfits and air kisses on people are key parts in the play of gestures, hyperbolic greetings, and "cool" demeanor. Fashion show participants are as much part of the show as the fashions themselves.

As the number of fashion weeks grows, attending becomes a matter of judging which shows have the greatest cachet or prestige for the participant. The visibility and instantaneity of fashion shows has been enhanced by live feeds, blogs, and interactive platforms. This has unsettled the hierarchy of the fashion media as fashion bloggers challenge the status of fashion journalists as the arbiters of fashion, transforming the mechanisms of taste-making.

Transformations in Fashion Retailing and Fashion Consumption

Transformations of the fashion industry and communication have impacted on fashion retailing. Online shopping has created a global marketplace and shortened timelines of fashion trends. While fashion weeks, online bloggers, influencers, and tastemakers are shapers of trends, streetstyle is also important, remaking the fashion retail landscape. Once dominated by department stores, specialist fashion boutiques, and chain stores in high streets, shopping precincts, and shopping malls, fashion retail now occurs across retail types and spaces. Fashion is now found also in shopping enclaves, "bohemian" urban spaces, "handmade" and craft markets, and design and creative precincts (Howard 2015). Traditional fashion retailers have adapted, introducing franchises, pop-up stores, concessions, and multi-retail sublets as omni-retailing mixes. Brick-and-mortar retailers have embraced online through attractive websites, "click and collect," in-store iPads, e-commerce and mobile commerce, and free returns. Equally, retailers engage with consumers digitally to build loyal communities of target consumers.

Diverse media and communication platforms have transformed fashion media and intersected with material forms. The expansion of the fashion industry in China is an exemplar of these changes (Finnane 2007; Wu 2009; Tsui 2009; Zhao 2013). While Shanghai has a long history as a fashion city, other cities including Beijing, Tianjin, Guangzhou, Chongqing, and Shenzhen are emerging. Eleven of the top 20 fashion cities are now in China. Consumer habits of Chinese are maturing as the country emerges as a design hub for luxury and designer fashion. As labor costs rise in China, mass apparel manufacture is moving to lower-cost countries. Despite the plethora of shopping malls and exclusive stores in Chinese cities, Chinese consumers prefer to shop online and mobile. Canny global designers and brands are launching collections in China and endorsing fashion shows, events, and exhibitions.

China illustrates how fashion is central to communicating and making visible the urban development by interplay between material and spatial formations and practices: "the urban is but one (albeit important) spatial articulation of an overall creative field whose extent is ultimately nothing less than global" (Scott 2010: 115). Of all the creative industries, fashion epitomizes the mediated city of today and imaginary cities of the future.

References

Anna, S. and Gronbach, E. (eds.) (2006) *Generation Mode*, Düsseldorf: Hatje Cantz.
Barnard, M. (2008) *Fashion as Communication*, Oxon and New York: Routledge.
Barthes, R. (2006) *The Language of Fashion*, trans. A. Stafford, A. Stafford and M. Carter (eds.), Sydney: Power Publications.
Benson, S. P. (1979) "Palaces of Consumption: Machine for Selling: the American Department Store, 1880–1940," *Radical History Review*, 21, pp. 199–221.
Black, S. (2008) *Eco-Chic: The Fashion Paradox*, London: Black Dog Publishing.
Bovone, L. (2005) "Fashionable Quarters in the Postindustrial City: The Ticinese of Milan," *City and Community*, 4(4), pp. 359–380.
Breward, C. (2003) *Fashion*, Oxford: Oxford University Press.
— (2004) *Fashioning London: Clothing in the Modern Metropolis*, Oxford: Berg.
Breward, C. and Gilbert, D. (eds.) (2006) *Fashion's World Cities*, Oxford: Berg.
Brown, S. (2010) *Eco Fashion*, London: Laurence King Publishing.
Craik, J. (2009) *Fashion: The Key Concepts*, Oxford: Berg.
Cramer, J. (2011) "Made to Keep: Product Longevity through Participatory Design," *Design Principles and Practice: An International Journal*, 5(5), pp. 437–445.
Crewe, L. (2017) *Geographies of Fashion: Consumption, Space, and Value*, London: Bloomsbury.
Curid, E. (2007) *The Warhol Economy: How Fashion, Art and Music Drive New York City*, Princeton, NJ: Princeton University Press.
Dallabona, A. (2014) "Narratives of Italian Craftsmanship and the Luxury Fashion Industry: Representations of Italianicity in Discourses of Production," in J. Hancock, G. Muratovski, V. Manlow, and A. Peirson-Smith (eds.) *Global Fashion Brands: Style, Luxury and History*, Bristol: Intellect, pp. 215–228.
Dei Ottati, G. (2014) "A Transnational Industrial Fast Fashion District: An Analysis of the Chinese Businesses in Prato," *Cambridge Journal of Economics*, 38, pp. 1257–1274.
Entwistle, J. and Rocamora, A. (2006) "The Field of Fashion Materialized: A Study of London Fashion Week," *Sociology*, 40(4), pp. 735–751.
Finnane, A. (2007) *Changing Clothes in China: Fashion, History, Nation*, Sydney: UNSW Press.

Fletcher, K. (2014) *Sustainable Fashion and Textiles*, 2nd edition, London: Earthscan.
Florida. R. (2012) *The Rise of the Creative Class: Revisited*, New York: Basic Books.
Gilbert, D. (2006) "From Paris to Shanghai: The Changing Geographies of Fashion's World Cities," in C. Breward and D. Gilbert (eds.) *Fashion's World Cities*, Oxford: Berg, pp. 3–32.
Hauge, A., Malmberg, A., and Power, D. (2009) "The Spaces and Places of Swedish Fashion," *European Planning Studies*, 17(4), pp. 529–547.
Howard, V. (2015) *From Main Street to Mall: The Rise and Fall of the American Department Store*, Philadelphia, PA: University of Pennsylvania Press.
Indvik, L. (2016) "Fashion Jobs: Find Out What They Really Pay," *Fashionista*, February 2, viewed July 4, 2017, https://fashionista.com/2016/02/fashion-jobs.
Jackson, T. and Shaw, D. (2006) *The Fashion Handbook*, London: Routledge.
Jansson, J. and Power, D. (2010) "Fashioning a Global City: Global City Brand Channels in the Fashion and Design Industries," *Regional Studies*, 44(7), pp. 889–904.
Lees-Maffei, G. and Fallan, K. (eds.) (2014) *Made in Italy: Rethinking a Century of Italian Design*, London: Bloomsbury.
Maloney, C. (2015) *The Economic Impact of the Fashion Industry*, Joint Economic Committee, United States Congress, February 6, accessed July 4, 2017, https://maloney.house.gov/sites/maloney.house.gov/files/documents/The%20Economic%20Impact%20of%20the%20Fashion%20Industry%20—%20JEC%20report%20FINAL.pdf.
Niessen, S., Leshkovich, A. M., and Jones, C. (eds.) (2003) *Re-orienting Fashion: The Globalization of Asian Dress*, Oxford: Berg.
Rantisi, N. (2003) "The Ascendance of New York Fashion," *International Journal of Urban and Regional Research*, 28(1), pp. 86–106.
— (2004) "The Designer in the City and the City in the Designer," in D. Power and A. Scott (eds.) *Cultural Industries and the Production of Culture*, London: Routledge, pp. 91–109.
Remy, N., Schmidt, J., Werner, C., and Lu, M. (2014) *Unleashing Fashion Growth City by City*, McKinsey and Co, viewed July 5, 2017, www.mckinsey.com/~/media/mckinsey/dotcom/client_service/marketing%20and%20sales/pdfs/unleashing_fashion_growth.ashx.
Rocamora, A. (2006) "Paris, Capitale de la Mode," in C. Breward and D. Gilbert (eds.) *Fashion's World Cities*, Oxford: Berg, pp. 43–54.
Santagata, W. (2004) "Creativity, Fashion and Market Behaviour," in D. Power and A. Scott (eds.) *Cultural Industries and the Production of Culture*, London: Routledge, pp. 75–90.
Scott, A. (1996) "The Craft, Fashion and Cultural Products Industries of Los Angeles: Competitive Dynamics and Policy Dilemmas in a Multisectoral Image," *Annals of the Association of American Geographers*, 86(2), pp. 306–323.
— (2010) "Cultural Economy and the Creative Role of the City," *Geografiska Annaler: Series B, Human Geography*, 92(2), pp. 115–130.
Segre Reinach, S. (2006) "Milan: The City of Prêt-à-Porter in a World of Fast Fashion," in C. Breward and D. Gilbert (eds.) *Fashions World Cities*, Oxford: Berg, pp. 123–134.
— (2014) "Italian Fashion: The Metamorphosis of a Cultural Industry," in G. Lees-Maffei and K. Fallan (eds.) *Made in Italy: Rethinking a Century of Italian Design*, London: Bloomsbury, pp. 239–251.
Shields, R. (ed.) (1992) *Lifestyle Shopping: The Subject of Consumption*, London: Routledge.
Simmel, G. (1903) "The Metropolis and Mental Life," in G. Bridges and S. Watson (eds.) *The Blackwell City Reader* (2002), Oxford: Blackwell, pp. 11–19.
— (1957) "Fashion," *American Journal of Sociology*, 62, pp. 541–548.
Skov, L. (2006) "The Role of Trade Fairs in the Global Fashion Business," *Current Sociology*, 54, pp. 764–783.
Smelik, A. (ed.) (2017) *Delft Blue to Denim Blue: Contemporary Dutch Fashion*, London: L. B. Tauris.
Steele, V. (1988) *Paris Fashion*, Oxford: Oxford University Press.
— (2003) *Fashion, Italian Style*, New Haven, CT: Yale University Press.
Stewart, M. (2005) "Copying and Copyrighting Haute Couture: Democratizing Fashion," *French Historical Studies*, 26(1), pp. 103–130.
Tsui, C. (2009) *China Fashion; Conversations with Designers*, Oxford: Berg.
White, N. (2000) *Reconstructing Italian Fashion*, Oxford: Berg.
Wilson, E. (1985) *Adorned in Dreams: Fashion and Modernity*, London: Virago Press.
Wilson, E. (2006) "Urbane Fashion," in C. Breward and D. Gilbert (eds.) *Fashion's World Cities*, Oxford: Berg, pp. 33–39.

Wu, J. (2009) *Chinese Fashion*, Oxford: Berg.
Zhao, J. (2013) *The Chinese Fashion Industry*, London: Bloomsbury.

Further Reading

Breward, C. and Gilbert, D. (eds.) (2006) *Fashion's World Cities*, Oxford: Berg.
Crewe, L. (2017) *Geographies of Fashion: Consumption, Space, and Value*, London: Bloomsbury.
Niessen, S. et al. (2003) *Re-Orienting Fashion: The Globalization of Asian Dress*, Oxford: Berg.

29
DIGITAL PUBLIC ART
Installations and Interventions

Martin Zebracki

Introduction

This chapter critically examines the digitally mediated roles and uses of artworks in urban public space and contemporary urban living. I particularly consider the ways in which everyday users re-appropriate "offline" material installations and remediate the urban condition through digital media practices and online interventions. *Public art* is a well-trodden terminological shorthand that commonly refers to publicly commissioned artworks designated for open places (usually beyond museums and galleries) with free, bodily physical access for all (see Miles 1997). However, this term is surrounded by an ongoing polemic about its contents, sites of production, and spaces and temporal frameworks for social engagement (Zebracki 2012, 2017c).

Cities are widely acknowledged to constitute breeding places for artists, creativity, and talents. Accordingly, they occupy the primary site for public art in foremostly placemaking practices that are aimed at representing local and national cultures, histories, and ideologies. Nevertheless, public art is neither neatly defined by nor confined to the physical boundaries of the city, as practices involve ideas, bodies, and matter that traverse space and time.

The proliferation of digital technologies in the networked urban society reveals another complicating factor in conceptualizing the urban condition and the "publicness" of public art (Marchese 2015; Zebracki 2017c). The "planetary urbanization" (Brenner and Schmid 2015) is increasingly channeled through the digital (Zebracki and Luger 2018). Digitally networked public art practices interconnect streets, private home spaces, formal and informal art markets, etc. through the World Wide Web. This segues into digital urbanity, a fluid, more-than-material condition of urban everyday life.

Despite the digital turn within the "geographical humanities" (geohumanities) and social sciences (Crang 2015; Ash et al. 2016), Rose (2016) contended that scholarship remains remiss in coming to grips with the digital mediation of cultural artifacts beyond their material environments. Hence, this chapter attends to digitally networked spaces as the locus for grappling with the relationships between cities, media, and everyday life. I do so through the specific lens of the roles and uses of public art installations and interventions to achieve greater clarity of their (lack of) mediated publicness in contexts of digital urbanity. In dovetailing urban geography to media scholarship, I specifically analyze how the digitally mediated geographies (the "know-whats," "know-wheres," and "know-whens") of public art have been reconfiguring the spaces of everyday urban life, while considering how both urban geography and media scholars have employed digital technologies as both sites and tools of research.

I first conceptualize urban public art in the digitally reconfigured/networked city—or the "Internet of Things." Second, I discuss do-it-yourself (DIY) modes for digital public art production and engagement. Third, I analyze the implications of digitally mediated public art practices for everyday sensemakings of the city. I end with reflections on the intersections of public art practices and digital citizenship and draw directions for further research.

Urban Public Art and the Internet of Things

What are the social and spatial implications of the digital for understanding urban public art practices and how do they integrate bodies and matter? These are some questions raised by actor-network theory (e.g., Latour 2005) and nascent post-structuralist, non-representational philosophies (e.g., Thrift 2008). These approaches have included humans and objects as equal entities and energies in understanding social relations and the social production of space. They have engendered fecund ways for querying the binaries between humans and objects, informing and mediating one another in powerful and productive relations.

The digital condition has queried what constitutes the materiality of real-world urban environments in the first place. The latter are co-constituted through the digital in multiuser, both offline and online, spaces within the networked society, where there is no neatly parallel ontogenesis of the material and digital. The experience of materiality has been intensified precisely because digitality is mediated through material artifacts. In digitally mediated environments, humans and objects marry (i.e., *cyborgs*, see Haraway 1991), where the interconnected amalgam of humans, techno-devices, and everyday (art) objects can be described as the Internet of Things (Graham and Haarstad 2011).

Digital culture particularly asks to revisit the bifurcated relationship between formal/commissioned and informal/unsolicited public art practices. Established art market agents and practitioners increasingly translate public artwork through digital media and, in so doing, play with novel material-digital, that is hybrid, parameters of the urban public sphere. Digital technologies have reconfigured conventional codes of both museum and public art practices in terms of institutional commissioning, public financing, procedures for "formal" consultation and "official" public participation, and the centrality of material objects. Accordingly, they have broken with the "fourth wall" to engage new and wider audiences. Beyond formal contexts of the art world, digital technologies have enabled new mediated social relations (e.g., online encounters and "artivism" beyond the gallery and public square), spatial practices and participation (e.g., free/cheap, unsolicited (re)appropriations of artworks by social media users), and aesthetics (e.g., digital mutations of material artworks through DIY media).

Strikingly, museums are increasingly more committed to curating online exhibitions, digital archiving, and experimenting with augmented reality-assisted tours to provide users with more immersive experiences of their art collection (see Paul 2016). Further, 3D-printed art is another emerging phenomenon, transforming digital design to physical, tactile artwork, or vice versa. This method has also been applied to bring cultural heritage back to material life. For example, the Institute for Digital Archaeology restored Palmyra's Roman arch, destroyed by the so-called Islamic State (IS), as 3D-printed replica in City Hall Park in New York in 2016 (Figure 29.1). This installation was followed by "digital feedback" over social media about the ethics of such additive manufacturing. While some perceived the 3D-printed sculpture as a tribute to Syrian antiquity, others took this "imported" public art piece as a token of digital colonialism (Bond 2016).

Figure 29.1 Digital Colonial Public Art? 3D-Printed Replica of Palmyra's Roman Arch, Destroyed by IS, on Display in City Hall Park, New York, 2016. User name and link blinded for confidentiality

Digital technologies may provide a powerful counterbalance to formal public art commissioning and practices. Their affordances have put everyday users in heightened capacities to encounter and disseminate public artwork in on-demand ways, spaces, and timeframes. A significant shift in focus has taken place from *functions*, centered around the artist's intention, toward *uses*, inscribing experiences and re-appropriations by everyday public users.

Stevens and Lossau (2015) originally applied this differentiation to "offline" urban public art. I here extend the notion of *uses* to contexts of digitally networked spaces (see Zebracki 2017a), which are shaped through *peer-to-peer* social media platforms such as Facebook, Twitter, and Instagram (i.e., Web 2.0; see John 2013). To varying degrees, social media are fraught with possibilities for re-appropriating, thus *co-creating*, extant material public artwork through traceable forms of engaging digital content (e.g., commenting, sharing), which comprise assemblages of text, image, and sound (Kidd 2014). Digital user (co-)creation, to some extent, has expanded the possibilities for gaining immersive experiences of the networked realities of urban space, art, and publicness. Therefore, it breaks with some of the static, cooperative motilities (Lofland 1998), or capacities of movement, of art engagers as known in offline public art worlds (see Vernet 2017).

Digitally networked public art involves multiple user environments, which are simultaneously more-than-material and more-than-digital within heterogeneous and somewhat elusive in-between spaces. This calls the definition of "the public" of public art into question (depending on the specificities of the arts of digital mediation). There are manifold thinkable examples. Users may take a snapshot of a physical public artwork in situ, edit the photo on the spot, and post the image along with an interpretative caption on one or multiple social networking sites. Then, they may have real-time interactions with other online users about co-created content of the original artwork in integrated digital forms (see multimediality in Rose 2016). Over time, other users may edit this content by the use of digital and online software and exchange mutated variants across multiple actual and digital sites, which they may do with entirely different intentions than the original artist and the first-time online poster. Where some users may act as active participants/editors/commenters in this process, others may perform as observers only.

This condition sheds new light on inter-communications, specifically the "stranger" relations, which revolve around urban public artwork. Warner (2005) problematized the aggregate of "the public": it is the multiplicity of different strangers across urban living spaces that constitutes the greater public. Hence, as acknowledged in political philosophy (e.g., Deutsche 1996; Mouffe 2007), public space does not pre-exist urban living but *becomes* as such through a multiplicity of oft-conflicting viewpoints and encounters that widely traverse social difference (e.g., sex, gender, sexuality, age, ethnicity, (dis)ability, religion, and geographical origin; see Zebracki 2017b). Therefore, following Warner (2005), the plural concept *publics* seems to be a more appropriate term to co-opt social difference in highly diverse city spaces.

So, how can we understand urban digital publics? In light of the merger of the material/digital, software/hardware, body/technology, humans/nonhumans, urban/non-urban, near/far, now/then etc., urban digital publics find themselves within fluid spatial, social, temporal, and actual/virtual realities of the Internet. Hence, urban digital publics are *distributed publics* (Hartley 2012; Gauthier 2015) in off- and online spaces; that is, spaces where digital multiuser environments overlay material environments (see "hybrid space" in De Souza e Silva 2004). Urban digital publics ambiguously adopt dynamic presences/absences of bodies and matter in the Internet of Things. They are dissipated over material places in and beyond the city as well as online through multiple social media accounts and within communication flows in real or asynchronous time patterns. Accordingly, they can reconfigure urban place attachments and query identities through DIY content engagement and curation.

DIY Urban Medium

Large strides have been made in developing scholarship and practices around urban digital geographies. A growing use of digital techno-devices in computing and statistical analysis has attended geography's quantitative revolution since the 1960s and in interview- and observation-based research on everyday experiences of urban life since the 1980s' qualitative turn (Zebracki and Luger 2018). Scholars and curators have increasingly applied Internet-based research methods and computer-mediated art to urban environments (Hewson and Stewart 2016; Pink et al. 2016). Digital and online technologies are no longer just *etic* ("outside") research tools where researchers, as "outside" onlookers, observe, "scrape," and analyze digital content. From an *emic* (i.e., auto-ethnographic) angle, they may act as "inside" social media users who contribute, and thereby are part of, digital user-created content (for example, through online community posting/messaging and interactive virtual gaming; see Boellstorff 2010). So, cyberspace itself has become foregrounded as site of research on everyday urban creative industries and public art practices (Zebracki 2017c).

The mechanical reproduction of artifacts (Benjamin [1936] 2008) has evolved to increasingly incorporate modes for digital reproduction. The contemporary digital age has implicated democratic and emancipatory waves. Techno-apparatuses have become accessible and affordable for large numbers of urban citizens, but undoubtedly not for all, which enable publics to *co-create* public artworks and "draw" their own city spaces (see do-it-together [DIT] and its variant do-it-with-others [DIWO] in Paul 2016). However, there remains a significant participation divide in digital culture across and within the urban Global North and South, owing to varying levels of digital literacies as well as authoritarian, territory-regulated restrictions to Internet usage (Reed 2014), such as in Turkey and China.

The bottom-up potential for engaging with, and co-creating, urban public art is a quintessential quality of socially networked, peer-to-peer environments. They have significantly reconfigured the binarisms between expert (artist) and layperson (amateur), between creator and engager, and between market structures and noncommercial user autonomy. *Situated knowledges* (see Haraway 1991), which are simultaneously conceptual (techne) and practice-based (episteme), are helpful in questioning creator–engager and researcher–researched positionalities as well as body–matter qualities. Barnes (2000: 743) conveyed that situated knowledges are "grounded in the physicality of specific human bodies and their artefacts." Material-based embodiment is nevertheless too narrow for grasping *digital* situated knowledges of how engagers become immersed in public art and how the spectacle and audience are reconfigured accordingly (see Courchesne 2002; Paul 2016).

Digitally networked embodiments involve dynamic, mobile, fluid, and ephemeral encounters between artwork and audiences, surfing and blending the binarisms of offline/actual and online/virtual spaces (Boellstorff 2010). Inspired by queer theory (e.g., Ahmed 2006; Boellstorff 2010), I render *que(e)rying* as critical semiotic device for studying public art in digitally networked space (Zebracki 2017c). This term involves a word play: it emphasizes the gerund of the verb "query" (to question), rather than the noun "queer," to move into "methodological activism" (Jones and Adams 2010: 203) and, accordingly, deconstruct conventionalisms and binarisms.

Kidd (2014) illustrated how digitally mediated art practices, involving DIY (co-)creation and dissemination of content, may be considered critical *interventions* into formal commissioning practices and the modus operandi of mainstream new media. Online users may, for instance, curate stories and images of public artworks to broadcast their own views assembled in text, image, and/or sound, thereby potentially relaying a vivid sense of "digital immediacy" to other users (Bell and Lyall 2005).

The DIY nature of digitally mediated engagements conceptually differentiates, "queries," urban public artwork along a material *installation* component and a digital *intervention* component. Extrapolating Radice et al.'s (2017: 288) argument on "offline" engagement with public art to digitally mediated environments, users may intervene online (e.g., through commenting and sharing), while the artist may be no longer in attendance and the original intentions for making the artwork might remain unknown to them. As such, the original artwork may "live on" and become digitally *mutated* (further beyond the artist's original conception and the artwork's material lifetime, if any), in the capacity of ongoing renditions within the computer-mediated urban art-space (where the real-world urban environment may serve as backdrop for the digital medium).

Sensemakings of Public Art in the Cyber-City

The digital mediation of public art provides new sensory insights into the spatialities and temporalities of its own materiality, if any, as well as of the urban condition altogether. Therefore, the operation of public art as digital urban medium and its sensory and affective impacts require some further scrutiny. The use of social networking sites for engaging and co-creating material-based urban public art, in a sense, abstracts the art from the physical urban environment, while it "stretches" the art and its urban locale throughout the digital public sphere. Thus, the material properties of public art and the urban environment have gained new senses and significance through technology-enabled contexts and digital practices. More than is sometimes acknowledged since the affective turn (see Anderson and Harrison 2012), the material has been increasingly intensified and, therefore, made (even) more relevant to user experience in the digitization of everyday urban life. Material artifacts (i.e., technological devices) perform as portals to access and mediate digitality, offering new senses of self/environment (Crang et al. 1999). The digital turn, therefore, needs to reinscribe the material dimension in its focus.

Mobile technological devices are particularly interesting in considering how they serve as screen spaces for navigating, registering, and re-appropriating public art in urban environments (see Verhoeff 2012). Mobile AR apps in particular may generate digital landscapes that are simultaneously portable, dynamic, and site-specific. For example, I have experienced first-hand how the GPS-based app *Lapse* (2016) attempted to construct an augmented reality journey through hidden art pieces in Miami. The app generates artwork in on-screen and site-specific urban environments. The spatial configurations of its AR installations allowed me to transform specific elements of the urban environment from static entities into more "liquid" forms through digital experience. That is to say, it may provide the user with augmented, real-imagined experiences, or "third space literacies" (Potter and McDougall 2017), of the digital urban condition. *Lapse*'s Word Cloud installation (Figure 29.2) presented insightful scripts to me, allowing me to wander the urban locale differently and imbue it with new meanings. Although user agency/autonomy was enabled, it felt somewhat limited, as I experienced that the app imprinted words in lieu of providing me with the technological ability to intervene and "write" on urban space myself.

Compared to socio-physical engagements with public art, a particularly important feature offered by digital technologies is the possibility for (systematically) creating and "saving" digital reproductions of public art content. They might relay specific *rememberings* of the content, site, and context as associated with the material artwork and its urban environment. Therefore, digitally mediated practices may be particularly conducive to re-enliven both art-matter and urban-matter (especially when the artwork is no longer in existence). However, the highly viral

Figure 29.2 Re-Wor(l)ding Urban Space with the Mobile Application *Lapse*, Miami. Shown is the author's screenshot of a GPS-based walk-through prose of the app component *The Writing*, Museum Park

digital image culture, and growing publicly accessible digital archives, might run up against a desire to *unremember*.

The digital re-incarnation of urban public artwork offers new opportunities for online users worldwide for not only remembering but also *re*-acting to original or digitally reproduced artwork. Re-actions can concurrently work out off- and online, where the digital/a-territorial is mutually attached to the material/territorial, thereby augmenting one another. My digital ethnographic study (Zebracki 2017c) on Paul McCarthy's controversial inflatable *Tree* in the city center of Paris in October 2014, notoriously known as "butt plug," is a case in point for articulating the affective dimensions of on- and offline translational public art practices. My study suggested that emotions as mediated over social media appeared to direct which content was wished to be remembered or forgotten by both online and offline publics. There was substantial discontent about the perceived anti-normative characteristics of this temporary inflatable: pornographic, anti-permanent, anti-classical, anti-sculptural, and anti-heteropatriarchal. Social media tempers flared, especially when an onlooker slapped the artist in his face during the unveiling and when vandals deflated the work just two days later.

Online commotion about *Tree*'s sex(uality)-inflected nature translated into some offline manifestations, both in favor of and against the artwork, which was instantaneously fed back to the global social media sphere. On- and offline interactions with the artwork appeared to inform discourses and actions *about* and *within* the urban sphere. Thus, digital interventions might hold powerful possibilities for reimagining everyday material urban space. *Tree*'s digital legacy still lives on after its material demolition. This case reveals how digital mediation iteratively turns the material installation into digital interventions, thereby preserving it as a "networked monument" (Gauthier 2015) of the digital age.

Another compelling example of how digital–actual urban public art spaces are lived is shown by the recent contestation over proposals by several US states to dismantle Confederate memorials. This was accompanied by a tug-of-war between alt-right, white-supremacist opposition and anti-fascist and anti-racism groups. Alt-right alliances demonstrated against the suggested removal of the statue of the Confederate General Robert E. Lee in the progressive college town of Charlottesville (see Stack and Caron 2017). They strategically did so not only in situ but also through disseminating controversial content over social media, which was promiscuously "liked" by online users with aligned radical and racist views. The demonstration was met with resistance by anti-fascists yet ended with alt-right violence directed at them, pursued by an iconoclastic outbreak played out in "real life" and online. Anti-fascist protesters dragged down the Confederate Soldiers Monument in Durham, North Carolina. This was an unmistakable sign of protest carried through by wide grassroots/netroots and artivist support (Figure 29.3), which alt-right groups consequently pushed back. This example shows how opposing offline and digital publics invested an urban public installation with different moral and political power and how they (ab)used the same installation through digital DIY interventions with real-world outcomes.

Reflections: The Arts of Digital Citizenship

This chapter has analyzed the dialectics of how the digital reconfigures engagement with art in urban space and how the urban condition is reconfigured by engaging art in digitally networked space. I have argued how they reveal the social, spatial, and temporal fluidities, or messiness, of digital public art. I have paid particular attention to how digital and online (mobile) technologies have impacted DIY practices, foremostly processes of *(co-)creation* over social media (i.e., Web 2.0), and re-activated both material and immaterial urban dimensions of the contents, sites, and contexts of public artwork. In different ways and to different degrees, such technologies

Figure 29.3 "Although It's Not About Monuments . . . Options Are Possible" (public post, Instagram, August 17, 2017). This artist proposed playful alternatives to dismantling Confederate statues from urban public spaces. User name and link blinded for confidentiality

have complemented the physical and digital, and augmented one another through cyborgian, more-than-human agencies and encounters.

Digital citizenship, defined by Mossberger et al. (2008: 1) as "the ability to participate in society online," is conducive to boosting ownership of, and *intervening* into, everyday (computer-mediated) urban environments. I have differentiated between material *installations* and digital *interventions*. I have used the former term to stress formally commissioned artworks in physical urban environments. I have used the latter term to explain the "digital modulation" of public art by how everyday publics co-create digital content of material public art within digitally networked space, and thereby might intervene into formal frameworks of public art practices (e.g., policymaking, commissioning, execution).

Although this difference is functional to my argument, I realize that the ontology of installations and interventions can be queried. Public art has the capacity to connect spaces of the city to the Internet and engage citizens in novel ways, while it is reconfigured and complicated by the ways in which it is "installed" in the digital context. The myriad of unsolicited art practices in the material urban public domain, such as graffiti writing, guerrilla art (e.g., yarnstorming), and performance-based artivism, might, similarly to my logic of user-created content online, be considered bottom-up interventions.

Based on some striking examples, I have illustrated how networked public art practices have informed actions and reactions that traverse the "here" and "there" in offline and online worlds. I have argued how digital and online technologies have expanded and deepened channels for interacting with urban art-matter, environments, and citizens and, as such, for creatively re-sensing and reshaping the urban condition (which may be ambiguously territorial and non-territorial). Public art as seen through the Internet of Things, or an Internet of bodies and (art) matter, has extended sites for engagements in "glocally" networked urban spaces. Such engagements sit along a continuum between, on the one hand, critical thinking and radical engagement and, on the other hand, cursory interest, sheer indifference, and "silly citizenship" (Hartley 2012). Dominant critiques in media studies pinpoint the latter condition by arguing that online activities do not necessarily instigate social transformations, profound interactions, and the development of deeper urban place identities. Rather, the democratic, participatory and hence inclusive potentials of the digital are considered highly limited (see Miller 2008; Carpentier 2011).

To this background, I encourage further research on how the complexity of digital urban sociospatial formations can be understood through public art as medium, particularly where its affective/experiential and inclusive participatory potentials and limitations are concerned. The digital has expanded and "accelerated" the agencies of publics for not only "reading" the urban environment as a text (which was the prevailing view of the "new" cultural geography of the 1980s-1990s), but also for experiencing it as an entity that is constituted through bodily, affective (re)actions. I welcome further comparative knowledge of the role of digitally mediated public art in formal/institutionalized spaces and contexts (e.g., spatial design, cultural policy, and institutional art programs) in juxtaposition with the roles and uses of public art as experienced in the informal, lived spaces across the on- and offline liminalities of the cyber-city. Deeper insights are needed into how the relationship between formal and informal agents in digital public art practices plays out in terms of social inclusiveness and, consequently, senses of publicness.

There remains a digital divide. A significant part of the publics are not (put) in an equal position, or "radius of action," to keep abreast of digital developments and to participate in digital urban culture and democracy (see Reed 2014), thereby falling (further) down the material "cracks" of the city. Research should critically address, and cultural policies should redress, how this digital divide is anchored in, and potentially reinforces, existing social and spatial inequalities in the city. Such concerted efforts of research and policy may provide greater insights into what digital public art practices may have in the offing for advancing more inclusive, and thus more "public," urban futures.

References

Ahmed, S. (2006) *Queer Phenomenology: Orientations, Objects, Others*, Durham, NC: Duke University Press.
Anderson, B. and Harrison, P. (eds.) (2012) *Taking-Place: Non-Representational Theories and Geography*, Farnham: Ashgate.
Ash, J., Kitchin, R., and Leszczynski, A. (2016) "Digital Turn, Digital Geographies?" *Progress in Human Geography*, 42(1), pp. 25–43.
Barnes, T. (2000) "Situated Knowledge," in R. Johnston, D. Gregory, G. Pratt, and W. Watts (eds.) *The Dictionary of Human Geography*, Oxford: Blackwell, pp. 742–43.
Bell, C. and Lyall, J. (2005) "'I Was Here': Pixilated Evidence," in D. Crouch, R. Jackson, and F. Thompson (eds.) *The Media and the Tourist Imagination: Converging Cultures*, London: Routledge, pp. 135–42.
Benjamin, W. ([1936] 2008) *The Work of Art in the Age of Mechanical Reproduction*, trans. J. A. Underwood, London: Penguin.
Boellstorff, T. (2010) "Queer Techne: Two Theses on Methodology and Queer Studies," in K. Browne, and C. Nash (eds.) *Queer Methods and Methodologies: Intersecting Queer Theories and Social Science Research*, London: Routledge, pp. 215–30.
Bond, S. (2016) "The Ethics of 3D-Printing Syria's Cultural Heritage," *Forbes*, September 22, www.forbes.com/sites/drsarahbond/2016/09/22/does-nycs-new-3d-printed-palmyra-arch-celebrate-syria-or-just-engage-in-digital-colonialism/#4eda8d0377db.
Brenner, N. and Schmid, C. (2015) "Towards a New Epistemology of the Urban?" *City*, 19(2–3), pp. 151–82.
Carpentier, N. (2011) "New Configurations of the Audience? The Challenges of User-generated content for Audience Theory and Media Participation," in V. Nightingale (ed.) *The Handbook of Media Audiences*, Malden, MA: Blackwell Publishing, pp. 190–212.
Courchesne, L. (2002) "The Construction of Experience: Turning Spectators into Visitors," in M. Reiser, and A. Zap (eds.) *New Screen Media: Cinema/Art/Narrative*, London: British Film Institute, pp. 256–67.
Crang, M. (2015) "The Promises and Perils of a Digital Geohumanities," *Cultural Geographies*, 22(2), pp. 351–60.
Crang, M., Crang, P., and May, J. (1999) *Virtual Geographies: Bodies, Space and Relations*, London: Routledge.
De Souza e Silva, A. (2004) "Mobile Networks and Public Spaces: Bringing Multiuser Environments into the Physical Space," *Convergence: The International Journal of Research into New Media Technologies*, 10(2), pp. 15–25.
Deutsche, R. (1996) *Evictions: Art and Spatial Politics*. Cambridge, MA: The MIT Press.
Gauthier, D. (2015) "Networked Monumental: Site, Production, and Distributed Publics: Online, and in Everyday Life," *Public Art Dialogue*, 5(1), pp. 17–54.
Graham, M. and Haarstad, H. (2011) "Transparency and Development: Ethical Consumption Through Web 2.0 and the Internet of Things," *Information Technologies and International Development*, 7(1), pp. 1–18.
Haraway, D. (1991) *Simians, Cyborgs, and Women: The Reinvention of Nature*, New York: Routledge.
Hartley, J. (2012) *Digital Futures for Cultural and Media Studies*, Oxford: Wiley-Blackwell.
Hewson, C. and Stewart, D. (2016) "Internet Research Methods," *Wiley StatsRef: Statistics Reference Online*.
John, N. (2013) "Sharing and Web 2.0: The Emergence of a Keyword," *New Media and Society*, 15(2), pp. 167–82.
Jones, S. and Adams, T. (2010) "Autoethnography Is a Queer Method," in K. Browne and C. Nash (eds.) *Queer Methods and Methodologies: Intersecting Queer Theories and Social Science Research*, London: Routledge, pp. 195–214.
Kidd, J. (2014) *Museums in the New Mediascape: Transmedia, Participation, Ethics*, Farnham: Ashgate.
Latour, B. (2005) *Reassembling the Social: An Introduction to Actor-Network-Theory*, Oxford: Oxford University Press.

Lofland, L. (1998) *The Public Realm: Exploring the City's Quintessential Social Territory*, Hawthorne, NY: Aldine de Gruyter.
Marchese, F. (2015) *Media Art and the Urban Environment: Engendering Public Engagement with Urban Ecology*, Dordrecht: Springer.
Miles, M. (1997) *Art, Space and the City: Public Art and Urban Futures*, London: Routledge.
Miller, V. (2008) "New Media, Networking and Phatic Culture," *Convergence: The International Journal of Research into New Media Technologies*, 14(4), pp. 387–40.
Mossberger, K., Tolbert, C., and McNeal, R. (2008) "Defining Digital Citizenship," in *Digital Citizenship: The Internet, Society, and Participation*, Cambridge, MA: MIT Press, pp. 1–20.
Mouffe, C. (2007) "Artistic Activism and Agonistic Spaces," *Art and Research: A Journal of Ideas, Contexts and Methods*, 1(2), www.artandresearch.org.uk/v1n2/mouffe.html.
Paul, C. (ed.) (2016) *A Companion to Digital Art*, Oxford: Wiley-Blackwell.
Pink, S., Horst, H., Postill, J., Hjorth, L., Lewis, T., and Tacchi, J. (2016) *Digital Ethnography: Principles and Practice*, London: SAGE.
Potter, J. and McDougall, J. (eds.) (2017) *Digital Media, Culture and Education: Theorising Third Space Literacies*, London: Palgrave, pp. 61–81.
Radice, M., Harvey, B., and Turner, S. (2017) "Pop-Up Ethnography and the Situated Cinema: Confronting Art with Social Science at the Winnipeg Festival of Moving Image," in M. Radice, and A. Boudreault-Fournier (eds.) *Urban Encounters: Art and the Public*, Montreal: McGill-Queen's University Press, pp. 269–93.
Reed, T. (2014) *Digitized Lives: Culture, Power, and Social Change in the Internet Era*, London: Routledge.
Rose, G. (2016) "Rethinking the Geographies of Cultural 'Objects' Through Digital Technologies: Interface, Network and Friction," *Progress in Human Geography*, 40(3), pp. 334–51.
Stack, L. and Caron, C. (2017) "State Leaders Call for Confederate Monuments to Be Removed," *The New York Times*, August 14, www.nytimes.com/2017/08/14/us/confederate-statue-kentucky.html.
Stevens, Q. and Lossau, J. (2015) "Framing Art and Its Uses in Public Space," in J. Lossau, and Q. Stevens (eds.) *The Uses of Art in Public Space*, London: Routledge.
Thrift, N. (2008) *Non-Representational Theory: Space, Politics, Affect*, London: Routledge.
Verhoeff, N. (2012) *Mobile Screens: The Visual Regime of Navigation*, Amsterdam: Amsterdam University Press.
Vernet, L. (2017) "Artwork as Strangers? Encounters with Two Monumental Artworks in Montreal," in M. Radice, and A. Boudreault-Fournier (eds.) *Urban Encounters: Art and the Public*, Montreal: McGill-Queen's University Press, pp. 25–50.
Warner, M. (2005) *Publics and Counterpublics*, New York: Zone Books.
Zebracki, M. (2012) "Engaging Geographies of Public Art: Indwellers, the 'Butt Plug Gnome' and Their Locale," *Social and Cultural Geography*, 13(7), pp. 735–58.
—— (2017a) "A Cybergeography of Public Art Encounter: The Case of *Rubber Duck*," *International Journal of Cultural Studies*, 20(5), pp. 526–44.
—— (2017b) "*Homomonument* as Queer Micropublic: An Emotional Geography of Sexual Citizenship," *Journal of Economic and Social Geography*, 108(3), pp. 345–55.
—— (2017c) "Queerying Public Art in Digitally Networked Space," *ACME: An International Journal for Critical Geographies*, 16(3), pp. 440–74.
Zebracki, M. and Luger, J. (2018) "Digital Geographies of Public Art: New Global Politics," *Progress in Human Geography*, https://doi.org/10.1177/0309132518791734.

Further Reading

Etzioni, A. (2015) *Privacy in a Cyber Age: Policy and Practice*, New York: Palgrave Macmillan.
Paul, C. (2016) "Augmented Realities: Digital Art in the Public Sphere," in Knight, C. and Senie, H. (eds.) *A Companion to Public Art*, Malden, MA: Wiley-Blackwell, pp. 205–25.
Pink, S. et al. (2016) *Digital Ethnography: Principles and Practice*, London: Sage.
Public Art Dialogue, Vol. 5 (2015) No. 1.

30
URBAN NIGHTLIFE CULTURES

Irina van Aalst

Introduction

Nightlife cultures are attracting increased attention in urban and cultural studies. The development of spatial clusters of clubs, bars, and restaurants has become a familiar governmental strategy to improve a city's image and stimulate the urban economy. Since de-industrialization, cities have increasingly turned their attention toward consumption (e.g., Bianchini 1995; Hall 2000; Van Aalst and Boogaarts 2002), during the day as well as at night to regenerate inner-city areas, to retain the middle and higher social classes, and to attract new visitors and tourists. However, in academic research, the bulk of attention has so far been paid to developments in the daytime.

In literature, arts, and film, the night has long been negatively valued—the night as opposed to day: evil versus good, danger versus safe, darkness and light, night falls and day rises. In academic writings, the night is often understood in ambivalent terms. The pioneer of night research, Murray Melbin (1987), found that people are much more alert in terms of encountering strangers during the "dark" hours. Yet the common realization of potential dangers seems to have contradictory consequences: "If not foe, then friend" (Melbin 1987: 73). People using the public space during night-time are aware of being in a special situation in which they may feel a sense of togetherness that can lead to unexpected moments of solidarity, friendship, and mutual assistance. Night-time tolerates forms of sociality and conviviality to emerge that are not normally encountered during daylight (Jayne et al. 2011). Night allows people to escape from the social structures of the day and lead a more alternative lifestyle, like that of an artist or writer (Gwiazdzinski 2005). More and more human activities are unfolding during the night, constructing a new domain of work and leisure. The distinction between day and night is becoming increasingly blurred in the 24/7 economy, where we are invited to consume all the time.

In literature and policy, there are generally two competing discourses about nightlife. On the one hand, the night is a space–time to be exploited commercially (night-time economy), emphasizing economic growth, job creation, adventure, sociability, tourism, and city promotion (Chatterton and Hollands 2002; Hubbard 2005; Helms 2008; Roberts and Eldridge 2009). On the other hand, nights are portrayed as space–times of transgressive and antisocial behavior. Moral panics focused on binge drinking, safety (Measham and Hadfield 2009; Talbot 2007), and social conflicts about noise and nuisance between residents and partygoers, who "live" at different rhythms (Van Liempt and van Aalst 2012). These downsides are foregrounded in the popular press when excesses in nightlife districts are filmed by security cameras and images of incidents are shared extensively via social media. Concerns about the personal security and wellbeing of consumers increasingly determine the "success" of these consumption spaces and the images of specific city centers. Common urban governmental responses have been "safe and healthy nightlife" policies and intensified surveillance, such as closed-circuit television (CCTV) systems, policing, and greater presence of private security staff in nightlife areas.

This chapter reviews various policy-related aspects of urban nightlife, such as technological and "soft" surveillance, moral panics, and gender, to deepen our understanding of how governance, cultures, and economies of urban nightlife produce the mediated city. More specifically, it shows that technologies and practices of communication are an integral part of these developments. First, it explores the rise of night-time economies; second, it focuses on governing the city after dark; and finally, it describes the global similarities and variations in urban nightlife.

The Rise of the 24-Hour City

The "colonization" of the night took place after the introduction of electric street lighting around 1880. Artificial lighting pushed back the frontiers of darkness, gave a great stimulus to the entertainment industry (Melbin 1987), opened up new urban spaces, and influenced the ambience and experience of the nightly times (Edensor 2013). The fear of being on the street after dark turned into an eager use of urban public spaces. Illuminated shop windows, extended store opening times, street lights, and entertainment make the city a 24-hour economy. Electric light helped nightlife bloom. The intensity of illuminated signs and screens on Broadway in New York City led to the nickname "Great White Way," a new landscape, a glittering multi-colored wonderland (Nasaw 1999: 6). Cities became more explicitly "communicative" through the use of screens and visual technologies that "mediate" the urban experience in many ways.

Since de-industrialization, concrete policies have been designed to regenerate post-industrial cities. When industry left, thousands of jobs were lost, factories were abandoned, parts of cities became empty, and perceived safety decreased (e.g., Minton 2009). Place-based production and industrial activities were terminated or replaced, leading to a loss of purpose and identity, especially in older industrial or harbor cities, such as the Ruhr area in Germany, Docklands in London, and waterfront areas in Rotterdam (Lovatt and O'Connor 1995; van Aalst and Boogaarts 2002). Families that could afford to move relocated to the suburbs. This was followed by the decentralization of commercial and retail activities to suburban areas. To a large extent, urban public encounters were displaced by electronic media; private suburban homes became "media centers" (e.g., McQuire 2008).

The "revalorization" of city centers and urban life started in the late 1970s or early 1980s (e.g., Harvey 1989). The shift away from their economic base in manufacturing and industry to service-oriented activities and the rise of footloose capital in this post-industrial economy were crucial to the re-emphasis on the prestige of urban centrality. This new "urbanity" centered on leisure, upmarket consumption, and prestigious offices and residential living. Then, in the 1980s, young upwardly mobile professionals ("yuppies") emerged as a significant component of society, and took over from the original, pioneer bohemian gentrifiers of the 1970s (Zukin 1989) as the main force behind the social upgrading of inner-city areas.

Against the background of place-based competition at the national and the international level, urban stakeholders place increasing value on the quality of life, and focus on the vibrancy and appeal of city centers as unique selling points in marketing and media campaigns. According to Zukin (1998: 825), "cities were no longer seen as landscapes of production, but as landscapes of consumption." What distinguished places from one another was the strength of their "consumptional identities" (Corner 1994). New theatres, museums, clubs, and festivals became critical elements in generating such place myths (Crewe and Beaverstock 1998), and they were used as instruments of urban regeneration projects and spatial planning (van Aalst and Boogaarts 2002) that were aimed at attracting media attention and bringing people back into the city to live, work, and enjoy themselves. A well-known example is the construction of the Guggenheim Museum in Bilbao (Spain), a visible landmark in the former industrial district that attracts almost a million visitors a year. By stimulating the "vitality and viability" of the 24-hour city center, policymakers aimed to attract visitors and residents back to the city during the evening and into the night.

This approach was highly influenced by cities in continental Europe that had been developing cultural policies to revitalize their urban nightlife since the late 1970s. Bianchini (1995: 121) identifies Rome's annual summer program of night-time cultural events as one of the first such initiatives. Following the launch of the *Nuit Blanche* ("Sleepless Night") in Paris in 2002, Light Night events, cultural festivals, and museum nights have spread to other European cities—for example, Copenhagen, Dublin, and Eindhoven—and North American cities, for instance New York. Features of these events are illuminations on buildings and light installations (Evans 2012). Late-night events and festivals operate at the interface of art and culture, the media, and tourism, and figure prominently in place promotion and marketing plans.

Further, bringing a more diverse cross-section of the population to the city center at night enhances safety and natural surveillance ("eyes on the street"; Jacobs 1961) and generates an opportunity to "double" the city's economy (Bianchini 1995: 124), or as Jacobs (1961: 259) stated, "a duplication of the most profitable use." The term "night-time economy," which is commonly used in British scholarly literature, refers to the activities in nightlife areas, in bars, and clubs, and to the cultural events that are given full scope in the context of urban entrepreneurialism to regenerate inner-city areas and to attract the middle and higher social classes to the city (e.g., see Shaw 2010; van Aalst et al. 2014).

Mediating the City After Dark

Concerns about the "dark" sides of the night-time economy in the public debate, media, and policy circles are related to the broader concerns of national and municipal governments about a lack of safety in public spaces after dark. Unhealthy environments created by excessive drinking and alcohol-fueled disorder in nightlife districts are widely believed to negatively affect a city's image and urban economy (Chatterton and Hollands 2002; Van Liempt 2015).

A key trend in governing the city after dark is an increased technological mediation of surveillance and policing (e.g., Van Liempt 2015). Real-time feedback from CCTV operators to police and bouncers on the ground is increasingly being implemented, as is the tracking of specific individuals as they move through urban public spaces. Interest in and the use of smart cameras and smart algorithms to handle and interpret data flows are also increasing (Timan and Oudshoorn 2012).

However, surveillance is no longer restricted to CCTV. Cities and police forces are experimenting with mobile cameras and cameras equipped with audio sensors. Since the introduction of personal media devices, especially mobile phones with cameras, public spaces have become flooded with devices that have the potential to act as surveillance technologies. Because of an increase in the functionality of these devices, more and more mobile cameras are being carried around by citizens, which leads to an increase in bottom-up recordings (movies/photos) of public spaces. These recordings can be publicly shared on local computers, between phones, or on the Internet, thus becoming a form of open-circuit television (OCTV) (Timan and Oudshoorn 2012). OCTV cameras configure citizens as active participants; surveillance is no longer solely in the hands of formal surveillance agents. But mobile camera devices are used for a wide variety of purposes, particularly for the leisurely recording and sharing of images. Partygoers constantly tweet and use social media to share and show their experiences in night-life districts with and to their peers. Camera phone practices in urban nightlife meditate, re-present, and reframe urban experiences; by using their mobile devices and sharing their experiences, citizens participate in unofficial place-marketing (Hjorth 2015).

More recently, social media have started to play a role in the organization of urban nightlife. By using the rapid organizational power of social media like Facebook, parties can be organized very quickly. In addition, there are underground parties and festivals whose venues are announced via social media only at the very last minute. These "raves" are held not in regulated and stylized places, but in disused tunnels or empty factories, and they are often illegal. At a more formal level, various media (e.g., free newspapers, like New York's *Village Voice*) provide partygoers with information about night-time events, as do video display screens in public transportation and lists of night-time activities posted in bars and clubs. Social media provide fans with an additional means to engage with their favorite DJs and musicians and are valuable to strengthen fan relationships.

Gendered Exclusion from Nightlife Areas

The 24-hour city and the public's desire to go out and have a good time at night grew not only as a result of the aforementioned broad economic changes, technological innovations, and urban restructuring, but also as a result of cultural factors and radically transformed lifestyle patterns (Hollands and Chatterton 2003). According to Bianchini (1995), the post-1968 emergence of new urban social movements, such as feminism, had an effect on the diversity of partygoers. To tackle the male dominance and sexual violence against women in the night-time city (Mackay 2014), women in the UK and the US hold nocturnal marches "Reclaiming the Night" (UK) or "Taking Back the Night" (US). It is a worldwide protest against sexual violence (see takeback-thenight.org) and a variety of women empowerment schemes have emerged in European, US, Latin American, and African cities. However, some have questioned whether these developments actually lead to more gender equality in the post-industrial city after dark.

Research by Roberts and Turner (2005) and Thomas and Bromley (2000) suggests that young women are particularly excluded from the late-night economy. Although young women are not a homogeneous category in terms of behavior, feelings of safety, experiencing freedom, etc., the literature on fear of crime in public spaces has shown that young women use a wide variety of tactics to negotiate such spaces (e.g., Pain 2000). In Dutch cities (Schwanen et al. 2012), there is a general underrepresentation of women in nightlife areas, especially later in the night (i.e., after 02:30). Women participate to a greater extent in the night-time economy during the busiest hours. Further, the research showed that women are more likely to be on the street alone only when the ratio of female to male visitors is higher (Schwanen et al. 2012). This aligns with Sheard's (2011) qualitative study among women in Leeds (UK), which found that they feel more confident and empowered when sites within the night-time economy are less male-dominated. Although diversity in nightlife areas grew in the aftermath of social change in the late 1960s, and postmodern urbanism is highly focused on the value of "difference," all kinds of (gender) inequalities have persisted (e.g., Massey 1994).

After the democratization of access to university, higher education expanded and student numbers increased (Chatterton and Hollands 2002). When students started to participate in night-time activities, some venues targeted students and young urban professionals through the pricing of entry and drinks, and by using online registration and members-only strategies (Böse 2005; Measham and Hadfield 2009). Although this promoted gender-based inclusion, at times it also affected the presence of other groups, like lower-class, nonwhite, and non-mainstream revelers (Chatterton and Hollands 2002). Concerns have been expressed that commercialization, branding, and the increase in surveillance and policing (securitization) have created urban nightlife environments that are increasingly predictable, sanitized, and secured to attract relatively riskless consumers (Talbot 2007), and that are particularly appealing to the creative class and young professionals in post-industrial and knowledge-based businesses (Florida 2002). These developments have resulted in the gentrification of nightlife areas and transformed the nature of the city's nightlife itself (Hae 2012).

In these nightscapes, "others"—non-consumers—are positioned as "strangers," people who need to be kept under surveillance and, in some cases, even removed from public spaces in contemporary cities (Coleman 2004). This "regulatory dilemma" (Hadfield et al. 2009) raises very specific management issues as well as a range of ethical questions. Research by Schwanen et al. (2012) suggests that the presence of more police in Dutch city centers after dark empowers women to move unaccompanied through a nightlife area, while reducing the inclination of ethnic youth groups to do so. In a college town in the Deep South of the US, Buford May (2014) found that there is racial disparity in the enforcement of dress codes, and that in nightlife, a variety of narratives and racial myths exist: "Black men are aggressive"; "Hip-hop clothing is not respectable attire"; and so on. At nightlife premises in the Netherlands, the discriminatory practices of door staff against youths of Moroccan, Turkish, or Surinamese/Antillean descent (the country's largest racial/ethnic minority groups) caused considerable public indignation in the 2000s. Although door policy is now regulated more strongly, many people of Arabic descent still feel discriminated against in the night-time economy (Boogaarts 2008). Schwanen and colleagues (2012: 278) indicate that nightlife spaces that are more diverse in terms of the ethnicity of the nightlife crowd are more intensely surveilled by the police.

Mediation of the Night by "Soft" Surveillance

Increasing tensions between nightlife visitors and the neighborhood lead to new forms of formal and informal governance in cities after dark through a mixture of public and private partnerships. The Dutch city of Rotterdam recently saw the introduction of *horeca* ("hotel/restaurant/cafe") stewards, a joint initiative of the city, the police, the nightlife industry, and venue owners. The stewards' tasks include preventing fights and helping visitors by steering them toward the night bus, taxi stand, or specific entertainment venues. These stewards are young people who are trained by the local authority and various partners, and whose main job is to intervene early to prevent trouble escalating into violence.

In many cities in the UK, there is a growing presence of "street pastors" in the night-time economy. These pastors are uniformed Christian volunteers who patrol nightlife areas at weekends to promote the safety of people who are on a night out. The first patrols were launched in London in 2003 and now operate in over 250 urban locations (Middleton and Yarwood 2015). Street pastors provide practical help and advice to those who are at risk of becoming involved in antisocial behavior or crime, and they take care of and listen to people who are mingling in public spaces. The pastors are sometimes guided to those in need by CCTV operators, the police, or door staff. They may also participate in police briefings or receive training from local authority partners. When in public space, street pastors try to distance themselves from the police in order to highlight that their role is not to regulate the night-time economy, but to offer independent help.

In response to growing tensions in Paris between the residents of inner-city areas and nightlife businesses, in 2011 an organization called *Pierrots de la Nuit* started performing mediation and counselling activities to prevent noise nuisance caused by people participating in nightlife activities in bars, clubs, and concert halls and during night festivals (see www.lespierrotsdelanuit.org). Their goal is to preserve the vitality of the Parisian night while respecting the living environment of the residents by means of artistic interventions in streets and squares. It is innovative in terms of combining artistic performances in public space and raising awareness among partygoers and the industry/entrepreneurs. The concept of the Pierrots has been replicated in Brussel and Barcelona, and other cities are showing interest.

Another example is the *nachtburgemeester* ("night mayor"), a management model pioneered in Amsterdam. The city elected its first night mayor in 2003 when nightlife was in crisis and perceived to be in decline (Roberts 2016). Amsterdam's night mayor now contributes to local policies that affect the night-time economy and acts on behalf of urban nightlife, promoting nightlife and representing local creative industries and the producers (venues) and consumers of nocturnal culture. The concept of the night mayor has now gone global: it has been replicated in London, Toulouse, and Zurich, and there are plans to introduce similar roles in Sydney and New York. Much like pastors in UK cities, these "mayors" act as mediators in the night, support development, and build bridges between different interest groups, such as entrepreneurs, municipality stakeholders, residents, visitors, and partygoers.

Nightlife Across the Globe

Urban nightlife research and studies on night-time economies have mainly focused on experiences and practices in Europe and the US. Although some issues, like increased commercialization and regulation, are global issues, there are local variations and differences between various cities across the globe.

In Singapore (Su-Jan et al. 2012) and Jakarta (Tadié and Permanadeli 2015), for example, international benchmarks have been adopted to demonstrate the modernization (i.e., Westernization) of nightlife. Also, in Chinese cities (Chew 2009), there seems to be a shift from a more culture-oriented nightlife to commercialized night-time activities, partly influenced by Western regeneration strategies in post-industrial cities (communicated by social media, TV, film, etc.). The emergence of "global" nightscapes refers to the way in which these local urban night spaces are sites of transnational flows constructed through globalization processes (Farrer 2008). It sometimes creates a form of nightlife that clashes with cultural values and religion. Islamic pressure regularly leads to governmental action in Indonesian cities like Jakarta to, for example, ban alcohol consumption in bars, clubs, and pubs. While Western cities exert stronger policing of nonwhite behavior, in some Islamic cities, public discourse is about removing "sin" from the central nightlife areas (Tadié and Permanadeli 2015). Many Chinese and Japanese cities have developed a specific nightlife practice: private rooms in clubs for karaoke television (KTV), where popular music can be played on televisions upon the request of patrons. KTV rooms have become common nightlife places because of the economic boom (Farrer 2008). Further, "tea pubs" (which serve non-alcoholic drinks) are popular among both young and older people who want to spend an evening with their friends.

Night markets are also part of the urban nightscapes of the Global South. In Taiwan, Hong Kong, Mumbai, Bangkok, and Seoul (Hou 2010: 111), these markets are evening events where street vendors congregate, selling clothing, food, and a range of other products. Buyers stroll through the market, taking in the atmosphere created by steam arising from woks and rice pans, vendors promoting their wares, loud music, and dense crowds (Yu 2004 in Pottie-Sherman and

Hiebert 2015). Dating back to eighth-century China, the night market phenomenon followed Chinese migration, first to Singapore, Malaysia, Indonesia, and Thailand, and more recently to Chinese diasporic communities in North American cities (Pottie-Sherman and Hiebert 2015). More and more night markets in Asia have been transformed from traditional economic spaces into touristic and leisure spaces.

In cities in Europe and the US, young people have been "colonizing" urban nights organized around food and alcohol consumption and entertainment for several decades, but this group is becoming increasingly diversified as a result of globalization and transnational mobilities. Alternative nightlife spaces, ethno-parties, Caribbean events, and the rise of Asian night markets in the Global North are examples of the impact of globalization on nightlife trends (e.g., Hou 2010; Pottie-Sherman and Hiebert 2015).

Conclusion

What happens during the night is more than just economy. It is about social encounters, the promise of inconsequential "fun," meeting other people, developing a sense of style, taste and self-presentation (music, clothing, make-up), and belonging to youth cultures. As we have seen, night-time cultures are highly communicative practices that operate along the axes of self-realization and danger, and provide opportunities for participation and policing. Nightlife spaces can have different meanings for different groups, and governing urban nightlife districts is mediated by the local context. This multiplicity and symbolism of nightlife and night cultures requires further research for a better understanding of the cultural, historical, and socio-economic differences among urban nightlife spaces across the world.

References

Bianchini, F. (1995) "Night cultures, night economies," *Planning Practice and Research*, 10(2), pp. 121–126.
Boogaarts, S. (2008) "Claiming your place at night: Turkish dance parties in the Netherlands," *Journal of Ethnic and Migration Studies*, 34(8), pp. 1283–1300.
Böse, M. (2005) "Difference and exclusion at work in the club culture," *International Journal of Cultural Studies*, 8, pp. 427–444.
Buford May, R. A. (2014) *Urban Nightlife: Entertaining Race, Class, and Culture in Public Space*, New Brunswick, NJ: Rutgers University Press.
Chatterton, P. and Hollands, R. (2002) "Theorising urban playscapes: Producing, regulating and consuming youthful nightlife city spaces," *Urban Studies*, 39(1), pp. 95–116.
Chew, M. (2009) "Research on Chinese nightlife cultures and night-time economies," *Chinese Sociology and Anthropology*, 42(2), pp. 3–21.
Coleman, R. (2004) "Images from a neoliberal city: The state, surveillance and social control," *Critical Criminology*, 12(1), pp. 21–42.
Corner, J. (1994) "Consumption editorial," *Media, Culture and Society*, 16, pp. 371–374.
Crewe, L. and Beaverstock, J. (1998) "Fashioning the city: Cultures of consumption in contemporary urban spaces," *Geoforum*, 29(3), pp. 287–308.
Edensor, T. (2013) "Reconnecting with darkness: Gloomy landscapes, lightless places," *Social and Cultural Geography*, 14(4), pp. 446–465.
Evans, G. (2012) "Hold back the night: Nuit Blanche and all-night events in capital cities," *Current Issues in Tourism*, 15(1–2), pp. 35–49.
Farrer, J. (2008) "Play and power in Chinese nightlife spaces," *China: An International Journal*, 6(1), pp. 1–17.
Florida, R. (2002) *The Rise of the Creative Class and How It's Transforming Work, Leisure, Community and Everyday Life*, New York: Basic Books.
Gwiazdzinski, L. (2005) *La Nuit, dernière frontière de la ville*, La Tour d'Aigues, l'Aube.

Hadfield, P., Lister, S. and Traynor, P. (2009) "This town's a different town today: Policing and regulating the night-time economy," *Criminology and Criminal Justice*, 9(4), pp. 465–485.

Hae, L. (2012) *The Gentrification of Nightlife and the Right to the City: Regulating Spaces of Social Dancing in New York*, New York: Routledge.

Hall, P. (2000) "Creative cities and economic development," *Urban Studies*, 37, pp. 639–649.

Harvey, D. (1989) "From managerialism to entrepreneurialism: The transformation in urban governance in late capitalism," *Geografiska Annaler Series B: Human Geography*, 71(1), pp. 3–17.

Helms, G. (2008) *Towards Safe City Centers? Remaking the Spaces of an Old-Industrial City*, Aldershot: Ashgate.

Hjorth, L. (2015) "Narratives of ambient play: Camera phone practices in urban cartographies," in M. Foth, M. Brynskov, and T. Ojala (eds.) *Citizen's Right to the Digital City*, Singapore: Springer.

Hollands, R. and Chatterton, P. (2003) *Urban Nightscapes. Youth Cultures, Pleasure Spaces and Corporate Power*, London and New York: Routledge.

Hou, J. (ed.) (2010) "'Night market' in Seattle: Community eventscape and the reconstruction of public space," in *Insurgent Public Space: Guerrilla Urbanism and the Remaking of Contemporary Cities*, New York: Routledge.

Hubbard, P. (2005) "The geographies of 'going out': emotion and embodiment in the evening economy," in J. Davidson, L. Bondi, and M. Smith (eds.) *Emotional Geographies*, Aldershot: Ashgate, pp. 117–134.

Jacobs, J. (1961) *The Death and Life of Great American Cities*, New York: Vintage.

Jayne, M., Valentine, G., and Holloway, S. (2011) *Alcohol, Drinking, Drunkenness: (Dis)Orderly Spaces*, Aldershot: Ashgate.

Lovatt, A. and O'Connor, J. (1995) "Cities and the night-time economy," *Planning, Practice and Research*, 10(2), pp. 127–134.

Mackay, F. (2014) "Mapping the routes: An exploration of charges of racism made against the 1970s UK reclaim the night marches," *Women's Studies International Forum*, 44, pp. 46–54.

Massey, D. (1994) *Space, Place and Gender*, Minneapolis, MN: University of Minnesota Press.

McQuire, S. (2008) *The Media City: Media, Architecture and Urban Space*, Thousand Oaks, CA: SAGE.

Measham, F. and Hadfield, P. (2009) "Everything starts with an 'e': Exclusion, ethnicity and elite formation in contemporary English clubland," *Adicciones*, 21(4), pp. 363–386.

Melbin, M. (1987) *Night as Frontier: Colonizing the World after Dark*, New York: Free Press.

Middleton, J. and Yarwood, R. (2015) "'Christians, out here?' Encountering street pastors in the post-secular spaces of the UK night-time economy," *Urban Studies*, 52(3), pp. 501–516.

Minton, A. (2009) *Ground Control; Fear and Happiness in the Twenty-First Century City*, London: Penguin Books.

Nasaw, D. (1999) *Going Out: The Rise and Fall of Public Amusements*, Boston, MA: Harvard University Press.

Pain, R. (2000) "Place, social relations and the fear of crime: A review," *Progress in Human Geography*, 24, pp. 365–387.

Pottie-Sherman, Y. and Hiebert, D. (2015) "Authenticity with a bang: Exploring suburban culture and migration through the new phenomenon of the Richmond night market," *Urban Studies*, 52(3), pp. 538–554.

Roberts, M. (2016) "What a 'night czar' can do to help nightlife survive," *The Conversation*, http://theconversation.com/what-a-night-czar-can-do-to-help-nightlife-survive-67253.

Roberts, M. and Eldridge, A. (2009) "Planning, urban design and the night-time city: Still at the margins?" *Criminology and Criminal Justice*, 9(4), pp. 487–506.

Roberts, M. and Turner, C. (2005) "Conflicts of liveability in the 25-hour city: Learning from 48 hours in the life of London's Soho," *Journal of Urban Design*, 10, pp. 171–193.

Schwanen, T., Van Aalst, I., Brands, J. and Timan, T. (2012) "Rhythms of the night: Spatiotemporal inequalities in the night-time economy," *Environment and Planning A*, 44, pp. 2064–2085.

Shaw, R. (2010) "Neoliberal subjectivities and the development of the night-time economy in British cities," *Geography Compass*, 4(7), pp. 893–903.

Sheard, L. (2011) "'Anything could have happened': Women, the night-time economy, alcohol and drink spiking," *Sociology*, 45, pp. 619–633.

Su-Jan, Y., Limin, H. and Chye Kiang, H. (2012) "Urban informality and everyday (night)life: A field study in Singapore," *International Development Planning Review*, 34(4), pp. 369–390.

Tadié, J. and Permanadeli, R. (2015) "Night and the city: Clubs, brothels and politics in Jakarta," *Urban Studies*, 52(3), pp. 471–485.

Talbot, D. (2007) *Regulating the Night: Race, Culture and Exclusion in the Making of the Night-Time Economy*, Aldershot: Ashgate.

Thomas, T. and Bromley, R. (2000) "City-centre revitalisation: Problems of fragmentation and fear in the evening and night-time economy," *Urban Studies*, 37, pp. 1403–1429.
Timan, T. and Oudshoorn, N. (2012) "Mobile cameras as new technologies of surveillance? How citizens experience the use of mobile cameras in public nightscapes," *Surveillance and Society*, 10(2), pp. 167–181.
Van Aalst, I. and Boogaarts, I. (2002) "From museum to mass entertainment: The evolution of the role of museums in cities." *European Urban and Regional Studies*, 9(3), pp. 195–209.
Van Aalst, I. Schwanen, T., and van Liempt, I. (2014) "Video-surveillance and the production of space in urban nightlife districts," in J. Van den Hoven, B. Koops, and H. Romijn et al. (eds.) *Responsible Innovation: The Ethical Governance of New and Emerging Technologies*. Dordrecht: Springer, pp. 315–335.
Van Liempt, I. (2015) "Safe nightlife collaborations: Multiple actors, conflicting interests and different power distributions," *Urban Studies*, 52(3), pp. 486–500.
Van Liempt, I. and van Aalst, I. (2012) "Urban surveillance and the struggle between safe and exciting nightlife districts," *Surveillance and Society*, 9(3), pp. 280–292.
Yeo, S. and Heng, C. H. (2014) "An (extra)ordinary night out: Urban informality, social sustainability and the night-time economy," *Urban Studies*, 51(4), pp. 712–726.
Zukin, S. (1989) *Loft Living: Culture and Capital in Urban Change*, New Brunswick, NJ: Rutgers University Press.
— (1998) "Urban lifestyles: Diversity and standardisation in spaces of consumption," *Urban Studies*, 35 (5–6), pp. 825–839.

Further Reading

Mateo, J. N. and Eldridge, A. (2018) (eds.) *Exploring Nightlife; Space, Society and Governance*, London: Rowman & Littlefield.
Melbin, M. (1987) *Night as Frontier: Colonizing the World after Dark*, New York: Free Press.
Van Liempt, I., van Aalst, I. and Schwanen, T. (2015) (eds.) *Geographies of the Urban Night*, Urban Studies special issue 52(3).

31
URBAN GAMING
Mobile Media, Spatial Practices, and Everyday Play

Ingrid Richardson

Introduction

Web-capable smartphones are rapidly becoming ubiquitous, and together with app-based media ecologies and the uptake of gamification strategies by businesses and developers, mobile games are now increasingly infused into many people's mundane day-to-day media and communication practices. As a number of media theorists have argued, the shift to mobile interfaces, together with the emergence of user-generated content creation, participatory media, and the proliferation of game elements in social media apps and services, have brought about a playful or "lusory sensibility" en masse.

This chapter explores the various modalities of mobile gaming and how mobile play is reshaping urban experience, from casual mobile games to location-based and augmented reality games. On the one hand, casual or "occasional" mobile games—played for minutes at a time and at irregular intervals—can be seen as a form of portable home entertainment that cocoons the player in public places. On the other hand, location-based augmented reality games that deploy navigational and image-capture technologies have the capacity to frame and mediate the ways we traverse, experience, share, and think about place; indeed, the digital mapping and representation of place increasingly pervades geosocial, interpersonal, and embodied experience in contemporary media culture. The chapter will conclude with a discussion of *Pokémon GO* as a significant "moment" in media history, through which we might critically interpret the entanglements of mobile media use, playful imaginaries, and games in quotidian urban life.

Casual Gaming in Public: The Mobilization of Private Space

Our interaction with mobile screens does not demand the dedicated attentiveness we give to other screens; indeed, "turning toward" them is often an in-the-moment practice (as we check for messages, social media posts, or a missed call) or measured in minutes (playing a few levels of *Angry Birds* while waiting for the train). In fact, even in the seemingly committed or immersive practice of gameplay, mobile phone engagement is characterized by interruption, and sporadic or split attention betwixt other activities. This has been recognized by the growing mobile phone game industry and its labeling of the "casual gamer," who plays at most for five minutes at a time and at irregular intervals. Casual mobile games are typified by interruptibility, where play becomes intertwined with everyday routines and fits into the existing patterns of daily life.

Within much game literature, casual games are typically described in terms of their properties; that is, they are designed for casual use, are easy to learn (e.g., simple puzzle, card, and word games), offer quick rewards in the form of virtual resources, and consist of levels of short duration. Thus, casual gaming is often understood as a mode of engagement that requires relatively low-level skills and only sporadic attention up to a threshold of around five minutes; those who play casual games describe the activity as peripheral, providing a "fun" and incidental distraction (Christensen and Prax 2012: 731). Yet as smartphones accompany us everywhere and anywhere, with an ever-growing app ecology populated by mobile games, it is clear that the somewhat pejorative term "casual" often works to disguise the substantial investments made by some casual gamers and oversimplifies an increasingly diverse and rapidly developing medium of gameplay (Taylor 2012). As Consalvo notes, the iPhone and subsequent smartphone touchscreens have put mobile gaming platforms "in the hands of millions of people who would never consider themselves gamers" (Consalvo 2012: 184). Like being "online," for many people playing games has become normalized, embedded in numerous other navigational, informational, productivity, and social media app-based activities within the mobile mediascape, and frequently embodied as part of urban dwellers' peripatetic and pedestrian movement through the built environment.

It has been argued that for many users, portable music devices such as the Walkman, iPod, MP3 player, and mobile phone afford the auditory privatization of public space, changing co-proximate behavior and the ongoing evolution of urban "micro-acoustic ecologies" (Helyer 2007) in different ways. In this cocooning of the self via the deliberate seclusion of auditory sense perception, as Bull has commented, "[m]ediated isolation itself becomes a form of control over the spaces of urban culture in which the 'minimal' self withdraws into a world small enough that it can exert almost total control over it" (Bull 2007: 9). Yet while MP3 players provide discrete sound bubbles or "sonorous envelopes" (Bull 2004: 290) that effectively allow the user to aurally suppress the urban soundscape, the mobile phone frequently works as a discontinuous and unpredictable device, puncturing time and the noise of the city, as users' contribute their own utterings of familiarity and intimacy in response to the constant irruptions of ringtones, bleeps, and alerts (see also Chapter 34, this volume). Nevertheless, as evidenced in a number of studies, much like listening to music, casual mobile gaming is often used to affect a mode of non-communicative co-presence when one is alone in public. To borrow from Goffman's useful analysis of pedestrian movement and interaction, the urban mobile gamer articulates a specific type of "gestural prefigurement" (Goffman 1972: 31–32), behaving in ways that accord with consensual and recognized modes of media distraction (much as book- or newspaper-reading on public transport is deployed and understood by others as do-not-disturb indicators).

When gameplay is situated in public places, the particular ways we engage with mobile games can determine (and are determined by) degrees of attention, practices of viewing, and the motility and mobility of the pedestrian body. Casual mobile gaming often takes place in the interstices of everyday life, in the gaps between productive and telic or goal-oriented activity. As noted by Hjorth and Richardson (2010), when the activity of casual mobile gaming in urban space takes place while waiting (for a friend, at a bus stop, or for a journey to end), it becomes a way of managing the corporeal agitation of impatience, aloneness, and boredom in public, enabling a mobilization of private space and privacy that can be deployed in situ while "being with others." The mobile device becomes co-opted into the corporeal labor of waiting, filling, and suturing the "dead" or "fractured" times and spaces that are "folded into everyday corporeal existence" (Bissell 2007: 281). Here, the activity of casual gaming enacts a particular kind of "face-work" in Goffman's (1972) sense, while at the same time maintaining a crucial peripheral awareness of one's spatial surroundings in readiness for the busy-ness of life to resume (see also Chapter 35, this volume). The transient and non-dedicated attentiveness required by the small screen and casual game—you can "switch off" but "not totally"—allows the user to both remain alert to the "arrival," which marks the end of waiting, yet able to avert their gaze from others and so cooperate in the tacit social agreement of non-interaction among strangers. For some, this kind of engagement with the mobile screen provides a means of safe seclusion from unwelcome interaction in potentially risky situations of co-present waiting, while remaining "open" or attentive to the proximity of that risk.

For Parikka and Suominen (2006) the "third place" between public and private space opened up by the mobile phone—in particular, via the use of mobile entertainment services, games, music and videos—demarcates a privatized space around the user, a habitual practice already common in the 19th century. They write:

> [W]hat is new in this division of space and creation of a place of one's own? Instead of seeing this solely as a trend of digital mobile culture, we argue that this is more a phenomenon that took off with the creation of modern urban space and the new paradigms of media consumption . . . [T]he pattern of mobile entertainment usage as the creation of a private sphere was already part of the railway culture of the nineteenth century—even if people consumed such media content as newspapers and books instead of digital entertainment.
>
> *(2006: n.p.)*

In this way, casual mobile gaming (among other mobile media practices) can be seen as a form of portable home entertainment that assists us in achieving occasional seclusion when in the presence of strangers. It is this closing-off that prompts Groening to comment that a society of "portable personal electronics is a society in which private space is as physically mobile as the populace and privacy itself is radically mobile" (2010: 1340). Similarly, Hjorth (2012) has argued that the mobile phone is frequently used as a micro-mobile home, allowing users to carry private space in their pockets and call upon it when needed. As I will suggest below, location-based gaming enacts and enables a quite different experience of space and place in urban environments by effectively opening up a hybrid space that coalesces geospatial location and online networks, converting urban spaces into collectively experienced playgrounds.

Location-Based Mobile Games: Transforming Urban Environments into Playspaces

Over the past decade, we have seen a proliferation of location-based games and playful apps that invite us to upload and share personal and local content in the moment, thereby enacting a hybrid, layered, and multifaceted experience of place, presence, and communication. As de Souza e Silva and Frith (2010) note, both the GPS-enabled iPhone and Google's Android operating system contributed to the popularization and commercialization of location-aware applications and location-based services, which typically provide situational information about the urban environment via online databases and media libraries, such that informational changes on the mobile screen impact upon the navigation and experience of physical space. Being online becomes enfolded inside present contexts and activities, like the embodied and itinerant acts of walking, driving, face-to-face communication, and numerous other material and embodied practices. Location-based mobile games, which integrate locational information or GPS data into the gameplay and mechanics, and augmented reality games, which further populate these geo-locative "real" places with interactive virtual objects seen through the camera view of one's mobile device, are theorized as particularly robust examples of this emergent hybrid ontology.

Historically, location-based games—referred to as urban games, big games, pervasive games, and mixed reality games—emerged out of avant-garde new media art, and involved creative experimentation with emerging media interfaces, platforms, and networks (see also Chapter 38, this volume). Such works deliberately sought to challenge or disrupt the mundane and familiar by transforming public spaces into playful places. Yet although location-based social games were once considered experimental in their enablement of geosocial play practices, they have more recently been mainstreamed (Wilken 2012), normalized, and commodified, part of the more general cultural shift toward gamification. This trend is exemplified by *Foursquare*, a playful app-based service (with a purported 30 million users) that integrates user-generated firsthand recommendations of "the best places to go" with wayfinding, friend networks, and consumer rewards.

Despite the cultural turn toward gamification, creators of urban and community games such as UK new media group Blast Theory continue to deliberately "hack" public space, inviting players to undergo a *de-familiarization* of their everyday mode of engagement with the urban environment. The integration of mobile location-based gaming into users' pedestrian experience also has this potential, enabling an intentional and playful resistance to the scripts of urban social life. Location-aware, augmented, and hybrid reality mobile games can transform urban spaces into participatory gameworlds that interrupt the more calculated instrumentality and intended functionality of the planned urban environment. Over 10 years ago, New York game designer Frank Lantz anticipated that we would see "large-scale, real-world games that occupy urban streets and other public spaces and combine the richness, complexity, and procedural depth of digital media with physical activity and face-to-face social interaction" (Lantz 2006: n.p.). Lantz, who was involved in such pivotal projects as *Pac-Manhattan*, understood that such games would play a key role in the future of gaming and fundamentally transform the urban experience; in some ways, this might describe the various effects of *Pokémon GO*, although, as I will suggest below, many have denounced the game for its facile representation of a complex and elaborate gameworld of significant conceptual and interactive depth.

Location-based mobile games also generate hybrid experiences of place and presence, requiring the player to integrate their own situated and embodied perception of the world with dynamic GPS-enabled information, embedded within an augmented and networked game reality. As Farman notes, mobile technologies have transformed the way many of us experience presence and absence, as we increasingly participate in collective form of "social proprioception," an ambient awareness of others perpetually co-present through networked media interfaces (2014: 386). As a number of theorists have observed, urban spaces are now filled with mobile media users who create communicative pockets of co-existing modalities of presence: co-located presence, telepresence, absent presence, distributed presence, and ambient presence, all of which demand different modes of embodied being-in-the-world (Ito and Okabe 2005; Hjorth and Richardson 2014). In this way, location-based mobile games and applications can be said to add a complex or layered *dimensionality* to place and space.

That is, the proliferation of such games, apps, and services, and their deployment within urban space, means that we need to rethink the spatial and place-based experience of being-in-public, as we increasingly integrate online information about the immediate environment into the patterns of urban life and peripatetic movement. Gordon and de Souza e Silva (2011) have argued that such hybrid practices generate what they term net-local public space or net localities, which describes the way people's embodied perception oscillates between that which is immediately present and that which is proximally distant or mediated. For many of us, social rituals and the experience of co-presence now commonly extend beyond the former, and "locality" or "being someplace" is contingently determined by both physical and digital proximity (2011: 56). Net-local public space describes the coalescence of those engaging in location-based activities with mobile devices, those (both co-present and online) participating in this network activity, and those non-participants who are co-located in the urban setting. For Pellegrino (2010), hybridity is the key word that describes the way participation is *co-constructed* in contemporary media culture. Gordon, de Souza e Silva, and Pellegrino use the term hybridity to refer to the way embodied perception is transformed as an effect of "changes in forms of co-presence," when "participation goes beyond physical co-presence and is experienced through multiple forms of proximity, both physical and virtual" (Pellegrino 2010: 99). Here, presence does not mean "being there" but rather what we experience is a "soft relationality," or the layering of presences (Speed 2010). As people's attentional foci become increasingly diversified and hybridized, the actual/virtual dichotomy previously used to differentiate between offline/online practices is thoroughly disassembled into a complex and dynamic range of modalities of presence.

Location-based mobile games also highlight the cultural specificity of network localities, online participation, and privacy. For example, the uptake of *Jiepang* in Shanghai, China reflects a Chinese notion of privacy that is informed by *guanxi* (social relations based on trust and reciprocal interpersonal obligations)—vastly different from Western concerns about surveillance and stalking in the context of *Foursquare*. As McCrea (2011) points out, individual and governmental patterns of mobile media ownership and use can have distinct trajectories; both consumption and production of media are very much informed by the local, and mobile gaming is played out differently across culturally diverse contexts, reinforcing the importance of considering situatedness and context in any analysis of games and cultural play (see Feldman in Further Reading). In what follows, I will discuss one recent example of location-based augmented reality mobile gaming, *Pokémon GO*, to highlight the hybrid and contextual nature of mobile play as it appropriates and transforms the urban environment into a ludic space.

Pokémon GO

Within the first weeks of its launch in July 2016, millions of people across several countries downloaded the *Pokémon GO* app onto their iOS and Android devices, and entered an augmented reality, wandering their neighborhoods and public spaces in search of Pokémon and PokéStops, and competing with other players at virtual Pokémon gyms. In this location-based hybrid reality, users are required to move through physical space as they tag, collect, trade, and battle for digital artifacts and player achievements, accessing a microworld through their smartphone via the digital overlay of game objects and virtual locations across the actual environment.

Through this augmented layering of the digital onto place, banal and familiar surroundings are transformed to become significant game loci. A Pokémon can be found and caught in one's own bathroom; a gym or PokéStop might be situated at the local library, cafe, or pub. The popularity of *Pokémon GO*—touted as the first ever *really* successful location-based game in terms of daily active users and revenue—has already been the subject of much criticism and celebration. The successes and failures of the game provide us as urban media researchers with an opportunity to explore and document the experience of en-masse location-based mobile gameplay. It is clear that the game and its uptake is situated within historical, social, and cultural contexts, bringing together decades of mobile media use, locative art practice, gaming, and Japanese culture.

For some, *Pokémon GO* is a positive experience—the gameplay evokes 20-something nostalgia (Surman 2009; McCrea 2017), encourages physical exercise, facilitates "genuine human-to-human interaction" (Wawro 2016), and effectively enhances players' sense of well-being and belonging (Vella et al. 2017). Yet as with mobile media and mobile games more generally, *Pokémon GO* can be flexibly deployed by users as a means to facilitate social interaction or as a "shield" to avoid engagement with others in public spaces. For others, the game forces us to reflect on the ongoing gendered, racial, socioeconomic, age-based, and bodily inequities of urban mobility that affect many of us on a daily basis (Isbister 2016). Frith (2017: 53) explores the "commercial potential of augmented reality," and how *Pokémon GO* can be used by businesses to attract foot traffic through the placement of "lures," revealing how digital "objects" can influence our movement and behavior in the physical world, as we enact the pedestrian labor of location-based gaming. Yet as Sicart (2017) warns, while *Pokémon GO* may open up new possibilities for design and play in urban augmented reality, we should be wary of the potential for corporate appropriation of public spaces enabled by the game.

As I have suggested, in a very fundamental way the mobile interface modifies what we pay attention to, what we "turn to" and face (and turn away from) in the everyday lifeworld, and the modalities and duration of that attentiveness. This is clearly evidenced by the wide-scale integration of casual mobile games such as *Candy Crush* and *Angry Birds* into the daily lives of many people (Keogh and Richardson 2017), but even more significantly and poignantly in players' involvement with location-based hybrid reality games such as *Pokémon GO*; games that require us to adopt an "as-if" structure of experience, moving through the environment "as if" it were game terrain or an urban playground. That is, *Pokémon GO* is not just a casual mobile game, for while we might play it in the midst of other daily activities, its mediatic affordances explicitly intervene with and modify those activities, impact upon our pedestrian trajectories, and alter our spatial interpretation and embodied affectual experience of urban life. As Colley et al. (2017: n.p.) suggest, there is evidence that games such as *Pokémon GO* may act as catalysts for large-scale changes in urban dwellers' destination choice or trip distribution. In other words, such games have the potential to incentivize "people to do something they rarely do: substantially change where they choose to go" (Colley et al. 2017: n.p.). Although it may be trivialized as "just a game," *Pokémon GO* reveals how many users' experience of public space is mediated by networked connectivity and increasingly "transformed through collisions of the digital and the urban" (Iveson 2016: n.p.).

As media become more mobile and playful, and games embed geo-locative data, users are increasingly interweaving everyday experience of place with playful virtual environments, transforming familiar neighborhoods and urban environments into ludic spaces. Players have tagged PokéStops, collected virtual rewards and fought battles in locations not intended for play—at museums, cemeteries, and historical sites—and in this way repurpose, defamiliarize, or resist the spatial logics and affective habitudes of regulated urban spaces. In large-scale augmented reality games such as *Pokémon GO*, the vast complexity of the physical and built environment is exploited as a fertile and manifold resource for game content, and players enact a kind of vernacular play that potentially challenges how such spaces may be formally circumscribed by local governments and city planners.

Lammes and Wilmott (2016) have explored the way location-based games such as *RunZombieRun* and others effectively "foreground the fluidity of mapping," such that "maps simultaneously function as (urban) navigational interfaces and gameboards," a description that can equally be applied to *Pokémon GO*. For Frith (2013), the way that mobile apps and map-based games interweave digital and physical information to create hybrid spaces impacts upon "spatial legibility," or the way urban environments appear as coherent and recognizable patterns. With developments in mobile technologies and the rise of collaborative platforms, making and sharing maps has taken on new playful and co-present dimensions. Yet we are also reminded of the inherently *spatial* and *mobile* nature of popular culture and media more generally, and how popular culture forms have always been "intimately, contingently and formatively co-implicated with/in everyday geographies" (Horton 2012: 11–12). In bringing together childhood and play studies with human geography, for example, Horton (2012) documents how his young research participants integrated Pokémon play into the structure of their mundane spatial practices and daily space-time routines, effectively remaking their homes, local shops, and neighborhoods as intervoled with the Pokémon universe.

Yet, it is also important to highlight the uneven ways people engage with the relationality of media and place, and in the context of mobile games, the embodied everyday politics of outside location-based play. When playing *Pokémon GO*, players' bodies are mobilized, empowered, and disempowered by their individual, collective, cultural, and corporeal *situatedness* in the world. That is, certain bodies have more latitude to deviate from "normalized" practices, while some—as Salen Tekinbaş (2017) argues—don't. Tekinbaş turns to the potential prejudice and marginalization that affects players of augmented reality games and mobile location-based apps such as *Pokémon GO*. That is, *Pokémon GO* requires users to explore their (sub)urban environment, enacting a form of gameplay that is underscored by issues of racial inequity and the relative freedom people have to move playfully through their neighborhoods and cities. Tekinbaş asks: what can *Pokémon GO* teach us about mobility, accessibility, race, and privilege? It is clearly more dangerous for some bodies to be in some places at certain times, and there is undoubtedly a hierarchy of risk at work that acts upon bodies differently, depending on age, gender, ethnicity, or social milieu. In their study of the racial and ethnic bias of *Pokémon GO*, Colley et al. (2017: np) examine how the game's data and code that "augments" reality often "reinforces preexisting power structures" and "geographic contours of advantage and disadvantage," as PokéStops and game resources are distributed more densely in wealthier areas with predominantly white non-minority populations.

The orchestration of playful performativity around urban cartographies has a long history that has been harnessed by *Pokémon GO* to new levels of mainstream uptake previously unheard of for urban games. On the one hand, this popularity highlights the powerful role of the playful in contemporary media, and the consolidation of decades of urban and hybrid reality gaming and place-making experimentation. On the other hand, we might argue that *Pokémon GO* players are narrowly goal-oriented, driven to collect and compete for virtual items as they engage in what is essentially a gamified activity—a simplified reduction of a popular but fairly complex trading game that was originally targeted at preteens. In this view, as appealing as it may be to contain and control an imaginary microworld, *Pokémon GO* is not an open-ended playground full of creative possibility, but rather a transformation of the local environment into a game resource, where urban loci are literally made relevant by the extent to which they are populated by virtual currency, game objects, and rewards. Nevertheless, regardless of players' perceptions and experiences, as affordances of ambient play (Hjorth and Richardson 2016), ludic augmented reality apps and games such as *Pokémon GO* are becoming increasingly diffused throughout everyday urban geographies and economies, affecting the embodied routines and interactions of city dwellers across the world.

Conclusion

This chapter has explored how both casual and location-based mobile gaming are instances of the way the "stuff" of media permeates everyday urban geographies. Through a critical analysis of these practices we can effectively reveal the relationality of (mobile) media, urban space, pedestrian practices, and play. I have explored how casual mobile gameplay is often used to demarcate a discrete space of one's own in busy public contexts, effecting a mobilization of private space. Although casual gameplay is often described as trivial and non-productive—an inconsequential activity residing in the interstices of more important everyday happenings—I suggest that such play is an indicator of emergent micro-practices of distraction among urban dwellers. Location-based mobile gaming, on the other hand, effectively conjoins pedestrian movement and emplacement in urban environments with geospatial data and online social networks, such that we engage in a kind of playful space-making that transforms the way we experience and attend to both the city and being with others. Each mode of gaming activates different ways of moving through (and resting in) the urban environment, and different patterns of sociability and interaction, dynamically transforming the way we experience our "being" and "doing" in the mediated urban world.

References

Bissell, D. (2007) "Animating suspension: waiting for mobilities," *Mobilities*, 2(2), pp. 277–298.
Bull, M. (2004) "'To each their own bubble': mobile spaces of sound in the city," in N. Couldry and A. McCarthy (eds.) *Mediaspace: Place, Scale and Culture in a Media Age*, London: Routledge, pp. 275–293.
— (2007) *Sound Moves: iPod Culture and Urban Experience*, London: Routledge.
Christensen, C. and Prax, P. (2012) "Assemblage, adaptation and apps: smartphones and mobile gaming," *Continuum: Journal of Media & Cultural Studies*, 26(5), pp. 731–739.
Colley, A., Thebault-Spieker, J., Lin, A. Y., Degraen, D., Fischman, B., Hakkila, J., Kuehl, K., Nisi, V., Nunes, N. J., Wenig, N., Wenig, D., Hecht, B. and Schoning, J. (2017) "The geography of Pokémon GO: beneficial and problematic effects on places and movement," *CHI 2017*, May 6–11, 2017, Denver, CO, USA.
Consalvo, M. (2012) "Slingshot to victory: games, play and the iPhone," in P. Snickars and P. Vonderau (eds.) *Moving Data: The iPhone and the Future of Media*, New York: Columbia University Press, pp. 184–194.
de Souza e Silva, A. and Frith, J. (2010) "Locative mobile social networks: mapping communication and location in urban spaces," *Mobilities*, 5(4), pp. 485–506.
Farman, J. (2014) "Creative misuse as resistance: surveillance, mobile technologies, and locative games," *Surveillance & Society*, 12(3), pp. 377–388, www.surveillance-and-society.org.
Frith, J. (2013) "Turning life into a game: Foursquare, gamification, and personal mobility," *Mobile Media & Communication*, 1(2), pp. 248–262.
— (2017) "The digital 'lure': small businesses and *Pokémon Go*," *Mobile Media & Communication*, 5(1), pp. 51–54.
Goffman, E. (1972) *Relations in Public: Microstudies of the Public Order*, Middlesex: Penguin Books.
Gordon, E. and de Souza e Silva, A. (2011) *Net Locality: Why Location Matters in a Networked World*, Malden, MA: Wiley-Blackwell.
Groening, S. (2010) "From 'a box in the theater of the world' to 'the world as your living room': cellular phones, television and mobile privatization," *New Media & Society*, 12(8), pp. 1331–1347.
Helyer, N. (2007) "The sonic commons: embrace or retreat?," *Scan: Journal of Media Arts Culture*, 4(3).
Hjorth, L. (2012) "iPersonal: a case study of the politics of the personal," in L. Hjorth, J. Burgess, and I. Richardson (eds.) *Studying Mobile Media: Cultural Technologies, Mobile Communication, and the iPhone*, London: Routledge, pp. 190–212.
Hjorth, L. and Richardson, I. (2010) "Playing the waiting game: casual mobile gaming," in H. Greif, L. Hjorth, A. Lasén, and C. Lobet-Maris (eds.) *Cultures of Participation: Media Practices, Politics and Literacy*, Berlin: Peter Lang, pp. 111–125.
— (2014) *Gaming in Social, Locative and Mobile Media*, London: Palgrave Macmillan.
— (2016) "Mobile games and ambient play," in M. Willson and T. Leaver (eds.) *Social, Casual and Mobile Games: The Changing Gaming Landscape*, New York: Bloomsbury, pp. 105–116.
Horton, J. (2012) "'Got my shoes, got my Pokémon': everyday geographies of children's popular culture," *Geoforum*, 43, pp. 4–13.
Isbister, K. (2016) "Why Pokemon Go became an instant phenomenon," *The Conversation*, July 16, 2016, http://theconversation.com/why-pokemon-go-became-an-instant-phenomenon-62412.
Ito, Mizuko and Okabe, Daisuke (2005) "Intimate connections: Contextualizing Japanese youth and mobile messaging," in R. Harper, L. Palen, and A. Taylor (eds.) *The Inside Text: Social, Cultural and Design Perspectives on SMS*, Dordrecht: Springer, pp. 127–145.

Iveson, K. (2016) "Pokémon GO and public space," *Cities and Citizenship*, August 17, http://citiesandcitizenship.blogspot.com.au/2016/08/pokemon-go-and-public-space.html.

Keogh, B. and Richardson, I. (2017) "Waiting to play: the labour of background games," *European Journal of Cultural Studies*, 21(1), pp. 13–25.

Lammes, S. and Wilmott, C. (2016) "The map as playground: location-based games as cartographical practices," *Convergence* (Online First), https://doi.org/10.1177/1354856516679596.

Lantz, F. (2006) "Big games and the porous border between the real and the mediated," *Receiver* 16, www.receiver.vodafone.com/16/articles/index07.html.

Licoppe, C. and Inada, Y. (2006) "Emergent uses of a multiplayer location-aware mobile game: the interactional consequences of mediated encounters," *Mobilities*, 1(1), pp. 39–61.

McCrea, C. (2011) "We play in public: the nature and context of portable gaming systems," *Convergence*, 17(4), pp. 389–403.

—— (2017) "*Pokémon*'s progressive revelation: notes on 20 years of game design," *Mobile Media & Communication*, 5(1), pp. 42–46.

Okabe, D. and Ito, M. (2005) "Personal, portable, pedestrian images," *Receiver* 13, www.receiver.vodafone.com/13.

Parikka, J. and Suominen, J. (2006) "Victorian snakes? Towards a cultural history of mobile games and the experience of movement," *Game Studies*, 6(1), http://gamestudies.org/0601/articles/parikka_suominen.

Pellegrino, G. (2010) "Mediated bodies in saturated environments: participation as co-construction," in L. Fortunati, J. Vincent, J. Gebhardt, A. Petrovcic, and O. Vershinskaya (eds.) *Interacting with Broadband Society*, Frankfurt am Main: Peter Lang, pp. 93–105.

Salen Tekinbaş, K. (2017) "Afraid to roam: the unlevel playing field of *Pokémon GO*," *Mobile Media & Communication*, 5(1), pp. 34–37.

Sicart, M. (2017) "Reality has always been augmented: play and the promises of *Pokémon GO*," *Mobile Media & Communication*, 5(1), pp. 30–33.

Speed, C. (2010) "Developing a sense of place with locative media: an 'underview effect'," *Leonardo*, 43(2), pp. 169–174.

Surman, D. (2009) "Complicating kawaii," in L. Hjorth and D. Chan (eds.) *Gaming Cultures and Place*, London: Routledge, pp. 179–193.

Taylor, T. L. (2012). *Raising the Stakes: E-Sports and the Professionalization of Computer Gaming*, Cambridge, MA: MIT Press.

Vella, K., Johnson, D., Wan Sze Cheng, V., Davenport, T., Mitchell, J., Klarkowski, M., and Phillips, C. (2017) "A sense of belonging: Pokémon GO and social connectedness," *Games and Culture* (Online First), https://10.1177/1555412017719973.

Wawro, A. (2016) "How did Pokémon GO conquer the planet in less than a week," *Gamasutra*, July 13, www.gamasutra.com/view/news/276955/How_did_Pokemon_Go_conquer_the_planet_in_less_than_a_week.php.

Wilken, R. (2012) "Locative media: from specialized preoccupation to mainstream fascination," *Convergence*, 18(3), pp. 243–247.

Further Reading

Feldman, B. (2018) "Agency and governance: Pokémon-Go and contested fun in public space," *Geoforum*, 96 (November), pp. 289–297.

Leorke, D. (2018) *Location-Based Gaming: Play in Public Space*, Singapore: Palgrave Macmillan.

Nijholt, A. (ed.) (2018) *Playable Cities: The City as a Digital Playground*, Singapore: Springer.

32
FROM SUBCULTURE TO SCENE
Urban Media Practices from Below

Geoff Stahl

Introduction

Urban media play a central role in determining how certain social forms take shape in the city. The inverse is also the case, as social forms in the city often determine the shape and scope of urban media. They are mutually constitutive and reliant upon one another. For many invested in the social and cultural life of the city, urban media serve multifarious functions, ranging from helping to circulate symbol-systems that foster and deepen a sense of belonging for members of a given group, providing creative opportunities and tools for producing cultural goods and commodities, drawing symbolic boundaries and maintaining the spaces in which they might flourish, to acting as vehicles that shape an understanding and experience of the city. Subcultures and scenes exemplify many of these characteristics in their use of urban media, and each gains its conceptual salience when considering how media function in relation to these distinctive sociocultural spaces and related practices as they take hold in the city.

While they are not restricted to being just urban phenomena, subcultures and scenes are often understood as specific collective responses to some of the problems and promises the city offers. Subcultures, a term with a more established pedigree in the social sciences, is tied to the emergence of modern sociology, with its particular focus on transformations affecting social life in late 19th-century European and early 20th-century American cities. From the early urban studies of the Chicago School to the critical case studies of the University of Birmingham's Centre for Contemporary Cultural Studies (CCCS), where the term subculture has been comprehensively developed and debated, and to more recent work on post-subcultures and scenes, the latter terms often deployed to deconstruct and challenge the dominance of the term subculture, the city serves as a vital context for their emergence and sustenance. The city produces, facilitates, and mediates (as well as mediatizes) spaces and practices where media and these social forms intermingle, and each informs each in a manner worthy of more consideration.

As terms designed to capture distinctive aspects of collective life in the city, the role of urban media in framing, shaping, and supporting subcultures and scenes is often un- or under-theorized. When social theorists have considered how these groups initially form, express their identity, as well as how they connect with one another, they have often only hinted at the role that media play, construing it as the lesser term in this relationship; there is scant research that treats all three terms, subculture/scene, media, and the city, with analytical or conceptual parity.

A brief overview of these terms as they emerged in social theory can highlight moments where the complementarity of the city, urban media forms and practices, as well as scenes and subcultures illustrates how they have helped define one another.

Origins of Subcultural Theory

Subcultural theory has its roots in the sociological theories of crime and deviance developed by Emile Durkheim in the late 19th century (1897), particularly in relation to his notions of social solidarity and *anomie* (normlessness). For Durkheim, the rise of secularization and urbanization pulled people out of more well-established institutional frameworks (the church and family) that connected individuals. New, uniquely urban institutions emerged in their stead as cities grew rapidly in the 19th century. Concomitant with the rise of rail travel and expanding employment opportunities through centralized industrialization, city centers brought together disparate individuals. This intensifying heterogeneity meant having to deal with life among strangers and foreigners, leaving many feeling anonymous, alienated, and adrift, unmoored from those earlier institutional anchor points. The response among certain segments of an expanding urban populous was to find other ways to give their lives meaning, to seek out alliances with those who shared similar interests. The possibility of associating freely provided novel sorts of opportunities and encounters in the city, including self-reinvention and new forms of solidarity. The creative and symbolic responses to the material conditions of this situation were embodied by the figure of the bohemian, a new urban type (Wilson 2000). The worlds they helped to cultivate and sustain, through a network of studio spaces and galleries, on the city's sidewalks, in bars and cafes, provided the cultural spaces that allowed this subaltern group to not only depict but also cast a critical gaze upon these new urban spaces through literature, poetry, essays, photography, and painting (Clark 2015). This was an urban demimonde whose creative and critical engagement with the demands of modern metropolitan life anticipated the sort of media-centered cultural spaces, with their own highly stylized acolytes, that would become a signature form of collective life found in cities henceforth (Seigel 1986; Bourdieu 1995).

However, for other citizens, limited means to access these rarefied worlds sometimes meant turning toward crime or underworlds riven with a moral code and social structure that challenged a normative worldview. For Durkheim, the latter move was better understood as a response to the alienating and atomizing impulses of the modern urban condition rather than as anything pathological. Crime and deviant behavior signaled a way forward, gestures pointing toward a new or different kind of moral universe. While Durkheim does not deal with media, his suggestion of crime and deviance as creative means of solving the alienating and anomic situation of the nascent modern city anticipates how certain subcultural groups would come to reply upon a repertoire of media forms as part of a distinctly urban survival kit.

Much of Durkheim's work carried over to the Chicago School of Sociology, members of which in the early decades of the 20th century first gave the term subculture its theoretical purchase (see Cressey on taxi dancers, 1932). Examining the social impact of rapid urbanization and immigration in what was then one of America's fastest growing cities, the body of work produced over the course of the first half of the 20th century did much to bring subcultures to the forefront of the sociological as well as the popular imaginary. Given its progressive politics and efforts at social reform (Lipman 2002), the School used a variety of media to document marginalized, "outsider" cultures, from gangs to taxi dancers to drug addicts, drawing from newspaper stories, police archives, and the commentary of participants as a means to explore the complex urban milieu then unfolding. Its founder, Robert E. Park (Park et al. 1967), was interested in marginalized groups and social segregation in the city. He also examined the role of the press in the city, through a style of sociological "reportage" (Lindner 1996), highlighting the rise of the metropolitan newspaper (and the tabloid press and "yellow journalism"). However, little of his work and that of others at the School explicitly explored how the media either framed deviance, crime, and delinquent behavior or how media might be used by these marginalized groups to make sense of their own situation. Media were understood as forces external to marginalized groups and drivers of public opinion, vehicles for instigating social discord and disorder. For Park and others at the School, urban newspapers and the rapid rise of outdoor advertising in civic spaces were tools of social control shaping perception of what was acceptable conduct in the city, the organs of a "new moral order" that underpinned civic life (Park et al. 1967: 223).

From the 1920s onward, subcultures appeared as a term describing a variety of marginalized groups in the city. It would become a more substantial part of the sociological lexicon, notably after the Second World War in the US and the UK, when issues of conformism, rebellious youth, and the influence of mass culture became objects of fascination for sociologists, the media, and the general public. Among the studies that sought to document postwar subcultures, the most sustained attempt to explore the relation of media to subcultures emerged in the early 1970s, through Stanley Cohen's (1972) studies on moral panics and folk devils in the UK. His analysis of Mods and Rockers, and their involvement in a number of seaside riots in the early 1960s, examined their framing by the media. For Cohen, the media, tabloid press, and televised reporting in particular, amplified the activities of the Mods and Rockers, labeling them in such a way that they were indelibly stigmatized as "folk devils" for mainstream newsreaders and viewers. The stories were meant to galvanize public opinion by promulgating media-generated moral panics that amplified and decontextualized certain behaviors and classed them as "deviant." These media representations were also internalized by these groups, allowing them to further amplify their own behavior in accordance to the stereotype. Cohen's studies analyze how the media functions as an ideological tool, reinforcing the prevailing view that subcultures were engaging in deviant, even criminal activity, ensuring their further marginalization; however, they are also significant because they offer an early account of how media work to give shape to the internal coherence of a subculture.

Some of Cohen's ideas about the media and representation would be taken up in the work of Stuart Hall and Tony Jefferson (1976), Dick Hebdige (1978), Angela McRobbie (1978), and others at the University of Birmingham's CCCS. Influenced also by Althusser, Gramsci, and other Marxist thinkers, they brought a class-based analysis to their studies of youth cultures. Informed also by the structuralism of Claude Levi-Strauss and the semiotics of Roland Barthes and Julia Kristeva, the CCCS analyzed the various homologies that allowed a subculture's seemingly disparate activities to cohere into something socially meaningful, a collective counterpoint to the dominant ideology. In examining the rituals, musical preferences, styles, and argot of select subcultures, emphasizing symbolic interventions such as refashioning of the detritus of the dominant culture into a spectacular style (the use of bin liners for clothing and baby pins as facial piercings among punks, for example), the CCCS produced accounts of how different subcultural groups "won space" through hegemonic struggles over meaning and value. They did this by creating a symbolic, often temporary, zone outside the dominant culture, deriving from its discarded elements a so-called "magical solution" to the "problem" of their structural exclusion from the mainstream.

Urban media appear in these accounts of subcultural practice, but their status as media is under-theorized. Music and fashion were ways in which solidarity and alterity were communicated sonically and visually, but they were rarely discussed as media. Other media crucial as forums for promoting music and other subcultural practices, serving as subcultural gatekeepers, such as 'zines (*Sniffin' Glue* and *Punk* were two key 'zines of the era), were never considered in any depth at the time. Media were narrowly understood as the press and mainstream television news, meaning a more nuanced reading of what constituted media practices in subcultures was an afterthought, rather than anything more fundamentally constitutive. A monolithic institution reinforcing a hegemonic worldview, the media was anathema to subcultures, doing its ideological work by co-opting their practices (commodifying their fashion and music) or by ideologically reframing them through media stories that sought to neutralize their threat by channeling their "noise" through more acceptable, familiar reference points (e.g., the family). An exception to this body of work can be found in the contemporaneous studies of Angela McRobbie (1978). Her focus on femininity, popular music, and young women's fascination with girl's magazines offered a more substantial engagement with the media *as* media, highlighting how gender gets constructed and how female readers, marginalized in the CCCS and its otherwise male-centered subcultures, were involved in media consumption in ways that suggested they were doing more than uncritically internalizing a dominant worldview.

McRobbie's work brought media consumption and the production of meaning on the part of its female consumers into the sphere of what was being referred to as subcultural studies. Sarah Thornton's (1996) work on UK club cultures in the mid-1990s further developed many of these points in a recalibrated form of subcultural theory. For Thornton, media were fundamental to how subcultures defined their exclusivity, where they plotted out a moral cartography of who was in and who was out, drawing upon Bourdieu (1995) to develop the term "subcultural capital" as the currency one accumulated to claim and maintain the status of insider "cool." Considering urban dance clubs and culture, Thornton's notion of different scales and types of media demonstrates how they bind together like-minded individuals, through small-run media such as zines (micro-media), niche media (*iD* or *Face*, in the UK), and how are articulated to and within larger hegemonic structures via mainstream mass media. Here, a broader understanding of the relevance of media can illuminate how they serve many valuable functions by contributing to the internal definition of a subculture. This offers an opportunity to reimagine subcultural theory in light of the specificity of sociospatial relations found in the city, made up as they are of often situational, temporary, as well as more resilient and longer-term, arrays of communicative channels and new forms of mediated connectivity. Subcultures draw upon a range of established, and prompt new, media forms and practices that require more expansive and productive considerations of how cities, media, and social forms such as subcultures (and scenes, as outlined below) are deeply interdependent.

Post-Subcultural Theory and Scenes

Thornton's revisions of subcultural studies anticipated what became known as post-subcultural theory (Muggleton and Weinzierl 2003; Bennett and Kahn-Harris 2004). This body of work challenged structuralist homologies that overemphasized coherence, stressed a modernist form of rupture, and valorized collective resistance and solidarity as articulated through spectacular style. Drawing from Baudrillard (1994) and others, in a postmodern world characterized by fragmentation, hybridity, heterogeneity, and a flattening-out of history, for post-subcultural theorists, style is just a play of surfaces, a highly mediated pastiche of previous subcultural practices. Originality as standard-bearer of subcultural authenticity loses its relevance, problematizing a politics based on the notion of collective resistance and readings of shared style as semiotically and semantically charged revolt. This approach is valuable for scrutinizing subcultural theory in light of the new challenges: the fraught and fruitful pluralisms of cosmopolitan spaces; how certain communities newly mediated through the Internet troubled what made subcultures still "sub"; and where boundaries between the material worlds of the city and the immaterial interactions afforded by online communities blurred or collapsed. However, as some have argued (Hesmondhalgh 2005; Blackman 2014), post-subcultural theory elides the internal coherence of group affiliations, placing greater emphasis on individual stylistic choices. This posits post-subcultural activities as subsumed by a neoliberal entrepreneurialism, making much of the literature a consumer-centered reformulation of subcultures, the latter a set of signifying practices in thrall to late capitalism, a fashionable form of false consciousness.

Reworkings of subcultural theory gained purchase in the *fin-de-siècle* sociological imagination by appearing at the conjuncture of two developments influencing social theory more generally: the "spatial turn" in the social sciences and the rise of the Internet. In the first of these, the spatial turn, a range of social theorists began to draw from humanistic and critical geography, such as the work of Yi-Fu Tuan (1977) and Doreen Massey (Massey et al. 1999), to explore issues of locality, place, and globalization. The second of these developments, the appearance of the Internet, also prompted concerns with space, locality, globalization, but with a renewed emphasis on networks, infrastructures, and their bearing on individual lives as well as the communality of new social worlds flourishing through and between these interfaces that mediate new forms of connectivity, both real and virtual (Castells 2001).

Recent considerations of the intersection of media, cultural spaces, and the collective life of the city have often relied upon the notion of scene to make sense of more informal social gatherings marked by heterogeneity, in contrast to the more formal coherence and homogenous nature of subcultures. Scene as a concept in social theory emerged at the same time that subcultural theory was being reconsidered and when the "spatial turn" was taking hold. While subcultural theory once scrutinized homologies that linked spaces, practices, and class position untainted by media, scene as a concept focuses more on the relations found between sociality and urban space where they become signature signs of a certain kind of urbanity. Will Straw (1991) suggests that scenes facilitate and even motivate particular set of relationships between individuals and institutions, determining how certain cultural practices relate to their own history and broader civic traditions, as well as how they absorb certain influences from elsewhere. The dynamic cross-fertilization of scenes imbues them with social energy, taking the form of distinctive sociospatial expression of a city's collective life. They offer the sense of an occasion enchanted times and places that cultivate a sense of "shared intimacy" (Blum 2003: 158), ensuring their distinction from the routines of everyday life. Scenes insulate and incubate creative activity, allowing the term conceptual traction among social theorists as it encompassed a range of activities associated with media production, distribution, and consumption.

Scenes also articulate social activity to urban spaces and thus can be construed as social media themselves. As Straw (2015) has argued, scenes can speed up or slow down cultural artifacts and media products as they move through the city, shaping the communicative channels through which they circulate. Scenes can also perform a custodial purpose, mediating how and what cultural commodities enter into circulation, or they may serve an archival function, determining which of these may be deemed of value enough to preserve. They also make visible and invisible certain aspects of the scene, mediating social behavior in the city, underpinning the city's civilizing function (Park et al. 1967), establishing ethical codes of conduct, framing urban experiences and expectations, as well as providing pedagogical prisms through which participants may come to understand not only themselves and others, but also the city itself (Straw 2015).

Scenes function as crucibles in which to develop, strengthen, and sustain a shared collective space and vision. They offer opportunities for unique forms of collaborations and projects, synergistic associations that can amplify the social power of the scene and deepen its shared value in and to particular places. The resulting dynamism feeds into an urban milieu that thrives on linking together bars, cafes, and workplaces, facilitating valuable day- and night-time economies the industriousness of which is another index of the vitality of the cultural life of the city (Stahl 2014). These activities can portend the transformation of a neighborhood. Berlin's new media scene, dubbed "silicon Allee," and based around Chausseestrasse in hip Prenzlauerberg, is populated by "digital bohèmes" and exemplifies these tensions (Brighenti and Mattiucci 2008). The same has been said of hipsters in many cities where their perceived dominance of certain neighborhood scenes, such as New York's Williamsburg (Schiermer 2014), Montreal's Mile End (Stahl 2010), and Berlin's Prenzlauerberg (Slobodian and Sterling 2013), has been framed as a new species of moral panic. Pilloried in various media as the most recent iteration of an urban folk devil, hipsters became a locus of anxiety regarding conspicuous consumption and were negatively construed as harbingers of neighborhood gentrification.

Social Media and Beyond

As data-, media-, and city-scapes have come to be deeply dependent upon one another over the last two decades, bound together courtesy of the rise of mobile media and the ubiquity of digital technologies, cultural spaces and the nature of their respective social activities have also been affected. Social media have afforded new ways of engaging with urban space individually and collectively, remediating old media and rendering new media seemingly indispensable to properly experiencing life in the city. Early adopters of these mobile media invested in collectively engaging with the city, evidenced in flash mobs (Brejzek 2010), urban exploration (Kindynis 2016), as well as street and graffiti artists (Snyder 2006). The specificities of digital technologies and novelty of social media enabled novel encounters in and with the city, producing new forms of socializing that re-enchanted civic space, through anything from momentary playful spectacles to longer-lasting interventions. They also allow individuals to connect with others surreptitiously, to appropriate and remediate urban space through trespassing and tagging, courtesy of the expanding number of interfaces and social media networks they use to produce, promote, document, disseminate, and make manifest their activities.

The discourse of novelty associated with new media gained its appeal as it allowed people to demonstrate their up-to-date-ness publicly, using civic spaces to creatively claim their social distinction, exemplifying the scenic power of what Alan Blum has called "being private in public" (Blum 2003: 157). The newness of social media and the proliferation of ubiquitous technologies have also altered how older media dedicated to the cultural life of the city function, shaping the social power of urban scenes. Weekly city magazines and alternative weeklies (Thornton's niche media) are a salient example of these changes. Emerging from the underground press of the 1960s (e.g., *Village Voice* and *L.A. Weekly*), urban weeklies services cater to specialized urban tastes not often reflected in mainstream media. While this includes political commentary on civic issues, most weeklies devote the majority of their content to the cultural life of the city, courtesy of interviews with artists, discussion of cultural issues, and a range of reviews, from films to theatre to music gigs to restaurants. They function as civic boosters whose cultural power is informed by how they share insider knowledge, implying degrees of intimacy with the inner machinations of the city (Anderson et al. 2012). Conveyed in this image of proximity to people, places, and power (political and cultural) is a vision of the city as an ethical space, structured around the health and vitality of its cultural spaces and social activities. The weekly mediates between the scene and the city, the tastes of its readers, and cultural gatekeepers, affirming for all a sense of shared interest and purpose in maintaining the value of the city-as-scene.

As social media began to encroach into territory once held by hardcopy weeklies, the latter reliant on classified sections and advertising for much of their revenue, their social and cultural relevance began to wane. Weeklies geared to service a broad-based group of aspirational urbanites saw many of their services redistributed and repurposed for smart devices and apps (Straw 2010). Selling and trading moved online, dating apps appeared, and restaurants, cafes, and bars were now reviewed online by customers, all relying on locative technologies and for user-generated content and input (see also Chapter 35, this volume). The centralization of cultural information in a hardcopy source parsed out on a weekly basis was replaced by digitalized services that thrived on immediacy. In this new paradigm of urban sociality, those engaged in the social and cultural life of the city, taking in bars, restaurants, music gigs, and its dating scene, are increasingly interpellated as prosumers, having at their disposal a feedback mechanism that registers their likes or dislikes, newly empowered as neoliberal entrepreneurs able to shape the social power of a scene.

Scenes are also subjected to other interests and forces, forms of collective life "from below" subject to appropriation by those who seek to sell cities "from above." The packaging of scenes through urban branding points to the fraught ways in which cultural spaces can get caught up in promotional imperatives to represent cities as "eventful" or "creative" hubs. In a competitive global setting where the symbolic economy has become an integral part of how cities imagine themselves on the world stage, and where the trope of the creative city (Florida 2005; Landry 2012) functions as a mantra for policymakers and other urban stakeholders, subcultures and, more pointedly, scenes come to resonate differently (Stahl 2014). "Scene" is lately a common rhetorical trope in urban policy, informing development, funding regimes and their support for lively cultural spaces. The social power of the scene is understood to have benefits for multiple stakeholders, from cultural producers and consumers to those who see its value as essential to a marketing arsenal geared toward fostering a sense of desirability, for foreigners and locals alike who may want to travel to or, more importantly, invest in these places.

The selling of the city as a space of eventfulness through forms of mediatization relies upon scenes to cultivate attractive atmospheres and demonstrate that they have the cultural resilience that appeals to those fantasies of sustainability central to the risk-averse imperatives of the private/public partnerships that have come to shape the cultural and experiential economies of cities (see also Chapter 24, this volume). Festival scenes, from film, music, and theatre, to restaurants and food trucks, are exemplars of the trend to maximize interest in a city's cultural vitality. Some cities have rehabilitated moribund city sectors into cultural precincts to further concentrate social activity around neighborhood hubs in an effort to consolidate (and monetize) scenic ambience, an effort enacted through policy and planning to choreograph social life and channel its energies into manageable zones. Cities making use of scenes as a part of their branding toolkit include Melbourne, Berlin, Liverpool, Toronto, and many others, which have come to market themselves as "music cities" (Baker 2017; Cohen 2017), offering package tours devoted to the histories of their scenes and establishing archives and museums to showcase their musical heritages to locals and tourists alike (Strong et al. 2017). Both subcultures and scenes are employed as an index of the sociality relied upon by cities jockeying for a position in a global marketplace, where cultural spaces are reduced not just to barometric signs of the health (or weakness) of a city's scenic life, but rendered a kind of currency in municipal, regional, and internationally focused cultural economies motivating what Jim McGuigan has called "cool capitalism" (2006).

References

Anderson, M., Guskin, E., and Rosenstiel, T. (2012). "Alternative Weeklies: At Long Last, a Move Toward Digital," *The State of the News Media 2012*.

Baker, A. (2017) "Algorithms to Assess Music Cities: Case Study—Melbourne as a Music Capital," *SAGE Open*, 7(1).

Baudrillard, J. (1994) *Simulacra and Simulation*, Ann Arbor, MI: University of Michigan Press.
Bennett, A. and Kahn-Harris, K. (2004) *After Subculture: Critical Studies in Contemporary Youth Culture*, London: Palgrave.
Blackman, S. (2014) "Subculture Theory: An Historical and Contemporary Assessment of the Concept for Understanding Deviance," *Deviant Behavior*, 35, pp. 496–512.
Blum, A. (2003) *The Imaginative Structure of the City*, Montreal: McGill-Queens University Press.
Bourdieu, P. (1995) *The Rules of Art: Genesis and Structure of the Literary Field*, trans. S. Emanuel, Stanford, CA: Stanford University Press.
Brejzek, T. (2010) "From Social Network to Urban Intervention: On the Scenographies of Flash Mobs and Urban Swarms," *International Journal of Performance Arts and Digital Media*, 6(1), pp. 109–122.
Brighenti, A. and Mattiucci, C. (2008) "Editing Urban Environments: Territories, Prolongations, Visibilities," in F. Eckardt, J. Geelhaar et al. (eds.) *Mediacity: Situations, Practices and Encounters*, Berlin: Frank and Timme, pp. 81–105.
Castells, M. (2001) *The Rise of the Network Society: The Information Age: Economy, Society, and Culture*, vol. 1, Hoboken, NJ: John Wiley and Sons.
Clark, T. J. (2015) *The Painting of Modern Life: Paris in the Art of Manet and His Followers*, Princeton, NJ: Princeton University Press.
Cohen, S. (1972) *Folk Devils and Moral Panics: The Creation of the Mods and Rockers*, London: MacGibbon and Kee.
— (2017) *Decline, Renewal and the City in Popular Music Culture: Beyond the Beatles*, London: Routledge.
Cressey, P. G. (1932) *The Taxi Dance-Hall: A Sociological Study in Commercial Recreation and City Life*, Chicago, IL: Chicago University Press.
Durkheim, E. (1951) *Suicide: A Study in Sociology* [1897], trans. J. A. Spaulding and G. Simpson, Glencoe, IL: The Free Press.
Florida, R. (2005) *Cities and the Creative Class*, London: Routledge.
Hall, S. and Jefferson, T. (eds.) (1976) *Resistance Through Rituals: Youth Subcultures in Postwar Britain*, London: Hutchison.
Hebdige, D. (1978) *Subculture: The Meaning of Style*, London: Methuen.
Hesmondhalgh, D. (2005) "Subcultures, Scenes or Tribes? None of the Above," *Journal of Youth Studies*, 8(1), pp. 21–40.
Kindynis, T. (2016) "Urban Exploration: From Subterranean to Spectacle," *British Journal of Criminology*, 57(4), pp. 982–1001.
Landry, C. (2012) *The Creative City: A Toolkit for Urban Innovators*, London: Earthscan.
Lindner, R. (1996) *The Reportage of Urban Culture: Robert Park and the Chicago School*, London: Cambridge University Press.
Lipman, P. (2002) "Making the Global City, Making Inequality: The Political Economy and Cultural Politics of Chicago School Policy," *American Educational Research Journal*, 39(2), pp. 379–419.
Massey, D., Allen, J. and Pile, S. (1999) *City Worlds*, New York: Routledge.
McGuigan, J. (2006) "The Politics of Cultural Studies and Cool Capitalism," *Cultural Politics*, 2(2), pp. 137–158.
McRobbie, A. (1978) "Working Class Girls and the Culture of Femininity," *Women Take Issue: Aspects of Women's Subordination*, pp. 96–108.
Muggleton, D. and Weinzierl, R. (2003) *The Post-Subcultures Reader*, London: Berg.
Park, R. E., Burgess, E. W., and Roderick, D. McKenzie (1967) *The City*, Chicago, IL: University of Chicago Press.
Schiermer, B. (2014) "Late-Modern Hipsters: New Tendencies in Popular Culture," *Acta Sociologica*, 57(2), pp. 167–181.
Seigel, Jerrold (1986) *Bohemian Paris: Culture, Politics, and the Boundaries of Bourgeois Life 1830–1930*, New York: Viking Penguin.
Slobodian, Q. and Sterling, M. (2013) "Sacking Berlin: How Hipsters, Expats, Yummies, and Smartphones Ruined a City," *The Baffler*, 23, pp. 138–146.
Snyder, G J. (2006) "Graffiti Media and the Perpetuation of an Illegal Subculture," *Crime, Media, Culture*, 2(1), pp. 93–101.
Stahl, G. (2010) "The Mile-End Hipster: Montreal's Modern Day Folk Devil," in B. Binder, M. Ege, A. Schwanhäußer, and J. Wietschorke (eds.) *Orte—Situationen—Atmosphären*, Frankfurt am Main: Campus Verlag, pp. 321–328.
— (2014) "Introduction," *Poor but Sexy: Reflections on Berlin Scenes*, Bern: Peter Lang, pp. 7–20.

Straw, W. (1991) "Systems of Articulation, Logics of Change: Communities and Scenes in Popular Music," *Cultural Studies*, 5(3), pp. 368–388.
— (2010) "Hawkers and Public Space: Free Commuter Newspapers in Canada," in B. Beaty, D. Briton, G. Filax, and R. Sullivan (eds.) *How Canadians Communicate III: Contexts of Canadian Popular Culture*, Athabasca: AU Press, pp. 79–93.
— (2015) "Some Things a Scene Might Be," *Cultural Studies*, 29(3), pp. 476–485.
Strong, C., Cannizzo, F. and Rogers, I. (2017) "Aesthetic Cosmopolitan, National and Local Popular Music Heritage in Melbourne's Music Laneways," *International Journal of Heritage Studies*, 23(2), pp. 83–96.
Thornton, S. (1996) *Club Cultures: Music, Media and Subcultural Capital*, Hanover, NE: Wesleyan University Press.
Tuan, Y. (1977) *Space and Place: The Perspective of Experience*, Minneapolis, MN: University of Minnesota Press.
Wilson, E. (2000) *Bohemians: The Glamorous Outcasts*, London: Tauris Parke Paperbacks.

Further Reading

Bennett, A. and Peterson, R. A. (eds.) (2004) *Music Scenes: Local, Translocal and Virtual*, Nashville, TN: Vanderbilt University Press.
Boutros, A. and Straw, W. (eds.) (2010) *Circulation and the City: Essays on Urban Culture*, Kingston and Montreal: McGill-Queens University Press.
Lindner, R. (2007) "The Cultural Texture of the City," The ESF-LiU Conference *Cities and Media: Cultural Perspectives on Urban Identities in a Mediatized World*, Vadstena; Sweden; 25–29 October 2006, no. 020, Linköping University Electronic Press.

33
DOCUMENTING URBAN NEIGHBORHOODS AND CLAIMING THE RIGHT TO THE CITY

Anita Bakshi

Introduction

The focus of this chapter is on mediated remembrance, particularly in the context of urban change as neighborhoods are affected by factors such as political fragmentation and division, economic decline, and gentrification. Investigated here are various means and strategies by which communities document and engage with the histories of their neighborhoods including collaborative mapping practices, archive creation, online repositories and games, art practices, and the provision of social services. Using a discussion of the "right to the city," I explore strategies that allow for the representation of more complex stories rather than one-dimensional or polarized versions. Both the right to the city and remembrance projects address salient issues of urban transformation—such as redevelopment, conflict, and gentrification—and can involve processes of regaining control through acts of appropriation and participation.

Urban Memory

It is important first to lay out connections between memory and the city, and to highlight the importance of urban space as a forum for projects of remembrance. The capacity of place physically to embody memory is a theme covered well by the work of philosopher Edward Casey (1987). Places can be embedded with meanings that are of significance to individuals, groups, or national communities, establishing the basic understanding of place as a "memory frame," as a background or setting for events and daily activities, such that people do not remember events in isolation, but rather as situated within particular landscapes or buildings. These sites link memories with temporal structures: "The 'when' and the 'where' are inextricably linked" (Casey 1987: 70).

The city is a framework for memories that are often collective, involving public life, social interaction, and group identities. Spaces of the city mediate events and their translation into memory. For Halbwachs, "every collective memory unfolds within a spatial framework" (1992: 40), and other scholars have described places as containers for remembrances related to community and social relationships (Low and Altman 1992; Hayden 1995). Several works have explored the connections between memory and the city, such as M. Christine Boyer's *The City of Collective*

Memory (1994), as well as more recent examples including *Memory Culture and the Contemporary City* (Staiger and Steiner 2009) and *Remembering, Forgetting, and City Builders* (Fenster and Yacobi 2010). In addition to scholarly and philosophical studies, autobiographical writings and literary explorations of the reciprocity between memory, imagination, and the city are important sources for studying and understanding this relationship. Orhan Pamuk's *Istanbul: Memories and the City* and W. G. Sebald's *Austerlitz* are excellent examples.

Place supports and frames memories, such that places are seen and experienced as they exist today, while at the same time memory and imagination work to allow access to the image of the place as it was in the past. Places can be important reserves of memory in environments where official histories are heavily imposed, often at the expense of other versions of the past, or in cities and neighborhoods that are being rapidly transformed through processes of redevelopment and gentrification. Urban memory plays a significant role in various urban conflicts at many scales. Memories often complicate or prolong conflicts. For instance, in Germany debates over memory and place in Berlin continue to be contentious even though the conflict has been "resolved" and the city is no longer divided. Imposed versions of history often manipulate and modulate memories related to the conflict and the populations involved. At the same time, personal memories gain increased importance in the attempt to maintain access to alternative versions of the past. In this context, spatial practices that harness memory become a critical part of a purposive reconstruction of the past. Concurrently, place-based memories can offer people a link to the past and connections to a sense of identity—one that may differ from national identity or from changes in meaning imposed on urban areas through redevelopment.

The Right to the City

There are important connections between urban memory (and the practices used for its mediation) and the "right to the city," a term first introduced by Henri Lefebvre in 1968. For David Harvey, "the right to the city is far more than the individual liberty to access urban resources: it is a right to change ourselves by changing the city." Yet it is usually "private or quasi-private interests" that reshape the city as a space for select groups (Harvey 2008: 38). Urbanist and political theorist Mark Purcell has pointed out that Harvey, as well as Manuel Castells, have interpreted Lefebvre's right to the city from a primarily economist perspective, whereby they understand the city as "mostly the result of capitalist production process" (Purcell 2013: 145). Purcell instead draws on Lefebvre's writings to make an important distinction. For Lefebvre, the right to the city referred to a more revolutionary project, one involving a movement *beyond* the state, operating through self-managed initiatives. In *The Production of Space*, Lefebvre wrote: "Any revolutionary project today, whether utopian or realistic, must, if it is to avoid hopeless banality, make the reappropriation of the body, in association with the reappropriation of space, into a non-negotiable part of its agenda" (quoted in Purcell 2013: 148).

I argue here that for projects of mediated remembrance this translates to participatory approaches that involve the reclamation and appropriation of urban space for a variety of embodied practices. Such approaches are required to create transformative projects that move beyond the cataloging of neighborhood histories. While such an accounting is important, it alone is not enough and can result in banal projects. It is especially salient for projects and efforts that operate in the context of the reconfiguration and redevelopment of urban space. The remainder of this chapter looks at such collective approaches whereby participatory urban repositories are created—interactive repositories of collective mappings, stories, and art. Such projects and approaches engage with the dynamic nature of urban citizenship.

According to Holston and Appadurai, the city is central to citizenship in important ways: "with their concentrations of the nonlocal, the strange, the mixed, and the public, cities engage most palpably the tumult of citizenship. Their crowds catalyze processes that decisively expand and erode the rules, meanings, and practices of citizenship" (Holston and Appadurai 1999: 2). In his later writings, Lefebvre argued for a new "contract of citizenship" with the radical extension of rights, including those to information, to difference, to self-management, and to the city (Purcell 2013: 146). Yet, Holston and Appadurai argue that contemporary notions of "liberal citizenship" refuse to acknowledge other identities—familial, cultural, ethnic, religious—in service of the abstract notion of belonging, thereby undermining "the sense of community on which it actually depends" (Holston and Appadurai 1999: 6–7). Such understandings of citizenship have implications for the right to the city, as certain practices are deemed unacceptable and disallowed.

Important means for expressing citizenship can be found in practices that document neighborhood histories and projects of community remembrance. While projects of remembrance will likely be less vocal than protests or political action campaigns, they nonetheless play an important role in claiming the right to the city and can be especially powerful means for counterposing vernacular conceptions of the past and present of the city with dominant state-authored projections. How can these "highly differentiated" identities and distinct neighborhood histories and memories be articulated? This must involve carefully crafting a process together with the communities and groups affected by the histories and memories that are being represented. The examples of such an interpretive role (Smith, Morgan, and Van der Meer 2003), outlined below, present strategies that practitioners might employ to work with communities and the fractures of history and memory within them. What is required is to consider the ethnographic present (Holston 1999) in the development of community projects, thereby creating a bridge to the data of social practice. This connection to praxis is essential for enabling interdisciplinary cooperation and developing more effective means of intervention. The examples I present illustrate the importance of such moves, as these projects and urban spaces become generators for establishing greater access to the city and incubating alternate forms of urban citizenship that go beyond existing limitations.

Projects of Appropriation and Participation

Projects of urban remembrance can be executed through a variety of media to develop repositories of varied composition, and I describe just a few examples here. Creating physical points of urban remembrance throughout the urban landscape in Boston, a community mural project in Boston's Roxbury and Dorchester neighborhoods allowed the local black youth to insert their voices into neighborhood narratives. The mural project serves to counter the stigmatization of the neighborhood in local media and popular perceptions and works to bolster local self-esteem. Including depictions of their struggles, as well as messages of hope, youth share narratives of encouragement with the wider neighborhood (Sieber, Cordeiro, and Ferro 2012).

Another project in Beijing, China took the form of a digital repository. The website www.oldbeijing.org (now maintained at a variety of other sites including www.oldbj.org) was created by the artist Zhang Wei in 2001, following his eviction from a *hutong* in central Beijing. The website presents a collection of old maps, images, and stories of this endangered urban typology. *Hutongs* are a network of narrow alleyways and courtyards that have formed the residential framework of old Beijing since the 13th century but are now being demolished at a rapid pace to make room for new developments (Jing, Allegretti, and McKay 2009). The website has been popular, recording around 20,000 daily hits as of July 2006 (Volland 2011: 188). A project in London brings together a digital repository with place-based performance. In 2005, The Red

Room, a radical theatre group, created the Hoxton Project. Working with local residents in the East London neighborhood of Hoxton, which has been experiencing rapid gentrification since the 1990s, the project explored "Hoxton's 'mythical' regeneration from the point of view of the people who live there, through a visual and oral montage of facts, fiction, and verbatim testimony" (Colombo 2009: 162). An oral history audio archive was created through interviews with over 30 local people, and the project culminated with a number of participatory "intimate walkabout performances" that moved audiences through neighborhood spaces while blending personal testimonies with fictional narratives.

Below, I describe a collaborative project that I developed in Nicosia, the divided capital city of Cyprus. This city has experienced that most radical of changes—the emphatic division into two political territories and the loss of its main urban center as a result of civil conflict. Nicosia is the capital of both the primarily Greek-Cypriot Republic of Cyprus, an EU member country, and the Turkish Republic of North Cyprus, a country that has been officially recognized only by Turkey. Here, I worked with communities on both sides of the divide to recover and to represent a common and shared history that had been obscured by the imposition of divergent national narratives. I used the practice of collaborative mapping: working with different participants, gathering information and stories, and then using these contributions to create visual renderings. This process allowed for many voices to come together on the same documents, creating a forum for putting dissenting voices in dialogue. The map became a "working table" (Corner 1999) upon which people could comment and remark upon others' stories and interpretations by proposing alternative versions, or adding to the story and complementing what others had said (Bakshi 2017; see Figure 33.1).

The project began with ethnographic fieldwork with shopkeepers who had at one time worked in the city's commercial center, an area that is now lost to the Buffer Zone that divides the city, inaccessible since 1974. I showed the shopkeepers maps and photographs that they could touch and point to. It was important to have a base capable of making tangible the ground of everyday life—the life that many had forgotten over the years or remembered in relation to nationalist narratives. The focus of the conversation was *not* on the conflict or the politics of contentious events. Rather the conversation began with simple questions: "What did your shop look like?"; "Where did you eat lunch?"; "Point to your shop"; and "Show me how you walked home every day." The use of the maps and photos created a bridge to the praxis of everyday life.

This work was presented as an exhibition, *Nicosia: Topographies of Memory*, at the Home for Cooperation in Nicosia's Buffer Zone in 2012 (see Figure 33.2). It was organized with the Association for Historical Dialogue and Research (AHDR) and was funded by the EU and the UNDP's Partnership for the Future program. The visual documents in the exhibition space were composed by different people, and the design of the exhibition and its composite maps and visual materials needed to make this absolutely clear. I employed various strategies, such as using different-colored text to mark the contributions made by various individuals and creating layered three-dimensional maps using clear acrylic. Archival photographs and family photos acquired from individuals are incorporated into the maps and drawings. Such visual strategies highlight that the maps are composed from multiple memories, emphasizing the fact that individuals remembered the same places in different ways. The maps were created over a period of two years of working together with individuals accessing their memories of a place more than four decades after its complete removal from the city; their remembrances were influenced by multiple forces, including starkly different renderings of the historical narrative (Bakshi 2016). These visual documents describe a shared urban life of which few traces remain, an urban citizenship that has been eroded by competing national narratives.

Figure 33.1 Discussion Over the Map
Photograph by author.

Figure 33.2 Topographies of Memory Exhibition
Photograph by author.

The exhibition was hosted by the AHDR in the Home for Cooperation (H4C), a "home" in the Buffer Zone. This is a space where people from all communities in Cyprus can engage with history and, perhaps even more importantly, connect with the present reality across the divide. The AHDR was established in 2003 by Greek-Cypriot and Turkish-Cypriot educators and researchers, focused mainly on creating alternative forums for the teaching of history. In 2007 they began the lengthy process of establishing the H4C with the purchase of a building: a former residential structure that ended up on the front lines of battle. Following the division of the city, it was left to slowly fall into disrepair in a no-man's land between two military checkpoints. Renovation began with EEA and Norway Grants, as well as funding from other international donors. After years of dealing with complicated technical and bureaucratic issues, including coordination with the UN and the two militaries, this building was officially re-opened in May 2011. The H4C provides a space for dialogue through hosting conferences and events. It houses a library, archive, offices, meeting rooms, and a very active cafe that has become a hotspot for informal meetings. Opportunities are provided for NGOs and individuals to design and implement innovative projects intended to enhance cross-cultural dialogue. As then AHDR president Chara Makriyianni stated at the building's inauguration: "The Home for Cooperation symbolizes the process and the outcome of cooperation and is, in itself, an example of how praxis driven by theory can result in great achievements." Today, they offer a broader range of programming that aims to bring in people who may not necessarily have much interest in bicommunal activities by hosting weekly salsa dance classes, live music nights, and an annual Buffer Fringe performing arts festival. They are continually seeking to expand their initiatives in Nicosia since, as the H4C's manager Marina Neophytou states, "when working at a community level, establishing a dynamic presence is essential in making long-term change."

Another important contribution of the AHDR has been the production of new approaches to the learning and teaching of history, always a contentious issue in Cyprus. Their *Nicosia is Calling* curriculum includes a series of booklets for students aged 11–16, which enable them to explore the historic walled city center through various activities. They are introduced to all aspects of the city's cultural heritage and to the many layers of history it embodies; neither Ottoman nor Hellenic history is privileged. This was translated into an online game in 2014 in order to expand the reach of the work. Daphne Lappa and Shirin Jetha of the AHDR describe their intentions for the online component of the *Nicosia is Calling* project:

> Being aware that we live in a society in Cyprus where people are still afraid to cross to the "other" side, where prejudices and hatred prevail and children especially are exposed to biased views of the past, was one of the major incentives to create an interactive educational game on Nicosia. We wanted to develop an educational platform that would provide young people with a fun way and an interactive tool in which they would learn about the past and present of the old city of Nicosia, its geography, its unique cultural heritage . . . What's more, all this could be done without having to rely on their teachers or schools, or even needing to leave their computer!
> *(https://mahallae.wordpress.com)*

The AHDR created another educational tool through the website showcasing their *Nicosia: The Story of a Shared and Contested City* project. This public history project aims to provide a historical overview of the city from 1878 to 1974. The website is organized through seven maps, ranging from an initial survey of Cyprus in 1885, to a number of maps from the Land Survey Department. These are embellished with demographic data and descriptions of political events, landmarks, and social and cultural events. The project aims to describe the many cultures and communities that have informed Nicosia throughout the years, and also includes narratives about homosexuality and gender dynamics in Cyprus. The AHDR seeks to challenge one-dimensional representations and offer a multi-perspectival visual narrative of the city's social life before and after the division, attempting conceptually to restore the city's unity and cultivate the sense of a shared city.

The Home for Cooperation is a space and a platform that allows for interdisciplinary work from a variety of different perspectives and interests. The space, programs, and projects provided by the AHDR serve to fill gaps in the existing infrastructure—cultural, social, architectural—to enable communities to engage with difficult pasts that continue to affect the present. The H4C creates a space that does not exist otherwise for Greek-Cypriots and Turkish-Cypriots, along with the other communities living in Cyprus, to meet, to learn each other's languages, and to engage in open dialogue. A space of engagement is created in a city that has been drastically reconfigured by division and political fragmentation. The large map of the old commercial center from the exhibition remains on the wall, providing information about aspects of the city's past. At the same time, active work and engagement with local histories occurs through performances and artistic interpretations like the Buffer Fringe Festival. Online resources, including archives, interactive maps, and games, allow for active engagement for a broader public, thereby connecting to the "data of social practice," and allowing for a right to a city that is also shared, not just divided.

Attending to a very different set of urban changes, a community project in Houston, Texas works to address the death of basic social safety nets, affordable housing, economic development programs, and creative programs and enterprises in the neighborhood. Project Row Houses (PRH) was established with the intent to serve as "a catalyst for transforming community through the celebration of art and African-American history and culture" (https://projectrowhouses.org). Created in 1993, this non-profit organization is based in Houston's northern Third Ward, one of the city's oldest African American neighborhoods. Twenty-two abandoned shotgun-style houses on a two-block site were renovated with the goal of establishing a creative and transformative presence (Kester 2011). Shotgun houses are a residential building typology common in the American South. They consist of narrow houses with doors at each end, and rooms stacked one after the other along this axis. It is a style that some architectural historians connect to Creole areas of New Orleans; others draw the origins back to Haiti and even to Africa (Joyner 2003: 25). The PRH houses are a distinctive presence, outlined in bright white paint, creating a sense of community in a neighborhood fragmented by patches of vacant lots. With a small amount of seed money from an NEA grant, artist Rick Lowe sought to refurbish these original homes for use as art spaces. In a neighborhood considered to be a "pocket of poverty" (Tucker 1995: 37) decline was approached through appropriation of space and self-management.

PRH works to shift the role of art from traditional studio practice to a force that can transform the social environment through neighborhood revitalization, historic preservation, community service, and youth education. Community services are provided through innovative programming such as Artists Rounds and Summer Studios Residency. They also organize "social safety nets," such as the Young Mothers Program, which provides housing and services for single mothers to raise their children in a creative, nurturing environment that "recall[s] the way communities used to be" (https://projectrowhouses.org).

Connections are made to the Third Ward's history and memories about the social structure that it had provided in the past. Rather than preserving historic structures as sites of visitation, they are utilized to do important work needed by residents today. Recognizing the economic aspect of keeping creative programs and enterprises viable, PRH hosts regular community markets to allow local artists to reach new audiences. They seek to build on the strong history of small businesses in the neighborhood, and expressly to "preserve this history by providing opportunities for entrepreneurs to experiment with business models, products, and showcases." Their efforts are an excellent example of how the intersections between art, architecture, heritage, and neighborhood development can be activated.

Guest curator Raquel De Anda describes how each artist involved in Round 44 in 2016 engaged with the urban landscape of Houston in efforts to integrate it into their work:

> Be it through phone conversations and email exchange, discussions around dinner tables, brainstorming strategies at coffee shops, or hosting skill share workshops in unexpected venues, each group asked questions about how their work would fit into the larger socio-political landscape of Houston, before initiating a course of action.
>
> (Project Row Houses 2016: 7)

Several homes were given over to the artists for transformation. Round 45 took place in 2017 with a series of installations collectively titled *Black Women Artists for Black Lives Matter at Project Row Houses*. Individual artists draw on the context of Houston, and PRH draws on the neighborhood's history and cultural heritage to address pressing current needs.

Community and neighborhood history is addressed by invited artists who interpret the geographical and historical context of the city and the neighborhood. Social services are provided that address current community needs by referencing the historic cultural and social structure. Documentation occurs through artistic practices, as well as community markets that keep them visible, ensuring continuity. In this way, PRH addresses major forces of urban change such as economic decline, fluctuating social conditions, and even gentrification. The last is a major barrier to access today for urban communities on the margins of desirable urban land. PRH has dealt with this problem by establishing the Row House Community Development Corporation, an affiliated organization that buys and renovates homes to create a larger pool of affordable housing. They work with developers to preserve space for community in the Third Ward (Kester 2011: 217). They have also bought a row house from an adjacent neighborhood, the Fourth Ward, and moved it to the PRH site. In that ward, upscale townhouses have replaced many of the historic row houses. Where the city and the National Register of Historic Places simply marked this history with a plaque, PRH deals directly with the pressures of development, and takes responsibility from the hands of urban "experts." The structure of the Community Development Corporation and the activities of PRH are excellent illustrations of the importance that Lefebvre places on appropriation and participation. Grant Kester refers to this project as "an act of appropriation that was both physical (the assertion of control over real property) and discursive" (Kester 2011: 213). This enables citizens to "de-alienate" urban space—as produced by capital, by systems of property, and through management by experts (Purcell 2013: 149)—and to reintegrate it with the social connections intrinsic to the place.

Conclusion

Through the provision of community spaces, economic programs, cultural events, or collaborative historical documentation, the projects discussed in this chapter engage with memory and history to serve as tools for active, vital transformation of present conditions. Straying outside the lines of disciplinary practices, they illustrate how practitioners can serve as "facilitators," "interpreters," and "sensemakers," together with communities. Collective repositories are created through the involvement of practitioners or scholars with certain skills: my facility with architectural knowledges and technologies, the artists that interpret Houston to develop art installations and practices, the educators and historians in Cyprus who create powerful forms of community engagement. This variety of perspectives allows for the expression and valorization of the "urban," which Lefebvre saw as distinct from the city. As Purcell summarizes, the urban involves

> inhabitants engaging each other in meaningful interactions, interactions through which they overcome their separation, come to learn about each other, and deliberate together about the meaning and future of the city. These encounters make apparent to each inhabitant their existence in and dependence on a web of social connections.
> (Purcell 2013: 149)

Such sites and repositories become available for interaction through a variety of means, including online archives and games or through visiting exhibitions and participating in events. These examples illustrate what becomes possible when disciplinary norms are left behind, and the focus turns to responding to the conditions and needs of the urban, and connecting to local praxis through participation and appropriation. As Lefebvre warns, the methods of distinct disciplines fall short when we seek to explicate or engage with the complexity of such conditions. What is required instead is the creation of hybrid forms of representation and engagement with community histories and memories. Such approaches can allow for the creation of vibrant and continually changing expression, creating living practices that link the past with the present.

References

Bakshi, A. (2016) "Trade and Exchange in Nicosia's Common Realm," in R. Byrant (ed.) *Shared Spaces and their Dissolution: Practices of Coexistence in the Post-Ottoman Sphere*, New York and Oxford: Berghahn.
— (2017) *Topographies of Memories: A New Poetics of Commemoration*, New York and London: Palgrave Macmillan.
Boyer, C. (1994) *The City of Collective Memory: Its Historical Imagery and Architectural Entertainments*, Cambridge, MA and London: The MIT Press.
Boym, S. (2001) *The Future of Nostalgia*, New York: Basic Books.
Casey, E. (1987) *Remembering: A Phenomenological Study*, Bloomington, IN: Indiana University Press.
Colombo, C. (2009) "Gentrification and Community Empowerment in East London," in L. Porter and K. Shaw (eds.) *Whose Urban Renaissance? An International Comparison of Urban Regeneration Strategies*, London and New York: Routledge.
Corner, J. (1999) "The Agency of Mapping: Speculation, Critique and Invention," in D. Cosgrove (ed.) *Mappings*, London: Reaktion Books.
Fenster, T. and Yacobi, H. (eds.) (2010) *Remembering, Forgetting, and City Builders*, Farnham: Ashgate Publishing.
Halbwachs, M. (1992) *On Collective Memory*, Chicago, IL: University of Chicago Press.
Harvey, D. (2008) "The Right to the City," *New Left Review*, 53, pp. 23–40.
Hayden, D. (1995) *The Power of Place: Urban Landscapes as Public History*, Cambridge, MA: MIT Press.
Holston, J. (1999) "Spaces of Insurgent Citizenship," in J. Holston (ed.) *Cities and Citizenship*, Durham NC: Duke University Press.
Holston, J. and Appadurai, A. (1999) "Cities and Citizenship," in J. Holston (ed.) *Cities and Citizenship*, Durham, NC: Duke University Press.
Jing, Y., Allegretti, G., and McKay, J. (2009) "Gathering Memories at the Battlefront: www.oldbeijing. org," in L. Porter and K. Shaw (eds.) *Whose Urban Renaissance? An International Comparison of Urban Regeneration Strategies*, London and New York: Routledge.
Joyner, B. (2003) *African Reflections on the American Landscape: Identifying and Interpreting Africanisms*, Washington DC: National Park Service, US Department of Interior.
Kester, G. (2011) *The One and the Many: Contemporary Art in a Global Context*, Durham, NC and London: Duke University Press.
Lefebvre, H. (1991) *The Production of Space*, trans. D. Nicholson-Smith, Oxford: Basil Blackwell.

— (2003) *The Urban Revolution*, Minneapolis, MN: University of Minnesota Press.
Low, S. and Altman, I. (1992) *Place Attachment: A Conceptual Inquiry*, New York and London: Plenum Press.
Project Row Houses (2016) *Round 44 Shattering the Concrete: Artists, Activists, and Instigators.*
Purcell, M. (2013) "Possible Worlds: Henri Lefebvre and the Right to the City," *Journal of Urban Affairs*, 36(1), pp. 141–154.
Sieber, T., Cordeiro, G., and Ferro, L. (2012) "The Neighborhood Strikes Back: Community Murals by Youth in Boston's Communities of Color," *City and Society*, 24(3), pp. 263–280.
Smith, L., Morgan, A., and Van der Meer, A. (2003) "Community-Driven Research in Cultural Heritage Management: The Waanyi Women's History Project," *International Journal of Heritage Studies*, 9(1), pp. 65–80.
Staiger, U. and Steiner, H. (eds.) (2009) *Memory Culture and the Contemporary City: Building Sites*, London: Palgrave Macmillan.
Tucker, S. (1995) "Artists and the Shotgun House: Houston's Project Row House," *Art Papers*, 19, p. 5.
Volland, N. (2011) "Taking Urban Conservation Online: Chinese Civic Action Groups and the Internet," in D. K. Herold and P. Marolt, (eds.) *Online Society in China: Creating, Celebrating, and Instrumentalising the Online Carnival*, New York: Routledge.

Further Reading

Bakshi, A. (2017) *Topographies of Memories: A New Poetics of Commemoration*, New York and London: Palgrave Macmillan.
Boyer, C. (1994) *The City of Collective Memory: Its Historical Imagery and Architectural Entertainments*, Cambridge, MA and London: The MIT Pres.
Kester, G. (2011) *The One and the Many: Contemporary Art in a Global Context*, Durham, NC and London: Duke University Press.

PART IV

Spaces and Practices of Daily Life in Mediated Cities

INTRODUCTION TO PART IV
Spaces and Practices of Daily Life in Mediated Cities

Zlatan Krajina and Deborah Stevenson

The extent to which daily living reproduces or also changes cities is a recursive concern in urban sociology. What makes it pertinent for urban media and communication debates is that practicing the city involves activating certain ideas about the city, while a considerable proportion of urban everyday life is linked with media practices in particular. These are a specific form of urban resource, at least in that they complicate a sense of place, stretching the space of action and imagination beyond physical location and creating further opportunities for intervention in the urban scene. Having demonstrated the urban origins of media institutions and communicative dimensions of urban design in the first, material dimensions and infrastructural aspects of urban media in the second, and the place of media economies, policies and cultures in post-industrial urban transformations in the third, in this, the fourth Part, we explore routine and recalcitrant principles of urban media life. Though placed in the final Part, daily uses of media in navigation and negotiation of urban spaces are as good a place to start in thinking about earlier issues.

As Hubbard puts it, "cities may be scripted, but our performances do not always follow the script" (2006: 126; see also Lane 2019). This important perspective gestures to the lasting relevance of de Certeau's (1984) model for exploring the urban as an unceasing interplay between politics of representation (strategies of control, the "concept-city") and multiplicity of reading (tactics of appropriation, such as disobeying, but not entirely rejecting, traffic signs). Cities are never accomplished, but are always in the making. When a section of urban space is physically constructed, it is further transformed by differential, intimate meanings, either by way of daily living (cf. Sinclair et al. 2002) or re-appropriation (e.g., squatting or communal gardening).

However, daily life is always more than the battle between strategies and tactics; it is where ideologies take effect and where societal pressures, shared imaginations and individual interventions coalesce with a promise to transform. This is why the everyday remains arguably most difficult to study; it is such only as long as it is perceived as ordinary and unproblematic, at which point its governing laws become difficult to track. As is familiar in human geography (Cresswell 1996; Sibley 1995), transgression or misuse of space can disturb the seemingly insignificant appearance of daily rounds in the city to the extent that the underlying, selective, logics of its order, pertaining chiefly to distinctions between insiders and outsiders, temporarily become visible and open to negotiation. Governing assumptions (e.g., proper uses of train stations for waiting) inform users' reactions to unlikely acts (e.g., "sleeping in") as inappropriate, rather than as signs of "a social problem (homelessness, racism)" (Cresswell 1996: 8, 9).

Contributors in this Part demonstrate ways in which urban media and communication articulates new formations of familiar issues concerning daily living: individuality and community, difference and identity, inhabitancy and protest, conviviality and segregation, criticism and transformation. The first group of chapters looks at how people's sensing, navigating and reading urban media environments inscribe differential meanings in those spaces, even if these practices remain invisible and without those involved being aware of their role in weaving manifold spaces of urban communication. In Chapter 34, Meri Kytö observes the reductive tendency of privileging sight in contrast to the "multimodal" nature of our sensing of the city. Bringing together cases as diverse as onomatopoeia and "sensory overload", and studies of personal stereo use, "masking" public spaces with white noise or deodorant and sensor-operated architecture, Kytö raises the issue of "sensory agency" as a political platform for negotiating the mediated city. Indeed, as we read in Jordan Frith's Chapter 35, the infusion of networked media (social, digital, locative) with urban practices such as walking transforms "spatial legibility". Urban places become physical-digital "hybrids", which serve users as resources in spatiotemporal orientation, presentation of self and wayfinding. Chapter 36, by Zlatan Krajina, complements the above arguments with the notion, drawn from media audience studies, that interaction is always wider than traces left online: reading urban media spaces is diverse and impossible to predict. People bring into interaction with their surroundings different, sometimes conflicting, elements of their "interdiscursive" identity formations (race, class, gender) that can take street intercourse in unlikely directions.

To understand such possibilities, the next set of chapters considers situations in which differential meanings of urban media space become the basis of publicly voiced claims and "communing". As Ilija Tomanić Trivundža and Mitja Velikonja show in Chapter 37, graffiti and street art historically helped certain groups compensate for "communicational deficit" in articulating issues and forms of expression not deemed legitimate otherwise but the specific visual vocabulary they produced was subsequently mobilized—first as documentation, then as self-promotion—in city branding. In Chapter 38, Tina Richardson further explores intended temporary disruptions of the urban order with a focus on DIY architecture, guerilla urbanism and place-hacking—from the Situationist International to "urban explorers" who redefine the meaning of "access" to guarded urban sites. In the urban world where most spaces have been privatized (Bridge and Watson 2003b), the creation of "situation"—such as converting a waiting area in a bank into a communal space—articulates mediation as reflection and practice as critique. Street traffic, a usual image of urban order, is the first to be disrupted, and symbolically significant places, such as central squares, the first to be occupied when rights, particularly the "right to the city", are claimed. In her overview of media-urban connections in protests, in Chapter 39, Tetyana Lokot highlights the physical/virtual nature of cases like NY Occupy movement and Euromaidan protests in Kyiv.

The last cluster of contributions considers ways in which urban media can be used for subaltern group constitution and identification. Attempts to map—and control—the multiplicity of urban living are as old as cities. First it may have been cinematic screening and maps and now it is also dashboards orchestrating real-time "big data" that seek to translate all aspects of urban living into information that could be used to create cities that are more manageable and orderly than before (cf. Shelton et al. 2015). However, any pursuit of order is relative to specific disorder thus created: repetitive removals of "slums" in European cities (previously working class, now Roma settlements) create disorder for their inhabitants for whom, though starved of resources, these spaces are a source of attachment (cf. Pile et al. 1999). In Chapter 40, Andrea Medrado considers the formation of communal solidarity, enacted in the streets as much as via social media, as resistance to acts of "militarization" by the state, as was the case with Rio de Janeiro's favelas in the wake of 2016 Olympics. In contexts where communities are defined by ethnic minority origin, urban community media, such as UK radio stations representing each group with separate slots, Medrado highlights, remain limited in reaching the wider milieu. Cultural difference (whether that of origin or taste) is never reducible to, but cuts across, physical and media spaces (Bridge and Watson 2003a; see also Amin 2006), and contact (encounter) among strangers, and its lack, remains the prime locus of differentiation and tension. In Chapter 41, Armond R. Towns turns to McLuhanite medium theory to deconstruct the racial construction of transport (freeway) facilities in American towns, particularly the ways in which escape routes during disasters such as hurricanes were less accessible to underprivileged black communities or how movements like #BlackLivesMatter used the same spaces to "take" unresolved issues of racism back "into streets". Steve Macek, in Chapter 42, also contrasts perspectives on daily life along the media–city axis, with a focus on representations of poverty in corporate media in American cities, which tend to reproduce initial, 19th-century moral panics in imperial cities about "underclass" areas as "dangerous", as opposed to attempts at alternative representations by grassroots and cooperative media, as exemplified in Nairobi and Caracas. In Chapter 43, Hollis Griffin looks at how the history of sexuality and gender portrays cities as spaces that promised marginal groups, such as sexual minorities, a safe space for identification and expression. As his reading of media programs on LGBT city tourism suggests, increased visibility has underpinned improved acceptance as well as articulating it as a narrowly defined token of consumption.

Reflecting on the difficulty of understanding the everyday as part of the complexity of knowing the mediated city, the final Chapter 44 by Simone Tosoni and Giorgia Aiello offers a critical overview of some of the methodological approaches and challenges, which scholars working in urban media and communication research have developed, seeking to consolidate different (urban and media) disciplinary conventions and specificities of the urban and the mediated. Perhaps some of those will also inspire our readers in formulating their studies to come.

References

Amin, A. (2006) "Public Space and Collective Culture", *City*, 12(1), pp. 5–24.
Bridge, G. and Watson, S. (2003a) "City Differences", in Bridge, G. and Watson, S. (eds.) *A Companion to the City*, Oxford: Blackwell, pp. 251–260.
Bridge, G. and Watson, S. (2003b) "City Publics", in Bridge, G. and Watson, S. (eds.) *A Companion to the City*, Oxford: Blackwell, pp. 369–379.
Cresswell T. (1996) *In Place/Out of Place: Geography, Ideology, and Transgression*, Minneapolis, MN: University of Minnesota Press.
De Certeau, M. (1984) *The Practice of Everyday Life*, Berkeley, Los Angeles, CA and London: California University Press.
Hubbard, P. (2006) *City*, London: Routledge.
Lane, J. (2019) *Digital Street*, New York: Oxford University Press.
Pile, S. et al. (1999) *Unruly Cities? Order/Disorder*, London: Routledge and Open University Press.
Shelton T. et al. (2015) "The Actually Existing Smart City'", *Cambridge Journal of Regions, Economy and Society*, 8, pp. 13–25.
Sibley, D. (1995) *Geographies of Exclusion: Society and Difference in the West*, London: Routledge.
Sinclair, I. et al. (eds.) (2002) *The Unknown City: Contesting Architecture and Social Space*, Cambridge, MA: MIT Press.

34
THE SENSES AND THE CITY
Attention, Distraction and Media Technology in Urban Environments

Meri Kytö

Introduction

Urban environments are complex clusters of mediated information and sensory experience. Focusing on the sensory enables us to ask new questions about older articulations of urbanity. How can the urban be understood through the senses? For example, how can we study the relationships between the city and media technologies by touch?

The following lengthy quote by the English writer and social critic Charles Dickens is from the first chapter of his book *Pictures from Italy* (1903). In the passage below, he describes traveling in a horse cart through France in 1844; I suggest you read it out loud:

> You have been travelling along, stupidly enough, as you generally do in the last stage of the day; and the ninety-six bells upon the horses—twenty-four apiece—have been ringing sleepily in your ears for half an hour or so; and it has become a very jog-trot, monotonous, tiresome sort of business; and you have been thinking deeply about the dinner you will have at the next stage; when, down at the end of the long avenue of trees through which you are travelling, the first indication of a town appears, in the shape of some straggling cottages: and the carriage begins to rattle and roll over a horribly uneven pavement. As if the equipage were a great firework, and the mere sight of a smoking cottage chimney had lighted it, instantly it begins to crack and splutter, as if the very devil were in it. Crack, crack, crack, crack. Crack-crack-crack. Crick-crack. Crick-crack. Helo! Hola! Vite! Voleur! Brigand! Hi! En r-r-r-r-route! Whip, wheels, driver, stones, beggars, children, crack, crack, crack; helo! hola! Charité pour l'amour de Dieu! crick-crack-crick-crack; crick, crick, crick; bump, jolt, crack, bump, crick-crack; round the corner, up the narrow street, down the paved hill on the other side; in the gutter; bump, bump; jolt, jog, crick, crick, crick; crack, crack, crack; into the shop-windows on the left-hand side of the street, preliminary to a sweeping turn into the wooden archway on the right; rumble, rumble, rumble; clatter, clatter, clatter; crick, crick, crick; and here we are in the yard of the Hotel de l'Ecu d'Or; used up, gone out, smoking, spent, exhausted; but sometimes making a false start unexpectedly, with nothing coming of it—like a firework to the last!

As heard in this excerpt, translating sensory experience to relatable and understandable language is a challenge. Here, the writer uses onomatopoeia (phonetical imitation) and repetition, and mixes several bodily notions (feeling tired and hungry, repetitious sounds, and the sudden change of them, shouts heard from outside and the all-encompassing wobble of the cart and people in it). Research into the sensory tackles the same challenges of terminology and thick description as the quote suggested. As sensory experience is very context-reliant and depends on cultural interpretation in order to be understandable via writing, the detail given to describe the actual phenomena at hand is important.

Dickens's 170-year-old example might seem a bit far off in a chapter discussing urban media but it rings true for most current residents of the small Nordic city I live in, Tampere (Finland). During winter, it gets dark at about three o'clock in the afternoon. As it is dark outside and the buses are well lit inside, it is difficult to see much else from the window than the reflection of one's own face. If the weather is wet, the reflections of street lamps and other electric signs get blurred. It is hard to know where exactly the bus is going and what the next stop is, especially when one has gazed upon one's gleaming smartphone and paid no attention to their surroundings during the trip. There is a destination display connected to GPS visible inside the bus, but often these are out of order. So how does one know when to alight in these kinds of conditions, if going to the city center? By the tremendous shake and rattle when the bus arrives at the old main street, Hämeenkatu, paved in cobble stone, a similar sensory cue that is embedded in the urban fabric in the Dickens description.

The Five Senses and More

The academic interest in the fields of social sciences and humanities toward the senses follows interest in the material and the corporeal. The discussion on the nature of sensory knowledge has roots in an old ontological dualism: Is human existence more mind than body? For the phenomenologist Maurice Merleau-Ponty, sensory perception is not an act of the mind but of the body, an act that connects us to the lived environment and thus constitutes it (Merleau-Ponty 1945). Another background for the interest in the sensory is the critique of the linguistic turn that happened during the 1970s in Western philosophy. According to the linguistic turn, the limits of one's language were seen as the limits of one's perceptions of the world. According to the anthropologist David Howes, to shift the focus from the mind to the body is an ideological revolution as perception is not just a matter of biology, psychology or personal history but also a matter of cultural information, heavy with social significance (2005: 3–4).

Contrary to popular assumption, there is a wider multitude of sensory modalities that extends beyond the classically defined (i.e., Western) five senses: touch, smell, sight, taste and hearing. Other senses that we use in everyday life include pain, temperature, balance, movement, vibration and various internal stimuli like hunger and thirst. Our senses "work" together and therefore, sensory experience is multimodal. The low beats in club music are both sound and tactile vibration. The taste of cinnamon is in the scent. One example of the interplay of the visual and sonic is demonstrated in the McGurk Effect, which shows that what we hear deeply influences what we see. Psychologists John MacDonald and Harry McGurk (1978) showed subjects a video with a person speaking syllables (like na, ta, ga, ka, na) but dubbed the audio track with different syllables. The subjects, who could well identify the syllables being spoken when not looking at the video, consistently misidentified the sounds when the video presented conflicting mouth movements. The striking point in this test is that knowing about the McGurk Effect and how it changes perception doesn't influence experiencing it, as one can experiment with various YouTube videos dedicated to demonstrating the effect.

Novel sensory phenomena are often related to new media technology. Studies in consumption of media technology have shown that in the processes of domestication (adapting and integrating new technology to familiar social processes and uses), commercialized and popularized technology (gadgets, tools, hardware and software) get new attributes and are molded into new practices and uses (see Morley 2000; Bakardjieva 2005). Some of the novel sensory phenomena such as electromagnetic hypersensitivity and ASMR ("autonomous sensory meridian response") have not as yet been scientifically explained but are nevertheless experienced and medicalized in everyday culture. Electromagnetic hypersensitivity is a claimed intolerance of electromagnetic fields produced by mobile phones, power lines and Wi-Fi, et cetera. The irritable presence of electricity is thought to produce the "Worldwide Hum" (2016), "an unusual low frequency sound, a low rumbling or droning sound that is louder at night than during the day, and louder indoors than outdoors". In the wake of the popularity of attention enhancing exercises like Buddhist meditation and mindfulness, the phenomenon of ASMR, in which tactile senses are aroused by binaural video recordings, has become popular on YouTube as well. The communities around producing and watching/listening to these intimate first-person-narrated videos report sensations of tingling and semi-erotic pleasure.

To question how stimuli become organized into internal mental models is to explore the mind as a kind of data-processing device, an assumption popular in cognitive psychology in the 1970s. This kind of thinking has strongly influenced the design of the algorithms for machine listening; a field of study of algorithms and systems for audio understanding by machine (for example, Bregman 1990). Anthropologist Tim Ingold (2000), inspired by work on visual ecology by James Gibson (1979) and ecology of the mind by Gregory Bateson (1973), admits the problematic status of biology in understanding perception as only a cognitive capability. Instead, he proposes that processes like thinking, perceiving, remembering and learning have to be studied within the contexts of people's relations with their environments. These skills are developed through practice and training and are thus as much cultural as they are biological (Ingold 2000: 170–171). With this argument in mind, the relationship between urban environments and media technology is embedded in situated knowledges, often tacit but then again often describable with adequate methods such as sensory ethnography. Studying the sensory often benefits from other kinds of research material that can be produced in an interview setting or a classic observation situation. Methods for sensory ethnography—reflexive and experimental processes like walking or mapping together, through which understanding, knowing and knowledge are produced—have been developed in many disciplines (Pink 2015). Simultaneously, dialogical knowledge production methods have been produced including co-authorship of research publications together with the subjects of research (Guilbault 2014).

Sensory Overload and Fragmentary Attention

Sensory annoyance in cities is a topic as old as cities themselves. In the Sumerian epic Gilgamesh dating from ca. 3000 BCE, there is a description of how "the uproar of mankind is intolerable and sleep is no longer possible by reason of the babel", resulting in the gods exterminating mankind by flooding the earth (Keizer 2010: 81). The narratives of sensory overload seem to repeat themselves more as the attributes of urbanity get stronger, and the denser and more populated the cities being written about become.

During the industrial age, the amount of technological infrastructure grew significantly. The quantity of street lamps, mobile music (gramophones) and traffic modified the sensory environment with the flow of light, sound and movement. To counterbalance the idea of continuous change, the French sociologist Henri Lefebvre (2004/1992) introduced a methodology called rhythmanalysis to better understand the production of urban space. Everyday patterns of movement, repetition, polyrhythmia (simultaneous conflicting rhythms) and isorhythmia (underlying repetitious rhythmic patterns) shed a light on the relationship between humans and the city as continuous weaving of the spatial and temporal fabric. Lefebvre reminds us of the diverse changes that happen between the collision of places (markets, streets, homes) and social relationships (neighbors, friends, family) (Simonsen 2004: 45).

In the classic texts of urban studies, the city home is depicted as a romanticized getaway place, a haven to which one retreats after a day of abundant psychological and sensory stimuli. For the sociologist Georg Simmel, writing at the beginning of the 20th century, all this coerces a city's inhabitants into being rational and instrumental in their social interactions, and to screen out much of the stimulus in order to be able to cope with it. All qualitative value is reduced to a measurable—and, as such, overwhelming—superficial tendency, developing an attitude Simmel called "blasé": an indifference and alienation from society and other people (Simmel 1950). This articulation of privacy as exclusion from public space was of course affordable only to a certain demographic, the male bourgeoisie, not inclusive of most women, children or staff who worked under the exhausted *Bürger*, the privileged citizen of the city. They did not have "a room of one's own" where they could shake off the urban ambience.

The irritation caused by the excess of urban stimuli was medicalized even before Simmel's essay. Neurasthenia—meaning mechanical weakness of the nerves with symptoms of fatigue, anxiety and high blood pressure—is a term that was first used in the 1820s and became popular at the second half of the 19th century. The causes of neurasthenia were firmly attributed to the outside world, to technological and social changes that drained the limited energy reserves of modern people. It was soon fashionable to be diagnosed as neurasthenic in America and Western Europe, a kind of *maladie á la mode* for intellectuals as melancholia had been during Romanticism (Schaffner 2016: 91–96).

The articulation between public and private space is highly relevant when tackling the urban. The built environment (houses, offices and apartments) acts as sensory regulator between the public and the private. The inside is safe from the natural forces, odors, the crush and din of the crowds. In the beginning of the 20th century, the need for isolation (and especially sonic isolation) began to take form in buildings that were padded with newly designed materials courtesy of a new engineering discipline, acoustics. Historian of technology Emily Thompson describes the non-reverberation of acoustic space as a form of modernity, the individual's exclusion from the urban:

> Just as modern technologies like pneumatic riveters, automobiles, and loudspeakers transformed the soundscape of city streets, so, too, did acoustical [sound absorbing] materials fundamentally transform the aural dimensions of interior space. These materials didn't simply eliminate the noises of the modern era, they additionally created a new, modern sound of their own. This sound was characterized first and foremost by its lack of reverberation; unprecedentedly absorptive materials created a sound that was clear and direct. In a culture preoccupied with noise and efficiency, reverberation became just another form of noise, an unnecessary sound that was inefficient and best eliminated.
>
> *(Thompson 2002: 171)*

During the 20th century, the regulation and design of the urban sensory realm continued in the lines of sanitation and hygiene. Deodorizing of not only individuals but also of spaces is a result of urban planning that has resulted in factories being situated away from city centers and areas of habitation. The electrification of vehicles will gradually reduce the century-old reign of the internal combustion engine. Masking is still a technique in use: recordings of the white noise of water fountains—practical as conversation masks in city parks—are played as masking sound effects by Japanese public *otohime* toilets. Also, the Paris metro has tried to mask and neutralize the odors of their trains with a scent called "Madelaine" (orange, lemon and lavender) and, following suit, Berlin metros have used perfumed scent in masking the mixture of smells considered unpleasant—the "wet umbrellas, body odor, unwashed dogs, kebab and currywurst, sometimes spilled beer or schnapps" (Spiegel Online 2008).

The regulation of the sensory environment is often a strategy of power in urban spaces. A much-debated gadget, the Mosquito anti-loitering device, is being used in public spaces in Britain, contrary to many critical voices. The product's website describes the gadget as "creat[ing] a sound detected only by younger people that becomes uncomfortable and intensley [sic] annoying encouraging then to move away from your property" (Compound Security Systems 2017). A more innocuous method than playing a high-frequency buzz is to run a playlist of Western classical music from the loudspeakers, which has been encouraged by the police authorities in Tampere in similar cases of "loitering youth". Needless to say, the Mosquito severely breaches teenagers' human rights of free movement and peaceful assembly, because it leaves no room for choice.

When they became portable, personal stereos became affordable and thus more common. The use of personal stereos opened up new possibilities for individuals to alter and design their own personal acoustic space. Sound studies scholar Michael Bull has studied the use of personal stereos and how it changes the experience of the urban environment (Bull 2000, 2007). Bull describes how using the iPod persuades the user into "auditory looking". The iPod users Bull has interviewed describe how they feel they are "not really there", but are solipsistic viewers shielded by their iPod from any truly reciprocal gaze from others in the city (Bull 2012: 201–202). The personalized musical environment has an aestheticizing potential as the contents of the iPod represent a repository of sensory and environmental stimuli, making the street mimic the different moods offered by the music playing on the iPod (Bull 2012: 203, 205).

This complex form of attention toward one's surroundings resonates with the claims made by art historian Jonathan Crary. Writing about the changing practices of vision during the second half of the 19th century, Crary states that attention had become a new and important subject within the modernization of subjectivity, something to be managed (Crary 1999: 17). Bull's research on personal stereos seems to extend this thought, as he notes various examples on how this management is also done in everyday sensory practices. As Malcolm McCullough writes in his book *Ambient Commons: Attention in the Age of Embodied Information*, the "experience of technology has changed so much since the industrial city and the heyday of print and broadcast media that it is time to reexamine the urban citizen's distraction" (McCullough 2013: 24). Distraction and fragmentary attention resulting from the use of mobile media technology is relevant in understanding the bodily and the affective experience of the mediated city. We may be looking at things without seeing them, or we may be listening to things and not only hear them. Changes in the levels of attention pose a challenge to the studies of the senses and the mediated city: is there a level of "adequate" sensory attention that would validate studying pervasive media in urban environments so it also includes low attention (Kassabian 2013)? These kinds of questions about human perception in the urban environment are currently being informed by the presence of growing sensory capabilities of technological perception—that is, ubiquitous sensor technology.

Sensors and the City

A sensor is an electronic component that detects events in its environment and relays that information for reception or response. Smart city infrastructures are based on sensor technologies that are coded to objects. Sensors detect weather conditions, count traffic and track water consumption. Sensors inside "smart buildings" detect when to lower the window shades, turn on lights, lock doors and open ventilation windows (see also Chapter 17, this volume). Background music in department stores is connected to sensors that measure the rhythms of the store: when there are more people (and hence, more background noise) the volume of the music goes up a notch and vice versa. In current urban environments, many sensory tasks previously only feasible for humans have been given over to sensors, like detecting the license plates of cars in parking lots, smoke detecting in department stores, and listening to noise levels at airports.

Code/space is where the production of space is infused with pervasive software and coded assemblages to such an extent that without them, it can't perform the spatial attributes expected of it. These kinds of spaces are reliant on network connectivity; this reliance can also be viewed as an advantage, since the systems operate with high utility, efficiency and productivity. For example, billing, ticketing, check-in, baggage routing, security screening, customs, immigration, air traffic control and airplane instrumentation work together to create coded infrastructures and coded processes that result in a coded assemblage that defines and produces airports and passenger air travel (Kitchin and Dodge 2011: 7–18; see also Chapter 15, this volume).

Code/spaces and sensor-activated software are often automated and as complex structures also have their weak points. If commercialized and brought to market prematurely, a recalibration of the features is often needed. Comedian Jake Yapp (2017) joked that speech recognition is by far the most fun technology one can currently have in the world of broadcasting: when on-air, you can hijack voice-activated gadgets of the audience by saying things like "Hey Siri, send my entire search history to 'Mum'". This remains to be tested, but as research at the Zhejiang University has shown, voice activation doesn't need to be audible to humans, only to the machines themselves. The researchers demonstrated that simple software modulating the voice commands to ultrasonic (+ 20 kHz) frequencies made it possible to activate Siri to initiate a FaceTime call on an iPhone or to even switch the phone to airplane mode (Zhang et al. 2017).

Technology keeps developing apace and surprising us with sensory inventions. Nevertheless, the question of the nonhuman sensory agency of ubiquitous technology is a larger set of philosophical conundrums that will puzzle people living in smart city constellations. According to philosopher Bruno Latour, it might be necessary to rethink the relationship between humans and nonhumans, object and subject (Latour 1993). Being a subject

> is not to act autonomously in front of an objective background, but to share agency with other subjects that have also lost their autonomy. It is because we are now confronted with those subjects—or rather quasi-subjects—that we have to shift away from dreams of mastery as well as from the threat of being fully naturalized.
>
> *(Latour 2014: 5)*

This is a political task "to distribute agency as far and in as differentiated a way as possible—until, that is, we have thoroughly lost any relation between those two concepts of object and subject that are of no interest any more" (Latour 2014: 16). The question Latour asks is above all ethical and radical in the sense that it not only questions human agency but also makes us ponder what nonhuman agency might be. These questions will be relevant in situations where sensory agency is handed over to intelligent sensory technology like face recognition software used with CCTV cameras, such as AnyVision, a real-time face and human recognition software for mass crowd events (Nvidia 2018).

What "looking and listening" (however these might be defined) sensors enable is relevant with respect to privacy and confidentiality. Philosopher Shoshanna Zuboff calls attention to the emergent logic of accumulation in the networked sphere she names surveillance capitalism. In her view, the work of surveillance redistributes and concentrates privacy rights to surveillance capitalists (such as Google and Facebook), who have many opportunities for secrets, unlike the individuals they surveil:

> many of their rights appear to come from taking others' without asking . . . Surveillance capitalists have skillfully exploited a lag in social evolution as the rapid development of their abilities to surveil for profit outrun public understanding and the eventual development of law and regulation that it produces. In result, privacy rights, once accumulated and asserted, can then be invoked as legitimation for maintaining the obscurity of surveillance operations.
>
> *(Zuboff 2015: 83)*

What makes up the commons in urban public code/space might need to be redefined. Malcolm McCullough shares Zuboff's concern about the frameworks of civil society, naming two focus points for urban resilience: liveability and socialization. McCullough acknowledges that "to go back to a world without pervasive computing"—continuously designed to be less obtrusive and more intuitive—"may be no more possible than going back to life before, say, electric lighting" (2013: 16). The challenge is to develop new cultural responses in the interface arts and for the information commons (McCullough 2013: 13–16). As humans adapt to technological contexts and different technologies (Ihde 2001), it will be interesting to see to what extent the relationship between the agencies of people and virtual agencies of media technologies will develop and interact and how the sensory abilities of media technology will continue to produce urban space.

References

Bakardjieva, M. (2005) *Internet Society. Internet in Everyday Life*, London: SAGE.
Bateson, G. (1973) *Steps to an Ecology of Mind*, London: Fontana.
Bregman, A. (1990) *Auditory Scene Analysis: The Perceptual Organization of Sound*, Cambridge, MA: MIT Press.
Bull, M. (2000) *Sounding Out the City: Personal Stereos and the Management of Everyday Life*, Oxford and New York: Berg.
— (2007) *Sound Moves: iPod Culture and Urban Experience*, London: Routledge.
— (2012) "The audiovisual iPod", in J. Sterne (ed.) *The Sound Studies Reader*, London and New York: Routledge.
Compound Security Systems (2017) viewed September 1, 2017, www.compoundsecurity.co.uk.
Crary, J. (1999) *Suspensions of Perception: Attention, Spectacle, and Modern Culture*, Cambridge, MA: MIT Press
Dickens, C. (1903) *American Notes for General Circulation and Pictures from Italy*, London: Chapman and Hall.
Drever, J. L. (2017) *The Case for Aural Diversity in Acoustic Regulations and Practice: The Hand Dryer Noise Story*, paper at the 24th International Congress of Sound and Vibration, London.
Gibson, J. (1979) *The Ecological Approach to Visual Perception*, New York and Howe: Psychology Press.
Guilbault, J. (2014) "Politics of ethnomusicological knowledge, production, and circulation", *Ethnomusicology*, 58(2), pp. 321–326.
Howes, D. (ed.) (2005) *Empire of the Senses: The Sensual Culture Reader*, New York and London: Berg.
Ihde, D. (2001) *Bodies in Technology*, Minneapolis, MN: University of Minnesota Press.

Ingold, T. (2000) *Perception of the Environment: Essays on Livelihood, Dwelling and Skill*, London and New York: Routledge.
Kassabian, A. (2013) *Ubiquitous Listening: Affect, Attention, and Distributed Subjectivity*, Berkeley, CA: University of California Press.
Keizer, G. (2010) *The Unwanted Sound of Everything We Want: A Book About Noise*, New York: Public Affairs.
Latour, B. (1993) *We Have Never Been Modern*, Cambridge, MA: Harvard University Press.
— (2014) "Agency at the time of the Anthropocene", *New Literary History*, 45.
Lefebvre, H. (2004) *Rhythmanalysis: Space, Time and Everyday Life*, trans. S. Elden and G. Moore, London and New York: Continuum.
MacDonald, J. and McGurk, H. (1978) "Visual influences on speech perception processes", *Perception and Psychophysics*, 24(3), pp. 253–257.
McCullough, M. (2013) *Ambient Commons: Attention in the Age of Embodied Information*, Cambridge, MA: MIT Press.
Merleau-Ponty, M. (1945) *Phénomènologie de la perception*, Paris: Gallimard.
Morley, D. (2000) *Home Territories: Media, Mobility and Identity*, London: Routledge.
Nvidia (2018) Metropolis Software Partners, viewed June 1, 2018, www.nvidia.com/object/metropolis-software-partners.html.
Pink, S. (2015) *Doing Sensory Ethnography*, London: SAGE.
Schaffner, A. (2016) *Exhaustion: A History*, New York: Columbia University Press.
Simmel, G. (1950) "The metropolis and mental life", in K. Wolff (ed.) *The Sociology of Georg Simmel*, Glencoe, IL: The Free Press.
Simonsen, K. (2004) "Spatiality, temporality and the construction of the city", in J. O. Bœrenholdt and K. Simonsen (eds.) *Space Odysseys: Spatiality and Social Relations in the 21st Century*, Aldershot: Ashgate.
Spiegel Online (2008) "The sweet smell of commuting—Berlin sniffs out new scent for local trains", viewed June 1, 2018, www.spiegel.de/international/zeitgeist/the-sweet-smell-of-commuting-berlin-sniffs-out-new-scent-for-local-trains-a-576589.html.
Thibaud, J.-P. (2003) "The sonic composition of the city", in M. Bull and L. Back (eds.) *The Auditory Culture Reader*, Oxford and New York: Berg.
Thompson, E. (2002) *The Soundscapes of Modernity: Architectural Acoustics and the Culture of Listening in America, 1900–1933*, Cambridge, MA: MIT Press.
Worldwide hum (2016) viewed September 1, 2017, https://hummap.wordpress.com/2016/04/22/the-competing-theories.
Yapp, J. (2017) *The Now Show*, Friday night comedy podcast, BBC, March 17.
Zhang, G., Chen, Y., Xiaoyu, J., Tianchen, Z., Zhang, T., and Wenyuan, X. (2017) "DolphinAttack: Inaudible voice commands, *CCS '17, Association for Computing Machinery*, https://doi.org/10.1145/3133956.3134052.
Zuboff, S. (2015) "Big other: Surveillance capitalism and the prospects of an information civilization", *Journal of Information Technology*, 30, pp. 75–89.

Further Reading

Classen, C. (1993) *Worlds of Sense: Exploring the Senses in History and Across Cultures*, London and New York: Routledge.
Diaconu, M. et al. (2011) *Senses and the City: An Interdisciplinary Approach to Urban Sensescapes*, Wien: Lit Verlag.
The Senses and Society Journal (2006–2017) London and New York: Taylor and Francis.

35
NAVIGATING HYBRID URBAN SPACES
Smartphones and Locative Media Practices

Jordan Frith

Introduction

Early Internet theory focused on dematerialized ideas of information. Science fiction authors and academic theorists talked extensively about people leaving their bodies behind to live in virtual worlds (Gibson 1983; Stephenson 1992), with cultural theorist Paul Virilio (1997) even positing that we may stop having physical sex. Nicholas Negroponte (1995) opposed the "world of bits" to the "world of atoms"; telecom companies ran commercials about the death of distance (*No More There* 1997). And as far as the urban goes, some experts in the 1990s wrote about the possible "death of cities" as people would be able to use new Internet technologies to connect from anywhere (Kolko 2000).

Of course, most of these early Internet predictions did not come true, at least not for the foreseeable future. People still interact face to face, they still engage in many forms of corporeal mobility, and most importantly for the purposes of this collection, cities did not die. In fact, cities matter more than ever and their importance has continued to rise even as the Internet has become more and more ubiquitous. Clearly, the digital information exchanged through the Internet did not make cities less important. Instead, something more interesting happened: digital information and physical space became merged in new ways (see also Chapter 21, this volume).

The merging of the digital and the physical has helped shape new experiences of urban spaces. This merging has contributed to the creation of what Adriana de Souza e Silva (2006) calls hybrid spaces, which are spaces in which physical location affects the digital information people access and the digital information shapes how people move through physical spaces (Frith 2015). In essence, physical location and digital information become co-constitutive, breaking down any remnants of a dichotomy between the materiality of spatiality and the supposed ethereality of digital information.

Hybrid spaces are not device-specific. Any merging of digital information with physical location can contribute to a hybridized form of urban space. However, much of the writing relating to hybrid spaces focuses on smartphone technology for a few main reasons. First, smartphones have become a widely adopted, in some countries almost ubiquitous, technology. Second, smartphones are mobile, meaning people can use them to access digital information while moving through physical space. And finally, smartphones have locative capabilities—including cellular triangulation, Wi-Fi triangulation, and GPS—that can provide the device with a precise physical location, enabling fine-grained retrieval of location-based information. Consequently, many mobile applications, commonly referred to as location-based services, now provide people with information based on their physical location. These apps include everything from weather applications to mapping application to social networking applications (see also Chapter 20, this volume).

Smartphones as locative media now often play an important role in how people understand urban spaces. They, drawing from the work of Paul Dourish and Genevieve Bell (2011), increase the "legibility" of urban spaces by providing an interface through which people can map routes, track mobility, find points of interest, and even find friends. The location-based information accessed through the smartphone becomes a new kind of place marker, a digital, often personalized version of the street signs and other physical markers that already impact the legibility of urban places. Consequently, the hybrid spaces created through the social practices of users and the locative affordances of smartphones become a new way of understanding how people negotiate mobility in urban milieus.

The impacts of smartphones as a form of urban media have been widely studied in mobile media research. For the purposes of this chapter, I will focus on three important strands of research that showcase how smartphones as locative media can alter urban legibility: (1) locative media and time/space coordination, (2) location information and the presentation of self, and (3) wayfinding through mobile mapping. The first two look at interpersonal uses of location sharing, while the final section discusses how research into mobile mapping can impact cognitive experiences of urban streets. As I show, all three areas are closely related and provide examples of how the hybridity of urban spaces has begun to shift experiences of the city.

Locative Media and Time/Space Coordination

Until relatively recently, periods of human mobility were accompanied by an inability to communicate with distant others. People could send letters while in transit, but by the time the letters reached their destination, the sender would not be in the same location. The same was true of the telephone and the Internet. People could call someone or email them to set up plans, but once they left that phone or computer, they were not able to maintain communication until arriving at another location with communication infrastructure.

A fundamental shift with adoption of the mobile phone came in the upending of the relationship between mobility and communication. Barry Wellman (2002) may have put it best when he argued that with fixed-line phones, people call places; with mobile phones, people call people. The fixed-line telephone was tied to a place, not a person. My home phone was my home phone, not *my* phone (it also belonged to the rest of my family), and if I was not home to answer it, I was not able to be reached. That changed with the mobile phone. For possibly the first time, people were able to remain in contact while traveling. No longer did time spent moving through the city mean time spent out of touch with absent others.

The ability to remain in contact with distant others through mobile phones contributed to a variety of social practices. For one, it let people remain tethered communicatively even while traveling, enabling new forms of "perpetual contact" (Katz and Aakhus 2002) and "connected presence" (Licoppe 2004). The mobile connections also let people focus on absent others, sometimes at the expense of paying attention to surrounding urban space, contributing to new forms of "absent presence" (Gergen 2002) or "telecocooning" (Habuchi 2005). However, possibly most important was the impact the mobile phone had on coordinating social activities.

Returning to the beginning of this section, before mobile phones, social coordination had to be determined in advance. If one person wanted to meet another at a cafe, those plans had to be established in fairly rigid terms over the phone (or using some other form of communication). Once the plans were set and the two parties left the house, the plans could not change until someone arrived at the final destination. The entire process of social planning shifted as mobile phones became ubiquitous. In effect, as Rich Ling (2004) argued, the rigidity of mechanical time lessened because people could remake plans on the fly and remain in contact while mobile to shift social engagements.

The shifts in coordination contributed to the growth of what Ling (2004) called "microcoordination," which refers to the ability to remake plans on the go. As he argued, people used mobile phones to lessen the need for strict planning, altering meeting times, location, and so forth at the last minute because of the ability to remain in contact while mobile. These new planning practices contributed to the lessening of the power of "mechanical time," which had dominated urban life for well over a century. As Georg Simmel (1950) speculated at the turn of the 20th century, if the clocks in Berlin all suddenly stopped, the social and economic life of the city would collapse. With industrialization, time had taken on a rigidity that became looser as mobile phones enabled people to remake plans on the fly and combat the rigidity of industrialized time with new forms of mobile communication.

These types of coordination then evolved further with the growth of a variety of location-sharing social applications. One of the first was the mobile service Dodgeball, which was created in 2000. Dodgeball enabled people to sign up for the service and send a text message with the user's location to Dodgeball. The service then sent that text out to the person's social network, letting everyone know about each member's location. In her qualitative work with Dodgeball users, Lee Humphreys (2007, 2010) found that people engaged in a form of social molecularity, in which they moved through the city in a kind of pack enabled by their Dodgeball usage.

Dodgeball was eventually superseded by more advanced location-based social networks (LBSNs) that took advantage of the Internet and locative capabilities of smartphones. The most popular LBSN—Foursquare[1]—let people form social networks through the application and then "check-in" to locations. Their check-ins were then shared with their friends, enabling people to provide a stream of their location information to friends.

The sharing of location information as a form of semi-mass communication contributed to some novel forms of coordination in urban spaces. Namely, the passive sharing of location information led to various forms of serendipitous coordination. For example, in interviews with Foursquare users, I found multiple examples of people meeting up because they happened to see a friend had checked in nearby (Frith 2012a, 2014). People also used LBSNs to further lessen the rigidity of planning, with some participants reporting that they would head out to a certain area of a city, check-in, and then just see which friends were nearby.

More traditional forms of mobile communication like voice calls and texting and newer forms, such as location sharing, all showcase how the smartphone works as a crucial piece of urban media. The city as a space of sociality is tied to the forms of mobile coordination with which people engage. Plans can be looser, getting stuck in traffic less catastrophic, and serendipity in social planning can increase. Coordination shifts as people gain the ability to engage in microcoordination. And with LBSNs, urban space as a social space also has the potential to become legible in new ways. By mapping out the locations of friends, people can view their spaces differently and choose locations based on where friends go. To some degree, this social form of legibility could have detrimental effects, contributing to new forms of homophily in which people only go places popular with people like them (Crawford 2007; Frith 2012b). But that kind of homophily is not a result of technology; it already happened long before smartphones. So, the legibility of social mapping can lead to new forms of serendipity, coordination, and legibility as people are able to view social networks on top of maps of urban spaces.

As a final note, location sharing can also enable safer forms of coordination for marginalized groups, while also disrupting existing social practices. Many members of the gay male community, for example, now use the mobile application Grindr to organize encounters. The application organizes results based on location, and the interface enables people to bypass some social surveillance found in almost all heteronormative societies (Licoppe et al. 2015). They can covertly coordinate encounters without taking the same level of risks that accompanied previous forms of social organization that sometimes took place in public spaces.

Location Information and the Presentation of Self

Erving Goffman (1959) wrote long before the growth of digital media. In fact, his writings were notable for their lack of focus on media of any kind, with one exception being a passage or two about the telephone. Nonetheless, Goffman became a key scholar used for understanding both the Internet and mobile communication. One of Goffman's main contributions was his writings on the presentation of self. He was a major figure in the dramaturgical approach to understanding social interactions, viewing interactions as a sort of play and the world the larger stage. As he argued, people operated on a backstage and frontstage, with the frontstage being the obvious performance of a certain type of self that depended on the audience and the social context.

Goffman's work was highly influential in Internet studies research, with scholars adopting Goffman's framework to examine how people present parts of themselves in different online contexts. Mobile communication scholars also adopted Goffman to analyze how people manage the frontstage/backstage dynamic of mobile voice calls (Rettie 2009). For example, which is front and which is back when someone engages in a conversation in a public place? Are both the surrounding area and the actual conversation frontstages? Clearly, mobile communication complicates how people present themselves, though research has shown that people engaged in voice calls and texting often do show awareness of the self they present to their surroundings (Humphreys 2005), despite some rather famous examples suggesting otherwise.

The presentation of self through mobile communication became more pronounced with smartphones as locative media. Now, location information has become a significant part of how people presented themselves to others on social media, contributing to what Raz Schwartz and Germaine Halegoua (2015) called the "spatial self." The spatial self revolves around how people use location information to construct identity. A few examples can showcase how this occurs and how it relates to smartphones as a form of urban media.

The first example is the photo map feature on Instagram. Instagram enables people to upload photos with location information attached. Photos with location information could then be placed upon a user's Instagram map, which becomes a spatial representation of someone's performance of self. All photos someone shares on social media present a certain self to an audience; people post good photos of themselves and post photos of events they are pleased they attended. For example, selfies have become a ubiquitous form of communication people use to communicate with their social network, and selfies often include locational markers in the background to highlight people's experiences. But adding actual locational metadata to these photos became a new addition to the identity people construct through Instagram, creating a new way to "overlay and interweave online and offline cartographies in different ways" (Hjorth and Pink 2014: 40) and shape identity.

The LBSNs discussed in the previous section are another example of how smartphones and location play into the presentation of self. When applications like Foursquare first came out, articles were written about using big data to track mobility patterns through check-ins. However, what these discussions often missed is that checking-in to locations is a selective, intentional process that is often used as a primary identity marker of the spatial self. Interviews with Foursquare users (Frith 2012a), for example, found that most users only shared location when they were somewhere they wanted to highlight to friends. They did not often check-in to highlight workplaces, gas stations, fast food, and the like. Instead, the check-in became an identity marker, a way to present oneself to a social network through digital markers of mobility.

The Instagram and Foursquare examples are specialized uses of location information to construct identity; however, at this point, location has found its way into many major social media tools (Wilken 2014). People can tag tweets with location; they can check-in to locations on Facebook to highlight parts of their lives; they can share location with their networks on review applications like Yelp. The locative capabilities of smartphones have become an increasingly important way people use urban areas to construct identity online and off. Sharing one's mobility to one part of a city over another is often a conscious choice, one made as a prime example of contemporary forms of the presentation of self. Location sharing also shows how urban locations can become intricately connected to issues of identity. More than ever before, the self that people present online is tied to specific location markers of digital information, representing a shift in how smartphones as urban media become tied to the hybridity of identity construction.

Wayfinding Through Mobile Mapping

The first two sections looked at smartphones as locative media from an interpersonal standpoint. However, it is likely that the most popular subset of location information does not involve connecting people to each other through location information. Instead, the most popular type of location-based service may be mapping services such as Google and Apple Maps (Mclellan 2013). Mobile mapping applications provide a new type of urban legibility and also impact how people understand and negotiate the city. To look at how, I will first discuss smartphones and mapping in terms of coordination before looking at urban memory and mapping.

Choosing routes through a city requires either prior knowledge or some kind of mapping technology. With paper maps, people often had to plan routes beforehand. Using a paper map, someone needed to know the general address of a location to plan a path. If one decided to add a second location without an address, the paper map is not much help. The same was true of maps people printed off the Internet using sites like Mapquest. To use Mapquest and print a route, someone needed to know where they were going before they left the house. The printed route would not be much good if one decided to add a trip to an extra location. Navigating the city either required wandering without a map or planning before one left home.

The time and place of mapping shifted with the widespread adoption of smartphones in much the same way social coordination shifted with mobile phones. With smartphones, people carry a map with them everywhere they go, a map that will plan their route and will not require they know a business's address. People who had to have routes traced before leaving the house now could map routes on the way, and importantly, they could add locations to their day more easily. In effect, the practices of navigating urban areas became more flexible and fluid. This flexibility is supported by the research of Troels Bertel (2013), who found that smartphone users were able to more easily reconfigure plans through the retrieval of spatial information. He labeled this process "flexible alignment" and showed how mobile mapping can significantly impact how one navigates and plans for trips through urban areas.

However, the question remains as to how mobile mapping impacts people's experience of the city. Research suggests that mobile mapping can negatively affect cognitive recall and impair people's ability to remember routes and landmarks. One study in particular suggests a difference in how various mapping media impacts urban recall. Ishikawa et al. (2008) used an interesting method for analyzing maps and cognitive impact. The researchers split participants into three distinct groups. The first group used a personal guide to walk them through the city of Kashiwa, Japan. The second group used a paper map to plan a route through the city. The third group used a turn-by-turn mobile mapping application for directions to their final destination. The researchers then compared each group to test the time it took to reach the final destination, estimations of time spent on the route, and recall of spatial information such as cardinal direction and landmarks.

The study found that the mobile mapping group took longer to arrive at the destination, did worse at recalling travel time, and performed worse on the cognitive recall tests about the urban space they moved through. As the authors summarize, "These results show that the GPS-based navigation system affects the user's wayfinding behavior and spatial understanding differently than do the maps and direct experience" (Ishikawa et al. 2008: 80). A different study using a similar methodology echoed that finding, arguing that

> A mobile map with automated position information (i.e., self-localization) essentially enables and possibly even encourages someone using it to switch off and to become the passive receiver of information, and as such does not support learning in a constructive manner.
>
> *(Willis et al. 2009: 108)*

Mobile mapping is obviously different from mobile coordination and self-presentation. However, when considered in terms of locative media, mobile mapping has similar consequences, impacting the legibility of urban space. Just as people are able to map friends to coordinate or create logs of their location to present to others, they are able to plot routes on the mobile interface of their smartphones, creating new ways of "reading" the city. The impacts, in some cases, may be negative, with mobile map users being less able to pay attention to and recall the urban spaces they move through. However, I want to conclude with a slight pushback on value judgments about mobile mapping applications.

Memory is complicated and closely related to the media people use. Socrates famously bemoaned the written language because he thought people would be less able to remember if they write things down. In fact, we offload memories all the time in a process called transactive memory. Transactive memory involves relying on something external to remember information (Sparrow et al. 2011). For example, I might rely on my mother to remember my father's birthday; she might rely on me to remember my brother's birthday. And the same process occurs with media. People may remember less when they know they can find the information quickly using a search engine. They might remember less about a route when they know they can easily retrieve the route on their smartphone. However, that offloading of memory, just like the offloading of social coordination, is not necessarily negative. Instead, it is an impact of the information retrieval of many forms of new media, one that should be judged in context and not using simplistic good/bad dichotomies.

Conclusion

At one point, people believed the Internet would grow in opposition to cities. Work would become decentralized, people would socialize online, and they would travel to virtual places rather than physical cities. None of that happened to any widespread degree. Instead, both the

Internet and cities are more important than ever, but they did not grow in opposition to one another. Instead, as this chapter has discussed, urban areas have merged with digital information to create new hybrid spaces. Digital information is increasingly shaped by physical location, and physical location is increasingly shaped by digital information.

The above sections looked at three examples of how smartphones as locative media impact experiences of urban space. I could have focused my attention elsewhere by discussing spatial search applications, geotagging, or route tracking, to name a few of many examples. But the three areas covered above—mobile coordination, the presentation of self, and wayfinding—all show how the hybridity of urban spaces have altered how some people navigate and experience urban environments.

Ultimately, the three areas I discussed all examine issues of spatial legibility. I argued that the way people "read" their surrounding space has started to change as they engage in new social practices and enter into new relationships with mobile devices. Space becomes more knowable as people can plot the location of friends, share their own location as an identity marker on Facebook, or map a route with Google Maps. The time and space of location sharing and mapping shifts as people engage with new technologically mediated experiences of exploration. As smartphones and locative media improve and we see the growth of future-oriented concepts such as Augmented Reality and the Internet of Things, it will become even more important for people to explore how urban spaces are increasingly mediated through access to digital information.

Note

1 In 2014, Foursquare moved its check-in functions to a standalone app called Swarm.

References

Bertel, T. F. (2013) "'It's like I trust it so much that I don't really check where it is I'm going before I leave': Informational uses of smartphones among Danish youth," *Mobile Media and Communication*, 1(3), pp. 299–313.
Crawford, A. (2007) "Taking social software to the streets: Mobile cocooning and the (an)erotic city," *Journal of Urban Technology*, 15(3), pp. 79–97.
Dourish, P. and Bell, G. (2011) *Divining a digital future*, Cambridge, MA: MIT Press.
Frith, J. (2012a) "Constructing location, one check-in at a time: Examining the practices of foursquare users," Dissertation [online], North Carolina State University, Raleigh, NC, http://repository.lib.ncsu.edu/ir/bitstream/1840.16/8064/1/etd.pdf.
— (2012b) "Splintered space: Hybrid spaces and differential mobility," *Mobilities*, 7(1), pp. 131–149.
— (2014) "Communicating through location: The understood meaning of the Foursquare check-in," *Journal of Computer-Mediated Communication*, 19(4), pp. 890–905.
— (2015) *Smartphones as locative media*, London, UK: Polity Press.
Gergen, K. (2002) "The challenge of absent presence," in J. Katz and M. Aakhus (eds.) *Perpetual contact: Mobile communication, private talk, public performance*, New York, NY: Cambridge University Press, pp. 227–241.
Gibson, W. (1983) *Neuromancer*, New York: Ace Books.
Goffman, E. (1959) *The presentation of self in everyday life*, New York, NY: Doubleday.
Habuchi, I. (2005) "Accelerating reflexivity," in M. Ito, D. Okabe, and M. Matsuda (eds.) *Personal, portable, pedestrian: Mobile phones in Japanese life*, Cambridge, MA: MIT Press, pp. 165–182.
Hjorth, L. and Pink, S. (2014) "New visualities and the digital wayfarer: Reconceptualizing camera phone photography and locative media," *Mobile Media and Communication*, 2(1), pp. 40–57.
Humphreys, L. (2005) "Cellphones in public: Social interactions in a wireless era," *New Media and Society*, 7(6), pp. 810–833.
— (2007) "Mobile social networks and social practice: A case study of Dodgeball," *Journal of Computer-Mediated Communication*, 13, pp. 341–360.

— (2010) "Mobile social networks and urban public space," *New Media and Society*, 12, pp. 763–778.
Ishikawa, T., Fujiwara, H., Imai, O., and Okabe, A. (2008) "Wayfinding with a GPS-based mobile navigation system: A comparison with maps and direct experience," *Journal of Environmental Psychology*, 28(1), pp. 74–82.
Katz, J. E. and Aakhus, M. (2002) *Perpetual contact: Mobile communication, private talk, public performance*, Cambridge, MA: Cambridge University Press.
Kolko, J. (2000) "The death of cities? The death of distance? Evidence from the geography of commercial Internet usage," in I. Vogelsang and B. Compaine (eds.) *The internet upheaval: Raising questions, seeking answers in communications policy*, Cambridge, MA: MIT Press, pp. 73–98.
Licoppe, C. (2004) "Connected presence: The emergence of a new repertoire for managing social relationships in a changing communication technoscape," *Environment and Planning D: Society and Space*, 22, pp. 135–156.
Licoppe, C., Rivière, C. A., and Morel, J. (2015) "Grindr casual hook-ups as interactional achievements," *New Media and Society*, 18(11), pp. 2540–2558.
Ling, R. (2004) *The mobile connection: The cell phone's impact on society*, San Francisco, CA: Morgan Kaufman.
McLellan, S. (2013) "The most popular app in the world is (envelope, please) . . . Google Maps!" *MediaPost*, www.mediapost.com/publications/article/207921/#axzz2jDS7kMYb.
Negroponte, N. (1995) *Being digital*, New York, NY: Vintage Books.
No More There (1997) viewed October 23, 2013, www.youtube.com/watch?v=ioVMoeCbrigand feature=youtube_gdata_player.
Rettie, R. (2009) "Mobile phone communication: Extending Goffman to mediated interaction," *Sociology*, 43(3), pp. 421–438.
Schwartz, R. and Halegoua, G. (2015) "The spatial self: Location-based identity performance on social media," *New Media and Society*, 17(10), pp. 1643–1660.
Simmel, G. (1950) *The sociology of Georg Simmel*, New York, NY: Free Press.
de Souza e Silva, A. (2006) "From cyber to hybrid: Mobile technologies as interfaces of hybrid spaces," *Space and Culture*, 3, pp. 261–278.
Sparrow, B., Liu, J., and Wegner, D. M. (2011) "Google effects on memory: Cognitive consequences of having information at our fingertips," *Science*, 333(6043), pp. 776–778.
Stephenson, N. (1992) *Snowcrash*, New York: Bantam Books.
Virilio, P. (1997) *Open sky*, London and New York: Verso.
Wellman, B. (2002) "Little boxes, globalization, and networked individualism," in M. Tanabe, P. Van den Besselaar, and T. Ishida (eds.) *Digital cities II: Computational and sociological approaches*, Berlin: Springer, pp. 10–26.
Wilken, R. (2014) "Places nearby: Facebook as a location-based social media platform," *New Media and Society*, http://nms.sagepub.com/content/early/2014/07/24/1461444814543997.abstract.
Willis, K. S., Hölscher, C., Wilbertz, G., and Li, C. (2009) "A comparison of spatial knowledge acquisition with maps and mobile maps," *Distributed and Mobile Spatial Computing*, 33(2), pp. 100–110.

Further Reading

Frith, J. and Saker, M. (2017) "Understanding Yik Yak: Location-based sociability and the communication of place," *First Monday*, 22(10), http://firstmonday.org/ojs/index.php/fm/article/view/7442.
Mattern, S. (2017) *Code and clay, data and dirt: Five thousand years of urban media*, Minneapolis, MN: University of Minnesota Press.
McCullough, M. (2004) *Digital ground: Architecture, pervasive computing, and environmental knowing*, Cambridge, MA: MIT Press.

36
MEDIA AUDIENCES IN THE URBAN CONTEXT

Zlatan Krajina

Introduction

A dominant aim across chapters in this volume has been to elucidate ways in which citizens read or make use of urban media to manage an array of necessary features of urban living, such as navigation of space, public events, domestic living, and political participation. Why would a concern with media audiences merit separate attention? Whether or not people can satisfactorily be seen as "media audiences" when they engage with urban media, it is under this rubric that the appreciation of context as a key source of differential uses and meanings of media was developed, and this is where future studies of urban media might find essential resources for grounded considerations of power and symbolic practice. In fact, connections between audience studies and urban sociology can be traced back to formative periods of modern urban living.

The establishment of "mass media" in the early 20th century coincided with urbanization and provided members of industrial or "mass" societies, who could not maintain direct contact with all others, with a source of "common sense." Shared points of interest such as news became key sources of spatiotemporal orientation for dispersed citizens. However, this mediated sense of belonging was only achievable through a (spatial and social) separation between "senders" of publicly relayed messages and privately constituted "receivers," who could, thus, interpret the same messages differently in diverse settings. This fundamental feature of technologically mediated communication meant that media could not merely serve to connect. Meaningful output (information, education, and entertainment) was only conceivable in specific, and not general, terms, thus articulating existing (or helping to develop) newer forms of social differentiation, like taste, class, race, gender, generation, and nation, as well as offering resources for social change. Studies of audiences sought to understand the circumstances of these different potential orientations of media communication and these insights remain extremely relevant for the study of urban media.

Meanwhile, audience studies has developed a focus on media consumption situated in the private realm, particularly concerning ways in which family and gender relations in the household are articulated through media use. Issues which have more to do with studying interactions with media in public, such as contingency of street situations and materiality of space (Krajina 2014), started to attract attention from audience scholars only recently, after media technologies penetrated public space in noticeable quantities, as part of the contemporary rise of service economy that privileges investment in communication infrastructures (Wi-Fi networks, billboards, public media events, etc.). Industrial (advertisers') interest in addressing "out-of-home" audiences and the increasing presence of media such as electronic billboards in public space will require audience studies to extend more ambitiously its principal site of investigation, the household, to the street, where media consumption continues, if in different forms, once people leave the house (see also Chapter 17, this volume). Urban studies, on the other hand, has seen limitations to its own prevalent focus on the street, whereby "the everyday rhythms of domestic life have rarely counted as part of the urban, as though the city stopped at the doorstep of the home" (Amin and Thrift 2002: 22). Urban studies has drawn some useful insights from audience studies, for instance to develop a deeper understanding of the significance of urban ICT systems (Crang et al. 2006) or branding strategies for ordinary citizens (Jansson 2003).

To support further efforts in extending the relevance and reach of audience research and intellectual scope of urban studies, in this chapter I revisit the heritage of audience studies through urban optics. I excavate the field's forgotten urban pedigree and advocate a firmer empirical hold of media consumption in public as a productive return to the urban origin of audience studies. By doing so, I also address urban scholars whom I hope to offer reasons for further engagement with insights from audience studies into how meanings of mediated spaces are negotiated and how urban living is interwoven with media practices. Urban scholarship on phenomena like reading outdoor advertising or "media façades," attending public (art or cinema) screenings, or partaking in "platform urbanism" tends to assume, rather than research, myriad important ways in which people negotiate cities alongside urban media, making the belated dialogue between urban and audience studies a timely opportunity.

"Urbanizing" Audience Research

The history of audience studies has been difficult, burdened by moral panics about the supposedly direct and damaging influence of media and complex intra-disciplinary battles. Morley's (1992: 71) metaphor of the pendulum that swings in different historical periods, signaling shifts of emphasis in research, synthesized these debates usefully by recognizing that some focused exclusively on the power of the producer (sender) and others on the power of the consumer (receiver). Contemporary audience curricula have consolidated around the recognition of the relative autonomy of both the producer and the consumer and the prevalent power of the producer (institutions such as the media, regulating bodies, etc.) in setting the agenda, even language, within which the conceivable range of different interpretations of the same events is imaginable in particular societies. This relationship between media and audiences as one of unstable equilibrium among unequal partners—as informed by the British cultural studies' uptake of Gramscian notions of hegemony—continues to make debates concerning audiences vital, despite the growing doubt about the adequacy of the term "audiences" for discussing daily life with the media (Ang 1996), particularly digital (Carpentier 2011). Other important assumptions in audience research, such as the primacy of cognition and humanist conception of action, have been challenged by calls for "non-representational" (Moores 2012) and "post-humanist" approaches (Rose 2017). I seek to complement these convincing interventions by bringing back into current debates certain insights which, despite their earlier origin, continue to have an empirical bearing on the understanding of inhabitancy of mediated urban space.

As Silverstone reminds us, urbanization made people seek a sense of security in spatiotemporal organization of life that was not of their own making (1993). As opposed to premodern settlements where space–time was defined by physical reach and familial relations, the environment produced by industrial infrastructures such as the mechanical clock, transport, functional building blocks, social distance, and specialized roles displaced the source of "ontological security" to the reassuring availability of things like "media texts on billboards, in newspapers, on television" that, with a host of others, amounted to "taken for granted seriality and spatiality of everyday life" (1993: 591–592). Social and political change brought about by democratization of education and consumption and civil rights movements made media representations of everyday life a site for comparison and reflection, replacing status given by birth with invention of lifestyle (Spasić 2004). The conception of modern everyday life as a sphere of oppression and monotony but also accomplishment (Highmore 2002) informed the understanding of media in modern society as a source of knowledge and a routine, often invisible, presence.

Nevertheless, it was concerns about media power that formulated public debates about the media, particularly during moments of crises such as the rise of fascism in Europe in the 1930s, the US "urban crisis" of the 1960s, the decline of the welfare state from the early 1980s, and the rise of populist neofascism in the 2010s. Facing the difficulty of grasping the troubling social scene, public debate has tended to deduce social problems from allegedly damaging work of *media*, as well as locating evidence in *urban* space. The renowned Institute of Social Sciences (the "Frankfurt School") pointed to massive migrations to cities as one important cause of popular consent to Hitler's rule, whereby workers were at once seen as exploited by the capitalist economic organization and blindly entertained by the "cultural industry" that was producing media as any other disposable commodity, intentionally preventing the enrichment of human spirit such as in "high art." The newly constructed "mass of gloomy houses and business premises in grimy, spiritless cities" made one "all the more subservient to his adversary—the absolute power of capitalism" (Adorno and Horkheimer 1979: 120). Media, it was believed (but not researched), had the power to inject messages and produce compliance with dominant ideology directly in the consciousness of the masses ("hypodermic needle model"), which no longer had resources, such as small group bonds, for defense.

As Scannell (2007: 9–10) recounts, on the other side of the Atlantic, the most rapidly increasing city, Chicago, saw urbanization conversely as a positive challenge, which invited the development of the then-new discipline, sociology, as a study of laws governing conviviality among strangers. The Chicago school's leading figure Robert Park praised the potential that newspapers had for serving as a conversation starter among strangers as a preamble to a healthy social organization (1955: 116, cited in Butsch 2011: 155). Led by the demand of the market for understanding the "influence" of messages on modifying voter and consumer behavior, New York-based sociologists like Lazarsfeld and Merton engaged in what was later recognized as "administrative/industrial" research. Though not abandoning the assumption of "influence" as initiated by the Frankfurt School (instead making it less direct and dependent on change of opinion), these sociologists discovered that life in cities actually supported the bulwarks of civic association against "influence." The "rediscovery of the primary group" made up of friendly or neighborly bonds provided a "shield" against media messages, with "opinion leaders" in each clique retelling (refracting) the message and thus challenging media power (the "two-step model," Morley 1992: 48).

The difficulty of coping with a subsequent 1960s crisis in American cities, characterized by a declining public culture, again was seen to point the media and their alleged power to modify behavior (Murdock 1997). The assumption that the televising of crime made certain viewers "vulnerable" (usually blacks, women, and children, defined as such by predominantly white, male, middle-class commentators) inflated moral panics and prompted not a sophistication of analysis but a retreat to laboratory investigations of effects such as those of mimicking a rewarded antisocial behavior as seen on TV (Livingstone 1996). Following the recognition that decontextualized correlating of causes and effects was misleading, some later attempts swung the pendulum to the opposite extreme, disregarding media power, and looking at how people positively used media to gain psychological "uses and gratifications" (such as self-realization) (Morley 1992). Other perspectives sought to understand long-term as opposed to immediate effects, and questioned how media "cultivated" certain beliefs, such as the world being a dangerous place, especially for those who, for lack of access to participation in society, spent more time watching television, which had tended to portray their group as likely victims (cf. Livingstone 1996).

The "neoliberal revolution" (Hall 2011), which underpinned the widescale distribution of media across national boundaries and coincided with decolonization, was famously observed by the then-new perspective of cultural studies as an opportunity to question historical (imperial) metanarratives and problematize issues of identity and difference. Cultural studies argued for the unstable relationship between media and audiences mentioned earlier. This model rejected decontextualized assumptions about "media effects" and demonstrated that all communication actually rests on an imminent disconnect between the signified and the signifier, a slip engendered by different definitions of their social situation that are available to different social groups involved in media production and consumption (Hall 1994). Thus, neither media have total power over meaning nor can audiences "misread" messages in just any imaginable way. Hall's famous "encoding/decoding" model, which remains canonical for contemporary audience studies, saw dominant conceptions of social reality, formed by specific contexts and historical conjunctures, as limiting frameworks for both media and audiences. Media draw from dominant social agenda and offer "preferred readings" of any social situation by closing off the potentially endless polysemy of texts through emphasis, phrasing, and selection ("encoding"). Audiences interpret the media ("decoding") from their own socially structured positions and assumptions, thus providing "preferred meanings" that usually neither entirely accept nor completely reject suggestions for the "correct" ("preferred") reading encoded in the message (Hall 1994).

"New audience studies" took Hall's challenge for thinking about media and audiences in a critical, circular, and non-deterministic manner and developed a grounded understanding of media consumption, which invalidated earlier theses about possibilities for prediction, generalization, or deduction of anyone's understanding of media from the media alone. Scholars such as Morley, Brunsdon, Gray, Hobson, Moores, Gillespie, Hermes, et al. explored how issues of class, gender, race, and patterns of urban living were articulated by differential forms of media use and assumptions about audiences inscribed in genres, texts, modes of address, and design of technologies. These ethnographic studies shared a commitment to appreciating context as constitutive rather than peripheral to meaning and the *urban* context played a vital, though not always well-explicated, role therein. These pioneering endeavors have made it widely accepted that meanings of any media will remain unknown until they have been researched in situ.

In Morley's anthological study of ways in which class informed different groups of interviewees' interpretations of the *Nationwide* TV magazine (1992), forms of urban living served to elucidate the central notion which emerged from this project, *interdiscourse* (intersectionality), which suggested that people's sensemaking mechanisms are overdetermined by a range of discourses (class, gender, race) that may not always work in concert. As Morley described it, a "white, male, working-class trade unionist" viewer might be "tied to a particular form of housing in the inner city, which has, since the war, been transformed before his eyes culturally by Asian immigrants, and the National Front comes closest to expressing his local chauvinist fears about the transformation of 'his' area," which makes him *accept* racism implied in dominant ("preferred") media coverage of racially defined street crime (1992: 127). Nevertheless, the viewer may as well, based on "his own experience of life in an inner-city area," *reject* the encoding of the police as "angels" (1992: 127). But as he subsequently turns to a sitcom that portrays a patriarchal family, his identification with "a working-class culture of masculinity" may invite him to *accept* dominant assumptions of the program (1992: 127).

Morley's subsequent study of "family television" made patterns of urban living a key factor, thus highlighting that the choice of a working-class area in South London, with nuclear families who had little access to social and geographic mobility, made significant difference as to the results of his project. The study suggested that gender relations intersected with those of class in encouraging different "modalities" of viewing ("distracted" for a housewife busy maintaining the household and "focused" for a man for whom the house is a place of rest) (1992: 199). In other important studies too, the urban served as formative background. Ang and Hermes (1996), for instance, noticed contrasting results of two studies, conducted in two different urban areas, on the reception of the same soap, *Dallas*, among female viewers. In her ethnographic study on video use among housewives, Gray (1992) had met the participants in a local video store (in an English town) where they exchanged recommendations and arranged group viewings, while Radway (1987) recruited her respondents among women fans of romance in a local bookshop (in a town in the American Midwest) which housewives used to frequent. In the former case, the "calculated ignorance" on how to use certain functions of the video recorder mediated the women's negotiation of the overall volumes of their household labor, and in the latter, the reading of the romance served the housewives as an escapist vehicle ("do not disturb" sign). Everywhere, the site of meaningful media consumption was urban everyday life, where media use, such as in Hermes' study of reading women's magazines, was mostly routine, "a fleeting, transient experience" (Hermes 1993). This experience was nonetheless significant in people's negotiations of what Moores (1993) defined as the "affordances and limitations" of daily life.

Though rarely leaving the house, research on media consumption rightly saw private and public realms as deeply connected. Private labor involved in technical efforts to connect the home with the great beyond, while maintaining guard of the symbolic order inside the house, tended to invite public speculation. According to Brunsdon (1997), the introduction of satellite dishes in the UK in 1980s functioned as a "non-verbal signifier of taste"; that is, preference for easy entertainment. The renunciation of dishes was publicly couched in terms of "controversy about siting" on protected buildings, much like with television antennae in the mid-20th century (1997: 151, 156, 160; see also Moores 1996). This criticism took the form of ideological struggle, as it typically came from upper-class commentators targeting houses in working-class districts and not in upmarket inner-city areas (Brunsdon 1997: 152).

More recently, authorities similarly disputed the installation of satellite dishes by diasporic audiences on façades of migrant neighborhoods in Western European cities as a worrying sign of the alleged withdrawal of migrants from shared host culture (Morley 2006: 282). Diasporic audience studies offered quite a different view. Gillespie's (1995) study on how media consumption articulated the intergenerational split among the Indian diaspora in Southall, UK provided evidence of the second generation's parallel familiarization with Indian culture via satellite TV and active search for recognition in British society via engagement with Western media. Robins and Aksoy's (2006: 97) studies of Turkish diasporic television audiences in London showed that the consumption of both local and satellite television, observed alongside their participants' daily attendance to ethnic shops, allowed those viewers to "make comparisons" among diasporic and host "cultural registers," thus acquiring a cosmopolitan perspective on the mediated world (see also Smets 2013).

Media technologies like radio and television may have been first exhibited in public spaces, but the household provided the central research site for audience studies. This preference was a historically specific intellectual response to the then-new developments such as postwar suburbanization of America or the construction of "the nuclear family" in postwar Britain as "the representative of the ideological (if not empirical) heartland of the television audience" (Morley 1992: 64, 78).

By analogy, to inquire about media consumption in public now concerns asking which sections of the media audience are more invited than others in particular cities (e.g., "young, upscale and affluent" in the UK; Krajina 2014: 23) to enjoy the advantages of physical (transnational travel without commitment) and symbolic (networking, "hyperactive") forms of mobility as the preferred modes of urban living. It will be important in this context to try to see how "home" and "out-of-home" modes of media consumption themselves interact and which tensions between the public and private they articulate, as has been attempted previously.

Studies of "domestication" of information and communication technologies (ICTs) worked with the assumption that households are "moral economies," involved in transactions of values within and beyond the home, whereby media articulate (connect) private and public realms through symbolic (e.g., scheduled programming) and material aspects (e.g., commodities appropriated as private furniture) (Hirsch 1992). In an exemplary study in this framework, which observed a middle-class North London-based family, Hirsch concluded that ICTs use articulated ways in which the life of the family "oscillates between an urban life of intensely hard work," which was bound with a variety of communication technologies, and "a rural, private, and cut-off life" (1992: 221). In a rare example of such cross-disciplinary consultation, geographers Crang et al. (2006) found relevance in the media domestication framework in their efforts to appreciate differences of ICT use in different neighborhoods in Newcastle-upon-Tyne, UK. The project differentiated among *degrees* of "intensity" and *styles* of use and recognized "episodic, often socially mediated, use" among residents of a poorer area and "pervasive use where the organizational power and tempo of life are more deeply mediated." Instead of merely reproducing crude narratives about the "urban digital divide," whereby access to "artefacts . . . [is] plotted against socio-demographic variables," the authors were able to provide a rather different, more nuanced, perspective of "multispeed urbanism" (Crang et al. 2006: 2552, 2668).

Media Consumption in Public and Urban Habitation: Seeking Place in Mediated Urban Space

Research on audiences in the digital context recognizes that "being a member of an audiences is no longer an exceptional event" (Abercrombie and Longhurst 1998: 68–69), but this relevant argument has regrettably swung the pendulum again. Having adopted the neoliberal reification of consumer choice, conceptions of digital audiences have tended to over-emphasize the power of the user (Couldry 2005). This strand of research has assumed not only that greater technical possibilities for interaction, such as posting or sharing content, made interaction more visible and researchable, but also that such audiences' activities exhausted their overall "activity," making previous, more invisible forms of differential engagement with media like television now curiously seem "passive" (Morley 2006). Critical assessments of such accounts remind us that traditional power relations between producers and consumers (e.g., commercial access, gatekeeping policies) and relevance of physical space (e.g., users' preference for interacting with those in geographical vicinity) are extended rather than abandoned in the virtual realm (Morley 2017). Further, people combine "old" and "new" media and medium-specific modes of engagement, thus making considerations of phenomena such as online civic engagement incomplete without considering other constitutive modalities like street talk. Even though "smart city" initiatives promote the installment of various sensors which read users' activity and respond, as well as interfaces with buttons which make the city seem more "participatory" (McCullough 2004: 74–86), visibility of action remains only one, arguably lesser, segment of interaction; for instance, as I show below, "not looking" at public screens likely comes from familiarity with their content rather than inactivity (Krajina 2014).

Structured primarily around the private gaze and the right to withdraw from public matters, rather than openness to engagement (Sennett 1993), media cities encourage users to take their sense of home with them as something "that attaches to the keypad of a mobile phone . . . a technological extension of the self" (Silverstone 2006: 242). A study by Brynskov et al. (2009: 157) in the area of "human–computer interaction" on people's "sensemaking" of a media façade in Aarhus, Denmark showed that passersby responded by intimately appropriating the public display, such as casting shadows or trying to figure out a narrative in the abstract imagery. In my own study (2014), done in two other different contexts and places, a moving image piece of pavement as part of a postwar promenade renovation in Zadar, Croatia and a one-off community art project in the regenerated area of East London also elucidated unexpected connections between private imagination and public intercourse. In both cases, ways in which locals gathered around imagery (imagining a "peaceful" conviviality previously damaged by the 1990s war in Zadar; displaying architecture threatened by urban regeneration as "immortal" in East London) articulated concerns about belonging and memory.

Thus, "interactivity" is more than the conceivable range of technical capacities for offering predetermined options (buttons) for audience response. As Bouman reminds us, "architecture has always been interactive. Even temples and churches . . . acquired their definitive meaning through use," such as manipulating the incoming light (1998). In the street, where public screens cannot be moved around or shut down, interaction takes less-material forms, including glancing and familiarizing (predicting types of ads in different places and thus making them less visible) or misusing (e.g., moving next to luminous standalone posters in darkened alleyways as "mini lighthouses" or gazing at billboards as fake points of interest to alleviate feelings of insecurity in the presence of strangers, Krajina 2014). Rather than a narrative to be viewed in isolation, public imagery tends to function as a scenographic element of the eventful space of the street that comes to matter to a passerby in moments of their simultaneous (episodical and contingent) dealing with the immediate street situation, thus contributing to their long-term sense of "at-homeness" (Krajina 2017). Interaction with urban media, inside and outside the home, is more about the intersecting *regimes of significance* (cognitive, embodied, experiential, situational, and biographical) and *textures of mediation* (symbolic, material, multisensory, responsive) than about any simplistic correlations between individual media and users' responses.

As opposed to the particular setup of film viewing in the cinema (a "night out" promising an uninterrupted, voyeuristic gaze of a single narrative in an ordered, darkened space), or frontal or immersive exhibition of artwork in galleries (Krajina 2016), interactions with public screens are more similar to ways in which household television historically developed its own specific "mode of address." TV constructed an uninterrupted flow of diverse programs where a distinctive use of sound (jingles) was devised to keep bringing the viewer assumed to be busy participating in domestic life back into interaction (Ellis 1982). Interactions in public too take the form of "encounters" with ceaseless video loops of brief and repetitive messages (Krajina 2014: 29). Producers assume their incidental viewers to be "intercepting" (Casetti 2013) the flow of information within the flows of street traffic. Spatial dimensions (distribution of media, their physical volumes, and representations of other spaces they offer) translate into strategic positions, both for producers, who place screens opposite the assumed flow of people's movement so as to "cut through" the cacophony of urban signage, and for pedestrians, who can negotiate the significance of the encountered image in the sightline, by moving around and looking away (Krajina 2014). And, as in the home, so in the street: there is no easy fit between codes. Certain passersby may, for instance, respond to the "hail" of billboard ads showing luxurious cars and misread them positively as promising signs of the neighborhood's overall facelift, and others may read the same ads negatively as anticipation of the imminent arrival of more affluent residents and gentrification of the area (Krajina 2014).

This rising interest in spatial dimensions of communication ("spatial turn") in media studies informed considerations of the mediated city as a complex of "multi-layered spatial configurations," from which vantage point people are seen as "simultaneously present—and act as audiences—in many different, often overlapping, spaces and social situations," such as walking past billboards, being engaged in a mobile phone conversation, or listening to music (Ridell 2015: 246–247). The more recent adoption of phenomenological perspectives on the significance of pre-cognitive dimensions of interaction (sensing, feeling) has helped expand somewhat reductive assumptions in urban studies that the pedestrian "reacts" (Walter Benjamin's conception of urban space as a land of "shock"), creates "cognitive maps" (Kevin Lynch's famous schema of paths, edges, nodes, landmarks, and districts), or, as "intuitively" assumed by the advertising industry, adopts one of several "modes" (e.g., rushing to work or being open to conversation; Cronin 2010). Repetitive sensing of media as relatively insignificant parts of street furniture can contribute to a sense of homeliness and place, which can emerge in any (physical or virtual) location endowed with repetitive practice (e.g., passing by) and intimate relevance (e.g., source of memory). In a study on the London Underground, a commuter, asked to produce an audio diary of his walking and interacting with endless posters, returned a nearly silent tape, explaining subsequently that the posters figured for him as ever-present signs of familiarity ("ontological security") (Krajina 2014). For daily navigators of urban environments, public screens largely remain invisible until they change significantly, provoking "locals" to seek adaptive responses (such as comparing the screen to what they knew before or elsewhere) and thus maintain familiarity with their everyday spaces, never as a finite but as "recursive" and temporary accomplishment (Krajina 2014).

Thus, it can hardly satisfy us to argue, with scholars like Joshua Meyrowitz or Marc Augé, that we no longer have a "sense of place" because our social activities such as holding a phone call and spaces like the bus have mixed in ways unimaginable before or to proclaim all patterned symbolic environments such as supermarkets or airports as disorienting "non-places," divorced from any sense of intimate or historical significance (see Moores 2012). As activities in physical space coalesce with those in networked space, "media uses" are increasingly recognized as "place-constituting activities" alongside other "possibly competing, place-making practices" (Moores 2012: 46). Particular configurations that emerge from the aligning (juxtaposition) of elements such as patriarchal codes of street behavior in a gentrifying neighborhood, or a feeling of personal outsideness whilst tripping over a ruptured sidewalk underneath luminous global advertising, are what makes particular urban places specific. Thus, future studies of media consumption, whichever the site of investigation, might do well by expanding the conventional notion of "dual" articulation of media (symbolic/material; public/private) with what Ridell (2015: 248) innovatively termed, reflecting on above developments, "triplet of non-representation-presentation-representation" or "urban triple articulation."

Conclusion

Through changing its perspectives on interaction with media, from issues of reception and decoding of media texts to matters of inhabitancy of media environments, audience studies has found urban settings significant, if usually unacknowledged, sites for defining its research problems as well as locating empirically informed accounts concerning the problematic relevance of media in modern daily life. Though both audience and urban studies define private and public realms as mutually implicated, a gradual rise of interest in public space for audience studies, on one hand, and in household living for urban studies, on the other, might further necessitate making issues like signification, interpretation, space, and infrastructure shared and transformative, rather than disciplinary and merely assumed concerns.

Audience studies has made it a commonplace that media tend to be used in ways unplanned by their producers and that media consumption provides unique insight into how difference, stability, and change are negotiated in everyday life. In private and public realms alike, any understanding of how the interaction of objects, signals, and bodies engenders new meanings of urban space will continue to depend on empirical engagement with citizens' differential practices of interaction. Addressed by a range of actors during daily rounds, citizens of mediated urban worlds find themselves pulled into everyday labor of translating sometimes radically diverse messages, physical structures, and presence of others into meaningful patterns, as they go on seeking place and visibility against the pleasures and pressures of social life in the city. Without empirical investigations of such vital situations, to paraphrase Strathern (1992: ix), all we are witnessing while merely observing people is people observing the city and, thus, leaving their transformative calibrations of city spaces, online and offline, forever unknown.

References

Abercrombie, N. and Longhurst, B. (1998) *Audiences: A Sociological Theory of Performance and Imagination*, London: Sage.
Adorno, T. W. and Horkheimer, M. (1979) *Dialectic of Enlightenment*, London: Verso.
Amin, A. and Thrift, N. (2002) *Cities: Reimagining the Urban*, Malden, MA: Polity Press.
Ang, I. (1996) *Living Room Wars: Rethinking Media Audiences for a Postmodern World*, London and New York: Routledge.
Ang, I. and Hermes, J. (1996) "Gender and/in media consumption," in Ang, I., *Living Room Wars: Rethinking Media Audiences for a Postmodern World*, London: Routledge, pp. 109–131.
Bouman, O. (1998) "Quick space in real time, part 3: Interactive architecture," *Archis*, 6, pp. 72–79.
Brunsdon, C. (1997) *Screen Tastes*, London: Routledge.
Brynskov, M. et al. (2009) "Staging urban interactions with media facades," *Human–Computer Interaction—INTERACT*, Heidelberg: Springer Verlag, pp. 154–167.
Butsch, R. (2011) "Audiences and publics, media and public spheres," in Nightingale, V. (ed.) *The Handbook of Media Audiences*, London: Wiley-Blackwell, pp. 149–165.
Carpentier, N. (2011) "New configurations of the audience? The challenges of user-generated content for audience theory and media participation," in Nightingale, V. (ed.) *The Handbook of Media Audiences*, London: Blackwell, pp. 190–207.
Casetti, F. (2013) "What is a screen nowadays," in Berry, C. et al. (eds.) *Public Space, Media Space*, London: Palgrave, pp. 16–40.
Couldry, N. (2005) "The extended audience: Scanning the horizon," in Gillespie, M. (ed.) *Media Audiences*, Maidenhead: Open University Press, pp. 183–222.
Crang, M. et al. (2006) "Variable geometries of connection: Urban digital divides and the uses of information technology," *Urban Studies*, 43(13), pp. 2551–2570.
Cronin, A. M. (2010) *Advertising, Commercial Spaces and the Urban*, Basingstoke: Palgrave Macmillan.
Ellis, J. (1982) *Visible Fictions: Cinema, Television, Video*, London: Routledge.
Gillespie, M. (1995) *Television, Ethnicity and Cultural Change*, London: Routledge.
Goggin, G. and Wilken, R. (2012) *Mobile Technology and Place*, London: Routledge.
Gray, A. (1992) *Video Playtime: The Gendering of a Leisure Activity*, London: Routledge.
Hall, S. (1994) "Reflections on the encoding/decoding model: An interview," in Cruz, J. and Lewis, J. (eds.) *Viewing, Reading, Listening: Audiences and Cultural Reception*, Boulder, CO: Westview Press, pp. 253–274.
— (2011) "The neo-liberal revolution," *Cultural Studies*, 25(6), pp. 705–728.
Hermes, J. (1993) "Media, meaning, and everyday life," *Cultural Studies*, 7(3), pp. 493–506.
Highmore, B. (2002) "Introduction: Questioning everyday life," in Highmore, B. (ed.) *The Everyday Life Reader*, London: Routledge, pp. 1–34.

Hirsch, E. (1992) "The long term and the short term of domestic consumption: an ethnographic case study," in Silverstone, R. and Hirsc,h E. (eds.) *Consuming Technologies: Media and Information in Domestic Spaces*, London: Routledge, pp. 194–210.

Jansson, A. (2003) "The negotiated city image: Symbolic reproduction and change through urban consumption," *Urban Studies*, 40(3), pp. 463–479.

Krajina, Z. (2014) *Negotiating the Mediated City: Everyday Encounters with Public Screens*, London: Routledge.

— (2016) "The alternative urbanism of psychogeography in the mediated city," in Humm, M. and Shaw, D. (eds.) *Radical Space*, London: Rowman & Littlefield, pp. 39–63.

— (2017) "From non-place to place: A phenomenological geography of daily life in mediated cities," in Rodgers, S. and Markham, T. (eds.) *Conditions of Mediation*, London: Peter Lang, pp. 161–171.

Livingstone, S. (1996) "On the continuing problems of media effects research," in Curran, J. and Gurevitch, M. (eds.) *Mass Media and Society*, 2nd ed., London: Edward Arnold, pp. 305–324.

McCullough, M. (2004) *Digital Ground: Architecture, Pervasive Computing, and Environmental Knowing*, Cambridge, MA: MIT Press.

Moores, S. (1993) *Interpreting Audiences: The Ethnography of Media Consumption*, London: Sage.

— (1996) *Satellite Television and Everyday Life*, Luton: John Libbey Media/University of Luton Press.

— (2012) *Media, Place and Mobility*, London: Palgrave Macmillan.

Morley, D. (1992) *Television, Audiences and Cultural Studies*, London: Routledge.

— (2006) *Media, Modernity and Technology*, London: Routledge.

— (2017) *Communications and Mobility: The Migrant, the Mobile Phone, and the Container Box*, London: Wiley-Blackwell.

Murdock, G. (1997) "Reservoirs of dogma: An archaeology of popular anxieties," in Barker, M. and Petley, J. (eds.) *Ill Effects*, London: Routledge, pp. 150–169.

Park, R. E. (1955) *Collected Papers of Robert Ezra Park: Vol. 3. Society*, Glencoe, IL: Free Press.

Radway, J. (1987) *Reading the Romance: Women, Patriarchy and Popular Literature*, London: Verso.

Ridell, S. (2015) "Exploring audience activities and their power-relatedness in the digitalised city: Diversity and routinisation of people's media relations in the triply articulated urban space," in Zeller, F. et al. (eds.) *Revitalising Audiences: Innovations in European Audience Research*, London: Routledge, pp. 236–260.

Robins, K. and Aksoy, A. (2006) "Thinking experiences: Transnational media and migrants' minds," in Morley, D. and Curran, J. (eds.) *Media and Cultural Theory*, London: Routledge, pp. 86–99.

Rose, G. (2017) "Posthuman agency in the digitally mediated city: Exteriorization, individuation, reinvention," *Annals of the American Association of Geographers*, 107(4), pp. 779–793.

Scannell, P. (2007) *Media and Communication*, London: Sage.

Sennett, R. (1993) *The Fall of Public Man*, London: Faber and Faber.

Silverstone, R. (1993) "Television and Ontological Security," in *Media, Culture and Society*, 15(4), pp. 573–598.

— (2006) "Domesticating domestication: Reflections on the life of a concept," in Berker, T. et al. (eds.) *Domestication of Media and Technology*, Maidenhead and New York: Open University Press, pp. 229–248.

Smets, K. (2013) "Diasporas and audience studies: A fruitful match? Reflections from a media ethnographic study on Turkish and Moroccan film audiences," *The Communication Review*, 16(1–2), pp. 103–111.

Spasić, I. (2004) *Sociologije svakodnevnog života*, Beograd: Zavod za udžbenike.

Strathern, M. (1992) "Foreword: The mirror of technology," in Silverstone, R. and Hirsch, E. (eds.) *Consuming Technologies: Media and Information in Domestic Spaces*, London and New York: Routledge, pp. vii-xiii.

Further Reading

Madianou, M. (2014) "Smartphones as polymedia," *Journal of Computer-Mediated Communication*, 19(3), pp. 667–680.

Ridell, S. and Zeller, F. (eds.) (2013) "Mediated urbanism: Navigating an interdisciplinary terrain," special issue of *International Communication Gazette* 75(5–6).

Ridell, S. and Tosoni, S. (2016) "Decentering media studies, verbing the audience: Methodological considerations concerning people's uses of media in urban space," *International Journal of Communication*, 10, pp. 1277–1293.

37
TEMPORARY INSCRIPTIONS
Exploring Graffiti and Street Art in the Age of Internetization of Everyday Urban Life

Ilija Tomanić Trivundža and Mitja Velikonja

Introduction

Even though humans have left their painted, inscribed, scratched, or applied traces on walls throughout history, it is only since the 1960s that the graffiti and street art scene was recognized as an urban media phenomenon. Philadelphia and New York became the capitals of what soon developed into, arguably, a globalized aesthetic and political practice. Graffiti began to be made and destroyed, appreciated and condemned across the urban world. Debates about the definition, the classification, and the political and artistic dimensions and limitations of graffiti have continued ever since. Curiously, despite this plethora of discussion, the theoretically informed, methodologically elaborated, comparative, and historically grounded scholarly literature on the subject is scarce. Prevalent are the sumptuously decorated "picture books" of graffitied cities or regions, presenting the great names of the local graffiti scenes (Keith Haring, Banksy, Obey, WK Interact, Laser 3.14, Swoon, etc.) or individual styles. An additional problem lies in the fact that the related but different concepts—*graffiti* and *street art*—are used randomly and uncritically. This chapter is divided into two broader thematic sections. The first, focusing on graffiti and street art as an urban medium of communication, begins by outlining their general traits and techniques, providing the basic definitional elements and outlining the most frequently used methodological approaches. We conclude the first section with a discussion on political dimensions of the two sets of practices. In the second thematic section, the focus shifts from graffiti/street art as a medium to the media and mediated communication of graffiti/street art. Here, both the complex role that the media have played in the denigration, promotion, and "mainstreamization" of the practice, as well as the changes resulting from the increase in mediated communication of graffiti/street art within the context of what is recognized as "internetization of everyday life," are outlined.

Traits, Types, and Techniques

Graffiti and street art are popular visual media for the expression of social belonging, personal presence, cultural choices, and political views in public urban space. They cohabitate with other modes of urban communication and are thought to express the writers' "right to the city" (Lefebvre 2000) or their entry, usually from the margins of society, into the public sphere, in their own manner. Graffiti and street art represent a specific two- or three-dimensional, usually illegal, visual expression in public space that is created to form a message, strike a conversation, and make a claim. They are found practically everywhere: on walls, pavements, bridges, underpasses, sports playgrounds, traffic signs, on and in means of public transport, in public toilets, in bus and railway stations, on park benches, in waiting rooms and schools, on trees, on locker doors, etc. Their main characteristics seem to be a specific aesthetic form, a site-specific interaction with the occupied surface, an implicit/explicit critique of the existing artistic and political institutions, a self-perceived non-acceptance and illegality, an intervention in public space, multi-modality, transience, polysemy, instantaneity, contagiousness, and anonymity. Ideal-typically, graffiti and street art can be divided into those that poetize the carrying surfaces and those that directly politicize them. Although they initially served as the medium of expression (and badge of merit) of very specific socio-demographic groups (youth, subcultures and scenes, or illegal groups), we will show in the subsequent part of this chapter that such "narrow" definitions are becoming increasingly hard to maintain because of ever greater "mainstreamization" of graffiti and street art and the proliferation of their practices.

To navigate the visual urban arena, some form of *graffiti* and *street art* classification can be helpful. Graffiti is made up of one- or multi-colored figurative or abstract wall paintings that are created with sprays, markers, various paints, chalk, etc. The main types include a *tag* (a graffiti-writer's pseudonym in the form of a logo), a *signature graffiti writing* (a graffiti-writer's longer "signature"), a *piece* (a more elaborate graffiti), a *throw-up* (a graffiti quickly made from stylized letters), a *burner* (an outstanding graffiti), a *roof-top* (a graffiti on a higher part of a building), an *end to end* (a graffiti that covers an entire car or wall), a *character* (a graffiti of a caricature character from popular culture or a stylized letter), a *wall of fame* (walls that feature the most perfected graffiti of the wider and local graffiti-writing scene alongside each other), a *battle* (graffiti-writers' battle on walls), as well as a *mural* in the technical sense (usually a legal painting on larger parts of buildings), and so on. A *black book* is, at the same time, a writer's notebook of impressions, a sketchbook, and a collection of the tags of other writers. A novice is called a *toy*, someone who creates many graffiti is a *bomber*, the one who only signs works with tags is a *tagger*, a maker of quality graffiti is a *piecer*, a writer who obsessively continues making graffiti even after he has been caught and penalized is a *fanatic*, a group of graffiti-writers is a *crew*, while the term *queen/king* or *master* is conferred only on the most perfected graffiti-writers of them all. As in all other subcultures, the "core" here differs from a variety of "scenes" that are aesthetically accepted, socially tolerated, ideologically seen as harmless, and increasingly commercially incorporated.

Street art developed a bit later, in the 1990s, originating from the graffiti-aesthetics and subculture and adopting the name *post-graffiti art*. Street art adds a third dimension to the two spatial ones; it inscribes messages not only onto but also into the urban space and uses a range of other tools. The best-known street art types are: *stencils, stickers, posters* (printed or unique); public installations and visual interventions (mosaics, wood engravings, various three-dimensional objects, illegal statuettes or reliefs made of metal, wood, concrete, plaster, plastic, tiles, fimo clay, snow, and a plethora of other materials); *scratchiti* and *scribbles* on public spaces (in trains and buses, in prison cells, on school and other benches); *latrinalia* (toilet wall writings); *arborglyphs* (cuts in trees), *petroglyphs* (cuts on rocks); *cuneiforms, chalk art, cut-outs*, and *paste-ups* (images cut out from paper and colored, possibly even collage images, that are then glued to public surfaces); *lock-ons* (installations locked onto public objects), and various other forms of visual interventions into given surfaces (scratching, perforating, hollowing, burning-out, imprinting or writing into fresh concrete, etc.). These techniques are constantly supplemented with new ones; thus, the diversity of this kind of street creativity, too, is endless.

Researching Graffiti and Street Art as Urban Media

Existing studies usually have three epistemological starting points. The first concerns the contextualization of graffiti and street art. The majority of studies, unfortunately, analyze these works in isolation from the spatial foundation onto which they are sprayed or glued—when, actually, it is only together that they form a complete message. Anti-government graffiti, for example, can be more effective if sprayed on a government building in the city center than elsewhere. Text and context are therefore necessary for proper interpretation. The second relates to the intentionality of graffiti and street art—they are made for a certain effect, either aesthetic or political. The third epistemological starting point is the understanding of the impact of graffiti on their social, political, and cultural environment. Here, we rely on Brecht's (2016) criterion of the political relevance of an art work: political relevance does not lie in what is invested in it but in the degree of its effect on or changes in the environment.

As all other emerging fields, graffiti studies has yet to create its own methodology. Since this is an interdisciplinary terrain at the crossroads of the visual cultural and media studies, subculture studies, and, in certain aspects, also of criminology and legal studies, the methods of research are suitably diverse. Furthermore, graffiti and street art can be studied from four "sites" of meaning production—the site of the context, the site of the graffiti-writer, the site of the graffiti content, and the site of the audience—each with its own respective methods. The context of graffiti can be studied using the historical-comparative method (e.g., Fredric Jameson, Walter Benjamin, the paradigm of the French *nouvelle histoire*, Alfred Radcliffe-Brown), semiotics (Georges Gurvitch, Eviatar Zerubavel), and autoethnography (e.g., Heewong Chang). When researching the site of the writer the methods of urban ethnography and participant observation, interviews, and the comparative method are especially useful. The majority of existing research deals with the site of graffiti itself, using the following methods: compositional interpretation, content analysis, the comparative method, and social semiology (Roland Barthes, Umberto Eco, Stuart Hall). Internetization not only brings about alternative ways of data collection (such as large-scale data harvesting from social networks and other publicly available online sources) but also introduces new methods into the graffiti researchers' toolkit, such as digital ethnography, digital observation, network analysis, and computer-assisted visual or geolocation analysis of large datasets which can be employed to study the practitioners, practices, and aesthetic elements. The site of the audience can be researched by methods from audience studies, such as interviews, participant observation, surveys, comparative studies, and last but not least, through action research (the aim of which is not only to study graffiti and street art but also to remove or alter the instances of hateful messages).

Political Dimensions of Graffiti and Street Art

Traditionally, graffiti and street art were mostly the media of individuals and groups with a communicational deficit (subpolitical groups, social and ethnic minorities, radical artists and social critics, etc.), "a weapon of the weak" in the words of James C. Scott (1985). Today, they are increasingly becoming the media of those in power, of popular and celebrity culture, consumerism, and high art—therefore of "affirmative character of culture," as defined by Herbert Marcuse (2009). Critics argue that graffiti is treading the path of gradual ideological, commercial, and aesthetic incorporation and commodification, trodden by other subcultures before it. From the radical otherness, it is becoming simply an acceptable diversity. This criticism is only partly justified: graffiti and street art can attack or support the existing condition; they can be used for aesthetic and political criticism or apology.

The dilemma regarding the political dimensions of graffiti and street art can be answered with the help of Rancière's (2004) "regimes of the arts" classification. Explicitly political graffiti agrees with the ethical regime of the arts that always pragmatically relates to someone or something outside the field of art. Graffiti is considered from the position of the intent, influence, or goal. Graffiti exhibited in the galleries and in the well-designed and expensive illustrated monographs follows the poetic or representative regime of the arts, which imitates the reality of the graffiti "out there" and presents it in an isolated "artistic" environment, meaning that it is evaluated and hierarchized according to the rules characteristic of a poetic regime. This aesthetic regime understands subcultural graffiti and street art to be inseparable from their "natural" environment—the walls and façades. It is founded on the perception of aesthetics or art as an autonomous form of social life. Unlike the political graffiti, the subcultural graffiti does not seem to be representing anything outside of itself and is not in the service of anything, but simultaneously builds its own aesthetic singularity and social autonomy. It is this sense of social autonomy that Rancière (2004) identifies as a political gesture. In short, the political dimensions of graffiti and street art are not only to be found in their explicit political statements, but also in the gesture of their creation and autonomous existence itself. To paraphrase Marshall McLuhan's famous argument (McLuhan and Fiore 1967/2001), graffiti as a medium is already the message.

Graffiti and the Media: From Denigration to Documentation to Mainstreamization

Both the initial global spread of graffiti in the 1980s and the popularization of street art at the turn of the 21st century have fundamentally relied not only on the nomadism of their practitioners but on the extensive presence of their work in a range of media, including photography books, magazines, documentary and feature films, music videos, and online (self)publishing. On the one hand, this multimedia presence was a product of the mainstream media coverage of the "graffiti phenomenon," which ranged from the predominantly negative coverage with the underpinnings of moral panic in the 1980s and 1990s (for discussions of graffiti as "urban plague" and "wars on graffiti" see, e.g., Ferrell 1996; Austin 2001; Kramer 2010; for connections of such campaigns to the questions of ethnicity, class, and race see, e.g., Morley 2000; Dickinson 2008) to the gradual acceptance of street art in the mainstream press since the turn of the 21st century (which instituted the differentiation between the "good" and "creative" [street art] and "bad" or "deviant" aerosol practices [graffiti/tagging]). On the other hand, a vibrant but far less documented alternative strand of graffiti showcasing and chronicling also simultaneously existed, in the form of photography books, graffiti magazines, social media, and documentary films that provided not only sympathetic but also visually telling accounts of this ephemeral form of public communication. Initially, the influential publications (e.g., Naar 1974, Cooper and Chalfant 1984, but also Brassaï 1961) and films (e.g., *Wild Style* (1983) and *Style Wars* (1983)) were not produced by the community of graffiti-writers but by engaged "outside" observers, who were typically not in direct or prolonged contact with the writers and crews.

By the mid-1980s, the community moved to "self-publishing" predominantly in the form of local or national graffiti magazines (such as the *International Graffiti Times* (USA), the *Aerosol Art Magazine* (UK), the *Bomber Magazine* (the Netherlands), the *Underground Productions* (Sweden), and the *Hype Magazine* (Australia), to name but a few examples), which were partially born out of a desire to share information and circulate works, and partly in response to the mainstream media's negative coverage and various municipal and transport authority "wars" against graffiti. Graffiti-related topics also featured prominently in other alternative culture zines, such as those of the punk movement and the emerging hip-hop culture. Jacobson (2015) notes that by the late 1990s these magazines—which were gradually evolving from fanzines into professional publications—became national hubs in an international network, offering an abundance of information to an increasingly interconnected, self-aware, and international community of writers. The speed and the scope of this information exchange intensified online, producing globally shared and locally adapted visual vocabularies, stylistic registers, and repertoires of expression as well as codes of conduct and skills. In the 1990s, publications on the subject became increasingly professionalized and frequently took the form of author monographs (either by writers and street artists or by photographers), which are typical of the art world, signaling the gradual adoption of graffiti into the cultural mainstream. A similar claim can be made about the popularity of documentaries, such as *Piece by Piece* (2005), *Bomb It* (2007), *Exit Through the Gift Shop* (2010), or *Graffiti Wars* (2011), which were produced in that period. The rise of the Internet and social media enabled not only new practices of image and information exchange (and the emergence of new cultural intermediaries) but also tipped the scales from professionalized production back to self-publishing—to the point that documentation and online presentation of one's own work has become a constitutive part of the current graffiti and street art production process (see also Chapter 29, this volume).

Admittedly, photography has always been a part of graffiti/street art production. Even before digital photography and networked media, writers would routinely photograph their work, keep photographic documentation of their creations, and show or exchange images with fellow writers. Photography is not simply the most convenient and accessible way to preserve these ephemeral works—often, it is the only way to document or exhibit them. Some of the works only ever exist as photographic images because of the speed of graffiti removal (e.g., a zero-tolerance policy against graffiti often implies removing graffiti within 24 hours, "bombed" train cars can be taken out of service to prevent public visibility, etc.). There is, however, a flip side to photography's positive relationship with graffiti/street art, since various other "interested parties" also rely on photographic mediation of graffiti. Apart from the writers, crews, fans, professional photographers, and researchers, extensive chronicling, systematic photographic documentation, and archiving is routinely produced by the police, municipal authorities, and graffiti removal contractors for the purposes of prosecution of writers and removal of graffiti/street art. Publicly available images are also increasingly scrutinized for the prosecution of writers.

Communication (Studies') Perspectives on Graffiti and Street Art

Graffiti and street art have long been at the periphery of media studies' interests. This changed fairly recently, as online visual (self)mediation became an inseparable part of the writing process and with the internet being the primary location for encountering graffiti and street art for many. The ubiquity of image-making and -sharing technologies in daily urban life and the "spatial" turn in media studies has triggered four wide areas of debate, namely: (1) the changing relationship between graffiti/street art and the physical space of the city; (2) the effects of photographic mediation on the production and reception of graffiti/street art; (3) the role of (new) cultural intermediaries; and (4) the subsequent transformation of the cultural and political status of graffiti/street art. These four dimensions are outlined in greater detail below.

The mediated communication of graffiti/street art on websites, blogs, and social network pages and accounts has greatly increased the visibility and accessibility of these works, but it comes with a heavy price—the loss of site-specificity. The often-expressed lamentation over the diminishing importance of the physical location and the dependency on the physical encounter with graffiti/street art originates in the understanding of graffiti as primarily a spatial practice—a communicative act related to (re)claiming, (re)mapping, and (re)imaging a city. Thus, for example, groups, such as gangs, political activists, and resistance movements, have long used graffiti, tagging, and murals to make spatial claims and engage in symbolic mappings or conquests of city space. The territorial nature of their practice is linked with the notions of power—with the city space seen as always being dominated by the political, administrative, and corporate interests (Irvine 2012)—which are simultaneously exposed and challenged by the illegal writing and its incidental encounter in the city. Online representations of graffiti and street art, it is argued, reduce the symbolic importance of the physical location, and give (undue) prominence to less encoded or less risky locations—a critique that often relies on the normative positions about politics of space and authenticity that predate the age of internetization.

The documentation and circulation of graffiti/street art in the form of photographic images prioritizes the object-centered perception and spectacle to a reflexive and critical interaction (for a dialogic approach to graffiti see Young 2013). Additionally, the performative aspects are undervalued (e.g., skills to access off-limits locations, physical fitness, risk management, etc.), thereby obscuring the fact that a finished piece is only a small part of a complex production process. Some authors (e.g., Glaser 2015) argue that photographic documentation often highlights the photographic aesthetics over the writing itself, to the extent that it guides the selection of (more photogenic) locations, adapts the piece size to display formats of mobile phone and computer applications and screens, and prioritizes the production of content that is photogenic or that achieves its full visual impact only as a carefully composed image (e.g., work that depends on observation from a particular vantage point).

While a certain level of negative influence of photography and online mediation on graffiti/street art is undeniable, recent writing on the subject tends to ignore the positive (creative) potential of this development, exemplified by street art animation (e.g., Blu's *Muto*), platform-specific work (e.g., @Lushlux), hybrid forms (e.g., GIF-iti), graffiti simulations, or through the use of photography rather than aerosol as the technique of expression (e.g., JR). This anxiety about the "corruptive" power of photography stems from a broader iconoclastic fear over the seductive power of images in Western societies (see, e.g., Mitchell 2005), which treats photographic images primarily as the dangerous storm troopers of the commodified society of spectacle and consumerism. This denigration of photography as an element of graffiti/street art is reminiscent of the debates surrounding photography and other practices of "claiming the city," such as urban exploration, in which it is dubbed, negatively, as "ruin porn" (see Chapter 38, this volume).

The notions of corruptive and parasitic aspects of photography also underline the frequently voiced objections regarding the growing mutual (inter)dependency between the writers and the (new) intermediaries, such as photographers, bloggers, and administrators of websites or social media accounts. Online platforms enable writers to have more control over their content (through self-presentation and self-promotion) and offer them potential for direct access to and interaction with the audience (followers on social media). It is not uncommon for famous street artists to have more than one million followers—e.g., Banksy 2.3m, JR 1.2m, OSGEMEOS 1.1m, and Shepard Fairey 1m followers on Instagram in summer 2018—and even the less renowned writers and artists tend to attract a following that is counted in several tens or hundreds of thousands of followers. The growing centrality of online mediation is often described by scholars as (unduly) shifting the power balance from the writers to the cultural intermediaries. The latter are increasingly seen as the decisive curatorial gatekeepers, notable experts, and ultimate trendsetters to whom the writers must turn for recognition and symbolic capital (e.g., Rushmore 2013; Glaser 2015). Moreover, the authors are keen to emphasize that the self-mediation efforts of the writers coexist within a plethora of self-presentation on social media, which further detaches the works of graffiti/street art from their original context and transposes them into wider networked flows of information, where they are forced to compete for attention under platform-specific algorithmic economies of attention. Under these conditions, graffiti/street art become objects of a double-layered mediation—first as visible representations, and second as invisible data (MacDowall 2016).

The above debates feed into a third broad topic that concerns the loss of graffiti/street art's critical charge due to its adoption by the art world, advertising industry, tourism, city branding, or career building (e.g., Abram 2008). Street art, in particular, is incorporated into the discourses of creative cities and globalized culture via notions of creativity, transgression, authenticity, and (aesthetic) innovation, fueling both the global tourism practices and local gentrification processes. While one strand of the debates focuses on macro-level commodification that triggers responses such as Blu's famous obliteration of his murals in Berlin and Bologna, another set of discussions highlights the connection between the online self-mediation practices and branding, i.e., the (self)promotion of the writers and street artists as (global) brands, resulting in commodification, commercialization, and fetishization of ephemeral and unsolicited public works, thereby diluting their critical subcultural charge. Banksy is both a paradigmatic and an extreme example of this process, exposing its deep-seated contradictions—ranging from city branding, guided tours, protective coating, and restoration to auction house sales, ultimately reaching the point where the sales potential of his works—through unauthorized removal of pieces—endangers their very existence in public space.

The media-savvy practitioners embrace this changed communicative ecology primarily for the many benefits it offers them: increased visibility, popularization and (global) reach, increased speed and accessibility of information, community building, potential for synchronous interaction, increased ability to curate or map their work, and, perhaps above all, documentation and preservation of work. The archiving potential, recognized already in the early days of the internet (the first online archive ArtCrimes was set up as early as 1994), has greatly evolved with Web 2.0 (intermediaries such as Wooster Collective), and culminates with the proliferation of social networks (e.g., there are currently over 2.3 million images tagged "street art" on Instagram and nearly three million on Flickr).

The ease of online publishing and circulation of works via photography and video has also brought about a new wave of vernacular chronicling, bringing the myriad narrations of origins and trajectories of various works to public awareness. It also enables the preservation of politically sensitive work in a digitalized form (e.g., the political murals of Cairo's Mohammed Mahmud street) that can still serve in the political struggle even after their physical removal.

Conclusion

Even though the field of media studies is not the primary domicile of (scholarly) debate about graffiti/street art, the tensions brought about by the increased mediation (or mediatization) of graffiti/street art are illustrative of the broader debates on the cultural and political status of these urban media practices. Graffiti and street art always exist at the intersection of multiple vernacular and institutional gazes, competing with the pre-existing regimes of visuality (corporate, administrative, artistic) that define both the legitimacy and legality of the practice. This is particularly visible in an ongoing debate about the legality and commodification of graffiti/street art.

In our view, two of the most significant contributions of media studies to the debates about graffiti/street art are the focus on the dynamism of the discursive-material struggles, and the skepticism regarding the deterministic and univocal view of the effects of communication technologies. Despite the mainstreamization, commodification, and co-optation, graffiti/street art still (co)creates critical political imaginaries and agonistic spaces in the mediated city (Mouffe 2007), as is vividly testified by the sprawl of murals and graffiti in Athens after 2008, in Libya, Egypt, and Tunisia after 2010, in Latin America during and after the dictatorships, and practically everywhere else in the world where groups with a communication deficit in the public sphere visually inscribe themselves into the public space.

References

Abram, S. (2008) "Komodifikacija ter komercializacija grafitov in street arta v treh korakih: od ulic prek galerij do korporacij," *Časopis za kritiko znanosti*, (36)231–232, pp. 34–49.
Austin, J. (2001) *Taking the train: How graffiti art became an urban crisis in New York City*, New York: Columbia University Press.
Brassaï (1961) *Graffiti*, Paris: Les Editions du Temps.
Brecht, B. (2016) *Me-ti: Book of interventions in the flow of things*, London, Oxford, New York, New Delhi, Sydney: Bloomsbury.
Cooper, M. and Chalfant, H. (1984) *Subway art*, New York: Henry Holt and Company.
Dickinson, M. (2008) "The Making of Space, Race and Place: New York City's War on Graffiti, 1970–the Present," *Critique of Anthropology*, 28(1), pp. 27–45.
Ferrell, J. (1996) *Crimes of style: Urban graffiti and the politics of criminality*, Boston, MA: Northeastern University Press.
Glaser, K. (2015) "The 'Place to Be' for Street Art Nowadays Is No Longer the Street, It's the Internet," *Street Art & Urban Creativity Scientific Journal*, (1)1, pp. 6–13.
Irvine, M. (2012) "The Work on the Street: Street Art and Visual Culture" in B. Sandywell and I. Heywood (eds.), *The Handbook of Visual Culture*, London & New York: Berg, pp. 235–278.
Jacobson, M. (2015) "The Dialectics of Graffiti Studies: A Personal Record of Documenting and Publishing on Graffiti Since 1988," *Street Art & Urban Creativity Scientific Journal*, 1(1), pp. 99–103.
Kramer, R. (2010) "Moral Panics and Urban Growth Machines: Official Reactions to Graffiti in New York City, 1990–2005," *Qualitative Sociology*, (33)3, pp. 297–311.
Lefebvre, H. (2000) *Writing on cities*, Oxford (UK), Malden (MA): Blackwell Publishers.
MacDowall, L. (2016) "#Instafame: Aesthetics, Audiences, Data" in K. Avramidis, and M. Tsilimpounidi (eds.), *Graffiti and street art: Reading, writing and representing the city*, London: Routledge, pp. 231–249.
Marcuse, H. (2009) *Negations: Essays in critical theory*, London: MayFlyBooks.
McLuhan, M. and Fiore, Q. (1967/2001) *The medium is the massage: An inventory of effects*, Corte Madera, CA: Gingko Press.
Mitchell, W. J. T. (2005) *What do pictures want?* Chicago, IL: University of Chicago Press.
Morley, D. (2000) *Home territories: Media, mobility and identity*, London: Routledge.
Mouffe, C. (2007) "Artistic Activism and Agonistic Spaces," *Art and Research*, 1(2), pp. 1–5.
Mubi Brighenti, A. (2010) "At the Wall: Graffiti Writers, Urban Territoriality, and the Public Domain," *Space and Culture*, 13(3), pp. 315–332.
Naar, J. with M. Kurlansky and N. Mailer (1974) *The faith of graffiti*, New York: Praeger Publishers.
Rancière, J. (2004) *The politics of aesthetics*, London, New York: Continuum.
Rushmore, R. J. (2013) *Viral art: How the internet has shaped street art and graffiti*, Self-published e-book. Available at: https://viralart.vandalog.com/read.
Scott. J. C. (1985) *Weapons of the weak: Everyday forms of peasant resistance*, New Haven, CT and London: Yale University Press.
Young, A. (2013) *Street art, public city: Law, crime and the urban imagination*, New York: Routledge.

Further Reading

Chaffee, L. G. (1993) *Political protest and street art: Popular tools for democratization in Hispanic countries*, Westport, CT and London: Greenwood Press.
Lovata, T. and Olton, E. (eds.) (2015) *Understanding graffiti: Multidisciplinary studies from prehistory to the present*, London and New York: Routledge.
Ross, J. I. (ed.) (2016) *The Routledge handbook of graffiti and street art*, London and New York: Routledge.

38
CREATING A SITUATION IN THE CITY
Embodied Spaces and the Act of Crossing Boundaries

Tina Richardson

Introduction: Constructing Situations

For Guy Debord and the Situationist International (1957–1972):

> The construction of situations begins beyond the ruins of the modern spectacle. It is easy to see how much the very principle of the spectacle—non-intervention—is linked to the alienation of the old world . . . The situation is thus designed to be lived by its constructors.
>
> *(Debord 2006: 40–41)*

It was the creating of situations that challenged the appearance of the everyday lived experience, and they believed this was an obligation. It was the quotidian, they felt, that enabled capital in the form of the spectacle to infiltrate the lives of the city dweller. For them, the spectacle was "where the tangible world is replaced by a selection of images which exist above it, and which simultaneously impose themselves as the tangible *par excellence*" (Debord 2005: 36, original italics). It was in the built environment that the spectacle was at its most prevalent, whereby it was manifested in such forms as advertising billboards, enticing shop windows, and public spaces dedicated to consumerism as a "pastime." Creating situations enabled a critique that intervened in material space and which could elicit resistance to the overriding forms that appeared as the sign of capital's dominance. One way that the Situationists resisted the spectacle was through the medium of their published materials, which often took the form of do-it-yourself (DIY) maps and architectural designs, reflecting their proposals for a unitary urbanism (a rather vague utopian approach to city dwelling that attempted to fuse play and functionalism), and their urban walking practice, psychogeography. For them psychogeography was "[t]he study of the specific effects of the geographical environment, consciously organized or not, on the emotions and behavior of individuals" (Situationist International 1996: 69).

However, decades prior to the Situationists the *flaneur* had been strolling the streets of Paris taking the position of a passive and detached observer of urban phenomena. The first description of the *flaneur* appeared in Baudelaire's *The Painter of Modern Life* (1863), providing Walter Benjamin with material for *The Arcades Project* (1927–1940), his unfinished research on the

Parisian arcades. At the same time, the Surrealists provided their contribution to urban walking practices and critique, with their ludic act of walking and its emphasis on psychoanalysis. Poet, writer, and Dadaist Louis Aragon wrote accounts of his Parisian walks in his text *Paris Peasant* (1926), offering his own affective response to the city spaces through the veil of sexual desire. Aragon's Paris appeared in the form of the boulevards that transformed the city in the late 19th and early 20th century. Overseen by Georges-Eugene Haussmann, the renovation turned an overcrowded and unsanitary space into an ordered place that epitomized the modernist metropolis of the time: one ready for the contemporary consumer that awaited it. Nevertheless, and predating this period, Jean-Jacques Rousseau is also often considered a *flaneur*: in *Confessions* (1782) he wrote about the act of walking and how it aided the process of philosophical enquiry.

It is not easy to pinpoint the exact moment that urban critique, in the form of moving about the city, became recognized as a form of analysis that could be applied to developed geographical space, and some theorists and writers will direct you to the work of William Blake, or even Daniel Defoe (see Merlin Coverley's *Psychogeography* [2006]). However, even if the contemporary creator of an urban situation cannot cite their original influence in regard to their own particular practice, what we do know is that the city has both fascinated and concerned us, in equal measure—since it first appeared as an urban agglomeration—and continues to today. Moreover, with today's available technology—which provides us with new tools to facilitate interconnectivity, multiple methods for expressing our affective responses to space, offering access to vast amounts of urban-related data, among many other things—we can become *bricoleurs* in our choice of methods that make up our urbanism toolbox. This enables us to read and rewrite the city in multiple ways, allowing us to express the heterogeneity of space and disseminate our findings like never before. The multiplicity of accessible methodologies can help us to see beyond the dominant discourse of the city, "whose surface is only its upper limit, outlining itself against the visible" (De Certeau 1988: 93).

This chapter will discuss the history of what appears under the general term of "urban critique" in its many incarnations, such as modern-day psychogeography, place-hacking, DIY urbanism, guerrilla urbanism, and urban exploration. By examining the act of placing one's body into the space under examination, we can begin to understand the dynamics that operate on us when crossing the material boundaries that appear in space, but also the symbolic ones that might be culturally formed in our psyche (such as ideas about who and who might not be allowed in certain spaces). Urban space is a mediated space that enables a form of reflexivity to take place when the individual engages with it in a critical way. The aesthetic and affective response that a person or group generates through the embodied process of the urban encounter momentarily changes the space to fit the subjectivity of those placing it under scrutiny. While this process can be undertaken and expressed in multiple ways depending on the approach undertaken, what is consistent across these alternative methods is a challenge to the taken-forgranted view that urban space is simply a neutral space that happens to appear as "the built environment"—something that is immovable and yet also innocuous. Urban critique, in whatever its form, provides an opportunity for the city to be examined at the micro level, through what Michel De Certeau describes as "spatial practices," which take the form of modes of resistance to an imposed way of life as it appears in "lived space" (1988: 96). These spatial practices allow one to question, and even challenge, the usual "rules of the highway," such as how we cross the road at a zebra or pelican crossing, or do not drive on the pavement.

By providing examples of the different forms of contemporary urban critique in regards to forming what can be described as situations, the discussion will focus on how some people actively seek to question the way urban space is manifest, and ask why it appears the way it does and whether we are able to challenge its seemingly fixed materiality. This chapter will provide an overview of these approaches and their mediated relationship with the practices of everyday life in mediated cities.

Urban Exploration

In 2016, a court case prevented four men from illegally climbing urban structures after images appeared of them carrying out these activities online (Batty 2016). However, this is not a new phenomenon. In 2008, the film *Man on Wire* (James Marsh) was released, which documented Philippe Petit's hour-long, illegal, high-wire walk between the Twin Towers in New York in 1974. This specific act predates our understanding of what today we describe as "urban exploration," which is now carried out by individuals known as UrbExers. One of the most well-known characters in this group of urban explorers is Bradley L. Garrett, who describes the practice as "recreational urban trespass" (2013: 27). UrbExers can practice anything from entering privately owned, decommissioned, industrial ruins to traversing corporate skyscrapers. Garrett (a cultural geographer) has himself climbed The Shard in London, and says of the younger generation of UrbExers that they "compete for attention and credibility online by combining their adventures with riskier activities such as base jumping, where people parachute from structures, and parkour, which involves navigating urban spaces by climbing, jumping, balancing and running through buildings" (Garrett cited in Batty 2016).

Garrett's book *Explore Everything: Place-Hacking the City* (2013) mostly examines the activist work of the London Consolidation Crew (of which Garrett was a member during this time) and their remapping of London. Their explorations took a vertical perspective, rather than a horizontal one, in examining this capital city—one that challenged the way that the city had historically been explored or viewed; for instance, entering abandoned London Underground tunnels. However, Garrett's book also covers cities further afield, such as Detroit in the United States and Nohra in Germany, and he blurs the line in regard to his own position as ethnographer and that of activist in many of the situations he discusses, acknowledging this by saying: "I have embedded myself in the community to see how people within it work and play, the rules they give themselves and the stories they tell" (2013: 4). Garrett also provides examples of some of the problems inherent in being in the space of "the other." Providing an example of his explorations in Eastern Europe, he states:

> There was a specific guilt that came with exploring Eastern Europe, arising from a clash of different value systems in regard to derelict space. Perhaps this is an indication of a larger continued tension between capitalism and communism: where East meets West, desire meets utility, nostalgia meets expectation and mobility meets place-making.
>
> *(2013: 63)*

In his own explanation of what urban exploration is, Garrett points us to the work of Jeff Chapman (aka Ninjalicious), who was a well-known Canadian UrbExer publishing what might be described as a manifesto for urban explorers: *Access All Areas* (2005). The book provides advice on locations for carrying out explorations and interventions, and even offers tips on how to get out of difficult situations. However, it is important to note that with urban exploration covering a wide spectrum of activities, not all approaches are considered to be as dangerous as those mentioned above. While exploring industrial ruins (ruinology) is often considered an UrbEx pursuit, it can also come under the rubric of psychogeography, which many may describe as a rather more "sedate" form of urban exploration, sitting on the cusp of these two forms of urban critique.

Ruinology (or "ruin porn," or even the rather more sanitized version, "ruin lust") is both the exploration and the (at times) scopophilic fascination with ruins. Popularized more recently in an exhibition called "Ruin Lust" at Tate Britain—see the associated publication: *Ruin Lust: Artists' Fascination with Ruins, from Turner to the Present Day* by Brian Dillon, Tate Publishing 2014—ruinology was also of interest to the Situationists. One of their less well-known (and rarely published in print form) maps features cut-up sections of a map of the Left Bank in Paris, alongside an image of Claude Lorrain's painting *Seaport with the Embarkation of Saint Ursula* (1641). While this particular painting of Lorrain's is not especially emblematic of the depictions of ruins that feature in many of his paintings, the Situationists were interested in his paintings of ruins, and while it may appear that their fascination was pornographic (ruin porn), it was far from it: "We have no predilection for the charms of the ruins" (Situationist International 1996: 45). As Tom McDonough explains in regard to the Situationists, the ruins are a spectacle which not only "reproduces power" but also repeats history, presenting it as something harmless (1994: 76). He also quotes them, saying that their "antipathy toward the 'charms of the ruins' was precisely an acknowledgement that those 'norms of abstract space' that construct public domain as evacuated were not 'charming' at all" (1994: 77).

Nevertheless, there are urban walkers who see ruins as something between these two positions—ruin porn being on one end of the spectrum and the aversion to their "charms" at the other end. In *Industrial Ruins: Space, Aesthetics and Materiality* Tim Edensor states: "In a conventional reading of the urban landscape, dereliction and ruin is a sign of waste and for local politicians and entrepreneurs, tends to provide stark evidence of an area's lack" (2005: 7). However, Edensor recognizes that these are spaces of heterogeneity in terms of "meaning and function" since the typical view of them being "useless" actually hides "the social, political and economic processes through which decisions about space and value are reached" (2005: 7). These concepts are also reflected in Patrick Keiller's 2011 film, *Robinson in Ruins*, where traces of past struggles appear in visual forms that continue to haunt the present. Hauntology is intrinsically linked to these forms of urban critique and can be especially attributed to both ruinology and a not dissimilar pursuit which appears under the heading of "bunkerology."

DIY/Guerrilla Urbanism

While some specialists on the urban scene are interested in acts that could be considered "grand gestures," there are also those that reflect the struggle of the everyday individual in regard to the claims they make on public space. These events take many forms, from the Occupy movement, beginning with the first protest in Wall Street, New York, in 2011, to more subtle, local actions such as yarn bombing. Jeff Hou says that these forms of DIY urbanism challenge the encroachment of private space into public space and "defy or escape the existing rules or regulations" (2010: 9). Hou examines DIY urbanism from around the world, including Filipina workers in Hong Kong who turned the ground floor of a bank into a community space (2010: 9) and the people of Mount Barker (Seattle, US) who saved their community garden from a private sale (2010: 10). Describing these areas as "insurgent public spaces," Hou states:

> From conversion of private homes into community third places to the occupation of streets for alternative uses, each of these acts may seem small and insignificant. But, precisely because these acts do not require overburdening investment or infrastructure, they enable individuals and often small groups to effect changes in the otherwise hegemonic urban landscapes.
>
> *(2010: 15)*

In his article "Do-It-Yourself Urban Design: The Social Practice of Informal 'Improvement' Through Unauthorized Alteration" (2014), Gordon C. Douglas looks at where urban interventions, like those above, intersect with design. Douglas's research has extended to include 14 cities and he orients their genesis in the 1960s-1970s (2014: 6). In his article, he provides examples of public interventions where the community have felt the local authorities have let them down in some aspect in regard to public space; for instance, the Highland Park Book Booth in Los Angeles, a re-appropriated telephone booth turned into a book depository (2014: 5), and the Urban Repair Squad of Toronto, who post stickers in subway stations saying "bikes allowed" in places where they are forbidden (2014: 18).

How we consider the "square movements" that have been taking place across the world in the last few years in regard to attempts by local people to hold on to their public spaces is worth investigating (e.g., the Gezi Park protests in Turkey in 2013). Stavros Stavrides asks: "Could we possibly understand the recent squares movement as an emergent form of such a contestation of dominant urban rhythms?" (2013: 44). He explains that "in the contemporary urban archipelago public space is space molded through rhythmicalities which sustain a state of normalized exception" and he suggests that the square movement, while not necessarily obliterating the power play of dominant forces in these spaces, nevertheless provides other options to local people, through "decentralization recentralization dialectics" and "coexisting initiatives" (2013: 45). Here, we can see new narratives available that work toward rewriting space form the position of the commons.

The variety of examples that appear under the rubric of DIY/Guerrilla Urbanism/Design demonstrates the breadth of creativity and the nuances within which these interventions operate. These multifarious interventions enable discussion on what can and cannot be placed under their title. For example, can the gravestone drawing shown in Figure 38.1 be considered graffiti or art, an urban intervention or a spontaneous act? One thing we can assume, though, is that this space was an embodied space at the time the artist made their mark, even if we are not certain of what they were trying to communicate to the viewer at the time.

In this section, we can see the variety of approaches to intervening in public (or private) space, ranging from what could be considered the ultra-masculine challenges to private space as demonstrated by the UrbExers, to the rather more aesthetic mediations such as yarn bombing and guerrilla gardening. What we will consider next is a form of urban critique that is both embodied and mobile: psychogeography.

Contemporary Mediated Psychogeographies

Most of the examples discussed so far do not look at the act of walking itself as a form of urban intervention or critique (not that one can easily separate the embodiment of placing oneself temporarily in that space in order to intervene in that moment, from the perambulatory action that takes you to that space in the first place). Nevertheless, it is the very process of walking that is the activist and/or critical aspect of psychogeography and enables a particular subjectivity to manifest on an immersive bodily level. This section will provide up-to-date examples of what could be termed psychogeographical events that relate directly to the act of creating moments (or situations) with regard to the body and its interactive relationship with the postmodern city. For a broader look at contemporary psychogeography in general, I direct you to my project *Walking Inside Out: Contemporary British Psychogeography* (2015).

Because of the multiplicity of walking practices that appear under the term "psychogeography" and also those that are not considered so by specific practitioners, it is best to be loose in our interpretation of the term and simply see it as a form of intentional walking that intervenes in space. Before we look at some examples it would befit us to consider psychogeography as a

Figure 38.1 Phoenix Drawing on a Gravestone in the Cemetery on the University of Leeds Campus in 2013

© Tina Richardson.

mode of communication. In his article, "The Alternative Urbanism of Psychogeography in the Mediated City," Zlatan Krajina quotes Raymond Williams in regard to materiality and culture:

> Psychogeographies produced by ordinary people during usual strolls though mediated urban space remind us how much "the modes of 'naturalisation' of . . . means of communicative production need to be repeatedly analysed and emphasised, for they are indeed so powerful, and new generations are becoming so habituated to . . . [this] reified mode."
>
> *(2016: 58)*

Krajina provides us with examples of ways that this "naturalization" can be challenged through the process of cultural-jamming-cum-psychogeography, whereby individuals can—as he provides in his example at Silicon Roundabout in London—reconsider their relationship with computerized advertising boards that proliferate in urban space today: the "negotiation of belonging in space via encounters with the changing surfaces of screens" (Krajina 2016: 46, 48). Advertisements are also considered by David Prescott-Steed in *The Psychogeography of Urban Architecture* (2013). He presents us with the *Lose Yourself in Melbourne* television advert (a city-sponsored tourist promotion), which he takes literally and uses as a springboard into a psychogeography of the city itself:

> If we take the *Lose Yourself in Melbourne* advertisement as a starting point, we can use it to map a trajectory from the past to the present, from the ideal to the material, from theory to practice, all the while changing what we see along the way.
>
> *(2013: 27)*

Prescott-Steed provides us with an academic's take on psychogeography in Australia; however, it is presented to the layperson in terms that make it accessible to everyone. One does not need to understand the theory of either the Situationists or that applied to contemporary psychogeography in order to partake in psychogeographical walks or events. Across the other side of the world, in the UK, the Museum of Walking arranges many immersive events that enable people to connect with their city. For example, in August 2017, there was an international sound walk that involved geolocation and performance. The event was launched at the Made of Walking International Festival in La Romieu, France, and was open to anyone. It involved utilizing methodologies from previous events from around the world that had already been undertaken and uploaded on a map by third parties. People could partake by clicking on the map to see the name and instructions of the previous event and could then create their own walk on Sound Walk Sunday (August 27, 2017). From Prague, there was a walk that included music and art. In Singapore, the "Umbrella for 2" walk enabled two individuals to listen to ambient sound played though the umbrella which utilized MP3 technology. On Sound Walk Sunday, people could choose from a multitude of past walks in order to create their own immersive situation anywhere in the world.

Another contemporary example is that of The Fourth World Congress of Psychogeography (4WCOP) who, surprisingly, have now had (only) three events, the last two both being called "The Fourth." This tongue-in-cheek reference to the playfulness of the Situationists is organized by academics and non-academics, and the annual conference includes both talks and walks that enable individuals to rewrite their city. Taking place in Huddersfield (UK) in 2017, there was a smell event by Witold van Ratingen: *Smells of the City: Scent, Modernity and Psychogeographical Perspectives*. This talk and walk highlighted the differences between smell in the built environment in regards to the modern and postmodern cities (for further discussion by a psychogeographer on smell and the city, see Henshaw, *Urban Smellscapes: Understanding and Designing Smell Environment*, 2014). Also included was an event that straddled the globe due to contemporary technology, such as the international event *Dérive Day*, organized by the developers of the Dérive App. This enabled walkers from around the world to use the same instructions given to them via the smartphone application, in their own particular city, demonstrating the contemporary way that the Situationist *dérive* (drift) has moved from one that creates a chance route using physical three-dimensional devices such as paper maps, to one where the digital/virtual can be employed to connect people across continents.

Neogeography and Mapping Situations

The process of (re)mapping, whether cognitive or physical, is often a key component in the lineage of psychogeography. The Situationists are well known for their *Naked City* maps and the Surrealists created their own maps of the world. Today, we have new technologies for mapping the spaces in which we move about. Often appearing under the umbrella of "neogeography," these modern tools can be used in conjunction with psychogeography and other urban critical practices in order to enable a deeper exploration of existing space, or in expressing local, subjective, or heterogeneous responses to space. Mark Graham explains how this works:

> All places are palimpsests. Among other things, places are layers of brick, steel, concrete, memory, history, and legend . . . The countless layers of any place come together in specific times and spaces and have bearing on the cultural, economic, and political characteristics, interpretations, and meanings of place.
>
> *(Graham 2010: 422)*

Psychogeography can utilize many tools as part of its practice, especially with regard to creating a chance route: from the basic rolling of a dice in order to decide direction to using maps from another city to walk your own. Part of the research for my own PhD thesis involved mapping the University of Leeds campus (Richardson 2014). On a number of walks over the summer with Leeds Psychogeography Group in 2009, we mapped our walks on the campus and in the immediate surrounding area with GPS software. By using OpenStreetMap, we then looked at the data uploaded by ourselves in conjunction with that uploaded by others (see Figure 38.2). The GPS signals, appearing as trails, creates the map itself, which is actually only white space containing dots where the signal is picked up and saved. Our own walks appear within the consolidation of trails you can see on this map, which also contain the routes of everyone else who has used the software and uploaded the data. Even though there is no pre-existing map outline on which these traces are placed, a map is formed out of them. Anyone familiar with the space can see the circumference of the campus, the main roads and, in one place, a zig-zag route taken between a row of terraced buildings.

These walks and the maps produced by them, whether intentional or not, place the practitioner bodily on the interface of physical and virtual space:

> This spontaneous (and remote) form of collaboration enabled walks to be woven across campus space, in a labyrinthine way, which were counter to the established paths. The participants (quite likely unknowingly) produced a rhizomatic space which responded to their own desires, but came together in the assemblage in the moment of making the online map, thus remapping the space itself.
>
> *(Richardson 2014: 200)*

Creating a Situation in the City

Figure 38.2 An Amalgamation of Dots That Reflected the GPS Location of Individuals Walking, Driving, or Cycling Around the Area Near the University of Leeds Campus at This Time

© Tina Richardson.

While we cannot see this space as what Marc Augé describes in his book *Non-Places: An Introduction to Supermodernity* (2008) as an absolute "world without frontiers" (2008: ix), in map form, it does appear as somewhat of a non-place, having nothing in it but the trails of the walker-participants. Augé explains that "the current globality consists of networks that produce homogenization and exclusion" but, also, do "not necessarily signify compartmentalization and separation" (2008: ix).

When exploring space, our interaction with this type of media can change our view and experience of that space as something solidly bounded are contained. Nevertheless, as Adam

Greenfield warns us in *Against the Smart City* (2013), we need to be careful with concepts that make us feel that the city is a seamless space, because using postmodern mobile devices that intervene in our connection with physical space "means that the user perceives no interruption in the flow of a technically mediated experience, even though the experience may be produced by the interaction of heterogeneous systems" (2013: 49). While this may not, at a cursory level, appear to be an issue, it follows that "the language of seamlessness implies that the hassles of everyday life have been mitigated by the intervention of powerful technologies, from whose complexity, in turn, the user has been carefully and deliberately shielded" (2013: 49).

However, and taking this into consideration, whichever complementary gadgets we choose to bring along with us on our urban explorations, the urban walker is also part of that toolbox inasmuch as they become a reflexive tool, responding to their environment, momentarily changing it, and themselves, at the same time. These types of tools, whether highly technological or not, can help us to turn space into place when used judiciously.

Conclusion: (Re)Constructing the City

It is apparent from this chapter alone how blurred the boundaries are among psychogeography, urban explorations, and DIY urbanism. Even though each of these forms of urban intervention has their own definition, often articulated by both academics and practitioners, we need to remain mindful that, in a way, it is their nebulous nature and the vagueness of their definitions that make them a malleable stratagem that can be appropriated by anyone who chooses to engage with their town or city. This is as important today as it has been at any time since the emergence of the modernist city:

> The idea of rewriting and remapping urban space has taken hold at a time when communicating with each other has never been easier (aided by the Internet and social networking). This has coincided with a geopolitical moment when people are aware they have a stake in a city that is diminishing before their eyes.
>
> *(Richardson 2015: 246)*

What is at stake can become apparent to the urban critic through the medium of their own bodies and through any interactive media that may appear in urban space or be used to observe and analyze it. However, what can easily be forgotten is our phenomenological relationship with the space itself, because the actual space also has a mediated relationship with something beyond itself and, therefore, so do we. This is not because of what appears in between oneself (as subject) and the built environment (as object), but because urban space is also a medium!

In his essay "The Origin of the Work of Art," Martin Heidegger explains how the Greek temple comes about. The temple, built by the citizens themselves, served to order their lives: it constituted the law and was the central point of political and sociocultural connections. As Heidegger states, it "makes visible the invisible" (2000: 89), because the temple represented the Gods and in its physical form illuminated the lives of the people. The temple formed the ground on which they led their daily lives; it became "the naming power of the word" (Heidegger 2000: 91). However, whilst the citizens had created the temple in order to house their Gods, over time, and through a process of cultural amnesia, they forgot that they had created the temple.

We, too, can forget that we created our cities. And while we may feel, in a phenomenological sense, that cities appear as something "out there" as opposed to us, being "in here" in our own separate internal worlds, we actually construct/reconstruct the city by changing our relationship with it, through "temporarily occupying and reimaging the spaces of the city" (Garrett 2013: 6).

When we engage with our cities in a different way than the quotidian of our everyday lives, we can cross thresholds which change both us and our cities, because "[g]oing beyond normally circumscribed boundaries forces one to think" (Garrett 2013: 8).

References

Althusser, L. (2006) "Ideology and Ideological State Apparatuses (Notes Towards an Investigation)," *Lenin and Philosophy and Other Essays*, trans. B. Brewster, Delhi: Aakar Books, pp. 85–126.
Augé, M. (2008) *Non-Places: An Introduction to Supermodernity*, London and New York: Verso.
Batty, D. (2016) "Urban Explorers Risking Lives and Arrest for Social Media Glory, Say Experts," *The Guardian*, viewed August 9, 2017, www.theguardian.com/uk-news/2016/mar/18/urban-explorers-arrest-social-media-base-jumper-free-running-parkour.
Coverley, M. (2006) *Psychogeography*, Harpenden: Pocket Essentials.
Debord, G (2005) *The Society of the Spectacle*, Detroit, MI: Black and Red.
— (2006) "Report on the Construction of Situations and on the International Situationist Tendency's Conditions of Organization and Action," in K. Knabb (ed.) *Situationist International Anthology*, Berkeley, CA: Bureau of Public Secrets, pp. 25–43.
De Certeau, M. (1988) *The Practice of Everyday Life*, trans. S. Rendall, Berkeley, Los Angeles, CA, and London: University of California Press.
Douglas, C. C. (2014) "Do-It-Yourself Urban Design: The Social Practice of Informal 'Improvement' Through Unauthorized Alteration," *City and Community*, 13(1), pp. 5–25.
Edensor, T. (2005) *Industrial Ruins: Space, Aesthetics and Materiality*, Oxford and New York: Berg.
Garrett, B. L. (2013) *Explore Everything: Place-Hacking the City*, London and New York: Verso.
Graham, M. (2010) "Neogeography and the Palimpsest of Place: Web 2.0 and the Construction of a Virtual Earth," *Tijdschrift voor Economische en Sociale Geografie*, 101(4), pp. 422–436.
Greenfield, A. (2013) *Against the Smart City*, New York: Do.
Heidegger, M. (2000) "The Origin of the Work of Art," in C. Cazeaux (ed.) *The Continental Aesthetics Reader*, Abingdon: Routledge, pp. 80–101.
Henshaw, Victoria (2014) *Urban Smellscapes: Understanding and Designing Smell Environment*, London: Routledge.
Hou, J. (2010) "(Not) Your Everyday Public Space," in J. Hou (ed.) *Insurgent Public Space: Guerrilla Urbanism and the Remaking of Contemporary Cities*, London and New York: Routledge, pp. 1–17.
Krajina, Z. (2016) "The Alternative Urbanism of Psychogeography in the Mediated City," in D. B. Shaw and M. Humm (eds.) *Radical Space: Exploring Politics and Practice*, London and New York: Rowman and Littlefield International, pp. 39–63.
McDonough, T. F. (1994) "Situationist Space," *October*, 67(Winter), pp. 58–77.
Prescott-Steed, D. (2013) *The Psychogeography of Urban Architecture*, Boca Raton, FL: BrownWalker Press.
Richardson, T. (2014) "The Unseen University: A Schizocartography of the Redbrick University Campus," University of Leeds, unpublished.
Richardson, T. (ed.) (2015) "Conclusion: The New Psychogeography," *Walking Inside Out: Contemporary British Psychogeography*, London: Rowman and Littlefield International, pp. 1–27.
Situationist International (1996) in ed. L. Andreotti and X. Costa (eds.) *Theory of the Dérive and Other Situationist Writings on the City*, Barcelona: Museu d'Art Contemporani de Barcelona.
Stavrides, S. (2013) "Contested Urban Rhythms: From the Industrial City to the Post-Industrial Urban Archipelago," *The Sociological Review*, 61(S1), pp. 34–50.
Stein, H. F. (1987) *Developmental Time, Cultural Space: Studies in Psychogeography*, Norman, OK and London: University of Oklahoma Press.

Further Reading

Roberts, L. (ed.) (2015) *Mapping Cultures: Place, Practice, Performance*, London and New York: Palgrave Macmillan.
Solnit, R. (2002) *Wanderlust: A History of Walking*, London and New York: Verso.
Wark, M. (2011) *The Beach Beneath the Street: The Everyday Life and Glorious Times of the Situationist International*, London and New York: Verso.

39
MEDIATED URBAN PROTEST
Practicing Dissent in Hybrid City Spaces

Tetyana Lokot

Introduction

Urban studies in its infancy was largely understood to cover urban planning and civil engineering, but came to encompass issues of politics and power (e.g., in the Northern American tradition, where issues of race, class and economic status were intrinsic to urban affairs and planning decisions). Today's mediated cities are complex environments where geographies, urban practices, technology, human interactions and politics meld together, and need to be studied as such.

Protest as a social and political phenomenon has always been closely tied with cities, especially as factors such as centralization of power in urban conglomerates and the general urbanization of the population came into play. But much of the early political, sociological and anthropological research on protests and urban protests paid little attention to the role of media in how protests are organized and how they play out in the city.

At the same time, the role of media—first mainstream, and later digital and networked—in protest mobilization and organization has been the focus of a number of scholars in communication and media studies. However, in this case media and their influence (and later, technologies and their affordances) have been the central focus of such research, without heeding the broader context of how these protest activities were mediated within urban spaces and everyday practices.

This chapter argues that the use of digitally networked media for civic action and protest must be analyzed within the broader context of mediated human activity in cities. Urban protest today occurs simultaneously online, offline and in urban spaces. This hybridity and multi-spatiality calls for an interdisciplinary approach to studying mediated urban protest, accounting for the urban environment as a digitally mediated spatial context, the platforms and technologies that mediate protest activity in the city, and the political and cultural context of dissent.

The chapter draws on the work of sociologist Henry Lefebvre (1996) and geographer David Harvey (2008) as well as the research by protest scholars such as Paolo Gerbaudo (2012) and Zeynep Tufekçi (2017), the work of researchers focused on networked activism, such as W. Lance Bennett and Alexandra Segerberg (2012), and media and politics scholars such as Andrew Chadwick (2013). This interdisciplinary literature allows for a richer, more diverse discussion of the evolution of urban-mediated protest research, incorporating work from different fields to better theorize about how dissent happens in mediated cities.

The chapter presents multiple case studies, many of them non-Western, to showcase the multifaceted canvas of mediated urban protests around the world. Case studies include the Gezi Park protests (Istanbul, Turkey), the Occupy Movement and its protests around the world, Tahrir Square protests (Cairo, Egypt) and other Arab Spring events, the Bolotnaya Square protests (Moscow, Russia) and the Euromaidan protests (Kyiv, Ukraine). These cases demonstrate the variety of protests in modern cities and underscore the need to combine the study of digitally augmented protest organization and contentious action with the study of the city itself as a spatially multiple yet material environment that is inextricably linked to urban protest activity.

Right to the City

Cities have always been understood as a cite of contestation, conflict and struggle for power, whether social, economic or political. Henry Lefebvre in his work *The right to the city*, first published in 1968, advocates for restructuring the power relations involved in the production of urban space. Lefebvre suggests that by claiming the right to the city, its citizens claim a broader "right to urban life" (Lefebvre 1996: 158) that allows them to structure both social relations and lived space within cities. It is only natural then that cities are where protest and contestation germinate, as citizens collectively seek to stake their claim to exert some measure of control and make decisions about how their city is built and shaped and how it lives. Harvey discusses the right to the city as a prime example of the exercise of collective power—a right to change ourselves as well as "to change and reinvent the city more after our hearts' desire" (Harvey 2012: 4).

The right to the city is also closely connected to the notion of citizenship, which is central to the act of protest. Purcell (2002) notes that Lefebvre combines the concept of a citizen with that of an urban denizen, a dweller of the city. For these citizens/inhabitants, claiming the right to their city involves two key rights: the right to participation in decision-making about the city, and the right to appropriation, i.e., the right to access, occupy and produce the material urban space they are embedded in (Purcell 2002). Certainly, such a theoretical approach to understanding the collective rights of urban citizens has applications beyond decisions and spaces within cities, and can also inform a broader politics of democratic participation in modern societies. It is no surprise, then, that cities continue to be the chosen locales for mass protest activity as an expression of political agency for engaged citizenry. But it is also evident that the collective dissent stretches far beyond claiming the right to the city and that urban protesters are fighting for a wide variety of social, political and economic transformations.

As frequent sites of protest activity, modern cities become focal points for the actions of protest movements that are often transnational (Köhler and Wissen 2003), yet concerned with how global issues are reflected in local contexts. Protesters often target representatives and headquarters of international institutions that are predominantly based in large megalopolises. Local and national authorities governing decision-making and exerting power in urban environments are also frequent targets of contentious action. In some cases, protests in cities may begin with a limited, explicitly urban agenda directly tied to rights claims to urban space, such as the threat to Istanbul's Gezi Park that led to mass protests in Turkey (Örs 2016; Gül et al. 2014) or the lack of affordable housing that led to the Israel 2011 protest movement (Marom 2013). But even such single-issue protests tend to develop to encompass broader problems and become more politically inclusive movements inviting civic action.

No matter the focus of urban protests, be it access to city infrastructure or opposition to illegal construction, the city inevitably becomes the stage where citizens contest hegemonic power and negotiate their collective demands. It is also where conflicts come to a head, often resulting in state-sanctioned violence or crackdowns on expressions of dissent. This embeddedness in the urban cityscape also has implications for how protests are interpreted, covered by or represented in the media and remembered. But in more material ways, today's multiply mediated cities and the multi-spatial practices and struggles of their inhabitants also shape how protest movements emerge and how their claims are developed and voiced. In other words, the mediatedness of urban life and the hybrid nature of urban spaces have a direct impact on how protest is practiced and experienced as a disruptive, but inevitable part of urban life.

Even though not all protests in urban locales might focus on explicitly hyperlocal issues of participation or appropriation, those involved in the act of protest nonetheless seek to remake their city: first, by embedding the claims and aims of the protest in the urban space they are co-producing; and second, by restructuring the mediated relations of power, access and information, grafted onto networks of relationships and the material and digital infrastructure of the city. Attempting to change their city through protest, the people seek to transform themselves, exercising "the freedom to make and remake" themselves and their cities (Harvey 2008: 24). In order for scholarly inquiry to capture those transformations in terms of agency, power relations and access to space, we must approach urban protest as a multi-dimensional, multi-spatial and multi-temporal assemblage (Davies 2012) of variously mediated spatial practices. Importantly, though, it is crucial to understand that the mediated nature of urban protests is not confined to the digital media realm and extends into various hybrid configurations where material and spatial aspects are just as central.

Protest and Digital Media

Just as the scholarship focused on urban spaces and urban life was at the outset mostly limited to fields such as geography or anthropology, the study of protest has in the past also been primarily the pursuit of scholars of sociology and political science. Traditionally, research on social movements, activism and protest focused on the cycles and frameworks of political mobilization (Tarrow 2011, 2013), as well as organizational structures of movements as institutions (e.g., McAdam et al. 1996; Davis et al. 2005). While these studies offered foundational theoretical concepts and models aimed at understanding collective action and contentious politics, the analyses rarely centered on the role of media in these processes. Rather, media technologies and their use were seen as supplementary rather than integral to protests and research often acknowledged only specific media forms, such as newspapers, television or other mainstream media channels (Mattoni and Treré 2014: 254) instead of adopting a more comprehensive approach.

After the advent of digital media, and especially technologies such as personal computing, mobile communication and social networking, scholars studying communications, politics and society have shifted their focus to exploring their role in political mobilization and civic participation processes. Both popular and academic views of the role of digital media range from cyberutopian to cyberdystopian and the democratizing potential of the internet and social media in particular remains a contentious issue (see also Chapter 21, this volume). Activists and governments in both democratic and authoritarian states find very different opportunities for action offered to them by these technologies. Still, there seems to be a certain scholarly fixation on digital media as both the field and the object of inquiry that results in a sort of platform fetishism around the power of communications technologies (Mattoni and Treré 2014).

More recent interdisciplinary research in the area strives for a more nuanced understanding of how digital media are entangled in the fabric of political participation, activism and protest. For instance, Chadwick (2013) demonstrates that "new" and "old" media platforms and practices co-exist and interact with each other as part of a complex hybrid media system, which also involves citizens, political bodies and other structures. On the other hand, Bennett and

Segerberg (2012) argue that the use of digital networked media by activists and protesters leads to a shift from collective to connective action, producing a new organizational pattern of action networks, where digitally enabled personal connections may emerge as an alternative to traditional political organizations and institutions. This kind of protest communication can connect a wider range of citizens and offer opportunities for more flexible, but ephemeral connections and mediate activist engagement via digital platforms. However, as Tufekçi (2017) cautions, social media and online networks can amplify protest movements as well as undermine their longevity, as they make speedy mobilization in protest movements easier while jeopardizing other elements of building dissent, such as sustainability and access to mainstream politics. Similarly, Lim (2014) argues that social movements today often emerge at the intersection of online and offline spaces: mobilization might occur on social media, but power is then contested and claims are made in urban public spaces, making the two dimensions interdependent.

From an urban media studies point of view, attending to the particulars of digital media's role in protest movements nonetheless preserves the fixation on media as the key element of an infinitely more complex environment of urban life. The use of any emerging media technologies is always rooted in the historical context of how power and movements are connected in particular spaces (Calhoun 1998), so understanding how activists and protesters use media to achieve their goals is predicated on a deeper understanding of spatial relations between those in power and the resistance. Responding to Morley's concerns about automatically canonizing new media as enabling protest or democratic development (Morley 2009), the opportunities for protest activity offered by digitally networked media, as well as their limitations, must be considered in a broader context of mediated human activity in cities.

Creating comprehensive scholarly frameworks for understanding the connections between media (and digital media in particular) and the work of modern social movements and protest groups is also hindered by the fragmented nature of social movement and protest studies (Mattoni and Treré 2014). Scholars working in this area tend to work on parallel tracks and draw on research from multiple fields such as political science, sociology, communication and internet studies, with little conceptual overlap, and this highlights the growing need for interdisciplinary work. Extending this logic further, in the study of urban-mediated protests, we must also account for the complex relationships between mediated protest practices and urban spaces, in order to tease out the significance of space, mobility and physical urban infrastructure in the modern practices of resistance. Communication networks augmented by digital technology often wrap around the existing practices and habits of urban denizens, embedding themselves in the city's structures and spaces to become only part of the everyday urban routines. Teasing out how these hybrid urban systems function in everyday and extraordinary circumstances should be the focus of research into urban-mediated protest.

Protest in Hybrid Urban Spaces

Morley's (2009) call for a "non-media-centric" approach that deals with both symbolic and material dimensions of lived reality is especially applicable to the urban media studies context, where the materiality of the city and its spaces is woven into the urban-mediated lived experience. The study of networked connections in largely symbolic terms can thus be made more meaningful when coupled with the analysis of more tangible social, infrastructural and geographical networks. Extending this concern with the materiality and spatiality of the mediated city, Tarantino and Tosoni (2013) call for an urban media studies that expands the liminal space between media-centered and place-centered approaches and looks at how the use of media by urban dwellers impacts their daily spatial practices. Such a practice-based approach focused on use scenarios is especially productive when analyzing the various tactics and activities of protesters operating in hybrid urban spaces, where concerns about connections, location and influence converge (see also Chapter 35, this volume).

A number of scholars have paid increasing attention to the role of mediated space in protest and activism. Nicholls (2008: 79) argues that the spatial geographies underlying social movement networks directly affect the relational dynamics in the movements depending on the locality/globality of the networks and contribute to the formation of "social movement space." Halvorsen (2012) further suggests that scholarly preoccupation with networks and networked spatialities often occludes the growing importance of material territories occupied by protesters in movements such as Occupy, leading some scholars to coin emergent protest modalities closely tied to the urban spaces claimed by protesters, such as protest squares (Patel 2013) or protest camps (McCurdy et al. 2016). Similarly, the notion of mobility as a symbolic idea of "access anywhere" becomes entangled with specific locations circumscribed by infrastructural concerns. Mobility, then, is defined in relation to urban spaces and how citizens move within them, but is also limited by those spaces where access to technology or connection to the network may be restricted or unavailable. The role of these various spatialities in contentious politics in cities is an important focus of scholarly study. Inevitably, the spatial and the social dimensions of social movement activity cannot be separated from each other (Martin and Miller 2003) as they impact each other in complex ways and must therefore be understood in concert.

Scholars focusing on protest, digital media and cities and operating in the interdisciplinary waters conducive to the productive study of contentious activity have generated a significant body of research that highlights key aspects of multiply mediated urban protest. Gerbaudo (2012) in his extensive field-based research calls for the need to understand exactly how the use of digital media and technologies resonates with street action and reshapes the repertoires of communication and contention for protesters from the Arab Spring to the Occupy movement. Georgiou (2013) also discusses the 2011 London riots and the Arab Spring events as examples of the amplified presence of marginalized groups on the city street and stresses that the mediated character of urban life contributed to the hyper-visibility of the local contestation on the global scale. The Occupy protest movement that began in 2011 in Zuccoti Park in the financial district of New York City emerges as one example of an urban-mediated protest that requires attention to both mediated connections and material spaces in order for its true nature to be revealed. As the protests against economic inequality spread worldwide, becoming multi-nodal and trans-urban (Georgiou 2013), scholars pointed to the powerful links between the mediated and the physical occupied space of the protests, embedded within high-traffic city areas, such as the Wall Street district in New York City. Reflecting on the networking logic of the Occupy Everywhere protests, Juris (2012) found that while activists used social media to connect individuals from different backgrounds and across cities, these connections actually contributed to the aggregation of protest participants within particular, especially visible urban physical spaces. Moreover, the geospatial characteristics of Occupy networks were reflective of the high-profile locations of the main protest action and this locale-oriented networked communication tended to reference activity around specific places and times (Conover et al. 2013). The urban street occupied by protesters became a representation of their civic and political concerns, but their mediated presence in this space also made visible the divisions they were rallying against. At the same time, being tuned into the mediated urban lifestyle granted protesters more control over their own visibility, allowing them to shape their occupation of the hybrid urban space along the lines of their political messages.

The combination of the tactics of occupying public space and making visible the presence of protesters in these spaces through multiple means is a common trend noted in the scholarship of urban protests. A stark example of this phenomenon is the Gezi Park protest in Istanbul, Turkey. Though initially the protest was aimed at saving the green park zone in central Istanbul from reconstruction, the occupied public space became a symbol of broader resistance against the Turkish authorities. The physical spaces of Gezi Park and nearby Taksim Square and their occupation by protesters turned into a nationwide protest movement, with the urban places of Gezi and Taksim coming to represent political opposition in a much broader context than the original resistance to city planning decisions (Gül et al. 2014). The idea of Gezi and of occupying public space such as a square or a park now serves a reference point for multiple resistance efforts in Turkish politics. Both mainstream media broadcasts and digital networks propagating images of the protest were important to the growth of participation in Gezi and Taksim action, but it was the hybrid urban space wherein the protest was simultaneously mediated through digital networks, public locations and citizen engagement with both that acted as a catalyst to rethinking the very concept of democratic deliberation. In fact, Örs (2016) argues that the Gezi protests were indicative of the change in how Istanbul residents engaged with public spaces, with the state and with each other in these spaces, reshaping the idea of democratic resistance as reclaiming both virtual and physical space for the public.

Existing public urban spaces such as parks and squares often serve as anchor points and arenas for protest activity, and often become eponymous with the protest itself: Tahrir Square in Cairo, Egypt was both a highly visible city landmark and a social media buzzword at the height of the resistance effort there (Tufekçi and Wilson 2012; Patel 2013). Often, though, citizens engaged in resistance seek to remake these urban spaces by claiming their own forms of ownership of these locations. McCurdy et al. (2016) provide one example of such appropriation of space by protesters in the form of protest camps. The camps, they argue, have a rich history and are not a new phenomenon, and yet, in a multiply mediated city, emerge as a particular space created specifically for enacting various repertoires of contention. These formations fuse together different infrastructures, practices and cultures, and rely on digital media and networks, but also certain routines and activities shaped by their place-based nature, to transmit and adapt tactical resistance mechanisms. Ukraine's Euromaidan protest serves as one example of a multiply mediated protest camp. Anchored in the central square in downtown Kyiv, the protest movement also set up its own camp-like infrastructure, creating and propagating a dissenting presence that was at once disruptive (tents in the city center, fires and burning tires) and at the same time conducive to deliberate and constructive action (field kitchen to feed protesters, a media center, technical support hubs and even a protest university with regular public lectures) (Lokot 2016). Euromaidan, like the Arab Spring protests, is sometimes dubbed a "Facebook revolution," but while digital media were part of the protest infrastructure, they were deeply embedded in, and connected to, the physically occupied and carefully constructed material scaffolding around the space of the protest in the city. When the action of Euromaidan was broadcast and shared through the media, the claims and confrontation were embodied in and represented by both the bodies and faces of protesting urban dwellers, and the soot-black tents, scuffed cobblestones and occupied public spaces of the city, rendering the city one with the protest.

As Georgiou notes, especially in highly mediated environments, human presence can itself be a form of political participation (Georgiou 2013), but it is both the presence of protesters in specific urban spaces and the affordances of digital media to make these spaces visible that contribute to global awareness and recognition of locally occurring expressions of dissent. The reaction of local authorities and law enforcement to the occupation and reinterpretation of public locations by protesters is also testament to the power of taking over a hybrid urban space. For instance, in Russia, the May 2012 OccupyAbay protest camp set up near the statue of Kazakh poet Abay in Moscow was significant not only because it drew a diverse group of active citizens from every political persuasion or because it represented a more static and stable continuation of the numerous but more ephemeral anti-government protest marches that preceded it (Volkov 2014). The speed with which the local law enforcement attempted to disband the resistance and remove the camp from public space (it only lasted from 9 to 16 May 2012 and was covered in much detail on social and mainstream media) is evidence that the Moscow authorities viewed such multiply mediated occupations of public space as attacks on their power and control over urban infrastructure and thus their control over the public as a whole. The combination of rhetorical presence and visibility in digital networks with physical presence and visible public disobedience in material urban space endowed the protest with a hybrid sort of power to capture public attention through multiple means and to be perceived as a threat to hegemonic rule in more than one sense.

Issers (2014) notes that this powerful multiply mediated disobedience tactic leads to the emergence of new "political toponymy," where the names of urban public spaces occupied by protesters come to represent the protests as a whole in public discourse and imagination. Examples of such toponyms include OccupyAbay and Bolotnaya Square in Moscow, Russia; (Euro)Maydan in Kyiv, Ukraine; Gezi Park and Taksim Square in Istanbul, Turkey; and Tahrir Square in Cairo, Egypt. How we talk about the protest, therefore, is closely connected to the spaces the protesters exist in. The evolution of such a toponymy is yet more evidence that any protest that originates within the hybrid spaces of modern cities is an amalgamation of mediated and spatial elements, digital and face-to-face interactions, material and virtual locales. Acts of resistance occupy both human imagination and public spaces in cities, airwaves and streets, and dissent is simultaneously mediated through social media updates and street art. Protesters claim the right to the hybrid city, where participation and appropriation are, like the city's denizens, at once online, offline and in the streets.

Conclusions

The chapter drew together the relevant aspects of technological mediation and materiality in the mediated city in the context of protest activity to demonstrate that both the infrastructure of the city and the media multiplexity of its citizens shape how contemporary protests are organized, made visible and perceived. Protest is thus seen as urban, emerging from the familiar spaces of the city, sometimes weaving extraordinary moments and sights into its daily fabric. At the same time, protest is seen as mediated, enmeshing material geographies of urban life and media use with extraordinary scenarios of mediation that also embed into the spaces and imaginaries of the city in protest.

The chapter situated mediated urban protest in the fairly recent urban media studies theoretical tradition, which seeks to bring together an interdisciplinary literature and to position itself at the intersection of more traditional fields. The chapter called for a de-centering of media and digital technology in protest studies, as well as anchoring the research in issues of spatial embodiment and presence—issues that, despite an overwhelming fixation on the digital, are very much present and relevant in urban protest studies. Further research is needed to examine urban protests as hybrid activity occurring in multiply mediated spaces, where material locations emerge as loci of representation of the ideal city (and the ideal citizen within it) and spaces where power is contested and reimagined, as protesters seek to change society, change the city—its material, digital and rhetorical shape—and, symbolically, change themselves within the city.

References

Bennett, W. L. and Segerberg, A. (2012) "The logic of connective action: Digital media and the personalization of contentious politics," *Information, Communication & Society*, 15(5), pp. 739–768.

Calhoun, C. (1998) "Community without propinquity revisited: Communications technology and the transformation of the urban public sphere," *Sociological Inquiry*, 68(3), pp. 373–397.

Chadwick, A. (2013) *The hybrid media system: Politics and power*, New York: Oxford University Press.

Conover, M. D. et al. (2013) "The geospatial characteristics of a social movement communication network," *PloS One*, 8(3), e55957.

Davies, A. (2012) "Assemblage and social movements: Tibet support groups and the spatialities of political organization," *Transactions of the Institute of British Geographers*, 37(2), pp. 273–286.

Davis, G. F. et al. (eds.) (2005) *Social movements and organization theory*, Cambridge, UK: Cambridge University Press.

Georgiou, M. (2013) *Media and the city*, Cambridge: Polity Press.

Gerbaudo, P. (2012) *Tweets and the streets: Social media and contemporary activism*, London: Pluto Press.

Gül, M. et al. (2014) "Istanbul's Taksim Square and Gezi Park: The place of protest and the ideology of place," *Journal of Architecture and Urbanism*, 38(1), pp. 63–72.

Halvorsen, S. (2012) "Beyond the network? Occupy London and the global movement," *Social Movement Studies*, 11(3–4), pp. 427–433.

Harvey, D. (2008) "The right to the city," *New Left Review*, 53, pp. 23–40.

Harvey, D. (2012) *Rebel cities: From the Right to the City to the Urban Revolution*, New York: Verso.

Issers, O. (2014) Политическая топонимика 2012: знаки текущего момента. *Вестник Омского университета*, 1(71), pp. 91–94.

Juris, J. (2012) "Reflections on #Occupy Everywhere: Social media, public space, and emerging logics of aggregation," *American Ethnologist*, 39(2), pp. 259–279.

Köhler, B. and Wissen, M. (2003) "Glocalizing protest: Urban conflicts and the global social movements," *International Journal of Urban and Regional Research*, 27(4), pp. 942–951.

Lefebvre, H. (1996) *Writings on cities*, Cambridge, MA: Blackwell.

Lim, M. (2014) "Seeing spatially: People, networks and movements in digital and urban spaces," *International Development Planning Review*, 36(1), pp. 51–72.

Lokot, T. (2016) *Augmented dissent: The affordances of ICTs for citizen protest (a case study of the Ukraine Euromaidan Protests of 2013–2014)* (Doctoral dissertation).

Marom, N. (2013) "Activising space: The spatial politics of the 2011 protest movement in Israel," *Urban Studies*, 50(13), pp. 2826–2841.

Martin, D. and Miller, B. (2003) "Space and contentious politics," *Mobilization: An International Quarterly*, 8(2), pp. 143–156.

Mattoni, A. and Treré, E. (2014) "Media practices, mediation processes, and mediatization in the study of social movements," *Communication Theory*, 24(3), pp. 252–271.

McAdam, D. et al. (eds.) (1996) *Comparative perspectives on social movements: Political opportunities, mobilizing structures, and cultural framings*, Cambridge, UK: Cambridge University Press.

McCurdy, P. et al. (2016) "Protest camps and repertoires of contention," *Social Movement Studies*, 15(1), pp. 97–104.

Morley, D. (2009) "For a materialist, non-media-centric media studies," *Television & New Media*, 10(1), pp. 114–116.

Nicholls, W. J. (2008) "The urban question revisited: The importance of cities for social movements," *International Journal of Urban and Regional Research*, 32(4), pp. 841–859.

Örs, İ. R. (2016) "Genie in the bottle: Gezi Park, Taksim Square, and the realignment of democracy and space in Turkey," in S. Benhabib and K. Volker (eds.) *Toward new democratic imaginaries: İstanbul seminars on Islam, culture and politics*, Springer, Cham, pp. 51–61.

Patel, D. (2013) *Roundabouts and revolutions: Public squares, coordination, and the diffusion of the Arab uprisings*, Paper presented at the annual meeting of the MESA. Retrieved from http://aalims.org/uploads/Patel.pdf.

Purcell, M. (2002) "Excavating Lefebvre: The right to the city and its urban politics of the inhabitant," *GeoJournal*, 58(2–3), pp. 99–108.

Tarantino, M. and Tosoni, S. (2013) "Introduction: Beyond the centrality of media and the centrality of space," *First Monday*, 18(11). Retrieved from http://firstmonday.org/ojs/index.php/fm/article/view/4953.

Tarrow, S. (2011) *Power in movement: Social movements and contentious politics*, Cambridge, UK: Cambridge University Press.
Tarrow, S. (2013) *Contentious politics*, Hoboken, NJ: Blackwell Publishing Ltd.
Tufekçi, Z. (2017) *Twitter and tear gas: The power and fragility of networked protest*, New Haven, CT: Yale University Press.
Tufekçi, Z. and Wilson, C. (2012) "Social media and the decision to participate in political protest: Observations from Tahrir square," *Journal of Communication*, 62(2), pp. 363–379.
Volков, D. (2014) «ОккупайАбай»-уличный протестный лагерь в Москве в мае 2012 года глазами его участников. *Вестник общественного мнения. Данные. Анализ. Дискуссии*, 1–2 (117), pp. 155–197.

Further Reading

Barassi, V. (2013) "Ethnographic cartographies: Social movements, alternative media and the spaces of networks," *Social Movement Studies*, 12(1), pp. 48–62.
Georgiou, M. (2013) *Media and the city*, Cambridge: Polity Press.
Gerbaudo, P. (2012) *Tweets and the streets: Social media and contemporary activism*, London: Pluto Press.

40
COMMUNITY, MEDIA, AND THE CITY

Andrea Medrado

Introduction: Visions of Community

Historically, the concept of community has occupied a prominent place in urban sociological thinking. When revisiting some of the debates that have revolved around it, Anthony Cohen criticizes how earlier urban sociologists tended to perceive community as a quality of social life that was intrinsic to rural society. Some of community's main attributes were assumed to be small, parochial, face-to-face, traditional, and conservative. Being in a community was assumed to entail interacting as persons who had comprehensive "personal knowledge of each other," as their relationships were underpinned by almost unbreakable ties of affinity and community (Cohen 2001: 25). Such perception is a legacy from canonical work such as that of Ferdinand Tönnies ([1887] 1963) who established a distinction between *gemeinschaft*, or community, and *gesellschaft*, or society, and Emile Durkheim's (1893) canonical distinction between organic and mechanical solidarity. These models, as well as those that followed, such as the "Darwinian" model of the Chicago school, responded to the rise of the urban society at the turn of the 20th century and recognized emerging forms of human association as rather technical outcomes of life in mass society. The idea of community was linked to notions thought to be characteristic primarily of rural societies, or familial, intimate, private, and informal bonds of affection. In contrast, mass and urban society was deemed largely anachronistic to communal solidarity; that is, public and rational, resting on depersonalized relationships, and specialized roles occupied in the industrial society.

As Simon Parker summarized, subsequent reflections revolved around defining what community is, and especially what community ought to be (2004: 97). A particularly relevant debate was that on the question of whether feelings of solidarity and social unity can be harnessed in densely populated urban core areas. In their celebrated study of *Family and Kinship in East London* ([1953] 1986), Michael Young and Peter Willmott offered a positive answer to this question, arguing for the recognition of what was elsewhere recognized as the "rediscovery of the primary group." For Young and Willmott, the view that cities might only lead to a blasé attitude of social withdrawal simply was not consistent with the experience of the working-class East End London subjects they studied (Young and Willmott 1992: xix, cited in Parker 2004: 75). Hebertz Gans also believed that a sense of community could thrive among central city populations who might as well enjoy the Gemeinschaft or villagelike quality of urban life

(Gans 1982, cited in Parker 2004: 77). Indeed, Jane Jacobs argued that density and diversity, combined with tolerable living conditions, are in fact essential components of urban community life (Jacobs 1992: 208, cited in Parker 2004: 79–80).

In other contexts, such as the Brazilian, Raquel Paiva proposed a more political understanding of community, whereby people can show acts of solidarity and form a community as politically engaged subjects in response to the shattering of their social fabric (Paiva 1998; Félix et al. 2017: 99). Indeed, later approaches sought to understand emergent communities based on shared interests and not necessarily a shared location, as was made possible by the media. As Jankowski and Prehn (2002) put it, communities can gather people who share "cultural, social or political interests," which can function as a key organizational principle, just as geographically circumscribed communities, such as villages, neighborhoods, towns, and even cities, are formed around location (Jankowski and Prehn 2002: 5).

This chapter discusses community, media, and the city, with particular attention to contingent community media practices in dangerous urban spaces in Brazil. I reaffirm the familiar argument that, despite the assumption that media supposedly allow citizens to live free from dynamics of locality and community, urban communities remain extremely important for debates about mediated cities. I also pay particular attention to the role that community media can play in the process of community building, as well as having relevance for people's belonging to the city. As I will show, rather than being reduced to documenting community folklore, different (offline and online) community media initiatives can serve citizens as practical (material) resources in their everyday lives structured by forms of inequality (see also Chapter 33, this volume). To explicate my arguments, I will draw from my previous research on community ("lamppost") radio's role in the everyday life of Pau da Lima (Medrado 2010) and my current research on how residents of favelas, marginalized by city authorities and mainstream media, make use of social media to create a network of solidarity and protection (Medrado and Souza 2015). Here, I refer to a broad definition of marginalization, which refers to the exclusion from participation from spheres of social life, leading to a state of economic, cultural or political disadvantage and deprivation (Keung, Li, and Song 2007). Finally, I will explore instances in which urban and community media are deeply intertwined as the latter represent important forms of "urban communication infrastructures" (Georgiou, Motta, and Livingstone 2016: 4–6).

Favela: Community as a Form of Resistance?

The favelas take their name from a robust plant that thrives in the arid Northeast, the region where most of the early immigrants who moved to Brazil's larger and wealthier cities came from. The etymological roots of the term "favela" matter because they present a deep symbolic dimension. The favelas are resilient plants that manage to stay alive against all odds, such as unfamiliar territories, unfavorable conditions, and recursive attempts to eradicate them. This is certainly also the case with the favela communities and their residents. Licia Valladares (2005) and Janice Perlman (1976) have addressed the ways in which the favela communities have historically defied urban policies which involved evictions, the "social cleansing" of favela areas, as well as the ingrained prejudices against favela residents. Here, Cohen's discussion of community proves once again helpful. He notes that the consciousness of community lay in shared perceptions of symbolic boundaries, which themselves are constitutive of communities as well as being constituted by people through interaction (2001: 13). Thus, it is crucial that we always begin with looking at the symbolic processes of the constitution of boundaries and that we focus on the "essentially symbolic nature of the idea of community itself, essentially enshrined in the concept of boundary" (Cohen 2001: 14). There is no community without rehearsed difference from other communities.

The urban context poses yet another important challenge; that is, a working contradiction. As Goldberger (2001) famously put it, the urban impulse is an impulse toward community, at different scales and in different forms. In important ways, the city represents the typical place for the flourishing of communities because it is thought to provide protection to its inhabitants. At the same time, residents of marginalized areas often have very distinct experiences of the wider city area, and the sense of protection can be coupled with a sense of insecurity and rejection. They are often subjected to discrimination, segregation, and even violence. Echoing previous historical examples such as Jewish ghettos in Europe during World War II, Loic Wacquant discusses the idea of neo-ghettoization in some of Chicago's deprived areas and Paris's lower-class districts, describing the condition of "advanced marginality." This condition is "fed by the fragmentation of wage labor, the reorientation of state policy away from social protection and in favor of market compulsion, and the generalized resurgence of inequality" (Wacquant 2014: 47). In the remainder of this chapter, I focus on precisely the impulse toward community as protection from within the dangerous city, or community formation as a mechanism of resisting oppression coming from both the neoliberal and authoritarian state, especially its surveillance policies.

What Makes It Community Media?

There has been an extensive debate about defining community media (Howley 2005). As Lewis (2006) has noted, the adoption of different terms has depended upon different historical and geographical contexts that "community media" stem from, such as "public access cable TV" in Canada and the United States (Berrigan 1977), "miners' radio" in Bolivia (O'Connor 1990), or "popular" media practices in Brazil (Gianotti 2016). Yet, despite this great variety of contexts and experiences, a few common points emerge: they are aimed at specific audiences, namely the communities in which the stations or initiatives are located or to which they speak regardless of location; and they are smaller-scale media (in contrast to mainstream media). Additionally, even in the context of niche markets and highly segmented Internet content and cable TV output, they are arguably better positioned to address the needs of the community than mainstream media.

In some cases, such as multicultural community radios, a greater plurality of viewpoints is recognized than in mainstream media. Salvatore Scifo (2016) conducted a study of how community radio was introduced as a third media sector in the United Kingdom, distinguished from both the public service and the commercial sectors. Unlike Brazil, a traditional immigration country that has gradually become an emigration area with a significant migratory reversal in the 1980s (Brzozowski 2012), in the UK, immigration remains at high levels. As Scifo suggests, one of the key concerns with community radio in the UK has been to cater for a culturally diverse society. He studied ALL FM, a radio station based in Manchester that catered for the catchment areas of Ardwick, a dense social housing area that had large numbers of refugees, Longsight, which had a thriving scene of Asian small and medium enterprises, and Levenshulme, which was also known for its significant cultural diversity (Scifo 2016: 217). In order to meet its multicultural purposes, ALL FM's strategy included:

> Putting in place a rotating playlist comprising Chart, Gold and Community (Asian, African, Irish and African Caribbean music) during breakfast and drive-time shows and programmes in foreign languages that include Somali, Farsi and Kashmiri shows, allegedly with a large following in their homeland and across the UK.
>
> *(ALL FM 2004: 26–27, cited in Scifo 2016: 218)*

However, running a multicultural community station was not devoid of challenges. Scifo notes, for instance, that as "the sense of communities of interest—based on ethnic groups, age groups or music genre—was arguably stronger than the sense of community of place, listeners often tuned in for specialist ethnic programmes." As a result, very few of them listened to the station continuously through the whole day (Scifo 2016: 216).

The issue of why people listen seems important to better understand the dynamics of communication in the relationship between communities and their media and the place of media technologies and practices in the constitution of communities like favelas. In what follows, I draw from my ethnographic reception study (2006–2010) of a community radio in a Brazilian impoverished community, Pau da Lima, which serves as a particularly relevant case because of its pronounced material and sensorial presence in the outdoor spaces of the neighborhood.

The Lamppost Radio and Its Urban Community

Pau da Lima is a large working-class neighborhood with several favela areas, within a district of approximately 25,000 inhabitants, located at the heart of Salvador, a city of 2.6 million inhabitants (Sistema de Informação Municipal de Salvador 2010). Pau da Lima's radio station "Pop Som" was founded in 1998 by a long-term resident, Edson Sales. It consisted of 22 loudspeakers attached to the lampposts in busy places, such as bus stops, grocery stores, and churches, hence the "lamppost radio" (*rádio de poste*) (see Figure 40.1). Although its programming was not broadcast via FM radio waves but, rather, by old-fashioned loudspeakers, the residents of Pau da Lima tended to perceive the lamppost radio as their "community radio station." One young resident, Ana Claudia, stated that:

> It is a community station because "Pop Som" addresses issues that are common problems in Pau da Lima, such as how to prevent dengue. I know and they know about these issues because we've lived here all our lives. We speak the same language. They sound like we sound.

Even if just consisting of public speakers, the lamppost radio contributed to fostering a sense of belonging among residents. For Clemência Rodriguez, this is a central feature of community media, which implies "becoming one's own storyteller, regaining one's own voice, reconstructing the self-portrait of one's own community and one's own culture" (2001: 3).

However, other opinions, such as that of an elderly woman who lived very close to one of the loudspeakers, reflected on some of the tensions involved in listening to the station:

> Sometimes they play annoying songs and I just have to listen to them . . . [But] they do open up for the community. My son is involved in a community theatre group and the presenters always mention stuff about it.

Her comments seem to contradict some of the academic perspectives on community radio. Several authors have written on how community radio, for instance, needs to entail democratic production processes with significant levels of participation from the communities involved (Hochheimer 1993). And, yet, listening to community radio via loudspeakers did not seem like something of an intensive democratic nature: listeners did not really have a choice but to listen and did not seem to be concerned about their participation in programming. Given the somewhat non-democratic nature of having to listen to the sounds being relayed by the public loudspeakers, let us return to our initial question here: what made the lamppost radio community radio?

Community, Media, and the City

Figure 40.1 Lamppost Radio "Pop Som," Pau da Lima, Salvador, Brazil
Photograph by Andrea Medrado.

My ethnographic research indicated that the sense of community was deeply linked to the issue of radio's presence. Residents largely shared the experience of relying on the lamppost radio in managing their daily rounds in the neighborhood. In spatial terms, the loudspeakers were strategically placed in places where they could be easily seen and heard. People within various age-ranges knew where the studio was located and appreciated the fact that its doors were always open. As indicated by my respondent, some community groups made extensive use of the lamppost radio as a campaigning resource because they could easily access the studio, talk to the presenters, and ask them to promote their events. I saw my respondent's son walking into the studio and handing in a piece of paper to the radio presenter who then immediately read an announcement about a community theatre play that would be happening on that weekend (Medrado 2010: 146). Whilst such practices of community building were not entirely democratic in normative terms, the lamppost radio gained importance as an everyday sonic presence in the community.

While the presence of the radio in the daily lives of residents supported their sense of belonging to the neighborhood, the lamppost radio also transformed their experience of the favela by augmenting their urban soundscape. This was well illustrated by the appreciation of another young resident, Nelson, for the radio's provision of what he refers to as "a soundtrack to the streets":

> I remember listening to good songs on the lamppost radio when I came back from school last year, around 5 or 6 o'clock. They had a programme, something about slow romantic songs. The music was good, calm, soothing, not noisy, usually *Música Popular Brasileira* (MPB) and it made me feel good coming home from a day at school.

In the loud environment of Pau da Lima's main avenue, a "calm" MPB song is a form of desired urban intervention by the community radio makers and a marker of Nelson's end of the day, representing a smooth transition from school to home. This resonates with some of Paddy Scannell's (1996) thoughts on the ontologically reassuring repetitiveness or "dailiness" of broadcasting. It appears that when it plays a soothing song at the end of a working day, "Pop Som" radio displays good knowledge of the daily routines of those moving around the neighborhood. The difference here from Scannell's reflections on the presence of public service broadcasting (BBC) in UK homes is that the "dailiness" of "Pop Som" does not refer to a domestic setting in a strict sense but rather to the sense of familiarity rehearsed in the streets. This, in turn, seems to confirm some of my respondents' perceptions that in order to be felt as "community," it is important that people who work at the station know intimately and reflect the perceived rhythms and characteristics of the neighborhood.

Community Media as "Community Infrastructures" in the Mediated City

So far, this chapter has analyzed the role that community radio can play in the processes of community building. In this section, I will focus on my current research on how residents of marginalized neighborhoods in Rio de Janeiro make use of social media as a resource for navigating daily life in a post-Olympic context. In 2018, Rio was facing the consequences of what many believe to be ill-conceived urban policies that aimed to prepare the city for the 2014 Soccer World Cup and the 2016 Olympics (see also Chapter 26, this volume). These can be summarized as: (a) the gentrification of impoverished areas that particularly affected the favelas located in the wealthy South Zone of the city; (b) segregation processes, such as the installation of walls to cover bordering areas of Favela da Maré and prevent visitors from the sights of poverty; and (c) the militarization of daily life as part of a larger government-sponsored program of "pacification" of the favelas, which involves a military-style occupation of selected areas (Comitê Popular da Copa e das Olimpíadas 2015).

Some of the questions that permeated the reconstruction of Rio for the Olympics included the state's projection of Rio as the marvelous city of beautiful landscapes and exotic attractions being marketed to global tourists. Indeed, there is a vast literature suggesting that a concern with the image of host cities is central to the study of mega events (Freitas et al. 2016). In practice, host urban spaces are remodeled and reconstructed so as to articulate in material space certain projected ideas. The problem is that such transformations do not necessarily meet the needs of the host city's inhabitants. Similar issues occurred in other cities, such as London, which hosted the Olympics in 2012. Phil Cohen, for instance, interviewed residents in the borough of Newham, East London, where he discovered that people worried that the social character of the area would change with the influx of affluent middle-class professionals (2013: 311–312).

In Rio's case, there was widespread anxiety about the need to achieve a greater control of the favela spaces. One of the most publicized of interventions that attempted this was the inclusion of Pacifying Police Units (UPPs) in several favela areas in Rio, a government-sponsored program that started in 2008 and is still being carried out today. In its earlier years, between 2008 and 2010, the so-called pacification program was praised by gains in public security, particularly in the upper-class neighborhoods. According to specialists interviewed by BBC Brazil at that time, the UPP project's main strength was to remove from drug traffickers the control over the favela communities (Carneiro 2010). However, confidence in the program was shortly after seriously hurt by allegations of human rights abuses by police officers (Watts 2014). According to the City of Rio's Defense of Human Rights Commission, in addition to accusations of police brutality, the violations included the harassment of residents, and the constant invasion of residents' homes. Additionally, Rio's public safety policies were driven by an overt militarization of daily lives in the favelas. According to Júlia Valente (2014), the term refers to the employment of military tactics and personnel, treating the favelas as enemy territories and criminalizing their entire population, particularly favelas' black youth.

In what follows, I draw from another favela case study, which explores how a group of favela activists appropriated social media as a daily resource to live in a post-Olympic militarized city. Since its launch in 2014, the Facebook page Maré Vive (www.facebook.com/Marevive) has managed to gather over 130 thousand likes and describes itself as "a community media channel produced collaboratively by residents." My in-depth interviews and ethnographic observations online and offline in 2017 suggest that Maré Vive adopted a community media profile by addressing neighborhood-specific issues having to do in particular with broader problems residents face, such as social inequality, racism, and police brutality. As is well known in urban studies, the neighborhood remains the basic spatial unit and organizational principle of urban communities. Historically, New York's Harlem has been a quintessential case in point. As Steve Pile et al. suggested, Harlem developed a double meaning, as a powerful global symbol of black urban culture, or "a global city within a global city," while also, for most of its history, being an economically deprived neighborhood in New York (Pile et al. 2005: 21).

In the Latin American context, many scholars have written about how the favelas have historically suffered from territorial but also academic stigmatization (Mooney 2005: 75) as well as being regarded as the homes of the dangerous classes and the sources of fear and anxiety in the city (Perlman 1976; Valladares 2005). Scholars writing in the 1930s until approximately the late 1960s (Agache 1930) specifically saw favelas as homes to "disorderly" people, crowded into "disorderly" places, and certainly not prone to constituting functional communities. Though such value-laden qualifications never entirely disappeared from public discourse, anthropologists such as William Mangin (1967) and Janice Perlman (1976) demonstrated various ways in which the favelas represented solutions to difficult social problems, such as providing housing for impoverished migrants. This paradigm shift allowed us to understand favelas as cohesive, organized places where mutual solidarity and community are frequent.

In order to assure the image of order for the international audience attending the Olympics in Rio, many security policies focused on subjecting favela residents to constant surveillance by the military police. Renata Souza (2017) refers to this phenomenon as the "militarization of daily life," which deeply affects the residents of Maré. Located in the North Zone of Rio de Janeiro, Maré is often referred to as a "complex of favelas" as there are 16 sub-areas within its boundaries. The problem is that different rival drug trafficking gangs control different areas. Thus, in order to make the favela safer for the World Cup, in April 2014, the authorities sent 2,700 army troops to occupy Maré (Roque 2014), which remained there until June 2015. During this period, accounts of human rights violations were frequent. After the military left the favela and the Government has not completed its plans to introduce a pacifying unit there, there have been frequent police operations in Maré. When these happen, residents, including elderly people and children, have to cope with intense gunfire exchanges, resulting in the closing of schools and a wide-ranging interruption of daily life. In response to this war zone-like context, the Facebook page Maré Vive posts several daily updates about the safety conditions of its various sub-areas, particularly when there are police operations taking place. Many posts enquire about the safety conditions in different areas of Maré and quickly find up-to-date information in the comment space from residents in different areas. Thus, residents who are on their way home in the favela can constantly check in to the page and hopefully avoid most dangerous areas, as illustrated by the following post (see Figure 40.2), which attracted 46 comments.

Maré Vive: Hey, people, good evening. How are we doing at the moment?
Comment 1: Maré Vive could be set up in an automatic mode and post every day the following sentence: be careful, resident, there is shooting in the "divisa" area.
Comment 2: That's a shame. Unfortunately, we need to live in this situation. I don't live in the divisa area [bordering area between Nova Holanda and Baixa], I am from Pinheiro, but it makes me sad and worried that you have to go through this. We have to ask for God's blessings and protection for everyone who's coming home.
Comment 3: Lots of shooting in the divisa area.
Comment 4: Shootings at this exact moment.

This extract of forms of community self-management via social media demonstrates the relevance of what Georgiou, Motta, and Livingstone referred to as communication infrastructures of daily life in mediated cities. The authors note that such infrastructures "can provide individuals with material and symbolic tools—assets—that help them manage everyday life, as well as access to resources to others in the locale" (2016: 7). Such resources can then be "summoned, mobilized, and appropriated by locals in developing networks of support and urban development" (2016: 7). Thus, as my study suggested, social media can offer digital avenues for residents of marginalized communities to negotiate security in spaces they traverse. "Communication infrastructures" become crucial assets, not only to address issues of belonging and participation in the community, but also as a vital resource for survival in spaces of urban conflict.

In Maré Vive, people made use of social media to help strengthen a sense of community belonging through acts of resistance to the imposed militarization of their daily spaces. In academic terms, resistance has been defined as an ability to challenge both traditional power structures—as in

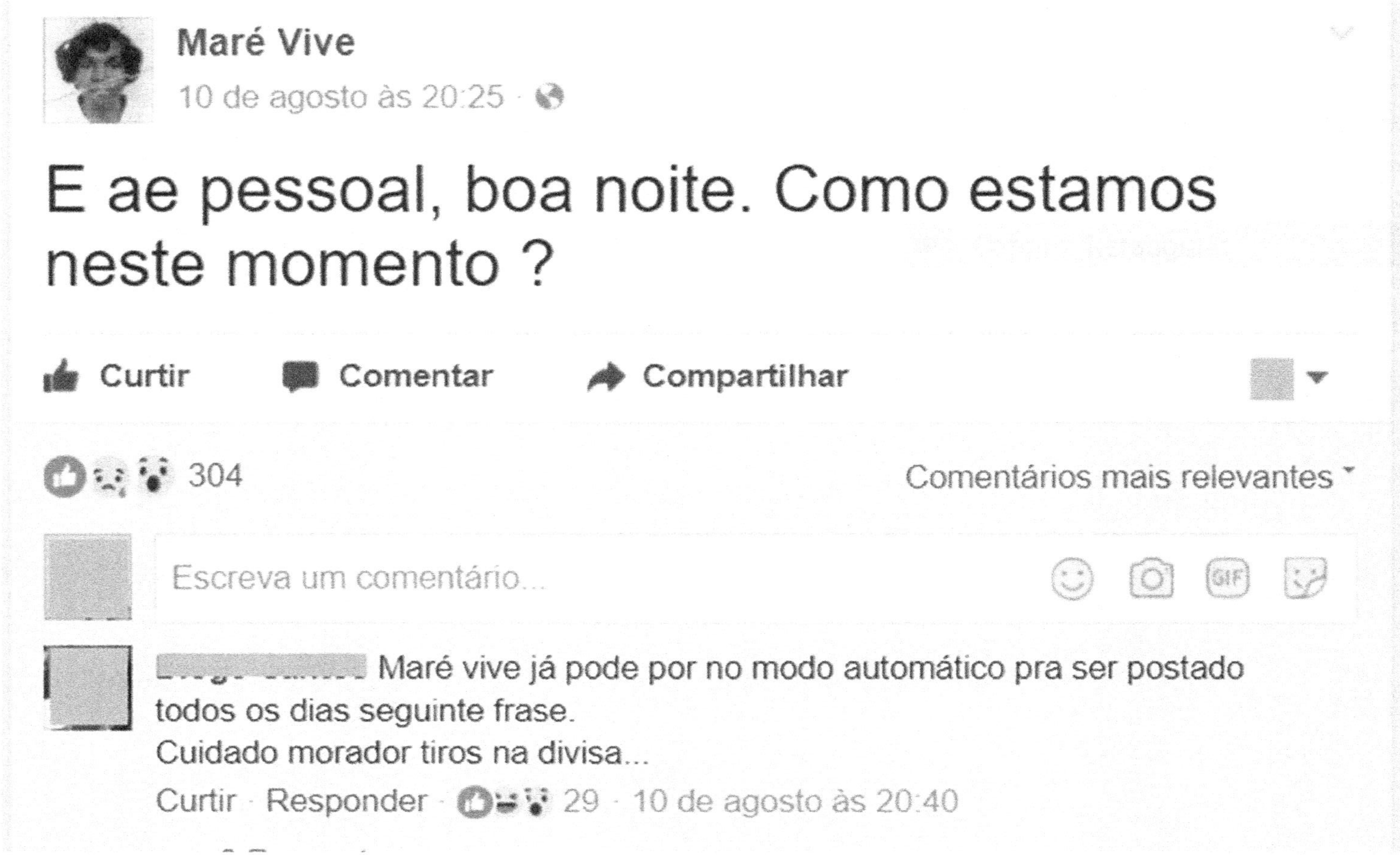

Maré Vive
10 de agosto às 20:25
E ae pessoal, boa noite. Como estamos neste momento ?
Curtir
Comentar
Compartilhar
304
Comentários mais relevantes
Escreva um comentário...
Maré vive já pode por no modo automático pra ser postado todos os dias seguinte frase.
Cuidado morador tiros na divisa...
Curtir · Responder · 29 · 10 de agosto às 20:40

Figure 40.2 Screen Capture, Facebook Fan Page Maré Vive, August 10, 2017

governmental, religious, and institutional—and hegemonic power structures—as in the Gramscian conception. In the favela, resistance refers to mobilizing communication resources as everyday life management assets used for the purposes of challenging the given conditions. People responded to harsh realities (a profound sense of insecurity) and lack of institutional support therein by sharing information, and showing care, hospitality, and resilience.

Concluding Thoughts

Communities matter in mediated cities. My research in the favelas indicates that the notion of community is still highly significant, and particularly so in a context of segregation, marginalization, and oppression, as was the case with Brazilian cities in the years prior to and following the 2014 Football World Cup and the 2016 Olympics. The affective dimensions of community, something I observed closely on the streets of Pau da Lima and the online spaces of Maré Vive, go hand in hand with political resistance. In this way, residents use different forms of offline and online media as resources to better manage everyday life and to affirm their identity as legitimate citizens who belong to and make important contributions to the city.

At the same time, as I showed, media can alter the nature of community living by incorporating a greater plurality of voices, as was the case with Manchester's ALL FM, by augmenting the neighborhood with their expansion into the soundscapes, as was the case of the lamppost radio, and into online spaces, as was the case with Maré Vive. In Pau da Lima, the soundscapes created by the lamppost radio helped create an enlarged neighborhood and showed the former's knowledge of the latter's daily urban rhythms. Finally, in Manchester, community manifested in terms of community of interest, based on ethnic groups, languages, and music genres, going beyond the geographic boundaries of the neighborhoods in the city.

References

Agache, A. (1930) *Cidade do Rio de Janeiro: Extensão, Remodelação, Embelezamento*, Rio de Janeiro: Prefeitura do Distrito Federal.
Berrigan, F. (ed.) (1977) *Access: Some Western Models of Community Media*, Paris: UNESCO.
Brzozowski, J. (2012) "International Migration and Economic Development," *Estudos Avançados* 26(75).
Carneiro, J. (2010) "UPPs Completam Dois Anos com Aprovação Alta e Planos de Expansão," BBC Brazil, December 20, viewed May 2, 2018, www.bbc.com/portuguese/noticias/2010/12/101216_rio_upps_2anos_jc.
Cohen, A. (2001) *The Symbolic Construction of Community*, London and New York: Routledge/Taylor and Francis e-Library.
Cohen, P. (2013) *On the Wrong Side of the Track? East London and the Post Olympics*, London: Lawrence and Wishart.
Comitê Popular da Copa e das Olimpíadas (2015) "Dossiê do Comitê Popular da Copa e das Olimpíadas: Olimpíada Rio 2016, os Jogos da Exclusão," viewed March 31, 2016, www.childrenwin.org/wp-content/uploads/2015/12/Dossie-Comit%C3%AA-Rio2015_low.pdf.
Durkheim, E. (1893) *De La Division Du Travail Social: Étude Sur L'Organisation Des Sociétés Supérieures*, Paris: Alcan.
Félix, C., Fragoso, M., and Pitasse, M. (2017) "Entre o Comunitário, o Popular e o Contrahegemônico: Limites Teóricos e Aproximações Cotidianas," *Questões Transversais Revista de Epistemologias da Comunicação*, 5(10), pp. 98–106.
Freitas, R., Lins, F., and Carmo, M. H. (2016) *Megaeventos, Comunicação e Cidade*, Rio de Janeiro: CRV.
Gans, H. J. (1982) *The Urban Villagers. Group and Class in the Life of Italian-Americans*, 2nd edition, London: The Free Press/Collier Macmillan Publishers.
Georgiou, M. (2013) *Media and the City: Cosmopolitanism and Difference*, Cambridge, Malden, MA: Polity Press.

Georgiou, M., Motta, W., and Livingstone, S. (2016) "Community Through Digital Connectivity? Communication Infrastructure in Multicultural London: Final Report," The London School of Economics and Political Science, London, UK, viewed August 7, 2017, http://eprints.lse.ac.uk/69587.

Gianotti, C. (2016) "Experiências em Comunicação Popular no Rio de Janeiro Ontem e Hoje: Uma História de Resistência das Favelas Cariocas. Núcleo Piratininga de Comunicação," *Fundação Rosa Luxemburgo*, 215.

Goldberger, P. (2001) "Cities, Places and Cyberspace," *Paul Goldberger Website*, viewed August 6, 2017, www.paulgoldberger.com/speeaches.php?speech=berkeley#articlestart.

Hochheimer, J. (1993) "Organising Democratic Radio: Issues in Praxis," *Media, Culture and Society*, 15(3), pp. 473–486.

Howley, K. (2005) *Community Media: People, Places and Communication Technologies*, Cambridge: Cambridge University Press.

Jacobs, J. (1992) *The Death and Life of Great American Cities*, New York: Vintage Books.

Jankowski, N. and Prehn, O. (eds.) (2002). *Community Media in the Information Age: Perspectives and Prospects*, Cresskill, NJ: Hampton Press.

Keung Wong, D. F., Li, C. Y., and Song, H. X. (2007) "Rural Migrant Workers in Urban China: Living a Marginalised Life," *International Journal of Social Welfare*, 16(1), pp. 32–40.

Lewis, P. (2006) "Community Media: Giving a Voice to the Voiceless," in P. Lewis and S. Jones (eds.) *From the Margins to the Cutting Edge: Community Media and Empowerment*, Cresskill, NJ: Hampton Press, pp. 13–39.

Mangin, W. (1967) "Latin American Squatter Settlements: A Problem and a Solution," *Latin American Research Review*, 2(3), pp. 65–98.

Medrado, A. (2010) "The Waves of the Hills: Community and Radio in the Everyday Life of a Brazilian Favela," PhD Thesis, University of Westminster, viewed August 3, 2017, http://westminsterresearch.wmin.ac.uk/8944/1/A_MEDRADO.pdf.

Medrado, A. and Souza, R. (2015) "As Transformações do Rio Pre-Olímpico: Ecos nas Paisagens Sonoras da Favela da Maré," *Revista Latinoamericana de Comunicación Chasqui*, 130, pp. 71–86.

Mooney, G. (2005) "Urban Disorders," in S. Pile, C. Brookes, and G. Mooney (eds.) *Understanding Cities: Unruly Cities?* London and New York: Routledge/Taylor and Francis e-Library, pp. 49–95.

O'Connor, A. (1990) "The Miners" Radio Stations in Bolivia: A Culture of Resistance," *Journal of Communications*, 40(1), pp. 102–110.

Paiva, R. (1998) *O Espírito Comum: Comunidade, Mídia e Globalismo*, Rio de Janeiro: Vozes.

Parker, S. (2004) *Urban Theory and the Urban Experience: Encountering the City*, London and New York: Routledge.

Perlman, J. (1976) *The Myth of Marginality: Urban Poverty and Politics in Rio de Janeiro*, Berkeley, CA, London: University of California Press.

Pile, S., Brook, C., and Mooney, G. (2005) *Unruly Cities?* London and New York: Routledge/Taylor and Francis e-Library.

Rodriguez, C. (2001) *Fissures in the Mediascape: An International Study of Citizens' Media*, Cresskill, NJ: Hampton Press.

Roque, A. (2014). "The Military Occupation of Maré Ahead of Brazil's World Cup," *Amnesty International Brazil*, April 8, viewed May 2, 2018, www.amnesty.org/en/latest/campaigns/2014/04/the-military-occupation-of-mare-ahead-of-brazils-world-cup.

Scannell, P. (1996) *Radio, Television and Modern Life*, Oxford: Blackwell.

Scifo, S. (2016) "The Origins and Development of Community Radio in Britain Under New Labour (1997–2007)," PhD Thesis, University of Westminster, viewed November 1, 2017, http://westminsterresearch.wmin.ac.uk/12210/1/Salvatore_SCIFO.pdf.

Sistema de Informação Municipal de Salvador (2010) População Residente (Habitantes), viewed July 20, 2019, www.sim.salvador.ba.gov.br/indicadores/index.php.

Souza, R. (2017) "O Comum e a Rua: Resistência da Juventude Frente à Militarização da Vida na Maré," PhD Thesis, Universidade Federal do Rio de Janeiro.

Tönnies, F. ([1887] 1963) *Community and Society*, London: Harper and Row.

Valente, J. (2014) "UPPs: Observações Sobre a Gestão Militarizada de Territórios Desiguais," *Revista Direito e Práxis*, 5(9), pp. 207–225.

Valladares, L. (2005) *A Invenção da Favela: Do Mito de Origem a Favela.com*, 1st edition, Rio de Janeiro: Editora FGV.

Wacquant, L. (2014) "Ghettos and Anti-Ghettos: The New Regime of Urban Marginality in the 21st Century," *City and Social Inclusion Monograph*, International Association of Educating Cities.
Watts, J. (2014) "Brazil to Order Army into Rio Slums as Violence Escalates Before World Cup," *The Guardian*, March 24, viewed August 2, 2017, www.theguardian.com/world/2014/mar/24/brazil-army-rio-slums-violence-world-cup.
Young, M. and Willmott, P. (1992) *Family and Kinship in East London*, London: Penguin.

Further Reading

Gordon, J. (2009) (ed.) *Notions of Community*, Oxford, Bern, Berlin, Bruxelles, Frankfurt am Main, New York, Wien: Peter Lang.
Valença, M., Cravidão, F., and Fernandes, J. A. (2012) *Urban Developments in Brazil and Portugal*, New York: Nova Science Publishers.

41
"THE STREET IS THE MESSAGE"
Racial Violence and the White Control of Mobility

Armond R. Towns

Introduction

Marshall McLuhan (2003) once famously argued that the "medium is the message." By this, he meant that the content of a medium, such as a television show, is often overexamined, but the physicality of the television itself also holds important meanings for the pace and scale of life in society. Relatedly, Richard Cavell (1999) posits McLuhan's argument that the medium is the message connects communication and media studies to geography. This is because, for Cavell, McLuhan considers the implications of media on conceptions of time and space. Conceptions of space and time, like media, are highly meaningful and have political implications. Yet, despite these political implications, McLuhan does little to acknowledge that the conceptions of space and time most dominate in Western societies structured racism, overwhelmingly centering the experiences of white, cis-gendered, middle-classed men.

The connection between space and racism is well documented in American inner cities. Freeways in the US have been constructed in ways that disproportionately destroy the homes of people of color in inner-city neighborhoods; Rodney King was pulled from his car and beaten in the streets of Los Angeles; a disproportionate number of black New Orleans Hurricane Katrina victims were stuck in the Ninth Ward because of both a lack of personal and public transportation; and New York City recently installed street surveillance cameras in the wake of 9/11. Relatedly, with the centrality of racism to the city streets, it makes sense that forms of protests often happen in those same streets. From the Great Migration and Civil Rights marches to #BlackLivesMatter blocking freeway traffic, the streets are full of meaning.

The streets are "media" in ways that hold racial implications. I argue that city streets are one mode of *mediating* our understandings of race. Space and mobility, inseparable on city streets, are highly contested and meaning-filled processes, especially when it comes to race. In this chapter, I examine two functions of the streets in the context of urbanity and race: (1) the streets reflect practices of wider institutional racism, which speaks to what Sarah Sharma and I (2016) call "the white control of mobility"; and (2) the same streets are sites where the resistance to such oppressions is located and also structured. Thus, this chapter proceeds by putting together disciplinary areas as diverse as black studies and materialist media studies to rethink the relation between urban geography, race, and media. It then moves into applying these areas of study to discussions that reveal the meaningfulness of the city street in relation to institutional racism as well as the meaningfulness of the city street for those who challenge said racism.

Black (Media) Studies

Although rarely read together, the work of black studies and materialist media studies has long been engaging in similar conversations about the interrelated materiality of space and politics. These different yet overlapping discussions provide me with the ingredients to develop a theoretical analysis of the urban street as one medium through which racialization processes are enacted. Thus, I seek to show the utility of both media studies and black studies, but also reveal some of their limitations when not considered together. First, while media studies addresses the materiality of space, it often does so in ways that have unconsidered racial implications (there are notable exceptions, such Jody Berland [2009], Jenny Burman [2010], and Sarah Sharma [2008]). And second, while black studies has developed a theorization of space, it does so largely without considering the media implications of space. Bringing the two together allows for a productive conversation about the relationship between city space, media, and race. And in line with the mobility studies turn in media studies (Sheller and Urry 2006; Packer 2008), black studies and media studies allow for an examination of the role of mobility in the production of racialized spaces as well. The street, then, is media in the sense that it structures racialized conceptions of who can and who cannot move through them freely.

First, media studies has largely addressed conceptions of space as a product of media technology in race-neutral ways. The works of McLuhan, James Carey, and Harold Innis stick out. Cavell (1999) argues that McLuhan should be considered a cultural geographer because McLuhan's own work consistently centers space. McLuhan notes that roads are an important medium of communication prior to the telegraph: "It was not until the advent of the electronic telegraph that messages could travel faster than a messenger. Before this, roads and the written word were closely interrelated" (McLuhan 2003: 127). Similarly, Carey makes the connection between transportation and communication, presumably only disrupted by the introduction of the electronic telegraph, which Carey argues "permitted for the first time the effective separation of communication from transportation" (2009: 157). For both McLuhan and Carey, then, space and media are intimately linked.

Of course, McLuhan and Carey build their theories off the work of Innis, who theorized all media as having either a time- or space-biased component. Time-biased media are those that last through time or, specifically, media that can survive for long time periods, such as stone and clay. These media are "heavy and durable and not suited to transportation" (Innis 2008: 33). But space-biased media traverse distances and thus are focused on efficient management of spaces. These media are concerned with the "dissemination of knowledge over space than over time"; as such, these media are often "light and easily transported" (Innis 2008: 33). Such media include paper and they are part of cultures transfixed by the rule of written law, making them "best suited to political and cultural control over distances, and . . . essential to the construction of empires" (Acland 2006: 173). According to Innis, space-biased media promote themes like nationalism and structure Western cultures of imperialism. In other words, space-biased media often lend themselves to the political control and organization of space. This literature offers useful analysis of the material implications of media, even as it lacks a discussion of how Western conceptions of time and space have racial implications.

A more explicit conversation on race and space can be found in black studies, although here media often drops out of the conversation. The work of Frantz Fanon (2004), for example, makes explicit connections between race and space, particularly Fanon's variants of nationalism in decolonial movements. For Fanon, some forms of nationalism reformulate colonization while others challenge it. Alvaro Reyes (2012) notes that Fanon's approach to space and nationalism exists because the objective reality of colonization begins as one structured on spatial/racialized segregation.

Thus, "there is a relay between the creation of the colonized as an epistemologically 'knowable' object and the spatial segregation, or locational 'fixing' of that object within the colony" (Reyes 2012: 14). These spatial, colonial relations do not easily die out with decolonial project, but are reformulated in ways that either maintain (neo)colonialism or structure radical movements against the continuance of former colonial relations.

Fanon makes distinctions between the new humanism that he sought to create and the "national bourgeoisie," a postcolonial spatial organization that could never fully end colonialism. Unlike the new, non-Western humanism that Fanon promotes, the national bourgeoisie was that white and nonwhite middle-classed population in the former colonies that "lulled itself into thinking that it can supplant the metropolitan bourgeoisie [the former colonial European power] to its own advantage" (Fanon 2004: 98). Thus, this national bourgeoisie was not *new* because it requires the maintenance of connection with the former colonizer to gain political and economic power. Here, Fanon notes that the national bourgeoisie are fabrications because they do not own the means of their own production and they have no way to accumulate capital, maintaining former colonial spatial relations in neocolonial contexts. Fanon, alternatively, sought a new humanism, not related to capitalist, colonial spatiality.

The works of Sylvia Wynter and Katherine McKittrick productively push Fanon's discussion of space into new arenas. Wynter (2003) articulates Western conceptions of space as rooted in Judeo-Christian conceptions of inhabitable versus uninhabitable zones. Thus, figures like Christopher Columbus and the Portuguese rounding the coast of South Africa were less Western European "discoveries" and more the reconceptualization of the Western self in ways that secularized thinking. The secularization of thought reframes European spatio-religious terms as spatio-racial ones, without acknowledging the overlap. McKittrick builds off Wynter to argue that processes of racial and sexual domination bleed into supposedly neutral academic fields. In a critique of Europe's assumed neutral mapping of the world, McKittrick asks: "how do Man's geographies get formulated, cast as natural truths, and become overrepresented? How does this politics of mapping, of making space, shed light on the repetitive displacement of the planet's nonwhite subjects?" (2006: 123). While Wynter leaves off with a discussion of the inhabitable and uninhabitable zones, McKittrick notes that these spatial concepts structure the discipline of geography's presumably neutral scientific project. Fanon, Reyes, Wynter, and McKittrick are all important for their examination of race and space, but they do not examine media, such as maps and transportation technologies, as important to conceptions of space.

In both media studies and black studies, there are political articulations of space as a construct. Media studies largely figures space as produced through a relationship to Western media technologies. Black studies figures its space in relation to the Western history of racial violence. However, both note the importance of the "West" as a construct that plays a significant role in structuring its conception of space as universal. The Western construct of space, as Doreen Massey (1994) has argued, is overwhelmingly passive and awaiting white male "intervention." Sarah Sharma and I examined this notion of intervention in our theorization of the "white control of mobility," which situates white, cis-gendered, middle-classed men as the central population that can traverse space without racial violence. The Western construct of space as passive and awaiting male intervention, for Massey, is for us premised on white male mobility through spaces as colonial and racial projects. Thus, Sharma and I noted that the mobility of nonwhite people has been structured by the mobility of, and the control of mobility by, white people. Whether it was colonialism, transatlantic slavery, or contemporary tourism culture, Sharma and I found that "certain people *become* white based on their autonomous mobility and the assumed right to move Others" (2016: 29). This navigation of space is often structured by "media": maps, writing, cars, and, for the rest of this chapter, streets.

From Freeways to Freedom

There are at least two engagements with the street as a space full of meaning that I analyze: (1) the streets articulate practices of systemic racism, by which I mean the street functions as a mediator of a country's approach to white and nonwhite bodies. Thus, the street is a contested site "in a culture governed by the dictates of the white control of mobility" (Sharma and Towns 2016: 40). And (2), the streets often structure challenges to oppressions, or there are alternative usages of the street. As many forms of racial violence happen through and on the street, it makes sense that resistance against that violence is mediated by city streets.

First, the processes of institutional racism as they relate to the street have been examined in various disciplines. These institutional effects have individual implications. The centrality of the white control of mobility, for example, was evident on the campus of my alma mater, UNC Chapel Hill, in 2015, as we received the tragic news that three Muslim students, Deah Shaddy Barakat, Yusor Mohammad, and Razan Mohammad Abu-Salha, were gunned down in their apartment by their neighbor, Craig Hicks. Reportedly, Hicks killed the three, execution style, over a disputed parking spot. The local and national news outlets promoted two discourses: first, some argued that Hicks engaged in a racially motivated hate crime that had nothing to do with the parking spot. And second, others argued that Hicks's actions were the same as "road rage," and the murders should not be made into a "racial issue." But, as Sharma and I argued, when viewed through a longer narrative of a white control of the mobility of people of color, "[t]hese murders had everything to do with a parking spot *and* everything to do with racialized hate" (2016: 39, emphasis added). Further, we noted:

> The parking spot, the road, and the sidewalk are extremely contested sites in a culture governed by the dictates of the white control over mobility. It is not just that these are the physical sites of the murders or because the ground is the backdrop upon which life unfolds. If they seem banal it is because the white control of mobility is exerted through automobiles, roads, sidewalks, gated communities, and parking lots—the everyday mechanisms of mobility. As we have argued, the control of mobility is central to exerting power and thus central to the re-creation of whiteness. In a culture governed by the white control over mobility, people of color are vulnerable when they park their cars, walk in the middle of the road, walk on the sidewalk, or just walk for that matter.
>
> (Sharma and Towns 2016: 40)

These murders should not be reduced to a "loss of sanity" by Hicks; rather, his actions are inseparable from the racialized meanings associated with space, driving, parking, and the street.

The white control of mobility that Hicks associated with the parking spot is backed by a history of systemic racism inscribed by, in, and on the city streets. City planner Robert Moses's racially motivated construction of New York City's freeways and overpasses provides just one example of the connection between streets and systemic racism (Kolitz and Ismail 2015), but he is no anomaly. In 1956, the National Interstate and Defense Highway Act was signed into law by then-US President Dwight D. Eisenhower. The bill was deemed necessary to make transportation between the east and west coasts as direct as possible, particularly during times of war. Yet, despite the Division of Highways' insistence that it routed freeways according to the "most direct and practical location" (Avila 2006: 207), a disproportionate amount of construction for these freeways went out of their way to cut through and destroy inner-city communities. Much like the current discourse of gentrification, the freeway construction was touted as of necessity for "urban renewal." It equally materialized a white control over mobility across space, by which the ability to destroy inner-city communities of color furthered the capability of white families to move in and out of the cities for employment. The freeway stands as the medium through which white people traverse space, on the one hand, and a further materialization of the dehumanization of people of color, on the other.

Relatedly, freeways and suburbs go hand in hand. Suburbanization assumed a right to mobility, one centrally structured around the capacity to own an automobile, to the right to reside in any neighborhood one wanted to, and the ability to access the benefits of freeways. Eric Avila details this process in Los Angeles, implying, while I argue, that the automobile and the freeway literally *mediated* the experience of different groups of people *out* of the inner city and *into* the suburbs. For Avila, this mobility was not neutral, but it led to the "privatization" of white ethnic Europeanness in ways that structured a new collective white identity. Thus, the ethnic and racial discrimination faced in the inner cities for being Irish, Jewish, or German mattered less if one could make it out of the cities and into the suburbs. The freeway *moved* Irishness into whiteness. Avila furthers this point by highlighting the limitations in many studies of white flight:

> Typically, *white flight* describes a structural process by which postwar suburbanization helped the racial resegregation of the United States, dividing presumably white suburbs from concentrations of racialized poverty. But the cultural corollary to this development has been overlooked. White flight entailed a renegotiation of racial and spatial identities, implying a cultural process in which an expanding middle class of myriad ethnic backgrounds came to discover itself as white.
>
> *(Avila 2006: 14, emphasis in original)*

The ability to move, and control movement, remade whiteness. And the freeway and car were central media for attaining this new, collective white identity.

The above actions make the street highly political. The street is not a neutral medium through which people navigate space; it is a contested medium through which racism (as well as other forms of oppression) functions. The street is also the medium through which people fight against racism. Similar to my usage of media, Robin Kelley argues that public transportation in Southern US cities during the Jim Crow era often functioned as "moving theatres" "that provide microcosms of race, class, and gender conflict that raged in other social spaces throughout the city (i.e., sidewalks, parks, and streets) but otherwise rarely found a place in the public record" (Kelley 1996: 62). As Kelley demonstrates, these forms of resistance were often not recorded in the Civil Rights public record because some of them did not match the popular narrative of black, nonviolent resistance. For example:

> Some [black male passengers] boldly sat down next to white female passengers and, often with knife in hand, challenged operators to move them. Others refused to pay their fare, or simply picked fights with bus drivers or white passengers. In the middle of the day on the Fourth of July, a black man riding the South Bessemer line pulled a knife on an operator after he was asked to move to the back of the bus. In another incident, a black passenger on the Ensley-Fairfield line boarded, moved the color dividers forward to increase space allotted to black passengers, and sat down next to a white man. The operator expelled him, but he reboarded on the return trip and this time "sat between two white men and began to laugh and make a joke about it." He was then moved bodily to the black section, but a few stops later approached the driver with an

open knife. Before the police arrived, he jumped out the window and escaped. When the bus returned later in the evening, he had the audacity to board again.

(Kelley 1996: 65)

The streets were "theatres," then, because they literally *mediated* the racial tensions of the city, as well as the forms of resistance that black people had at their disposal throughout the city. This mirrors other research on the street as a fundamental site where racial, sexual, and gendered differences emerge (Jacobs 1992; Cresswell 1998; Ahmed 2000; Ruddick 2013).

Another example of using the street as a medium through which people fight against racism occurred in Selma, Alabama in 1965. That year, a group of black protesters planned to walk in the middle of the street from Selma to Montgomery to voice their grievances to then-Governor George Wallace, who was infamously known for promoting the maintenance of racial segregation in the US South. Before they could make it, they were violently greeted by police in riot gear. This violent attack of white police on largely black protesters was captured on camera:

For fifteen minutes, ABC viewers saw [county sheriff Jim] Clark's posse and Alabama state troopers outfitted with gas masks and truncheons beat, gas, and brutalize a procession of black demonstrators who had crossed over the Edmund Pettus Bridge with the intention of marching to Montgomery to protest their disenfranchisement to Governor George Wallace.

(Bodroghkozy 2012: 116)

For these protesters, the street was not solely a space of protest, but also, along with the television camera, the medium through which white people in the US were forced to acknowledge racial divisions.

Also, it should not be shocking that the Black Panther Party, an antiracist, socialist organization in the US during the mid-20th century, often shut down city streets. After the police murder of Richmond, California resident Denzil Dowell, cofounders Huey Newton and Bobby Seale "quickly organized a street-corner rally to talk with community members about Denzil Dowell's case and explain their organization's program, especially their position on community self-defense" (Bloom and Martin Jr. 2013: 54). Fifteen Panthers gathered in front of a liquor store in North Richmond and their presence began to garner attention from walkers and drivers who pulled over to hear what the Panthers were saying: "Cars stopped, and traffic began backing up," and even as a police car tried to pass,

[a] number of cars pulled out of the way to let his car through, but one man refused to move, and the officer got stuck in the swelling traffic jam and had to stay there in his car observing the rally until it ended.

(Bloom and Martin Jr. 2013: 55)

The Party's influence on street protests has lived on in other contemporary protests, such as digital media recordings of police actions. Similarly, one of the Party's most effective tactics was to "police the police," which involved Party members listening to police scanners and driving behind police cars in Oakland, California. If an officer pulled over a black motorist, the Party members would be there to remind the motorist of his or her rights and to prevent the police officers from overstepping their boundaries. In a similar manner, protesters today have been inspired by, or taken to the streets themselves, with the help of video footage of police brutality. Digital media, then, are helping to archive city life in ways that may not receive the mainstream attention it deserves. Thus, while many white people were shocked to see the videotape of Rodney King being beaten in the streets of Los Angeles by white police officers, many black and brown people were not. King's beating, and the lack of acquittal of the white police officers involved, led to the 1992 LA Rebellion—not unlike the 1965 Watts Rebellion, which also involved police violence against a black man in the street. Both the 1965 and 1992 events involved white people engaging in violently aggressive controls of black automobile movement on city streets. King is but one example. Networked and social media allow for an even higher proliferation of similar images, as many city residents have cell phone video capability in their back pockets. As I have noted elsewhere, these video images cannot be viewed as inherently "saving" anyone (Towns 2015), but they are important for constructing as well as archiving the street as a medium of protest, as a contemporary mode of "policing the police."

Perhaps unsurprisingly, many of the recorded instances of racial violence on the street take to the street—the same medium through which the white control of mobility is enacted. The tactic of blocking freeway traffic the Panthers enacted has regained much life in contemporary forms of struggle with groups like #BlackLivesMatter. These tactics have led people like Atlanta Mayor's Kasim Reed to argue that "Dr. King would never take a freeway" (Theoharis 2016). This statement, as Jeanne Theoharis argues, flies in the face of the above history. In addition, it continues a too-simplistic narrative of "correct" versus "incorrect" forms of protest, where some ask for quantifications of "how blocking traffic ends racism or police brutality." Such a question is an oversimplification because it ignores the long connection between racism, mobility, and space—a connection that #BlackLivesMatter did not make but white supremacy did. The more interesting thing, I argue, is that whether in California (Hamilton 2016), Minnesota (Badger 2016), or Virginia (WRIC 2016), when #BlackLivesMatter blocks freeway traffic it disrupts the white control of mobility and discussions of racial supremacy that flow from the freeway into other everyday spaces like sidewalks, schools, and malls. #BlackLivesMatter disrupts the "temporal order" of things (Sharma 2014) by which drivers used to efficiency on the road (e.g., arriving home within 30 minutes after work) are denied that presumably normal capitalist mode of traversing space. In the process, drivers of all races are "inconvenienced" and must stop on the freeway to consider the black body, as per oppression, as central to their inconvenience. These blocks in traffic are educational. They "inconvenience" drivers returning to the suburbs (and with gentrification, going back to the city) for a few hours; while "inconvenience" is not strong enough of a word to describe what happens to the persons and families of Michael Brown, Renisha McBride, Eric Garner, and Sandra Bland. Of course, Brown was killed while jaywalking, McBride was killed after crashing her car, Garner was killed for standing on the street, and Bland was "found dead" in her cell after a traffic violation turned violent. Each died on the move, on the street. Why would the protests of their deaths not follow suit?

These instances are not reducible to the US, but structure Western society. In the United Kingdom, police brutality has disproportionately impacted black people, such as Sheku Bayoh, Sarah Reed, and Mark Dugan, whose 2011 police murder "sparked riots across the country that summer" (Bangura 2016). And in early 2017 in the streets of Paris, a black man identified only as Theo was stopped for an "identity check" by the police and, according to investigators, beaten and "accidentally" anally raped by a police officer's baton (Elizalde 2017). This incident sparked antiracist protests throughout the streets of Paris. In this context of the white control over mobility, the street is not surprisingly the medium through which rebellion occurs.

Conclusion

The street is the message. This argument is twofold. First, the street is often representative of histories of racial oppression. The policing of the street and their material layout (white mobility) are often structured on the history of dehumanizing specific bodies. Relatedly, the street can be used in alternative manners that outline the racism that structures them. Similarly, Fanon (1994) notes in *A Dying Colonialism* that Algerian Muslims took over the radio from the French and used it for their own purposes. Thus, radio waves have functioned both as maintainers of empires and critiques of imperialism. It is not shocking that city streets function in a similar manner: they are media that are always open to alternative usages that may not be in the purview of those in power. Within this context, we can further reexamine the relations between media, mobility, and race. Rather than solely considering race through media representations of the city, such as in film or television shows, we can theorize the material implications of media on transforming conceptions of time and space, which articulate difference with an array of raced, classed, gendered, and sexual implications.

References

Acland, C. (2006) "Harold Innis, Cultural Policy, and Residual Media," *International Journal of Cultural Policy*, 12(2), pp. 171–185.

Ahmed, S. (2000). *Strange Encounters: Embodied Others in Post-Coloniality*, London: Routledge.

Avila, E. (2006) *Popular Culture in the Age of White Flight: Fear and Fantasy in Suburban Los Angeles*, Berkeley, CA: University of California Press.

Badger, E. (2016) "Why Highways Have Become the Center of Civil Rights Protest," *The Washington Post*, www.washingtonpost.com/news/wonk/wp/2016/07/13/why-highways-have-become-the-center-of-civil-rights-protest/?utm_term=.a360f9150558.

Bangura, S. (2016) "We Need to Talk about Police Brutality in the U.K.," *The Fader*, www.thefader.com/2016/03/29/police-brutality-uk-essay.

Berland, J. (2009) *North of Empire: Essays on the Cultural Technologies of Space*, Durham, NC: Duke University Press.

Bloom, J. and Martin, W. (2013) *Black Against Empire: The History and Politics of the Black Panther Party*, Berkeley, CA: University of California Press.

Bodroghkozy, A. (2012) *Equal Time: Television and the Civil Rights Movement*, Champaign, IL: University of Illinois Press.

Burman, J. (2010) "Suspects in the City: Browning the 'Not-Quite' Canadian Citizen," *Cultural Studies*, 24(4), pp. 200–213.

Carey, J. (2009) *Communication as Culture*, London: Routledge.

Cavell, R. (1999) "McLuhan and Spatial Communication," *Western Journal of Communication*, 63(3), pp. 348–363.

Cresswell, T. (1998) "Night Discourse: Producing/Consuming Meaning on the Street," in N. Frye (ed.) *Images of the Street: Planning, Identity and Control in Public Space*, London: Routledge.

Elizalde, E. (2017) "Black Man's Injuries after Alleged Sodomy with Baton by French Police Officers Were Accident, Investigators Say," *The New York Daily News*, www.nydailynews.com/news/world/black-man-allegedly-raped-french-officers-accidental-article-1.2968919.

Fanon, F. (1994) *A Dying Colonialism*, New York: Grove Press.

— (2004) *Wretched of the Earth*, New York: Grove Press.

Hamilton, M. (2016) "Protesters with Black Lives Matter Shut Down 405 Freeway in Inglewood," *The Los Angeles Times*, www.latimes.com/local/lanow/la-me-ln-protest-inglewood-20160710-snap-story.html.

Innis, H. (2008) *The Bias of Communication*, Toronto: University of Toronto Press.

Jacobs, J. (1992) *The Death and Life of Great American Cities*, New York: Vintage.

Kelley, R. (1996) *Race Rebels*, New York: The Free Press.

Kolitz, D. and Ismail, A. (2015) "The Lingering Effects of NYC's Racist City Planning," *Hopes and Fears*, www.hopesandfears.com/hopes/now/politics/216905-the-lingering-effects-of-nyc-racist-city-planning.

Massey, D. (1994) *Space, Place, and Gender*, Minneapolis, MN: University of Minnesota Press.
McKittrick, K. (2006) *Demonic Grounds: Black Women and the Cartographies of Struggle*, Minneapolis, MN: University of Minnesota Press.
McLuhan, M. (2003) *Understanding Media*, Corte Madera, CA: Gingko Press.
Packer, J. (2008) *Mobility Without Mayhem*, Durham, NC: Duke University Press.
Reyes, A. (2012) "On Fanon's Manichean Delirium," *The Black Scholar*, 42(3–4), pp. 13–20.
Ruddick, S. (2013) "Constructing Difference in Public Spaces: Race, Class, and Gender as Interlocking Systems," *Urban Geography*, 17(2), pp. 132–151.
Sharma, S. (2008) "Taxis as Media: A Temporal Materialist Reading of the Taxi-Cab," *Social Identities*, 14(4), pp. 457–464.
— (2014) *In the Meantime*, Durham, NC: Duke University Press.
Sharma, S. and Towns, A. (2016) "Ceasing Fire and Seizing Time: LA Gang Tours and the White Control of Mobility," *Transfers*, 6(1), pp. 26–44.
Sheller, M. and Urry, J. (2006) "The New Mobilities Paradigm," *Environment and Planning A*, 38, pp. 207–226.
Theoharis, J. (2016) "MLK Would Never Shut Down a Freeway, and 6 Other Myths about the Civil Rights Movement and Black Lives Matter," *The Root*, www.theroot.com/mlk-would-never-shut-down-a-freeway-and-6-other-myths-1790856033.
Towns, A. (2015) "That Camera Won't Save You! The Spectacular Consumption of Police Violence," *Present Tense*, 5(2), pp. 1–9.
WRIC (2016) "Black Lives Matter Protesters Shut Down Virginia Freeway, 13 Arrested," *NBC4*, http://nbc4i.com/2016/07/19/black-lives-matter-protesters-shut-down-virginia-freeway-13-arrested.
Wynter, S. (2003) "Unsettling the Coloniality of Being/Power/Truth/Freedom: Towards the Human, After Man, its Overrepresentation—An Argument," *CR: The New Centennial Review*, 3(3), pp. 257–337.

Further Reading

McKittrick, M. and Woods, C. (2007) *Black Geographies and the Politics of Place*, Brooklyn, NY: South End Press.
Shabazz, R. (2015) *Spatializing Blackness: Architectures of Confinement and Black Masculinity in Chicago*, Champaign, IL: University of Illinois Press.
Urry, J. (2007) *Mobilities*, Cambridge, UK: Polity Press.

42
LIVING IN THE DISADVANTAGED END OF "DUAL CITIES"
Understanding the Urban Poor and the Precariat

Steve Macek

Introduction

This chapter examines the various ways the dominant corporate media have represented, framed, and made sense of the poverty, economic precarity, slums, and increasing inequalities of wealth and income that are such salient features of contemporary neoliberal cities around the globe. Such representations are important because they influence debates around public policies concerned with issues like persistent urban poverty (Gilens 1999). The chapter also explores the grassroots media that the oppressed, economically and racially marginalized populations of these cities have produced "from below" in response to dominant media narratives. It begins by examining the recent global trend toward widening economic inequality and its impact on cities before moving on to dissect how these developments have been portrayed in the media.

Planet of Slums

By the end of the first decade of the 21st century, for the first time in human history, the majority of the world's population lived in urban areas. Virtually all of the future growth in the earth's population is projected to take place in cities. A sizable segment of those residing in the planet's burgeoning metropolitan centers find themselves inhabiting "the disadvantaged end" of the city, zones marked by concentrated poverty, unemployment, crowding, inadequate infrastructure, and substandard housing (see Davis 2006 and UN-Habitat 2016: 13–14).

While the economic fortunes of much of the earth's population have improved slightly in recent years, the rapid urbanization of the past few decades has also been accompanied by rising inequalities of wealth and income and worsening conditions for the poorest urban dwellers. Beginning in the 1970s, capitalist elites and their political allies in one country after another initiated a campaign to deregulate business, crush trade unions, liberalize international trade, privatize government services, and shrink spending on the social services; known as "the Washington Consensus" or "neoliberalism," this campaign has further exacerbated the gap between the rich and the rest. The extent of this widening divide is shocking indeed.

According to an Oxfam report, in 2015, the 62 wealthiest individuals on the planet collectively owned the same wealth as 3.6 billion people, half the global population (Oxfam 2016: 2). Moreover, in 2017, the richest 10% of the world's adults owned some 88 % of all global assets (Credit Bank Suisse 2017: 9).

The economic polarization associated with the neoliberal era has hit workers and the poor especially hard. While the rich have seen their annual incomes soar, earnings for low-wage workers have actually fallen over the past 20 years (Oxfam 2016: 12–14). Over 1.4 billion workers worldwide—and over half of all workers in developing countries—are in "vulnerable" or "precarious" forms of employment that are insecure, informal, often part-time or short-term, poorly paid, and typically performed in undesirable working conditions (International Labor Organization 2017: 2). Economist Guy Standing estimates that fully one quarter of the world's adult population can be counted among the ranks of the "precariat"—meaning that they work jobs of limited duration, have limited employment protection, and have "no sense of career, no sense of occupational identity" in sharp contrast to earlier generations of workers who saw themselves as part of the "industrial proletariat" (Standing 2011: 24). On top of this, despite a decade of uninterrupted economic growth, global unemployment remains relatively high (at 5.7%) a decade after the economic meltdown of 2008 (International Labor Organization 2017: 1). While the share of the world's population living in poverty overall has been on the decline for decades, 783 million workers, 29% of the global workforce, are still among the "working poor," meaning they earn less than $3.10 in US dollars per day (International Labor Organization 2017: 7).

Rampant job insecurity and the growing disparity between the affluent and the impoverished have had a profound impact on cities and urban life. The United Nations reports that roughly 75% of urban areas across the globe have experienced an increase in income inequality over the past 20 years (UN-Habitat 2016: 15). The sheer extent of economic inequality in three so-called global metropolises—New York City, Chicago, and London—is illustrative. In 2014, the richest 5% of New York City households earned 88 times as much as the poorest 20%, and some 1.7 million New Yorkers, a fifth of the city's inhabitants, lived below the US poverty line (Roberts 2014). As of 2016, more than 1.3 million Chicagoans were officially classified as poor and the child poverty rate in the city exceeded 33% (Ihejirika 2016). Further, according to one estimate, the wealthiest 10% of London households currently own 52% of the city's wealth while the bottom 50% own just 5.3% (Trust for London 2017).

Of course, economic inequality is even more pronounced in the emerging megacities of the Global South. For instance, in Rio de Janeiro, Brazil, the average household income of the most affluent 10% of households in 2011 was 58 times that of the bottom 10% of households (Euromonitor 2013). In rapidly urbanizing Nigeria, the number of people living in poverty soared from 69 million in 2004 to 112 million in 2010 while, during the same time span, the number of millionaires in the country rose by 44% (Akinwotu and Olukoya 2017).

The trends described above are evidence of the worldwide emergence of "dual cities." Originally coined by Manuel Castells, the notion of the "dual city" draws attention to the way the restructuring of the global economy has contributed to growing spatial segregation of socio-economic classes within major metropolitan centers (although even supporters of the concept admit that the dual city metaphor to some degree over-simplifies complex urban social realities) (Castells and Mollenkopf 1991). Perhaps the most visible manifestation of the rampant economic polarization of recent years has been the development of vast slums in the sprawling urban agglomerations of South America, Africa, and Asia. Slums can be defined as crowded settlements of informal or poorly constructed housing, usually without adequate sanitation and infrastructure, whose residents typically lack formal land tenure. The United Nations estimates that some 881 million people inhabit such areas in the developing world alone (UN-Habitat 2016: 3). Since 1970, slums throughout the developing world have expanded at a faster rate than the cities of which they are a part (Davis 2006: 17). In Mumbai, India, roughly 42% of the city's 20 million residents live in slums (Phadke 2015). As Mike Davis put it in his *Planet of Slums*, "instead of cities of light soaring toward heaven, much of the twenty-first century city squats in squalor, surrounded by pollution, excrement and decay" (Davis 2006: 19).

Covering the Urban Underclass

The rise of the "dual city" and the economic vulnerability endured by the disadvantaged people it houses are the direct result of powerful economic trends aided and abetted by neoliberal government policies. Yet journalistic discourse about the urban poor, the urban working class, slums, and slum dwellers typically fixates not on the structural or institutional causes for rising inequality and deprivation, but on the deviant behavior and allegedly defective values of the disadvantaged themselves.

The commercial news media's propensity for framing the urban poor and working class as morally defective or dysfunctional has a long history. Mid-19th-century British writer Henry Mayhew's pioneering series of newspaper articles on working-class residents of London uncovered the squalor in which they lived and was generally sympathetic to their plight. Yet, Mayhew also viewed his subjects' troubles as due, at least partially, to their own ignorance, laziness, and bad habits. For instance, he claimed that "costermongers"—those who make their living selling things on the street—"taken as a body, entertain the most imperfect idea of the sanctity of marriage" and that "the notion of morality among these people agrees strangely . . . with those of many savage tribes" (Mayhew 1985: 42–43). Nor was Mayhew alone in constructing the urban working class as dysfunctional and potentially barbarian. In his muckraking 1890 tract *How the Other Half Live*, reformer and early photojournalist Jacob Riis exposed the horrific living conditions in the dank tenements of New York City's Lower East Side, yet he still insisted that a sixth of the more than 1.5 million destitute residents of the city were "unworthy" paupers, "frauds," and "professional beggars" (Riis 1914: 224). Throughout the late 19th and early 20th century, newspapers across the world consistently represented big city slums and their residents as alien, degenerate, and a threat to civilization and framed campaigns by police and public health officials to address the problems of the slums as "crusades against heathen territories" (Mayne 1993: 208). While there have been historical junctures when the mainstream news media have broken with the dominant interpretation of destitute urbanites as shiftless and immoral—notably during the Civil Rights and welfare rights insurgencies of the 1960s—these moments have been few and far between.

Several studies of contemporary news coverage of the urban poor in Europe, the US and the Global South have found that such reporting often distorts or obscures the structural causes of economic deprivation and frequently frames the poor as "abnormal," "defective," "disorderly," and "threatening." Such framing serves to justify ideologically the neoliberal assault on social welfare programs and the intensification of policing directed at disadvantaged urban communities. In the UK, the press has tended to blame the underprivileged for their economic misfortunes and, to some degree, for the weakness of the national economy (Golding and Middleton 1982). In the US, research has found that news media coverage of what politicians in the 1980s took to calling "the urban underclass" reinforces negative stereotypes about the economically disadvantaged and inaccurately portrays America's poor as overwhelmingly African American (Gilens 1999; see also Chapter 21, this volume).

Jairo Lugo-Ocando's investigation of the way global journalism represents those in poverty across the developing world concludes that the poor are consistently positioned in the news as "other," as different and inferior, and often depicted as "passive" victims of circumstances (Lugo-Ocando 2015). He also found that reporting by international news outlets like CNN and the BBC on stories about the poor in Africa and Latin America often failed to consult even a single named source from the affected communities and is typically "articulated through the voices of Westerners" (Lugo-Ocando 2015: 62). Moreover, he noted that Western news accounts about growing economic inequality and poverty in the Global South often omit any reference to their structural causes. The fact that the poor are rarely if ever the focus of routine journalism—less than 1% of stories covered by mainstream American news outlets, according to one study (Froomkin 2013)—makes the distorted nature of the few stories the media does carry about the urban poor that much more influential.

Research on the news media's coverage of specific impoverished urban neighborhoods confirms the overall pattern outlined above. Thus, for instance, one study of British TV news reporting on the extremely deprived inner-city district of Handsworth in Birmingham, UK found that the neighborhood attained visibility in the national British media mainly in connection to a series of riots and in the context of its very high crime rate (Cottle 1994: 236). Through its repeated portrayal in connection with crime and mayhem, "Handsworth and its associated communities have become charged with meaning and stigmatized as deviant, other, and outside normal boundaries of behavior and morality" (Cottle 1994: 239). Similarly, James Ettema and Limor Peer's study of newspaper coverage of different areas of Chicago demonstrates the mainstream news media's tendency to criminalize economically depressed inner-city neighborhoods. Ettema and Peer compared newspaper stories about two very different neighborhoods that appeared in Chicago's two main dailies, *The Chicago Tribune* and *The Sun-Times*: Austin, an impoverished, majority-African American community on Chicago's West Side, and Lincoln Park, an affluent, mostly white community on Lake Michigan near the city's downtown. Their analysis revealed that 69% of stories about the Austin area were framed "in terms of a social problem" while only 34% of stories about Lincoln Park were framed this way (Ettema and Limor 1996: 839). Indeed, the dominant image of Austin constructed by the city's two main daily newspapers as "crime-ridden and drug-infested" stood in stark contrast to the more sanguine image constructed of the upscale Lincoln Park neighborhood despite the fact that the latter actually had a higher incidence of reported crime in the period under study (Ettema and Peer 1996: 840).

The Urban Poor on Screen: Movies and TV

The depiction of the urban poor in contemporary commercial movies and scripted television programs typically replicates the conservative ideological assumptions that underwrite mainstream journalistic discourse about urban poverty and slums. In Hollywood movies and in commercially oriented films produced by other national film industries, the poor are inevitably constructed as either predatory criminals, abject victims, or pathological parasites and their communities are portrayed as chaotic and dangerous. The violence and crime associated with the "mean streets" of the slums in such films is transformed into a titillating and terrifying spectacle for a viewer assumed to be middle class. One of the few major longitudinal studies of representations of poverty in American movies, which analyzed 299 films about poverty and homelessness produced from 1902 through 2015, found that the poor in these films were consistently represented as either "objects of fear" or "objects of pity" and that "when movies try to explain why people are homeless or poor, the causes are generally rooted in individual failure or a dramatic, tragic event," while the larger social and economic forces that cause mass impoverishment were largely ignored (Pimpare 2017: 291). On occasion, films and television programs that project a more complicated, sympathetic, and nuanced picture of indigent city dwellers—usually produced independently on relatively low budgets and intended for niche audiences—have gotten some distribution and praise from critics.

The overarching patterns in screen depictions of the slums and the urban underclass can be illustrated by a closer analysis of three representative texts: a typical Hollywood crime thriller (*Street Kings*), an international hit movie set in a Mumbai slum (*Slumdog Millionaire*), and a "social realist" crime series that aired on American cable television (*The Wire*).

David Ayer's 2008 crime thriller *Street Kings* typifies Hollywood's tendency to sensationalize and spectacularize the violence and suffering that has accompanied the growing economic and social polarization of the world's major cities. Set in present-day Los Angeles, the film tells the story of a rogue LAPD Vice Squad detective Tom Ludlow (played by Keanu Reeves) whose investigation of the murder of his estranged former partner, Terrence Washington, uncovers a vast criminal conspiracy involving his own commanding officer. Ludlow's quest takes him on a grim tour of the lower-class "underside" of LA. Hunting for Washington's killer, he first stops in a blighted, graffiti-covered Latino neighborhood where he chases a gang member through trash-strewn alleys and later, he visits a ghetto neighborhood where he brutally interrogates a heavily tattooed gangster.

As is typical of Ayer's LA crime thrillers (*Training Day* [2001], *End of Watch* [2012]), violence and criminality are depicted in *Street Kings* as an inescapable feature of the poor and working-class areas of the city. Virtually everyone Ludlow encounters in his journey through these neighborhoods is a vicious outlaw, an addict, or a victim. As Ludlow prowls the mean streets of the city, the audience's expectation of his next violent showdown with some suspect or another adds to the film's suspense. And the ensuing fight scenes—including shootouts using machine guns—are always shot, staged, and edited to be dramatic, exciting, and extremely bloody.

As is often the case in Ayer's movies, many of the police officers in *Street Kings* are just as morally compromised as the lower-class thugs they police. Despite this unflattering image, cops—the heroic-yet-flawed character of Ludlow, Washington, an officer helping Ludlow named Disco—are the only people in the film with any redeeming qualities who are not completely helpless; the audience is invited to identify with them. As such, *Street Kings* ultimately presents spectators with what amounts to a cop's perspective on LA's low-income communities of color, one that sees these neighborhoods as literally hostile terrain.

While not as bleak as *Street Kings*, British director Danny Boyle's *Slumdog Millionaire* (2008) also sensationalizes its run-down setting for the voyeuristic pleasure of its (presumably Western, white, well-to-do) viewers. Winner of the 2008 Oscar for Best Picture, the movie tells the story of an orphaned former street urchin from the slums of Mumbai named Jamal Malik who, thanks to his wits and good luck, manages to win the Indian version of the TV game show, "Who Wants to Be a Millionaire," and reunite with his lost childhood sweetheart, Latika. Through a series of flashbacks that trace his improbable path to victory on the gameshow, the audience is shown the ordeals Jamal, his brother Salim, and Latika must endure to survive the horrors that surround them. Images of the squalor and overcrowding of Mumbai's slums have long been a staple of Indian gangster and social realist films. However, Boyle departs from these cinematic precursors by adopting a style that is anything but social realist, dazzling the audience with bright colors, rapid montage, and high-energy camera work. Throughout, viewers are bombarded with vivid shots of ragged mobs, filthy public toilets, alleyways, brothels, rickety shacks, and giant garbage heaps that flow past at a dizzying rate.

Some critics have labeled Boyle's aestheticized vision of urban poverty in this movie "poverty porn." Indeed, simply by virtue of its stunning visuals, *Slumdog* does tend to "glamorize" the horrific conditions out of which Jamal climbs, making them "look appealingly exotic and exciting for Western movie audiences" (Hanrahan 2015: 107). Entirely absent from the film is any kind of systematic examination of the political and economic factors responsible for Mumbai's massive informal settlements. As novelist Arundahti Roy has argued, the film "decontextualizes poverty" and, in the process, "makes India's poverty a landscape, like a desert or a mountain range, an exotic beach, god-given, not man-made" (Roy 2009). But perhaps just as importantly, the fantasy plot—with its focus on an individual character who rises from rags to riches against the odds—underestimates the considerable structural barriers preventing real-life Jamals from escaping their plight.

While most popular screen representations of slums and ghettos have overwhelmingly shared the sensationalism and obsession with urban pathology evident in *Street Kings* and *Slumdog Millionaire*, there have been notable exceptions. The HBO series *The Wire* (2002–2008), set in contemporary Baltimore, won critical acclaim for its extended exploration of the economic and racial divides cleaving the American city and its sympathetic, detailed, and nuanced depiction of the African American residents of the city's impoverished ghetto neighborhoods (see also Chapter 5, this volume). Created by former crime reporter David Simon, the series is a social realist variation on the police procedural which, in the first season, follows a group of detectives investigating a number of unsolved killings they suspect are tied to a drug dealing operation being run by a gang out of a public housing project. Over the course of its five seasons, the series examines the struggles of dockworkers working at Baltimore's port, the corruption plaguing city politics, Baltimore's failing public schools, and the decline of the city's main newspaper. Unlike *Street Kings*, *The Wire* does not center its narrative exclusively on the police or on law enforcement's view of the city and its problems. Rather, throughout the series, street-level drug peddlers, unemployed workers, homeless drug addicts, children living in foster homes, and embattled school teachers are given equal screen time with police detectives and none of them are stereotyped, glamorized, demonized as monsters, or transformed into objects of pity.

More significantly, unlike most screen explorations of the lives of the so-called urban underclass, *The Wire* always situates the struggles encountered by its destitute and working-class characters in the context of broader institutional failures (such as the disappearance of blue-collar jobs, inadequate social services, and underfunded schools). As Sherryl Vint has argued, the series is "distinct from other police dramas in its focus on the systematic problems of racism and poverty in America" (Vint 2013: 5). For example, in Season Four, one central storyline concerns a character, Dukie Weems, who is the child of drug addicts and is failing at school. Though a caring teacher helps him to improve his academic performance temporarily, by the end of the season, a combination of misfortunes and bureaucratic obstacles causes him to drop out; his family is evicted from their apartment and he is forced to sell drugs on the street. Dukie's story arc makes it clear that at every step of the way he has been let down by bankrupt or dysfunctional social institutions (such as the school system and state-run child protective services) that should have protected him.

Ultimately, *The Wire* puts the dual city on display not to frighten or titillate but to condemn the injustice and inequality upon which it is based and to awaken in the audience a desire for social reform. David Simon and several contributing writers to *The Wire* point to the show's examination of inner-city crime as embodying an argument for abolishing America's "war on drugs" and the mass incarceration of African American youth that it has enabled (Simon et al. 2008: 50). But the series is not only an indictment of the American criminal justice system; it is also a sweeping indictment of neoliberal capitalism and the harm it has inflicted on the vulnerable (Vint 2013: 102). As Simon himself explained, the overarching theme of the series is that "raw, unencumbered capitalism . . . devalues human beings" (Talbot 2007). In mainstream commercial media, such self-consciously anti-capitalist explorations of urban poverty are rare indeed.

A Voice for the Excluded: Poor People's Media

Corporate media representations of life on the "disadvantaged end" of the global city are not the only ones. Community-controlled, not-for-profit grassroots media provide a platform for voices, ideas, and perspectives that are routinely excluded from mainstream media. The proliferation of slums across the globe has been accompanied by an explosion of media created by and for the urban poor. Though typically short-lived and often lacking in financial resources, these organizations produce content that offers an alternative to, and often directly contests, representations of the poor and the working class produced by the media outlets owned and managed by elites.

Consider the case of Pamoja 99.9 FM, a noncommercial, volunteer-run community radio station serving Kibera, a desperately poor informal settlement of more than one million people located on the outskirts of Nairobi, Kenya. Pamoja—the Swahili word for "together"—was founded by former BBC journalist Muchiri Kioi in 2007 to focus on "the day-to-day aspects of life in Kibera" consistently ignored by mainstream news organizations (Kopecky 2007). Funded by donations from the founders, the occasional grant, and equipment donated by dissident politicians, the station airs a mixture of music programming (mostly reggae, hip-hop, and East African music), public service announcements, and BBC news dispatches together with locally produced news and public affairs programming addressing issues of concern to the slum's youth. Topics discussed on such shows range from drugs, teen pregnancy, and HIV/AIDS to the environment and women's issues. During the rioting and ethnic clashes that rocked Kibera following the disputed December 27, 2007 presidential election, Pamoja promoted a message of peace. It also became "a clearing house for the sort of basic information that people would need after a hurricane or other natural disaster" (Baldauf 2008). As one of the station's staff members, Mohammad Abubakr, remarked, "so many people in the ghetto have no way to express themselves . . . through radio, we can reach them" (Baldauf 2008).

The very existence of an outlet like Pamoja FM poses a challenge to Kenya's dominant, elite-controlled commercial mass media, to the politicians such media support, and to the mainstream media's derogatory and distorted representations of the marginalized and disadvantaged residents of shantytowns like Kiberia. Not surprisingly, the station's founders had considerable difficulty obtaining a broadcast license from government officials (who regarded the station as too closely allied with opposition politician Raila Odinga). It took two and a half years of bureaucratic wrangling with the Communications Commission of Kenya before the license was granted (Kopecky 2007).

The government resistance encountered by Pamoja FM is typical of the kind of repression that often greets media created by the urban poor. The trials endured by community broadcaster Mbanna Kantako in the US illustrate the lengths to which the state will go to suppress such outlets. In 1987, Kantako—a blind African American tenants' rights activist living in a racially segregated public housing project in Springfield, Illinois—set up a studio and small transmitter in his apartment to share community news with other residents. Using the call letters WTRA (for Tenants' Rights Association), Kantako broadcast illegally and called his one-man station Black Liberation Radio. He played "uncensored songs by Ice T, NWA, Public Enemy and other then-controversial hip-hop groups that spiced messages of defiance with plenty of four-letter words" (Rushton 2013). He also relayed tenants' complaints about the administration of the housing project and aired reports about police brutality against the project's largely African American residents. Springfield police complained to the Federal Communication Commission. In 1989, an FCC official accompanied by a Springfield police officer visited his studio and demanded that he stop broadcasting. That was the beginning of a series of confrontations between Kantako and federal broadcast regulators. He has been subject to FCC fines, which has refused to pay. In 2000, US Marshalls seized his radio equipment in a raid that Kantako broadcast live and, later, a federal judge issued a restraining order to push him off the air (Rushton 2013). As recently as 2011, he had received threatening letters from the FCC (Human Rights Radio 2011). Yet, Kantako's station, now called Human Rights Radio, continues to broadcast news about, and for, his community in defiance of regulators.

On very rare occasions, media made by the urban poor and working class has received government support, enabling it to reach larger audiences (see also Chapter 40, this volume). Following the political ascendancy of Hugo Chavez and his Bolivarian socialist movement in 1999, Venezuela's National Assembly passed laws ensuring the right of public access to television and radio and providing government funding for community broadcast outlets. By 2011, the country had nearly 1,200 noncommercial public and community media outlets, many of them broadcasting programming produced directly by community reporters, documentarians, and video producers. A number of these outlets are explicitly dedicated to empowering and amplifying the voices of the urban poor and working class.

For instance, Vision Venezuela TV (ViVe) is an independent, cooperatively run public television station founded in 2004 in the capital city of Caracas that airs content such as documentaries on housing and a narrative series called *Historias de Vida* about community organizing (Artz 2015: 234). ViVe organizes video production training through neighborhood organizations and workers' councils and directly collaborates with community videographers on all its programming. Another noncommercial community television station in Caracas, Ávila TV, airs a combination of news, public affairs, and creative programming produced by and for the city's youth, all with a "hip-hop sensibility" and socialist political commitments. Ávilia's telenovelas ("soap operas") focus on the lives of working-class Caracas families and contain "political overtones with not-so-subtle barbs at the opposition for undemocratic obstruction and the government for not championing working class interests" (Artz 2015: 237).

Conclusion

With soaring economic inequality continuing to structure the world's burgeoning metropolises, it is likely a growing share of the global population will be forced to reside in slums and other economically marginalized urban enclaves. The elite-owned press and corporate screen media have provided the public with mostly distorted, lurid, and stereotyped representations of this reality. This matters because the way media define social issues like urban poverty shapes public policy debates about the best ways of addressing these issues (Gilens 1999). But the rise of community-controlled noncommercial media like Pamoja FM and ViVe TV creates opportunities for the urban poor and working class to speak out in their own voices about the conditions in which they live and perhaps gives them an opportunity to intervene directly in policy debates that impact their lives.

References

Akinwotu, E. and Olukoya, S. (2017) "'Shameful' Nigeria: A country that doesn't care about inequality," *The Guardian*, July 18, www.theguardian.com/inequality/2017/jul/18/shameful-nigeria-doesnt-care-about-inequality-corruption.

Artz, L. (2015) *Global Entertainment Media: A Critical Introduction*, London: Wiley-Blackwell.

Baldauf, S. (2008) "Positive radio brings calm to tense Kenya slum," *Christian Science Monitor*, January 11, www.csmonitor.com/World/Africa/2008/0111/p01s02-woaf.html.

Castells, M. and Mollenkopf, J. (eds.) (1991) *Dual City: Restructuring New York*, New York: Russell Sage Foundation.

Cottle, S. (1994) "Stigmatizing Handsworth: Notes on reporting spoiled space," *Critical Studies in Mass Communication*, 11(3), pp. 231–256.

Credit Suisse (2017) *Global Wealth Report 2017*, Zurich: Research Institute, http://publications.credit-suisse.com/index.cfm/publikationen-shop/research-institute/global-wealth-report-2017-en.

Davis, M. (2006) *Planet of Slums*, London and New York: Verso.

Ettema, J. and Limor, P. (1996) "Good news from a bad neighborhood: Toward an alternative to the discourse of urban pathology," *Journalism and Mass Communication Quarterly*, 73(4), pp. 835–856.

Euromonitor International (2013) "World's largest cities are the most unequal," http://blog.euromonitor.com/2013/03/the-worlds-largest-cities-are-the-most-unequal.html.

Froomkin, D. (2013) "It can't happen here: Why is there so little coverage of Americans struggling with poverty?" *Nieman Reports* (Winter), http://niemanreports.org/articles/it-cant-happen-here-2.

Gilens, M. (1999) *Why Americans Hate Welfare*, Chicago, IL: University of Chicago Press.

Golding P. and Middleton, S. (1982), *Images of Welfare: Press and Public Attitudes to Poverty*, London: Blackwell Publishers.

Hanrahan, F. (2015) "The poverty tour: Life in the slums of Mumbai and Manila as seen in Danny Boyle's *Slumdog Millionaire* and Merlinda Bobis's *The Solemn Lantern Maker*," *Atlantis: Journal of the Spanish Association of Anglo-American Studies*, 37(1), pp. 101–119.

Human Rights Radio (2011) "Welcome to the Human Rights Radio Network," www.humanrightsradio.net.

Ihejirika, M. (2016) "More children in Illinois living in poverty than before the recession," *Chicago Sun-Times*, June 24, http://chicago.suntimes.com/politics/more-children-in-illinois-u-s-living-in-poverty-than-before-recession.

International Labour Organization (2017) *World Employment Social Outlook*, Geneva: International Labour Office.

Kopecky, A. (2007) "Slum community radio hits the airwaves," *The Daily Nation*, August 18.

Lugo-Ocando, J. (2015) *Blaming the Victim: How Global Journalism Fails Those in Poverty*, London: Pluto Press.

Mayhew, H. (1985) *London Labour and the London Poor*, London: Penguin Books.

Mayne, A. (1993) *The Imagined Slum: Newspaper Representation in Three Cities 1870–1914*, Leicester, London, and New York: Leicester University Press.

Oxfam. (2016) "An economy for the 1%," *Oxfam Briefing Paper No. 210*, January 18, www.oxfam.org/sites/www.oxfam.org/files/file_attachments/bp210-economy-one-percent-tax-havens-180116-en_0.pdf.

Phadke, M. (2015) "Slum redevelopment: SRA to acquire land with slum clusters from private trusts," *Indian Express*, November 22, https://indianexpress.com/article/cities/mumbai/slum-redevelopment-sra-to-acquire-land-with-slum-clusters-from-private-trusts.

Pimpare, S. (2017) *Ghettos, Tramps and Welfare Queens: Down and Out on the Silver Screen*, New York: Oxford University Press.

Riis, J. (1914) *How the Other Half Lives: Studies Among the Tenements of New York*, New York: Charles Scribner's Sons.

Roberts, S. (2014) "Gap between rich and poor in Manhattan is greatest in the U.S., Census finds," *New York Times*, September 17, www.nytimes.com/2014/09/18/nyregion/gap-between-manhattans-rich-and-poor-is-greatest-in-us-census-finds.html.

Roy, A. (2009) "Caught on film: India 'not shining'," *Dawn.com*, www.dawn.com/news/921599.

Rushton, B. (2013) "Keeping it real: Mbanna Kantako is still on the air," *Illinois Times*, April 25, http://illinoistimes.com/article-11283-keeping-it-real.html.

Simon, D., Lehane, D., Pelecanos, G., Price, R., and Burns, E. (2008) "Saving cities, and souls," *Time Magazine*, March 17, p. 50.

Standing, G. (2011) *The Precariat: The New Dangerous Class*, London and New York: Bloomsbury Academic.

Talbot, M. (2007) "Stealing life: The crusader behind *The Wire*," *The New Yorker*, October 22, www.newyorker.com/magazine/2007/10/22/stealing-life.

Trust for London (2017) "Wealth Distribution," www.trustforlondon.org.uk/data/wealth-distribution.

UN-Habitat (2016) *World City Report 2016: Urbanization and Development- Emerging Futures*, Nairobi, Kenya: UN-Habitat, https://unhabitat.org/wp-content/uploads/2014/03/WCR-%20Full-Report-2016.pdf

Vint, S. (2013) *The Wire*, Detroit, MI: Wayne State University Press.

Further Reading

Krstić, I. (2016) *Slums on Screen: World Cinema and the Planet of Slums*, Edinburgh: Edinburgh University Press.

Macek, S. (2006) *Urban Nightmares: The Media, the Right and the Moral Panic over the City*, Minneapolis, MN: University of Minnesota Press.

Mayne, A. (2017) *Slum: The History of a Global Injustice*, London: Reaktion Books.

43
THE POLITICS OF SEXUALITY IN MEDIATED CITIES

Hollis Griffin

Introduction

There are strong parallels between the ways that cities facilitate the formation of sexual minority communities and the ways that audiences composed of sexual minorities are courted by the media industries. Cities bring people together in public space: crowds coalesce in streets, communities concentrate in neighborhoods, and strangers bump into each other on public transit (Simmel 1903). Purchasing a drink or a meal, paying a cover charge at a club, or buying a membership pass to a community center provide people with avenues for circulating in spaces where sexual minorities congregate. In essence, cities bring people together, allowing them to make contact with others like themselves (Bell and Valentine 1995; Meeker 2003). The media industries also bring people together. Movies, television programs, and online content represent particular desires, life experiences, and habits of mind shared by members of audiences. In an increasingly niche-oriented marketplace, sexual minorities are a much sought-after demographic among media companies (Gross 2001; Aslinger 2009; Griffin 2017). Thus, movies, television programs, and online content provide sexual minorities with new opportunities to convene around media forms created especially for them.

Media forms made for sexual minorities narrate the practices, institutions, and cultures associated with same-sex desire. As a result, the representation of cities is often a key component of these media (Griffin 2017). All representations of sexual minorities refract same-sex desire through the characteristics of a given medium. So, when movies, television programs, and online content depict city life, they do it in ways that are consistent with how particular genres are used to tell stories, or how various modes of financing are employed to produce and distribute content (Lotz 2007). At the same time, representations of sexual minorities invoke more ideas than they contain, suggesting universality through particular signifiers and modes of address that downplay or just erase the differences between diverse groups of people.

After reviewing key debates about sexual identities and the city as a space of both oppression and freedom, I look at the role played by media in the construction of the city as such space. Specifically, I explore how the travel-themed television series *Round Trip Ticket* (Various, 2005–2009) and *Bump!* (Various, 2004–2013) construct LGBT neighborhoods as spaces of consumption for sexual minority audiences. These representations draw upon a long history of such neighborhoods, which have, for centuries, provided safe harbor and opportunities for community building for sexual minority people. The programs construct some sense of diversity in representing these neighborhoods insofar as each episode's segments showcase a variety of different places to go and see. *Round Trip Ticket* and *Bump!* provide viewers with opportunities for armchair travel, bringing them close to places they might not encounter through other means. Even so, that variety cannot accommodate the complexities of sexual minorities' experiences of public space. The programs suggest that the pleasures of consumption are equally available to all viewers and, as I demonstrate, that is not necessarily the case. The programs are consistent with the economic mandates of production companies, television networks, and advertisers insofar as they represent cities and their LGBT neighborhoods in consumer-friendly ways (Fursich 2002). Segments feature hosts and correspondents patronizing certain businesses, buying particular products, and participating in specific cultural milieux. All cities are home to neighborhoods where minority communities of all kinds gather. Such neighborhoods provide people with feelings of freedom and belonging that they do not often enjoy outside of these spaces. In *Round Trip Ticket* and *Bump!*, the desire to be among like-minded others is represented as a need that can be satisfied in the marketplace. The programs paint consumption as providing a means for the self-actualization of sexual minority viewers and an avenue for their participation in communities of people like themselves. In doing so, *Round Trip Ticket* and *Bump!* cast sexual desire and consumer desire as mutually informing pursuits, connecting sexual minorities in the audience with those on screen via constructions of city life that foreground the pleasures of buying and consuming commodities.

Cities and Sexual Minorities

Cities provide many attractions, employment opportunities, and community-building resources to people who experience same-sex desire. They feature a simultaneous dispersal and concentration, wherein the spatial practices of cities are such that sexual minorities can be found throughout urban locales but cluster in particular places. Henri Lefebvre defines "spatial practices" as the processes through which relations of production are situated in social space. These practices construct certain locales as being "desirable or undesirable; benevolent or malevolent; sanctioned or forbidden to particular groups" (Lefebvre 1991: 33). So, for example, while sexual minorities and their communities can be found throughout New York City, they have a long history of concentrating in the Greenwich Village area (Chauncey 1994). The 1969 Stonewall riots have made the neighborhood a symbol of the fight for LGBT equality. The neighborhood provides sexual minorities with a sense of safety but it has also worked to insulate them from the rest of the city. One result is a racial segregation that makes the neighborhood far whiter than the city itself is. Similar patterns of dispersal, concentration, and racial disparity can be found in cities throughout the world, as in Paris and London, where neighborhoods like the Marais and Soho are associated with sexual minorities but these populations and the various institutions (businesses, public services) that serve them can be found throughout the locales. Spatial practices are historical in nature, so the dispersals and concentrations of sexual minorities in cities shift and morph over time. For example, the technology boom of the 1990s increased the cost of living in historically LGBT neighborhoods in San Francisco, especially the Castro. As a result, San Francisco's sexual minority communities have increasingly migrated beyond city limits, especially to the neighboring city of Oakland (Boyd 2003). Similarly, Schöneberg has long been a neighborhood associated with sexual minorities in Berlin. But the development of the art and nightlife scenes in Friedrichshain and Kreuzberg have made these neighborhoods hubs for sexual minorities in the early decades of the 21st century as well.

In historical research on cities and sexual minorities, scholars argue that the rise of wage labor associated with the Industrial Revolution enabled people who experience same-sex desire to work and, thus, live outside of family units and associated constraints on behavior (D'Emilio 1993; Houlbrook 2005). Thus, the rise of manufacturing in the late 19th century allowed people to build lives and communities around same-sex desire. For that reason, cities are often configured as key aspects of sexual minority identities and communities. Industrialization and wage labor mark a discursive shift from more dispersed experiences of same-sex desires to the organization of these desires into personal identities and broader communities. Even so, issues of gender, race, and class mitigate an easy understanding of the relationship between cities and same-sex desire, because these combine with sexual identities in many conflicting ways (Halberstam 2005). Thus, while city life is often a constitutive feature of many sexual minority lives and communities, it operates differently for subjects from different identity groups (Chauncey 1994).

The experiences of sexual minorities who also identify as racial and ethnic minorities call into question an understanding of cities as enabling a linear emergence from the closet. In his ethnographic research on men of the Dominican diaspora who have sex with men in New York City, Carlos Decena states that many of his interview subjects depend on immigrant and familial networks to help them find housing and steady work (Decena 2011). These material needs and the resources that the men use to meet them constrain their ability to build lives around same-sex desire. As a result, living in New York City does not facilitate the subjects' "coming out" in the traditional sense of that term, where one makes his/her sexual desires public knowledge simply upon communicating them to others. Instead, the subjects' same-sex desires function as open secrets where there is only a tacit understanding between the men and their families regarding same-sex desire. Decena found that family members are aware of the men's same-sex desires but those desires are not often a topic of discussion in the context of the home. Even so, Decena's subjects are not "in the closet." Rather, unspoken understandings among family members enable these men to move between familial and immigrant networks and the networks of sexual minorities they meet in other contexts. In that sense, city life does not free these men from their families entirely. At the same time, families do not impinge on the men's ability to realize their desires in any uniform way. In some sense, their families facilitate the men's same-sex desires by providing them with stability in their home and work lives.

Geosocial networking applications—or "mobile apps," as they are called in many places—are a prominent feature of city life for sexual minorities. Mobile apps like Grindr, Scruff, and Growlr help men who have sex with men make interpersonal connections safely in the urban spaces of heteronormative societies. While there are a handful of mobile apps that target female users, these technologies are few in number and not nearly as prevalent as those that target men (Murray and Sapnar Ankerson 2016). Further, these technologies foreground sex and gender binaries in ways that limit the ways that transgender people might use them (Griffin 2017). As these facts highlight, sex and gender also shape sexual minorities' experiences of cities. Scholars conducting research on sexual minorities and cities often frame their arguments through a binary understanding of sex and gender because of the profound structural differences in how cultures understand male and female desire (Kennedy and Davis 1993; Tang 2011). People's experiences of cities are profoundly affected by such beliefs and mores, as well as the conditions and norms that emerge from them. Across a variety of different cultures and locations, men enjoy greater access to public spaces and institutions than women do, and women bear more burdens in the private sphere. Thus, social anxieties regarding feminine propriety and gendered divisions of labor prevent an easy equation of male and female experiences of cities.

Even so, sexed and gendered dynamics of power at work in cities do not necessarily eliminate the potential for women to build communities there. For instance, in her ethnographic research on lesbians in Hong Kong, Denise Tang found that her subjects actively sought out bonds with lesbians and had access to spaces that facilitated that. At the same time, Tang's subjects faced struggles in asserting their sexual autonomy because so many of them live with family members. Some of the women have these living arrangements because of cultural norms regarding sex and gender. But scarcity related to government land allocation plays a related role in her subjects' ability to live outside of family homes. Tang found that her subjects often have to live with families because it is so difficult to find housing in Hong Kong. So many of the women have to maintain these living arrangements, even when they have the means to do otherwise. Social norms present another difficulty, as well. In Hong Kong's cultural imaginary, marriage is the route to a home of one's own. So, experiencing same-sex desire can be an issue of considerable tension between lesbians and their families, for a variety of reasons. Yet, much like Decena's subjects, these facts do not push Tang's subjects "into the closet." Rather, the women's same-sex desires necessitate particular negotiations with family members regarding their autonomy. Several of Tang's subjects reported that financial stability increased the respect they receive from their parents, giving the women more leeway to pursue connections with other lesbians around the city.

Sex and gender shape sexual minorities' experiences of cities in ways that often create lesbian communities beyond the confines of city areas more traditionally associated with sexual minorities. While the Marais has long been associated with queer Paris, another part of the city, Montmartre, has been home to several spaces important to lesbian communities at various points in time (Sibalis 1999). In Hong Kong, Tang reports that her subjects were more likely to seek out lesbians in neighborhoods less firmly connected to sexual minorities, like Tsim She Tsui and Mong Kok, than they were in areas more widely associated with sexual minorities, like Soho and Lan Kwai Fong. Tang found that the high cost of living in Hong Kong makes city institutions that cater to lesbians precarious. H20 and Red, two commercial venues that served lesbians in Hong Kong in the 1990s, were forced to close as a result of rising rents. These economic concerns have a considerable impact on the formation of lesbian communities in many different cities. For instance, two businesses that played important roles in the formation of lesbian communities—Rubyfruit in New York and Star Gaze in Chicago—closed as a result of the high cost of real estate in both cities (Griffin 2017).

The closure of businesses that serve sexual minorities highlights the relationship between community formation and the forces of gentrification, the process by which developers push out existing (poorer) residents and businesses to generate more profit from city land. On one hand, the practices associated with gentrification often involve the closure of businesses and displace less advantageous populations in ways that foreclose on the enactment of identities and communities related to same-sex desire (Delany 2001). On the other hand, gentrification generates additional possibilities for the formation of communities in the form of new attractions, new public spaces, and new patterns of commerce. In both Toronto and Sydney, economic transformations precipitated the dispersal of sexual minorities in neighborhoods historically associated with them (Nash and Gorman-Murray 2014). At the same time, in both cities, these conditions gave rise to new enclaves elsewhere. Thus, city spaces in which sexual minorities congregate are as much a part of gentrification as they are outside of it. In that sense, the relationship between commerce and sexual minorities forged in cities features a profound double movement of enactment and erasure.

The difficulties of romanticizing what cities have to offer to sexual minorities become especially problematic when considering issues related to transgender. Public spaces like bars and clubs that cater to sexual minority consumers can provide transgender people with places to congregate comfortably and safely. But those institutions can feature forms of gender policing that make transgender consumers feel unwelcome and unsafe, as well (Doan 2004). Further, while cities provide employment opportunities for many people, transgender people experience forms of discrimination that people with more normative identities do not. Research on transgender workers at call centers in cities in the Philippines found that these workers are often segregated within workspaces: clustered away from the more central spaces of doing business in ways that animate exploitative hierarchies (David 2015).

Having charted the complexities in how the urban plays out in the negotiation of sexual identities, I now focus on how communication practices inform that process. Whether television representation or smartphone usage, media spaces tend to replicate much of what goes on in the city but also give rise to unexpected twists. When cities are represented on *Round Trip Ticket* and *Bump!*, the complexities of the lives of sexual minorities who live there fall out of focus. The travel-themed programs target sexual minority audiences by framing cities in ways that foster feelings of freedom and belonging. At the same time, the programs smooth over the disparate experiences of diverse populations. The programs cast city life as unproblematically enabling, universally helping people pursue and realize their same-sex desires. Through modes of address that intertwine consumption and cultural membership, the programs construct cities as arenas for tacitly politicized modes of consumption. *Round Trip Ticket* and *Bump!* champion difference and then actively work to minimize it.

Consuming the City in Travel-Themed Television

On programs like *Round Trip Ticket* and *Bump!*, cities are articulated as signs to be consumed (Urry 2002). Segments detail various leisure and entertainment opportunities available to sexual minorities in different locations, courting viewers through a hybrid mode of address that mixes reportage and promotion. The programs employ narrative strategies that attempt to create a sense of community between on-air talent and viewers in the audience. A host's direct address to the camera forges an intimate relationship with viewers, as though they are a friend sharing a story about their travels to a particular city. Through this mode of narration, *Round Trip Ticket* and *Bump!* mediate a relationship between people in the audience and those depicted on screen by attempting to make the differences between the places inhabited by viewers at home and the cities depicted on screen exciting but also harmless. In summary, the programs construct cities so that they are different enough to be interesting to viewers but not different enough to be off-putting for them. As such, they become one point of reference for visitors seeking same-sex pleasures.

Across the segments that comprise each episode, *Round Trip Ticket* and *Bump!* construct a sense of variety in which the segments showcase a range of different sexual minorities in each city. Voiceover narration presents this construction of variety as evidence of the diversity of experiences available to sexual minorities in different cities. The programs combine commodity pleasures with a touch of political commentary, casting travel as a way for sexual minorities to find others like themselves (Sender 2005). *Round Trip Ticket* is produced specifically for the US-based cable television network Logo. Each episode uses interviews and location footage to highlight a different urban destination: New York City, Paris, San Francisco, and Berlin. By highlighting the interactions between the host and correspondents, episodes of *Round Trip Ticket* take viewers on a friendly, guided tour of neighborhoods associated with sexual minorities.

Individual episodes aggregate multiple clips: interviews, site visits, stock footage. Segments enumerate the features of a given city, offering them to audiences as a list of attractions they might seek out there. On *Round Trip Ticket*, transitions between segments are interspersed with kinetic graphics; animated cityscapes flash across the screen in black, white, and pink, an aesthetic that unites the program's tropes of urbanness and sexual identity. Every episode opens with the host defining the series as "a passport to how LGBT people are living, loving, and changing the world." Cutting back and forth between segments hosted by a cast of gender diverse and somewhat racially diverse correspondents, *Round Trip Ticket* features television "talk" that is constructed as being spontaneous (Corner 2000). The host's voiceover and reports by the correspondents convey information about the cities as though it is special knowledge. The program uses interviews to draw on the direct knowledge of locals, positioning them as experts. By doing so, *Round Trip Ticket* articulates the interviewee's experiences of a given city as being universal and their opinions about living there as fact.

Both programs foreground LGBT neighborhoods in their depiction of cities. Each episode's multiple segments offer viewers a range of different perspectives on the neighborhoods, constructing a sense of variety that attempts to underline the program's claims to represent an authentic vision of a city locale. The host's voiceover tries hard to convey the program's open-mindedness about the diversity within sexual minority communities. Crucially, though, the program downplays the differences between viewers (Aslinger 2009). Instead, it emphasizes the merits of distinctiveness and suggests a commonality between the experiences that sexual minorities have in various cities. *Round Trip Ticket*'s Mexico City episode illustrates the ideological issues that attend the rendering of cultural difference as an opportunity for consumption. The episode starts with a sequence in which shots depict people shopping, walking down streets, eating in restaurants, and riding bicycles. The voiceover is relatively dissonant in that the host tells viewers about the prevalence of poverty in the city and discusses the anti-LGBT sentiments that people from the Global North often associate with Latin American countries. But the voiceover concludes cheerfully; the host tells viewers that a new generation of sexual minorities in Mexico is working "to give people a voice" in civic affairs.

The program gestures to socio-economic and cultural issues in Mexico City but reins in that discussion with optimistic sentiments about the sexual minorities who live there. This segment cuts directly to a second segment that introduces a young man through voiceover. The voiceover identifies the interviewee as "José, an average Mexican citizen," who is then shown walking down the street in on-location footage that is similar to the episode's opening montage. In the sequences that follow, sound elements cut between the correspondent's voiceover and José's comments. Visual elements illustrate the pair as they walk down city streets and into stores and cafes. In voiceover, the correspondent reveals that the area is known as La Zona Rosa, a neighborhood that is home to many businesses that court sexual minority consumers. The pair discuss the neighborhood and its attractions but the segment segues into an exchange in which the correspondent questions José about the perceptions of Mexico in the Global North. The correspondent asks José about the Mexican Government's efforts to push businesses that serve sexual minorities out of La Zona Rosa during the 1990s. The correspondent also asks if José has been victimized by the hypermasculinity that many people in the Global North associate with Latin American men. About both issues, José says: "you just need to be yourself." He answers the correspondent's query about the city's cultural climate by telling him growing up gay in Mexico is "so much fun." In this way, the interview constructs the city as featuring liberal sexual mores rooted in the practices of commerce. It defuses anxieties that the locale might precipitate among viewers in the Global North. Finally, it leaves aside any possibility that female experiences of Mexico City and La Zona Rosa might diverge considerably.

Couched in feelings of open-mindedness and personal agency, *Round Trip Ticket* simultaneously paints cities as commodity pleasures to be consumed by audiences in the Global North and assures them that they will feel safe and welcome there. Additional segments in *Round Trip Ticket*'s Mexico City episode feature a brief interview with a lesbian restaurateur who owns a bar called "Pussy." The final segment includes an interview with a DJ at Club Living, a dance club that caters to gay men. Over short clips of sleekly designed dance floors, lounge spaces, and state-of-the-art media equipment, the DJ identifies similarities between the Mexico City club and venues that cater to gay men in cities in the Global North. Yet Escalante believes that there is a key difference between Mexico City and cities in the Global North, arguing that Mexico needs to pay as much attention to issues that affect sexual minorities as other cities do. It is a telling moment insofar as *Round Trip Ticket* suggests, in some sense, that tourists from the Global North might help modernize Mexico.

Like all episodes of *Round Trip Ticket*, the Mexico City episode illustrates how the program strains to manage the friction caused by its dialectic between the general and the particular. That tension becomes most visible in episodes where sexual minorities who live in cities in the Global South are framed for audiences who live in the Global North (Puar 2007). As a whole, *Round Trip Ticket* seeks to alleviate white anxieties and soothe middle-class sensibilities, which I discussed in the first part of the chapter, with a neoliberal "can-do," individualistic spirit rooted in commodity consumption. But when the program offers viewers an inside look at Mexico City, *Round Trip Ticket*'s limited vision casts the city and the people who live there as alluring yet also alien. Matters of diversity within sexual minority communities are left aside entirely.

Like *Round Trip Ticket*, *Bump!* uses a range of segments to construct a varied portrait of sexual minority life in one city per half-hour episode. The program is produced via a partnership between two Canadian companies: Pink Triangle Press, an LGBT media conglomerate, and Peace Point Entertainment Group, a television production company. *Bump!* began airing in 2004 on OUTtv, a Canadian television network that courts sexual minority viewers. The program was distributed to similar television networks in several different countries: the US, first on here! and then on Logo, in France on Pink TV, in Israel on EGO, in Germany on TIMM, and in the Netherlands on OutTV. In addition to watching *Bump!* on television, viewers can download individual episodes or watch them streaming online, and many are also available for sale on DVDs that are bundled by geography. For instance, *Bump! American Northeast* collects episodes featuring New York, Philadelphia, and Washington while *Bump! Great Britain* includes episodes that detail London, Manchester, and Brighton. Furthermore, *Bump!* has a smartphone application that allows viewers to download information detailed in episodes directly to their mobile phones. *Bump! Mobile Guides* provide links that enable users to access local websites and publications, find hotels and restaurants, and locate sites of specific interest to sexual minority travelers.

While similar in tone to Logo's *Round Trip Ticket*, *Bump!*'s mode of production alters the program's mode of address and, thus, its depictions of cities and sexual minorities. Although the hosts' accents allude to *Bump!*'s Canadian production, the program is made for a global viewership, so its aesthetics and narratives feature "transparency" or "zero-degree style" (Olson 1999). These terms refer to a narrative and formalist paradigm employed by media companies that attempts to make content more accessible to differently located audiences. The program's use of this paradigm is a structuring element of each episode. *Bump!* does not include as many interviews with locals and episodes do not involve multiple correspondents. Rather than *Round Trip Ticket*'s playful banter between hosts and reporters, *Bump!* episodes focus on the host alone. The result is a mode of address that streamlines its representation of cities so that they might be legible to viewers in a vast array of viewing contexts. Where *Round Trip Ticket* features local figures and businesses, *Bump!* segments are more likely to inform viewers where they can find global brands that they buy and use at home. *Bump!* also differs from *Round Trip Ticket* in its use of stock footage rather than location shooting. It uses voiceover narration more heavily as well.

The Madrid episode is similar to other installations of *Bump!* in that the city is constructed so that the tensions of cultural difference are raised and then soothed by the host's performance. In one segment, the lesbian host patronizes a salon that serves sexual minorities. She interacts with staff by emphasizing her poor mastery of Spanish miming to the store's employees in an exaggerated fashion for the purposes of comedy. This moment epitomizes the show's overall tone: disparities regarding identity seemingly disappear in the host's performance. The segment defuses still more tension when the host is brusquely rebuffed after attempting to flirt with a straight female employee, an interaction also played for comedy. The segment closes with the host turning to the camera in order to perform her embarrassment with a funny face to entertain the audience. As a whole, the segment raises and then resolves issues related to difference. It alleviates the tensions associated with same-sex desire in heteronormative cultures by articulating the host's desires as just another part of her comedic performance.

Bump! dispenses with local perspectives from city residents almost completely. In the program's Madrid episode, the host walks through a department store and narration cuts between different shots of signage for international fashion brands, including Diesel, Camper, and Adidas. Such iconography is familiar to the program's global audience, constructing cities in ways that tangle commodity consumption and cultural belonging without lingering on details that are unique to the city. The episode closes with a series of short sequences that depict the host drinking and dancing in different bars and nightclubs around Madrid. Rather than feature a single business, the sequence cuts quickly between shots of multiple locations, marking transitions with each business's name and website address. This footage includes minimal interactions with city residents. Instead, it focuses on the host as she mugs for the camera, drinks at bars, and dances in clubs around Madrid. Like *Round Trip Ticket, Bump!* constructs a city as a consumer-friendly playground for people who experience same-sex desire. The program constructs some sense of variety within the city but never points to any diversity within sexual minority communities. Although *Round Trip Ticket* injects some local knowledge into its representation of city life, *Bump!* dispenses with it completely. In doing so, the program highlights how a global marketplace for media created for sexual minority viewers depicts cities but ends up erasing their particularities.

Connecting Cities and Their Representations

The labor and leisure opportunities afforded by cities can provide people with the means to build lives around same-sex desire. In that sense, the broad structural conditions that characterize consumer capitalism play a significant role in the formation of sexual identities and communities. That process is made concrete in travel-themed television programming created for and circulated to sexual minorities. In these programs, cities become objects of consumption in narratives that articulate sexual desire through consumer desire. *Round Trip Ticket* and *Bump!* both demonstrate the role that cities often play in communities composed of sexual minorities. As with all representations, the fidelity between the signifiers seen in media texts and the signifieds to which they refer is always necessarily limited. Even so, the differences between them reveal a great deal of insight: the programs' representations of cities bracket or merely leave aside most of the tensions and complexities that characterize life there, collapsing race, gender, and class differences in the name of cultural inclusion that favors consumption. Though historically, expansion of niche markets contributed to the visibility of LGBT identities, consumption-based media such as the above homogenize cities and the sexual minorities who circulate in them.

Yet the differences between *Round Trip Ticket* and *Bump!* highlight different aspects of the relationship between consumption, cities, and sexual minorities. *Round Trip Ticket* suggests notions of community through the host's interactions with correspondents and locals. In contrast, *Bump!*'s single host casts cities as locations where individuals might circulate and consume freely, independent of the people who actually live in those places. In its reliance on stock footage, *Bump!* foregrounds the consumer brands associated with transnational capitalism at the expense of attention to unique aspects of a given location. In the similarities between the two programs, the role of commerce in facilitating sexual minority identities and communities is readily apparent. In the differences between them, the constraints placed on those identities and communities become apparent as well. The programs construct cities in ways that foreground the feelings of freedom and belonging that LGBT neighborhoods make available to people. In that sense, *Round Trip Ticket* and *Bump!* provide audiences with a look at how sexual minorities around the world gather in urban space, suggesting to viewers that they are part of a global community composed of others like themselves. Even though the narrative strategies employed by travel-themed television simplify the dynamics of power that shape those communities, *Round Trip Ticket* and *Bump!* provide evidence of how sexual minorities have gathered in cities for centuries.

References

Aslinger, B. (2009) "Creating a Network for Queer Audiences at LOGO TV," *Popular Communication*, 7(2), pp. 107–121.
Bell, D. and Valentine, V. (eds.) (1995) *Mapping Desire: Geographies of Sexualities*, New York: Routledge.
Boyd, N. A. (2003), *Wide-Open Town: A History of Queer San Francisco to 1965*, Berkeley, CA: University of California Press.
Chauncey, G. (1994) *Gay New York: Gender, Urban Culture, and the Making of the Gay Male World, 1890–1940*, New York: Basic Books.
Corner, J. (2000) *Critical Ideas in Television Studies*, New York: Oxford University Press.
David, E. (2015) "Purple-Collar Labor and Queer Value at Global Call Centers in the Philippines," *Gender and Society*, 29(2), pp. 169–194.
Decena, C. (2011) *Tacit Subjects: Belonging and Same-Sex Desire among Dominican Immigrant Men*, Durham, NC: Duke University Press.
Delany, S. (2001) *Times Square Red, Times Square Blue*, New York: NYU Press.
D'Emilio, J. (1993) "Capitalism and Gay Identity," in H. Abelove, M. A. Barale, and D. M. Halperin (eds.) *The Lesbian and Gay Studies Reader*, New York: Routledge, pp. 467–476.
Doan, P. (2004) "Queers in the American City: Transgendered Perceptions of Urban Space," *Gender, Place, and Culture*, 14(1), pp. 57–74.
Fursich, E. (2002) "Packaging Culture: The Potential and Limitations of Travel Programs on Global Television," *Communication Quarterly*, 50(2), pp. 204–226.
Griffin, F. H. (2017) *Feeling Normal: Sexuality and Media Criticism in the Digital Age*, Bloomington, IN: Indiana University Press.
Gross, L. (2001) *Up from Invisibility: Lesbians, Gay Men, and the Media in America*, New York: Columbia University Press.
Halberstam, J. (2005) *In a Queer Time in Place: Transgender Bodies, Subcultural Lives*, New York: NYU Press.
Houlbrook, M. (2005) *Queer London: Perils and Pleasures in the Sexual Metropolis, 1918–1957*, Chicago, IL: University of Chicago Press.
Kennedy, E. and Davis, M. (1993) *Boots of Leather, Slippers of Gold: The History of a Lesbian Community*, New York: Routledge.
Lefebvre, H. (1991) *The Production of Space*, Cambridge: Blackwell.
Lotz, A. (2007) *The Television Will Be Revolutionized*, New York, NYU Press.
Meeker, M. (2003) *Contacts Desired: Gay and Lesbian Communications and Community, 1940s–1970s*, Chicago, IL: University of Chicago Press.
Murray, S. and Sapnar Ankerson, M. (2016) "Lez Takes Time: Designing Lesbian Contact in Geosocial Networking Apps," *Critical Studies in Media Communication*, 33, pp. 53–69.

Nash, C. and Gorman-Murray, A. (2014) "LGBT Neighbourhoods and 'New Mobilities': Towards Understanding Transformations in Sexual and Gendered Urban Landscapes," *International Journal of Urban and Regional Research*, 38, pp. 756–772.

Olson, S. (1999) *Hollywood Planet: Global Media and the Competitive Advantage of Narrative Transparency*, New York, Routledge.

Puar, J. (2007) *Terrorist Assemblages: Homonationalism in Queer Times*, Durham, NC: Duke University Press.

Sender, K. (2005) *Business Not Politics: The Making of the Gay Market*, New York: Columbia University Press.

Sibalis, M. (1999) "Paris," in D. Higgs (ed.) *Queer Sites: Gay Urban Histories Since 1600*, New York: Routledge.

Simmel, G. (1903/2002) "The Metropolis and Mental Life," in G. Bridge and S. Watson (eds.) *The Blackwell City Reader*, Oxford and Malden, MA: Wiley-Blackwell.

Tang, D. (2011) *Conditional Spaces: Hong Kong Lesbian Desires and Every Day Life*, Hong Kong: Hong Kong University Press.

Urry, J. (2002) *The Tourist Gaze*, Thousand Oaks, CA: SAGE.

Further Reading

Arroyo, B. (2016) "Sexual Affects and Active Pornographic Space in the Networked Gay Village," *Porn Studies*, 3(1), pp. 77–88.

Brown, G. and Browne, K. (eds.) (2016) *The Routledge Research Companion to Geographies of Sex and Sexualities*, New York: Routledge.

Manalansan IV, M. F. (2018) "Restless Urban Meanderings: Mournful Flânerie in Troubled Times," *GLQ: A Journal of Lesbian and Gay Studies*, 24(1), pp. 42–44.

44
METHODOLOGICAL APPROACHES IN URBAN MEDIA AND COMMUNICATION RESEARCH

Simone Tosoni and Giorgia Aiello

Introduction

Over the last two decades, the study of urban media and communication has witnessed an upsurge of empirical research, characterized by a plurality of methodological perspectives on how the urban, communication, and mediation ought to be conceived, and consequently also by the adoption of a vast array of research methods.

Whilst a valuable asset, this multiplicity of perspectives may contribute to the establishment of a number of over-specialized approaches, thus fragmenting the field further and hindering the development of a shared debate. In this final chapter, we aim to help readers find their way through the field's main methodological heuristics, as a way to both foster internal dialogue and offer guiding principles for urban media and communication scholars to develop their empirical research. For this purpose, we distinguish three main strands of research within urban media and communication studies: approaches that consider the city as *content* of communication, as a *context* of media engagement, and as a *medium* of communication (Aiello and Tosoni 2016).

Cities as Content of Communication

The first strand of research sits at the intersection of the humanities and social sciences, addressing media representations of the city and considering them as constitutive of urban phenomena. As James Donald claims, there may be "no such thing as a city"; rather, we ascribe coherence to the multiplicity and diversity of "historically and geographically specific institutions, social relations of production and reproduction, practices of government, forms and media of communication, and so forth" (1992: 422) that interact in and ultimately also produce the space that we come to define as "city". Instead, the city ought to be considered as an imagined environment, not unlike the now widespread idea that the nation is an "imagined community". This imagining, Donald argues, is as relevant as "the material determinants of the physical environment" (1992: 422) to understand the city. It is in this sense that scholars working in this area focus on "[t]he discourses, symbols, metaphors and fantasies through which we ascribe meaning to the modern experience of urban living" (1992: 422). However, within this particular research strand, there are three main broad types of inquiry.

The first type focuses on representations of urban localities, cities, and urban processes in specific media texts, genres, or in the production of an author. These representations are explored in relation to media as diverse as literature (Lehan 1998), comics (Davies 2017), videogames (Anable 2013), and web documentaries (Holmes 2017), but also tourist brochures and guidebooks (Gilbert 1999; Siegenthaler 2002), and through interpretative methodologies that are strictly connected to the specificities of the *corpus* of texts under study. Particular attention is devoted to the relationship between cinema and the city, insofar as these are seen as "the most important cultural form—cinema—and the most important form of social organization—the city—in the 20th century (and, for the time being at least, the twenty-first century)" (Shiel 2001: 1; for an overview of cases, see Chapter 3, this volume). While this first type of inquiry has for long been centered on a single medium, recent research on place (Govers and Go 2009) and city branding (Dinnie 2010) has contributed to updating its methodological framework so as to include transmediality and multimodal representations (Paganoni 2015).

The second type of inquiry shifts the analytical focus from specific representations to broader logics and ideologies underpinning the media representation of cities. These ideological biases are traced, first of all, in relation to the content found in mainstream media discourse. Steve Macek (2006) has, for example, underlined how media discourse has promoted moral panic over the American city, by systematically depicting inner cities as morally decayed and uncontrollably violent and thus also promoting the adoption of reactionary social policies and surveillance techniques. Moreover, some scholars have integrated the analysis of mainstream media discourse with the analysis of people's everyday interactions with the media. Myria Georgiou (2013) has, for example, shown how media can support "liberatory" forms of cosmopolitanism, notwithstanding the neoliberal and market-oriented values informing mainstream media discourse. Another approach here focuses on media representations by integrating an analysis of their content with an investigation of their enunciative strategies. For example, Deborah Epstein Nord (1995) traces the typical semiotic enunciator of the Victorian city in 19th-century literature—the "invisible but all-seeing novelist effacing all of himself but his voice in the evocation of an urban panorama" (1995: 1)—back to the well-known figure of Baudelaire and Benjamin's *flaneur*. Yet, "if the rambler or *flaneur* required anonymity and the camouflage of the crowd to move with impunity and to exercise the privilege of the gaze", Nord reveals the concealed gendered nature of this enunciative subject by highlighting that "the too-noticeable female stroller could never enjoy that position" (1995: 4).

Through a similar approach, though focusing on visual representations of the city, Scott McQuire (2016) has shown how, historically, attempts to visually represent the modern city have been informed by two main semiotic strategies: the all-encompassing view from above exemplified by aerial photography, and the street view typical of the photo series, which is able to represent life in cities and urban transformation in a more fine-grained, yet fragmented way. These two strategies, he argues, have converged in the representational strategies of contemporary *geomedia* (e.g., Google Street View).

Finally, a computational approach sets out to detect representational patterns in large bodies of images and videos, for example pictures of cities and localities posted on social media. As an example, Nadav Hochman, Lev Manovich, and Mehrdad Yazdani (2014) have addressed "the relation between physical places and their social media representations [analyzing 28,419] social media photos that were tagged and shared on Instagram during the street artist Banksy's month-long residency in New York, October 2013" (2014: 1).

The third type of inquiry within this research strand focusing on the city as content deals with issues related to urban data visualization; that is, graphical representations for the analysis and communication of data about cities. Over the last decade, this topic has gained momentum because of the growing importance of big data in public debates, academic analyses, and the institutional management of urban issues (Drucker 2014). That said, data visualization is not just a technical process, nor is it a transparent window into information about cities and the urban. Rather, data visualization inevitably entails multiple layers of mediation, including the transposition of observable world phenomena into the data sources underpinning visualizations, the translation of such data into imagery, and the transformation of visual imagery into "the socially, culturally, and historically specific 'ways of seeing' engendered in the data visualization" (Gray et al. 2016: 229; see also Chapter 22, this volume). To develop a reflexive understanding of the inevitable bias implied in these forms of mediation, scholars in the field—who are often also active in the development of applied and experimental data visualization projects—advocate forms of critical literacy rooted in disciplines like visual, cultural and urban studies, geography, semiotics, aesthetics, and cartography, together with computer science. Visual analysis is often complemented with empirical methods like interviews, ethnography, and document analysis to shed light on data visualization production, usage, and reception practices.

Rob Kitchin's collaborative work, for example, employs participant observation, ethnography, and an analysis of archived correspondence to address the politics of data and design in the Dublin Dashboard, a website visualizing data about the city of Dublin that was built by two members of the research team (Kitchin, Maalsen, and McArdle 2016). In a similar vein, though with an experimental design approach, Simeone and Patelli (2016) involved different stakeholders—architects, urban planners, managers, scholars, and companies—to assess "if these end users considered meaningful the results of the social media analyses as performed and visualized by Urban Sensing" (2016: 261), an EU-funded project researching urban issues through social media analysis and visualization.

Cities as Contexts of Media Engagement

A second research strand addresses the city as a context of media engagement, aiming to shed light on the relationship between media usage and urban daily life, or the plurality of practices and routines that unfold within and across urban spaces (Graham 2004).

Stemming from the ethnographic tradition within audience studies, this strand of research attempts to extend scholars' analytical focus beyond the limits of the household, where it had been firmly confined until last decade, notwithstanding some notable exceptions (i.e., Lemish 1982; McCarthy 2001). As empirical research agendas are updated to include squares, streets, parks, cafes, or public transit, scholars are called to reflect on the peculiar *urban* nature of these public and semi-public places—a theoretical and methodological issue that remained by and large implicit in the studies of the private space of the household. *Hybrid space* (de Souza e Silva 2004; Frith 2012), *netspace* (Willis 2016), or *net locality* (Gordon and de Souza e Silva 2011) are only some examples of the methodological concepts proposed by scholars from different backgrounds to describe the intertwining of urban physical space, embodied place experience, and media-related practices.

Regarding the empirical methods employed to investigate this relationship, a key role is played by ethnographic observation, used alone or with other qualitative methods, mostly in-depth interviews. Not rarely, scholars back up their observations with the analysis of audio diaries (Krajina 2014) or video excerpts (Licoppe and Figeac 2015), recorded by them or by interviewees, sometimes with experimental recording devices designed for the purpose. These ethnographic approaches differ according to what can be called the "extension" and "intension" of the observation.

The extension of the observation refers to the breadth and the type of the portion of reality under study, and for the ethnographic approach, it depends on the definition of the ethnographic field. Scholars tend to define the extension of their empirical studies through three different lenses. First, with a media-centric approach, by focusing on a communication device (e.g., portable MP3 players, see Bull 2013), a platform (e.g., Foursquare, see Humphreys and Liao 2013), or a service (e.g., SMS/mobile texting services, see Kasesniemi and Rautiainen 2002), and by observing their usage across the different sites where they are actually engaged by people; second, with a site-centric approach, where scholars limit their observation of people's media engagement to a specific urban public or semi-public locality (e.g., Internet use in Wi-Fi cafes, see Hampton and Gupta 2008; mobile phones in the Tokyo underground, see Sugiyama 2013); and third, scholars who adopt a practice-centric approach focus on a social practice and investigate how it unfolds across different urban sites, involving different media-related activities. These practices can be "widely dispersed among different sectors of social life" (Schatzki 1996: 91), such as walking (Van Den Akker 2015) or driving (Haddington and Rauniomaa 2011), or they can be "more complex practices found in and constitutive of particular domains of social life" (Schatzki 1996: 98). Among these practices, defined as *integrative*, we find both ordinary everyday practices (Tosoni and Ridell 2016) and more specialized work-related practices, like media production (Rodgers, Barnett, and Cochrane 2014).

These different ways of defining the extension of the observation entail different adaptations of the ethnographic approach. On the one hand, scholars tailor the technicalities of the observation to the specificities of the sites of engagement, according to what Zlatan Krajina (2014) calls *methodological site-specificity* (2014: 51). On the other hand, especially when adopting a media- and practice-centric approach—where media engagement is observed across different urban contexts and/or mobilities—scholars tend to adapt their methods of observation in ways that are inspired by multi-sited ethnography (Marcus 1995), and mobile methods of inquiry (Büscher, Urry, and Witchger 2011; Manderscheid 2014).

The intension of the observation refers to the specific elements of the portion of reality under study that must be paid attention to, and depends on the theoretically informed objectives of the study and by the sensitizing concepts included in the researcher's methodological framework. Sensitizing concepts serve to bring some elements of the object under study to the forefront, thus inevitably overlooking others in the background (Blumer 1954) and constraining the researcher's perception and understanding. The study of media engagement in urban contexts is strongly influenced by a phenomenological conceptualization of space (Tosoni 2016), derived from phenomenological geography via the ethnographic tradition in audience studies. This is a methodological framework that has its linchpin in the distinction between space and place, where places are made out of space by repeated contacts that result in habituation, in the endowment of symbolic meanings, and in the development of affective attachments (Cresswell 2011). Media engagement in urban space is an integral part of these repeated practices of *place-making* (de Souza e Silva and Sheller 2015), which cannot be properly understood without a specific attention to media.

Recent research attempts to extend the intension implied by this methodological framework in three distinct, yet interrelated directions. First of all, by developing a dialogue with non-representational theories in human geography (Thrift 2008; Anderson and Harrison 2010) and, therefore, taking into account all the forms of bodily habituation and affect that contribute to define one's relationship to a particular place and its material elements (Moores 2012; see also Chapter 10, this volume). Second, this focus on embodiment resonates with the call within visual anthropology to develop a sensitivity to multisensoriality (Pink 2006). Here, the main aim is to extend the understanding of how media-engaged subjects experience urban space to the role played by other senses (Mattern 2008; Pink 2007; see also Chapter 34, this volume). Third, in dialogue with post-structuralist geographies (Murdoch 2006), there is also an attempt to extend the phenomenological conceptualization of space into a relational one (Jones 2009; Tosoni 2016) in order to grasp the interplay between the materiality of space, its symbolic meaning, and the practices of embodied subjects (Tosoni and Tarantino 2013; Timeto 2015). Therefore, space is conceived as possessing a processual and heterogeneous ontology, as it emerges dynamically from the uninterrupted interplay of material, symbolic, and pragmatic elements.

Cities as Media

Finally, a third strand focuses on the city as a *medium*. Drawing from the traditions of semiotics and rhetorical studies, it considers the urban built environment as a form of mediation in its own right, and aims to understand how "the urban" communicates—both from a symbolic and material standpoint (Aiello 2011). From this point of view, the physical qualities of cities mediate the everyday lives of both individuals and communities, as the urban built environment is a major observable manifestation of the "power-filled social relations" (Massey 1999: 21) that both constrain and enable a range of actions and practices among urban dwellers.

At the same time, the urban built environment can also be seen as a form of mediatization, as it is often used as a form of currency that is exchanged through media-like urban planning materials and promotional websites for tourism and real estate, for example. Often, this is done from the top down, in that global and second-tier cities alike are increasingly fashioned to project a desirable "world-class" image through photogenic cityscapes and lifestyle-oriented planning initiatives such as creative and cultural districts or waterfront developments (see also Chapter 24, this volume).

Within this broader approach to the city as a medium, it is possible to outline two main bodies of research, which are set apart by distinctive, though compatible, methods. These are critical and material rhetoric, on the one hand, and social semiotics and multimodality, on the other.

Critical rhetoric scholars have focused mainly on how "the material spaces of the everyday" (Dickinson 2002: 6) contribute to shaping specific ways of being and forms of identification. Here, the urban built environment is seen as a rhetorical inducement and an understanding of urban space as a whole is key to gaining critical insight into how particular subjectivities, actions, and/or forms of civic engagement are summoned by our surroundings. This perspective is rooted in US scholarship on material rhetoric and, particularly, the work of Carole Blair. Her argument that "being there" (Blair 2001)—that is, being where the "text" under study is located—is fundamental when analyzing paintings in museums or monuments in cities has shaped this field as a whole. As Blair and Michel (2000) claim, this kind of analysis focuses much less on "issues of symbolism" than "on the performative dimension of the site" (2000: 40).

When it comes to rhetorical scholarship focusing specifically on the urban and the suburban, the work of Greg Dickinson is particularly prominent. Dickinson's writing on spaces of memory and authenticity such as American old towns and main streets points to relationships between consumer culture, the urban built environment, and everyday performances of the self (Dickinson 1997). Likewise, he examines the spatial rhetorics and placemaking tropes that interpellate suburban dwellers in ways that, much in a Foucauldian way, compel them to become productive enacters of all-American values and social structures (Dickinson 2015).

To account for the importance of affect (Massumi 2002) and embodiment in the analytical process, Dickinson and Aiello (2016) reconstruct the state-of-the-art in rhetorical approaches to the urban built environment as a methodological framework that they summarize as "being through there". In doing so, they articulate the significance of both being in the presence of the materiality of the site(s) under study (e.g., to appraise their various textures, as in Aiello 2011 and Aiello and Dickinson 2014), and of moving through space with one's whole body and senses, at times in different directions and at different rates (e.g., in a car vs. on foot).

Scholars whose work is grounded mainly in British and Australasian critical discourse analysis and social semiotics see the urban "landscape" as a deployment of semiotic resources, which are typically examined as manifestations of major discursive structures and power relations. These semiotic resources are multimodal, ranging from writing and imagery to sound and texture. However, a focus on language has been historically dominant in this area of inquiry, with many scholars focusing their empirical efforts on researching "linguistic landscapes", which Landry and Bourhis (1977) originally defined as "[t]he language of public road signs, advertising billboards, street names, place names, commercial shop signs, and public signs on government buildings" in "a given territory, region, or urban agglomeration" (1977: 25). This is still a thriving perspective, particularly among linguists and sociolinguists interested in researching power relations among different ethnolinguistic groups in multilingual societies, together with the relationship between local identities and globalizing forces tied to consumption, tourism, and politics (see Gorter 2006; Shohamy et al. 2010; see also Chapter 2, this volume).

That said, in the early 2000s, Ron Scollon and Suzie Wong Scollon (2003) developed a broader approach known as *geosemiotics*, which they defined as "the study of the social meaning of the material placement of signs and discourses and of our actions in the material world" (2003: 2). In studying a variety of "texts" displayed in public, Scollon and Wong Scollon highlight the importance of examining both their emplacement and indexicality; that is, their physical location in space and their material relationship with their context and functions. Their geosemiotic framework is made of three key analytical dimensions, each covering one of the major semiotic systems that are at work in the making of a "place". As a semiotic system, *interaction order* refers to the ways social relationships between different human actors are organized in space, and how these actors behave in each other's presence. *Visual semiotics* is somewhat narrowly defined as "the ways in which pictures (signs, images, graphics, texts, photographs, paintings, and all of the other combinations of these and others) are produced as meaningful wholes for visual interpretation" (Scollon and Wong Scollon 2003: 8). Finally, *place semiotics* refers to the meanings of spatial organization itself, in particular in relation to the uses of different kinds of space, which, for example, may be private or public, or else frontstage or backstage.

The Scollons' approach has greatly influenced further developments in discursive and semiotic approaches to space and place (see Lou 2014; also, Gendelman and Aiello 2010). In this vein, Adam Jaworski and Crispin Thurlow (2010) have extended and replaced the notion of "linguistic landscapes" with that of "semiotic landscapes" to encompass the breadth of research on the "textual mediation or discursive construction of place and the use of space as a semiotic resource in its own right" (2010: 1).

From a methodological standpoint, the two approaches to studying the city as a medium outlined here are germane as well as complementary. Both perspectives emphasize the entanglement of the symbolic with the material and, thanks to their emphasis on multisensoriality and multimodality, both perspectives also lend themselves to an investigation of under-researched aspects of urban communication such as smell- and soundscapes.

Conclusions

So far, attempts to integrate these three main strands of research have been fairly sporadic. Yet, the combination of symbolic meanings conveyed by the city as a medium and of its representations as content plays a key role in molding those placemaking practices that are at the center of research on the city as a context of media engagement. Similarly, people experience the city as a medium while being engaged in media-related activities, and with an understanding of urban locales that is often derived from media representations of cities. Through our modest attempt to summarize and define the key methodological heuristics of current empirical research in the field, we hope to highlight how a systematic dialogue between the three major approaches outlined in this chapter could prove to be fruitful for the development of a more nuanced approach to researching urban media and communication. By the same token, this final chapter is ultimately meant to work as an invitation for other scholars in the field to contribute further to cross-methodological dialogue and collaboration.

References

Aiello, G. (2011) "From wound to enclave: The visual-material performance of urban renewal in Bologna's Manifattura delle Arti", *Western Journal of Communication*, 75(4), pp. 341–366.

Aiello, G. (2013) "From wasteland to wonderland: The hypermedia(tiza)tion of urban regeneration in Leeds' Holbeck Urban Village", *First Monday*, 18(11), http://firstmonday.org/ojs/index.php/fm/article/view/4957/3789.

Aiello, G. and Dickinson, G. (2014) "Beyond authenticity: A visual-material analysis of locality in the global redesign of Starbucks stores", *Visual Communication*, 13(3), pp. 303–321.

Aiello, G. and Tosoni, S. (2016) "Going about the city: Methods and methodologies for urban communication research—Introduction", *International Journal of Communication*, 10(2016), pp. 1252–1262.

Amin, A. and Thrift, N. (2002) *Cities: Reimagining the urban*, Cambridge, UK: Polity.

Anable, A. (2013) "Playing (in) the city: The warriors and images of urban disorder", in G. Papazian and J. M. Sommers (eds.) *Game On, Hollywood!: Essays on the Intersection of Video Games and Cinema*, Jefferson, NC: McFarland, pp. 86–100.

Anderson, B. and Harrison, P. (2010) *Taking-place: Non-representational theories and geography*, Farnham, Surrey; Burlington, VT: Ashgate.

Blair, C. (2001) "Reflections on criticism and bodies: Parables from public places", *Western Journal of Communication*, 65(3), pp. 271–294.

Blair, C. and Michel, N. (2000) "Reproducing Civil Rights tactics: The rhetorical performances of the Civil Rights Memorial", *Rhetoric Society Quarterly*, 30(2), pp. 31–55.

Blumer, H. (1954) "What is wrong with social theory?" *American Sociological Review*, 19(1), pp. 3–10.

Bull, M. (2013) "Privatizing urban space in the mediated world of iPod users", in C. Berry, J. Harbord, and R. O. Moore (eds.) *Public space, media space*, Hampshire, New York: Palgrave Macmillan, pp. 248–264.

Büscher, M., Urry, J., and Witchger, K. (eds.) (2011) *Mobile methods*, London, New York: Routledge.

Cresswell, T. (2011) "Place", in J. A. Agnew and J. S. Duncan (eds.) *The Wiley-Blackwell Companion to Human Geography*, Malden, MA: Wiley-Blackwell, pp. 235–244.

Davies, D. (2017) "'Comics on the main street of culture': Alan Moore and Eddie Campbell's From Hell (1999), Laura Oldfield Ford's Savage Messiah (2011) and the politics of gentrification", *Journal of Urban Cultural Studies*, 4(3), pp. 333–360.

de Souza e Silva, A. (2004) "Mobile networks and public spaces: Bringing multiuser environments into the physical space", *Convergence: The International Journal of Research into New Media Technologies*, 10(2), pp. 15–25.

de Souza e Silva, A. and Sheller, M. (eds.) (2015) *Mobility and Locative Media. Mobile communication in hybrid spaces*, London, New York: Routledge.

Dickinson, G. (1997) "Memories for sale: Nostalgia and the construction of identity in Old Pasadena", *Quarterly Journal of Speech*, 83(1), pp. 1–27.

Dickinson, G. (2002) "Joe's rhetoric: Starbucks and the spatial rhetoric of authenticity", *Rhetoric Society Quarterly*, 32(4), pp. 5–27.

Dickinson, G. (2015) *Suburban dreams: Imagining and building the good life*, Tuscaloosa, AL: University of Alabama Press.

Dickinson, G. and Aiello, G. (2016) "Being through there matters: Materiality, bodies, and movement in urban communication research", *International Journal of Communication*, 10(2016), pp. 1294–1308.

Dinnie, K. (ed.) (2010) *City branding: Theory and cases*, Basingstoke; New York: Palgrave Macmillan.

Donald, J. (1992) "Metropolis: The city as text", in K. Thompson and R. Bocock (eds.) *Social and cultural forms of modernity: Understanding modern societies*, Cambridge: Polity, pp. 418–470.

Drucker, J. (2014) *Graphesis: Visual forms of knowledge production*, Cambridge, MA: Harvard University Press.

Frith, J. (2012) "Splintered space: Hybrid spaces and differential mobility", *Mobilities*, 7(1), pp. 131–149.

Gendelman, I. and Aiello, G. (2010) "Faces of places: Façades as global communication in post-Eastern bloc urban renewal", in A. Jaworski and C. Thurlow (eds.) *Semiotic landscapes: Language, image, space*, London, UK: Continuum, pp. 256–273.

Georgiou, M. (2013) *Media and the city: Cosmopolitanism and difference*, Cambridge: Polity.

Gilbert, D. (1999) "'London in all its glory—or how to enjoy London': Guidebook representations of imperial London", *Journal of Historical Geography*, 25(3), pp. 279–297.

Gordon, E. and de Souza e Silva, A. (2011) *Net locality: Why location matters in a networked world*, Chichester, UK: John Wiley and Sons.

Gorter, D. (ed.) (2006). *Linguistic landscape: A new approach to multilingualism*, Clevedon: Multilingual Matters.

Govers, R. and Go, F. (2009) *Place branding: Glocal, virtual and physical identities, constructed, imagined and experienced*, Basingstoke; New York: Palgrave Macmillan.

Graham, S. (2004) "Beyond the 'dazzling light': From dreams of transcendence to the 'remediation' of urban life: A research manifesto", *New Media and Society*, 6(1), pp. 16–25.

Gray, J., Bounegru, L., Milan, S., and Ciuccarelli, P. (2016) "Ways of seeing data: Toward a critical literacy for data visualizations as research objects and research devices", in S. Kubitschko and A. Kaun (eds.) *Innovative methods in media and communication research*, Basingstoke; New York: Palgrave Macmillan, pp. 227–252.

Haddington, P. and Rauniomaa, M. (2011) "Technologies, multitasking, and driving: Attending to and preparing for a mobile phone conversation in a car", *Human Communication Research*, 37(2), pp. 223–254.

Hampton, K. N. and Gupta, N. (2008) "Community and social interaction in the wireless city: Wi-fi use in public and semi-public spaces", *New Media and Society*, 10(6), pp. 831–850.

Hochman, N., Manovich, L., and Yazdani, M. (2014) "On hyper-locality: Performances of place in social media", *Proceedings of 2014 International AAAI Conference on Weblogs and Social Media (ICWSM)*.

Holmes, T. (2017) "Giving visibility to urban change in Rio de Janeiro through digital audiovisual culture: A Brazilian web documentary project and its circulation", *Journal of Urban Cultural Studies*, 4(1–2), pp. 63–85.

Humphreys, L. and Liao, T. (2013) "Foursquare and the parochialization of public space", *First Monday*, 18(11), http://firstmonday.org/ojs/index.php/fm/article/view/4966.

Jaworski, A. and Thurlow, C. (eds.) (2010) *Semiotic landscapes: Language, image, space*, London and New York: Continuum.

Jones, M. (2009) "Phase space: Geography, relational thinking, and beyond", *Progress in Human Geography*, 33(4), pp. 487–506.

Kasesniemi, E.-L. and Rautiainen, P. (2002) "Mobile culture of children and teenagers in Finland", in J. E. Katz and M. Aakhus (eds.) *Perpetual contact: Mobile communications, private talk, public performance*, Cambridge: Cambridge University Press, pp. 139–169.

Kitchin, R., Maalsen, S., and McArdle, G. (2016) "The praxis and politics of building urban dashboards", *Geoforum*, 77, pp. 93–101.

Krajina, Z. (2014) *Negotiating the mediated city: Everyday encounters with public screens*, London, New York: Routledge.

Landry, R. and Bourhis, R. (1977) "Linguistic landscape and ethnolinguistic vitality: An empirical study", *Journal of Language and Social Psychology*, 16, pp. 23–49.

Lehan, R. (1998) *The city in literature: An intellectual and cultural history*, Berkeley, CA: University of California Press.

Lemish, D. (1982) "The rules of viewing television in public places", *Journal of Broadcasting*, 26(4), pp. 757–781.

Licoppe, C. and Figeac, J. (2015) "Direct video observation of the uses of smartphones on the move: Reconceptualizing mobile multi-activity", in A. de Souza e Silva and M. Sheller (eds.) *Mobility and locative media: Mobile communication in hybrid spaces*, London; New York: Routledge, pp. 48–64.

Lou, J. J. (2014) "Locating the power of *place* in *space*: A geosemiotic approach to context", in J. Flowerdew (ed.) *Discourse in context*, London: Bloomsbury, pp. 205–223.

Macek, S. (2006) *Urban nightmares: The media, the right, and the moral panic over the city*, Minneapolis, MN: University of Minnesota Press.

Manderscheid, K. (2014) "Criticising the solitary mobile subject: Researching relational mobilities and reflecting on mobile methods", *Mobilities*, 9(2), pp. 188–219.

Marcus, G. E. (1995) "Ethnography in/of the world system: The emergence of multi-sited ethnography", *Annual Review of Anthropology*, 24, pp. 95–117.

Massey, D. (1999) "Imagining globalisation: Power-geometries of time-space," in M. Hoyler (ed.) *Power-geometries and the politics of space-time: Hettner-Lectures 1998 with Doreen Massey* (Vol. 2, pp. 9–23). Heidelberg, Germany: Department of Geography, University of Heidelberg.

Massumi, B. (2002) *Parables for the virtual: Movement, affect, sensation*, Durham, NC: Duke University Press.

Mattern, S. (2008) "Silent, invisible city: Mediating urban experience for the other senses", in F. Eckardt et al. (eds.) *Mediacity: Situations, Practices and Encounters*, Berlin: Frank & Timme, pp. 155–176.

McCarthy, A. (2001) *Ambient television: Visual culture and public space*, Durham, NC: Duke University Press.

McQuire, S. (2016) *Geomedia: Networked cities and the future of urban space*, Malden, MA: Polity Press.

Moores, S. (2012) *Media, place and mobility*, Basingstoke; New York: Palgrave Macmillan.

Murdoch, J. (2006) *Post-structuralist geography: A guide to relational space*, London: SAGE Publications Ltd.

Nord, D. E. (1995) *Walking the Victorian streets: Women, representation, and the city*, Ithaca, NY: Cornell University Press.

Paganoni, M. (2015) *City branding and new media: Linguistic perspectives, discursive strategies and multimodality*, Cham: Springer Nature.

Pink, S. (2006) *The future of visual anthropology: Engaging the senses*, London: Routledge.

Pink, S. (2007) "Sensing Cittàslow: Slow living and the constitution of the sensory city", *The Senses and Society*, 2(1), pp. 59–77.

Rodgers, S., Barnett, C., and Cochrane, A. (2014) "Media practices and urban politics: Conceptualizing the powers of the media-urban nexus", *Environment and Planning D: Society and Space*, 32(6), pp. 1054–1070.

Schatzki, T. R. (1996) *Social practices: A Wittgensteinian approach to human activity and the social*, Cambridge; New York; Melbourne: Cambridge University Press.

Scollon, R. and Wong Scollon, S. (2003) *Discourses in place: Language in the material world*, London: Routledge.

Shiel, M. (2001) "Cinema and the city in history and theory", in M. Shiel and T. Fitzmaurice (eds.) *Cinema and the city: Film and urban societies in a global context*, Oxford; Malden, MA: Blackwell, pp. 1–18.

Shohamy, E., Ben-Rafael, E., and Barni, M. (eds.) (2010). *Linguistic landscape in the city*, Bristol: Multilingual Matters.

Siegenthaler, P. (2002) "Hiroshima and Nagasaki in Japanese guidebooks", *Annals of Tourism Research*, 29(4), pp. 1111–1137.

Simeone, L. and Patelli, P. (2016) "Urban sensing: Potential and limitations of social network analysis and data visualization as research methods in urban studies", in S. Kubitschko and A. Kaun (eds.) *Innovative Methods in Media and Communication Research*, London: Palgrave, pp. 253–272.

Sugiyama, S. (2013) "The muted mobile in Tokyo", in S. Tosoni, M. Tarantino, and C. Giaccardi (eds.) *Media and the city: Urbanism, technology and communication*, Newcastle-upon-Tyne: Cambridge Scholars Publishing, pp. 105–119.

Thrift, N. (2008) *Non-representational theory: Space, politics, affect*, London, UK: Routledge.

Timeto, F. (2015) "Locating media, performing spatiality: A nonrepresentational approach to locative media", in R. Wilken and G. Goggin (eds.) *Locative media*, London: Routledge, pp. 94–106.

Tosoni, S. (2016) "Addressing 'captive audience positions' in urban space: From a phenomenological to a relational conceptualization of space in urban media studies", *Sociologica*, 9(3).

Tosoni, S. and Ridell, S. (2016) "Decentering media studies, verbing the audience: Methodological considerations concerning people's uses of media in urban space", *International Journal of Communication*, 10(2016), pp. 1277–1293.

Tosoni, S. and Tarantino, M. (2013) "Space, translations and media", *First Monday*, 18(11), http://firstmonday.org/ojs/index.php/fm/article/view/4956/3788.

Van Den Akker, R. (2015) "Walking in the hybrid city: From micro-coordination to chance orchestration", in A. de Souza e Silva and M. Sheller (eds.) *Mobility and locative media: Mobile communication in hybrid spaces*, London; New York: Routledge, pp. 33–47.

Willis, K. S. (2016) *Netspaces: Space and place in a networked world*, London; New York: Routledge.

Further Reading

Aiello, G. and Tosoni S. (eds.) (2016) "Going about the city: Methods and methodologies for urban communication research", Special section of the *International Journal of Communication*, 10(2016).

Hartmann, M. (2013) "From domestication to mediated mobilism", *Mobile Media and Communication*, 1(1), pp. 42–49.

Lynch, K. (1960) *The image of the city*, Cambridge, MA: MIT Press.

INDEX

Locators in *italics* refer to figures. Named beginning 'Mc' are filed under 'Mac'. Initials are used for author first names whereas full names are used for historic or celebrity figures.

#BlackLivesMatter 443
24-hour cities 327–328

Aarhus, Denmark, sensemaking 393
Abercrombie, Patrick 242
Abidjan, Côte d'Ivoire 70
"aboutness" 69
Ackoff, R. 138
acoustics 374–375
address systems 166–168
advertising *see* branding cities; outdoor advertising
aeroplanes 38
affect 471
"agora coalition" 98
agoras, mobile 100–101
Aiello, G. 471
air pollution 131, 215, 222; apathy and trust 221–222; controversial communication 217–222; social production of space 216–217
air quality indexes (AQIs) 217–222, *219*
airplanes 38
Aksoy, A. 391
algorithm bias 231–232
ALL FM 427
Alphabet 133–134
Althusser, L. 24
Amin, A. 5, 107–108, 111
Amsterdam: lighting 157; nightlife 331
analogue coding 178
Anderson, B. 16, 175
anonymity online 226
anthropology of mediation 204, 205
appropriation, urban memory projects 355–361
Arab Spring 180–181, 417, 420, 421

Aragon, L. 406
archaeology of the media city 9, 13–21
architecture: acoustics 374; DIY architecture 368; national ideologies 143–146, 152–153; semiotics of urban space 26; Situationists 405; tourism 271; *see also* media architecture
archives 136–137
art: digital citizenship 321–324; DIY urban medium 318–319; Internet of Things 315–317; in public spaces 253, 314–315; sensemaking 319–321; street art 368; tourism branding 268
artificial light *see* lighting
"assemblies of infrastructures" 206
Association for Historical Dialogue and Research (AHDR) 356–360
Astana, Kazakhstan 150–152
Athens, as cultural capital 276
Athens Summit 276
audience studies 387–388; *see also* media audience studies
Augé, M. 33, 394, 413
augmented reality 319–321, 337–341
automation, smart homes 187–188
autonomous sensory meridian response (ASMR) 373
Ayer, David 450

Babylon 174, 176
"background relations" 188
Bagehot, W. 66, 67, 71
Bakhtin, M. M. 24
Baldwin, C. 159, 160
Balibar, É. 24

Baltimore, Maryland: algorithm bias 231–232; *The Wire* 57–58, 451
Banham, R. 101
Banksy (street artist) 403
Barcelona, Olympic Games 268
Barthes, R. 26
Bassett, C. 110
Baudelaire, C. 122, 405–406, 467
Baudrillard, J. 78, 347
bazaars 90
BBC, MediaCityUK 259–260
Beck, U. 119
behavioral geography 23, 29
Beijing: air pollution 221–222; *ParticipationPlus* 297–299; ring roads 101; urban memory project 355
Belfast, TV production 61
Benjamin, W. 15, 18, 50–51, 54, 55, 69–70, 405–406
Bennett, W. L. 416, 418–419
Berlin: cinema 52–53; new media scene 349
Bertel, T. 383
Bianchini, F. 328
big data 468
bike-sharing platforms 300
"Bilbao effect" 271
billboards *see* outdoor advertising
Birmingham, UK: Centre for Contemporary Cultural Studies 344, 346; media coverage 449; TV production 62–63
Black Panther Party 442–443
black studies 438–439; *see also* race
Blow-Up 53, 54
Blu (street artist) 403
Blum, A. 349
bodily habituation 469–470
Bordwell, David 50–51
Bosnia and Herzegovina, national ideologies 144, 147
Boston, urban memory project 355
Bouman, O. 393
boundary crossing 406, 412–414
Bourdieu, P. 24, 71, 347
Bourhis, R. 471
Boyer, M. C. 239, 240, 242
Boyle, Danny 450–451
brain as computer 138
branding cities 265, 268–272, 350; cities as media 470; fashion industry 307; *see also* tourism
"brandscape" 270–271
Brazil, outdoor advertising 80
bricoleurs 406
British colonization 208
British television soaps 61
broadcasting *see* radio; television
Brunsdon, Charlotte 48
Brynjolfsson, E. 294

Bucharest, *Arc de Triumf* 143
Budapest, consumption-centered urban restructuring 92
built environment: acoustics 374; cities as media 470; glass as building material 10; Situationists 405
Bump! 456–457, 460–464
"bunkerology" 408
bustling cities 107–108

Caché 52–53, 54
Cairo, Tahrir Square protests 417, 421
Calvino, I. 243
Cambridge, UK 231
capital 10–11, 170–171
capital cities: capitals of culture scheme 251, 252, 274–281; fashion capitals 305, 309; national ideologies 143, 150; relocation of Kazakhstan's capital 150–152
capitalism 11; "cool capitalism" 350; inequality 451; postmodernist models of urban space 32–33; surveillance 377
capitals of culture scheme 251, 252, 274–281
Caracas, Venezuela 204–205, 209–212
Cardiff, TV production 61
Carey, J. 165, 438
Carpo, M. 294–295
Carr, Nicholas 188
Casetti, F. 39
Casey, E. 353
Castells, M. 24, 26–27, 227, 244, 447
casual games 335–337, 340; *see also* gaming
cathode-ray tubes (CRTs) 36–37
Cavell, R. 437
CCTV: cinema 52; journalistic placemaking 69; nighttime 328–329; police 197; sensors and the city 377
Celik Rappas, I. 61–62
Central and East European (CEE), consumption-centered urban restructuring 85, 88–92
Centre Pompidou, Paris 293
Chadwick, A. 416, 418
Chapman, J. 407
Chávez, Hugo 210, 453
Chicago: inequalities 449; urbanization 388–392
China: fashion industry 311; LED lighting 162; location-based mobile games 339; nightlife 331, 332; *ParticipationPlus* 297–299; urban memory project 355
Choay, F. 31–32
cinema 10; in cities 46–50; historical context 17–18; in India 3; *Man on Wire* 407; modernity 50–51; and photography 46–48; poverty 449–451; surveillance 51–54; time context 54–55
cinematic spectatorship 40
cities: centrality of concept 129; cinema in 46–50; communication 1–2; as computers 134–136,

138–139; as content of communication 466–468; definition 1, 3; intellectual field 48–50; LGBT neighborhoods 457–460, 463–464; and media 2–4, 9; as media 470–471; media engagement 468–470; population living in 225; sexual minorities 457–460; on television 60–61; tourism 267–269
citizen as concept 180
citizen journalists 70–71
citizenship: art 321–324; "right to the city" 355, 417
citizensourcing 228–231
city slogans 269
city spaces as media 129–132
"cityness", cinema 48, 54
Clemens, J. 42
co-creation: art in public spaces 317, 318–319, 321–323; community media-making 210–212, 427–434; location-based mobile games 339
Cohen, A. 195–196, 346, 425
Colangelo, D. 39
collective intelligence 228
co-location 257
colonial era: cultural heritage 315, *316*; media and social change 208
command, smart homes 189–190
commercialization of public space 77–81; *see also* outdoor advertising
communication: air pollution 217–222; cities 1–2; cities as content of 466; graffiti and street art 401–403; media and urban formation 180–183; media cities 119; urban change 177–180
the communicative in urbanity 1
community: as concept 425–426; cyber urbanism 226–227; favelas 426–427; lamppost radio 428–430; media-making 210–212, 427–434
community space 408–409
computational methods 138, 244–245
computers, cities as 134–136, 138–139
connectivity, global cities 176
consumer culture: historical context 76–77; outdoor advertising 77–79
consumption 11; fashion industry 310–311; nighttime 326, 327–328; in public and urban habitation 392–394; semiotics of urban space 29–30
consumption-centered urban restructuring 84–85; further research 92; understanding cities as scenes and objects of consumption 86–88; urban change and the production of consumption spaces 88–92
"controllable domesticity" 18
convergence media 257
The Conversation 53, 54
"cool capitalism" 350
"core-peripheral" media industry 258
The Cosby Show 60

cosmopolitanism 116
cosmopolitanization 119, 122
courier drones 300
Crary, J. 244, 375
Crawshaw, C. 266
creating situations *see* Situationists
creative cities: and media cities 255–263; street art 403
creative class 251, 255–256, 258, 279
creative industries 251–254; cultural capitals scheme 277–279; cultural policies 279–280; fashion 304–311; Manchester, UK and Shanghai, China 256, 258, 259–262; tourism branding 268–269
crime surveillance 196, 198–199, 200–201; *see also* police
critical political economic approach 86, 87
Croatia's Homeland War 145, 146–150
cultural capitals scheme 251, 252, 274–281
cultural clusters 251
cultural context: creative industries 251; graffiti and street art 399; nightlife 326–327; and space 438; television 58–59; urban strangers 121–122
cultural geography, semiotics of urban space 23
cultural identity 3
"cultural materialism" 24
cultural studies 390
"cultural turn" 87–88, 92
"culturalist" approaches 88
culturalist model 32
curation, municipal archives 136–137
Curtin, Michael 61
cyber urbanism 225; digital governance and citizensourcing 228–231; infrastructures 227–228; intersections of urban space, cyberspace, and democratic potential 225–227; online public sphere 231–232
cybernetics, urban planning 243

dangerousness 198–199
data: graphical representations 467–468; online public sphere 231–232; "science of cities" 244–245; urban planning 236
de Certeau, M. 107, 108–111, 112, 367
de Souza e Silva, A. 379
Debord, G. 405
debt, post-digital cinema 51–52
Decena, C. 458
delivery drones 300
Dell'Aria, A. 40
democracy: citizensourcing 228–231; cyber urbanism 225–227; and participation 2–3; social media 180–181
demographics: 19th century 15; outdoor advertising 78–79
denizens 180, 181
density of public space 301
Detroit, lighting 161

Dickens, Charles 49, 61, 66, 71, 371–372
Dickinson, G. 470–471
digital citizenship 321–324
digital coding 178–180
digital divide 253
digital governance 228–231
digital isolation 226
digital media: art 314–315; media cities 13, 19–20; mobility 99–100; outdoor advertising 78; participation 131; protest movements 416, 418–419; proximity-connectivity nexus 99; smart homes 185–187
digitalized human capital 230–231
dimming lights 161–162
display technology 293–294
DIY architecture 368
DIY urban medium 318–319
DIY urbanism 408–409
Dodgeball service 381
domestic *see* everyday; home
domestic automation 187–188
Donald, J. 466
Douglas, G. C. 409
driving, as mobility 110–111
drones 300
"dual city" 447–448
Dubai, architecture 271
Durkheim, E. 288, 345

Eco, U. 26–27
Edensor, T. 408
election data 231
electricity: lighting 158–159; media cities 17–18; smart meters 188
electromagnetic hypersensitivity 373
"electronic presence" 10
"electronic presentation" 10
Eliot, T. S. 138
Elliott, A. 102–103
employment *see* labor markets; precarious employment
"end of tourism" 267
Enlightenment
Enlightenment, modernist models of urban space 32
"entrepreneurial cities" 269
entrepreneurialism 269–270
environment *see* air pollution
Environment Agency, UK 199
Epstein, R. 138
ethics, subjectivity in the media city 123–124
ethnicity: nightlife and discrimination 330; outdoor advertising 80; sexual minorities 458; suburbanization and telecommunications 169–171; urban strangers 121–122
ethnography: art in public spaces 321; cities as context of media engagement 468–469; media-making 429–430; mediation 205

Ettema, J. 449
European Union: common European identity 274–281; creative industries 252; cultural capitals scheme 251, 252, 274–281
Europeanization of the city 251
events: mobilities 284–285; splintered urban experiences 289–290; tourism 268; urban leisure 283; venues 285–289; watching, being, and making 283–284
everyday: consumption-centered urban restructuring 86–87; graffiti and street art 397; media representations 389; mediation 116; spaces and practices of daily life 367–369
extensibility 168–169

façades 292–294, 299, 393
Facebook: favela activism 431; instant mobilization 100; media clusters 257; surveillance 194, 196
Facebook revolutions 180–181, 421
face-to-face communication 13, 19, 176, 257
fandom 285
Fanon, F. 438, 439
fashion capitals 305, 307, 309
fashion industry 252–253, 304–305; design and labor 308–309; diversification of fashion media 310; fashion capitals and weeks 305, 307, 309; identity 304–305; mediated cities 304, 306–307; networking and placemaking 306–307; retail and consumption 310–311
fashion weeks 309
favelas 426–427, 428–431
feet 107–111
Feifer, M. 267
femininity, outdoor advertising 79–80
festivals 268, 350
field spaces, journalism 70–72
figurative symbolism 177
film viewing *see* cinema; television
flagship stores 270
flanerie: and consumer culture 77; fashion industry 304; journalism 69–70; Situationists 405–406; television 57; urban strangers 116, 121–123
Florence: city spaces as media 129; fashion industry 307
Florida, R. 255–256, 259
Foster, Norman 271
Foucault, M. 195, 265–266
Foursquare 383
Fourth World Congress of Psychogeography (4WCOP) 411–412
fragility of cities 51
"freedom of choice" 51–52
freeway systems 101, 437, 438, 440–441
Frith, J. 289
Fritzsche, P. 68
futures, precautionary surveillance 199–200

gamification 335, 338
gaming 335–342; casual gaming in public 335–337; location-based mobile games 337–341
Gans, H. 425–426
Garden City movement 237, *238*
Garrett, B. L. 407
gas lighting 157–158
"gaze": media consumption in public and urban habitation 392–394; tourism 265–266
Geddes, P. 237, 239, 242, 243
gender: nighttime exclusion 329–330; outdoor advertising 79–80; semiotics of urban space 30; sexual minorities 458–459; smart homes 189, 190–191; subcultures 347; surveillance of women 201–202
General Purpose Technologies (GPTs) 294, 300
gentrification: sexual minorities 459; tourism 268–269; TV production 62
geographic context: local journalism 72, 73; meaning of 109; mediation and difference 117; television 60; *see also* human geography
geography's quantitative revolution 318
geomedia 19–20, 467
Georgiou, M. 420, 421, 467
geosemiotics 471
geosocial networking apps 458
Gerbaudo, P. 416
Gezi Park protests (Istanbul, Turkey) 417, 421
Giddens, A. 16
Glasgow, regeneration 276, 279
glass as building material 10
global, "mobilities turn" 97
global cities 130; creation of 170–171; meaning of 174–175; media clusters 258; mediation 174–177, 183; tourism 265
Global North: journalism 73; LGBT neighborhoods 461–462
Global South: citizensourcing 229; inequality 447, 449; journalism 73; LED lighting 162; nightlife 331–332; social change 131
globalization 175, 182–183; *see also* global cities
Goffman, E. 382
Goldberger, P. 427
Google: media clusters 257; surveillance 194; urban planning 245
Gottdiener, M. 33
governance, digital 228–231
GPS software 337–338, 380, 384, 412, *413*
graffiti 368, 397, 403–404; communication perspectives 401–403; definition 398; media portrayal 400–401; political dimensions 399–400; studies of 399; subcultures 80, 398, 399–401; traits, types, and techniques 397–398
Graham, M. 412
Greece: Greek democracy 236; Thessaloniki's urban design 27–30

Greimas, A. J. 27
grid, telecommunications 168–169
guerrilla urbanism 408–409
Guggenheim Museums 271

habitation: hands and feet 107–113; as lineal 113–114; spatial organization 108–113
Haeusler, M. 292–293
Hague Summit 275
Hall, S. 24–26, 49, 390
Halvorsen, S. 420
HandM 306
hands 107–113
Harvey, D. 32–33, 169, 269–270, 354, 416
hate speech 226
Haussmann, Baron Georges-Eugène 239–240, 242, 243, 406
Health and Safety Executive (HSE) 199
Hébrard, E. 27, 28, 30
Heidegger, M. 414
Henkin, D. 67
heritage: postwar/post-socialist transition 145–146; urban monuments 143–145, 148–150
Hicks, Craig case 440
higher education 329–330
high-wire walking 407
hipsters 349
historical context: air pollution 217; consumption-centered urban restructuring 85, 86; contradictory role of the media in the formation of cities 175–177; forms of communication across human history in relation to urban change 177–179; informatic metaphors 134–135; media as contradictory forces in the process of urban formation 180–183; media cities 15–20; municipal archives 136–137; outdoor advertising 76–77
Hitler, Adolf 143
HIV/AIDS 79–80
Hollywood 61
home: mediated cities 185; smart homes 185–192; suburbanization and privacy 186; "urbanizing" audience research 390–392
Homeland War, Croatia 146–150
Hou, J. 408
Houston, Texas, urban change 360–361
Howard, E. 237
Hoyler, M. 3
Huhtamo, E. 38
human association 1, 2
human capital 230–231
human geography: air pollution 216; mobility 97; non-representational theories 469; semiotics of urban space 23, 26; transgression 367
Humphreys, L. 226–227
Hussmann, H. 39
Huxley, T. 239

hybrid spaces 379–380, 419–422, 468
hygiene 374–375

identity: European 275–276, 277; fashion industry 304–305; networked self 102–103; and place 253–254; surveillance 194
Ihde, Don 188
illuminant technology 293–294
"imageability" 27
incandescent light bulbs 158–162
India: film viewing 3; precapitalist models of urban space 31
industrial cities 15–16
Industrial Revolution 458
inequality: Global South 447; and urbanization 446–447; *see also* poverty
inflight entertainment 38
informatic metaphors 134–135
information: air pollution 218–222; the case against "information processing" 138–139; collective intelligence 228; informatic metaphors 134–135; informational ecologies 136–138; pollution 131; smart cities 236; surveillance 194, 198, 202; *see also* knowledge
information and communication technologies (ICTs): air pollution 218–221; domestication 392; media clusters 256–257
information literacy 137
information processing 138
informational ecologies 136–138
infrastructure: community media 430–434; cyber urbanism 227–228; digital age 300; media and social change 206–212; media as 129–132; media cities 117, 118; telecommunications 165–171; urban monuments 143–145, 148–150
Ingold, T. 109, 110, 113, 373
"inhabitant knowledge" 110
Innis, H. 438
insecurity, post-digital cinema 51–52
Instagram 265, 382
instant mobilization 100
institutions: consumption-centered urban restructuring 86–87; media cities 118
intellectual technologies 168
interaction order 471
interactivity 392–394
interdisciplinarity 3
Internet access 225, 229–230
Internet of Things 187, 315–317
internetization 399
intersectionality, outdoor advertising 79–80
IP addresses 167
Iran, outdoor advertising 80
Ishikawa, T. 384
Islamabad, Pakistan, citizensourcing 229

Issers, O. 422
Istanbul: Gezi Park protests 417, 421; TV production 61–62

Jacobs, J. 196, 243, 426
Jakarta, nightlife 331
Jameson, F. 32
Jankowski, N. 426
Jansson, A. 266–267
Jenkins, H. 257
Jensen, O. B. 100, 102
Jiménez, A. 228
journalism 66–67, 72–73; as a culture of public circulation 67–69; field spaces 70–72; placemaking 69–70; poverty 448–453; subcultures 345–346

Kaniss, P. 68
Kashiwa, Japan, navigation study 384
Kayhan, S. 61–62
Kazakhstan, relocation of capital city 150–152
Keiller, P. 408
Kelley, R. 441–442
Kenya, Pamoja FM 452–453
Kidd, J. 318
King, R. 437
Kitchin, R. 468
Kittler, Friedrich 167
Klingmann, A. 270–271
knowledge: city spaces as media 129; consumption-centered urban restructuring 85; "inhabitant knowledge" 110; situated knowledges 318; surveillance 199; *see also* information
Kozinets, R. 270–271
Krajina, Z. 3, 40, 411, 469
Krauss, R. 40
Kyrgyzstan, outdoor advertising 80

labor markets: creative class 251, 255–256, 258, 259; fashion industry 308–309; media clusters 258–262; precarious employment 447
lamppost radio 428–430
landline phones 380
landmarks 253–254; tourism 270
Landry, R. 471
landscapes *see* urban landscapes
Lantz, F. 338
Lavedan, P. 27, 28
Le Corbusier 242–243
LED technology 161–162, 293, 294, 297–299
Ledrut, R. 32
Leeds, UK, gendered exclusion in nightlife 329
Lefebvre, H. 24, 119, 216, 228, 354, 362, 374, 416, 417, 457
legal context, outdoor advertising 81
leisure *see* urban leisure

lesbians 458–459
Lévy, P. 228
Lewis, P. 427
LGBT neighborhoods: in cities 457–460, 463–464; on television 456–457, 460–463
libraries, municipal archives 137
lighting 130; historical context 156–163; illuminant technology 293–294; nighttime 130, 160, 327; nineteenth century artificial light 157–159; twentieth century modernity 159–161; twenty-first century LEDs 161–162; *see also* nighttime
Ling, R. 381
linguistic turn 372
literature representations 49, 61
live events *see* events
liveness *see* realtime
Liverpool, UK: cultural capitals scheme 277, 278, 279; television soaps 61
local: globalization 182–183; the home 186; media's role 181–182; "mobilities turn" 97
local journalism 71–72, 73
locatability 166–168
location, meaning of 109; *see also* geographic context; navigation of the city; place
location-based mobile games 337–341
location-based social networks (LBSNs) 381–383
London: algorithm bias 232; cinema 53–54; in Dickens 49; fashion industry 305, 308; global cities 174–175; historic lighting 157, 158; journalistic field spaces 71; journalistic placemaking 69; symbolic context 119; television soaps 61; urban memory project 355–356; urban planning 242
Los Angeles: fashion industry 308–309; freeway system 101; lighting 160–161; *Street Kings* 450
Lugo-Ocando, J. 448–449
Lyft 171
Lynch, K. 27–29

McAfee, A. 294
McCullough, M. 38, 137–138, 228, 377
MacDonald, J. 372
McDonough, T. 408
Macedonia, national ideologies 145
Macek, S. 467
McFedries, P. 134
McGurk, H. 372
McKittrick, K. 439
McLuhan, M. 15–16, 437, 438
McQuire, S. 38–39, 467
McRobbie, A. 347
Madrid, sexual minorities 463
Magee, L. 178–180
Man on Wire 407
Manchester, UK: ALL FM 427; from creative city to media city 256, 258, 259–260, 262; creative industries 251–252

Mangin, W. 431–432
Manovich, L. 39
mapping 383–384; neogeography 412–414; psychogeography 405, 409–412; *see also* navigation of the city
Marcuse, H. 399
Maré Vive, social media 431–434
Marxism, structural 24
"Marxist sociological poetics" 24
masculinity, outdoor advertising 79–80
Massey, D. 97, 118, 119, 348, 439
material, semiotics of urban space 24
material context, consumption-centered urban restructuring 87
Mattern, S. 38, 129
Mayhew, H. 448
Medellín, Columbia, citizensourcing 229
media: and cities 2–4, 9; cities as 466; cities as context of engagement with 468–470; social change 204–212
media architecture 292–294, 301; post-screens 300; screens 294–299
media as urban infrastructure 129
media audience studies 368, 387, 394–395; media consumption in public and urban habitation 392–394; "urbanizing" audience research 388–392
"media capital" 61
media cities: "big city life" 15–17; and creative cities 255–263; digital 13, 19–20; electricity 17–18; futures 20–21; inventing 13–14; mediation and difference 117–119; suburban 18–19; *see also* subjectivity in the media city
media clusters: local creative milieus 256–259; Manchester, UK 256, 258, 259–260, 262; Shanghai, China 256, 258, 260–262
media events 19
media façades 292–294, 299, 393
media technology 3
MediaCityUK 259–260
mediated cities: fashion industry 304, 306–307; the home 185; surveillance 200
mediation 5; and difference 117–119; disciplinary context 204; everyday 116; global cities 174–177, 183; smart homes 190–191; social 206
mediatization 284, 288–289
Medvedev, P. N. 24
Melbin, M. 326
memory: meaning of 353–354; transactive 384; *see also* urban memory
Merleau-Ponty, M. 111–112, 113
metaphors: brain as computer 138; city as computer 134–136, 138–139; informatic metaphors 134–135
methodological approaches in urban media and communication research 466; cities as content

of communication 466–468; cities as contexts of media engagement 468–470; cities as media 470–471
methodological site-specificity 469
"metropolitan journalism" 71
Mexico City: monument 143; sexual minorities 461–462
Meyrowitz, J. 394
Miami, *Herald's* newsrooms 70
"micro-coordination" 381
"middle space", the home 186
migrants, as urban strangers 121–122
Mihye, A. 300
Milan, fashion industry 305, 307
Mitchell, W. 226
mobile agoras 100–101
mobile capital 171
mobiles *see* smartphones
"mobilities turn" 96–98, 102
mobility 11; digital technology and the city 99–100; events 284–285; protest movements 420; space and racism 438, 439–441; *see also* transportation
modernist models of urban space 31–32
modernity: cinema 50–51; cities as computers 134–135; lighting 159–162; television 58–59; tradition/modernity dichotomy 205
modernization 15, 29, 50
monuments *see* urban monuments
moral panics: graffiti 400; live events 285; media discourse 467; nighttime 326–327; subcultures 346, 349
More, Thomas 236, 244
Morley, D. 113, 388–391, 419
Moscow, OccupyAbay 421–422
Mosquito anti-loitering device 375
multiplicity of reading 367
multisensoriality 469–470
Mumbai, *Slumdog Millionaire* 450–451
Mumford, L. 13, 135, 136
municipal archives 136–137
museums 137, 315
music venues 287

nachtburgemeester 331
The Naked City 60
national ideologies 152–153; Astana, Kazakhstan 150–152; capital cities 143, 150; Croatia's Homeland War 145, 146–150; postwar/post-socialist transition 145–146; urban monuments 143–145
national media, location in cities 71–72
naturalist model 32
navigability 166–168
navigation of the city 379–380, 384–385; location information and the presentation of self 382–383; locative media and time/space coordination 380–382; wayfinding through mobile mapping 383–384
neofascism 389
neogeography 412–414
neohellenism 30
"neoliberal revolution" 390
neoliberalism: inequality 446–447; media and social change 208–209
net locality 468
netspace 468
network society 205, 244
networked self 102–103
networking, fashion industry 306–307
neurasthenia 374
"new journalism" 71
"new mobilities turn" 97
New Orleans: journalistic field spaces 72; TV production 61, 62
New York: algorithm bias 232; citizensourcing 229, 230; city spaces as media 129; fashion industry 305, 308–309; global cities 174–175; graffiti and street art 397; journalistic placemaking 69; Occupy Movement 420; Palmyra's Roman arch 315, *316*; *Rear Window* 53, 54; sexual minorities 458; space and racism 437; spatial organization 108–111; television 57, 60–61; tourism 269, 270
Newcastle, incandescent light bulbs 159
newspapers 66, 68, 73, 345–346; *see also* journalism
newsrooms 70, 73
Nicholls, W. J. 420
Nicosia, Cyprus 356–360
Nietschke, O. 293, 301
Nigeria: film industry 209; outdoor advertising 79–80
Nightcrawler 160–161
nighttime: 24-hour cities 327–328; artificial light 130, 160, 327; club subcultures 347; economies of 253, 326, 328, 331–332; gendered exclusion 329–330; mediating the city 328–329; nightlife cultures 326–327; surveillance 328–329, 330–331
Nold, C. 100–101

object of consumption 86
Occupy Movement 417, 420, 421–422
OccupyAbay 421–422
Olympic Games: events and tourism 268; social media in Rio 430–434
"on the move" 96
OpenStreetMap 412
oral communication 177, 178, 181
organists 111–113
Orkhestra 295–297, *296*
outdoor advertising 11, 76; commercialization 77–79; historical context 76–77;

intersectionality 79–80; psychogeography 411; public space 77–78; regulation and social acceptance 81; remediation 78–79
overmodernity 33

Paiva, R. 426
Pamoja FM 452
panoptic cities 195–200
Papastergiadis, N. 43
Parikka, J. 337
Paris: Centre Pompidou 293; fashion industry 305, 308, 310; flanerie 406; global cities 174–175; lighting 157; nightlife 331; police and racism 443; *The Skywalk Is Gone* 54–55; *Tree* (art installation) 321; Triumphal Arch 143; urban planning 239–242, *241*
Park, R. E. 68, 345–346
Parker, S. 425
parkour 407
participation: the city as a political space 98–99; co-creation of art 317, 318–319, 321–323; digital 131; instant mobilization 100; media consumption in public and urban habitation 392–394; urban memory projects 355–361
ParticipationPlus 297–299, *298*
Peaky Blinders 62–63
Peeping Tom 53
Peer, L. 449
Pennsylvania, algorithm bias 231–232
Perlman, J. 426, 431–432
personal stereos 375
Philadelphia: address systems 167; graffiti and street art 397
phones *see* landline phones; smartphones
photography: and cinema 46–48; graffiti and street art 401, 402–403; tourism and image 265–267; urban planning 242
pianists 111–113
place: diminished sense of 394; and identity 253–254; meaning of 109; "mobilities turn" 97; networked self 102–103; semiotics of urban space 26–27; urban memory 354
place semiotics 471
placemaking: fashion industry 306–307; journalism 69–70
planning *see* urban planning
planning and design 2
play: casual gaming in public 335–337; location-based mobile games 337–341; smart homes 191; *see also* urban leisure
Pokémon GO 339–341
police: algorithm bias 231–232; patrol systems 170; precautionary surveillance 199–200; and racism 443; surveillance 196, 197
policies, outdoor advertising 81
political context: citizensourcing 228–231; the city as a political space 98–99; digital interfaces 99–100;

graffiti and street art 399–400; online public sphere 231–232; *see also* protest movements
political economy: critical political economic approach 86, 87; semiotics of urban space 24–26
politics of representation 367
pollution *see* air pollution
"possessive spectatorship" 11–12
postcolonialism 208, 439
post-graffiti art 398; *see also* street art
post-industrial urbanism 251–254, 327
postmodernism 144
postmodernist models of urban space 32–33
post-socialist transition 11; consumption-centered urban restructuring 85, 88–92; national ideologies 145–146
post-subcultural theory 347–349
"post-tourism" 267
poverty: media portrayal 446, 449–453; slums 446–448; urban underclass 448–449
power, media representations 389
Poznań, Poland 78
Prague, psychogeography walks 411
precapitalist models of urban space 31
precarious employment 447
precariousness of city life 51–52
precautionary surveillance 199–200
Prehn, O. 426
Prescott-Steed, D. 411
Price, C. 293
print 178
privacy 339; gaming in public 336–337; the home 186; media consumption in public and urban habitation 392–394; social media 349
production: consumer culture 77; consumption-centered urban restructuring 88–92; media clusters 257, 257–262, *259*; semiotics of urban space 24–26, *25*, 27–29
production of media: journalistic placemaking 69; television 61–63
progressivism, outdoor advertising 79, 80
progressivist model 32
Project Row Houses (PRH) 360–361
projectors 292–293
property *see* real estate
protest movements 416–417, 422; Arab Spring 180–181, 417; the city as a political space 98–99; digital media 416, 418–419; hybrid spaces 419–422; "right to the city" 417–418; social media in Rio 430–434; "square movements" 409, 417; on the street 442–443
proximity-connectivity nexus 99
"psycho-geographic" maps 243–244
psychogeography 405, 409–412
public space: art 253, 314–315; the city as a political space 98–99; digital interfaces 99–100; DIY/guerrilla urbanism 408–409; media

consumption 392–394; online public sphere 231–232; outdoor advertising 77–78; urban exploration 267, 407–408
publicness, journalism 67–69
Purcell, M. 354, 362

quantitative revolution 318

race 444; black studies 438–439; nightlife and discrimination 330; outdoor advertising 80; space and racism 437; violence and freedom 440–443
radio: Abidjan 70; community media 427–430; poor people's media 452–453
radio dispatch 170
Rantisi, N. 308
re-actions 321
real estate: creative industries 268; event venues 285–286; Shanghai, China 261, 262
realtime: digital networks 20; events 283–290; futures 20–21; television 19
Rear Window 53, 54
recessions, post-digital cinema 51–52
regionalism, urban planning 239–240
regulation, outdoor advertising 81
religion, outdoor advertising 80
remediation, outdoor advertising 78–79
remembrance 353–354
representation: cities and media 467; media power 389; politics of 367; poverty 446, 449–453; street art and graffiti 400–401
representation/signification 3
retail: fashion industry 310–311; shopping malls 89–90, 305
Reykjavik, Iceland, citizensourcing 229
Rheingold, H. 228
rhythmanalysis 374
"right to the city" 354–355; citizenship 355, 417; graffiti and street art 397–398; protest movements 417–418
Riis, J. 448
Rio de Janeiro 430–434
road systems 101, 437, 438
Robins, K. 10, 226, 391
robots, smart homes 187–188, 189
Rodriguez, C. 428
Romanticism, modernist models of urban space 32
Rome, Ancient 178
Rose-Redwood, Reuben S. 167
Rotterdam, nightlife 330
Round Trip Ticket 456–457, 460–464
ruin porn/ruin lust 408
ruinology 408

Salford, television soaps 61
Salvador, Brazil 428–430
same-sex *see* LGBT neighborhoods

San Francisco: cinema 53, 54; sexual minorities 457
sanitation 374–375
Sao Paulo, outdoor advertising 81
Sassen, S. 170
satellite dishes 391
Saunders, P. 186
Scannell, P. 288, 389
scenes: post-subcultural theory 347–349; social media 349–350; subcultures 344
Schlesinger, P. 278, 279
Schmidt, F. 230
"science of cities" 244–245
Scifo, S. 427–428
Scollon, R. 471
Scollon, S. W. 471
Scott, J. C. 167, 399
screens 10, 36–37; digital interfaces in public space 99–100; gaming in public 335–336; live events 283–284, 286; media architecture 294–299; media consumption in public and urban habitation 392–394; outdoor advertising 78; post-screens 300; technology 293; television 59–60; urban/rural 38; *see also* urban screen media
search engine manipulation 231–232
"Second Machine-Age Architecture" 294, 300, 301
Segerberg, A. 416, 419
Selma, Alabama 442
semiotic approaches, consumption-centered urban restructuring 86
semiotics of urban space: consumption 29–30; epistemological considerations 23; methodological approaches 471; modelling 31–33; as place 26–27; political economy 24–26; production 24–26, 25, 27–29
Senatus Populusque Romanus (SPQR) 180
Sennett, R. 120, 123
sensemaking: art 319–321; media façades 393
senses 368, 371–373; multisensoriality 469–470; overload and fragmentary attention 373–375; sensors and the city 376–377; smellscapes 412
Serbia, national ideologies 144–145, 147
Sex and the City 57
sexism, outdoor advertising 79–80
sexual minorities 456–457; in cities 457–460; connecting cities and their representations 463–464; consuming the city in travel-themed television 460–463
Shane, P. 226
Shanghai, China: from creative city to media city 256, 258, 260–262; creative industries 251–252
Sharma, S. 171, 437, 439
Sherlock Holmes 16
shopping malls: consumption-centered urban restructuring 89–90; fashion industry 305
Sidewalk Labs 133, 245
Siegel, G. 40

sight (as sense) 368
Silverstone, R. 388–389
Simmel, G. 15, 120, 122, 123, 159–160, 304, 374, 381
Singapore: nightlife 331; psychogeography walks 411
situated knowledges 318
Situationist International 405
Situationists 405–407; DIY/guerrilla urbanism 408–409; neogeography and mapping situations 412–414; psychogeography 409–412; re-constructing the city 414–415; urban exploration (UE) 407–408
The Skywalk Is Gone 46–48, 54–55
slow cinema 46–48, 54
Slumdog Millionaire 450–451
slums: clearance in Paris 239–240; community media-making 426–427, 428–431; and urbanization trends 446–448
smart cities: building cities from scratch 133–134; digital networks 20; futures 21; post-digital cinema 51
smart homes 185–187; automation 187–188; command 189–190; future trajectories 191–192; mediating exteriorities 190–191; play 191
smart meters 188
smartification 187
smartphones: art in public spaces 319; casual gaming in public 335–337; events 286–289; location-based mobile games 337–341; navigation of the city 380–384
smellscapes 412
Smíchov, Prague 89–90
social acceptance, outdoor advertising 81
social change: centrality of city 129; Global South 131; urban media 204–212
social class: creative class 251, 255–256; "middle space" 186; outdoor advertising 80; semiotics of urban space 30; telecommunications 170–171; underclass 448–449
social field 71
social forms 344
social media: art in public spaces 321; democracy 180–181; nightlife 329; Rio de Janeiro 430–434; subcultures 349–350
"social movement space" 420
social production of space, air pollution 216–217
social semiotics 28–29
social space 24
sociosemiotics 27–29
Soja, E. 243
solar lighting 162
solidarity, media cities 118
Sorkin, M. 98
Souza, R. 432
Soviet Union, urban monuments 143–144

space: air pollution and social production 216–217; city spaces as media 129–132; consumption-centered urban restructuring 84–85, 87, 90, 92; everyday life 367–369; human geography 26; location-based mobile games 337–341; meaning of 109; mobile agoras 100–101; "mobilities turn" 97; outdoor advertising 78; protest movements 420–421; and race 437, 438–439; sensors and the city 376–377; social 24; tourism 265–267; urban critique 406; *see also* public space; semiotics of urban space; time-space
"space-as-text" 10, 23
"space-in-text" 10, 23
spaces of flow 244
"spatial legibility" 368, 385
spatial organization, hands and feet 108–113
spatial overabundance 33
"spatial turn" 85, 87, 92, 348
spectatorship 40
sport venues 287
"square movements" 409, 417
Srinivas, L. 3
starchitects 271
Stevenson, D. 3
Stiegler, B. 13
Stonewall riots 457
strangeness 116
strangers 116, 119–123, 121–123; art in public spaces 317; cyber urbanism 226–227; nightlife 330; nighttime 326
street art 368, 397, 403–404; communication perspectives 401–403; definition 398; media portrayal 400–401; political dimensions 399–400; studies of 399; subcultures 80, 398, 399–401; traits, types, and techniques 397–398
Street Kings 450
street pastors 330
street vendors 331–332
streets: artificial light 157; consumption-centered urban restructuring 90–92; hands and feet 109–111; race and space 441–443
"stretched situations" 102
"structural Marxism" 24
struggle 131
Struppek, M. 41
student nightlife 329–330
subaltern digital media users 121–122
subcultural capital 347
subcultures 253, 344–345; fashion industry 304; graffiti and street art 80, 398, 399–401; journalism 345–346; origins of subcultural theory 345–347; post-subcultural theory and scenes 347–349; social media 349–350
subjectivity in the media city 116–117, 119–121; ethical predicament 123–124; mediation and difference 117–119; strangers 121–123

suburbanization: the home 186; media cities 18–19; mobile dispatch 169–171
suburbs, television 59, 68
Sudnow, D. 112–113
Suominen, J. 337
surveillance 130–131; cinema 51–54; crime 196, 198–199, 200–201; futures 199–200; meaning of 194–195; mediated cities, synoptic cities 200; nighttime 328–329, 330–331; panoptic cities 195–200; power 202; precautionary 199–200; sensors and the city 376–377; smart homes 190; of women 201–202
surveillance capitalism 377
Susik, A. 40
Swan, Joseph 159
Sweden, HandM 306
symbolic context: consumption-centered urban restructuring 87; world cities 119
symbolism, figurative 177
synoptic cities 200
systems approach, urban planning 243

Tahrir Square protests (Cairo, Egypt) 417, 421
Taipei, *The Skywalk Is Gone* 46–48, 54–55
Takism Square protest 421
Tang, D. 459
Tarantino, M. 419–420
taxi drivers 171
technology: building cities from scratch 133–134; lighting 157–162; media façades 292–294; modernity and the suburb 59; sensors and the city 376–377; surveillance and cinema 52–54; surveillance in the city 196–197; telecommunications 165–171; urban planning 131–132
Tekinbas, S. 341
telecommunications 171–172; extensibility 168–169; locatability 166–168; mobile capital 171; navigability 166–168; suburbanization 169–171; and transportation 165–166
telegraphy 178
television 11; and the city 57–58; the city on 60–61; community media-making 210–212; crime 200–201; historical context 18–19; LGBT neighborhoods 456–457, 460–463; live events 283–284, 288, 289; modernity 58–59; outside the domestic 59–60; poverty 449–451; production 61–63; satellite dishes 391; suburbs 59, 68; "urbanizing" audience research 390–392; *see also* cinema
Thailand, citizensourcing 229–230
"the uncanny" 49–50
Thessaloniki, urban design 27–30
Thompson, E. 374
Thompson, F. 138
Thornton, S. 347

Thrift, N. 5, 107–108, 110–111
time context: cinema 54–55; journalism 68–69; locative media 380–382; of media 438; media as contradictory forces in the process of urban formation 181; *see also* nighttime
time-space 11; "geomedia" 19–20; navigation of the city 380–382; urban planning 244
Timor Leste, Dili 182
Tokyo: fashion industry 308; global cities 174–175
Tönnies, F. 425
Toronto, taxi drivers 171
Tosoni, S. 419–420
tourism: branding and promotion 265, 269–272; cities 267–269; "end of tourism" 267; image and space 265–267; "post-tourism" 267; surveillance 198
Townsend, A. 226
tradition/modernity dichotomy 205
transactive memory 384
transgender 459–460
transportation: the city as a political space 98–99; consuming the city in travel-themed television 460–463; density of public space 301; digital technology, mobilities, and the city 99–100; events 284–285; mobile agoras 100–101; "mobilities turn" 96–97, 96–98; the networked self 102–103; "on the move" 96; and telecommunications 165–166
Treaty of Rome 275
Tree (art installation) 321
Trollope, Fanny 156
Tuan, Y. 109–110, 348
Tufekçi, Z. 416, 419
Turkey, TV production 62; *see also* Istanbul
Turkle, S. 226
typists 111

Uber 133–134, 171
underclass 448–449
UNESCO 251
United Kingdom, police and racism 443; *see also individually named cities*
United States: online public sphere 231–232; outdoor advertising 76–77; television 58–59; *see also individually named cities*
upskirting 202
urban: centrality of concept 129; definition 3
urban critique 406–407; DIY/guerrilla urbanism 408–409; neogeography and mapping situations 412–414; psychogeography 409–412; re-constructing the city 414–415; urban exploration 407–408
urban design, semiotics of urban space 27–29
urban ecology 72
urban economy 2
urban experience and community 2

urban exploration (UE) 267, 407–408; *see also* tourism
urban formation 180–183
urban landscapes 252; branding cities 269–272; methodological approaches 470–471; outdoor advertising 77; *see also* space
urban leisure: event mobilities 284–285; gaming 335–342; splintered urban experiences 289–290; venues 285–289; watching, being, and making the event 283–284
urban memory 61–62, 353–354; projects of appropriation and participation 355–361; "right to the city" 354–355
urban monuments 143–145, 148–150, 315–323
urban planning: building cities from scratch 133–134; fragmented views 243–245; postmodernist models of urban space 33; precapitalist models of urban space 31; smart cities 236–237; technology 131–132; visions of the city 237–243
urban regeneration: cultural capitals scheme 275–276; tourism 268–269
urban screen media 36–37, 42–43; abundance of 37–40; aesthetic category 41–42; meaning of 37–38
urban semiotics 23; *see also* semiotics of urban space
urban subjectivities *see* subjectivity in the media city
urbanization: audience studies 389; human association 2; media platforms 14; and slums 446–448
UrbExers 407
Urry, J. 97, 102–103, 265–266
utility poles, telecommunications 168–169
utopia 236–238

Valladares, L. 426
van Es, K. 288
Venezuela 204–205, 209–212
Venice, outdoor advertising 81
Venkatesh, S. 118
Venturi, R. 5
Verhoeff, N. 40
Vidler, Anthony 49–50

violence, racial 437, 440–443
virtual reality 251
visibility 12
Vision Venezuela TV (ViVe) is 453
visual semiotics 471
visualization of data 467–468
voice command 189
Vukovar, Croatia 147–150, *151*

walking 107–111, 406, 411–412; *see also* flanerie
Warner, M. 226
Washington Consensus 446–447
Watson, A. 3
wayfinding through mobile mapping 383–384
Webster, F. 226
Wellman, B. 380
Western construct of space 439
"white control of mobility" 438, 439–441
white flight: race and space 441; telecommunications 169–171; television 59
Wiethoff, A. 39
Williams, P. 186
Williams, R. 24, 59, 411
Willmott, P. 425
The Wire 57–58, 451
Wollen, Peter 50
""word-of-mouth mobilization" 100
world cities: symbolic context 119; tourism 265; *see also* global cities
writing, historical context 177–178
Wynter, S. 439

Y Combinator 133
Yondr 287, 289
Young, M. 425
Youngblood, G. 39
Yugoslavia: dissolution 147; national ideologies 144, 146

Zagreb, national ideologies 146, 150
zoning, semiotics of urban space 28
Zuboff, S. 377
Zuckerberg, Mark 191
Zukin, S. 62, 87, 121, 327–328